NAOKI URASAWA'S
20th CENTURY BOYS

VOL 22
THE BEGINNING OF JUSTICE

With the cooperation of
Takashi NAGASAKI

NAOKI URASAWA'S 20th CENTURY BOYS

PROFILES

Just one week until the final virus is released, and time is running out!! Will the 20th Century Boys be able to save humanity?!

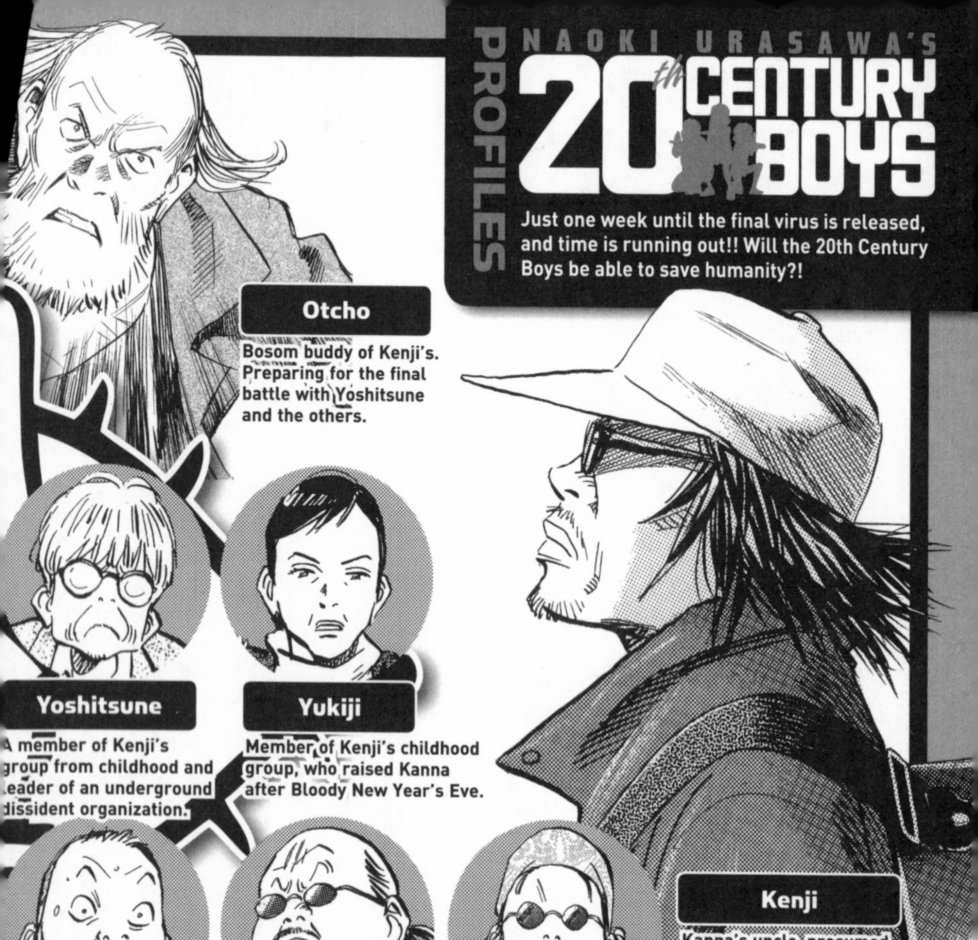

Otcho

Bosom buddy of Kenji's. Preparing for the final battle with Yoshitsune and the others.

Yoshitsune

A member of Kenji's group from childhood and leader of an underground dissident organization.

Yukiji

Member of Kenji's childhood group, who raised Kanna after Bloody New Year's Eve.

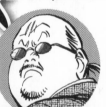

Kenji

Kanna's uncle, presumed dead on Bloody New Year's Eve, who has miraculously returned.

Keroyon

Member of Kenji's group from childhood who brought the vaccine developed by Kiriko to Tokyo.

Maruo

Member of Kenji's group from childhood and manager of nationally revered singer Haru Namio.

Konchi

Member of Kenji's group from childhood who played Kenji's song on his radio station and made it a huge hit.

The Friend then becomes leader of the world, but is assassinated in 2015 by a member of the Friends organization. Incredibly, the Friend comes back to life at the Expo 2015 opening ceremony, just in time to shield the Pope from an assassin's bullet. Deified by the world for this miracle, the Friend then orders the dispersal of a killer virus around the world, resulting in the destruction of the world as we know it...

Now, three years later, the Friend is President of the World. His plans for the total annihilation of humanity plow ahead. He goes on national radio and confesses to masterminding the diabolical events of the past, and then announces that he will destroy the world in one week. Knowing the only safe spot on earth is the Expo venue, Kanna plans a big music festival there. As the final battle looms, Kenji returns to Tokyo!!!!

H CENTURY BOYS

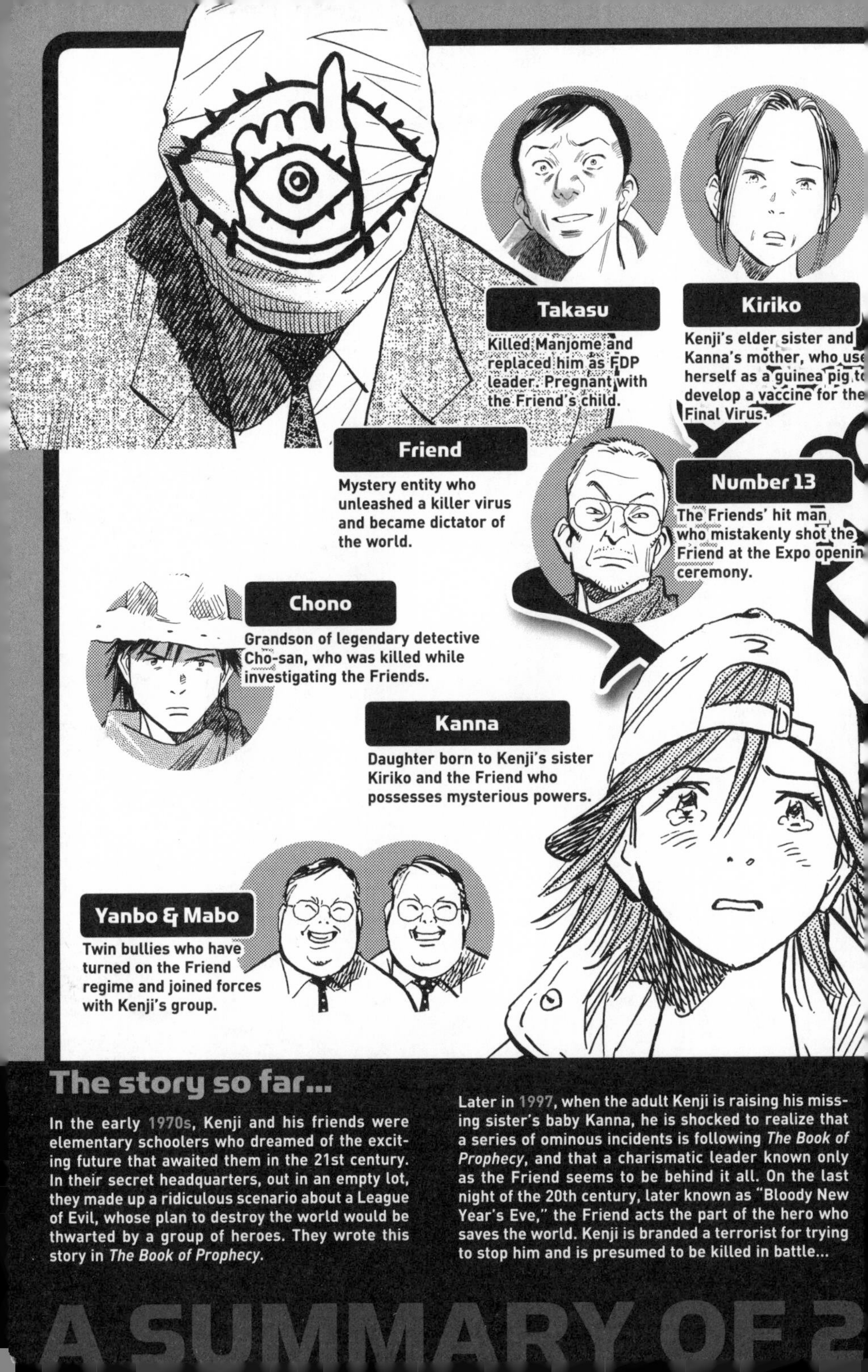
Takasu
Killed Manjome and replaced him as FDP leader. Pregnant with the Friend's child.
Kiriko
Kenji's elder sister and Kanna's mother, who use herself as a guinea pig to develop a vaccine for the Final Virus.
Friend
Mystery entity who unleashed a killer virus and became dictator of the world.
Number 13
The Friends' hit man who mistakenly shot the Friend at the Expo openin ceremony.
Chono
Grandson of legendary detective Cho-san, who was killed while investigating the Friends.
Kanna
Daughter born to Kenji's sister Kiriko and the Friend who possesses mysterious powers.
Yanbo & Mabo
Twin bullies who have turned on the Friend regime and joined forces with Kenji's group.

The story so far...

In the early 1970s, Kenji and his friends were elementary schoolers who dreamed of the exciting future that awaited them in the 21st century. In their secret headquarters, out in an empty lot, they made up a ridiculous scenario about a League of Evil, whose plan to destroy the world would be thwarted by a group of heroes. They wrote this story in *The Book of Prophecy*.

Later in 1997, when the adult Kenji is raising his missing sister's baby Kanna, he is shocked to realize that a series of ominous incidents is following *The Book of Prophecy*, and that a charismatic leader known only as the Friend seems to be behind it all. On the last night of the 20th century, later known as "Bloody New Year's Eve," the Friend acts the part of the hero who saves the world. Kenji is branded a terrorist for trying to stop him and is presumed to be killed in battle...

A SUMMARY OF 2

CONTENTS
VOL 22
THE BEGINNING OF JUSTICE

NAOKI URASAWA'S
20th CENTURY BOYS

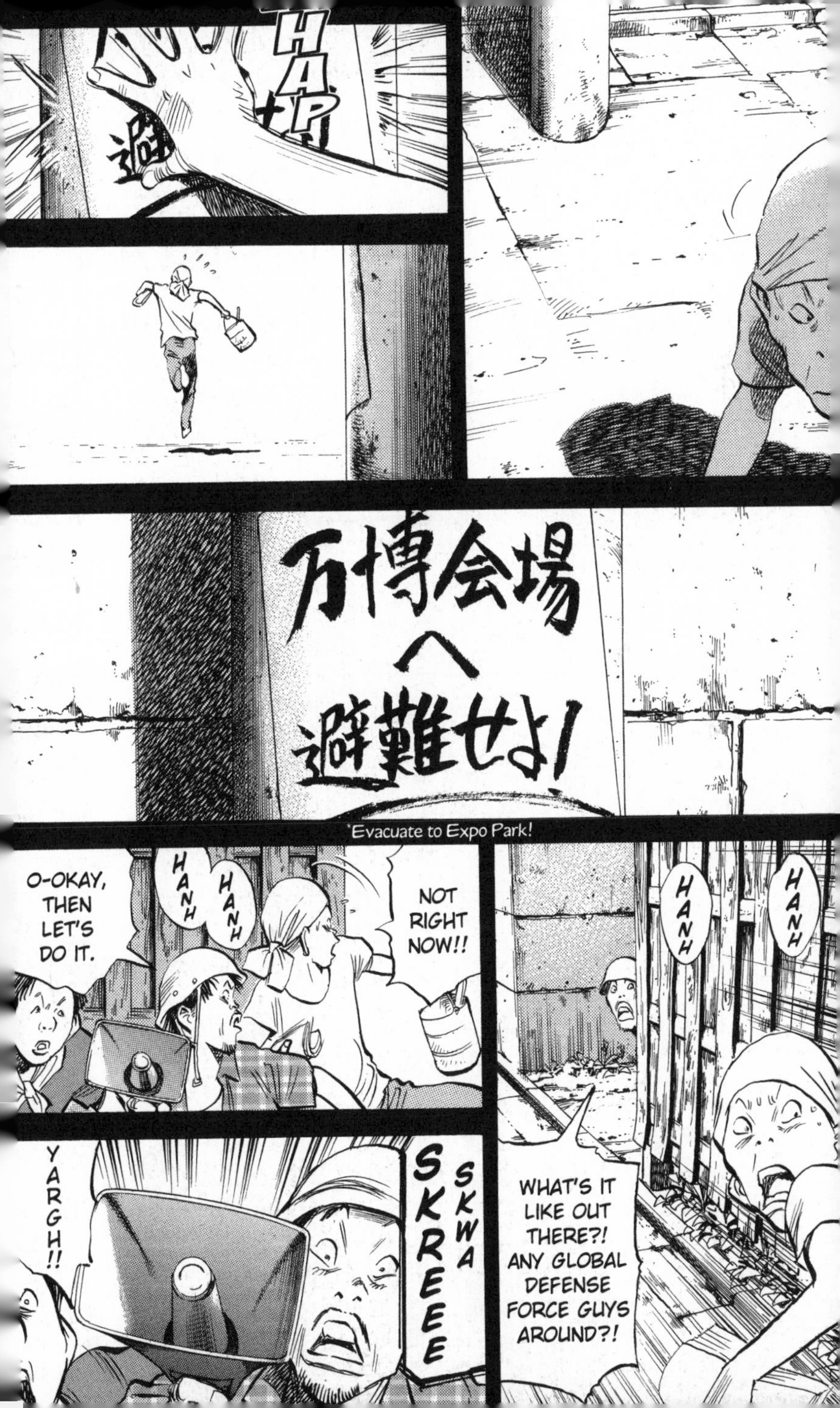
HAP
万博会場へ避難せよ!
*Evacuate to Expo Park!
HANH
HANH
WHAT'S IT LIKE OUT THERE?! ANY GLOBAL DEFENSE FORCE GUYS AROUND?!
NOT RIGHT NOW!!
HANH
HANH
O-OKAY, THEN LET'S DO IT.
SKWA
SKREEEE
YARGH!!

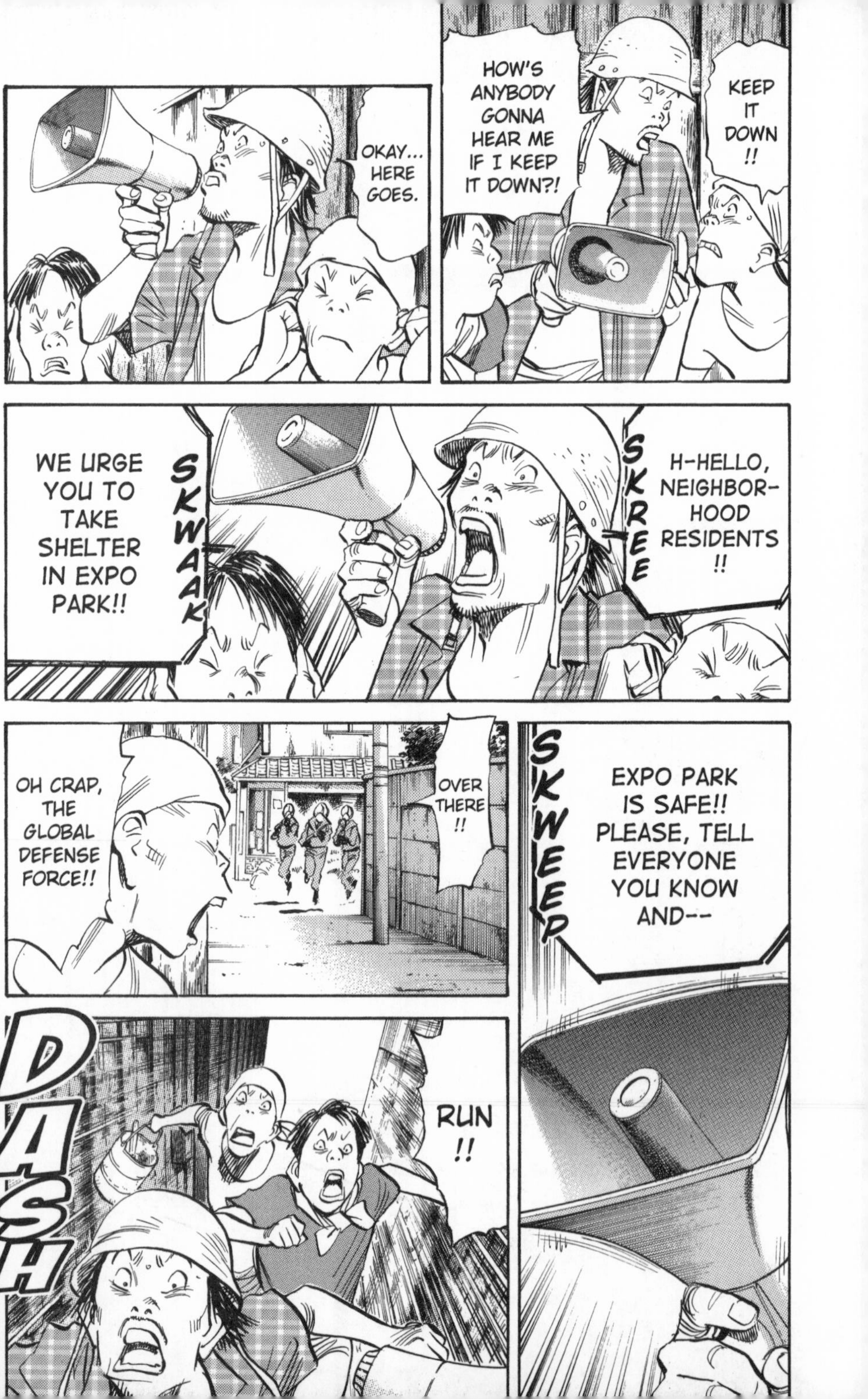
KEEP IT DOWN!!
HOW'S ANYBODY GONNA HEAR ME IF I KEEP IT DOWN?!
OKAY... HERE GOES.
SKREE
H-HELLO, NEIGHBOR-HOOD RESIDENTS!!
SKWAAK
WE URGE YOU TO TAKE SHELTER IN EXPO PARK!!
SKWEEP
EXPO PARK IS SAFE!! PLEASE, TELL EVERYONE YOU KNOW AND--
OVER THERE!!
OH CRAP, THE GLOBAL DEFENSE FORCE!!
RUN!!
DASH

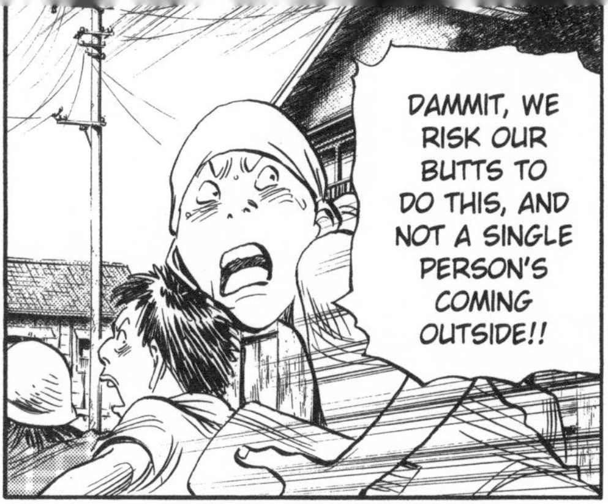
DAMMIT, WE RISK OUR BUTTS TO DO THIS, AND NOT A SINGLE PERSON'S COMING OUTSIDE!!

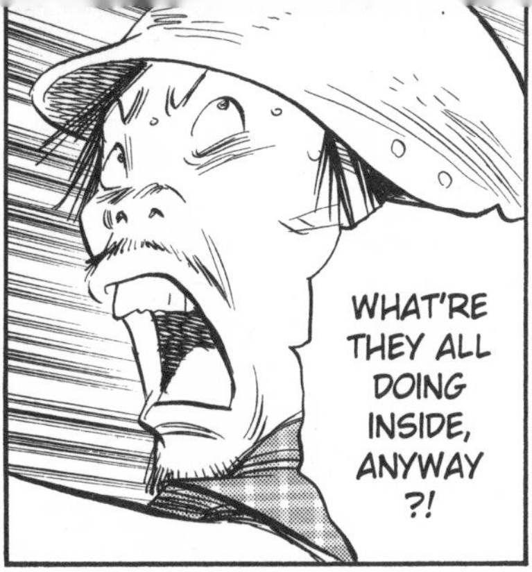
WHAT'RE THEY ALL DOING INSIDE, ANYWAY ?!

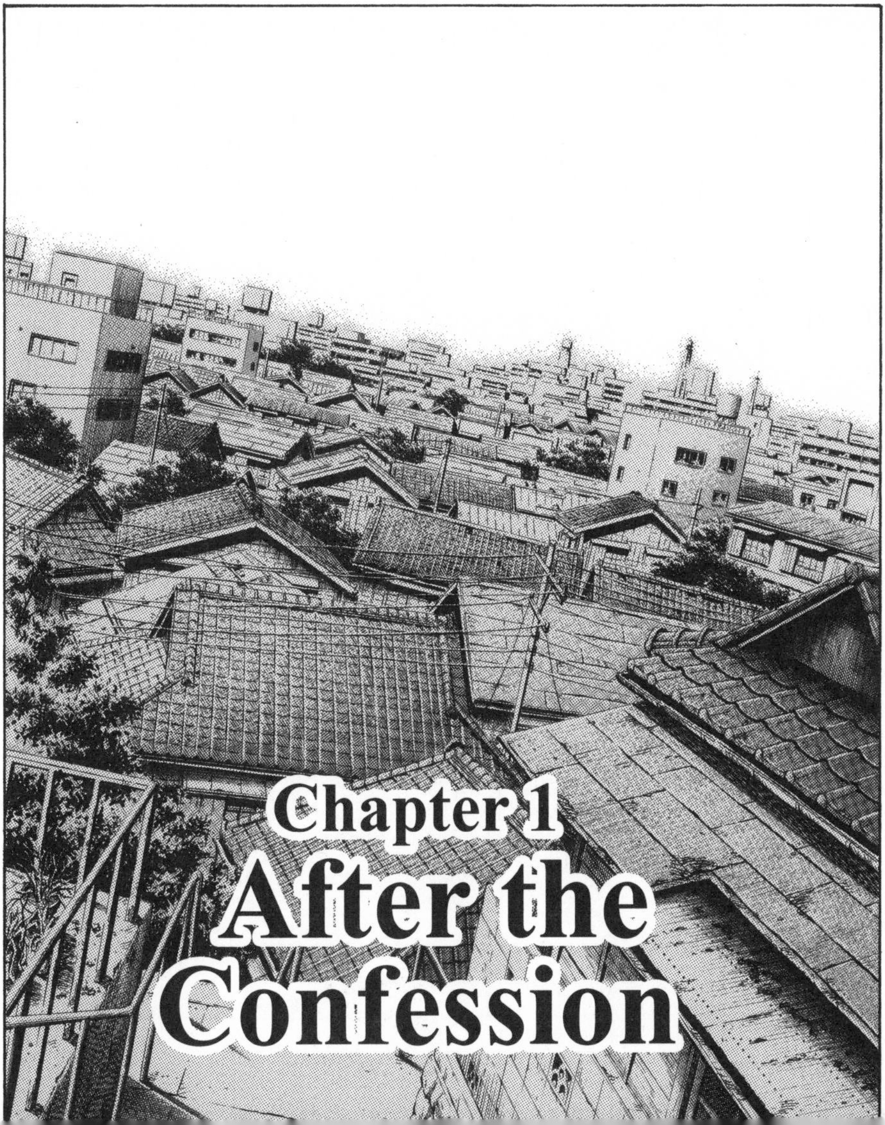
Chapter 1
After the Confession

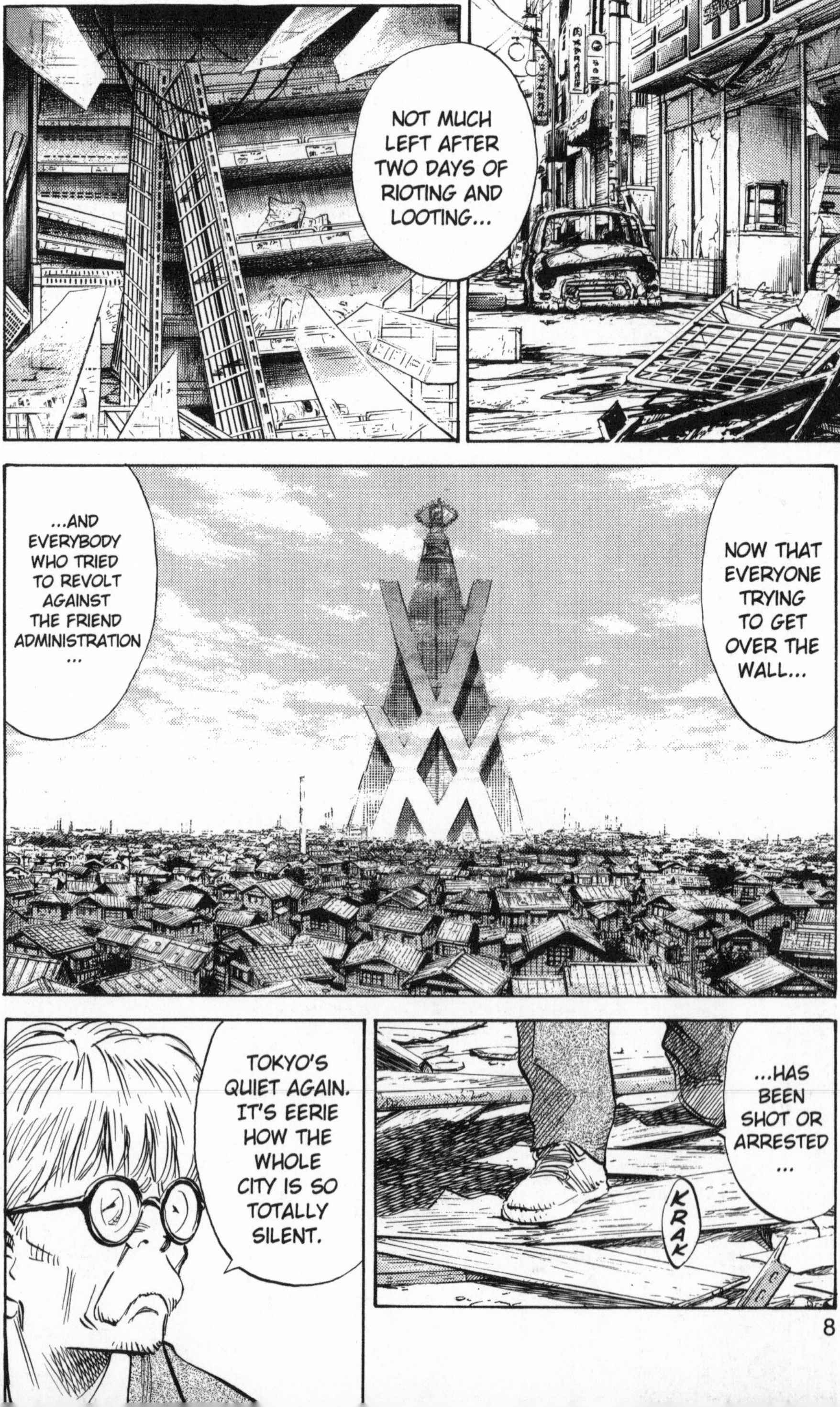
NOT MUCH LEFT AFTER TWO DAYS OF RIOTING AND LOOTING...
NOW THAT EVERYONE TRYING TO GET OVER THE WALL...
...AND EVERYBODY WHO TRIED TO REVOLT AGAINST THE FRIEND ADMINISTRATION ...
...HAS BEEN SHOT OR ARRESTED ...
KRAK
TOKYO'S QUIET AGAIN. IT'S EERIE HOW THE WHOLE CITY IS SO TOTALLY SILENT.

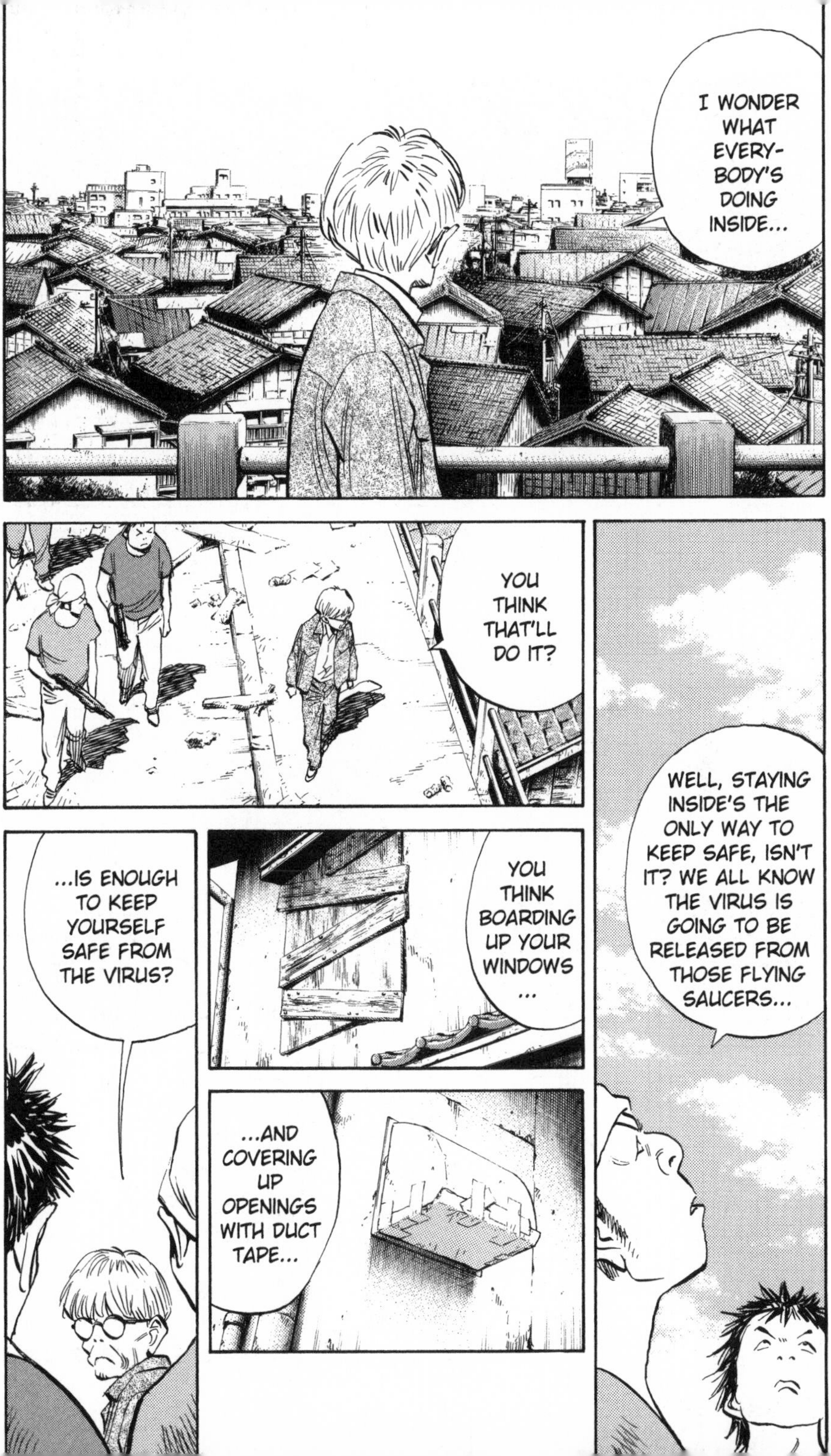
I WONDER WHAT EVERY-BODY'S DOING INSIDE...
WELL, STAYING INSIDE'S THE ONLY WAY TO KEEP SAFE, ISN'T IT? WE ALL KNOW THE VIRUS IS GOING TO BE RELEASED FROM THOSE FLYING SAUCERS...
YOU THINK THAT'LL DO IT?
YOU THINK BOARDING UP YOUR WINDOWS ...
...AND COVERING UP OPENINGS WITH DUCT TAPE...
...IS ENOUGH TO KEEP YOURSELF SAFE FROM THE VIRUS?

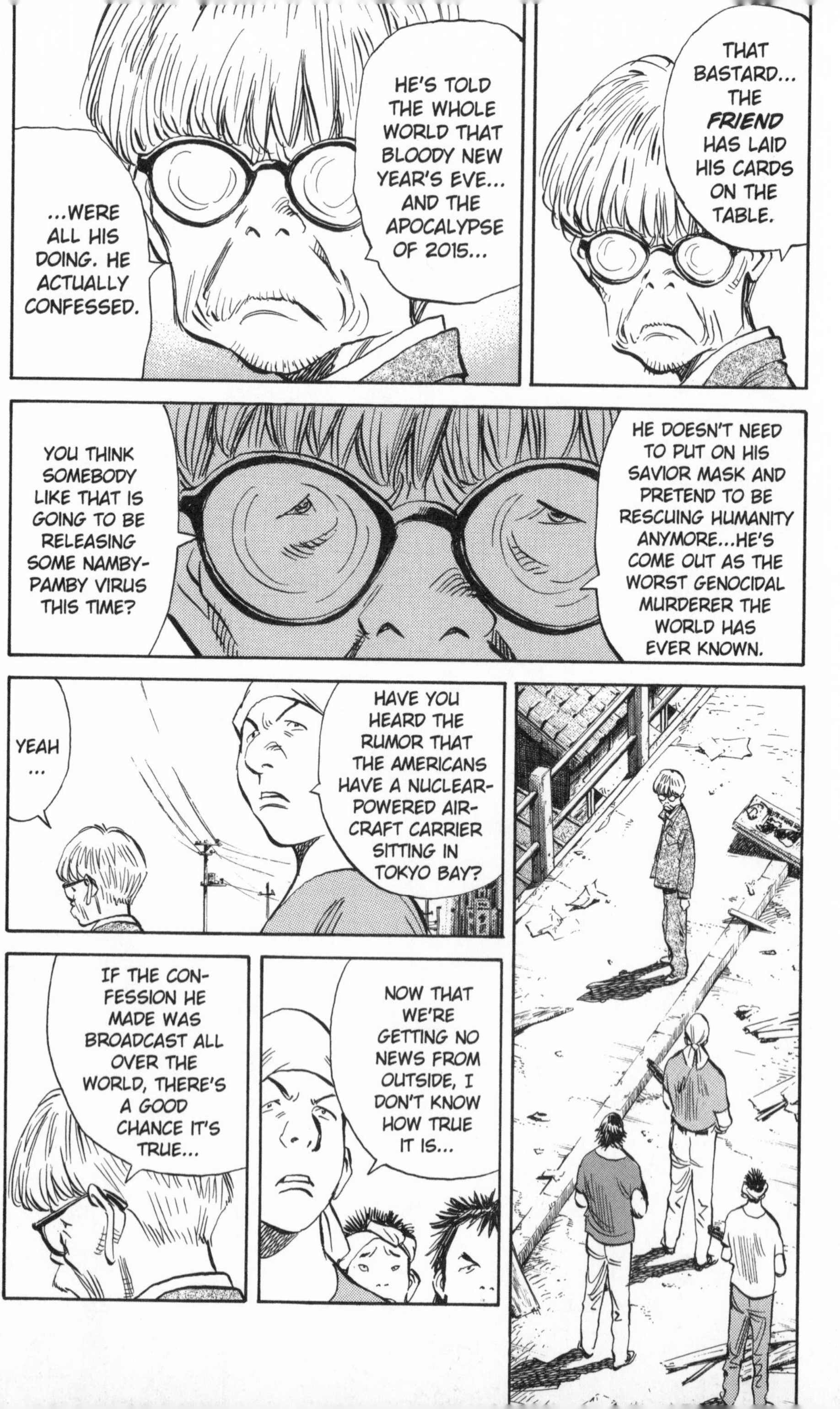
THAT BASTARD... THE *FRIEND* HAS LAID HIS CARDS ON THE TABLE.
HE'S TOLD THE WHOLE WORLD THAT BLOODY NEW YEAR'S EVE... AND THE APOCALYPSE OF 2015...
...WERE ALL HIS DOING. HE ACTUALLY CONFESSED.
HE DOESN'T NEED TO PUT ON HIS SAVIOR MASK AND PRETEND TO BE RESCUING HUMANITY ANYMORE...HE'S COME OUT AS THE WORST GENOCIDAL MURDERER THE WORLD HAS EVER KNOWN.
YOU THINK SOMEBODY LIKE THAT IS GOING TO BE RELEASING SOME NAMBY-PAMBY VIRUS THIS TIME?
HAVE YOU HEARD THE RUMOR THAT THE AMERICANS HAVE A NUCLEAR-POWERED AIRCRAFT CARRIER SITTING IN TOKYO BAY?
YEAH...
NOW THAT WE'RE GETTING NO NEWS FROM OUTSIDE, I DON'T KNOW HOW TRUE IT IS...
IF THE CONFESSION HE MADE WAS BROADCAST ALL OVER THE WORLD, THERE'S A GOOD CHANCE IT'S TRUE...

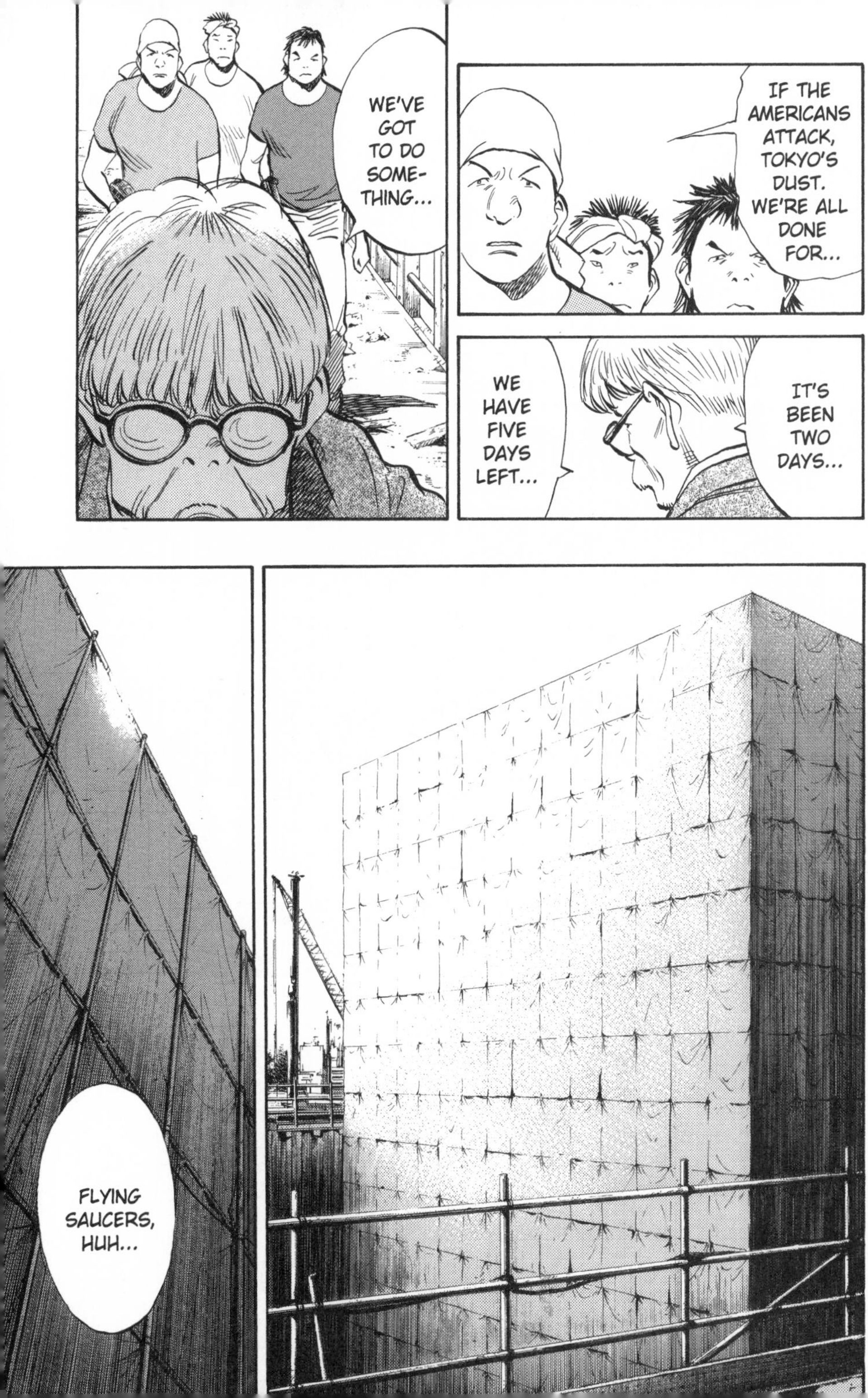
IF THE AMERICANS ATTACK, TOKYO'S DUST. WE'RE ALL DONE FOR...
IT'S BEEN TWO DAYS...
WE HAVE FIVE DAYS LEFT...
WE'VE GOT TO DO SOME-THING...
FLYING SAUCERS, HUH...

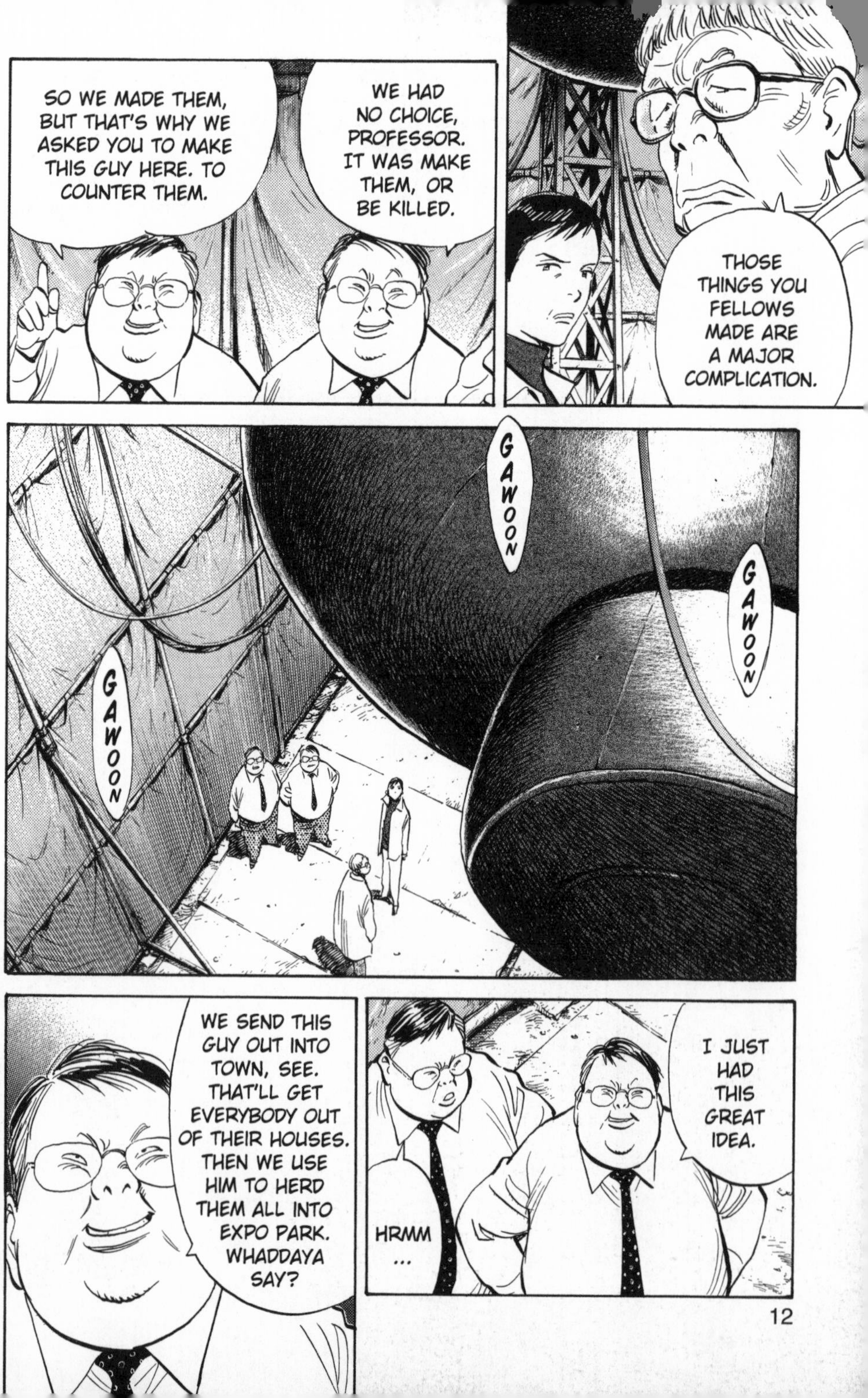
THOSE THINGS YOU FELLOWS MADE ARE A MAJOR COMPLICATION.
WE HAD NO CHOICE, PROFESSOR. IT WAS MAKE THEM, OR BE KILLED.
SO WE MADE THEM, BUT THAT'S WHY WE ASKED YOU TO MAKE THIS GUY HERE. TO COUNTER THEM.
GAWOON
GAWOON
GAWOON
I JUST HAD THIS GREAT IDEA.
HRMM ...
WE SEND THIS GUY OUT INTO TOWN, SEE. THAT'LL GET EVERYBODY OUT OF THEIR HOUSES. THEN WE USE HIM TO HERD THEM ALL INTO EXPO PARK. WHADDAYA SAY?

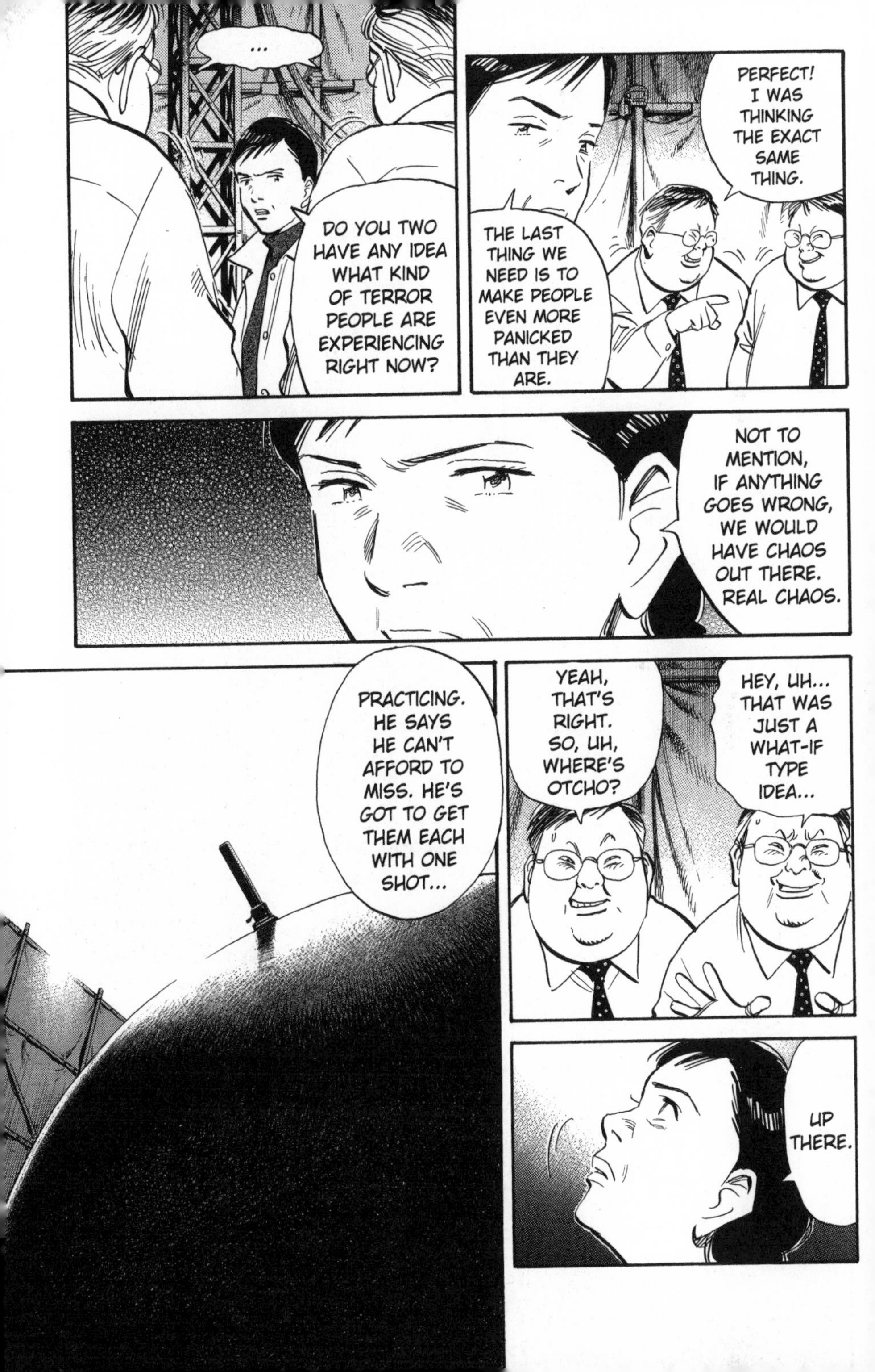
PERFECT! I WAS THINKING THE EXACT SAME THING.
THE LAST THING WE NEED IS TO MAKE PEOPLE EVEN MORE PANICKED THAN THEY ARE.
...
DO YOU TWO HAVE ANY IDEA WHAT KIND OF TERROR PEOPLE ARE EXPERIENCING RIGHT NOW?
NOT TO MENTION, IF ANYTHING GOES WRONG, WE WOULD HAVE CHAOS OUT THERE. REAL CHAOS.
HEY, UH... THAT WAS JUST A WHAT-IF TYPE IDEA...
YEAH, THAT'S RIGHT. SO, UH, WHERE'S OTCHO?
UP THERE.
PRACTICING. HE SAYS HE CAN'T AFFORD TO MISS. HE'S GOT TO GET THEM EACH WITH ONE SHOT...

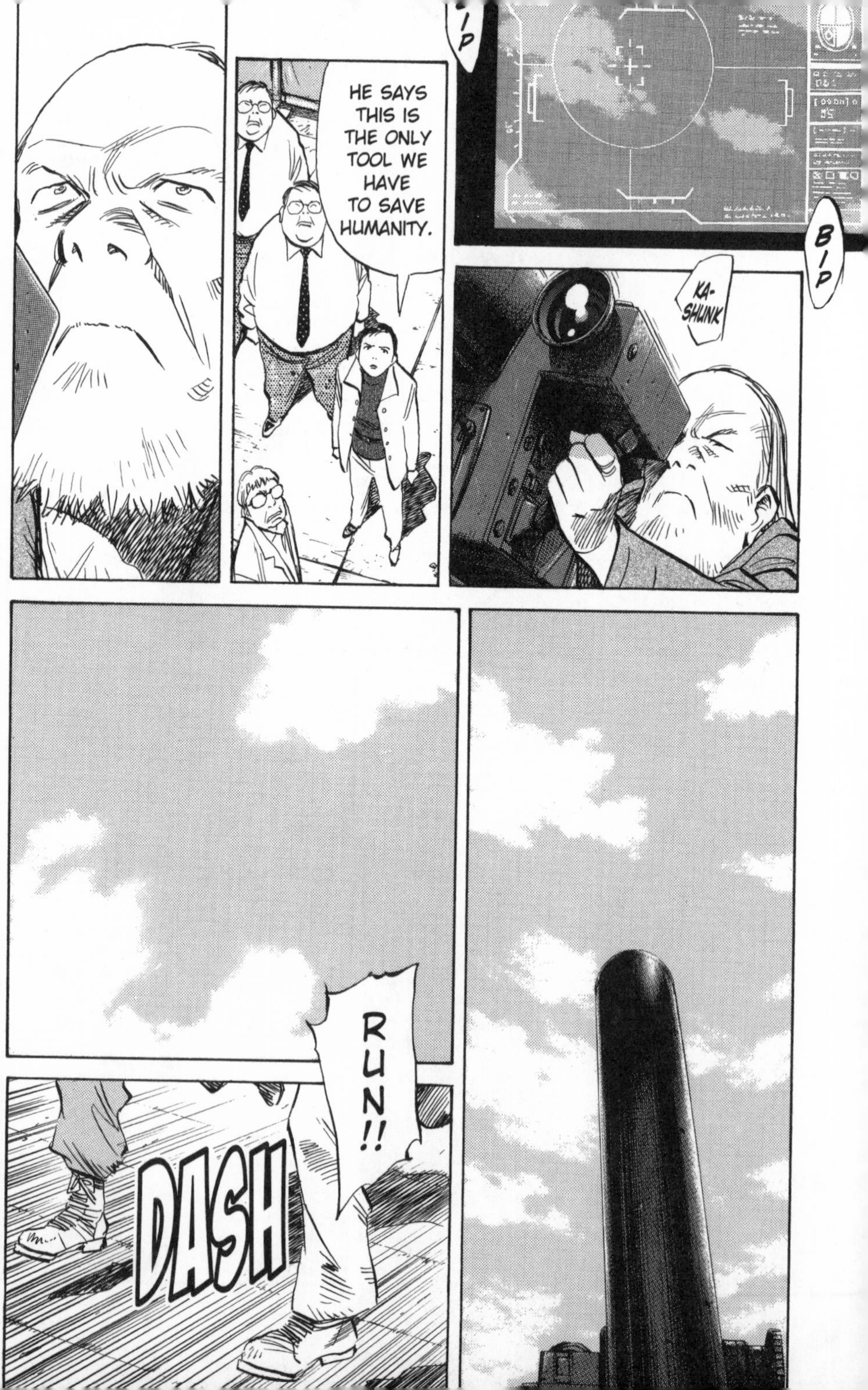
BIP
KA-SHUNK
HE SAYS THIS IS THE ONLY TOOL WE HAVE TO SAVE HUMANITY.
RUN!!
DASH

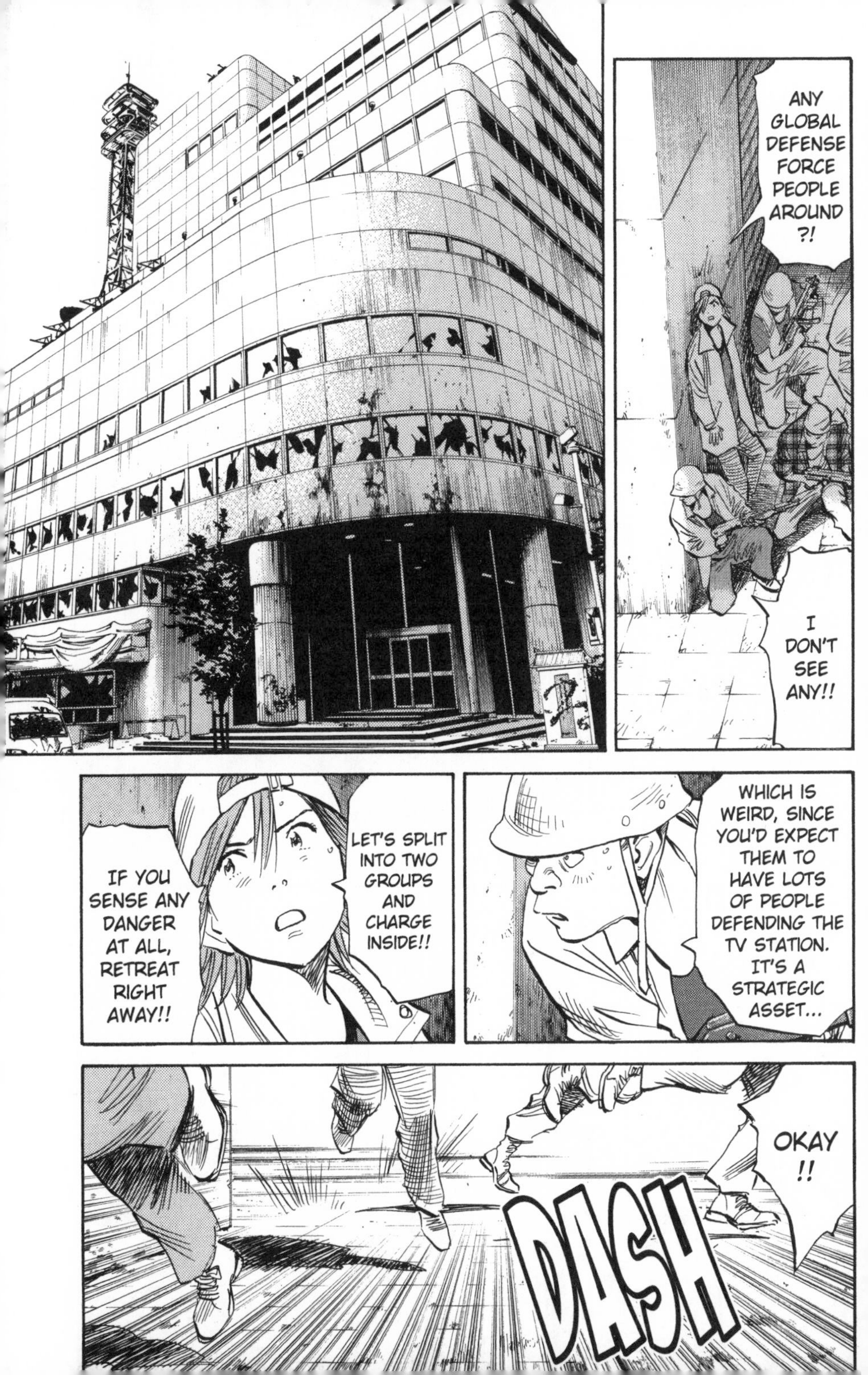
ANY GLOBAL DEFENSE FORCE PEOPLE AROUND?!
I DON'T SEE ANY!!
WHICH IS WEIRD, SINCE YOU'D EXPECT THEM TO HAVE LOTS OF PEOPLE DEFENDING THE TV STATION. IT'S A STRATEGIC ASSET...
LET'S SPLIT INTO TWO GROUPS AND CHARGE INSIDE!!
IF YOU SENSE ANY DANGER AT ALL, RETREAT RIGHT AWAY!!
OKAY!!
DASH

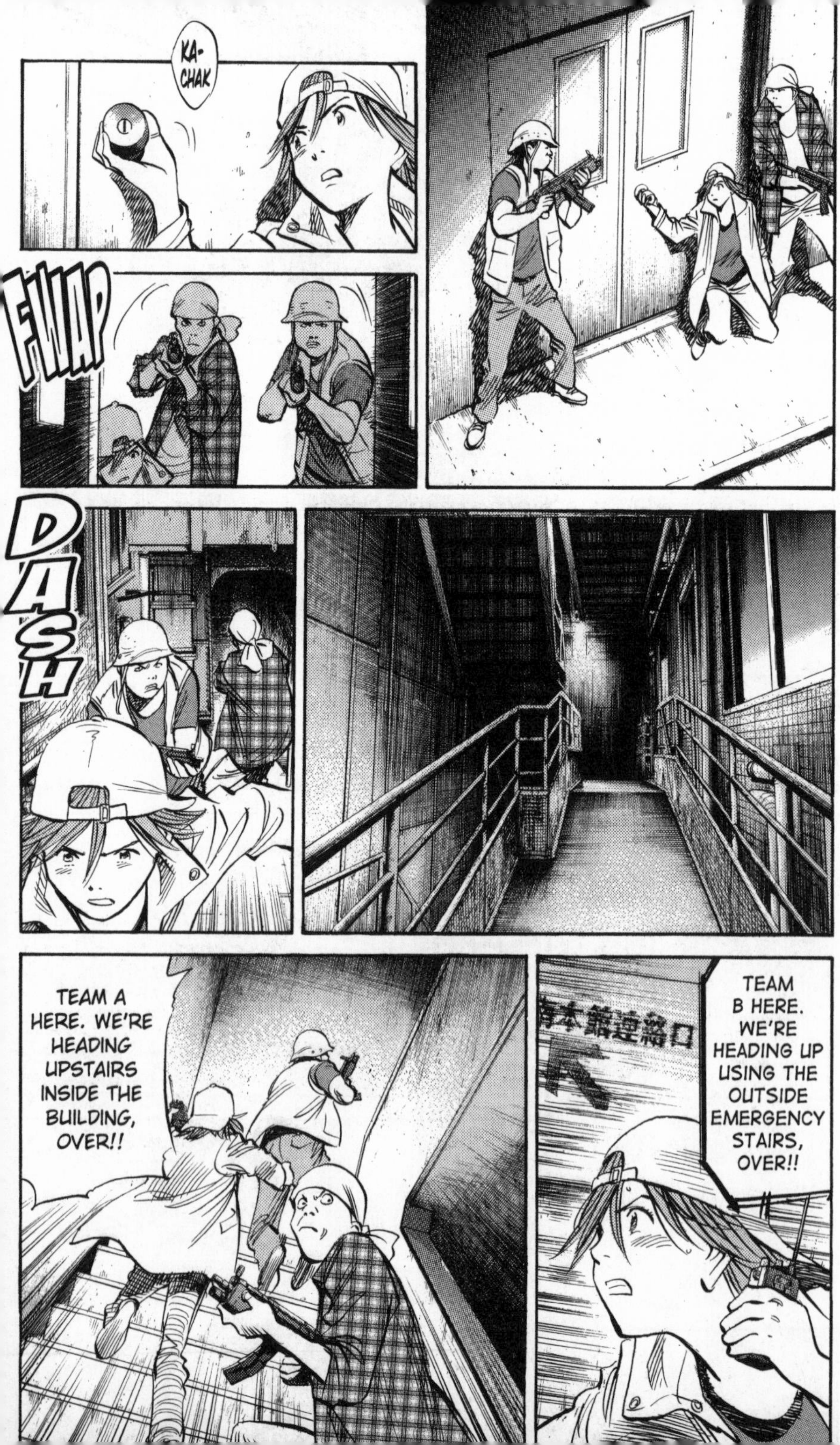
KA-
CHAK
FWAP
DASH
TEAM B HERE. WE'RE HEADING UP USING THE OUTSIDE EMERGENCY STAIRS, OVER!!
TEAM A HERE. WE'RE HEADING UPSTAIRS INSIDE THE BUILDING, OVER!!

?!

HYEE!!

←Cスタ

*Studio C

LOOKS LIKE THE BROAD-CASTING EQUIPMENT IS UN-DAMAGED...

GLOBAL DEFENSE FORCE SOLDIERS...

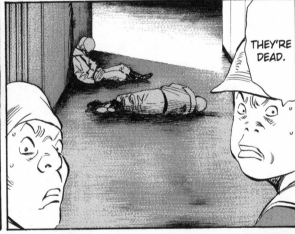

THEY'RE DEAD.

!!

KLAK

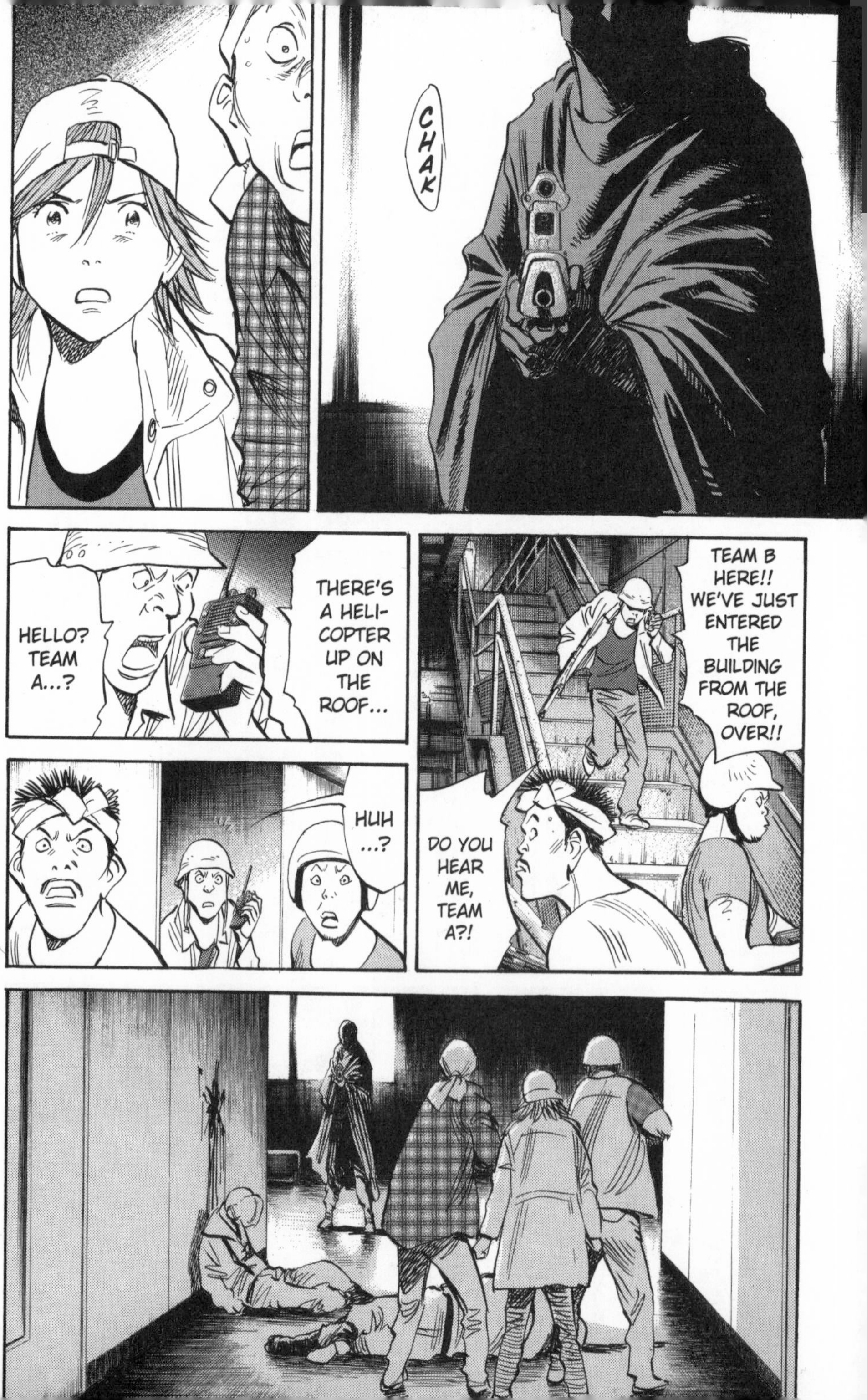
CHAK
TEAM B HERE!! WE'VE JUST ENTERED THE BUILDING FROM THE ROOF, OVER!!
DO YOU HEAR ME, TEAM A?!
THERE'S A HELI-COPTER UP ON THE ROOF...
HELLO? TEAM A...?
HUH ...?

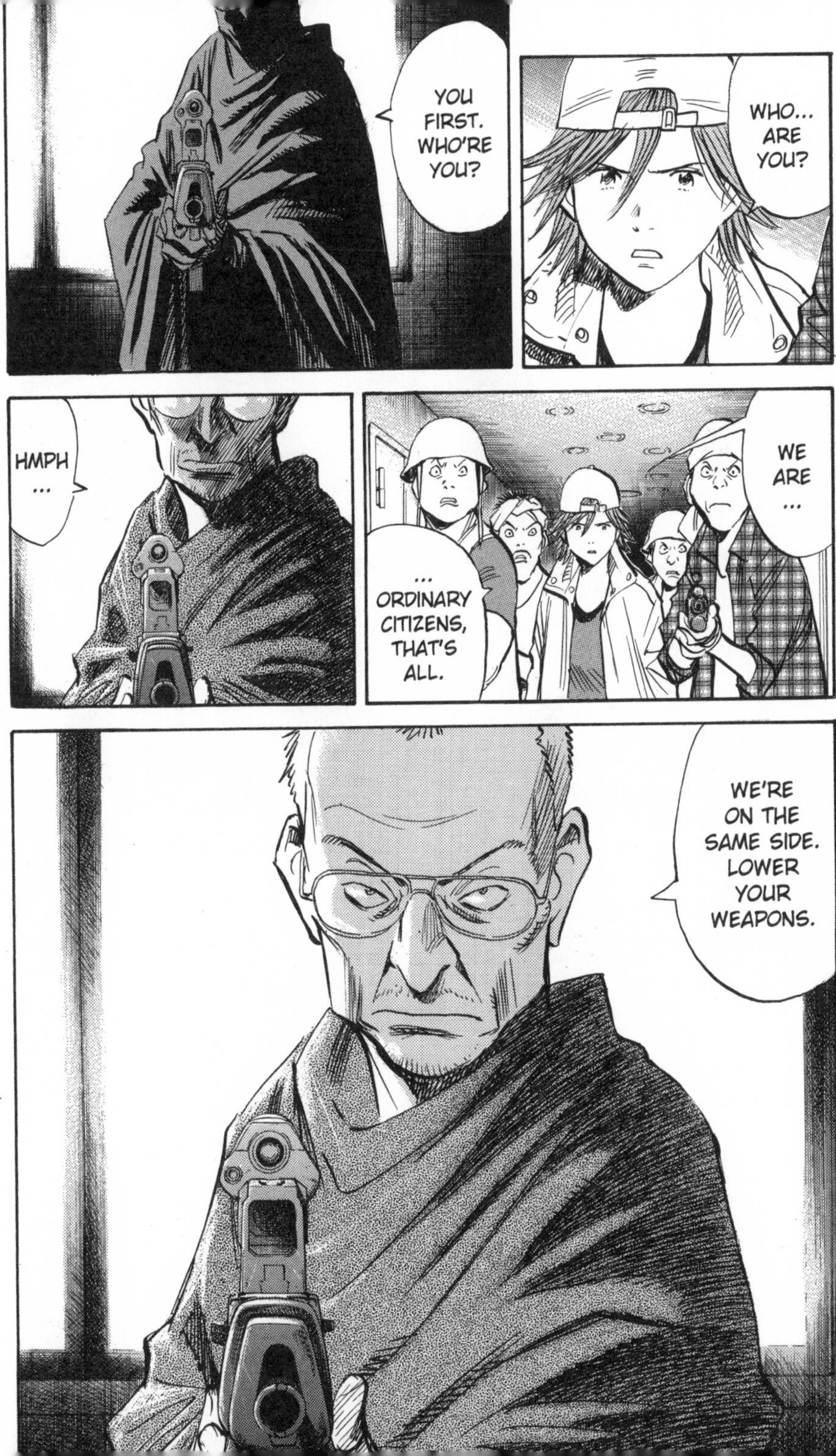
WHO... ARE YOU?
YOU FIRST. WHO'RE YOU?
WE ARE ...
... ORDINARY CITIZENS, THAT'S ALL.
HMPH ...
WE'RE ON THE SAME SIDE. LOWER YOUR WEAPONS.

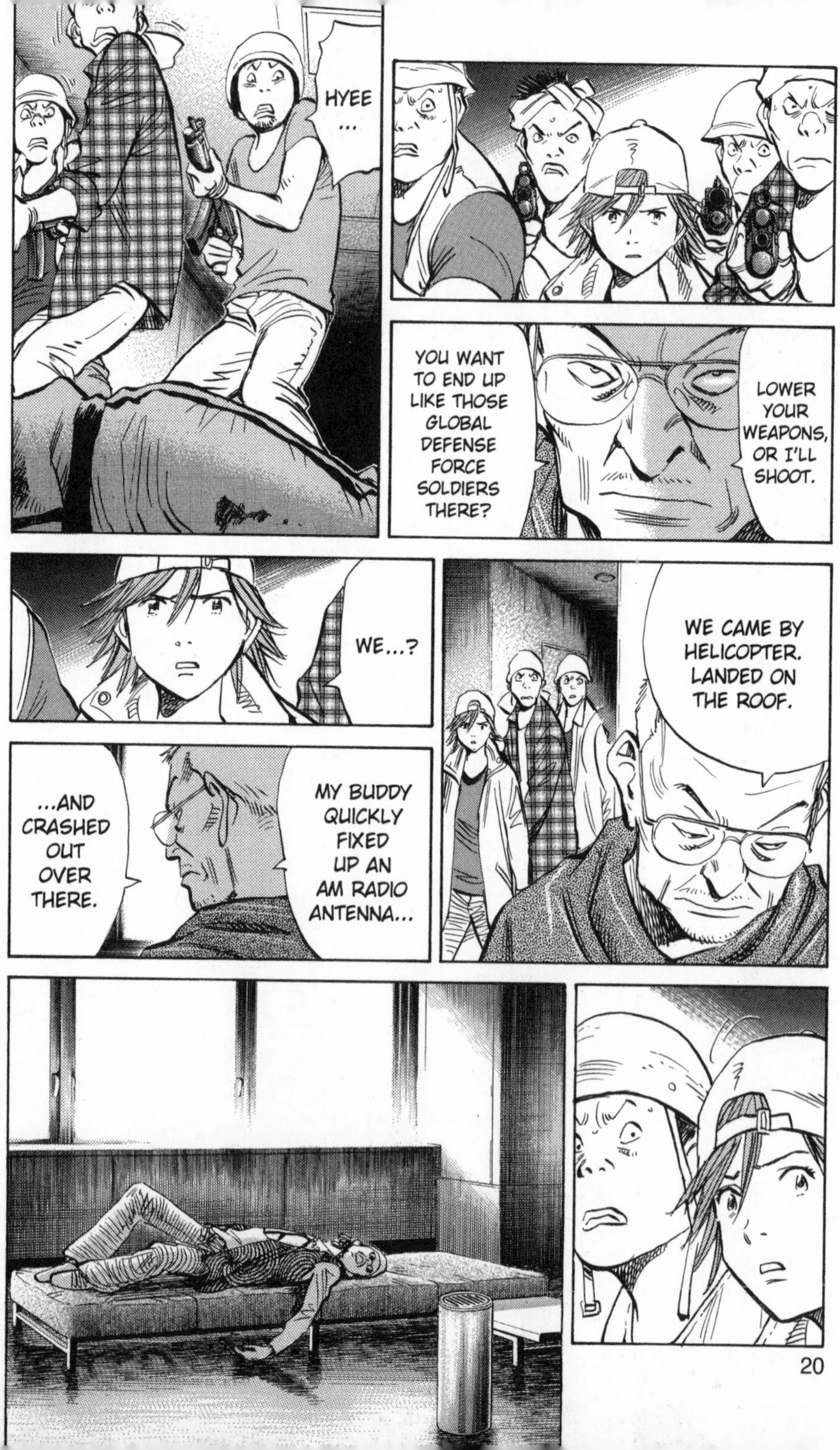
LOWER YOUR WEAPONS, OR I'LL SHOOT.
YOU WANT TO END UP LIKE THOSE GLOBAL DEFENSE FORCE SOLDIERS THERE?
HYEE ...
WE CAME BY HELICOPTER. LANDED ON THE ROOF.
WE...?
MY BUDDY QUICKLY FIXED UP AN AM RADIO ANTENNA...
...AND CRASHED OUT OVER THERE.

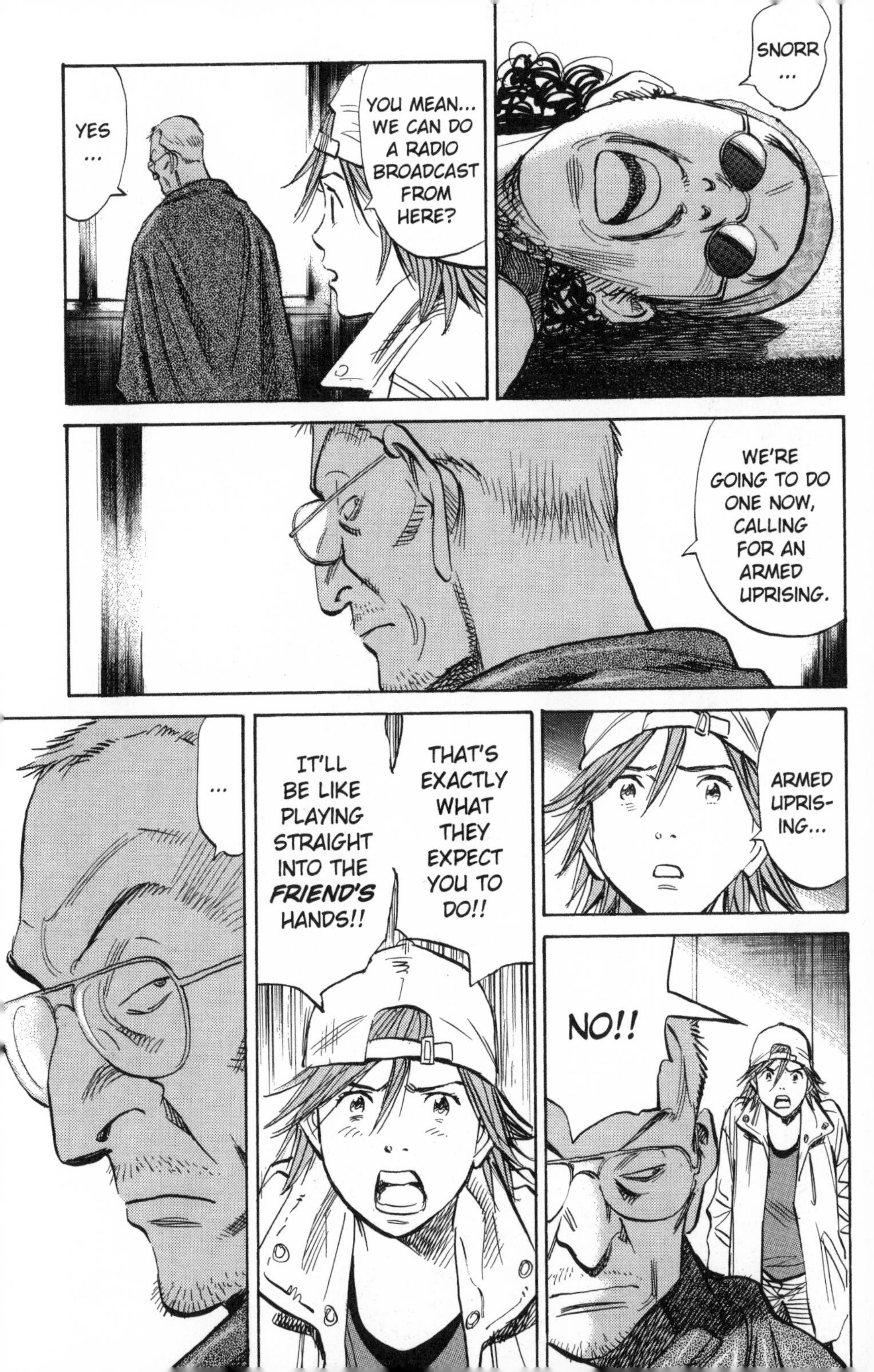
SNORR ...
YOU MEAN... WE CAN DO A RADIO BROADCAST FROM HERE?
YES ...
WE'RE GOING TO DO ONE NOW, CALLING FOR AN ARMED UPRISING.
ARMED UPRIS-ING...
NO!!
THAT'S EXACTLY WHAT THEY EXPECT YOU TO DO!!
IT'LL BE LIKE PLAYING STRAIGHT INTO THE *FRIEND'S* HANDS!!
...

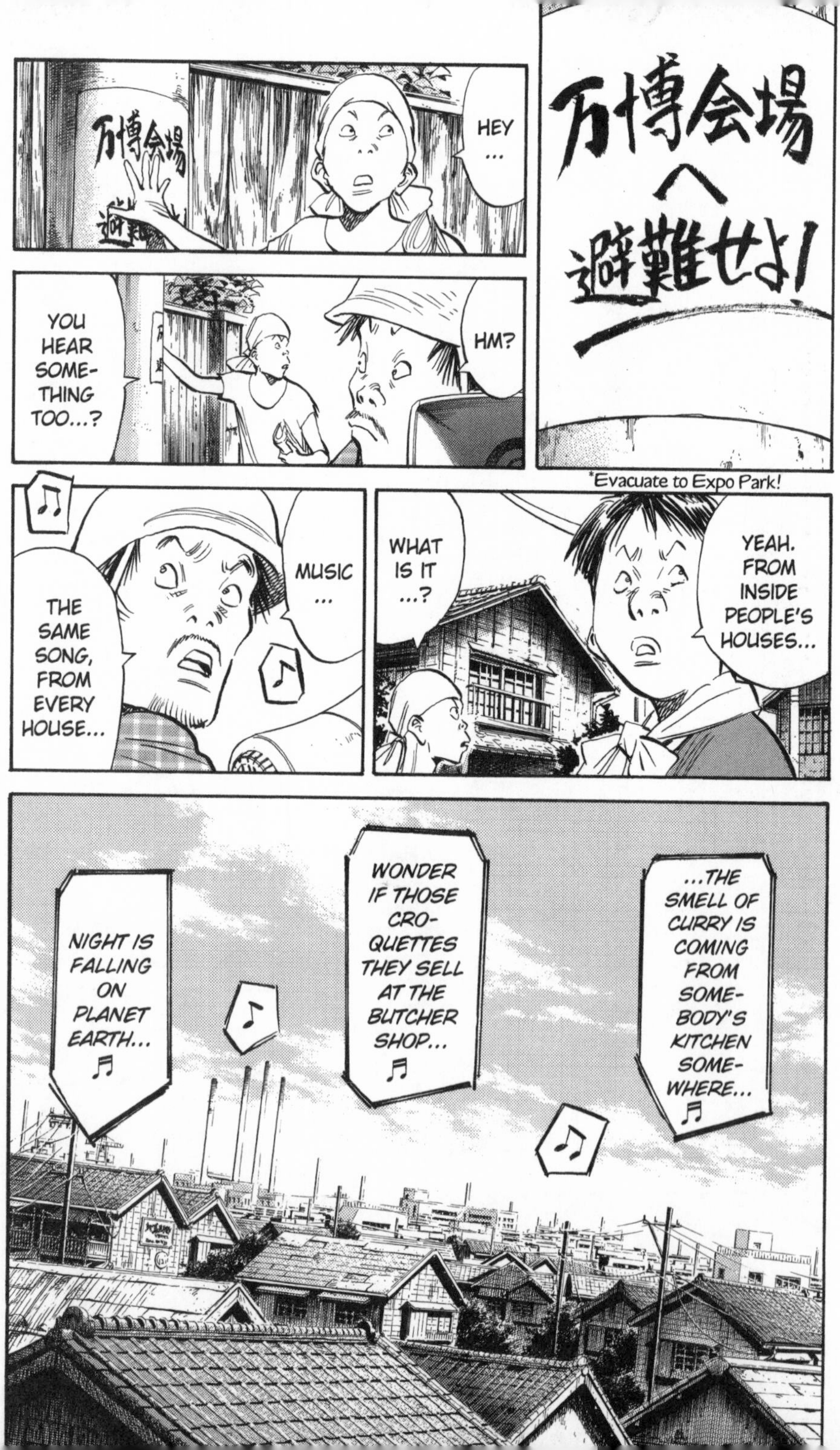
万博会場へ避難せよ!
HEY ...
HM?
YOU HEAR SOMETHING TOO...?
YEAH. FROM INSIDE PEOPLE'S HOUSES...
WHAT IS IT ...?
MUSIC ...
THE SAME SONG, FROM EVERY HOUSE...
...THE SMELL OF CURRY IS COMING FROM SOMEBODY'S KITCHEN SOMEWHERE... ♫
WONDER IF THOSE CROQUETTES THEY SELL AT THE BUTCHER SHOP... ♫
NIGHT IS FALLING ON PLANET EARTH... ♫
*Evacuate to Expo Park!

Chapter 2 Final Song

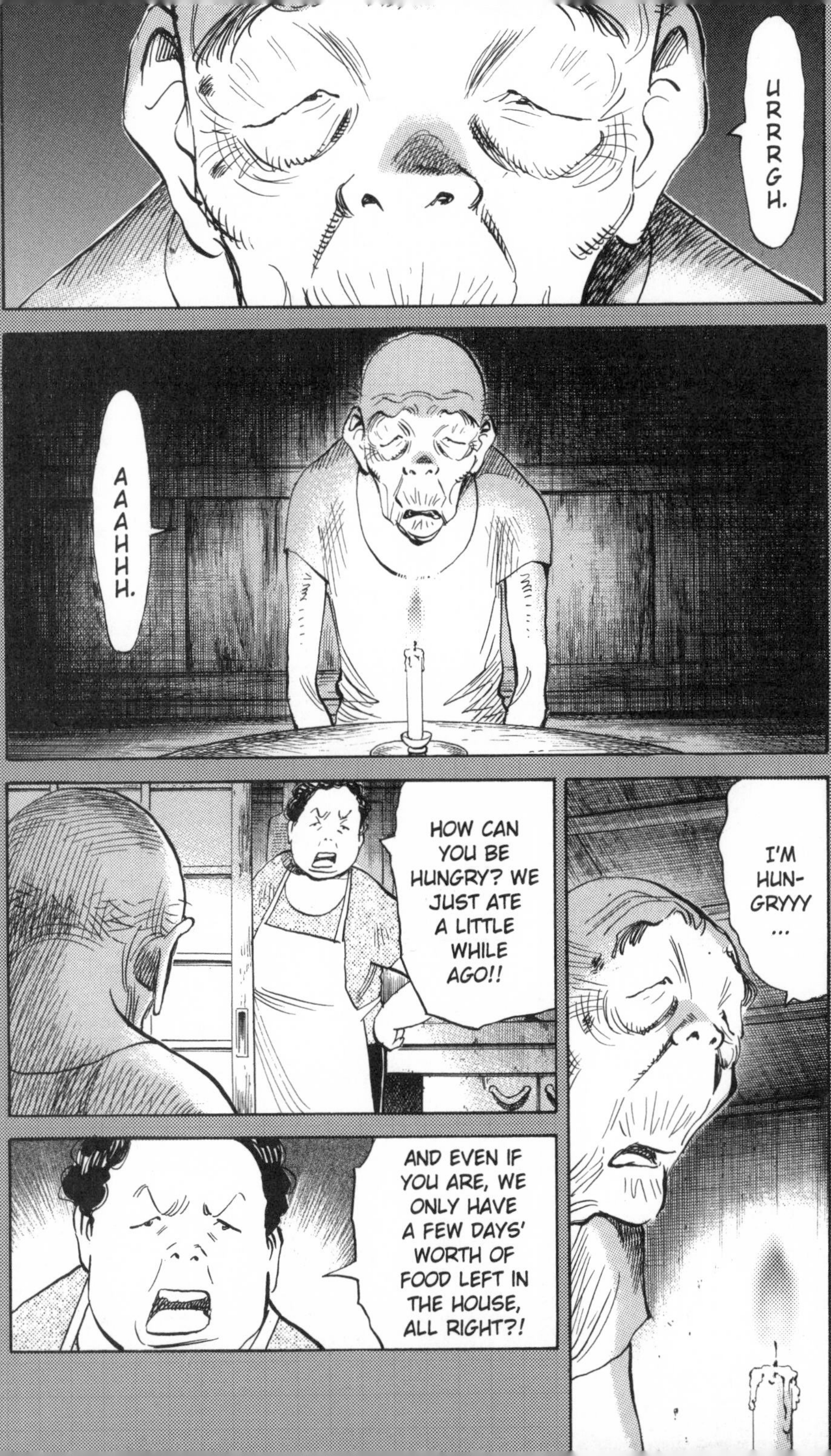
URRRGH.
AAAAHHH.
I'M HUN-GRYYY ...
HOW CAN YOU BE HUNGRY? WE JUST ATE A LITTLE WHILE AGO!!
AND EVEN IF YOU ARE, WE ONLY HAVE A FEW DAYS' WORTH OF FOOD LEFT IN THE HOUSE, ALL RIGHT?!

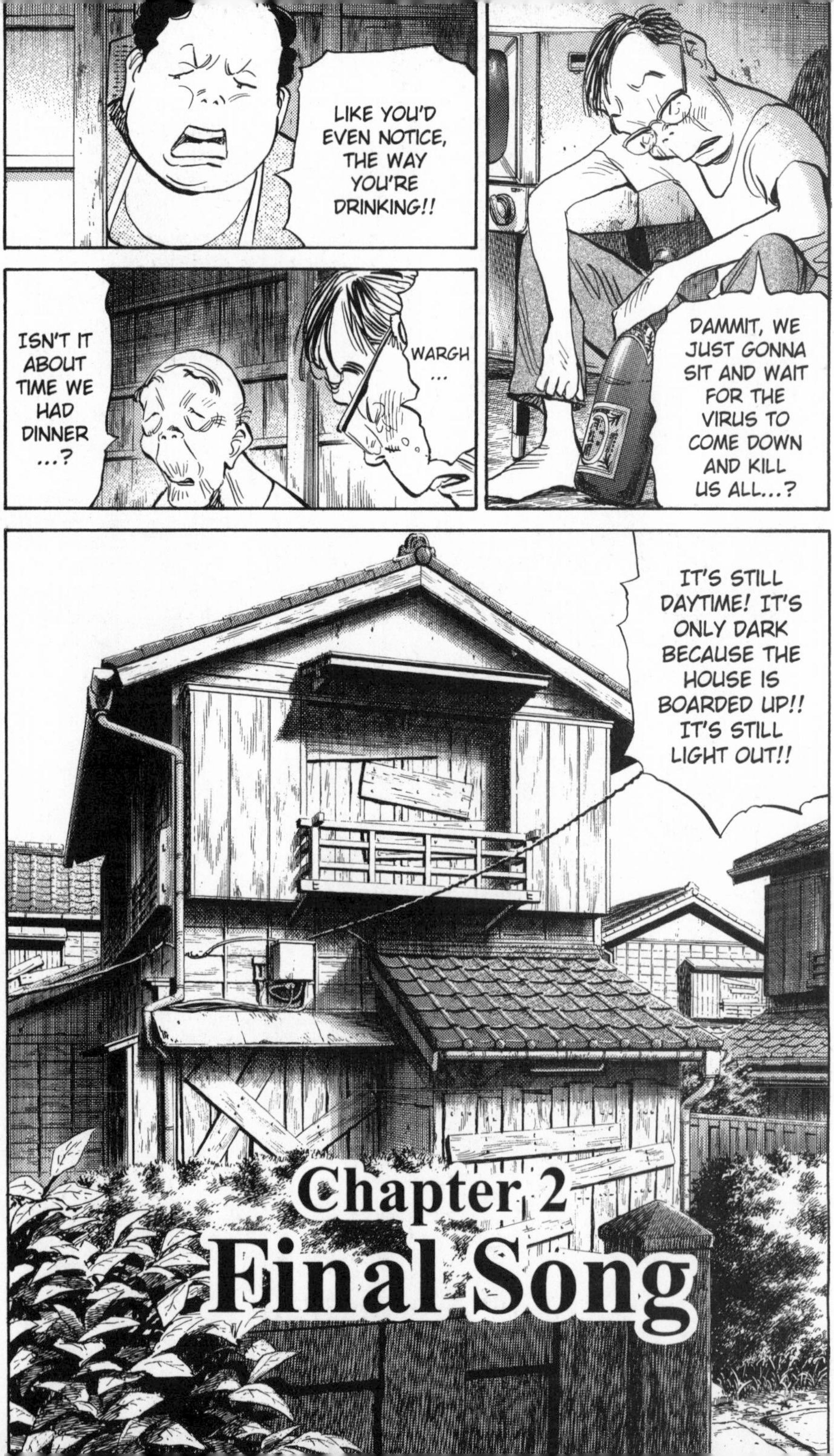
DAMMIT, WE JUST GONNA SIT AND WAIT FOR THE VIRUS TO COME DOWN AND KILL US ALL...?
LIKE YOU'D EVEN NOTICE, THE WAY YOU'RE DRINKING!!
WARGH...
ISN'T IT ABOUT TIME WE HAD DINNER...?
IT'S STILL DAYTIME! IT'S ONLY DARK BECAUSE THE HOUSE IS BOARDED UP!! IT'S STILL LIGHT OUT!!
Chapter 2
Final Song

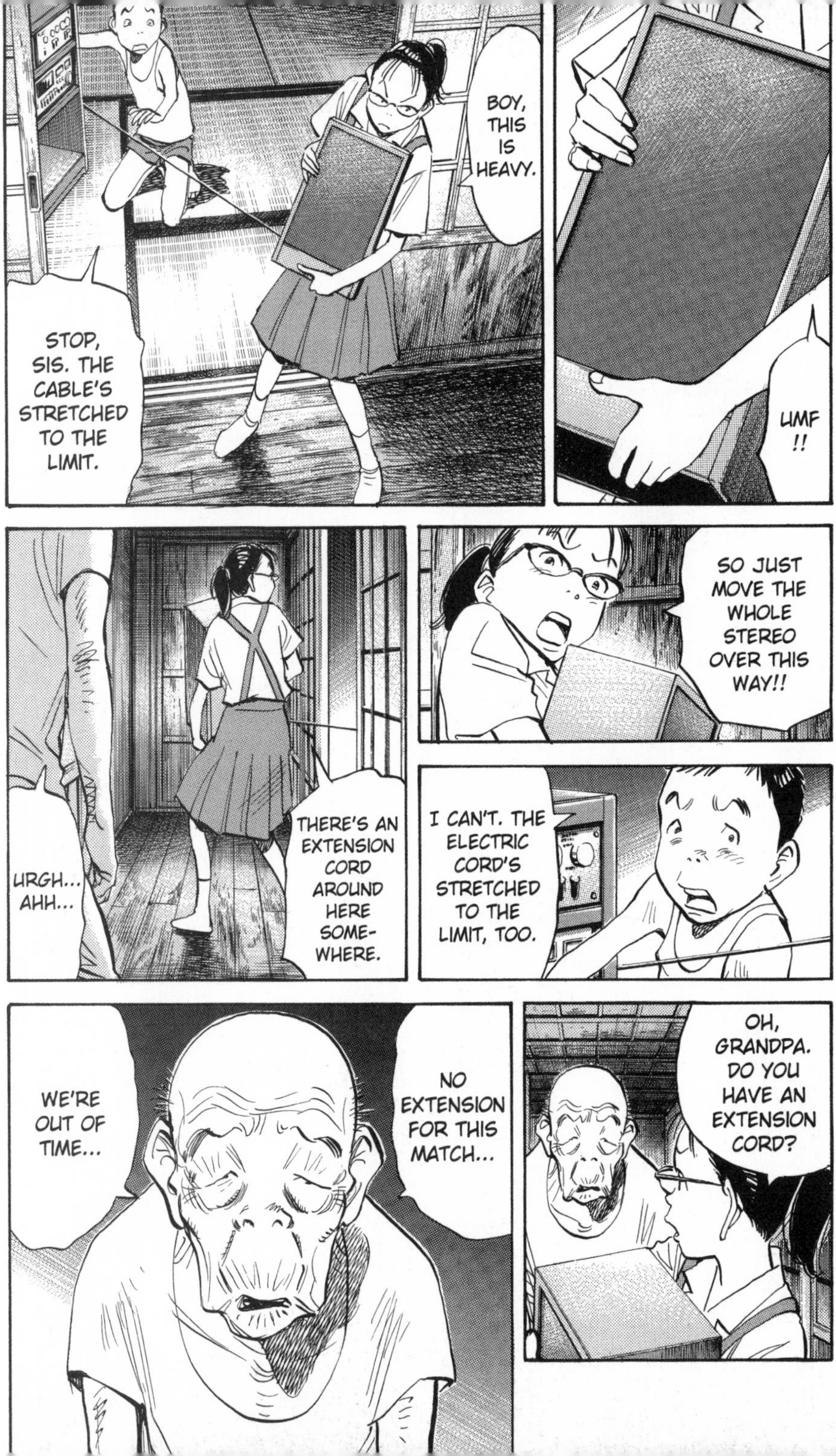
UMF !!
BOY, THIS IS HEAVY.
STOP, SIS. THE CABLE'S STRETCHED TO THE LIMIT.
SO JUST MOVE THE WHOLE STEREO OVER THIS WAY!!
I CAN'T. THE ELECTRIC CORD'S STRETCHED TO THE LIMIT, TOO.
THERE'S AN EXTENSION CORD AROUND HERE SOME-WHERE.
URGH... AHH...
OH, GRANDPA. DO YOU HAVE AN EXTENSION CORD?
NO EXTENSION FOR THIS MATCH...
WE'RE OUT OF TIME...

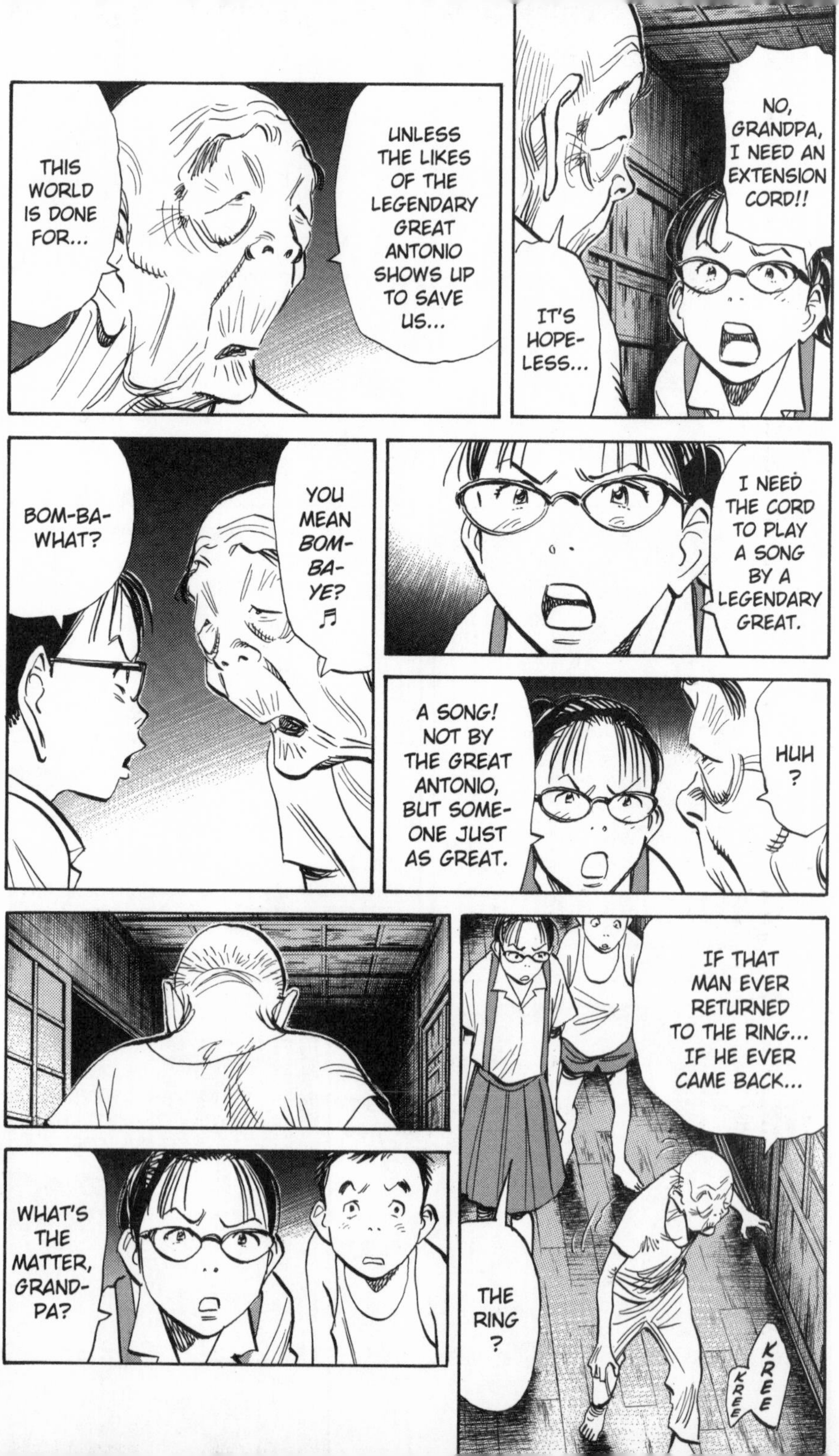
NO, GRANDPA, I NEED AN EXTENSION CORD!!
IT'S HOPE-LESS...
UNLESS THE LIKES OF THE LEGENDARY GREAT ANTONIO SHOWS UP TO SAVE US...
THIS WORLD IS DONE FOR...
I NEED THE CORD TO PLAY A SONG BY A LEGENDARY GREAT.
HUH?
A SONG! NOT BY THE GREAT ANTONIO, BUT SOME-ONE JUST AS GREAT.
YOU MEAN BOM-BA-YE? ♬
BOM-BA-WHAT?
IF THAT MAN EVER RETURNED TO THE RING... IF HE EVER CAME BACK...
THE RING?
KREE
KREE
WHAT'S THE MATTER, GRAND-PA?

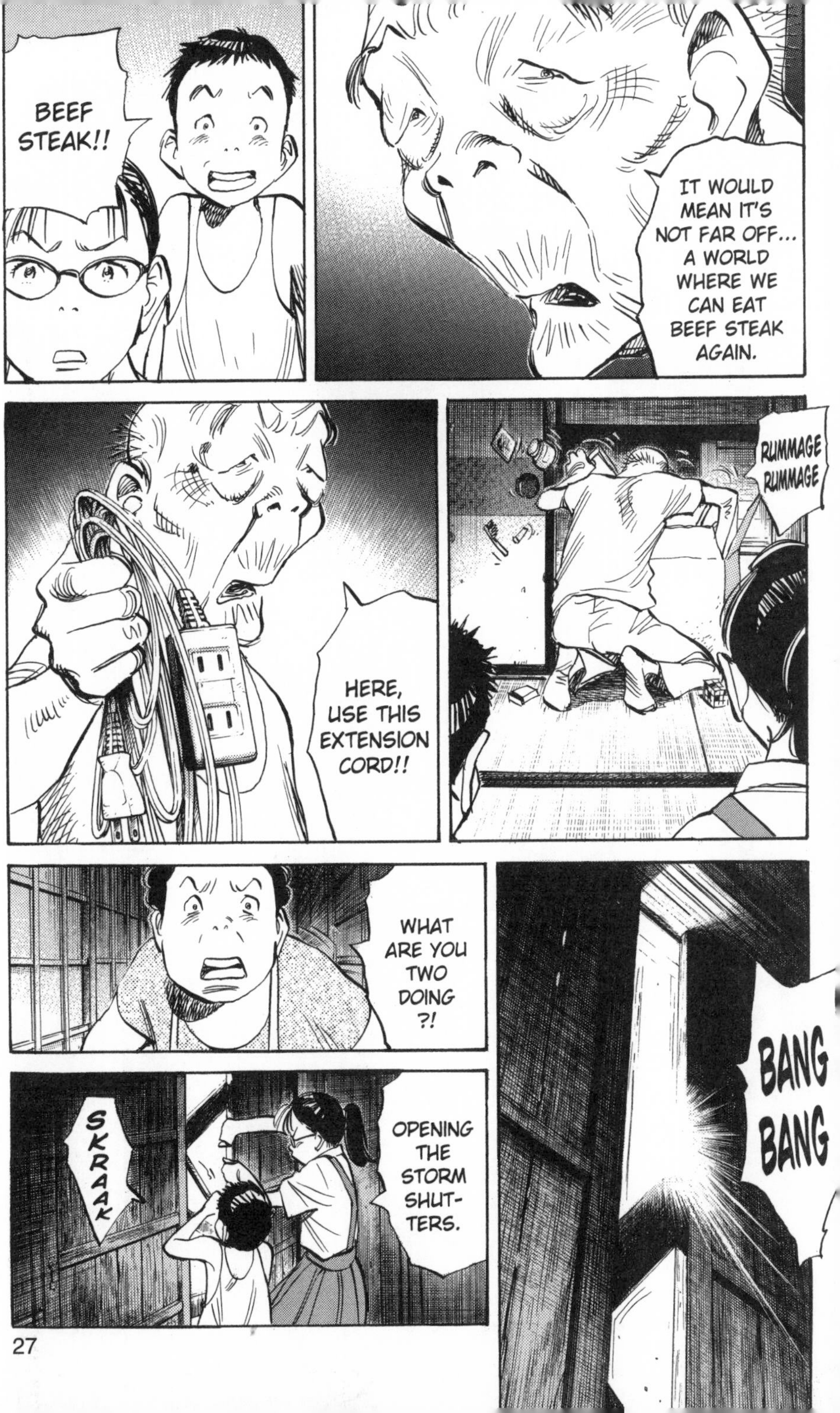
IT WOULD MEAN IT'S NOT FAR OFF... A WORLD WHERE WE CAN EAT BEEF STEAK AGAIN.
BEEF STEAK!!
RUMMAGE RUMMAGE
HERE, USE THIS EXTENSION CORD!!
BANG BANG
WHAT ARE YOU TWO DOING?!
OPENING THE STORM SHUT-TERS.
SKRAAK

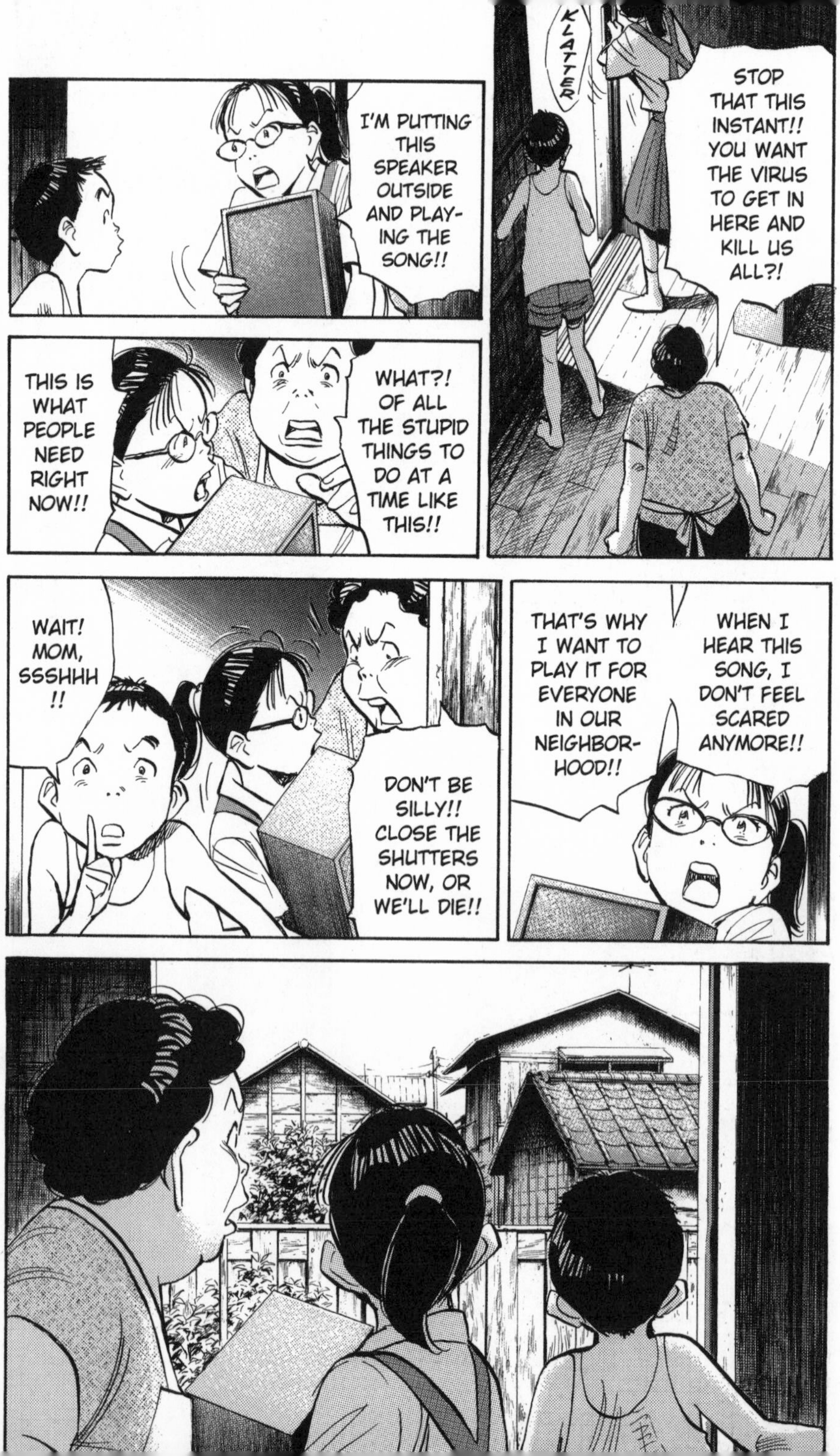
KLATTER
STOP THAT THIS INSTANT!! YOU WANT THE VIRUS TO GET IN HERE AND KILL US ALL?!
I'M PUTTING THIS SPEAKER OUTSIDE AND PLAY-ING THE SONG!!
WHAT?! OF ALL THE STUPID THINGS TO DO AT A TIME LIKE THIS!!
THIS IS WHAT PEOPLE NEED RIGHT NOW!!
WHEN I HEAR THIS SONG, I DON'T FEEL SCARED ANYMORE!!
THAT'S WHY I WANT TO PLAY IT FOR EVERYONE IN OUR NEIGHBOR-HOOD!!
DON'T BE SILLY!! CLOSE THE SHUTTERS NOW, OR WE'LL DIE!!
WAIT! MOM, SSSHHH!!

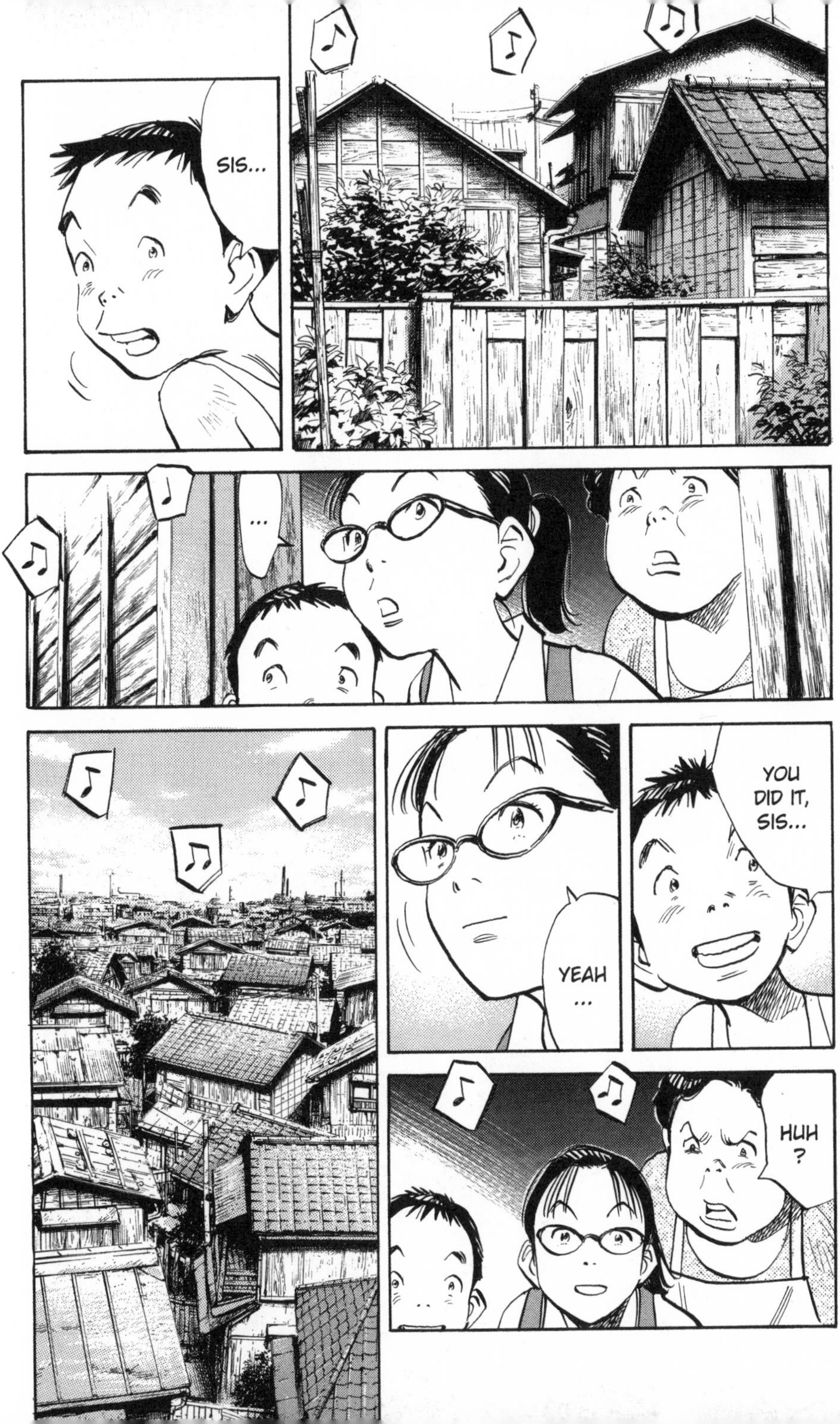
SIS...
...
YOU DID IT, SIS...
YEAH ...
HUH ?

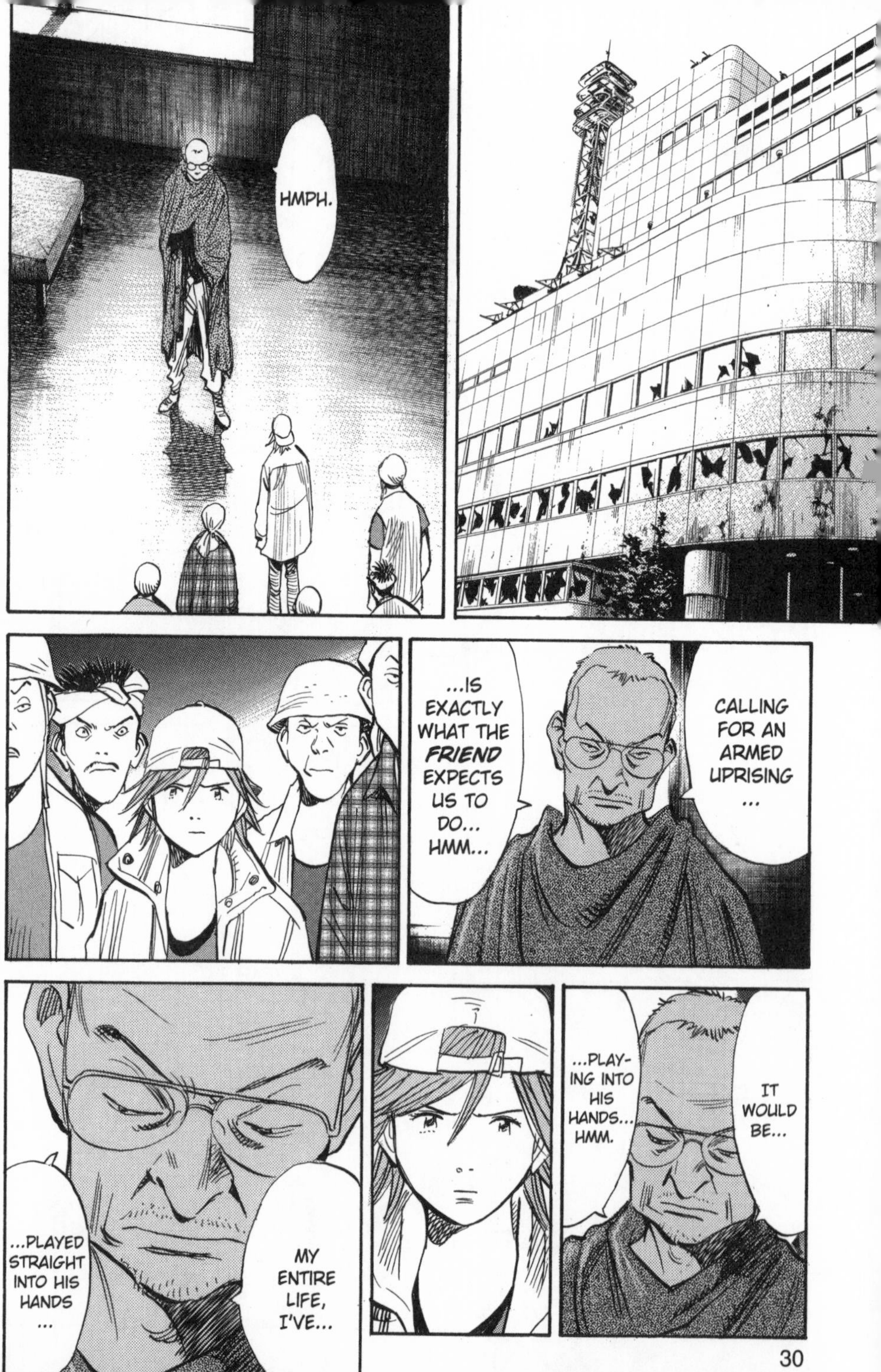
HMPH.
CALLING FOR AN ARMED UPRISING ...
...IS EXACTLY WHAT THE *FRIEND* EXPECTS US TO DO... HMM...
IT WOULD BE...
...PLAY-ING INTO HIS HANDS... HMM.
MY ENTIRE LIFE, I'VE...
...PLAYED STRAIGHT INTO HIS HANDS ...

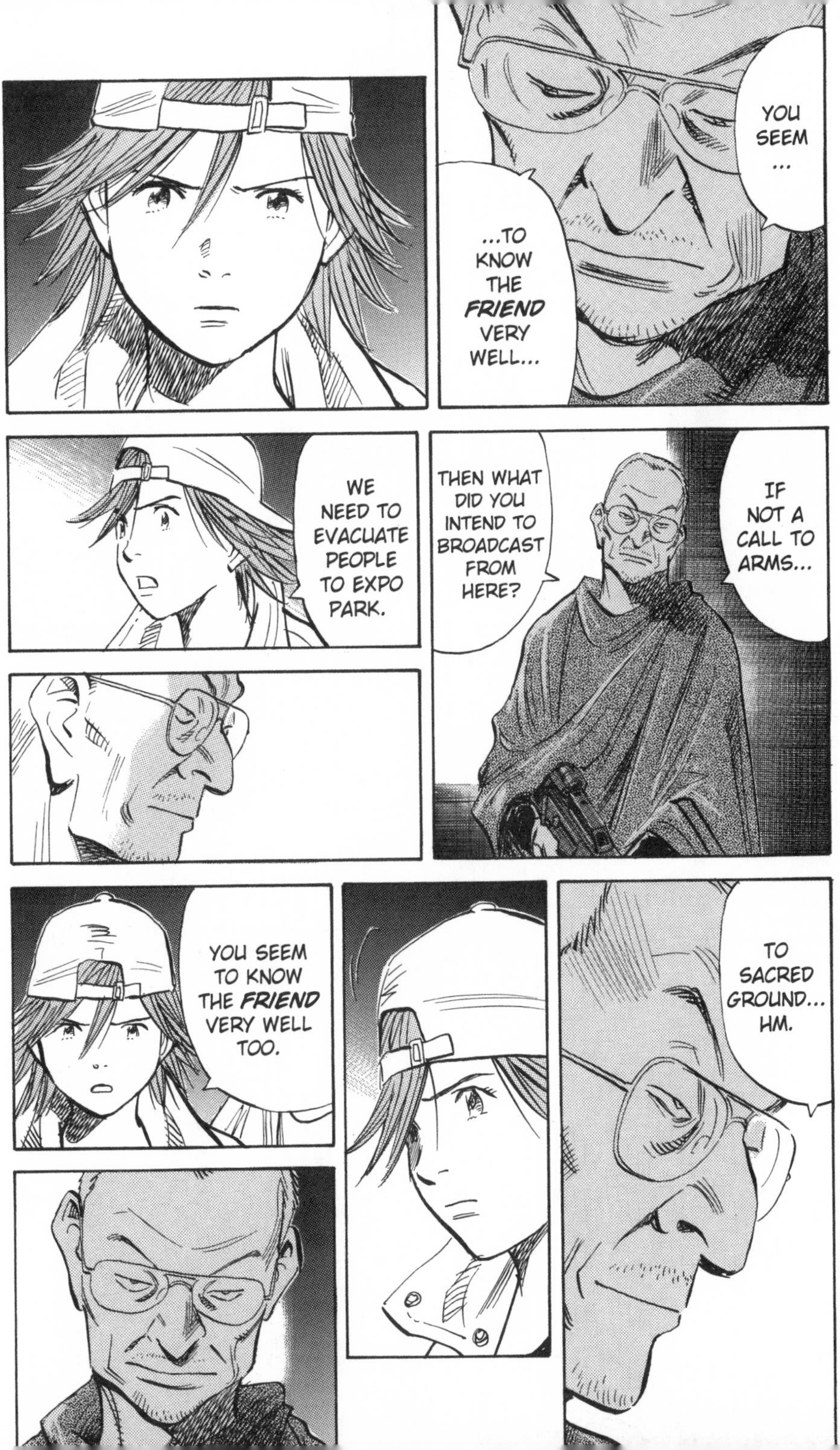
YOU SEEM ...
...TO KNOW THE *FRIEND* VERY WELL...
IF NOT A CALL TO ARMS...
THEN WHAT DID YOU INTEND TO BROADCAST FROM HERE?
WE NEED TO EVACUATE PEOPLE TO EXPO PARK.
TO SACRED GROUND... HM.
YOU SEEM TO KNOW THE *FRIEND* VERY WELL TOO.

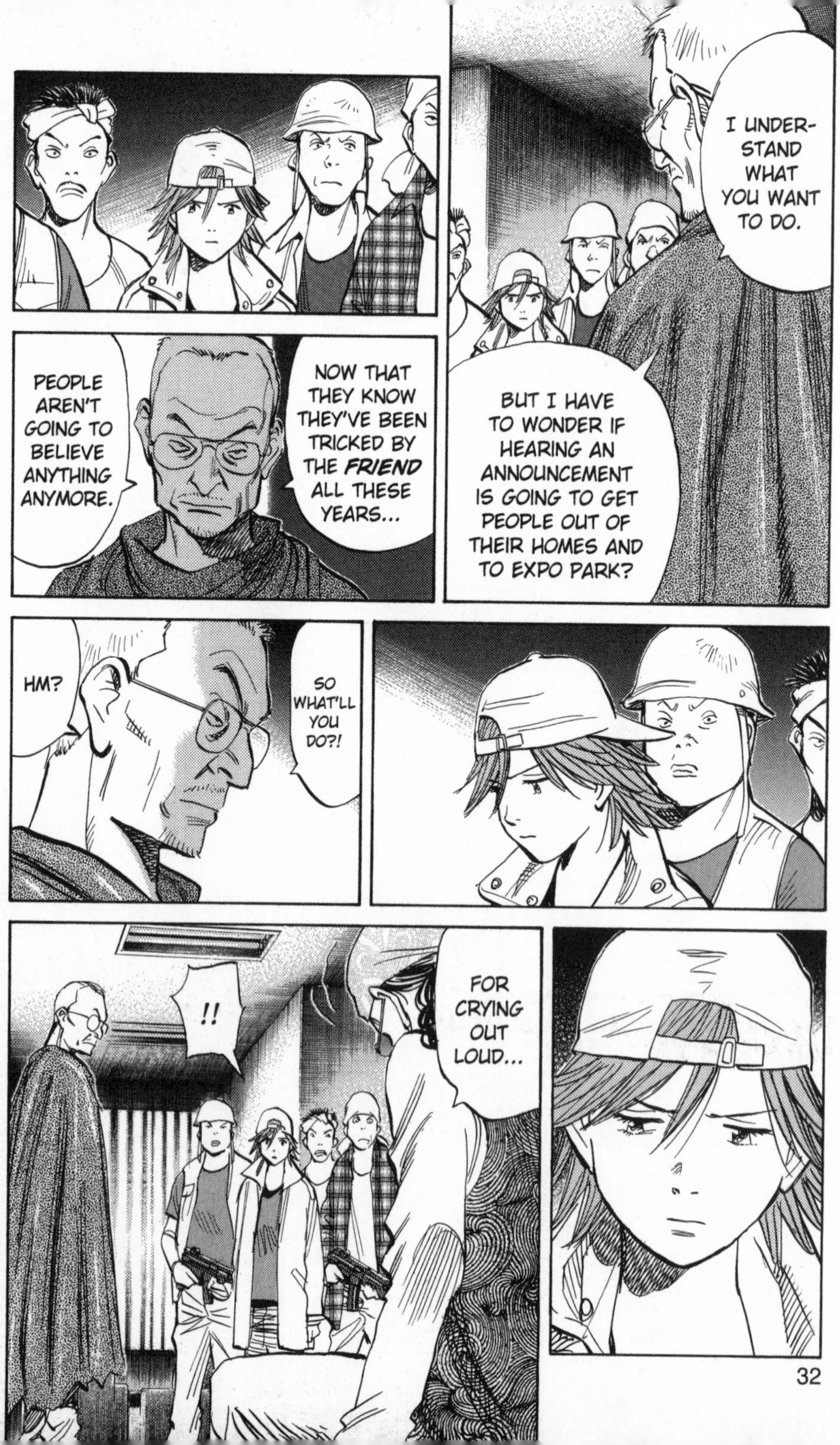
I UNDER-STAND WHAT YOU WANT TO DO.
BUT I HAVE TO WONDER IF HEARING AN ANNOUNCEMENT IS GOING TO GET PEOPLE OUT OF THEIR HOMES AND TO EXPO PARK?
NOW THAT THEY KNOW THEY'VE BEEN TRICKED BY THE *FRIEND* ALL THESE YEARS...
PEOPLE AREN'T GOING TO BELIEVE ANYTHING ANYMORE.
SO WHAT'LL YOU DO?!
HM?
FOR CRYING OUT LOUD...
!!

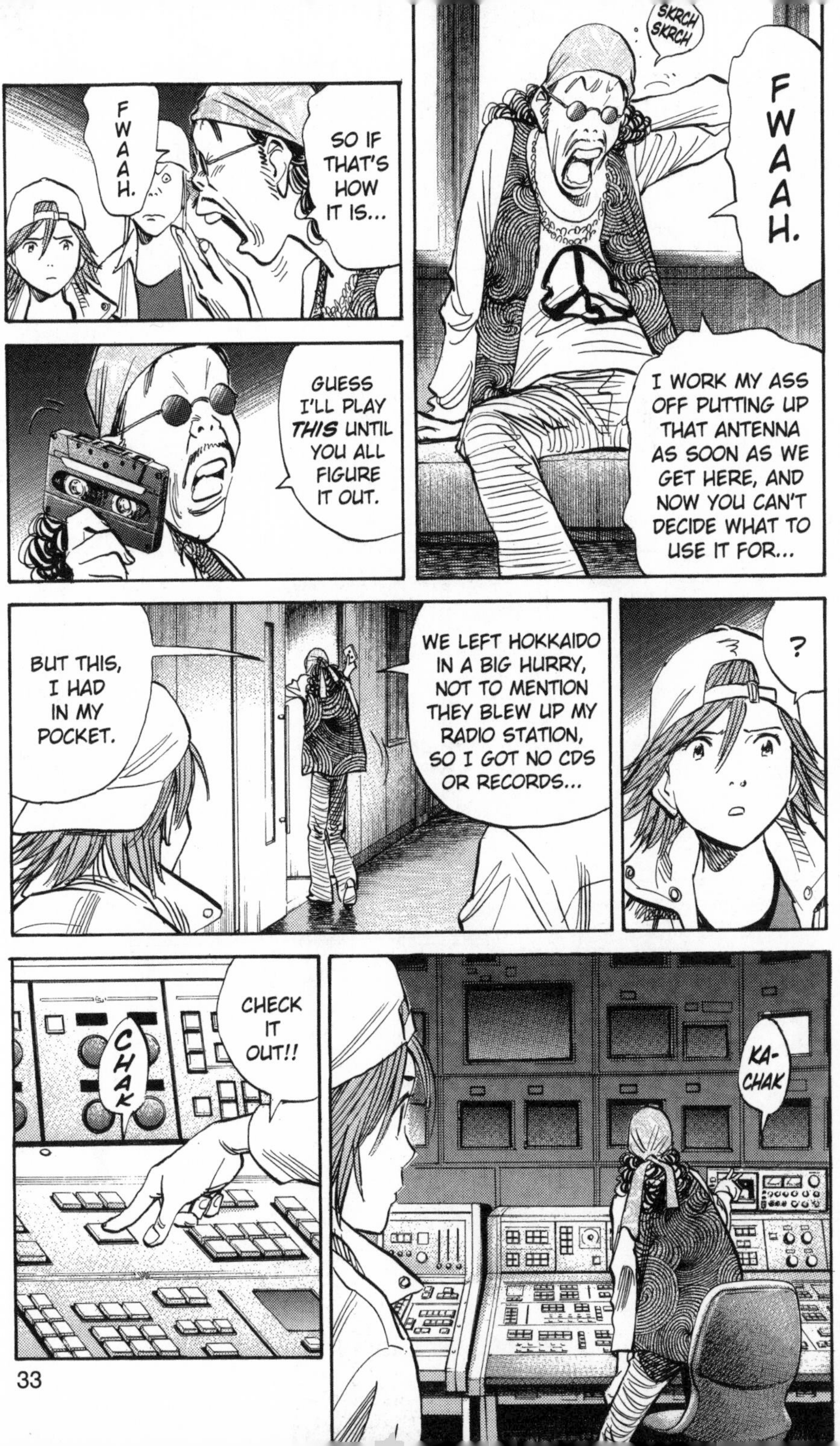
SKRCH SKRCH
FWAAH.
I WORK MY ASS OFF PUTTING UP THAT ANTENNA AS SOON AS WE GET HERE, AND NOW YOU CAN'T DECIDE WHAT TO USE IT FOR...
SO IF THAT'S HOW IT IS...
FWAAH.
GUESS I'LL PLAY *THIS* UNTIL YOU ALL FIGURE IT OUT.
?
WE LEFT HOKKAIDO IN A BIG HURRY, NOT TO MENTION THEY BLEW UP MY RADIO STATION, SO I GOT NO CDS OR RECORDS...
BUT THIS, I HAD IN MY POCKET.
KA-CHAK
CHECK IT OUT!!
CHAK

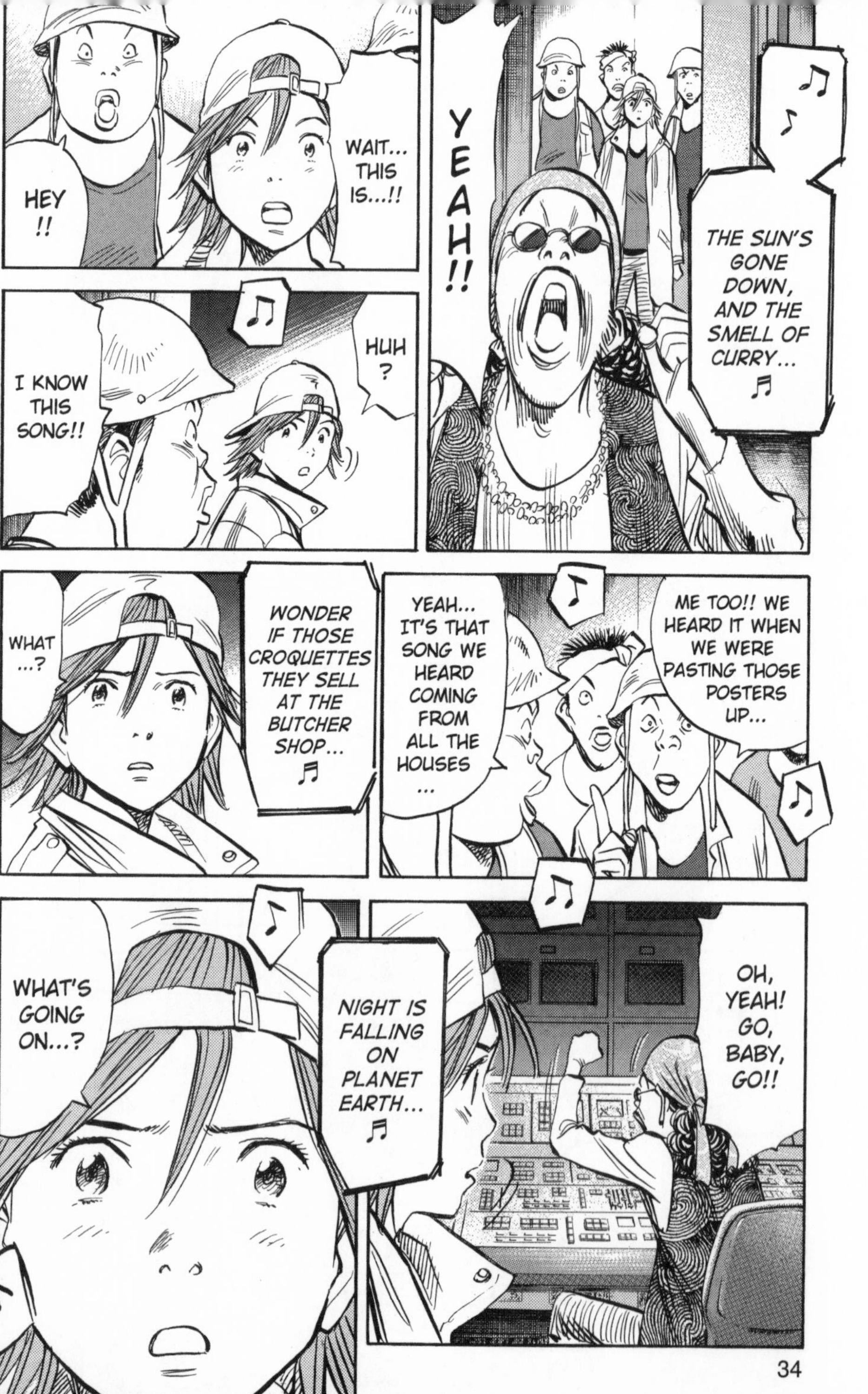
THE SUN'S GONE DOWN, AND THE SMELL OF CURRY...
YEAH!!
WAIT... THIS IS...!!
HEY!!
HUH?
I KNOW THIS SONG!!
ME TOO!! WE HEARD IT WHEN WE WERE PASTING THOSE POSTERS UP...
YEAH... IT'S THAT SONG WE HEARD COMING FROM ALL THE HOUSES...
WONDER IF THOSE CROQUETTES THEY SELL AT THE BUTCHER SHOP...
WHAT...?
OH, YEAH! GO, BABY, GO!!
NIGHT IS FALLING ON PLANET EARTH...
WHAT'S GOING ON...?

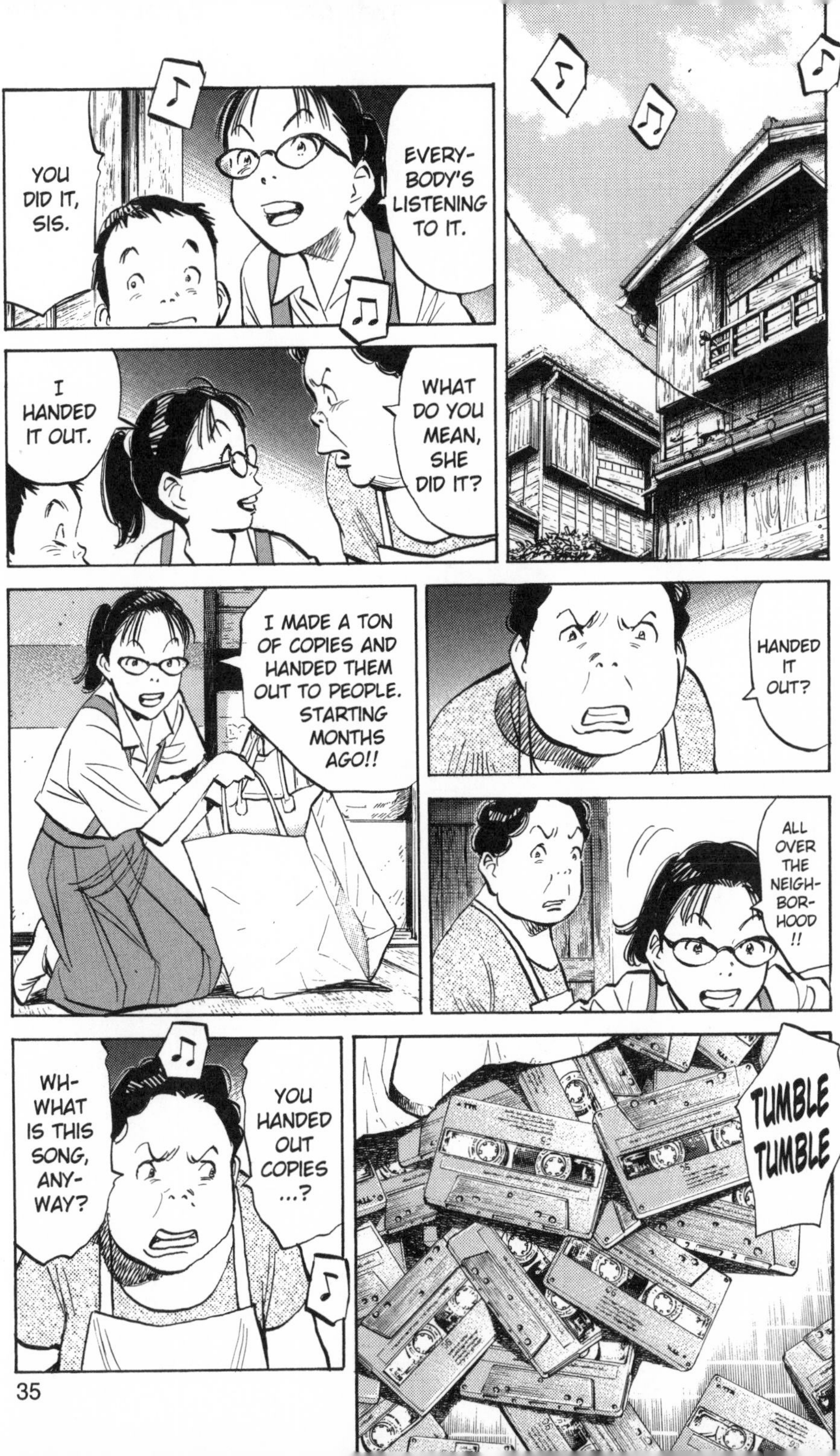
EVERY-BODY'S LISTENING TO IT.
YOU DID IT, SIS.
WHAT DO YOU MEAN, SHE DID IT?
I HANDED IT OUT.
HANDED IT OUT?
ALL OVER THE NEIGH-BOR-HOOD!!
I MADE A TON OF COPIES AND HANDED THEM OUT TO PEOPLE. STARTING MONTHS AGO!!
TUMBLE TUMBLE
YOU HANDED OUT COPIES ...?
WH-WHAT IS THIS SONG, ANY-WAY?

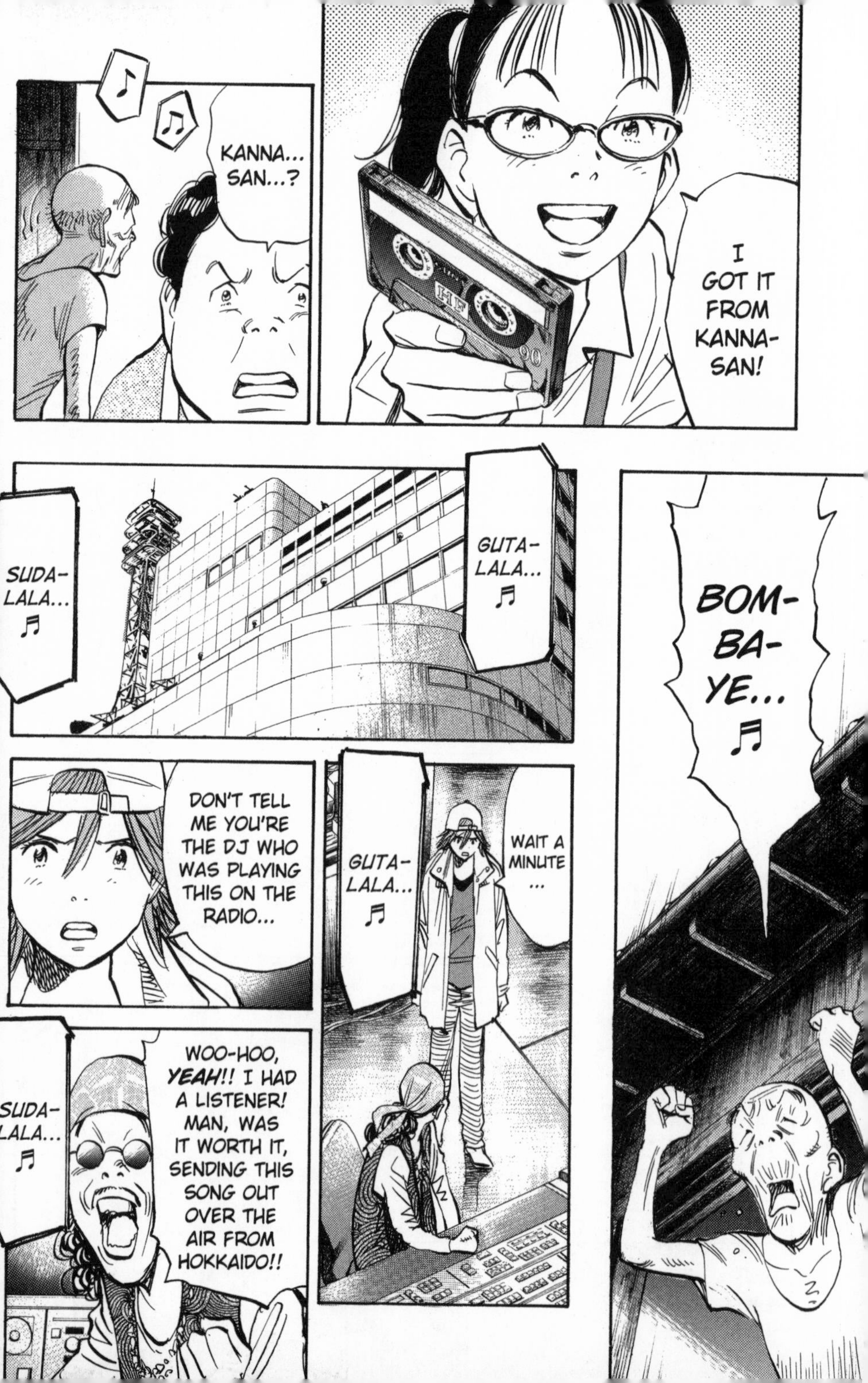

I GOT IT FROM KANNA-SAN!
KANNA... SAN...?
BOM-BA-YE... ♬
GUTA-LALA... ♬
SUDA-LALA... ♬
WAIT A MINUTE ...
GUTA-LALA... ♬
DON'T TELL ME YOU'RE THE DJ WHO WAS PLAYING THIS ON THE RADIO...
WOO-HOO, ***YEAH***!! I HAD A LISTENER! MAN, WAS IT WORTH IT, SENDING THIS SONG OUT OVER THE AIR FROM HOKKAIDO!!
SUDA-LALA... ♬

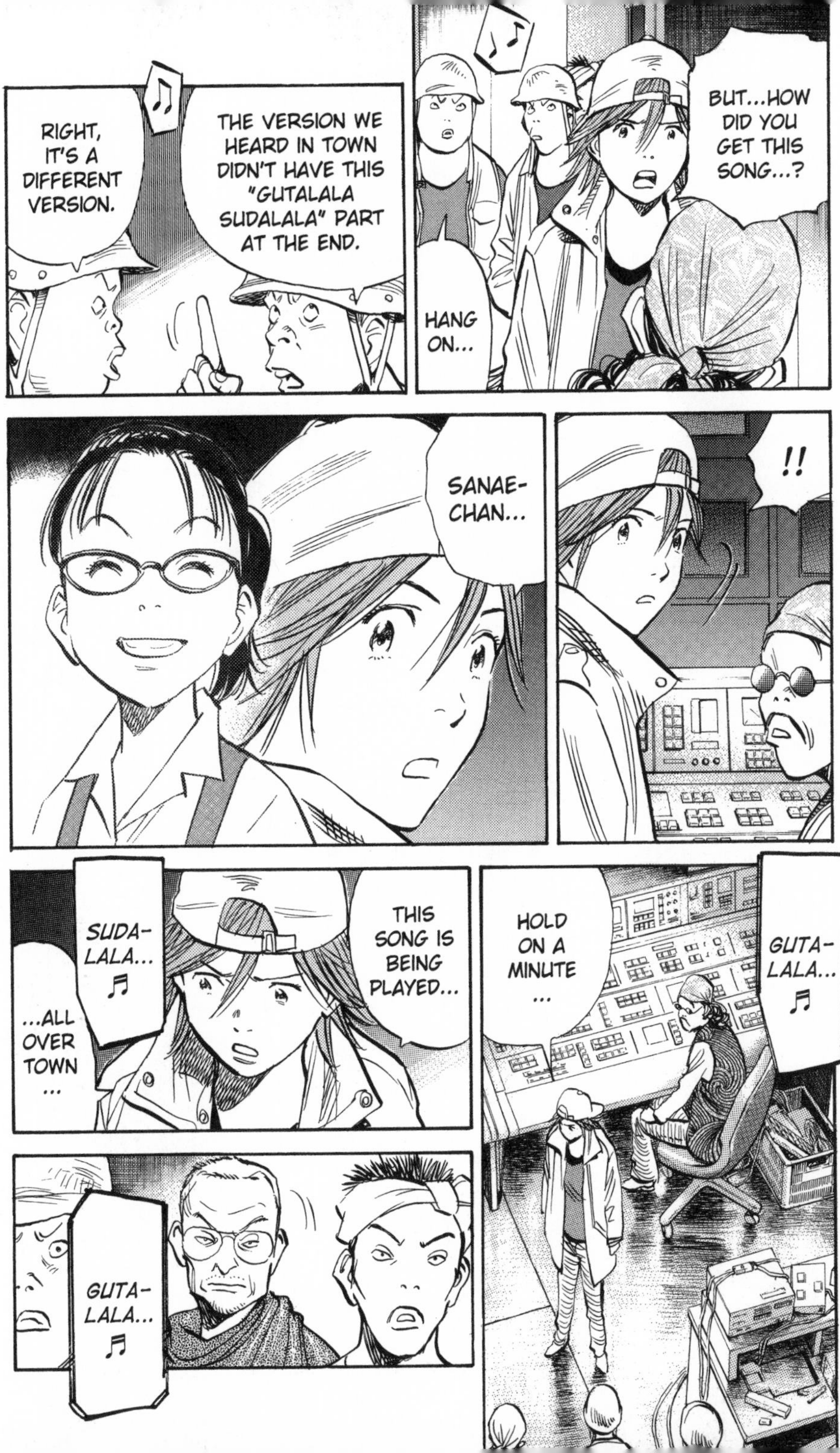
BUT...HOW DID YOU GET THIS SONG...?
HANG ON...
THE VERSION WE HEARD IN TOWN DIDN'T HAVE THIS "GUTALALA SUDALALA" PART AT THE END.
RIGHT, IT'S A DIFFERENT VERSION.
!!
SANAE-CHAN...
GUTA-LALA... ♬
HOLD ON A MINUTE ...
THIS SONG IS BEING PLAYED...
SUDA-LALA... ♬
...ALL OVER TOWN ...
GUTA-LALA... ♬

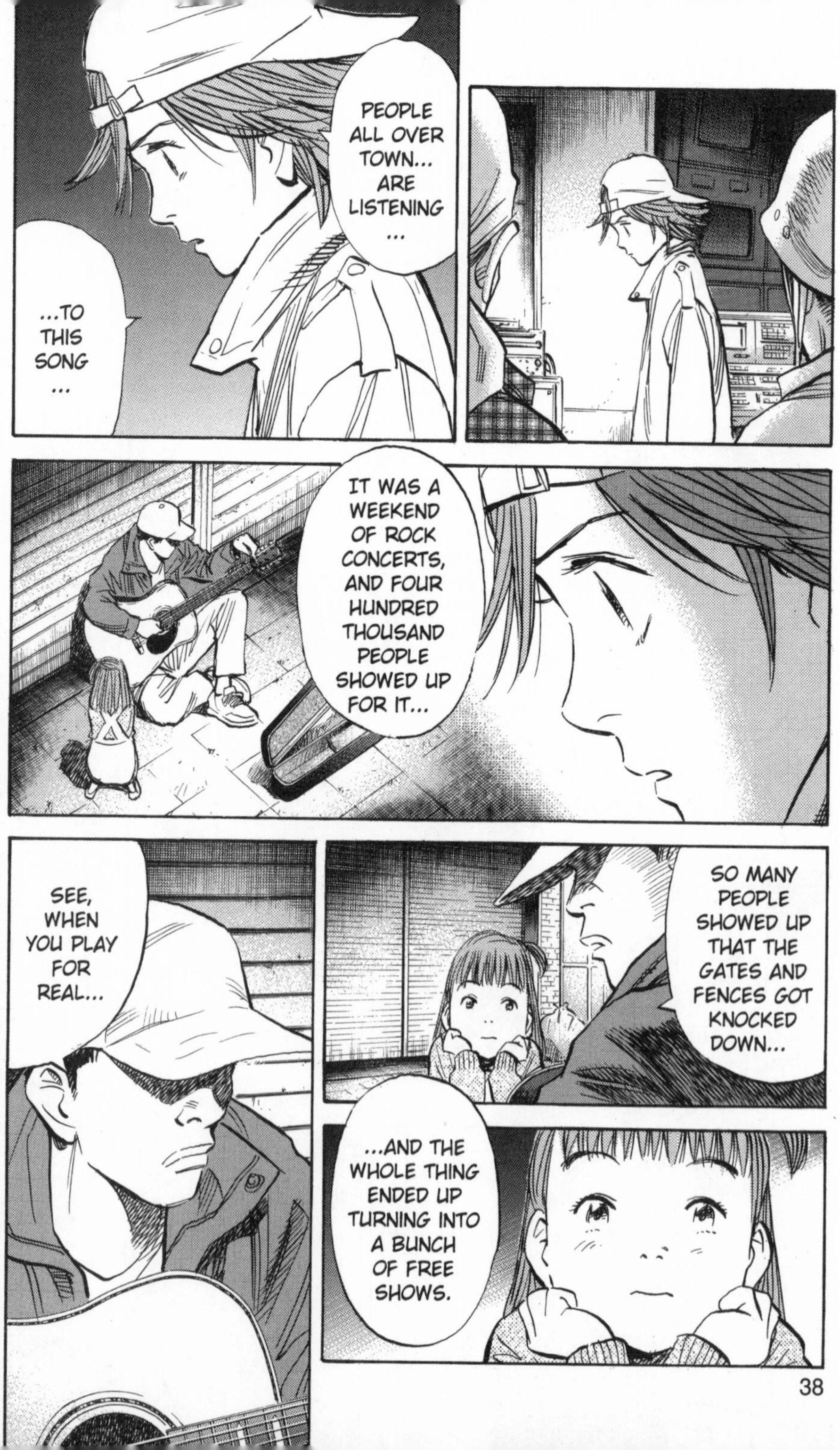
PEOPLE ALL OVER TOWN... ARE LISTENING...
...TO THIS SONG...
IT WAS A WEEKEND OF ROCK CONCERTS, AND FOUR HUNDRED THOUSAND PEOPLE SHOWED UP FOR IT...
SO MANY PEOPLE SHOWED UP THAT THE GATES AND FENCES GOT KNOCKED DOWN...
...AND THE WHOLE THING ENDED UP TURNING INTO A BUNCH OF FREE SHOWS.
SEE, WHEN YOU PLAY FOR REAL...

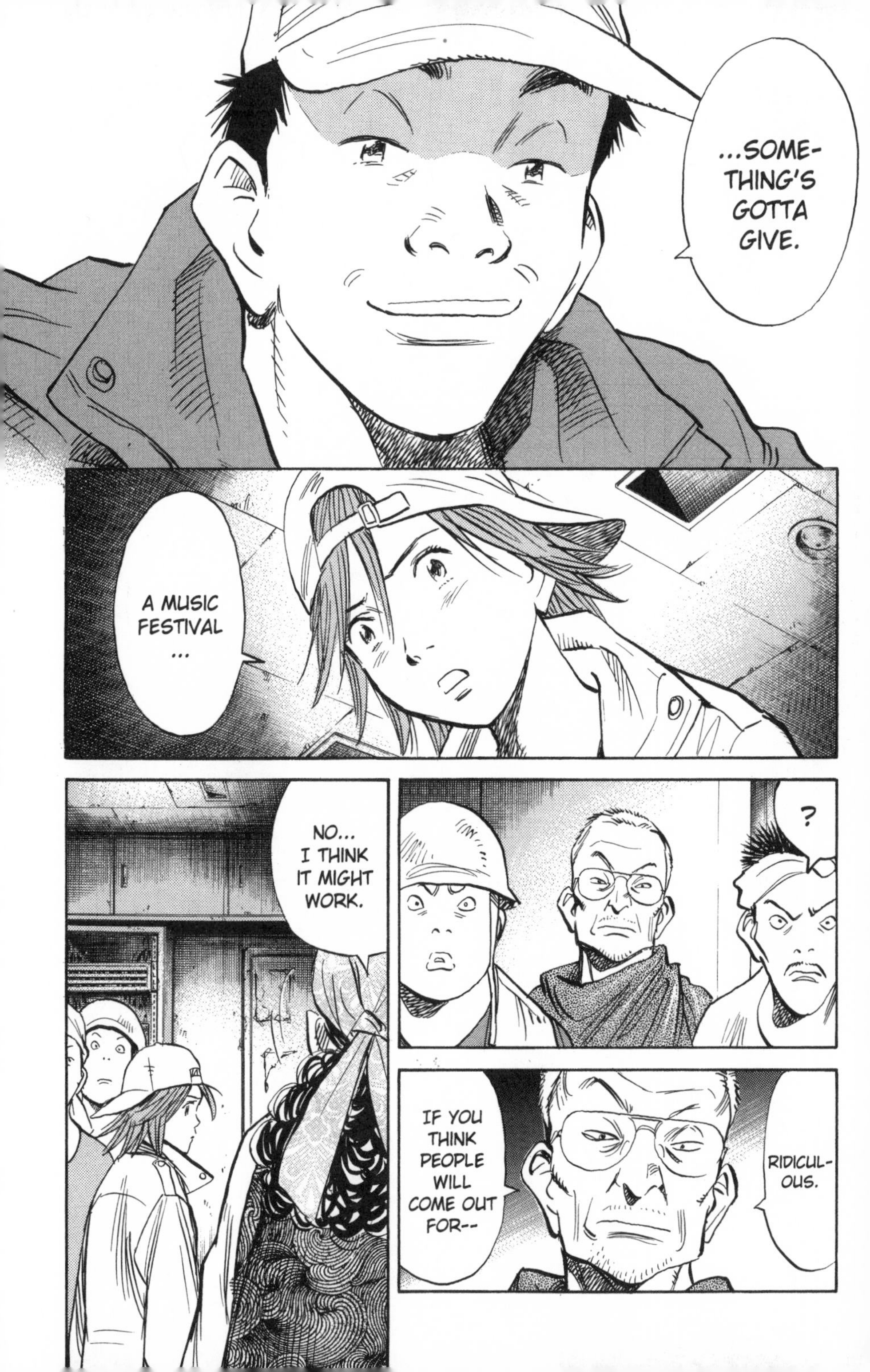
...SOME-THING'S GOTTA GIVE.
A MUSIC FESTIVAL ...
?
RIDICUL-OUS.
IF YOU THINK PEOPLE WILL COME OUT FOR--
NO... I THINK IT MIGHT WORK.

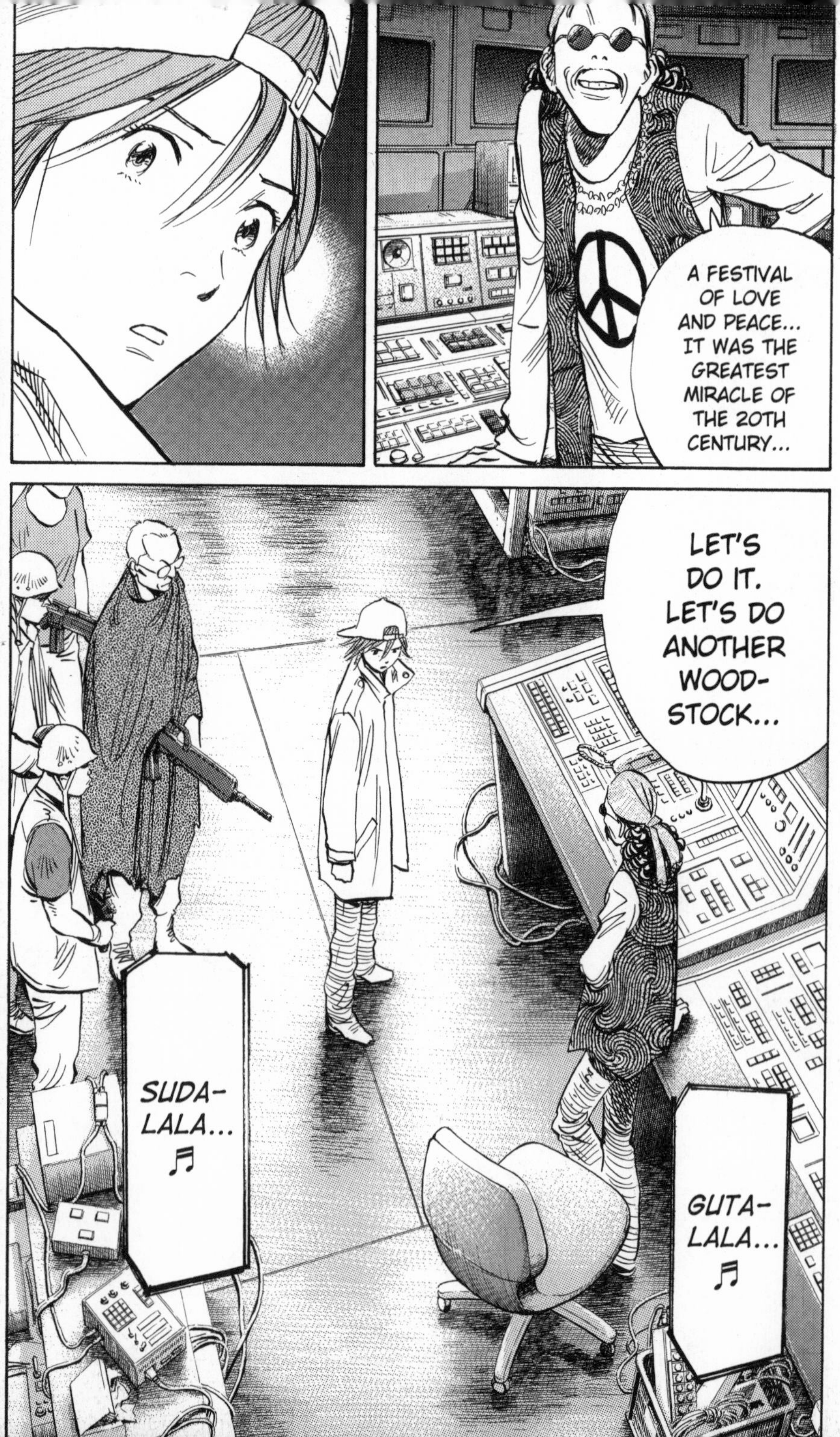
A FESTIVAL OF LOVE AND PEACE... IT WAS THE GREATEST MIRACLE OF THE 20TH CENTURY...
LET'S DO IT. LET'S DO ANOTHER WOOD-STOCK...
SUDA-LALA... ♬
GUTA-LALA... ♬

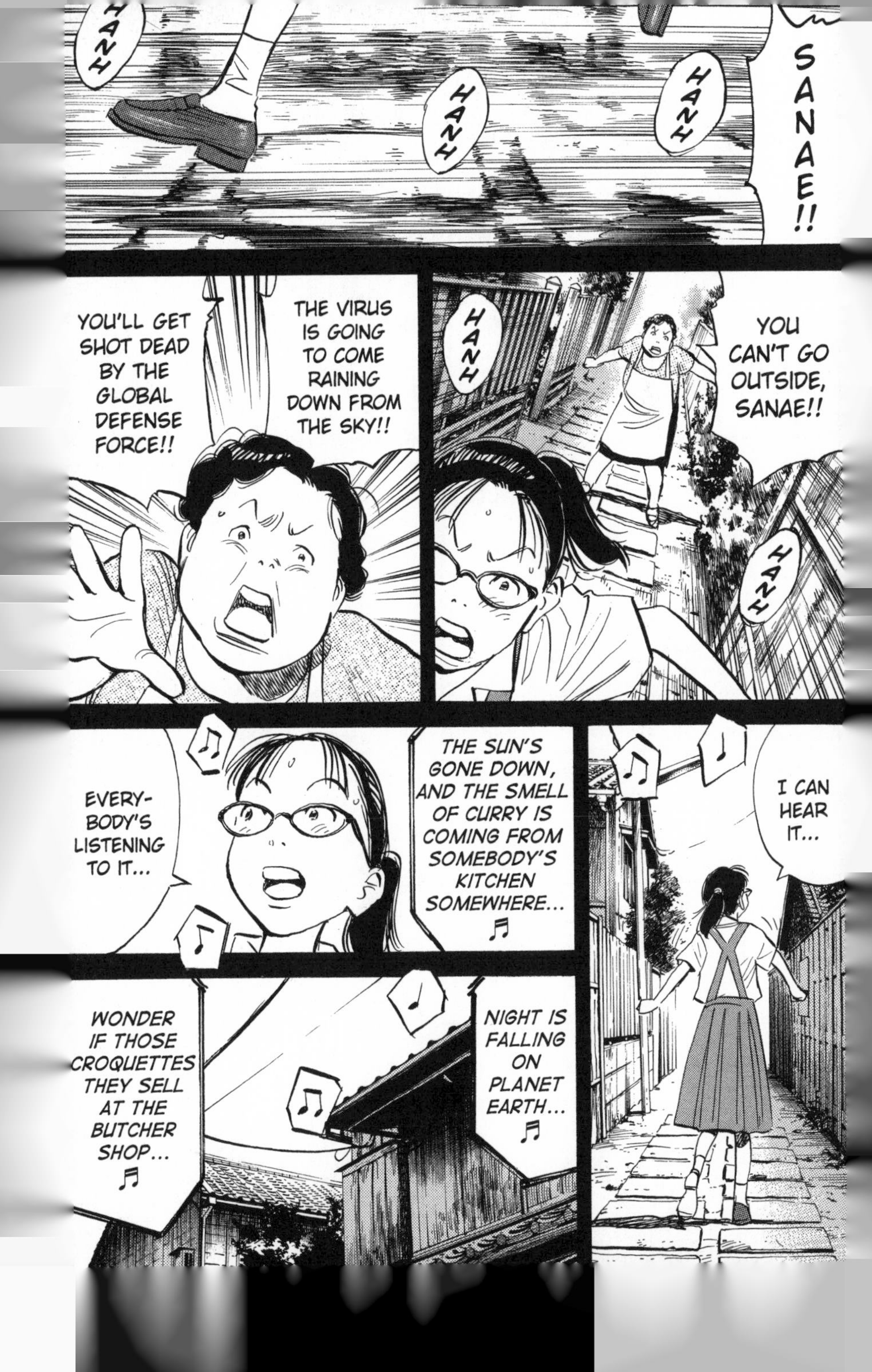
SANAE!!
HANH
HANH
HANH
YOU CAN'T GO OUTSIDE, SANAE!!
HANH
HANH
THE VIRUS IS GOING TO COME RAINING DOWN FROM THE SKY!!
YOU'LL GET SHOT DEAD BY THE GLOBAL DEFENSE FORCE!!
I CAN HEAR IT...
THE SUN'S GONE DOWN, AND THE SMELL OF CURRY IS COMING FROM SOMEBODY'S KITCHEN SOMEWHERE... ♬
EVERY-BODY'S LISTENING TO IT...
NIGHT IS FALLING ON PLANET EARTH... ♬
WONDER IF THOSE CROQUETTES THEY SELL AT THE BUTCHER SHOP... ♬

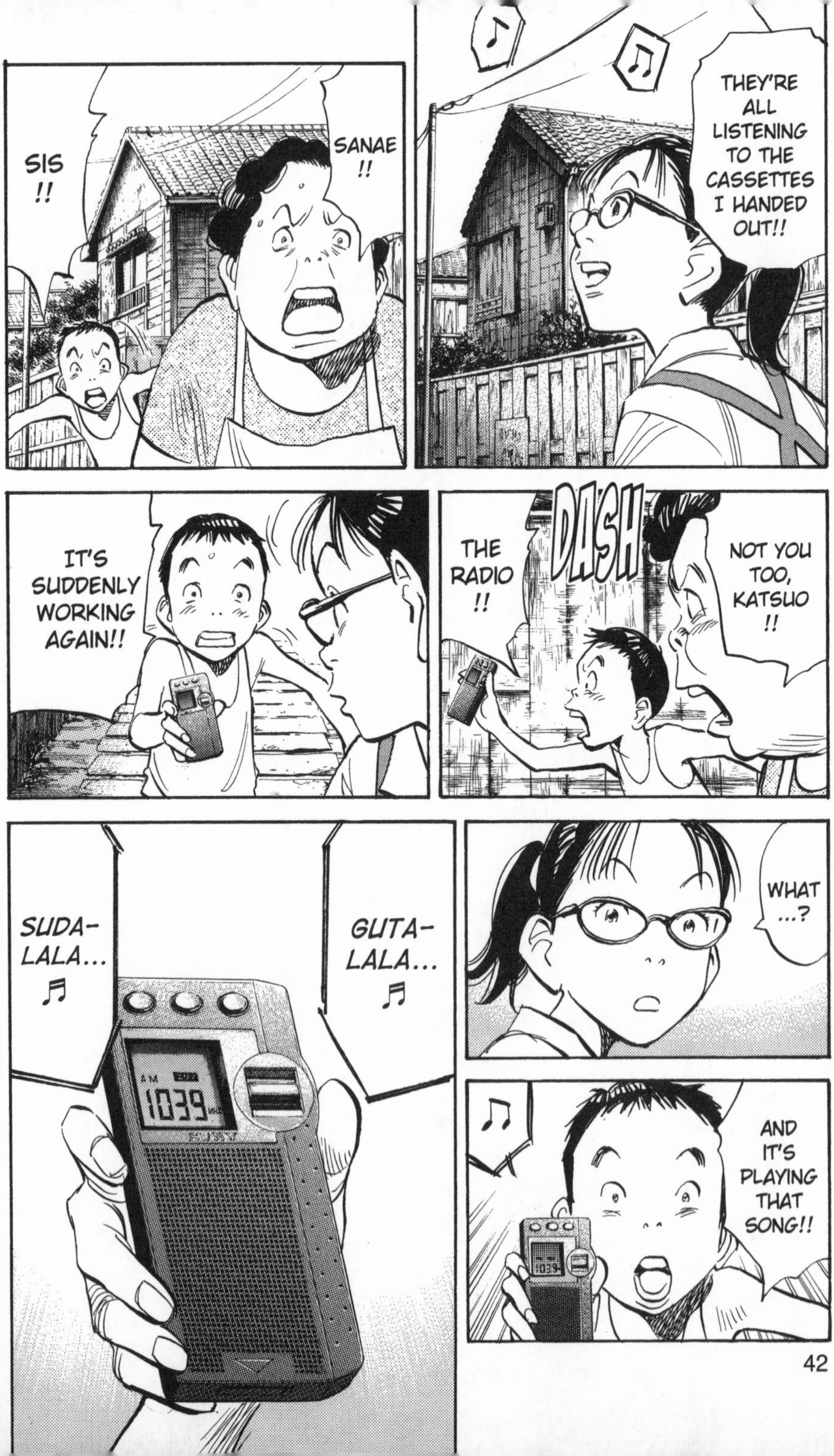
THEY'RE ALL LISTENING TO THE CASSETTES I HANDED OUT!!
SANAE !!
SIS !!
NOT YOU TOO, KATSUO !!
DASH
THE RADIO !!
IT'S SUDDENLY WORKING AGAIN!!
WHAT ...?
AND IT'S PLAYING THAT SONG!!
GUTA-LALA...
SUDA-LALA...

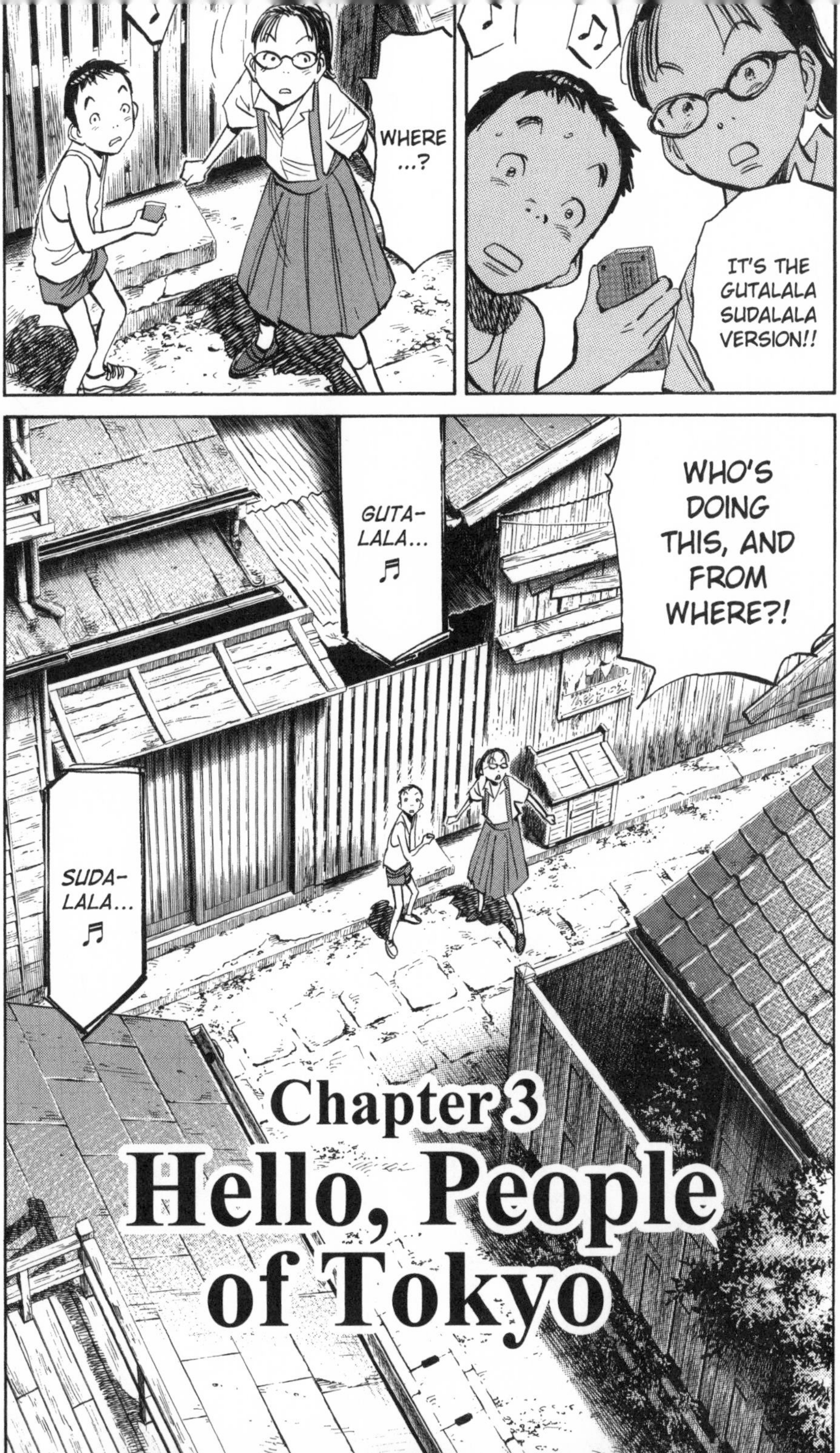
IT'S THE GUTALALA SUDALALA VERSION!!
WHERE ...?
WHO'S DOING THIS, AND FROM WHERE?!
GUTA-LALA... ♬
SUDA-LALA... ♬
Chapter 3
Hello, People of Tokyo

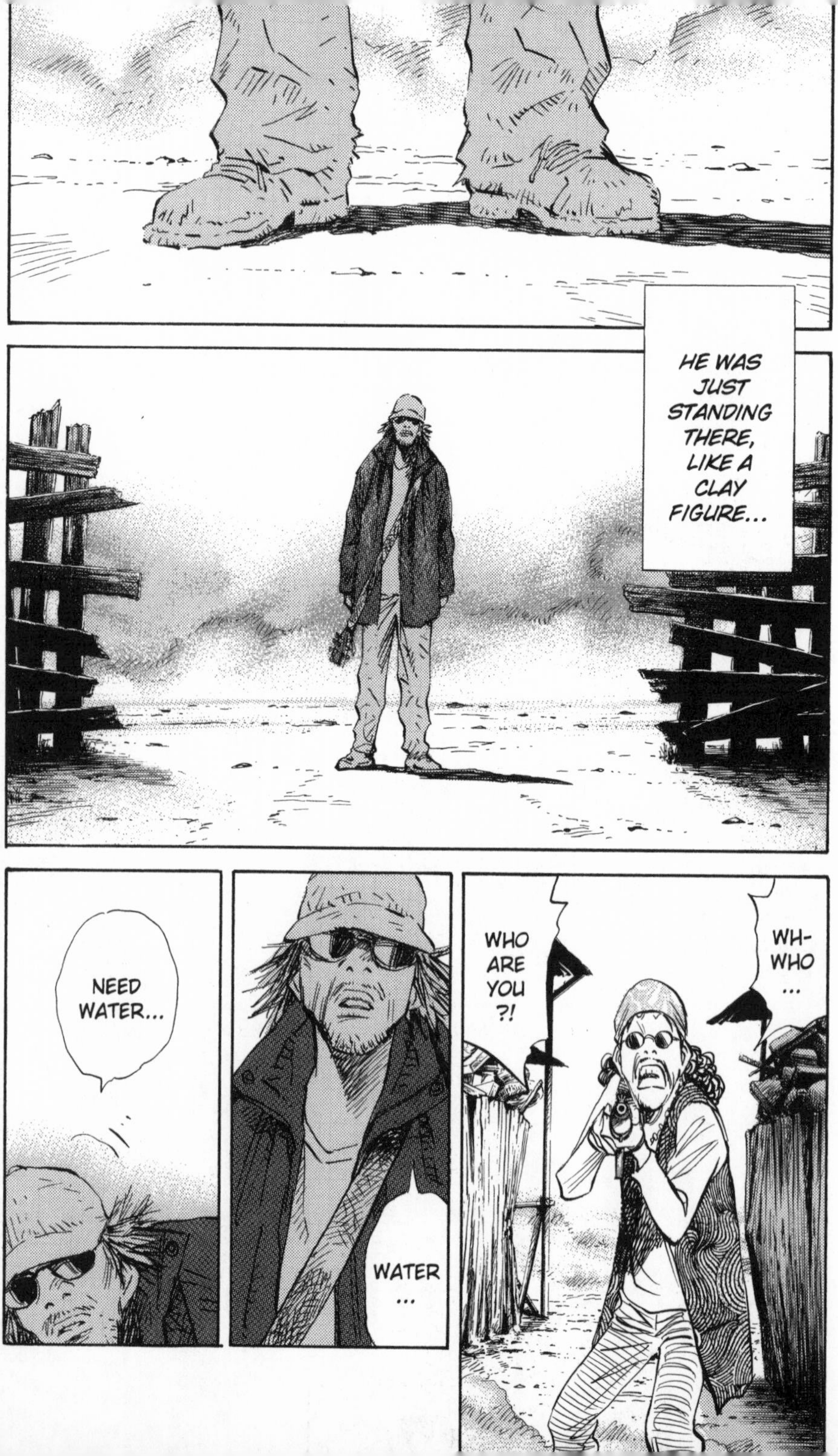
HE WAS JUST STANDING THERE, LIKE A CLAY FIGURE...
WH- WHO ...
WHO ARE YOU ?!
WATER ...
NEED WATER...

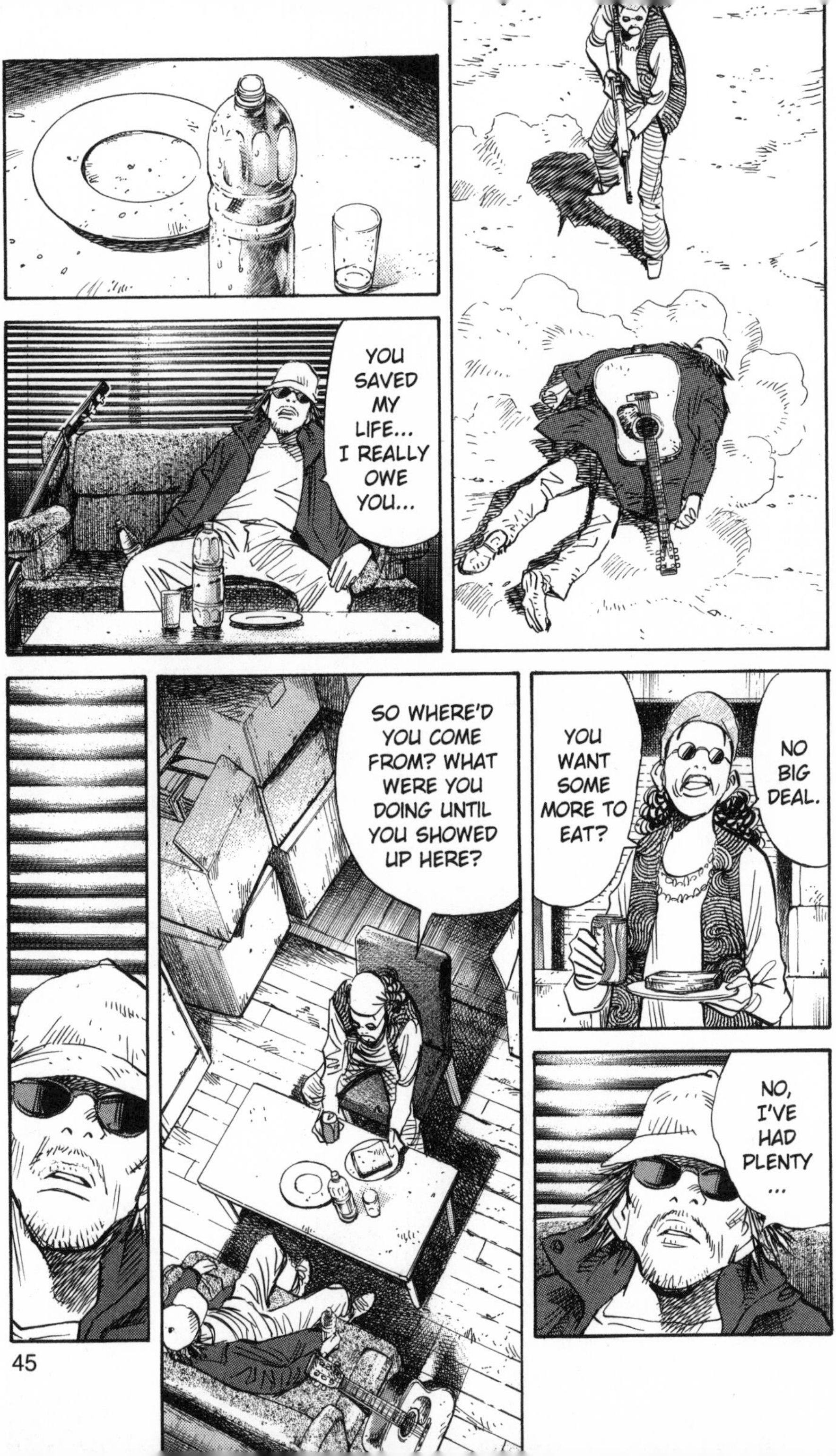
YOU SAVED MY LIFE... I REALLY OWE YOU...
NO BIG DEAL.
YOU WANT SOME MORE TO EAT?
NO, I'VE HAD PLENTY ...
SO WHERE'D YOU COME FROM? WHAT WERE YOU DOING UNTIL YOU SHOWED UP HERE?

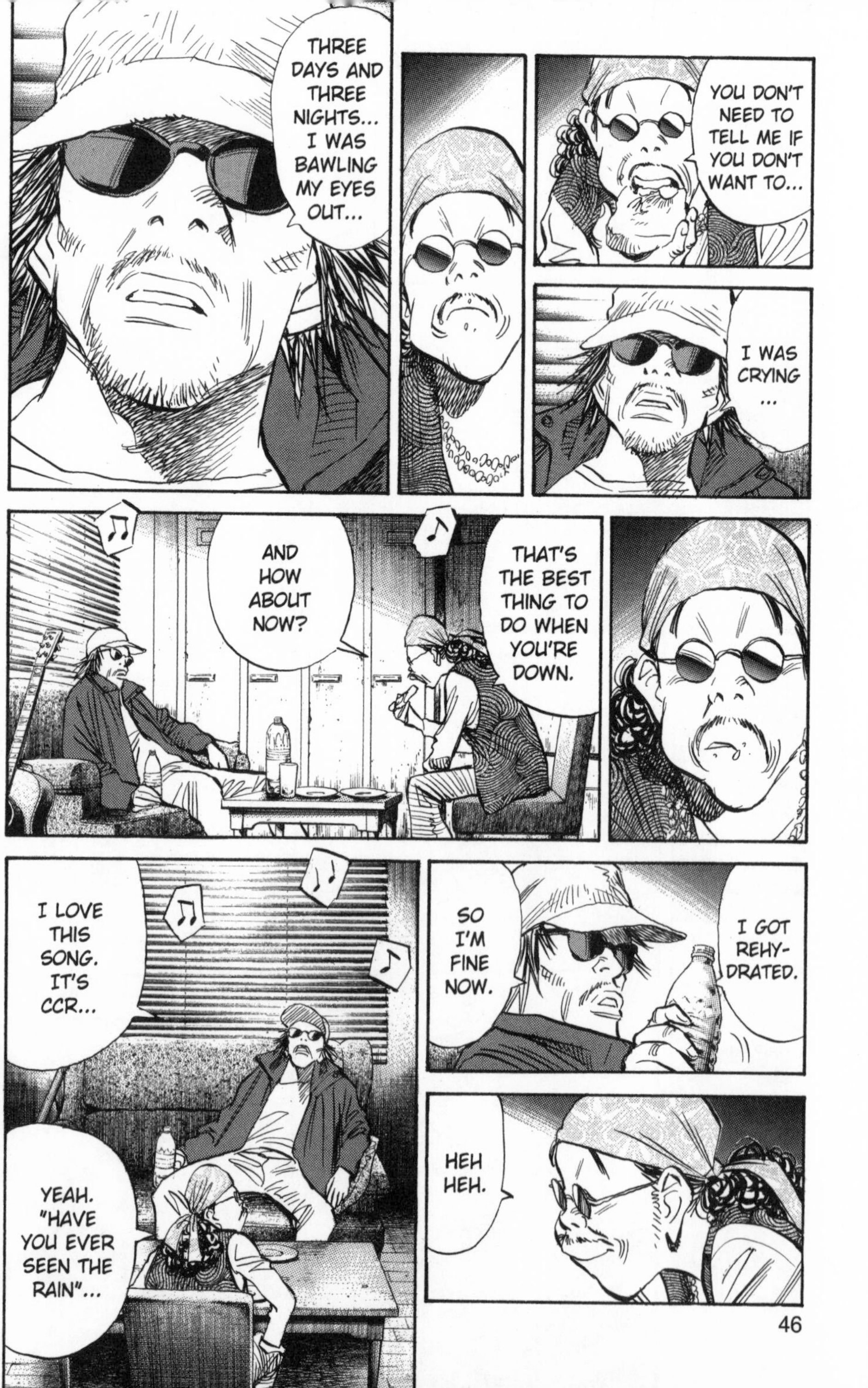
YOU DON'T NEED TO TELL ME IF YOU DON'T WANT TO...
I WAS CRYING ...
THREE DAYS AND THREE NIGHTS... I WAS BAWLING MY EYES OUT...
♫
♪
THAT'S THE BEST THING TO DO WHEN YOU'RE DOWN.
AND HOW ABOUT NOW?
I GOT REHY-DRATED.
SO I'M FINE NOW.
HEH HEH.
♪
♫
♪
I LOVE THIS SONG. IT'S CCR...
YEAH. "HAVE YOU EVER SEEN THE RAIN"...

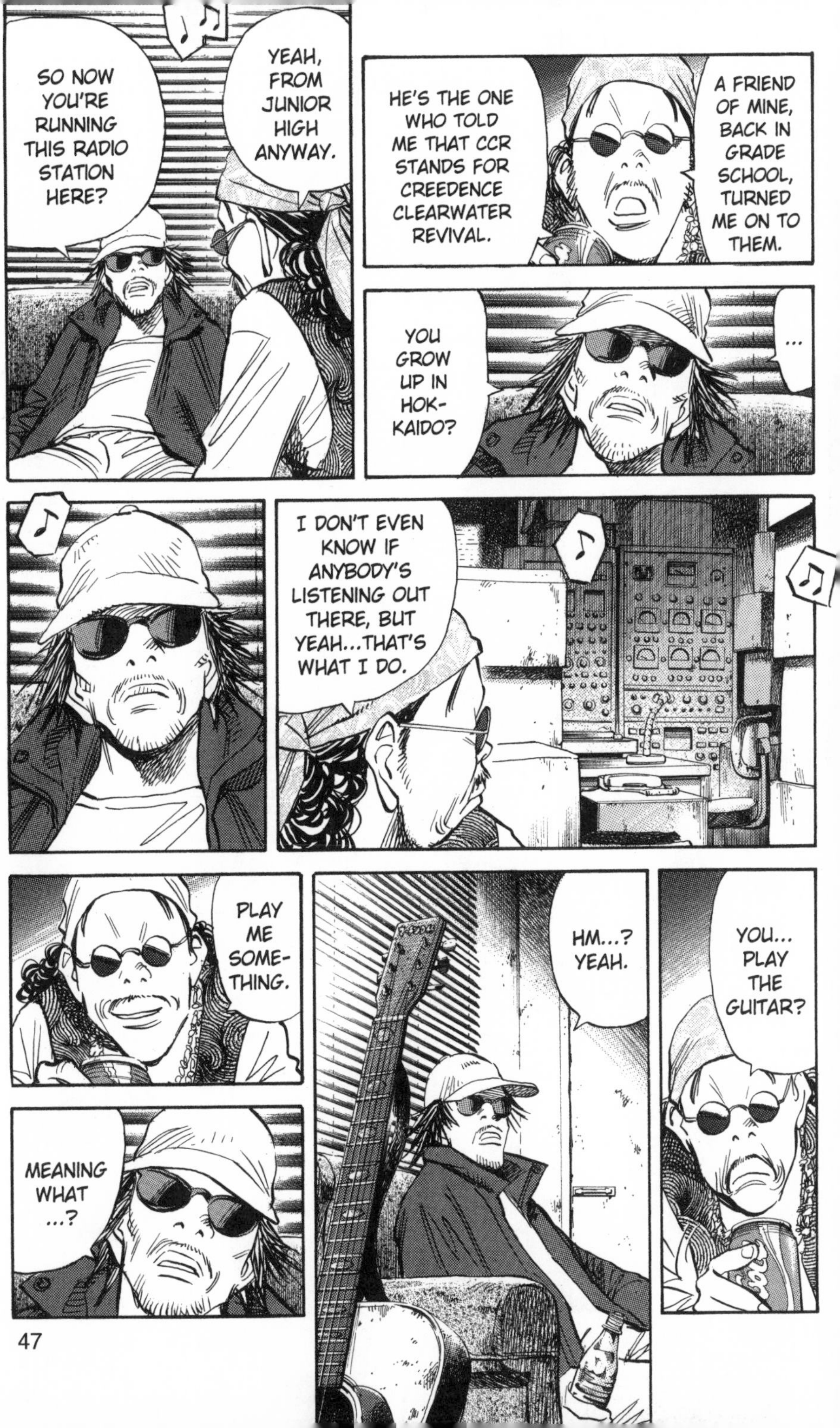
A FRIEND OF MINE, BACK IN GRADE SCHOOL, TURNED ME ON TO THEM.
HE'S THE ONE WHO TOLD ME THAT CCR STANDS FOR CREEDENCE CLEARWATER REVIVAL.
...
YOU GROW UP IN HOK-KAIDO?
YEAH, FROM JUNIOR HIGH ANYWAY.
SO NOW YOU'RE RUNNING THIS RADIO STATION HERE?
I DON'T EVEN KNOW IF ANYBODY'S LISTENING OUT THERE, BUT YEAH...THAT'S WHAT I DO.
YOU... PLAY THE GUITAR?
HM...? YEAH.
PLAY ME SOME-THING.
MEANING WHAT ...?

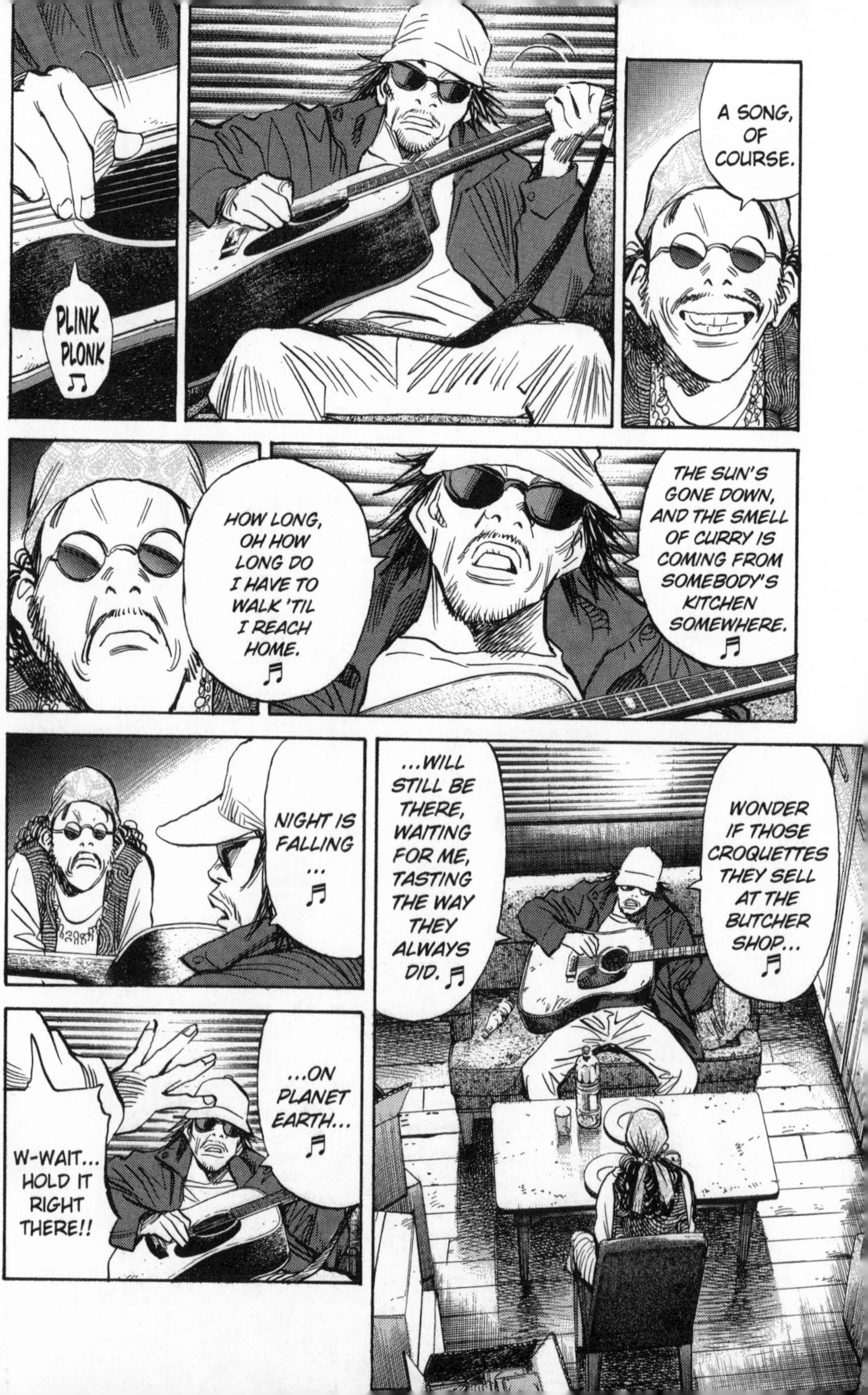
A SONG, OF COURSE.
PLINK PLONK ♫
THE SUN'S GONE DOWN, AND THE SMELL OF CURRY IS COMING FROM SOMEBODY'S KITCHEN SOMEWHERE. ♬
HOW LONG, OH HOW LONG DO I HAVE TO WALK 'TIL I REACH HOME. ♬
WONDER IF THOSE CROQUETTES THEY SELL AT THE BUTCHER SHOP... ♬
...WILL STILL BE THERE, WAITING FOR ME, TASTING THE WAY THEY ALWAYS DID. ♬
NIGHT IS FALLING ... ♬
...ON PLANET EARTH... ♬
W-WAIT... HOLD IT RIGHT THERE!!

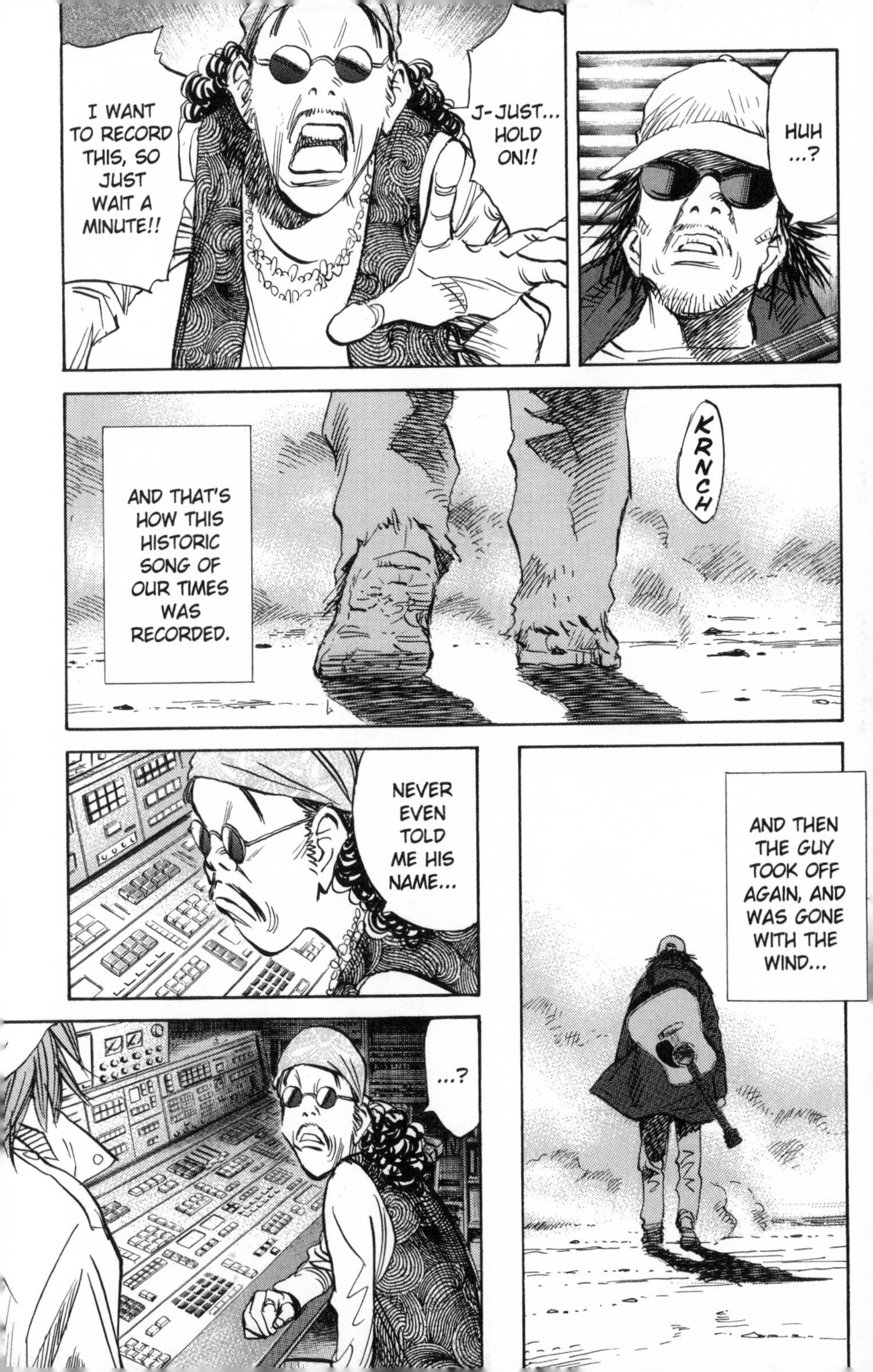
HUH ...?
J-JUST... HOLD ON!!
I WANT TO RECORD THIS, SO JUST WAIT A MINUTE!!
KRNCH
AND THAT'S HOW THIS HISTORIC SONG OF OUR TIMES WAS RECORDED.
AND THEN THE GUY TOOK OFF AGAIN, AND WAS GONE WITH THE WIND...
NEVER EVEN TOLD ME HIS NAME...
...?

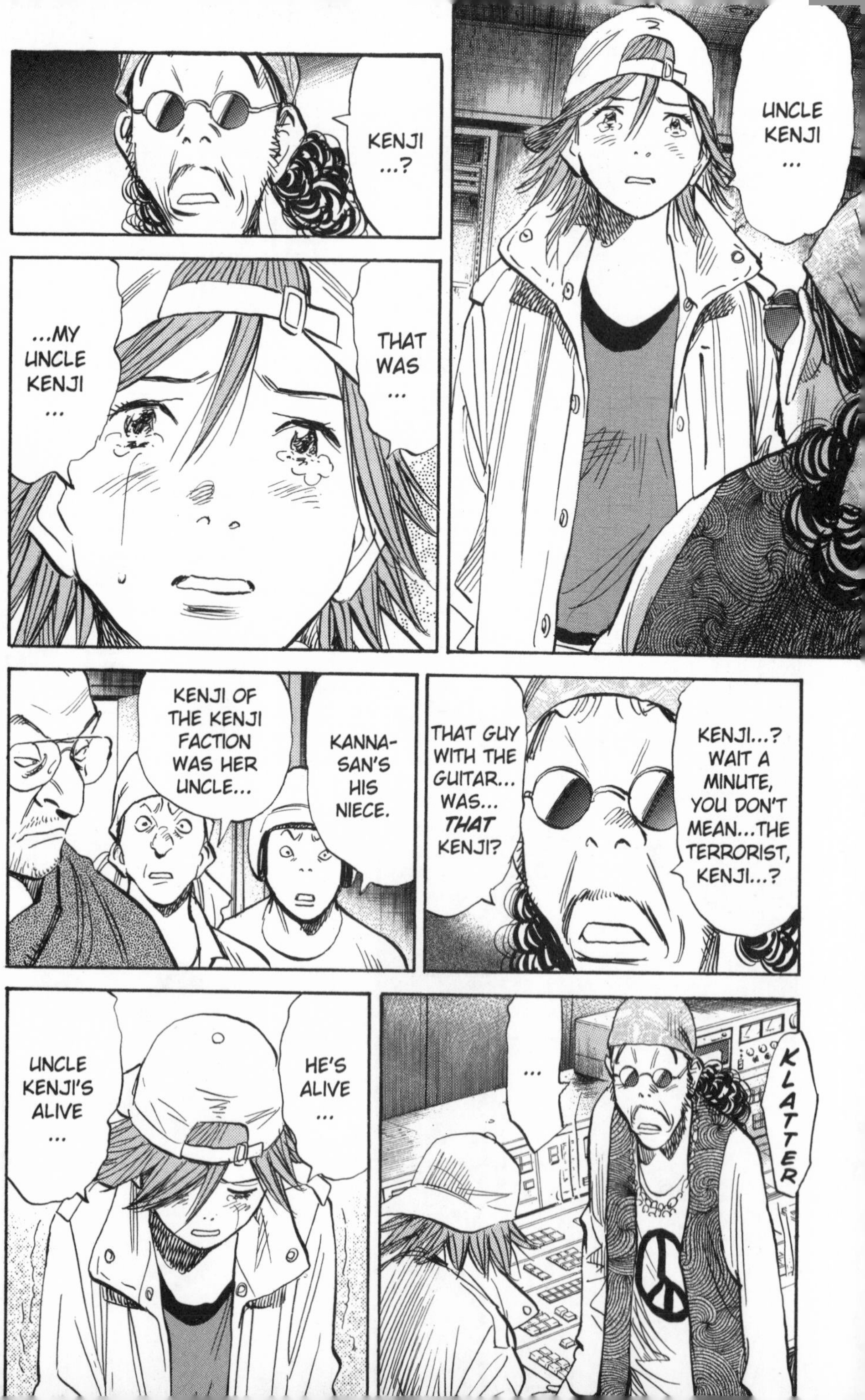
UNCLE KENJI ...
KENJI ...?
THAT WAS ...
...MY UNCLE KENJI ...
KENJI...? WAIT A MINUTE, YOU DON'T MEAN...THE TERRORIST, KENJI...?
THAT GUY WITH THE GUITAR... WAS... *THAT* KENJI?
KANNA-SAN'S HIS NIECE.
KENJI OF THE KENJI FACTION WAS HER UNCLE...
KLATTER
...
HE'S ALIVE ...
UNCLE KENJI'S ALIVE ...

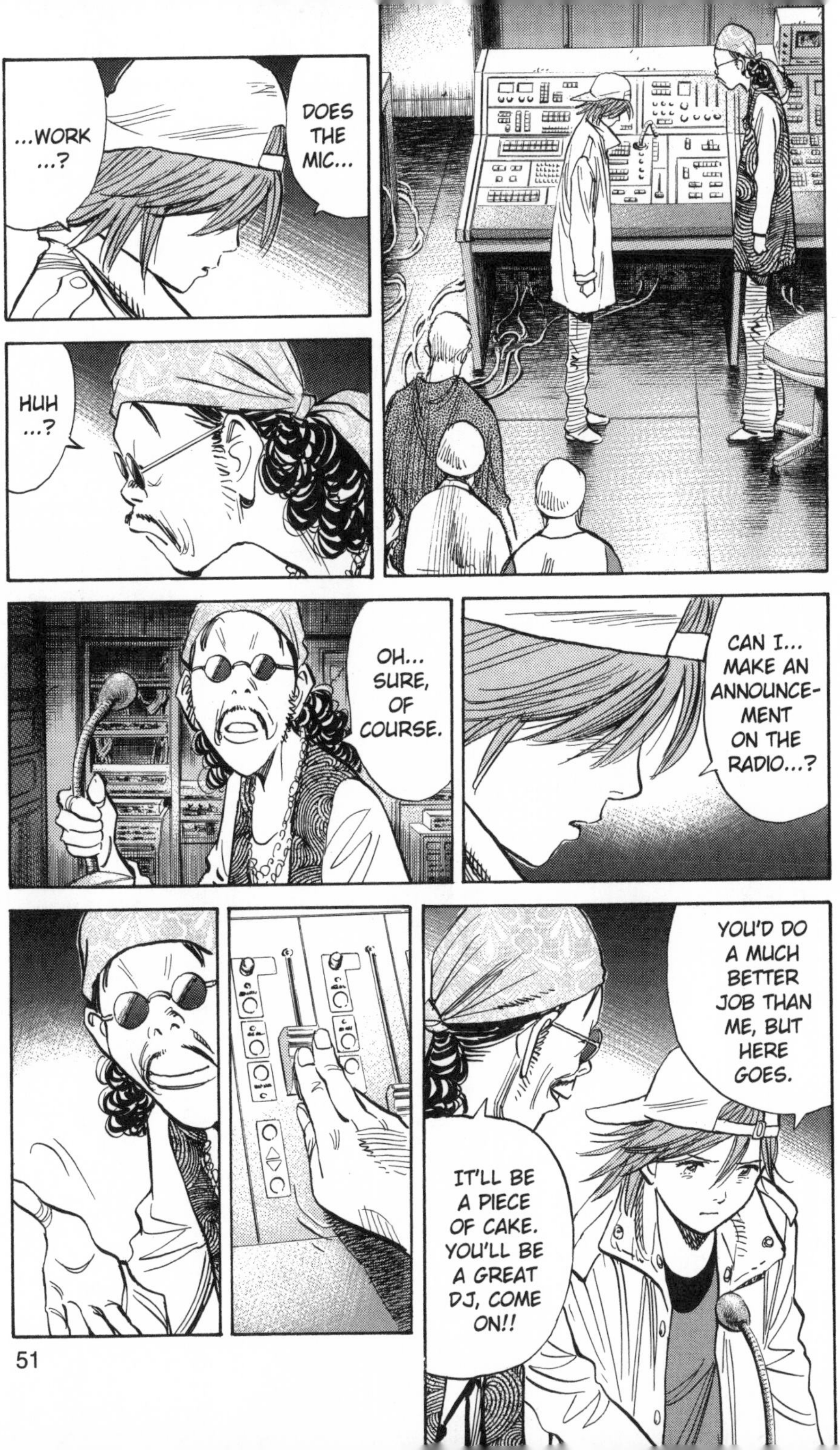
DOES THE MIC...
...WORK ...?
HUH ...?
CAN I... MAKE AN ANNOUNCEMENT ON THE RADIO...?
OH... SURE, OF COURSE.
YOU'D DO A MUCH BETTER JOB THAN ME, BUT HERE GOES.
IT'LL BE A PIECE OF CAKE. YOU'LL BE A GREAT DJ, COME ON!!

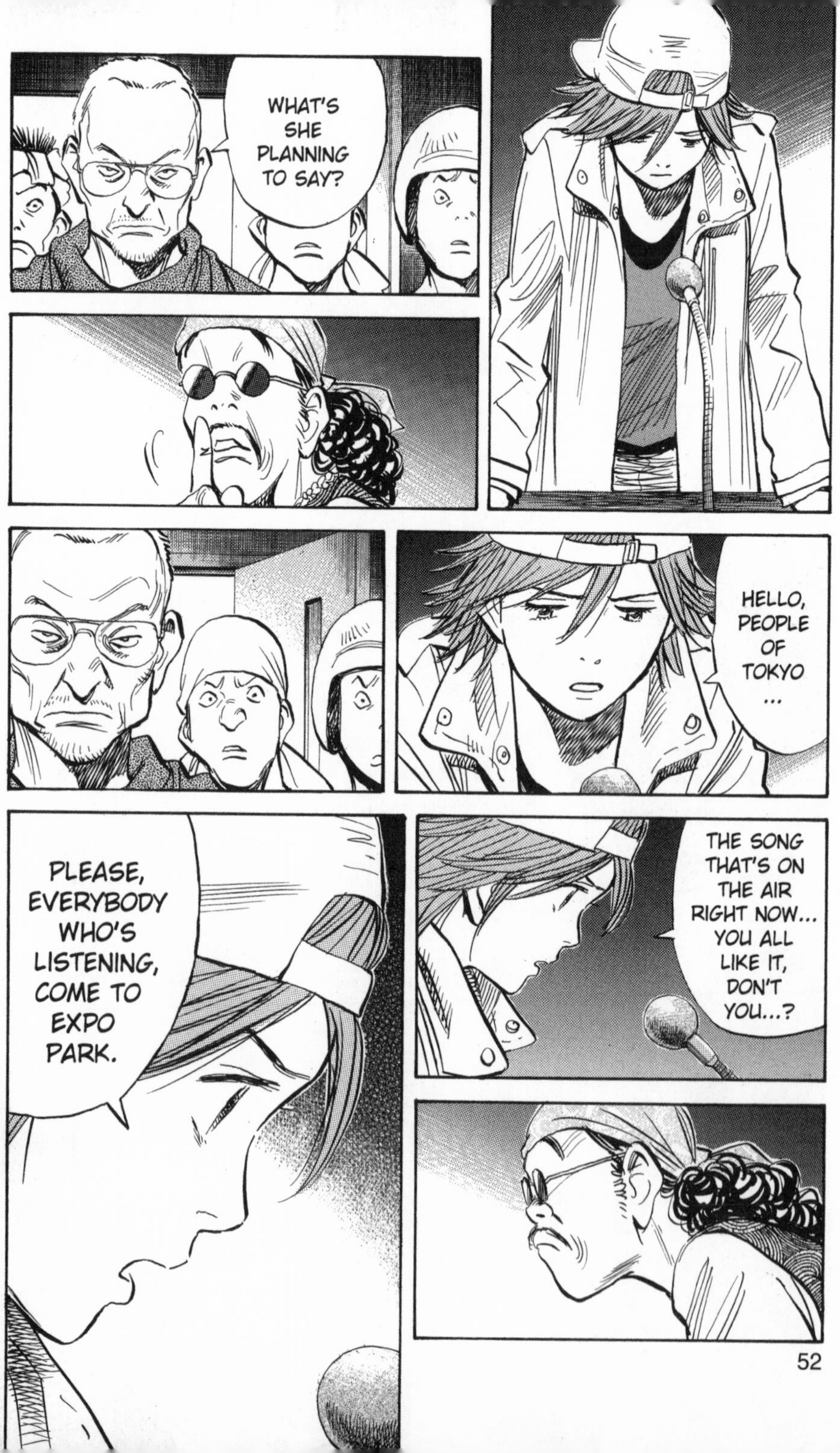
WHAT'S SHE PLANNING TO SAY?
HELLO, PEOPLE OF TOKYO ...
THE SONG THAT'S ON THE AIR RIGHT NOW... YOU ALL LIKE IT, DON'T YOU...?
PLEASE, EVERYBODY WHO'S LISTENING, COME TO EXPO PARK.

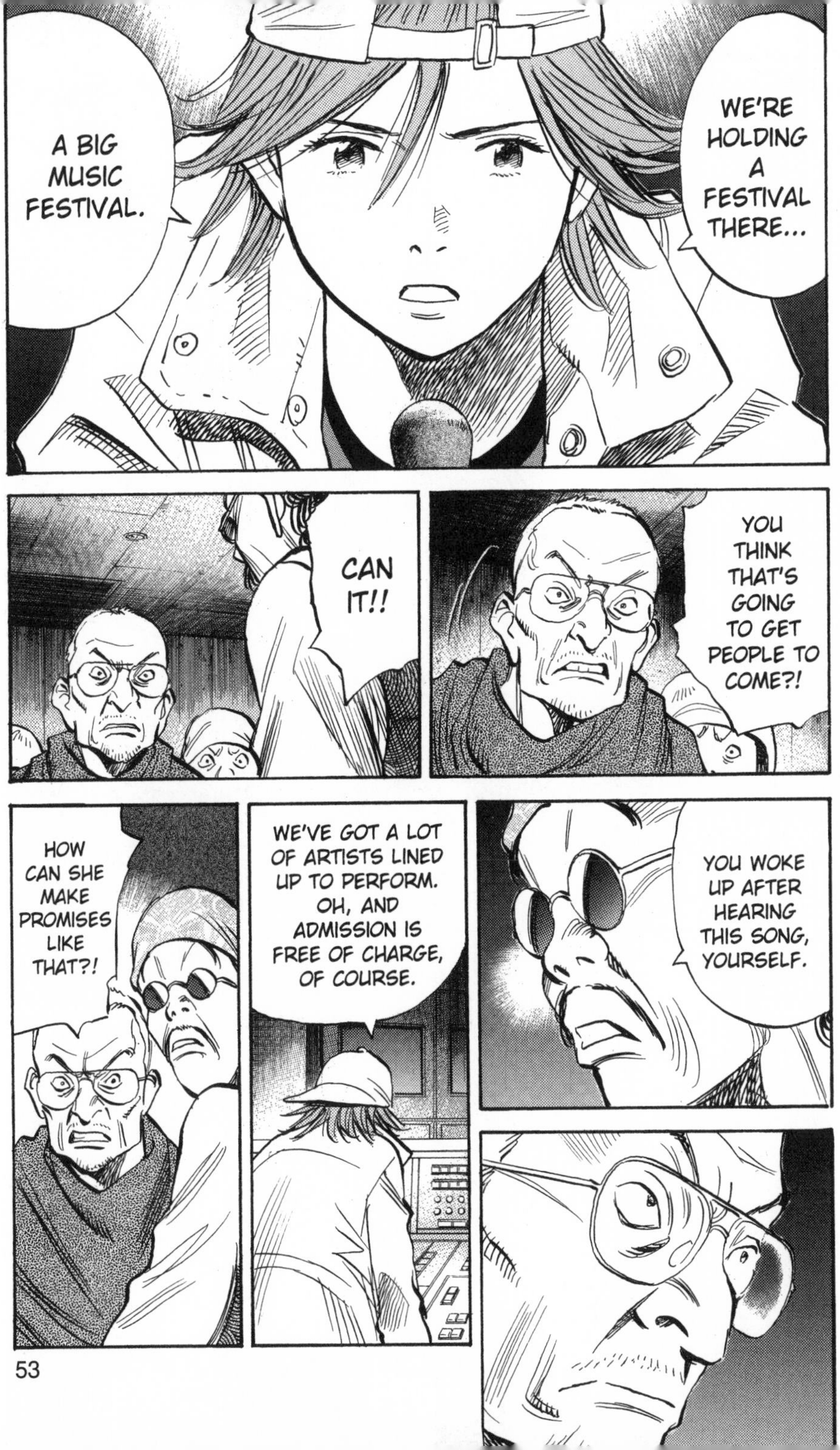
WE'RE HOLDING A FESTIVAL THERE...
A BIG MUSIC FESTIVAL.
YOU THINK THAT'S GOING TO GET PEOPLE TO COME?!
CAN IT!!
YOU WOKE UP AFTER HEARING THIS SONG, YOURSELF.
WE'VE GOT A LOT OF ARTISTS LINED UP TO PERFORM. OH, AND ADMISSION IS FREE OF CHARGE, OF COURSE.
HOW CAN SHE MAKE PROMISES LIKE THAT?!

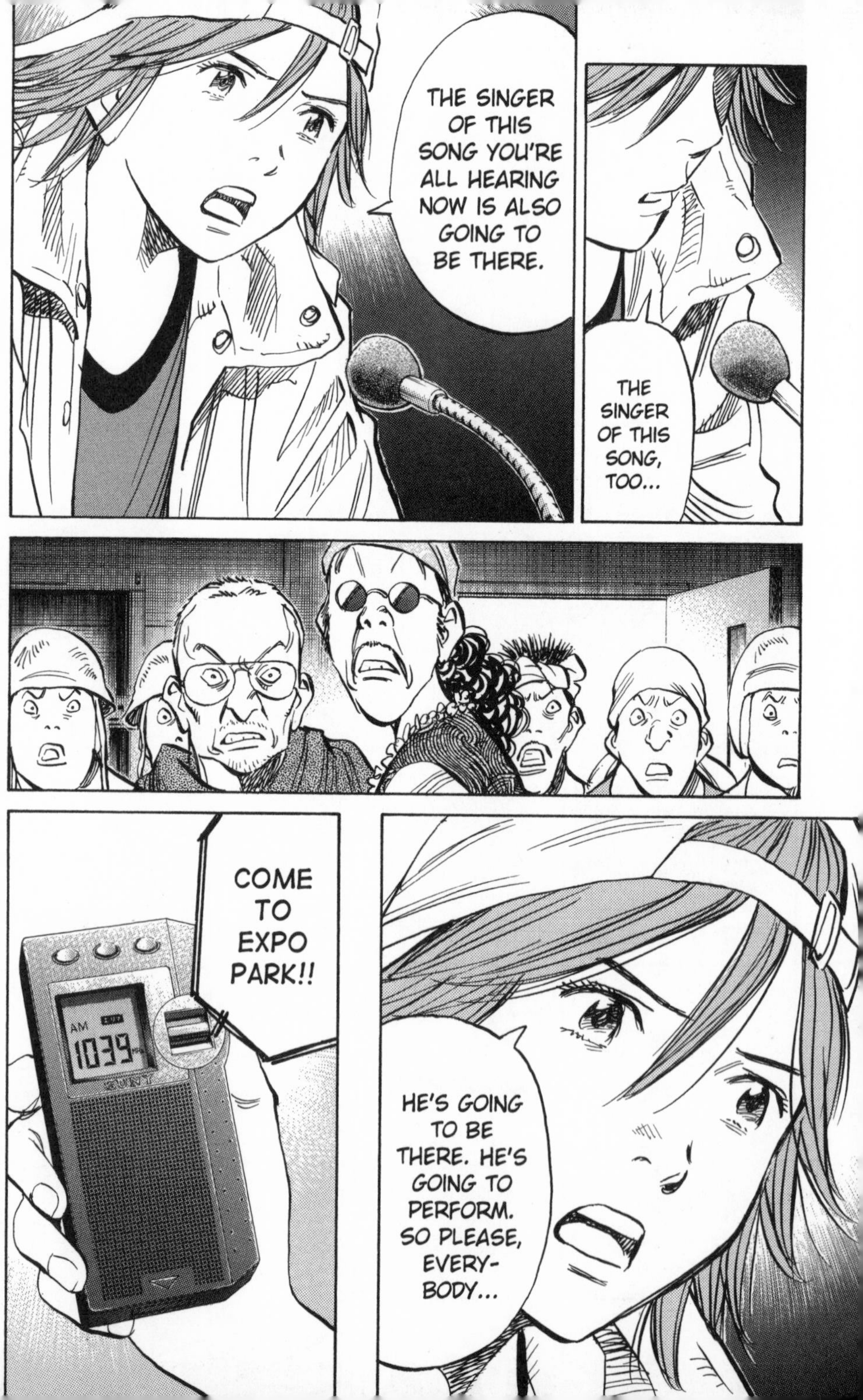
THE SINGER OF THIS SONG, TOO...
THE SINGER OF THIS SONG YOU'RE ALL HEARING NOW IS ALSO GOING TO BE THERE.
HE'S GOING TO BE THERE. HE'S GOING TO PERFORM. SO PLEASE, EVERY-BODY...
AM 1039
COME TO EXPO PARK!!

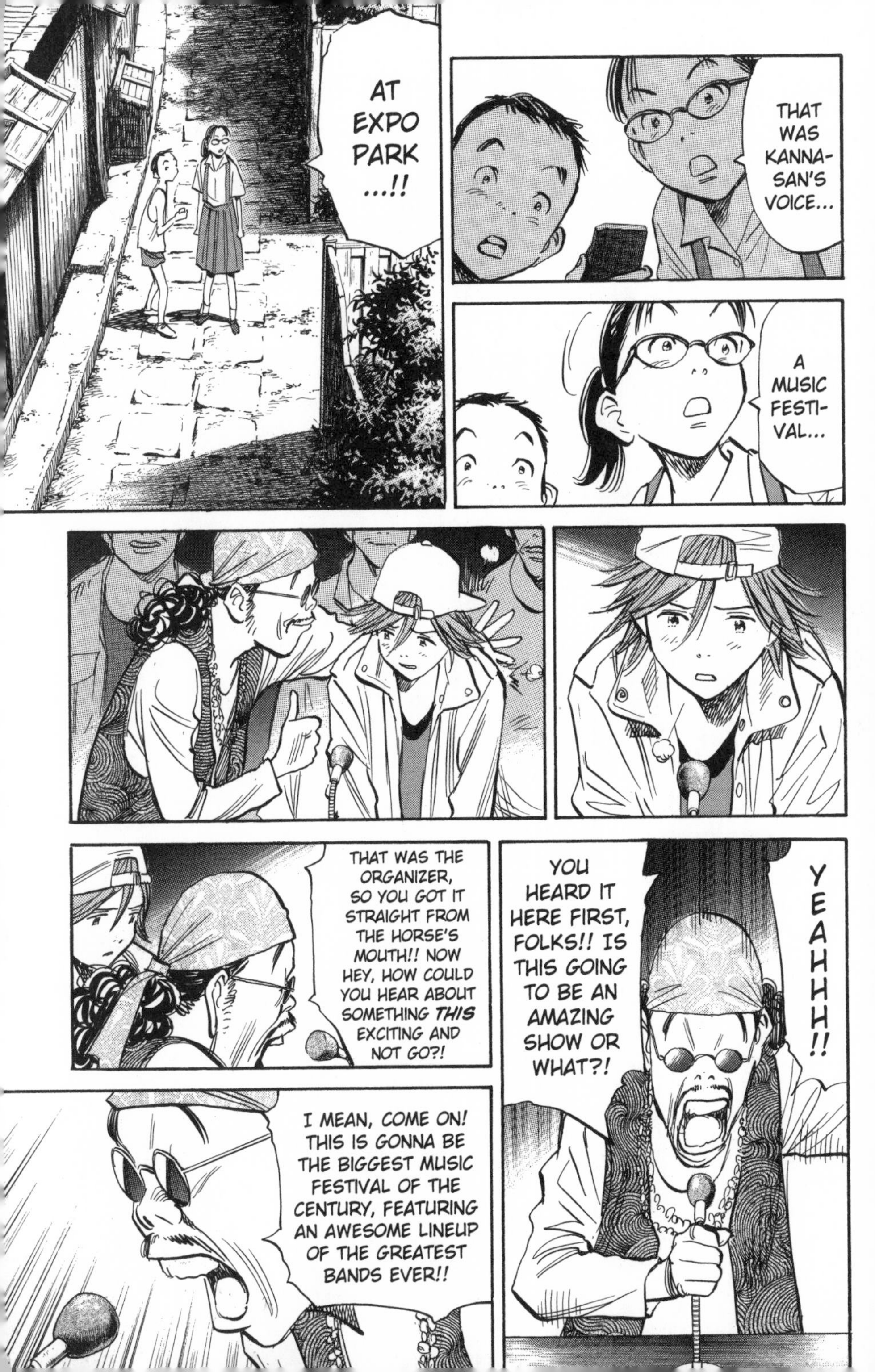
THAT WAS KANNA-SAN'S VOICE...
A MUSIC FESTIVAL...
AT EXPO PARK ...!!
YEAHHH!!
YOU HEARD IT HERE FIRST, FOLKS!! IS THIS GOING TO BE AN AMAZING SHOW OR WHAT?!
THAT WAS THE ORGANIZER, SO YOU GOT IT STRAIGHT FROM THE HORSE'S MOUTH!! NOW HEY, HOW COULD YOU HEAR ABOUT SOMETHING *THIS* EXCITING AND NOT GO?!
I MEAN, COME ON! THIS IS GONNA BE THE BIGGEST MUSIC FESTIVAL OF THE CENTURY, FEATURING AN AWESOME LINEUP OF THE GREATEST BANDS EVER!!

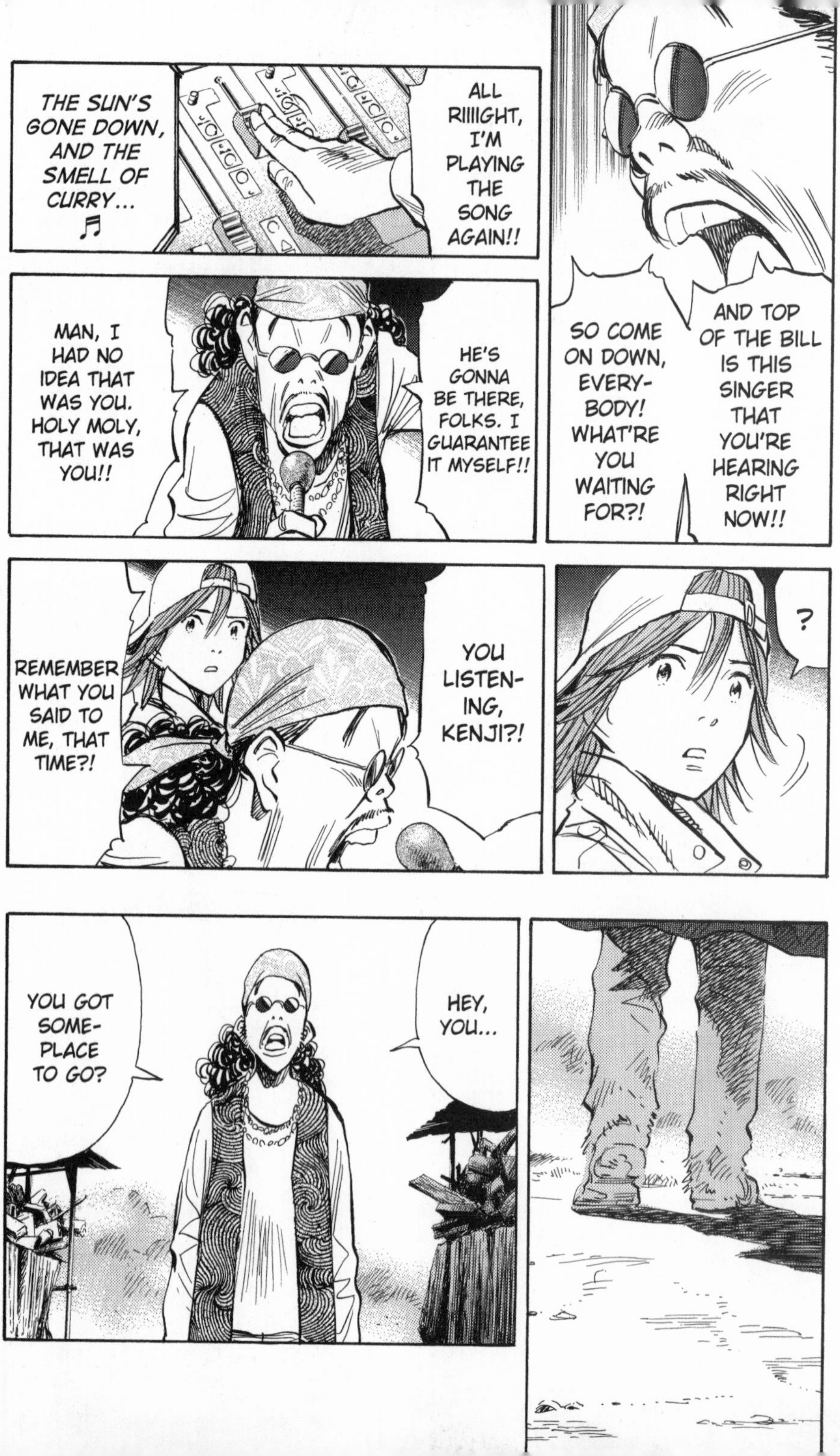
AND TOP OF THE BILL IS THIS SINGER THAT YOU'RE HEARING RIGHT NOW!!
SO COME ON DOWN, EVERY-BODY! WHAT'RE YOU WAITING FOR?!
ALL RIIIIGHT, I'M PLAYING THE SONG AGAIN!!
THE SUN'S GONE DOWN, AND THE SMELL OF CURRY... ♬
HE'S GONNA BE THERE, FOLKS. I GUARANTEE IT MYSELF!!
MAN, I HAD NO IDEA THAT WAS YOU. HOLY MOLY, THAT WAS YOU!!
?
YOU LISTEN-ING, KENJI?!
REMEMBER WHAT YOU SAID TO ME, THAT TIME?!
HEY, YOU...
YOU GOT SOME-PLACE TO GO?

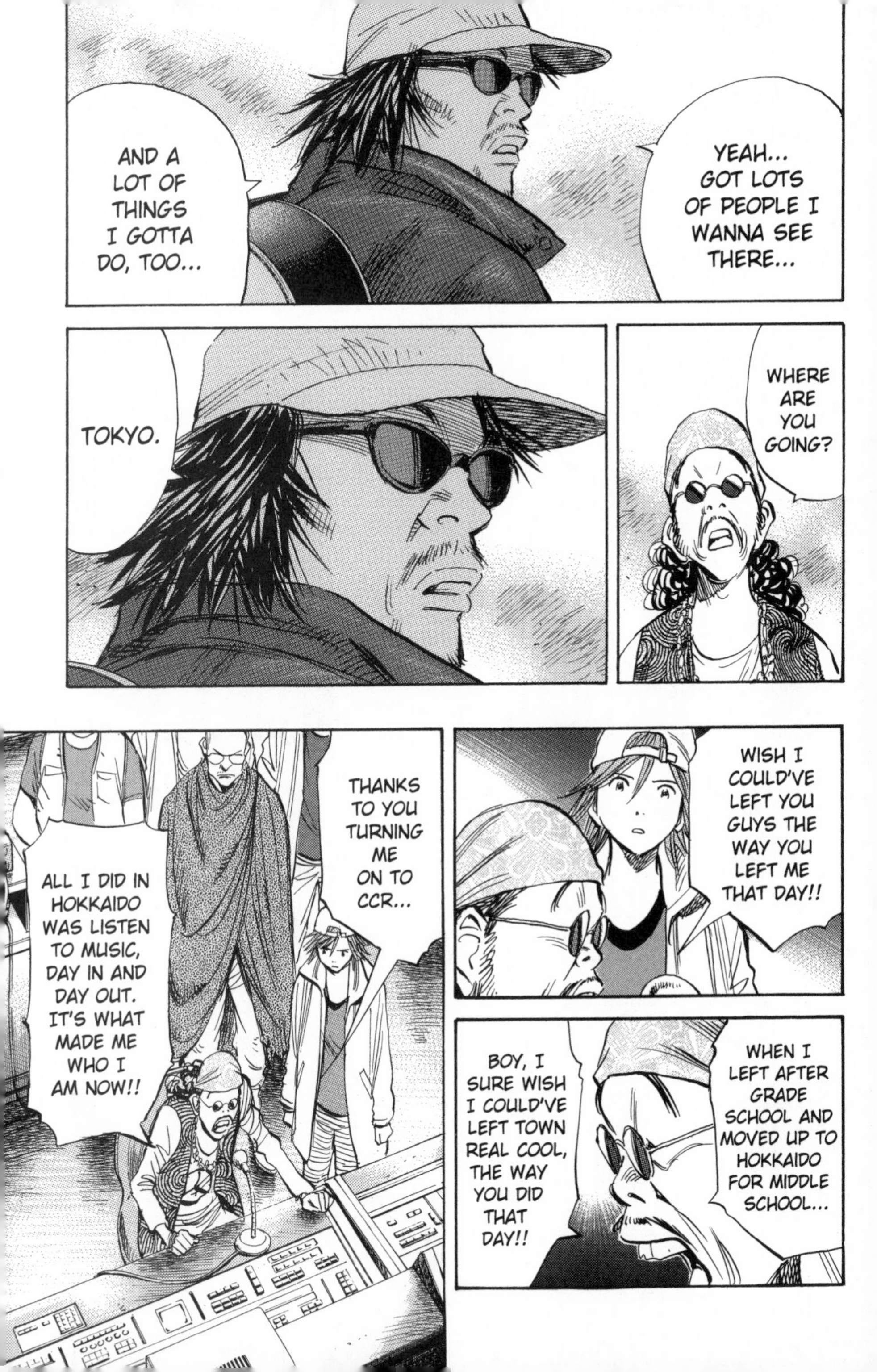
YEAH... GOT LOTS OF PEOPLE I WANNA SEE THERE...
AND A LOT OF THINGS I GOTTA DO, TOO...
WHERE ARE YOU GOING?
TOKYO.
WISH I COULD'VE LEFT YOU GUYS THE WAY YOU LEFT ME THAT DAY!!
WHEN I LEFT AFTER GRADE SCHOOL AND MOVED UP TO HOKKAIDO FOR MIDDLE SCHOOL...
BOY, I SURE WISH I COULD'VE LEFT TOWN REAL COOL, THE WAY YOU DID THAT DAY!!
THANKS TO YOU TURNING ME ON TO CCR...
ALL I DID IN HOKKAIDO WAS LISTEN TO MUSIC, DAY IN AND DAY OUT. IT'S WHAT MADE ME WHO I AM NOW!!

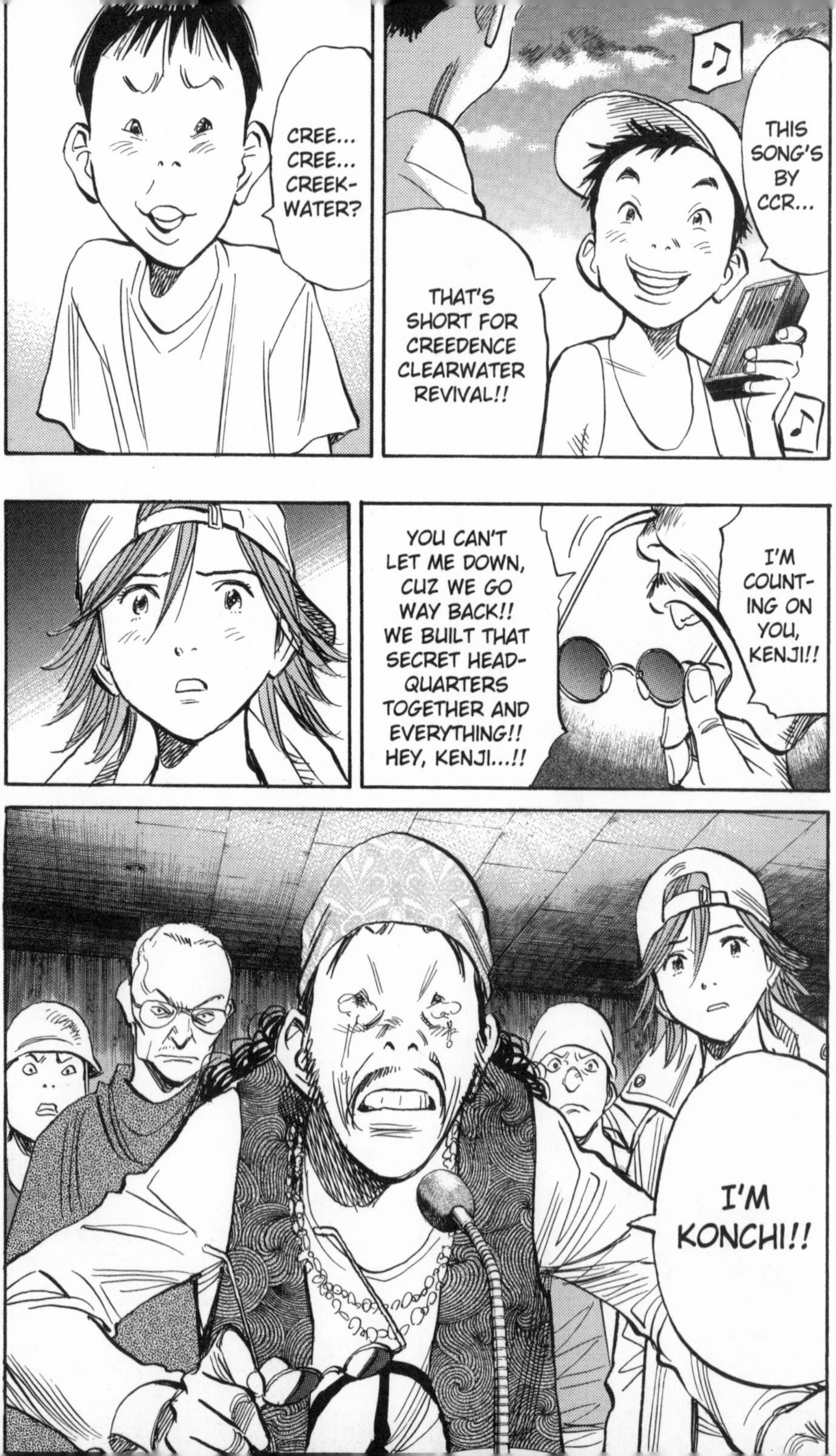
THIS SONG'S BY CCR...
THAT'S SHORT FOR CREEDENCE CLEARWATER REVIVAL!!
CREE... CREE... CREEK-WATER?
I'M COUNT-ING ON YOU, KENJI!!
YOU CAN'T LET ME DOWN, CUZ WE GO WAY BACK!! WE BUILT THAT SECRET HEAD-QUARTERS TOGETHER AND EVERYTHING!! HEY, KENJI...!!
I'M KONCHI!!

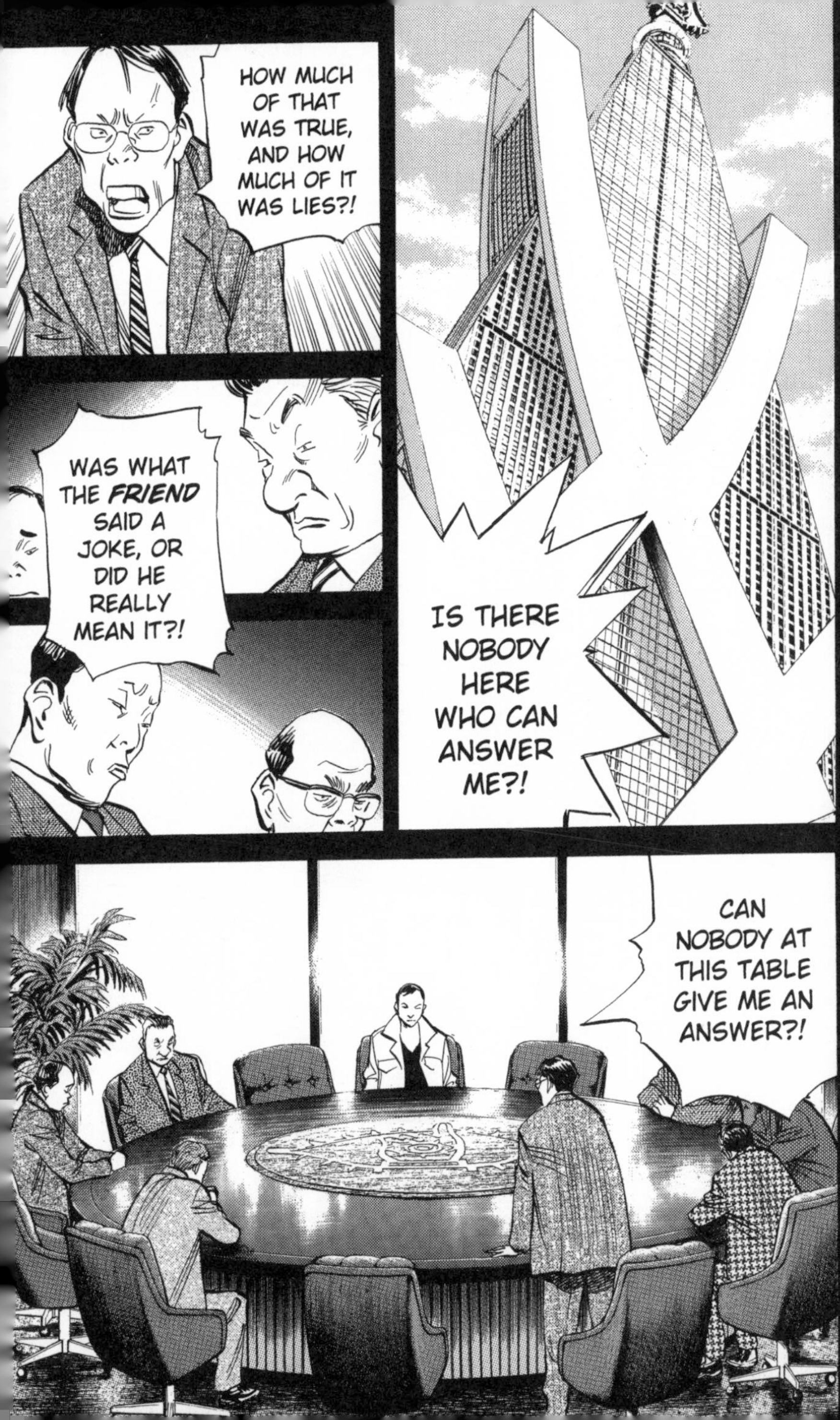
IS THERE NOBODY HERE WHO CAN ANSWER ME?!
HOW MUCH OF THAT WAS TRUE, AND HOW MUCH OF IT WAS LIES?!
WAS WHAT THE *FRIEND* SAID A JOKE, OR DID HE REALLY MEAN IT?!
CAN NOBODY AT THIS TABLE GIVE ME AN ANSWER?!

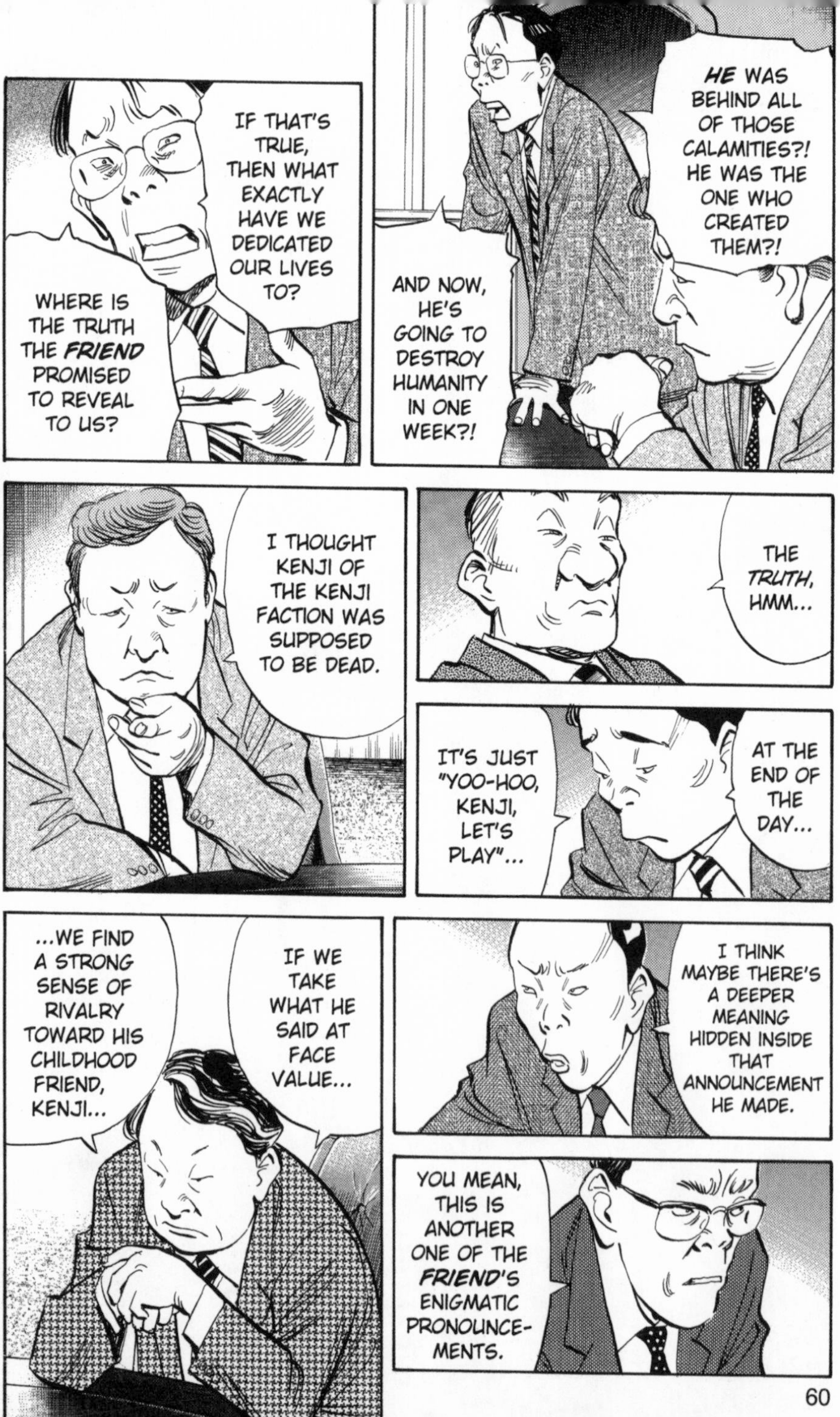
HE WAS BEHIND ALL OF THOSE CALAMITIES?! HE WAS THE ONE WHO CREATED THEM?!
AND NOW, HE'S GOING TO DESTROY HUMANITY IN ONE WEEK?!
IF THAT'S TRUE, THEN WHAT EXACTLY HAVE WE DEDICATED OUR LIVES TO?
WHERE IS THE TRUTH THE ***FRIEND*** PROMISED TO REVEAL TO US?
THE *TRUTH*, HMM...
AT THE END OF THE DAY...
IT'S JUST "YOO-HOO, KENJI, LET'S PLAY"...
I THOUGHT KENJI OF THE KENJI FACTION WAS SUPPOSED TO BE DEAD.
I THINK MAYBE THERE'S A DEEPER MEANING HIDDEN INSIDE THAT ANNOUNCEMENT HE MADE.
YOU MEAN, THIS IS ANOTHER ONE OF THE ***FRIEND***'S ENIGMATIC PRONOUNCE-MENTS.
IF WE TAKE WHAT HE SAID AT FACE VALUE...
...WE FIND A STRONG SENSE OF RIVALRY TOWARD HIS CHILDHOOD FRIEND, KENJI...

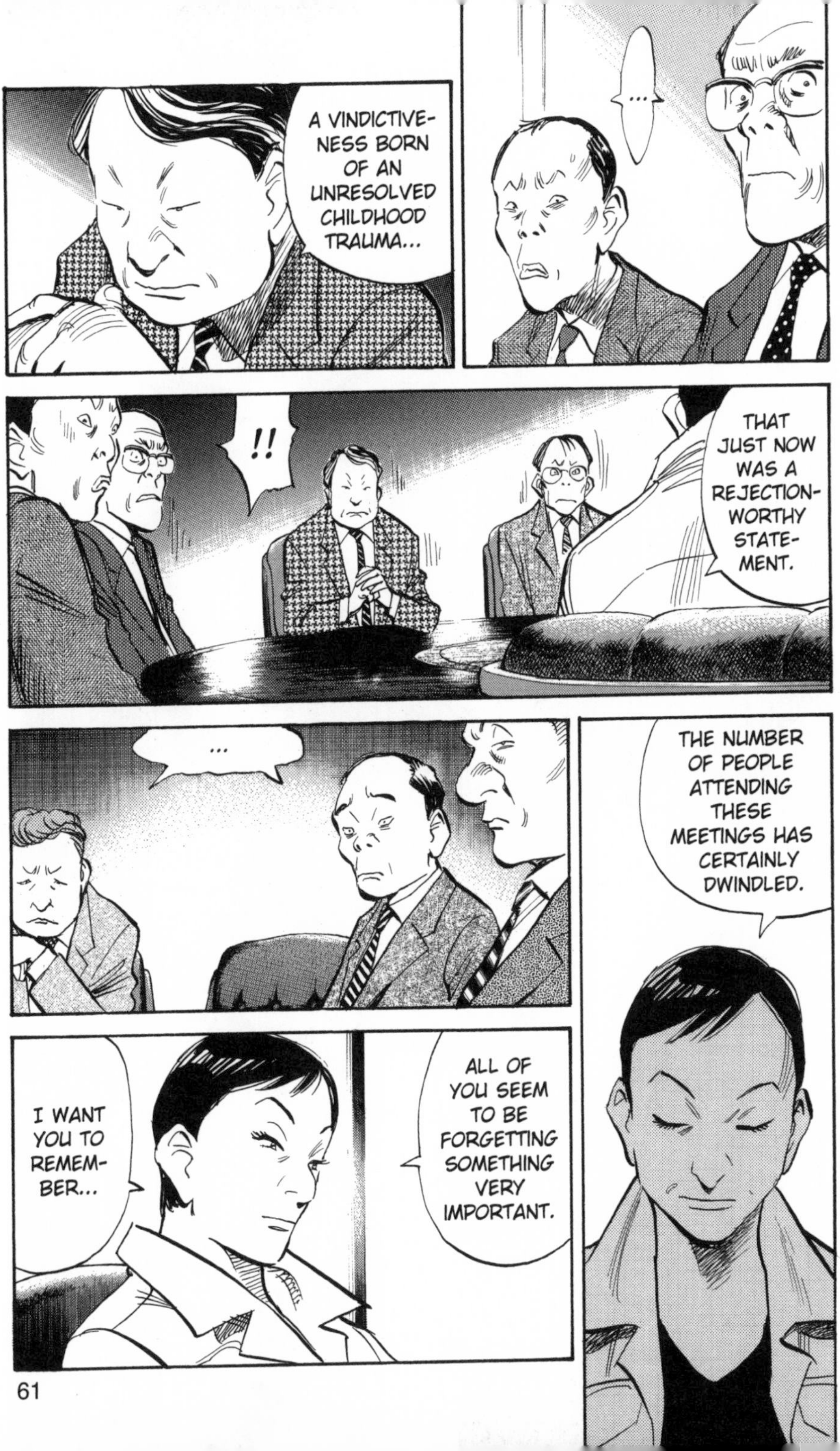
...
A VINDICTIVENESS BORN OF AN UNRESOLVED CHILDHOOD TRAUMA...
THAT JUST NOW WAS A REJECTION-WORTHY STATEMENT.
!!
THE NUMBER OF PEOPLE ATTENDING THESE MEETINGS HAS CERTAINLY DWINDLED.
...
ALL OF YOU SEEM TO BE FORGETTING SOMETHING VERY IMPORTANT.
I WANT YOU TO REMEMBER...

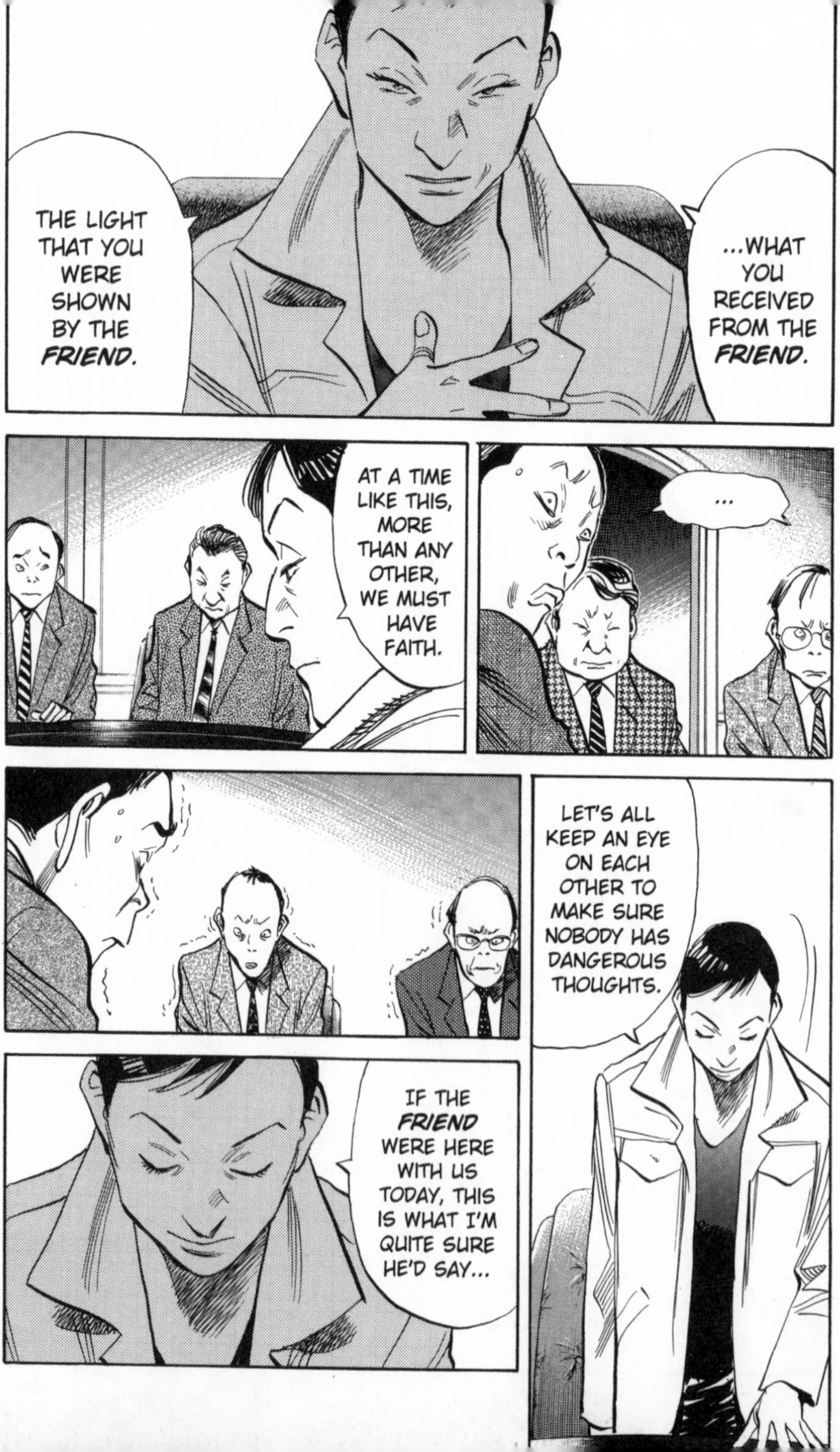
THE LIGHT THAT YOU WERE SHOWN BY THE FRIEND.
...WHAT YOU RECEIVED FROM THE FRIEND.
...
AT A TIME LIKE THIS, MORE THAN ANY OTHER, WE MUST HAVE FAITH.
LET'S ALL KEEP AN EYE ON EACH OTHER TO MAKE SURE NOBODY HAS DANGEROUS THOUGHTS.
IF THE FRIEND WERE HERE WITH US TODAY, THIS IS WHAT I'M QUITE SURE HE'D SAY...

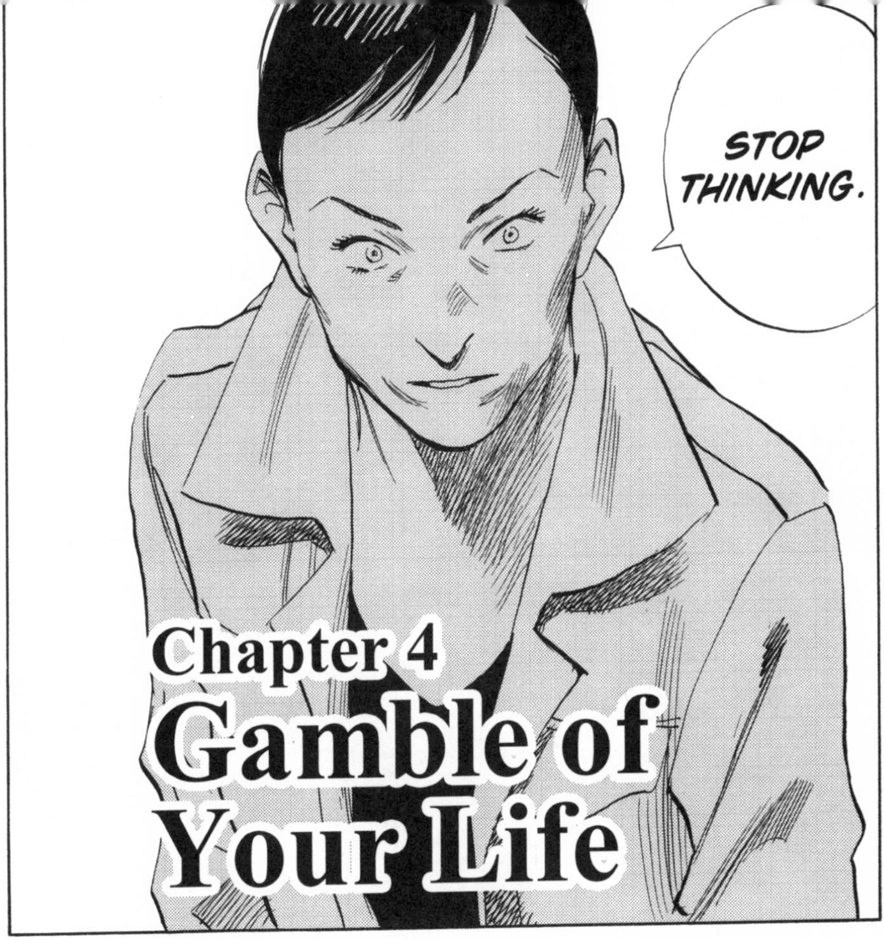
STOP THINKING.

Chapter 4
Gamble of Your Life

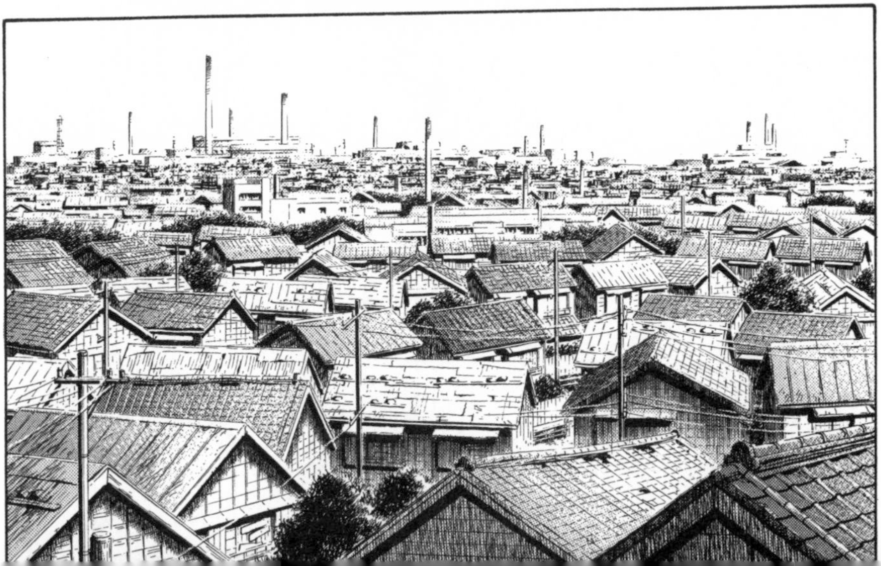

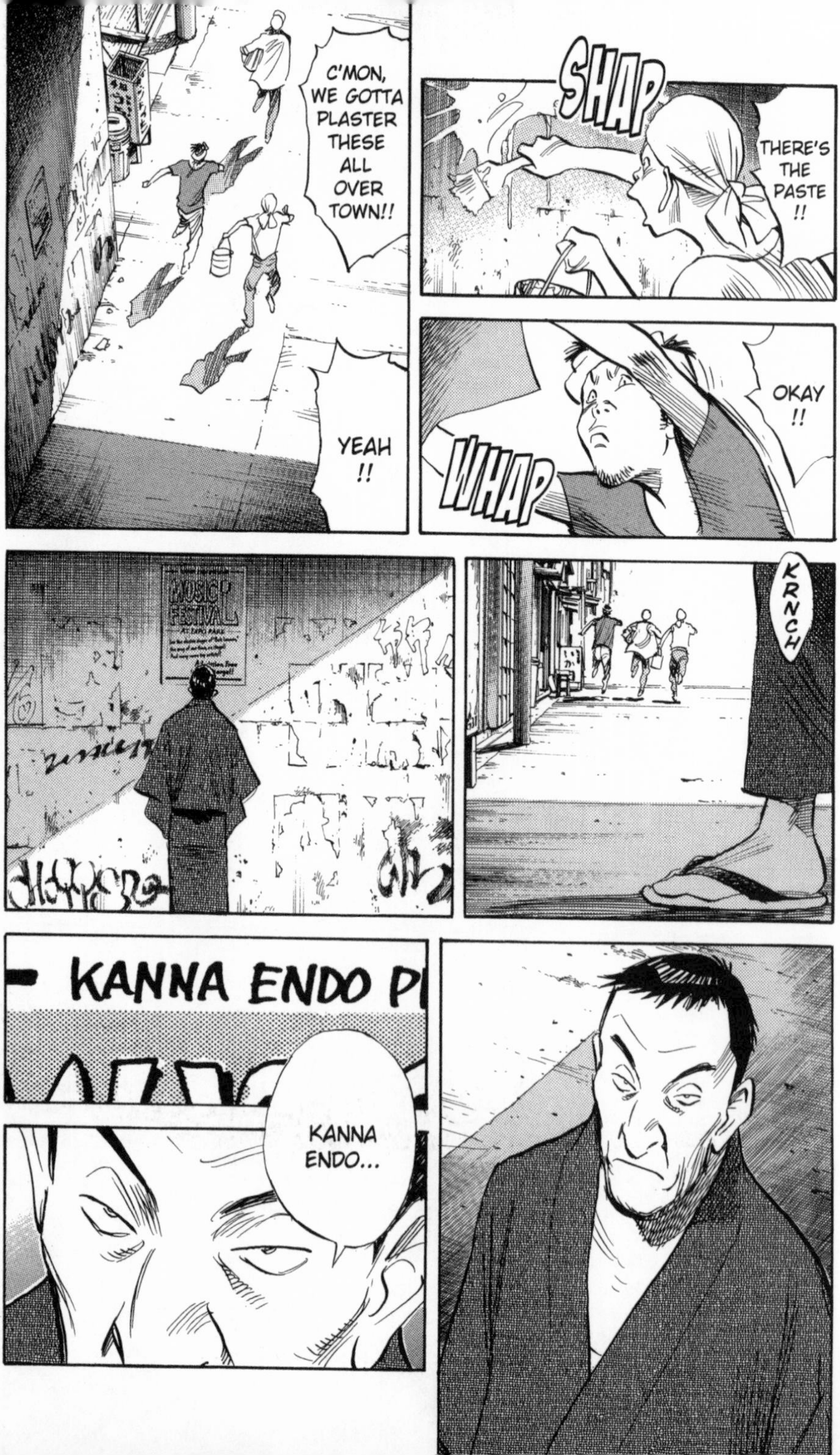
SHAP
THERE'S THE PASTE !!
WHAP
OKAY !!
C'MON, WE GOTTA PLASTER THESE ALL OVER TOWN!!
YEAH !!
KRNCH
MUSIC FESTIVAL
KANNA ENDO P
KANNA ENDO...

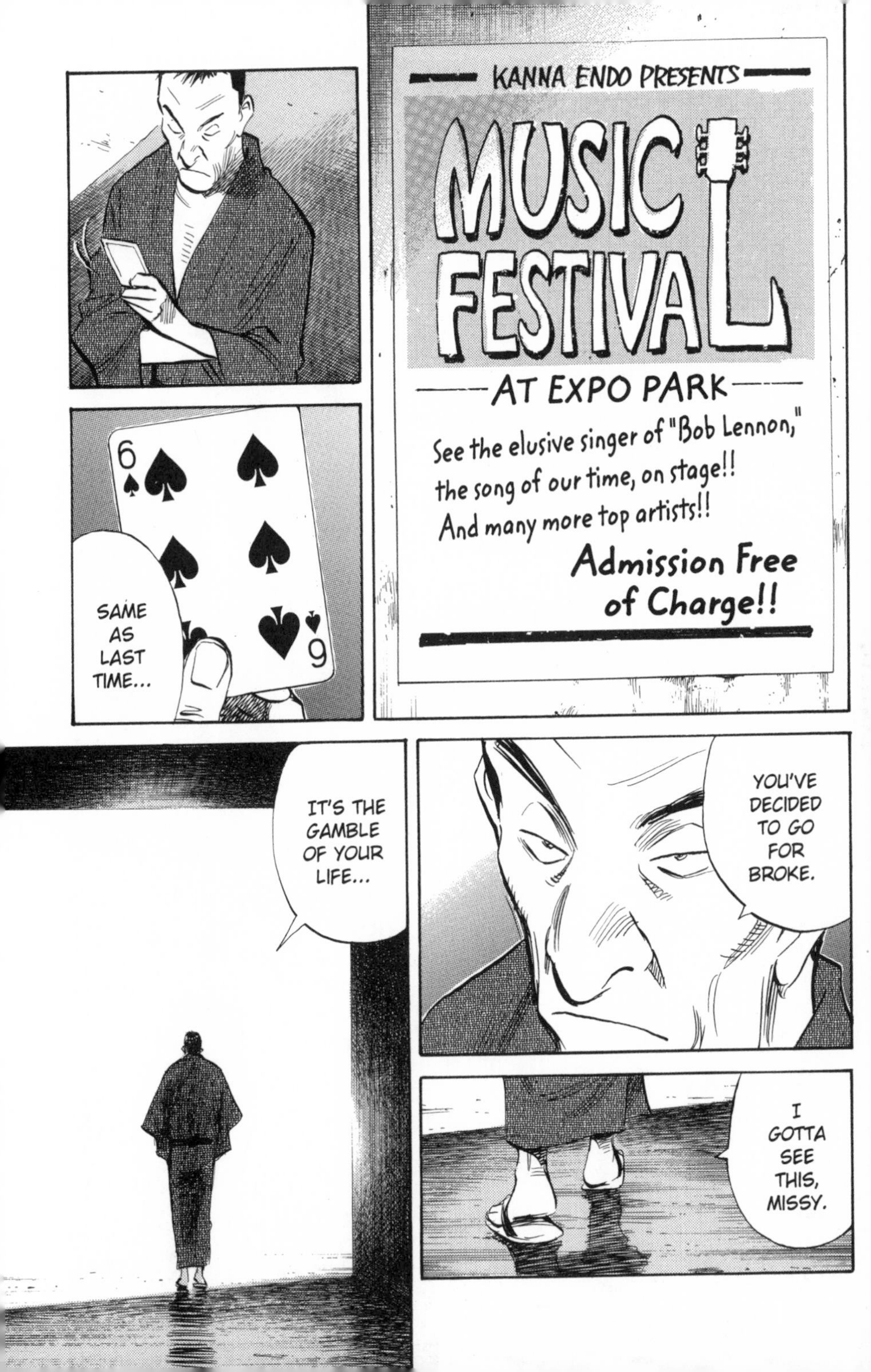
KANNA ENDO PRESENTS
MUSIC FESTIVAL
AT EXPO PARK
See the elusive singer of "Bob Lennon," the song of our time, on stage!! And many more top artists!!
Admission Free of Charge!!
SAME AS LAST TIME...
YOU'VE DECIDED TO GO FOR BROKE.
I GOTTA SEE THIS, MISSY.
IT'S THE GAMBLE OF YOUR LIFE...

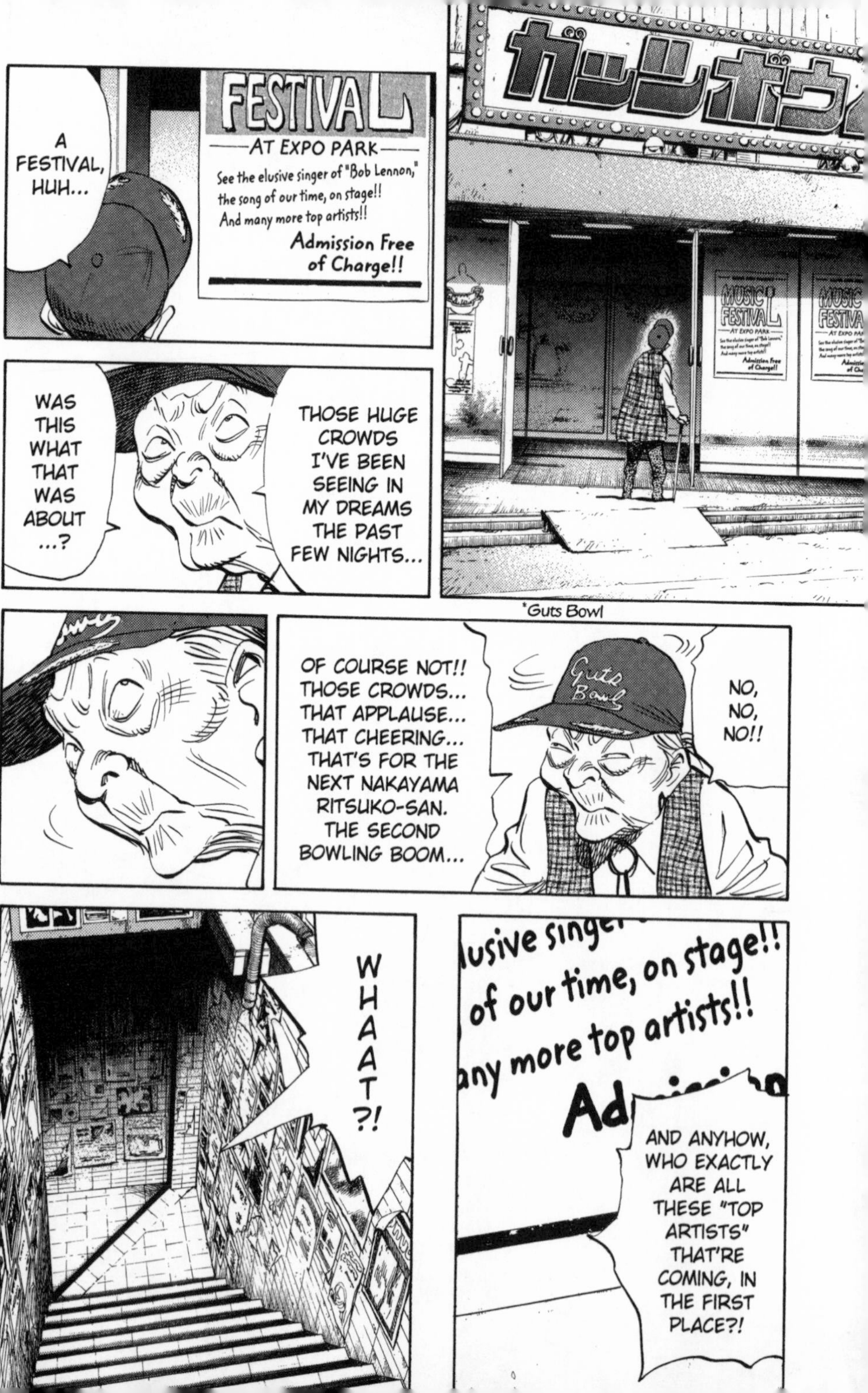
ガッツボウ
MUSIC FESTIVAL
AT EXPO PARK
MUSIC FESTIVAL
AT EXPO PARK
*Guts Bowl
FESTIVAL
AT EXPO PARK
See the elusive singer of "Bob Lennon," the song of our time, on stage!! And many more top artists!!
Admission Free of Charge!!
A FESTIVAL, HUH...
THOSE HUGE CROWDS I'VE BEEN SEEING IN MY DREAMS THE PAST FEW NIGHTS...
WAS THIS WHAT THAT WAS ABOUT ...?
NO, NO, NO!!
Guts Bowl
OF COURSE NOT!! THOSE CROWDS... THAT APPLAUSE... THAT CHEERING... THAT'S FOR THE NEXT NAKAYAMA RITSUKO-SAN. THE SECOND BOWLING BOOM...
lusive singer
of our time, on stage!!
any more top artists!!
Ad
AND ANYHOW, WHO EXACTLY ARE ALL THESE "TOP ARTISTS" THAT'RE COMING, IN THE FIRST PLACE?!
WHAAAT?!

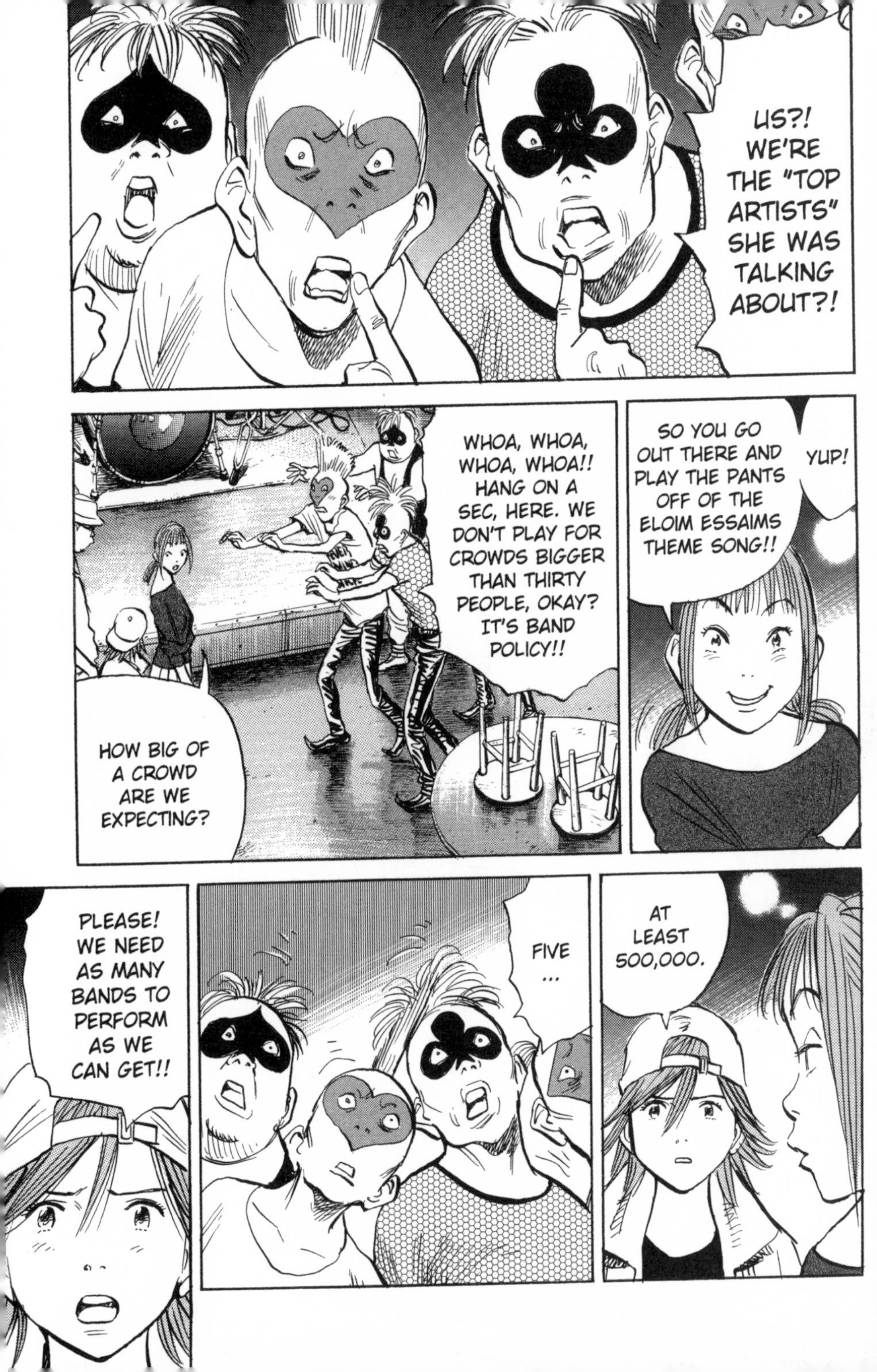
US?! WE'RE THE "TOP ARTISTS" SHE WAS TALKING ABOUT?!
SO YOU GO OUT THERE AND PLAY THE PANTS OFF OF THE ELOIM ESSAIMS THEME SONG!!
YUP!
WHOA, WHOA, WHOA, WHOA!! HANG ON A SEC, HERE. WE DON'T PLAY FOR CROWDS BIGGER THAN THIRTY PEOPLE, OKAY? IT'S BAND POLICY!!
HOW BIG OF A CROWD ARE WE EXPECTING?
AT LEAST 500,000.
FIVE ...
PLEASE! WE NEED AS MANY BANDS TO PERFORM AS WE CAN GET!!

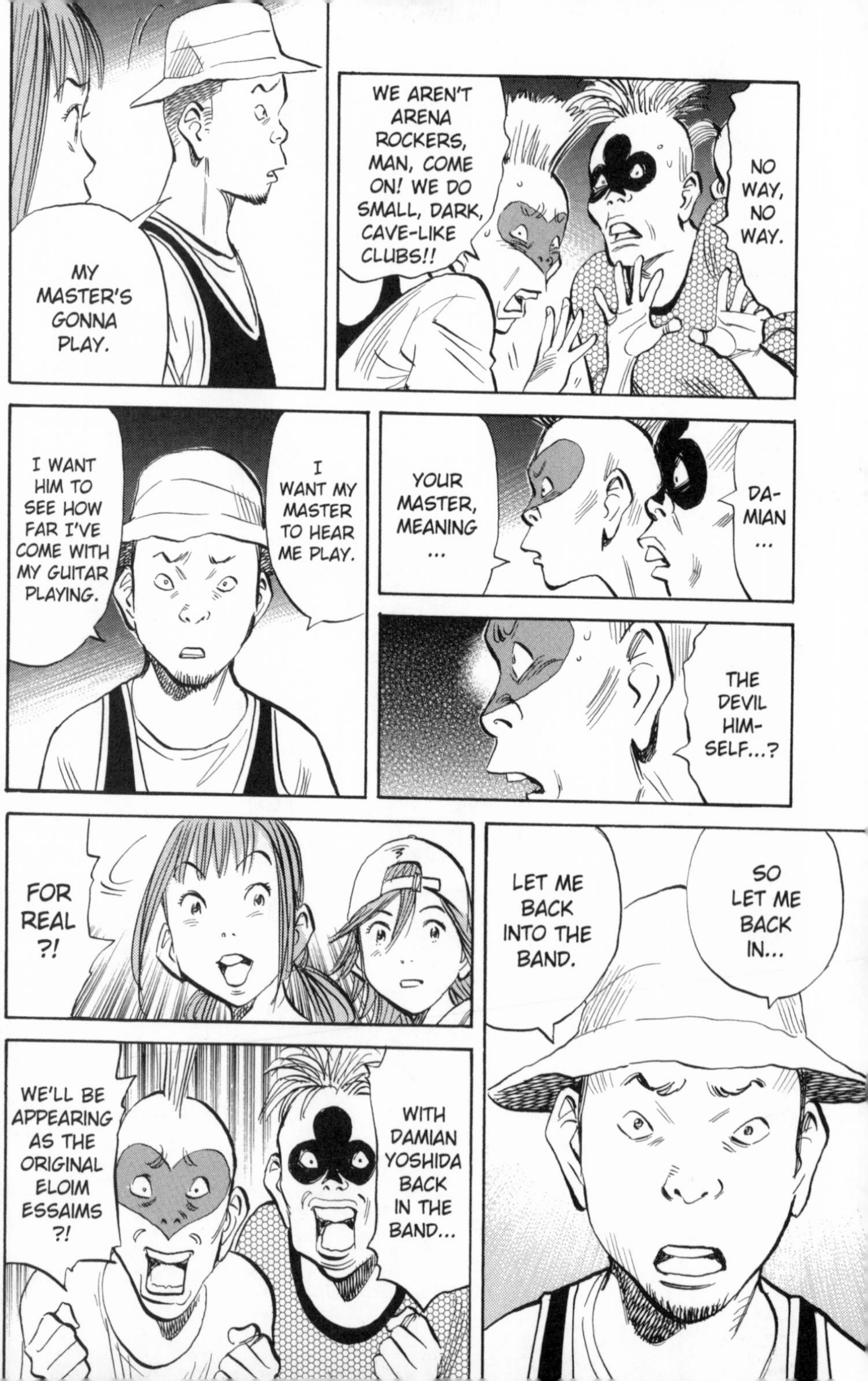
NO WAY, NO WAY.
WE AREN'T ARENA ROCKERS, MAN, COME ON! WE DO SMALL, DARK, CAVE-LIKE CLUBS!!
MY MASTER'S GONNA PLAY.
DA-MIAN...
YOUR MASTER, MEANING...
THE DEVIL HIM-SELF...?
I WANT MY MASTER TO HEAR ME PLAY.
I WANT HIM TO SEE HOW FAR I'VE COME WITH MY GUITAR PLAYING.
SO LET ME BACK IN...
LET ME BACK INTO THE BAND.
FOR REAL?!
WITH DAMIAN YOSHIDA BACK IN THE BAND...
WE'LL BE APPEARING AS THE ORIGINAL ELOIM ESSAIMS?!

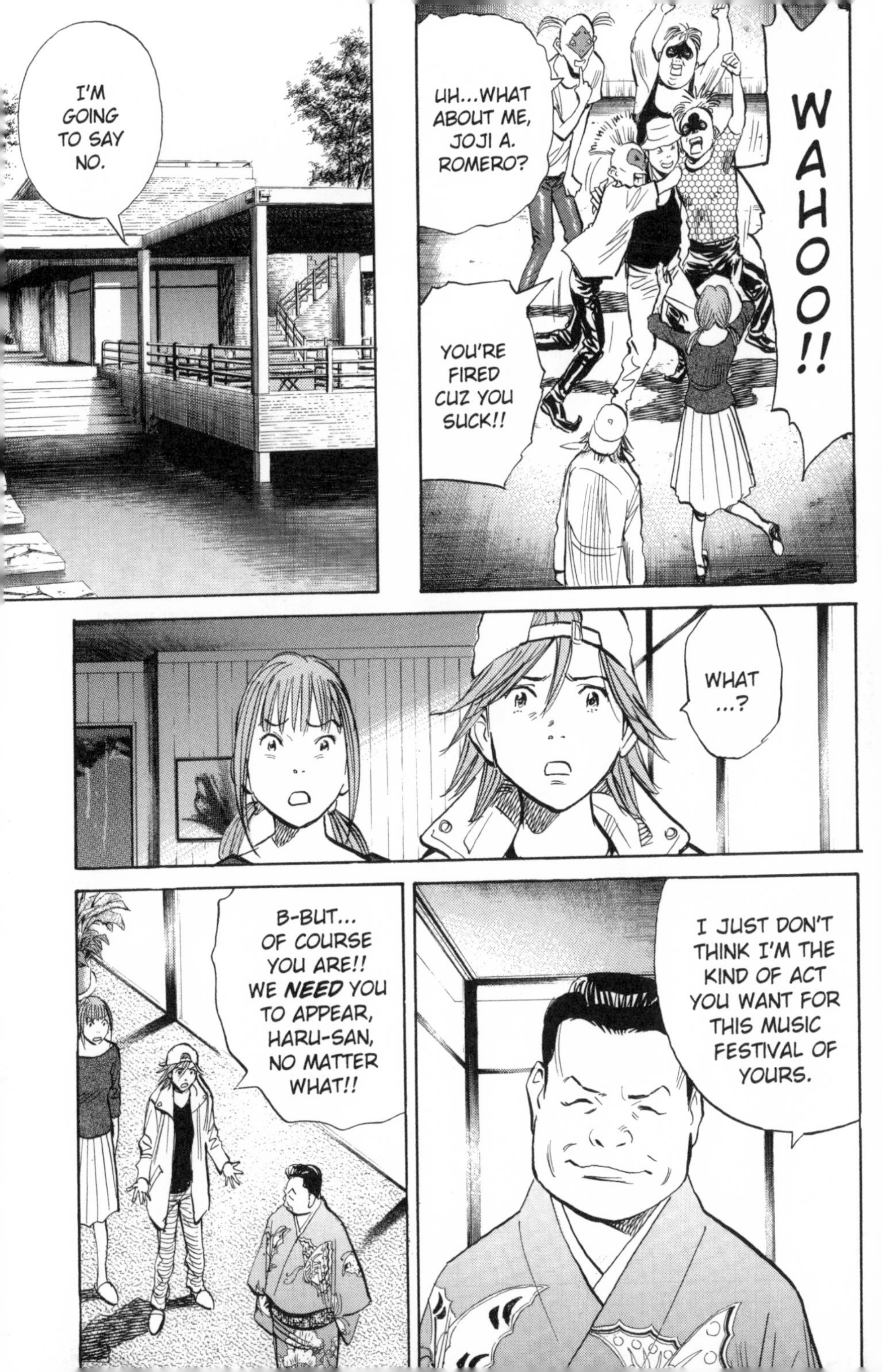
WAHOO!!
UH...WHAT ABOUT ME, JOJI A. ROMERO?
YOU'RE FIRED CUZ YOU SUCK!!
I'M GOING TO SAY NO.
WHAT ...?
I JUST DON'T THINK I'M THE KIND OF ACT YOU WANT FOR THIS MUSIC FESTIVAL OF YOURS.
B-BUT... OF COURSE YOU ARE!! WE NEED YOU TO APPEAR, HARU-SAN, NO MATTER WHAT!!

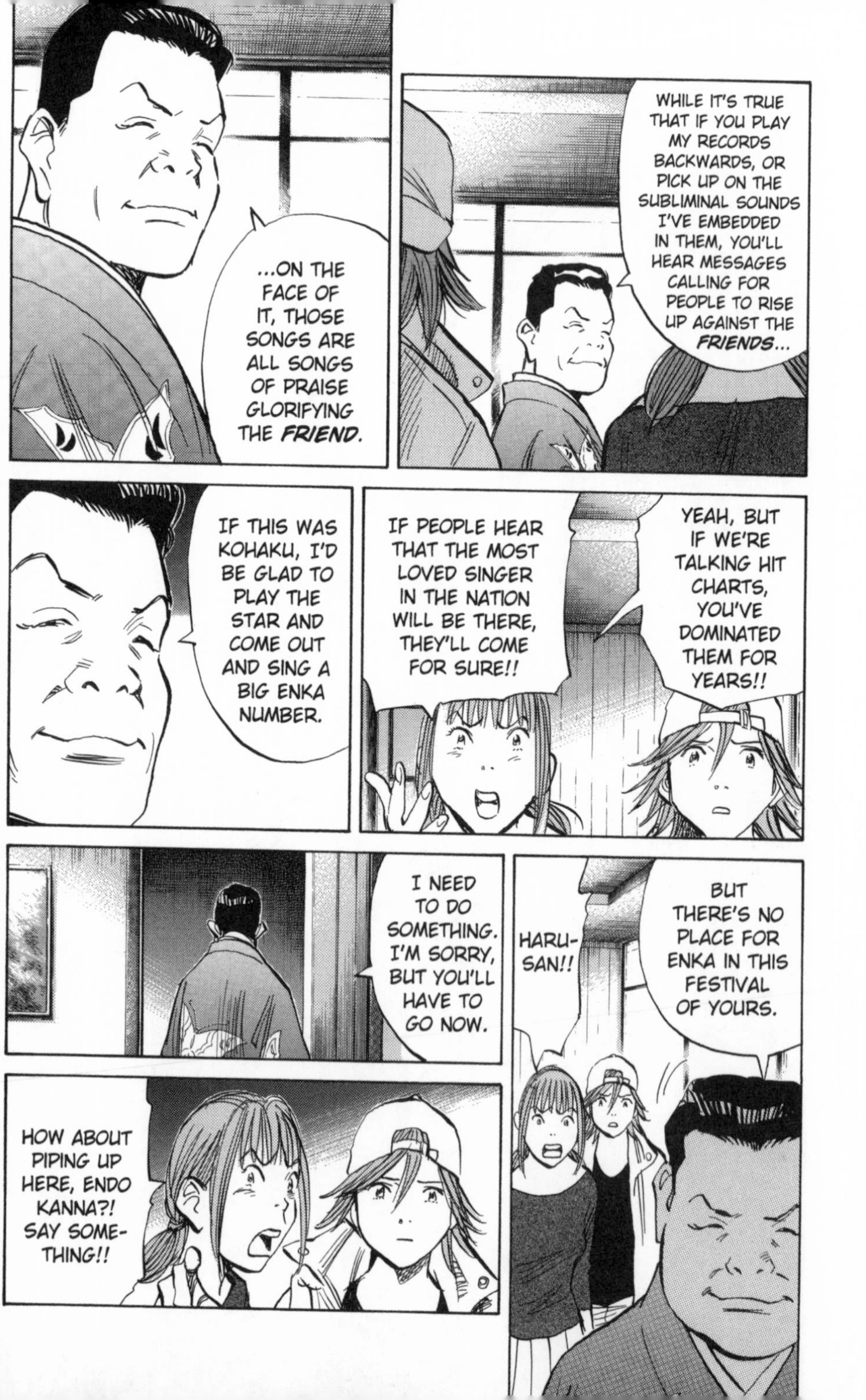
WHILE IT'S TRUE THAT IF YOU PLAY MY RECORDS BACKWARDS, OR PICK UP ON THE SUBLIMINAL SOUNDS I'VE EMBEDDED IN THEM, YOU'LL HEAR MESSAGES CALLING FOR PEOPLE TO RISE UP AGAINST THE *FRIENDS*...
...ON THE FACE OF IT, THOSE SONGS ARE ALL SONGS OF PRAISE GLORIFYING THE *FRIEND*.
YEAH, BUT IF WE'RE TALKING HIT CHARTS, YOU'VE DOMINATED THEM FOR YEARS!!
IF PEOPLE HEAR THAT THE MOST LOVED SINGER IN THE NATION WILL BE THERE, THEY'LL COME FOR SURE!!
IF THIS WAS KOHAKU, I'D BE GLAD TO PLAY THE STAR AND COME OUT AND SING A BIG ENKA NUMBER.
BUT THERE'S NO PLACE FOR ENKA IN THIS FESTIVAL OF YOURS.
HARU-SAN!!
I NEED TO DO SOMETHING. I'M SORRY, BUT YOU'LL HAVE TO GO NOW.
HOW ABOUT PIPING UP HERE, ENDO KANNA?! SAY SOME-THING!!

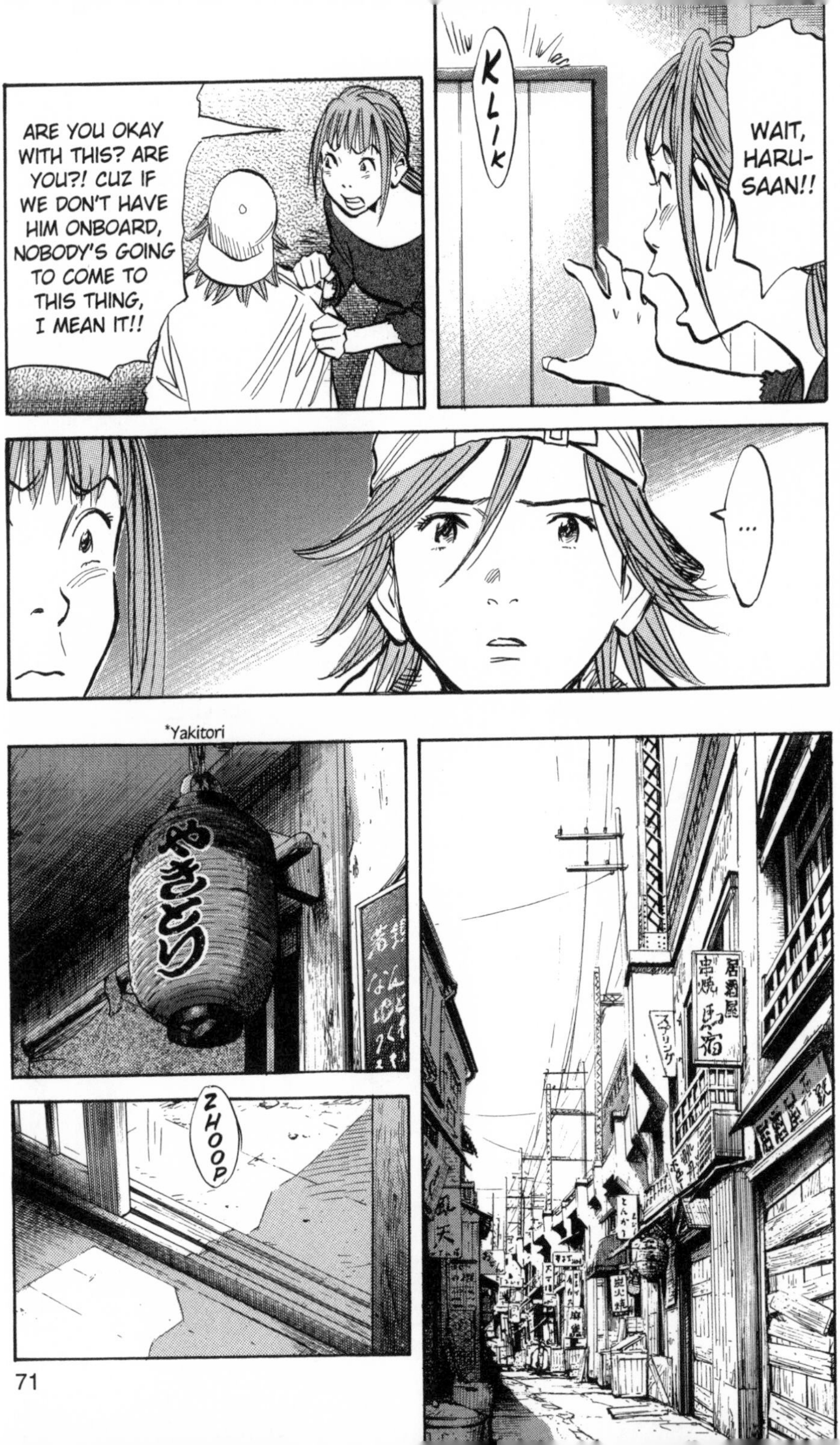
KLIK
WAIT, HARU-SAAN!!
ARE YOU OKAY WITH THIS? ARE YOU?! CUZ IF WE DON'T HAVE HIM ONBOARD, NOBODY'S GOING TO COME TO THIS THING, I MEAN IT!!
...
*Yakitori
やきとり
ZHOOP

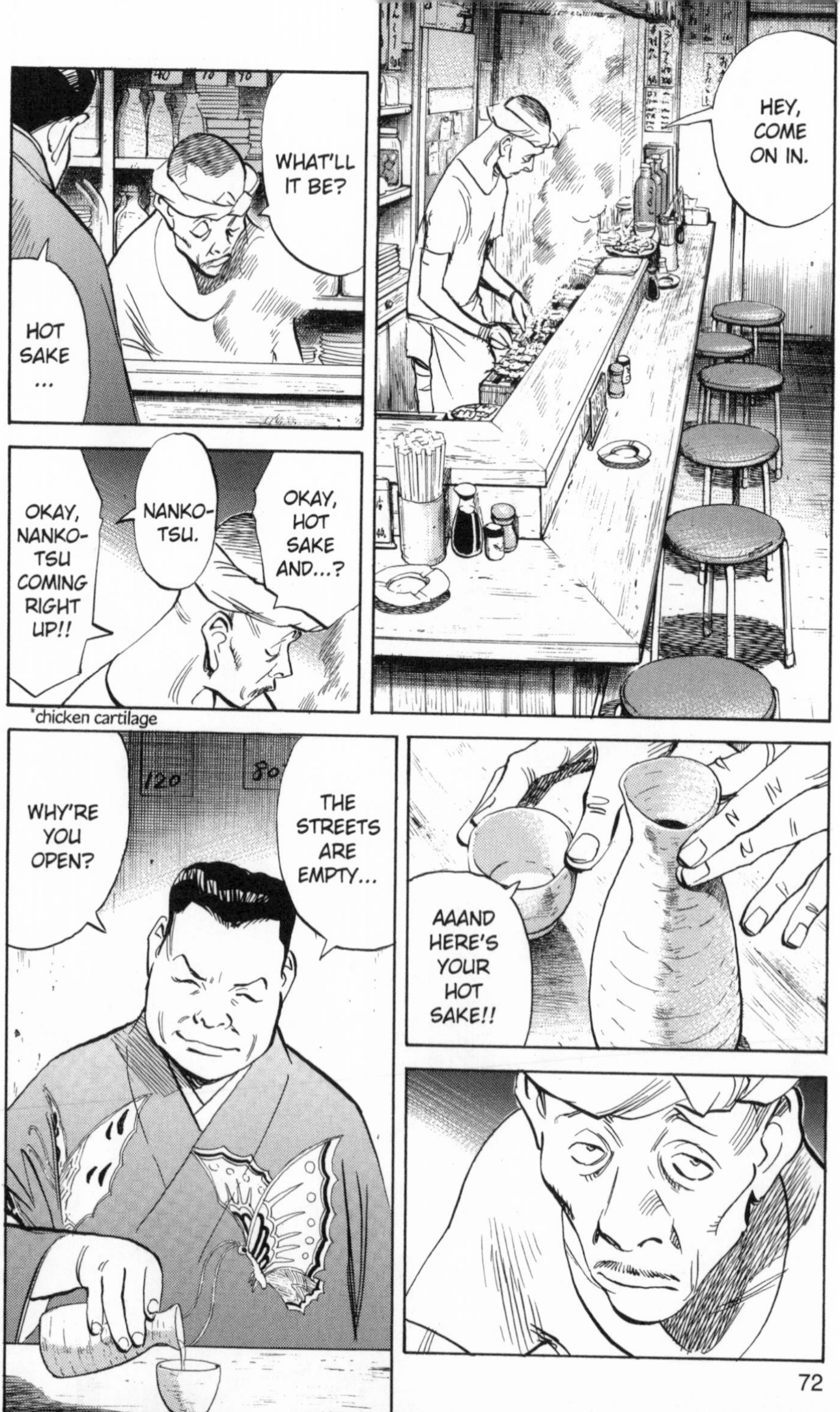
HEY, COME ON IN.
WHAT'LL IT BE?
HOT SAKE ...
OKAY, HOT SAKE AND...?
NANKO-TSU.
OKAY, NANKO-TSU COMING RIGHT UP!!
AAAND HERE'S YOUR HOT SAKE!!
THE STREETS ARE EMPTY...
WHY'RE YOU OPEN?

*chicken cartilage

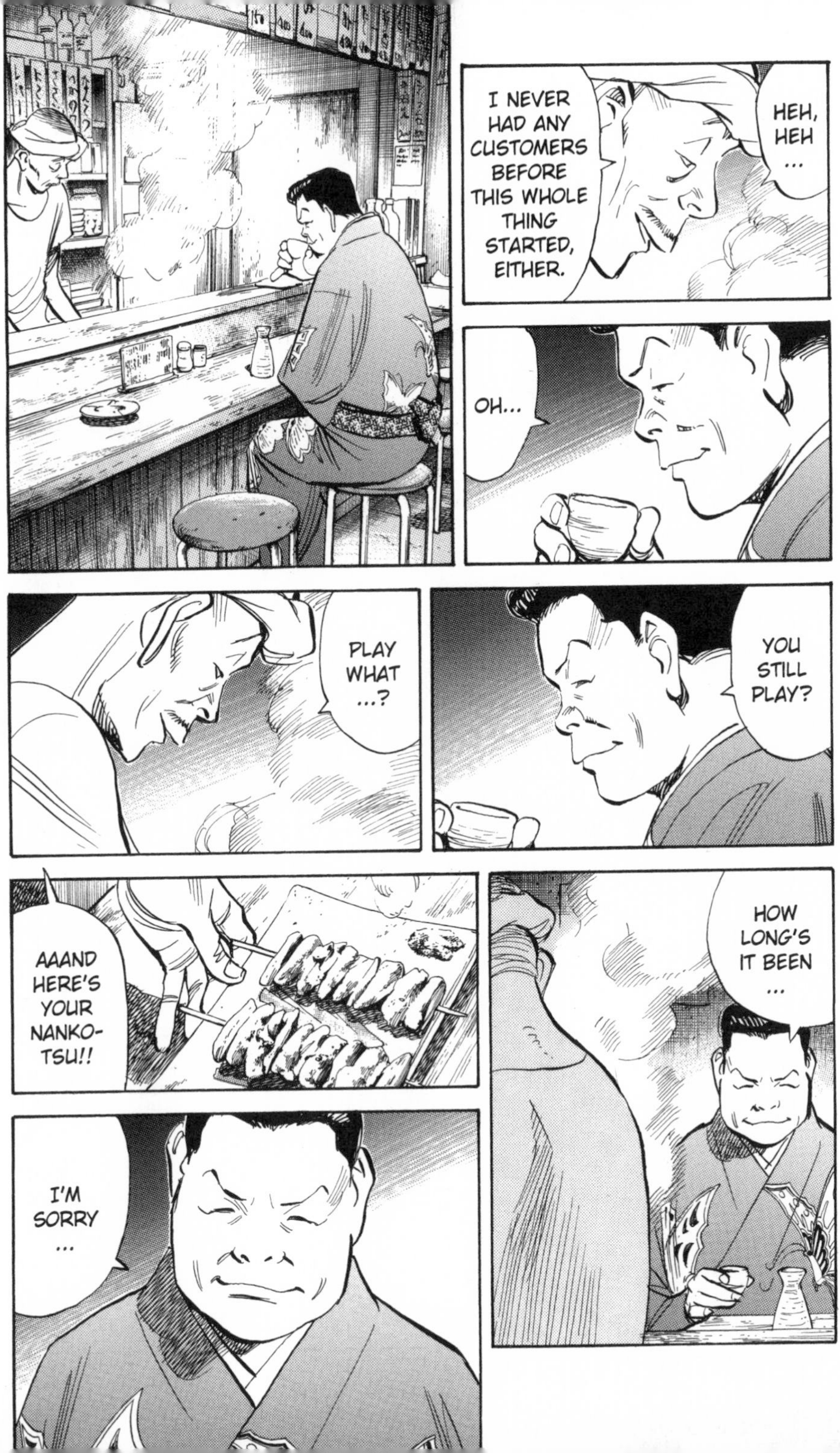
HEH, HEH ...
I NEVER HAD ANY CUSTOMERS BEFORE THIS WHOLE THING STARTED, EITHER.
OH...
YOU STILL PLAY?
PLAY WHAT ...?
HOW LONG'S IT BEEN ...
AAAND HERE'S YOUR NANKO-TSU!!
I'M SORRY ...

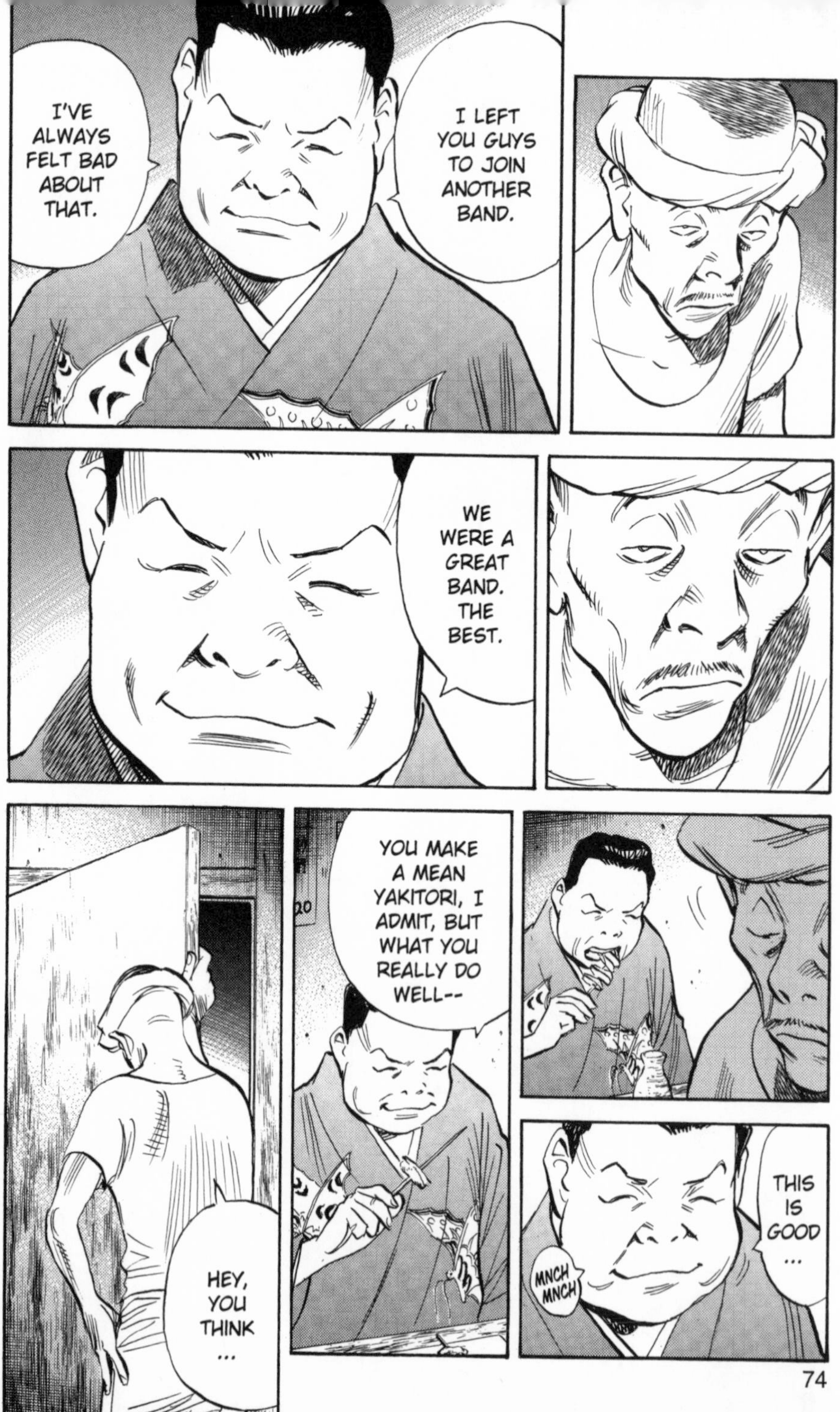
I LEFT YOU GUYS TO JOIN ANOTHER BAND.
I'VE ALWAYS FELT BAD ABOUT THAT.
WE WERE A GREAT BAND. THE BEST.
MNCH MNCH
THIS IS GOOD ...
YOU MAKE A MEAN YAKITORI, I ADMIT, BUT WHAT YOU REALLY DO WELL--
HEY, YOU THINK ...

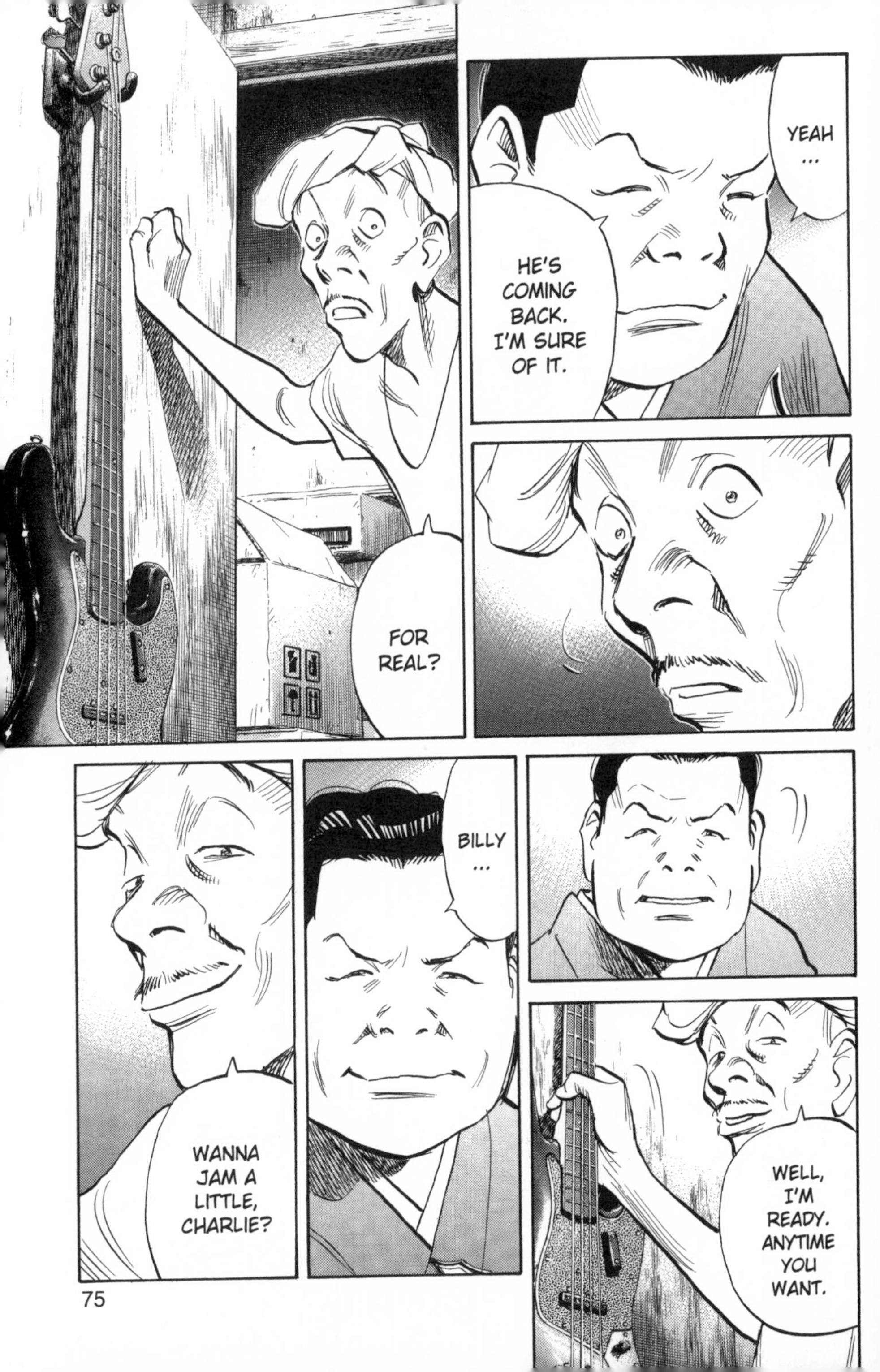
YEAH ...
HE'S COMING BACK. I'M SURE OF IT.
FOR REAL?
WELL, I'M READY. ANYTIME YOU WANT.
BILLY ...
WANNA JAM A LITTLE, CHARLIE?

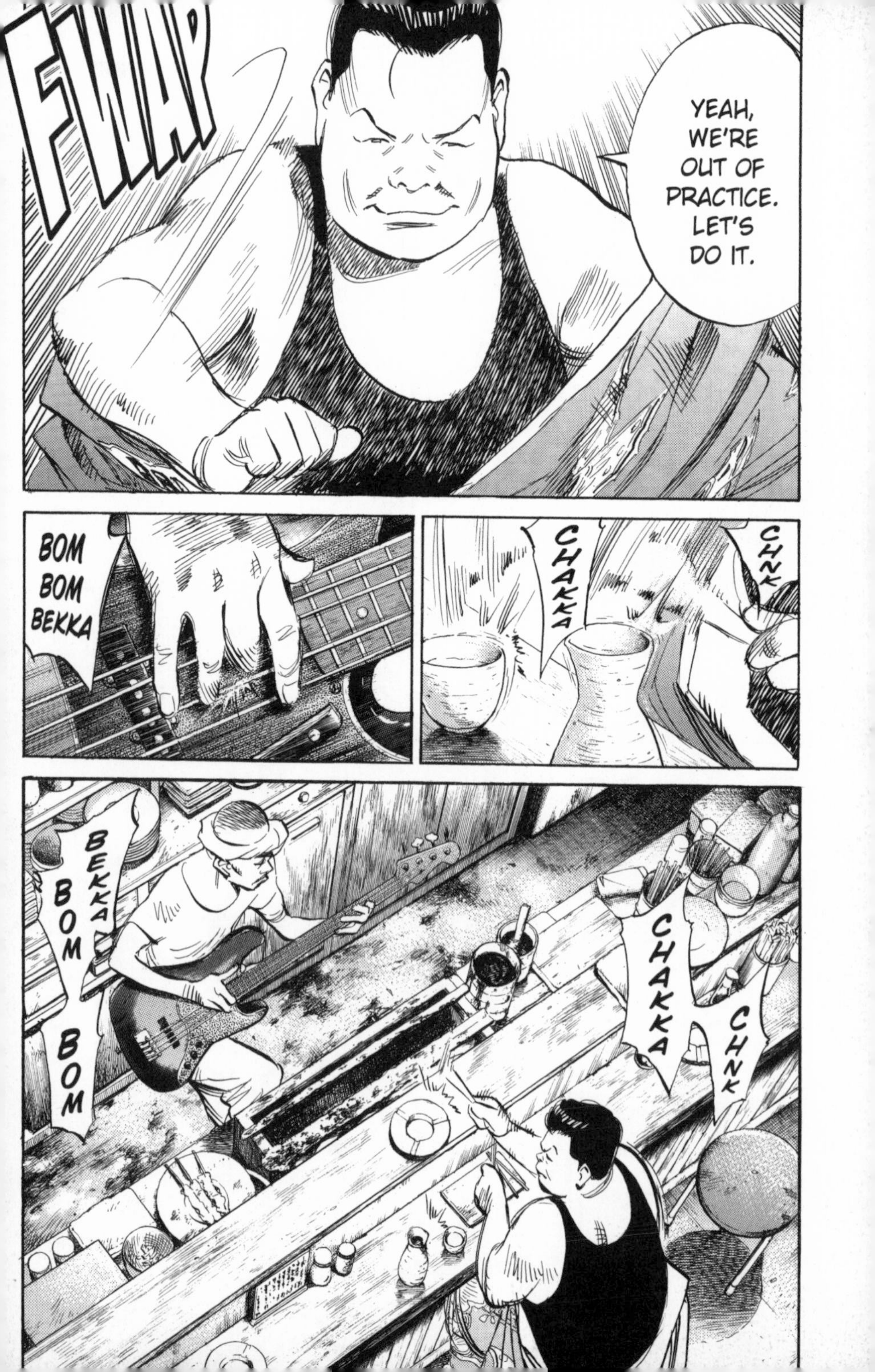
FWAP
YEAH, WE'RE OUT OF PRACTICE. LET'S DO IT.
CHNK
CHAKKA
BOM BOM BEKKA
CHAKKA
CHNK
BEKKA BOM
BOM BOM

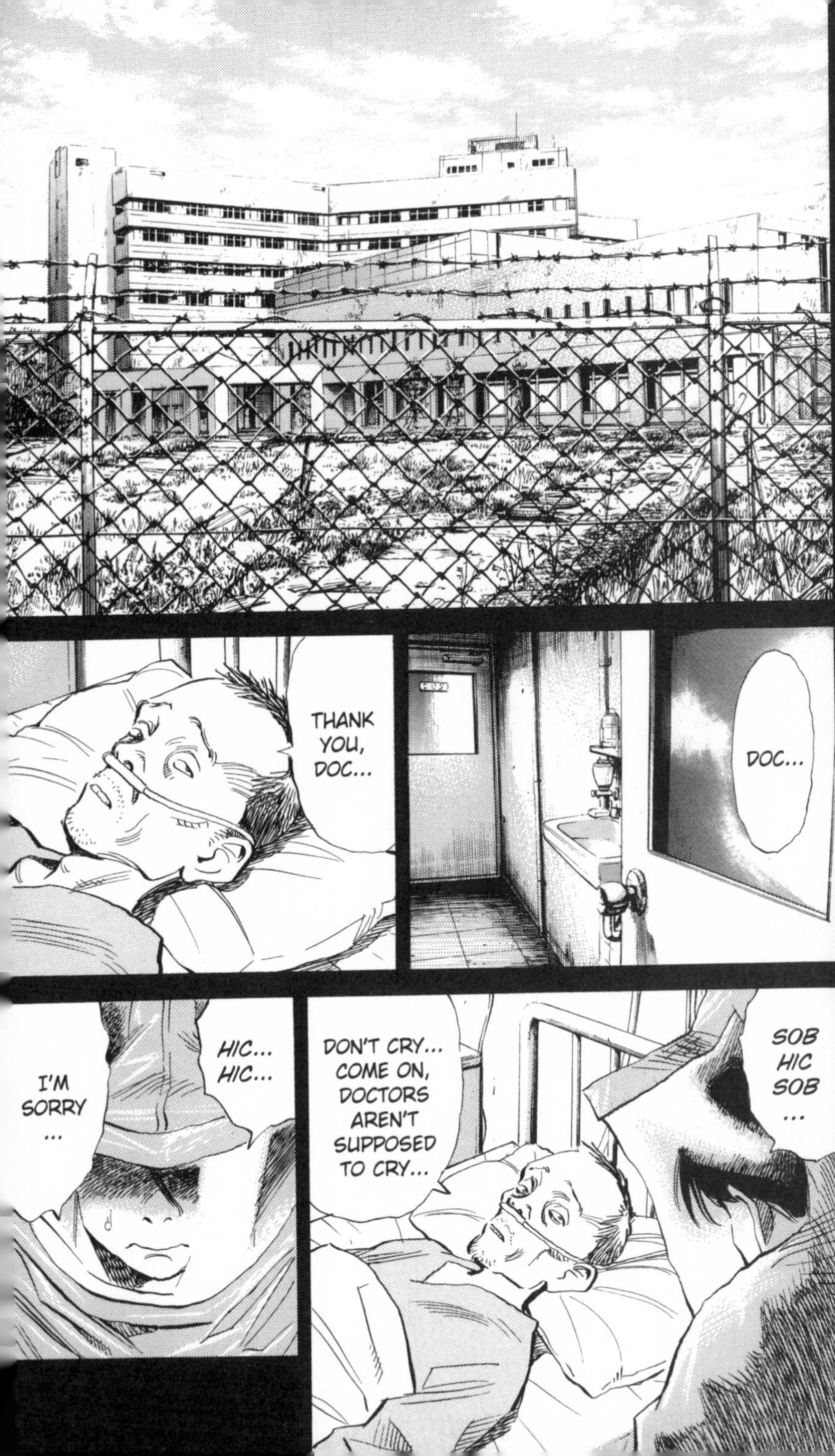
DOC...
THANK YOU, DOC...
SOB HIC SOB ...
DON'T CRY... COME ON, DOCTORS AREN'T SUPPOSED TO CRY...
HIC... HIC...
I'M SORRY ...

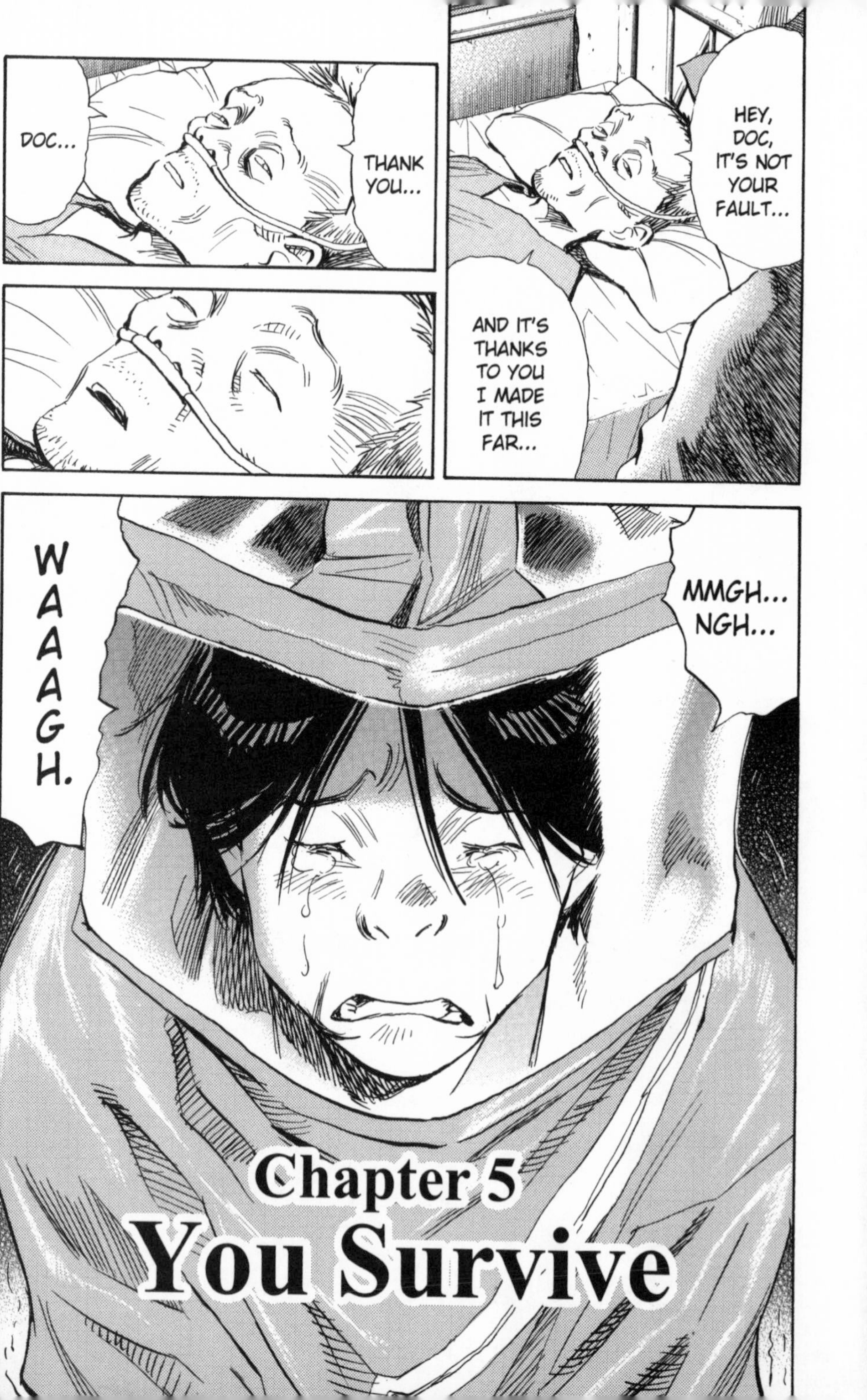
HEY, DOC, IT'S NOT YOUR FAULT...
AND IT'S THANKS TO YOU I MADE IT THIS FAR...
THANK YOU...
DOC...
MMGH... NGH...
WAAAAGH.
Chapter 5
You Survive

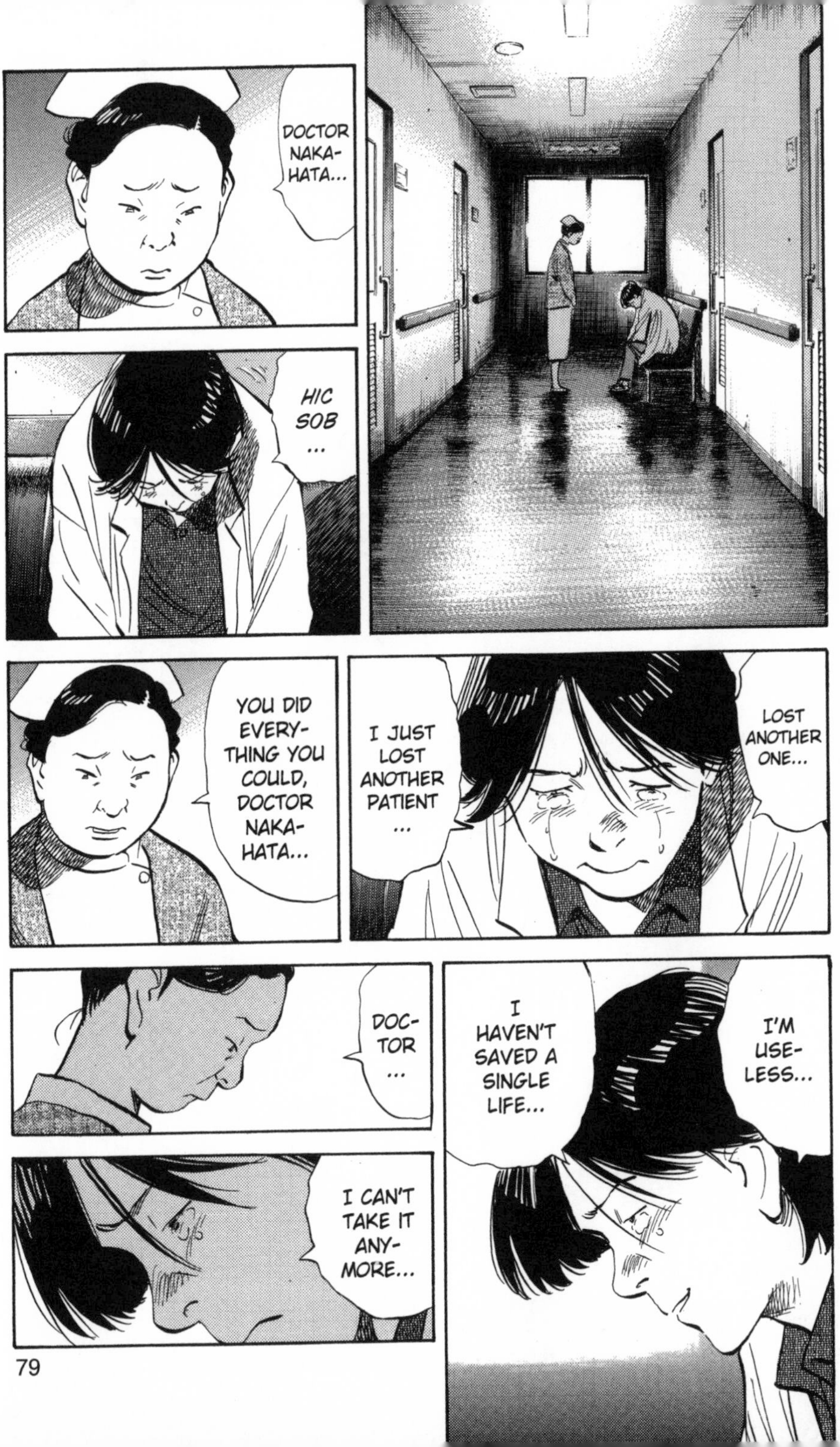
DOCTOR NAKA-HATA...
HIC SOB ...
LOST ANOTHER ONE...
I JUST LOST ANOTHER PATIENT ...
YOU DID EVERY-THING YOU COULD, DOCTOR NAKA-HATA...
I'M USE-LESS...
I HAVEN'T SAVED A SINGLE LIFE...
DOC-TOR ...
I CAN'T TAKE IT ANY-MORE...

I CAN'T SIT HERE AND WATCH PEOPLE DYING LIKE THIS ANYMORE !!

I'M SORRY...

YOU TAKE A BREAK, YASUDA-SAN. YOU NEED IT...

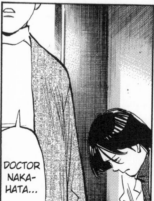

DOCTOR NAKA-HATA...

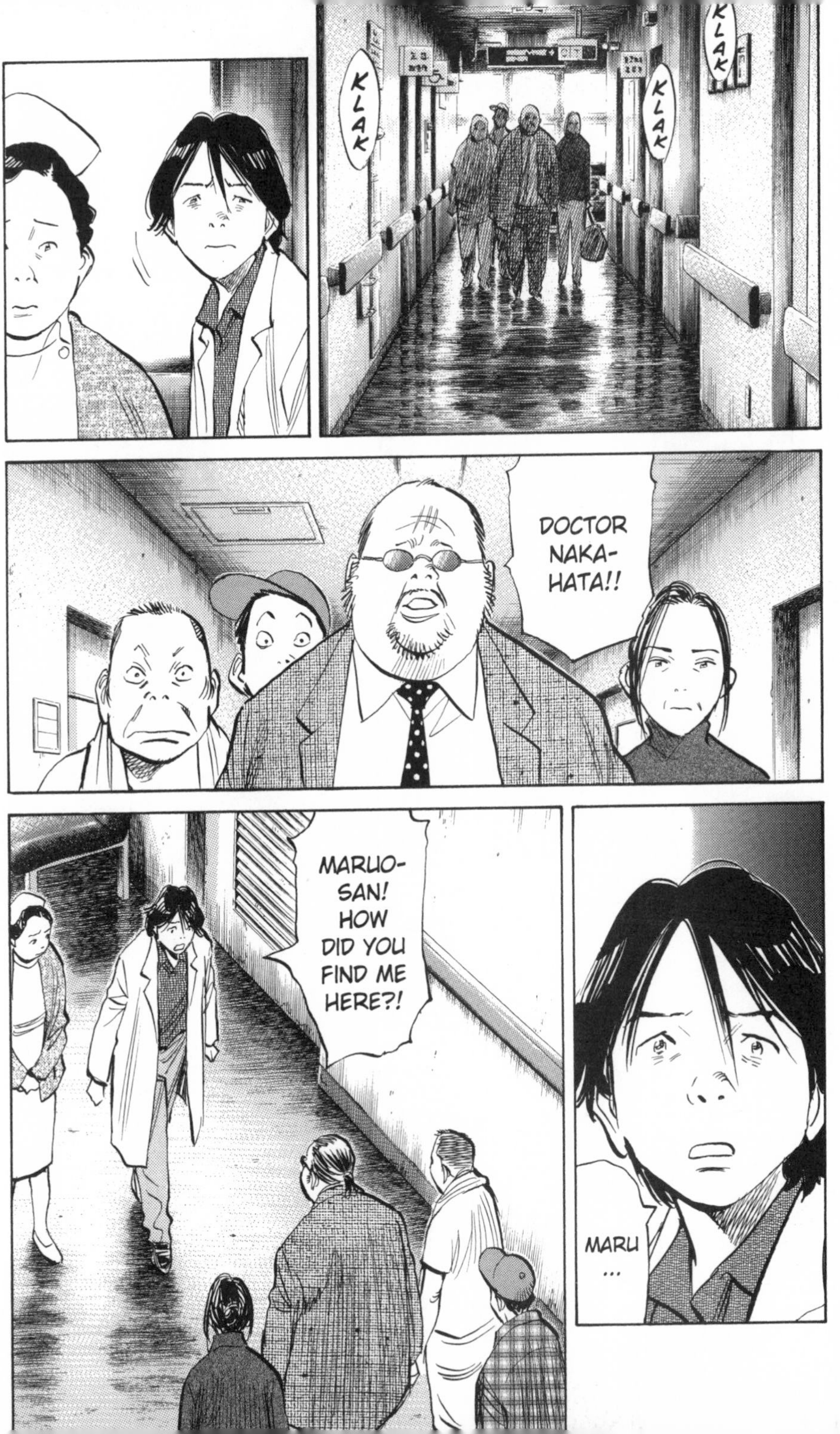
KLAK
KLAK
KLAK
DOCTOR NAKA-HATA!!
MARU ...
MARUO-SAN! HOW DID YOU FIND ME HERE?!

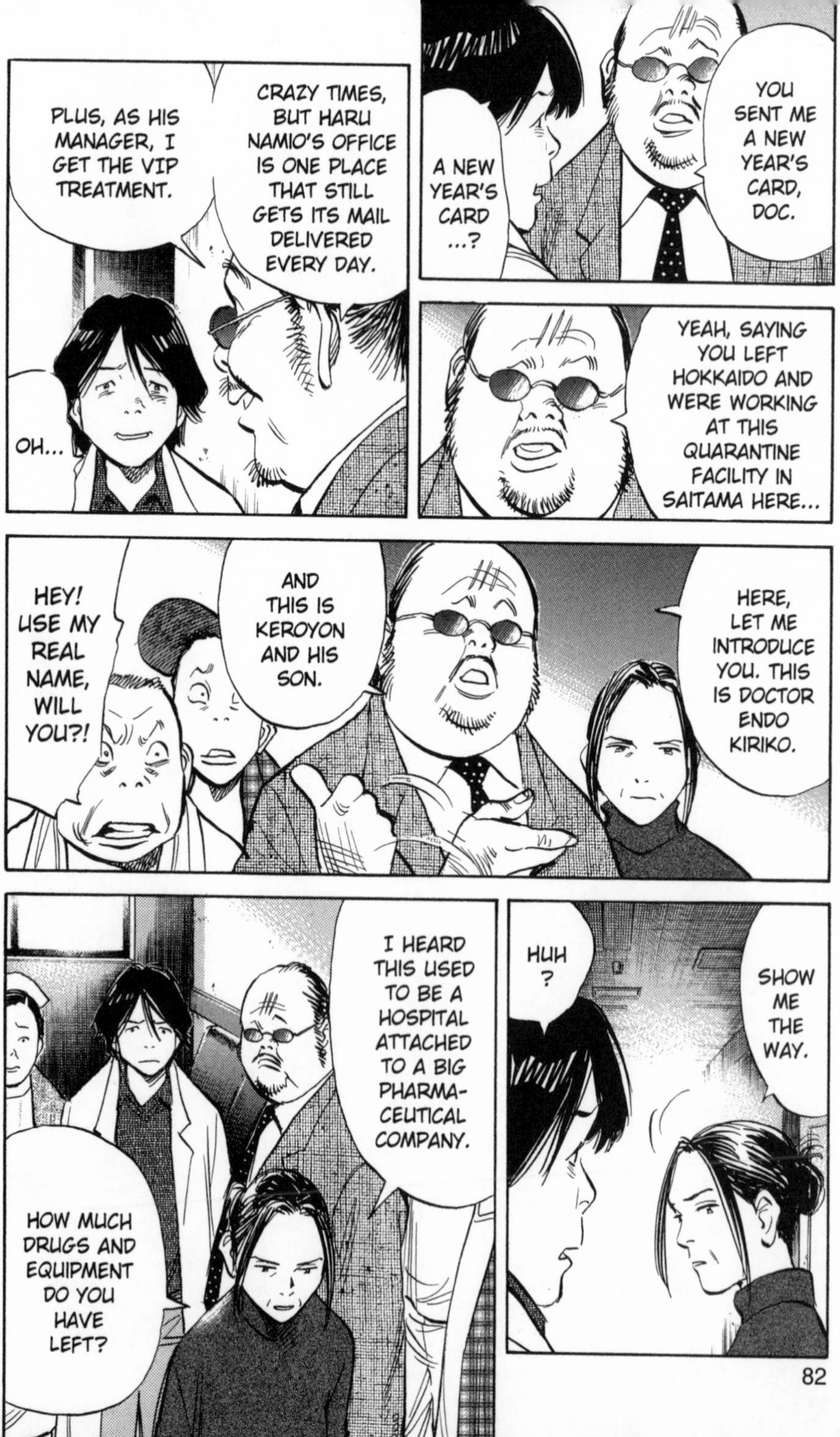
YOU SENT ME A NEW YEAR'S CARD, DOC.
A NEW YEAR'S CARD ...?
YEAH, SAYING YOU LEFT HOKKAIDO AND WERE WORKING AT THIS QUARANTINE FACILITY IN SAITAMA HERE...
CRAZY TIMES, BUT HARU NAMIO'S OFFICE IS ONE PLACE THAT STILL GETS ITS MAIL DELIVERED EVERY DAY.
PLUS, AS HIS MANAGER, I GET THE VIP TREATMENT.
OH...
HERE, LET ME INTRODUCE YOU. THIS IS DOCTOR ENDO KIRIKO.
AND THIS IS KEROYON AND HIS SON.
HEY! USE MY REAL NAME, WILL YOU?!
SHOW ME THE WAY.
HUH ?
I HEARD THIS USED TO BE A HOSPITAL ATTACHED TO A BIG PHARMA-CEUTICAL COMPANY.
HOW MUCH DRUGS AND EQUIPMENT DO YOU HAVE LEFT?

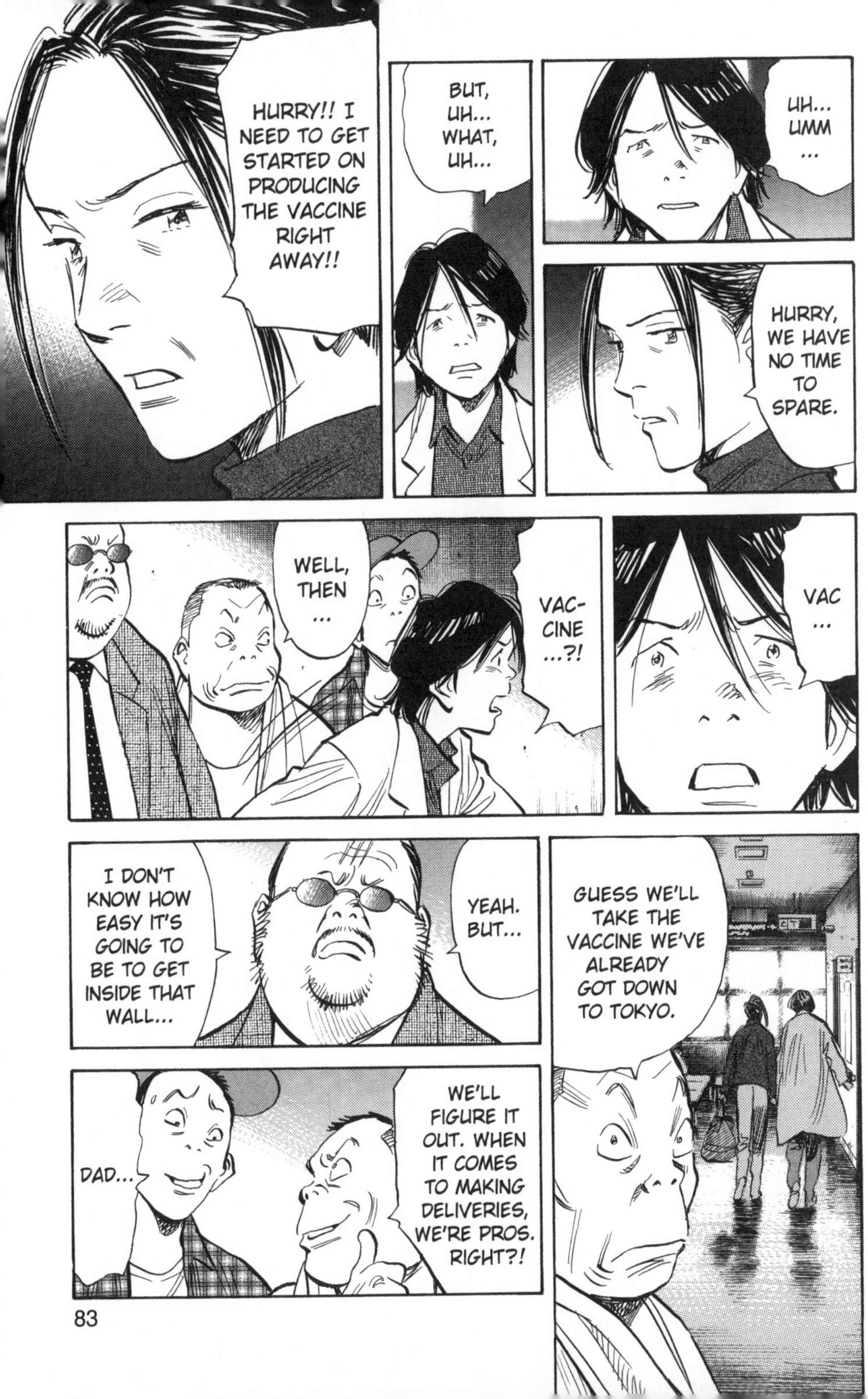
UH... UMM ...
HURRY, WE HAVE NO TIME TO SPARE.
BUT, UH... WHAT, UH...
HURRY!! I NEED TO GET STARTED ON PRODUCING THE VACCINE RIGHT AWAY!!
VAC ...
VAC-CINE ...?!
WELL, THEN ...
GUESS WE'LL TAKE THE VACCINE WE'VE ALREADY GOT DOWN TO TOKYO.
YEAH. BUT...
I DON'T KNOW HOW EASY IT'S GOING TO BE TO GET INSIDE THAT WALL...
WE'LL FIGURE IT OUT. WHEN IT COMES TO MAKING DELIVERIES, WE'RE PROS. RIGHT?!
DAD...

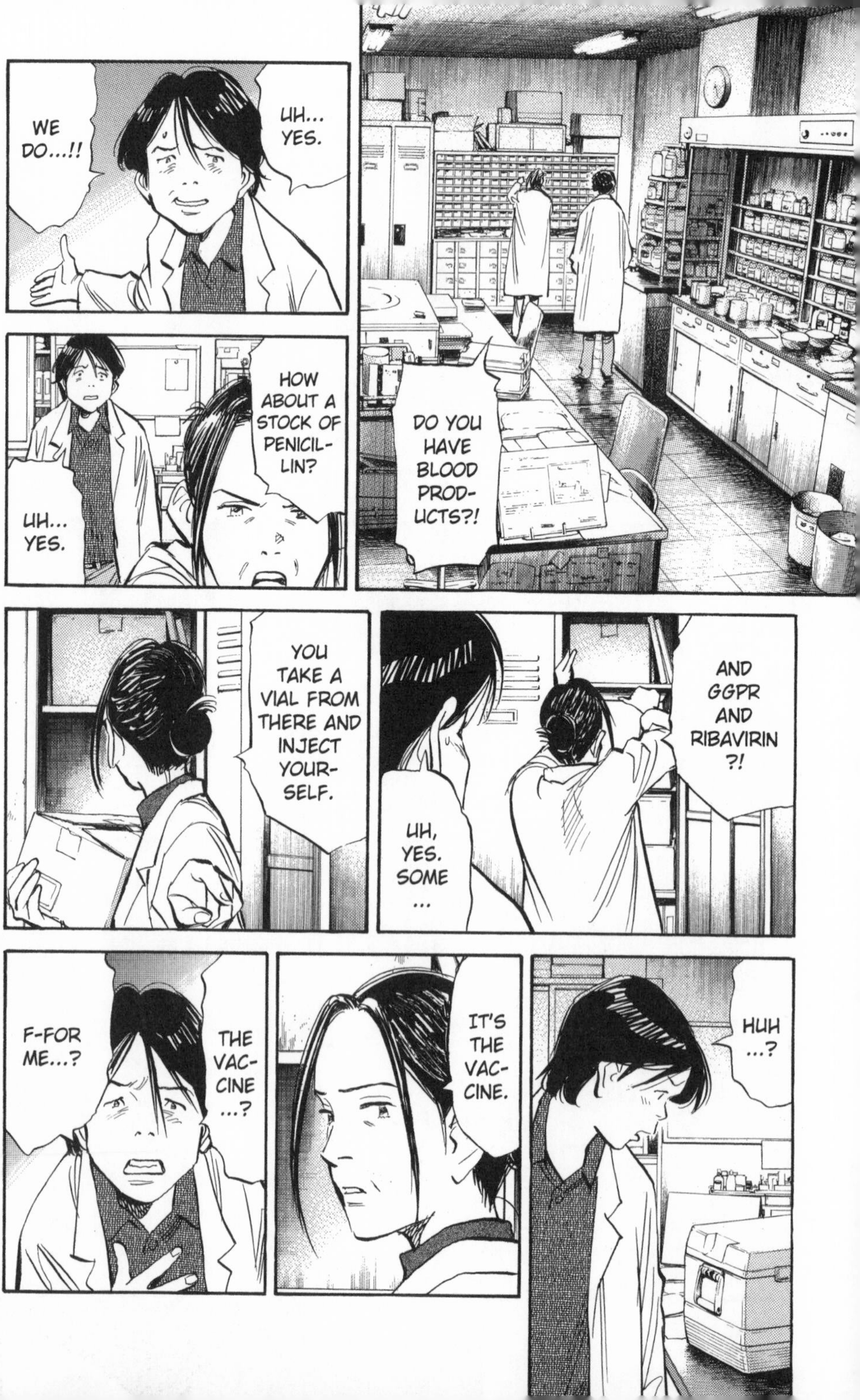
DO YOU HAVE BLOOD PRODUCTS?!
UH... YES.
WE DO...!!
HOW ABOUT A STOCK OF PENICILLIN?
UH... YES.
AND GGPR AND RIBAVIRIN?!
UH, YES. SOME...
YOU TAKE A VIAL FROM THERE AND INJECT YOURSELF.
HUH...?
IT'S THE VACCINE.
THE VACCINE...?
F-FOR ME...?

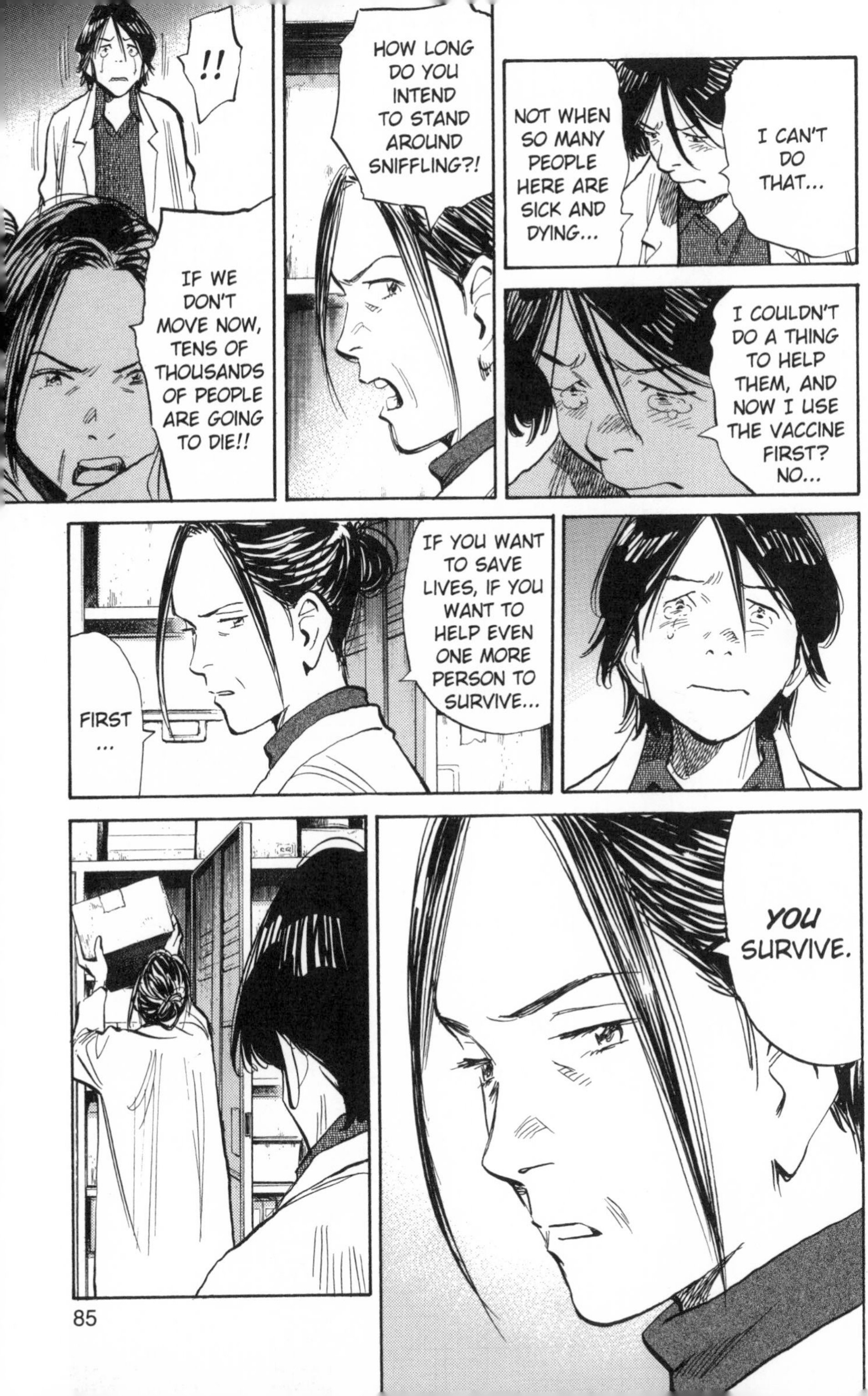
I CAN'T DO THAT...
NOT WHEN SO MANY PEOPLE HERE ARE SICK AND DYING...
I COULDN'T DO A THING TO HELP THEM, AND NOW I USE THE VACCINE FIRST? NO...
HOW LONG DO YOU INTEND TO STAND AROUND SNIFFLING?!
!!
IF WE DON'T MOVE NOW, TENS OF THOUSANDS OF PEOPLE ARE GOING TO DIE!!
IF YOU WANT TO SAVE LIVES, IF YOU WANT TO HELP EVEN ONE MORE PERSON TO SURVIVE...
FIRST ...
YOU SURVIVE.

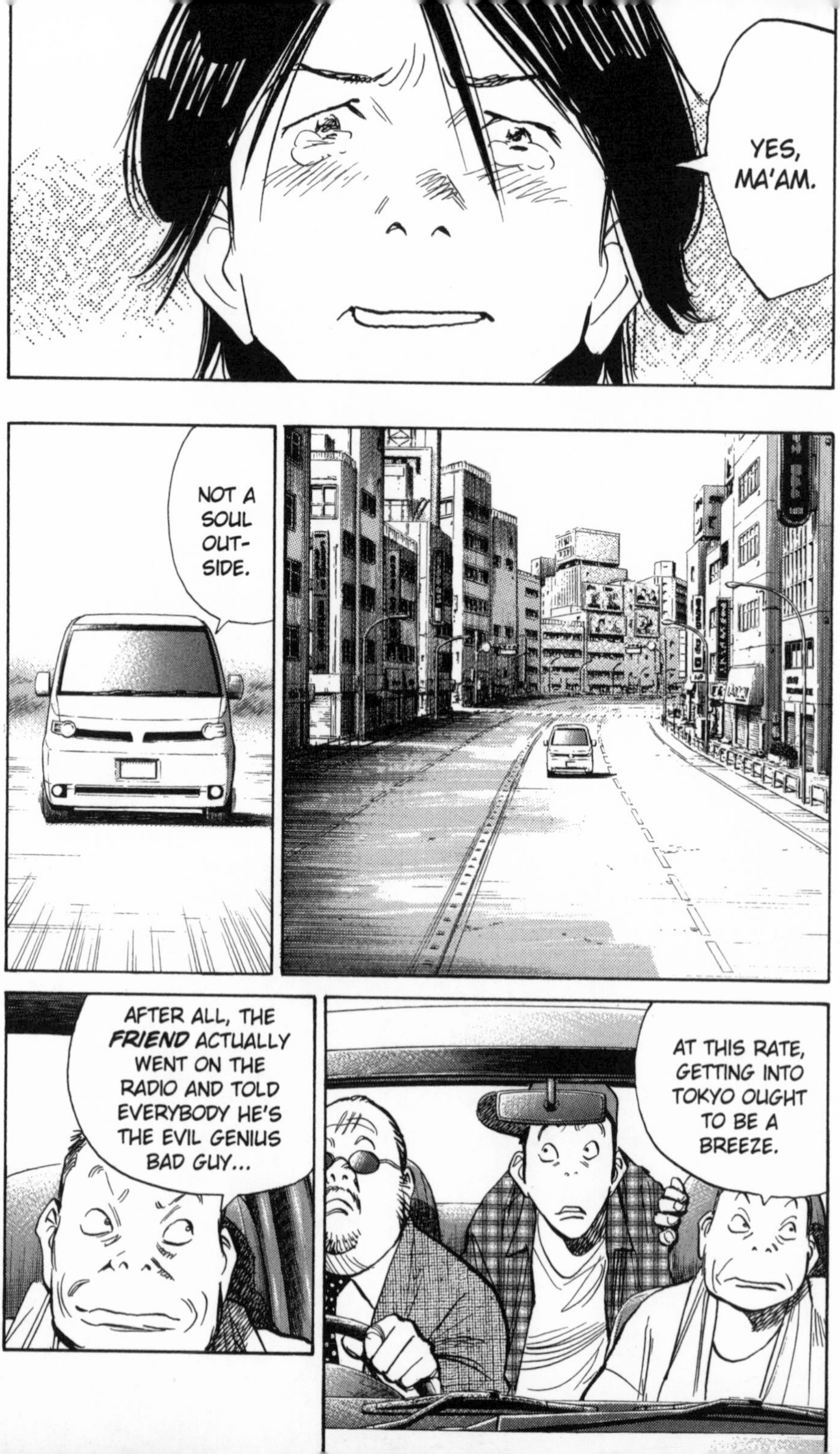
YES, MA'AM.
NOT A SOUL OUT-SIDE.
AT THIS RATE, GETTING INTO TOKYO OUGHT TO BE A BREEZE.
AFTER ALL, THE ***FRIEND*** ACTUALLY WENT ON THE RADIO AND TOLD EVERYBODY HE'S THE EVIL GENIUS BAD GUY...

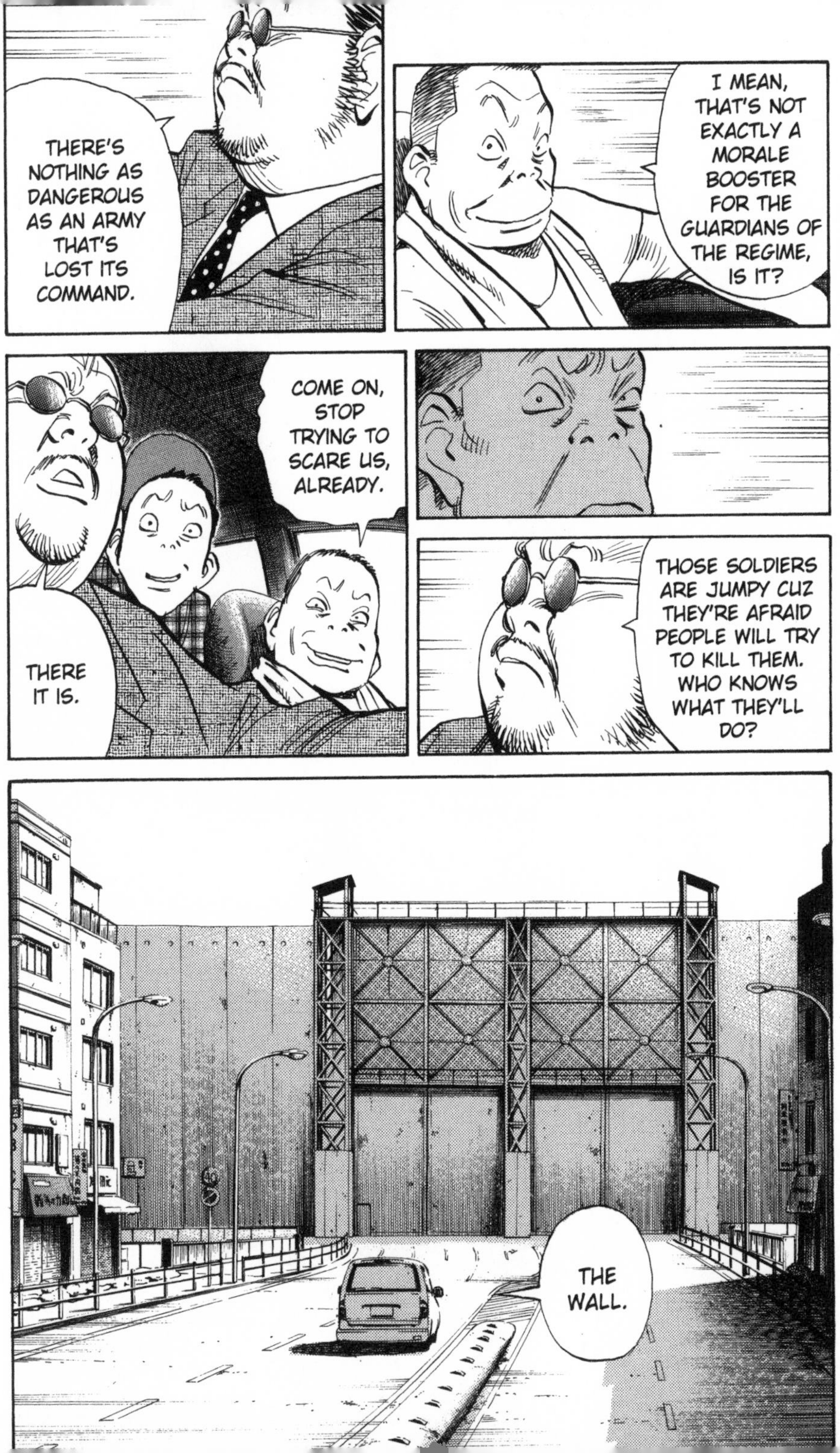
I MEAN, THAT'S NOT EXACTLY A MORALE BOOSTER FOR THE GUARDIANS OF THE REGIME, IS IT?
THERE'S NOTHING AS DANGEROUS AS AN ARMY THAT'S LOST ITS COMMAND.
THOSE SOLDIERS ARE JUMPY CUZ THEY'RE AFRAID PEOPLE WILL TRY TO KILL THEM. WHO KNOWS WHAT THEY'LL DO?
COME ON, STOP TRYING TO SCARE US, ALREADY.
THERE IT IS.
THE WALL.

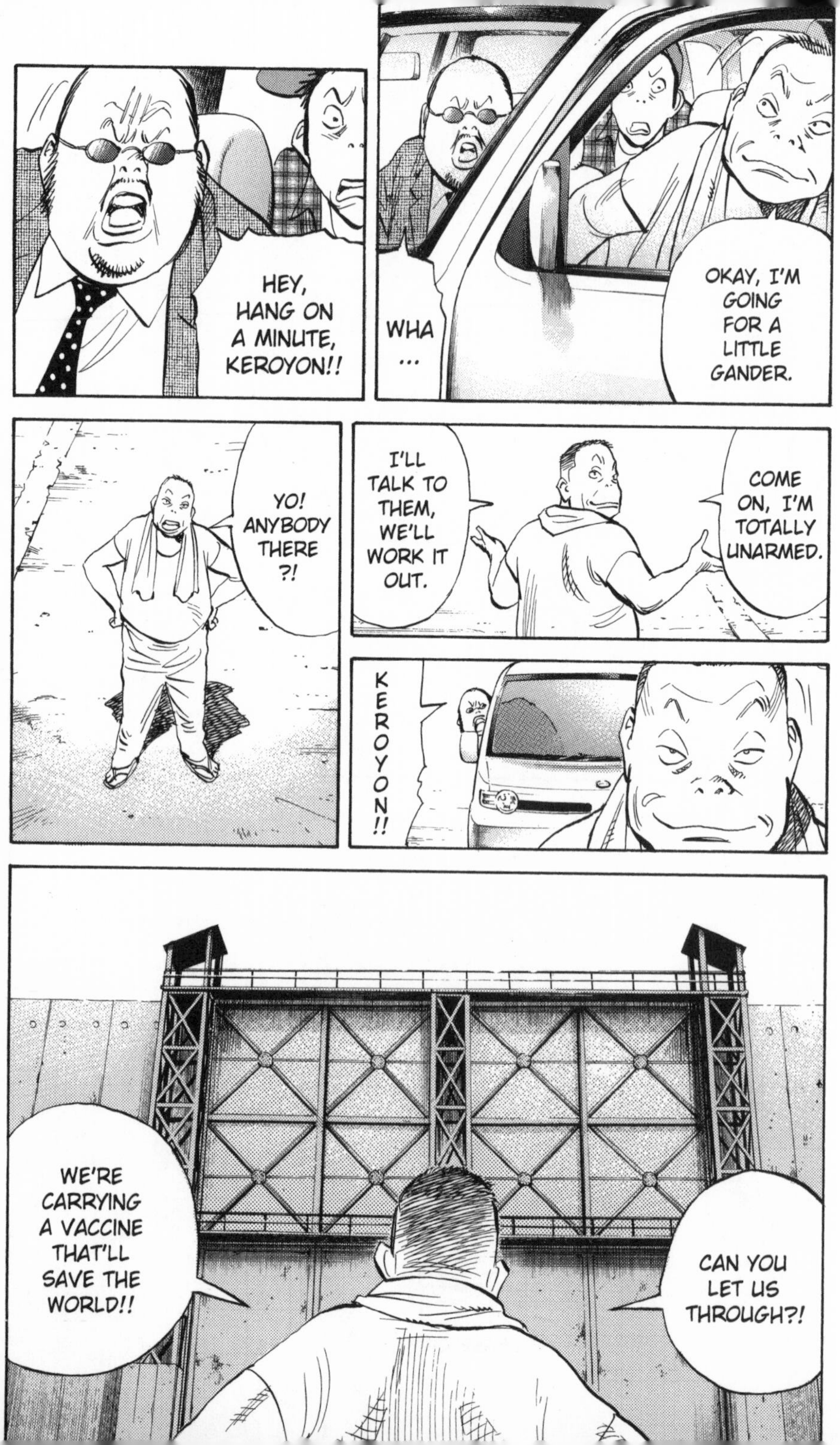
OKAY, I'M GOING FOR A LITTLE GANDER.
WHA ...
HEY, HANG ON A MINUTE, KEROYON!!
COME ON, I'M TOTALLY UNARMED.
I'LL TALK TO THEM, WE'LL WORK IT OUT.
KEROYON!!
YO! ANYBODY THERE ?!
WE'RE CARRYING A VACCINE THAT'LL SAVE THE WORLD!!
CAN YOU LET US THROUGH?!

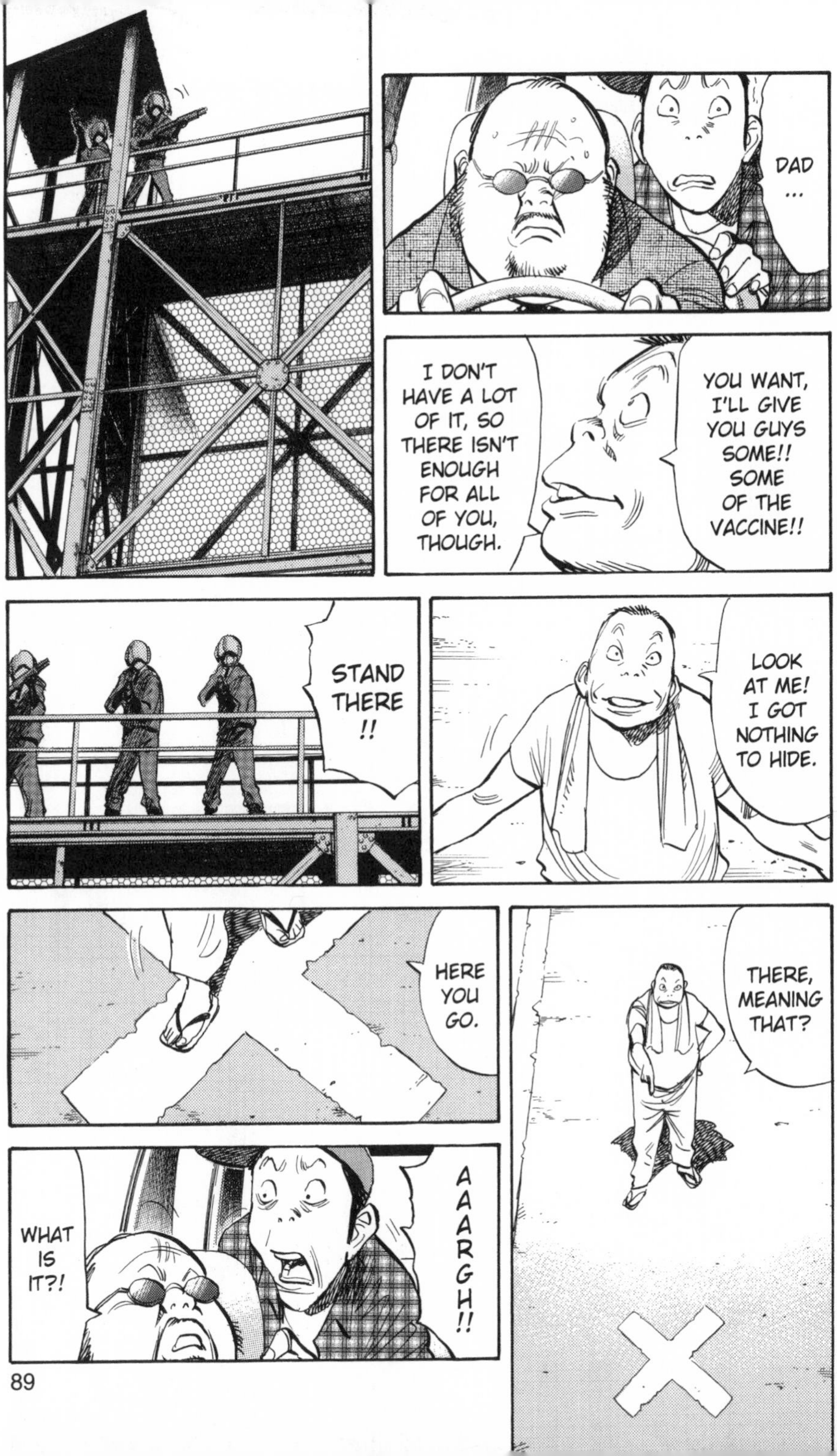
DAD ...
YOU WANT, I'LL GIVE YOU GUYS SOME!! SOME OF THE VACCINE!!
I DON'T HAVE A LOT OF IT, SO THERE ISN'T ENOUGH FOR ALL OF YOU, THOUGH.
LOOK AT ME! I GOT NOTHING TO HIDE.
STAND THERE !!
THERE, MEANING THAT?
HERE YOU GO.
AAAARGH!!
WHAT IS IT?!

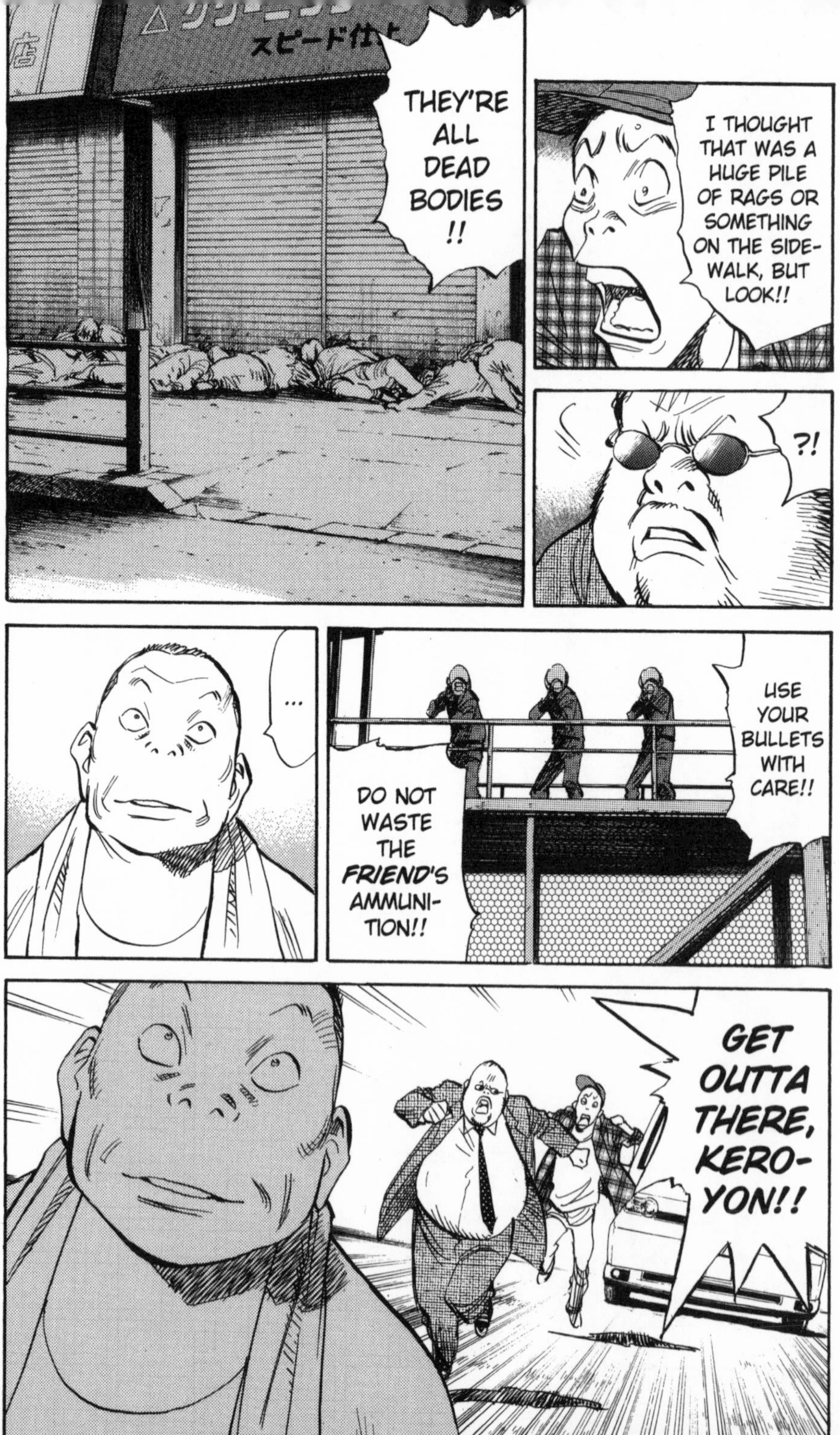
I THOUGHT THAT WAS A HUGE PILE OF RAGS OR SOMETHING ON THE SIDE-WALK, BUT LOOK!!
?!
スピード仕上
THEY'RE ALL DEAD BODIES !!
USE YOUR BULLETS WITH CARE!!
DO NOT WASTE THE FRIEND's AMMUNITION!!
...
GET OUTTA THERE, KERO-YON!!

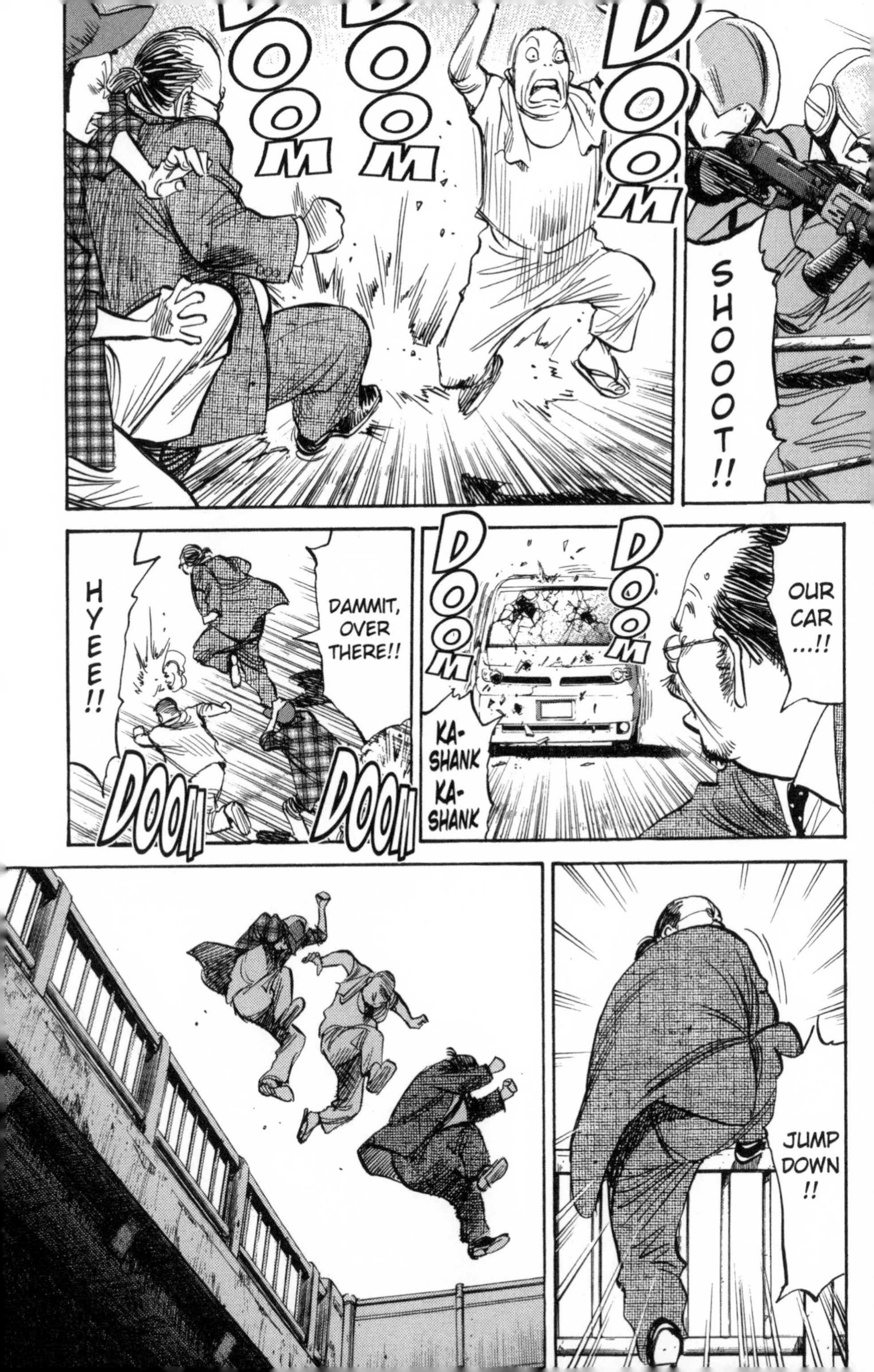
SHOOOOT!!
DOOM
DOOM
DOOM
OUR CAR ...!!
DOOM
DOOM
KA-SHANK KA-SHANK
DAMMIT, OVER THERE!!
HYEEE!!
DOOM
DOOM
JUMP DOWN!!

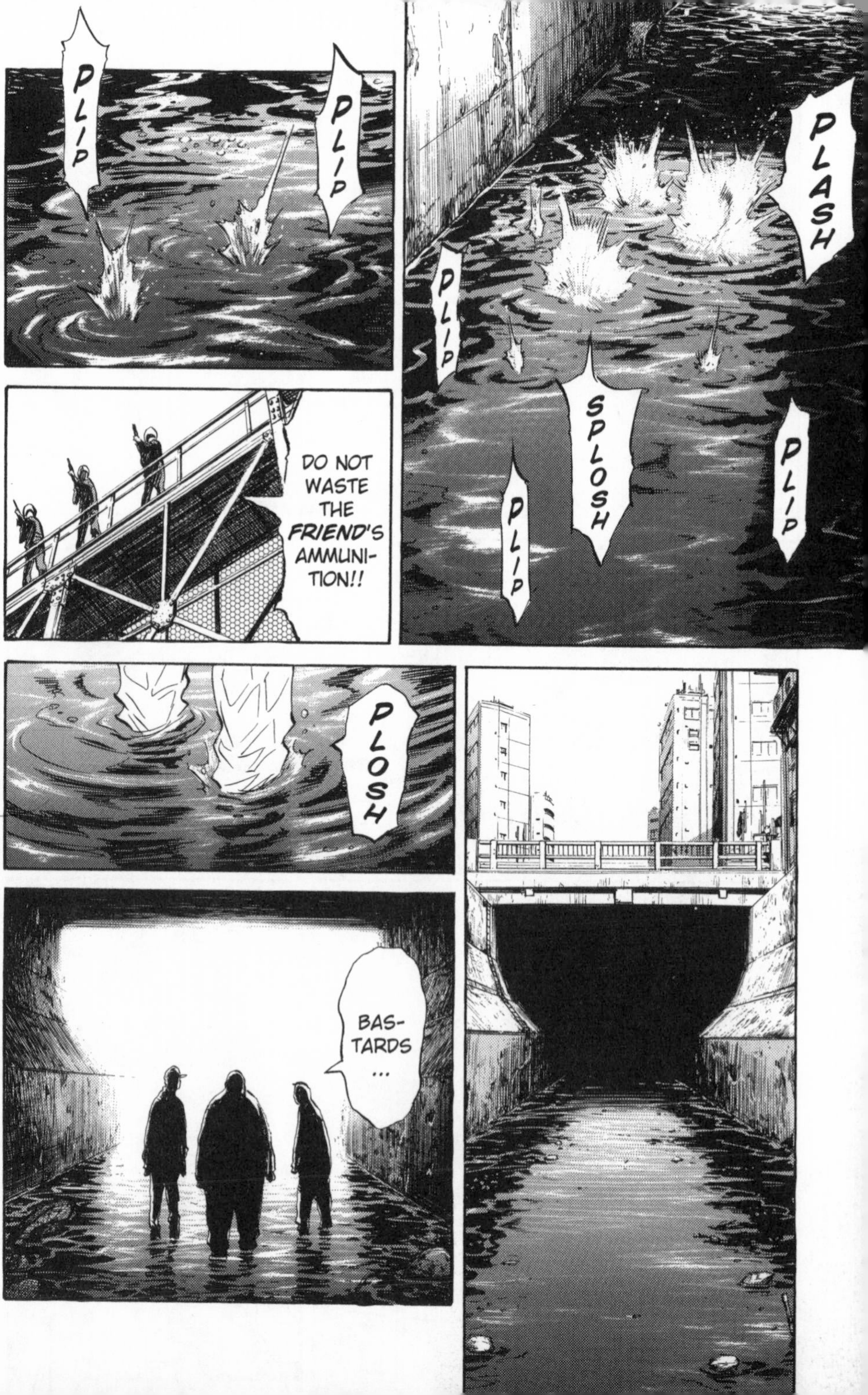
PLASH
PLIP
SPLOSH
PLIP
PLIP
PLIP
PLIP
DO NOT WASTE THE FRIEND'S AMMUNITION!!
PLOSH
BASTARDS...

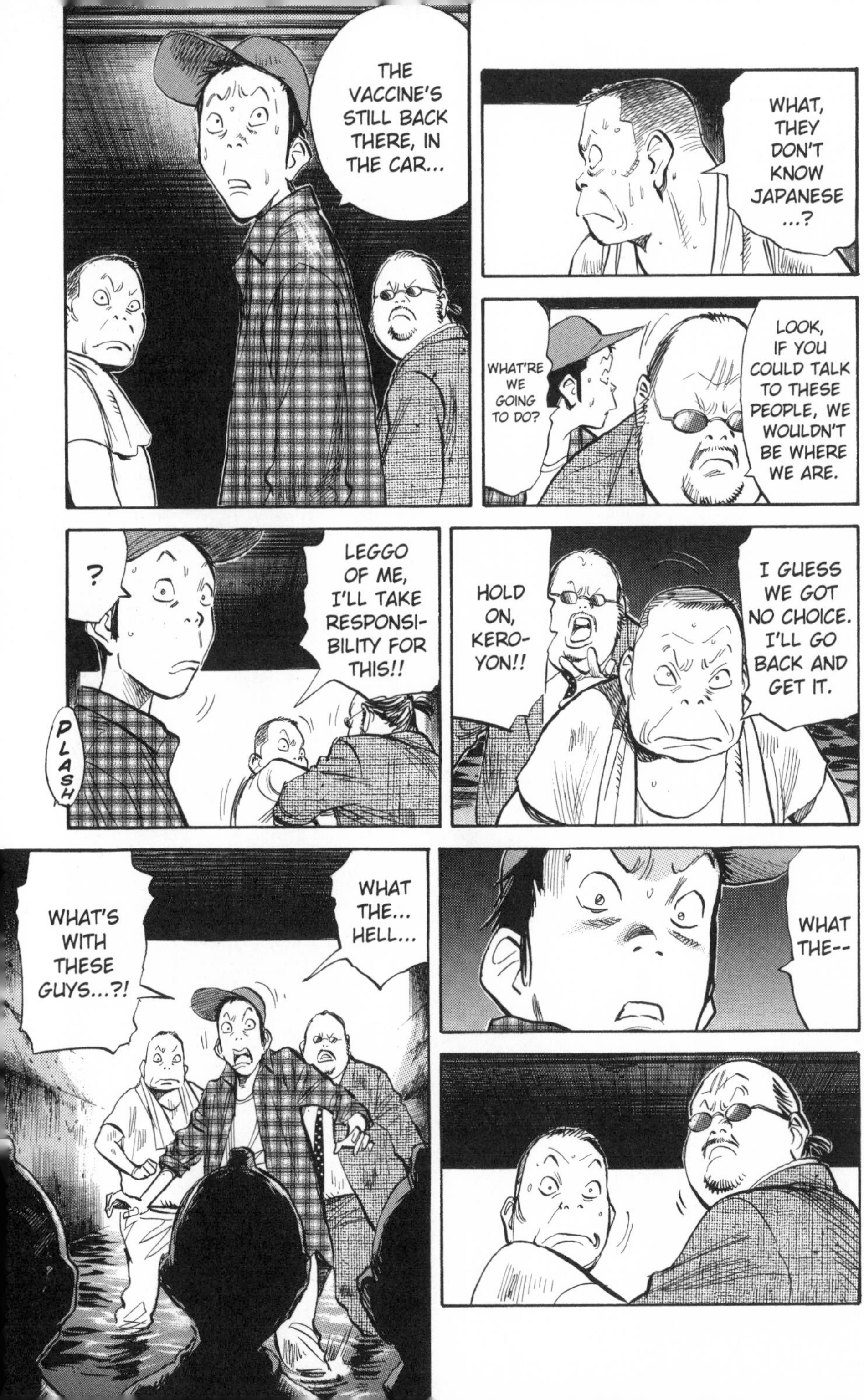
WHAT, THEY DON'T KNOW JAPANESE ...?
LOOK, IF YOU COULD TALK TO THESE PEOPLE, WE WOULDN'T BE WHERE WE ARE.
WHAT'RE WE GOING TO DO?
THE VACCINE'S STILL BACK THERE, IN THE CAR...
I GUESS WE GOT NO CHOICE. I'LL GO BACK AND GET IT.
HOLD ON, KERO-YON!!
LEGGO OF ME, I'LL TAKE RESPONSI-BILITY FOR THIS!!
?
PLASH
WHAT THE--
WHAT THE... HELL...
WHAT'S WITH THESE GUYS...?!

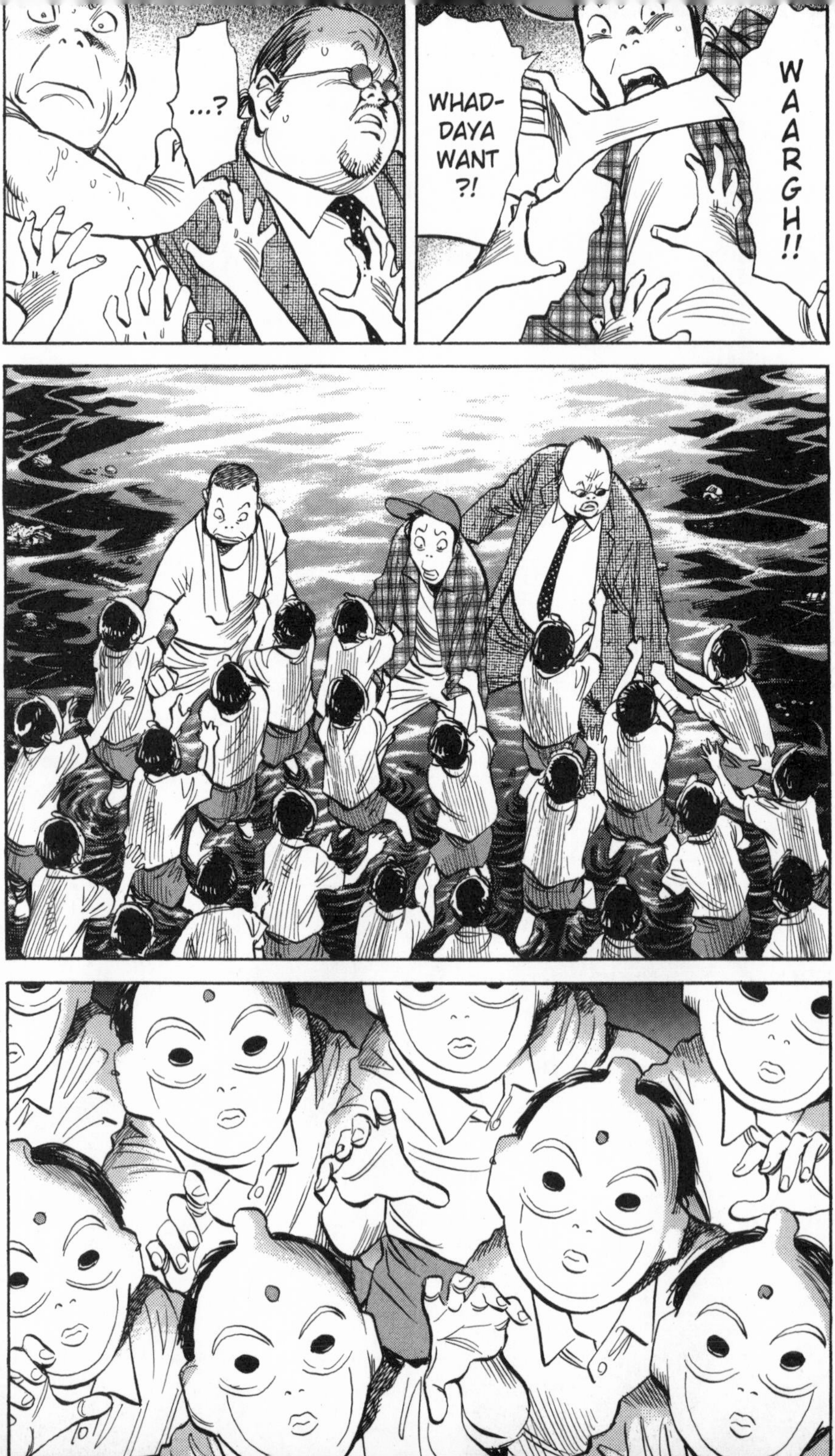
WAARGH!!
WHAD-DAYA WANT ?!
...?

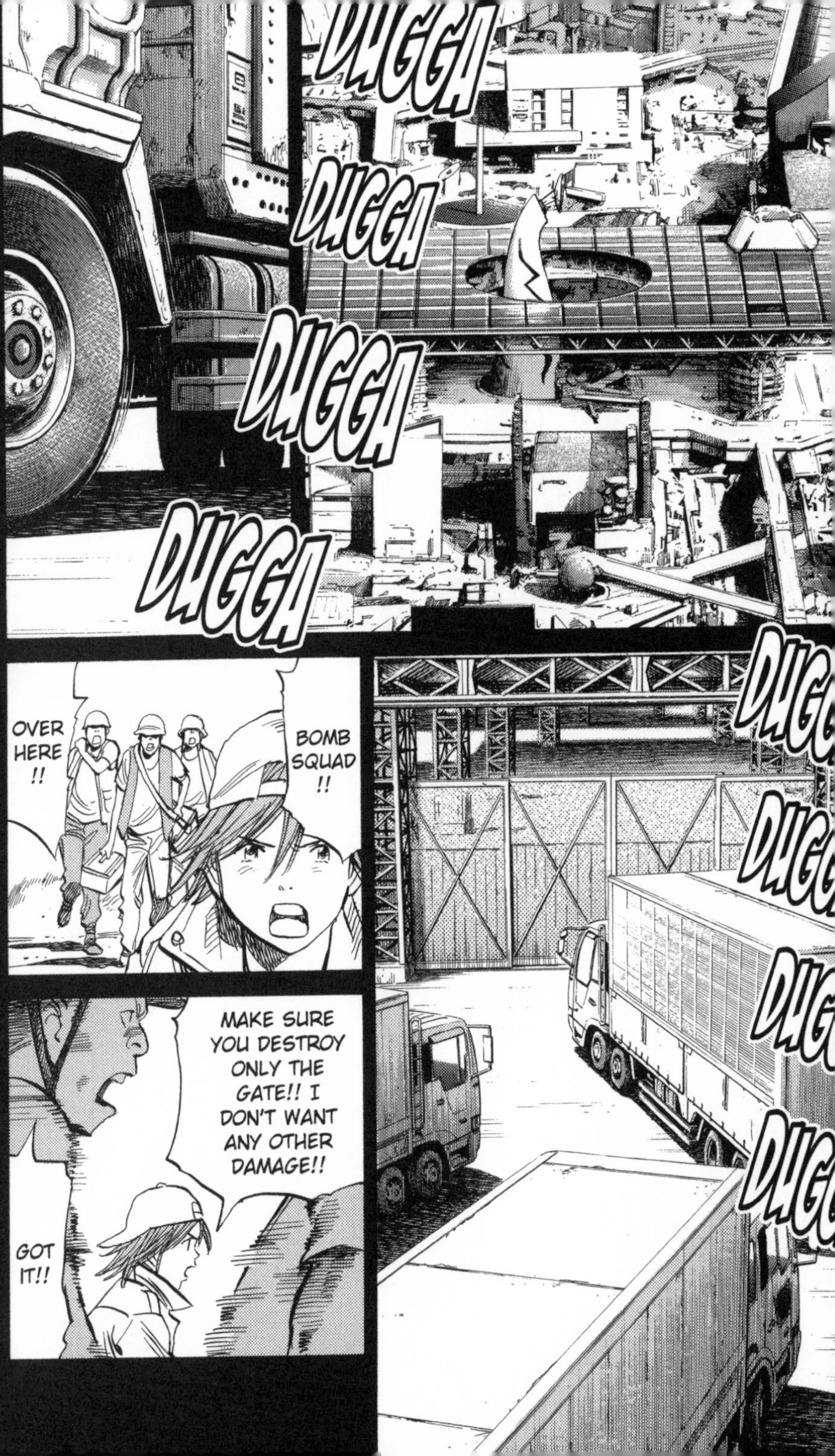
DUGGA
DUGGA
DUGGA
DUGGA
DUGG
DUGG
DUG
DUG
BOMB SQUAD!!
OVER HERE!!
MAKE SURE YOU DESTROY ONLY THE GATE!! I DON'T WANT ANY OTHER DAMAGE!!
GOT IT!!

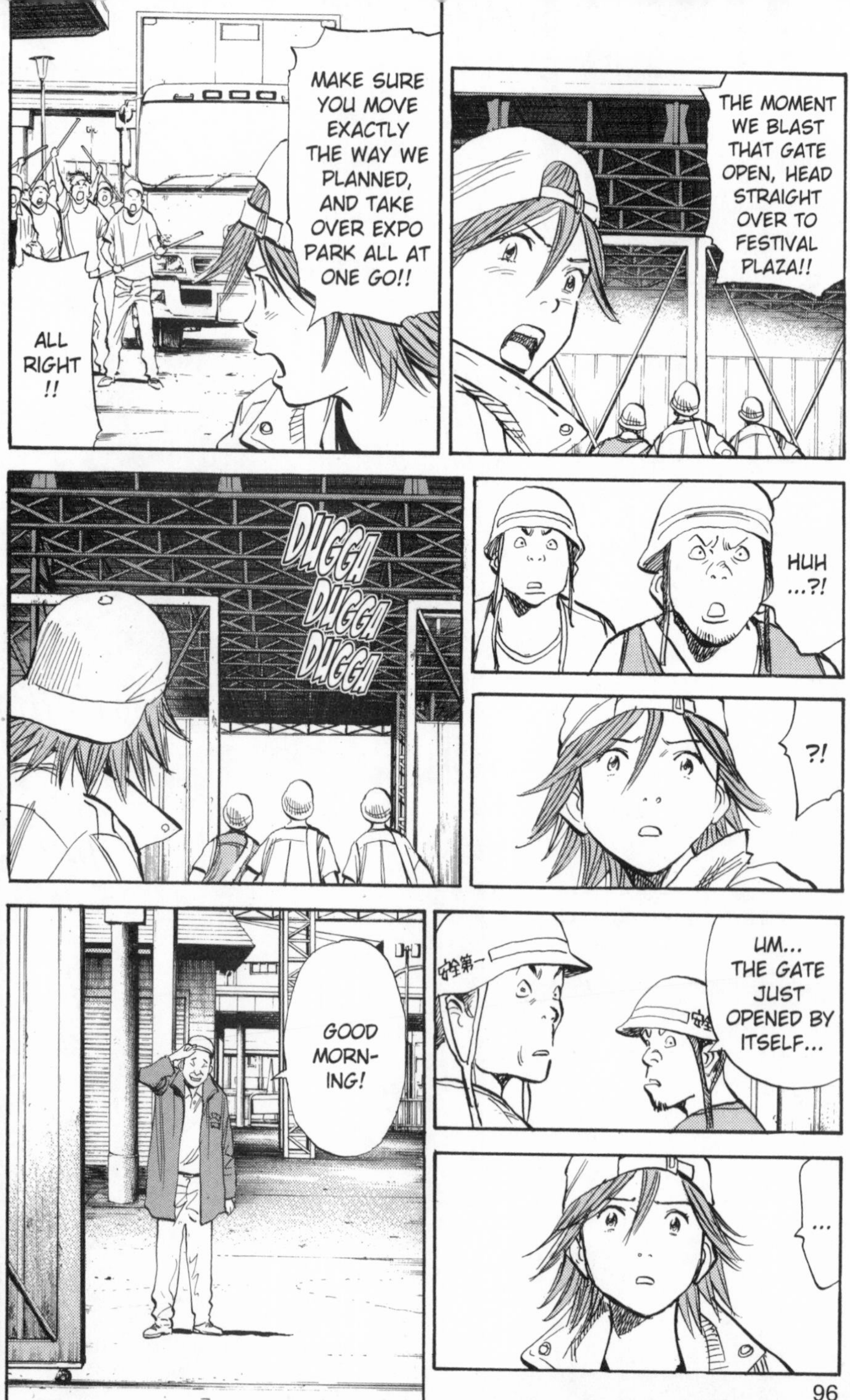
THE MOMENT WE BLAST THAT GATE OPEN, HEAD STRAIGHT OVER TO FESTIVAL PLAZA!!
MAKE SURE YOU MOVE EXACTLY THE WAY WE PLANNED, AND TAKE OVER EXPO PARK ALL AT ONE GO!!
ALL RIGHT !!
HUH ...?!
?!
DUGGA DUGGA DUGGA
UM... THE GATE JUST OPENED BY ITSELF...
...
GOOD MORNING!

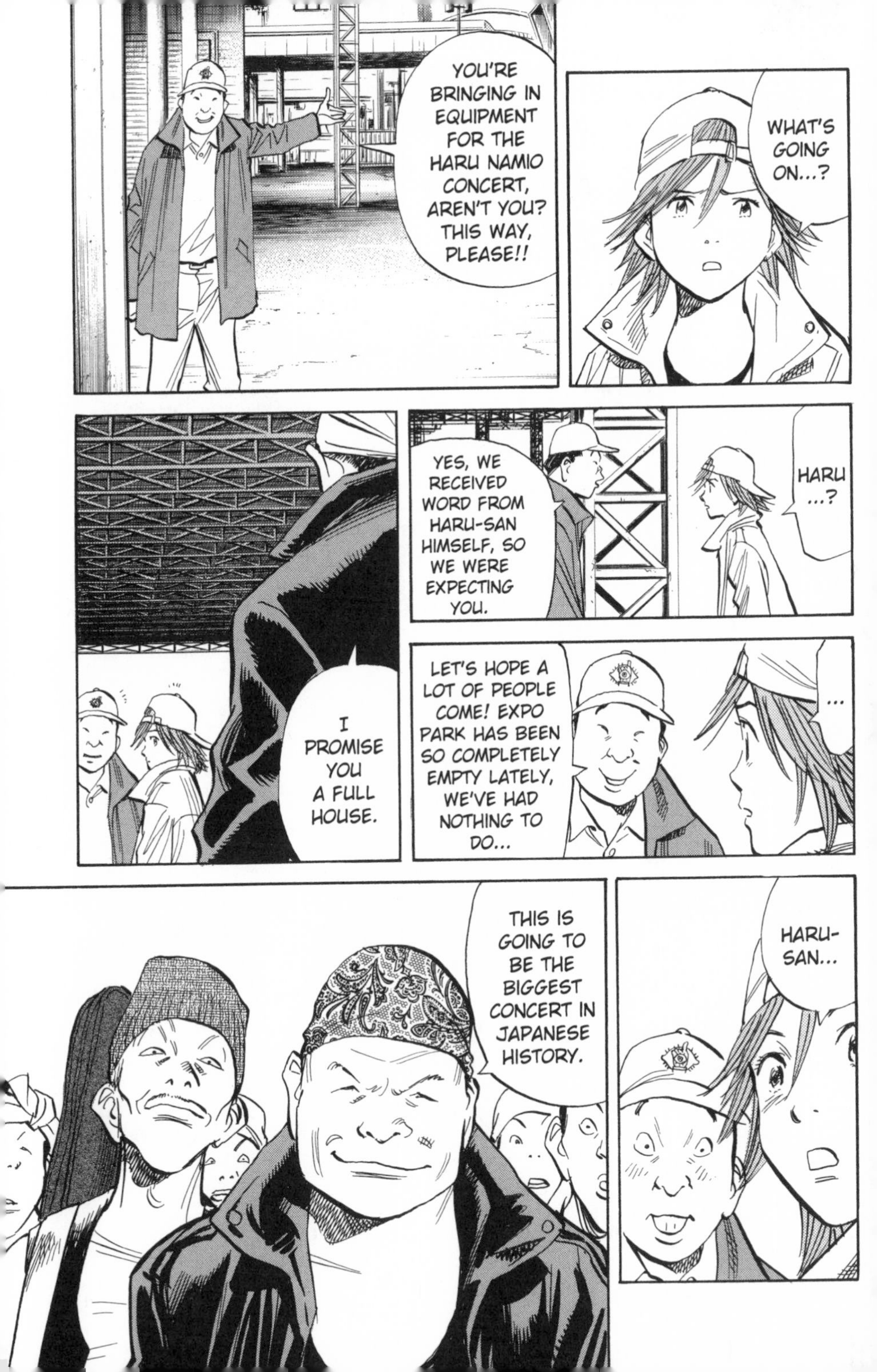
WHAT'S GOING ON...?
YOU'RE BRINGING IN EQUIPMENT FOR THE HARU NAMIO CONCERT, AREN'T YOU? THIS WAY, PLEASE!!
HARU ...?
YES, WE RECEIVED WORD FROM HARU-SAN HIMSELF, SO WE WERE EXPECTING YOU.
...
LET'S HOPE A LOT OF PEOPLE COME! EXPO PARK HAS BEEN SO COMPLETELY EMPTY LATELY, WE'VE HAD NOTHING TO DO...
I PROMISE YOU A FULL HOUSE.
HARU-SAN...
THIS IS GOING TO BE THE BIGGEST CONCERT IN JAPANESE HISTORY.

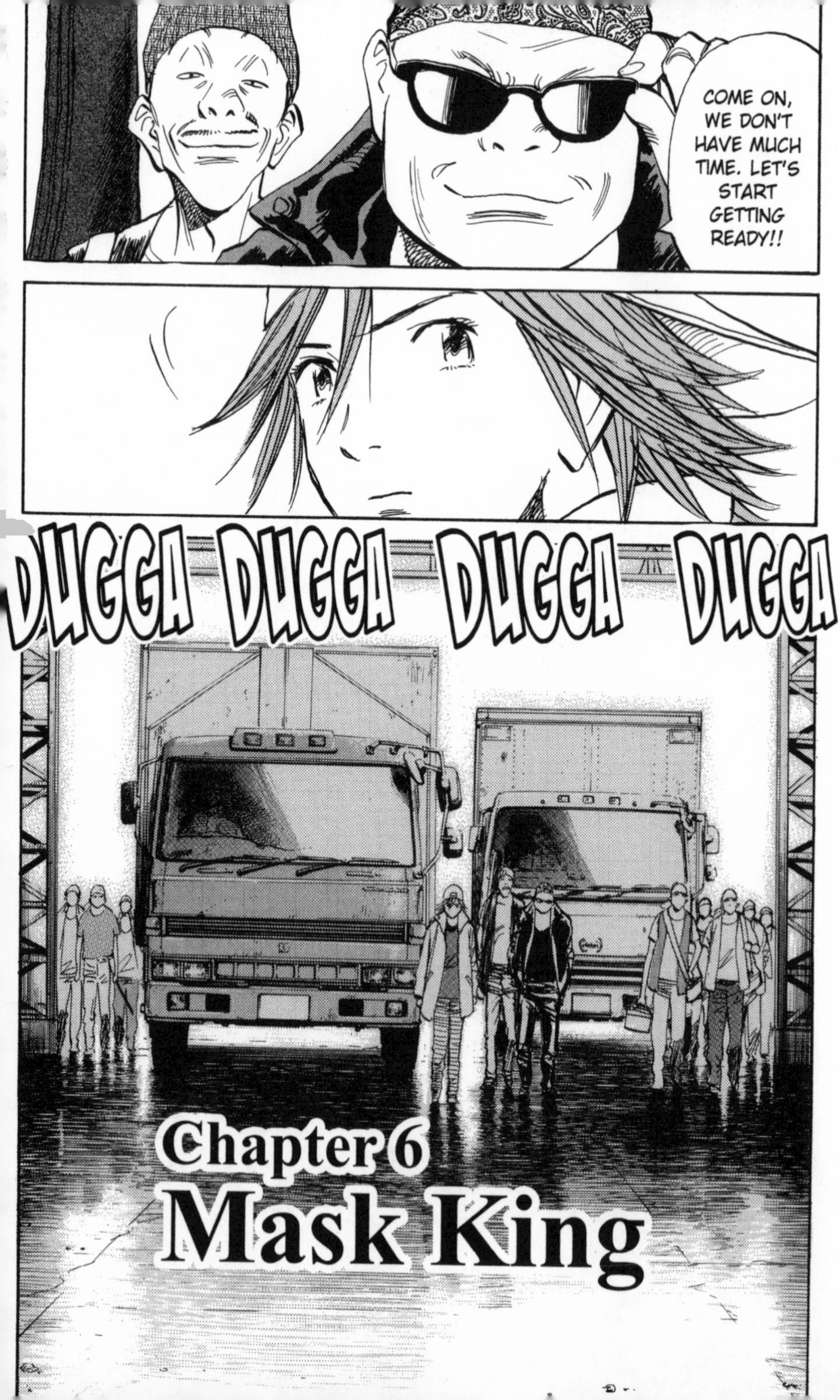
COME ON, WE DON'T HAVE MUCH TIME. LET'S START GETTING READY!!
DUGGA DUGGA DUGGA DUGGA
Chapter 6
Mask King

WH-WHAT'S THE STORY... WITH YOU KIDS?

DAD...

...

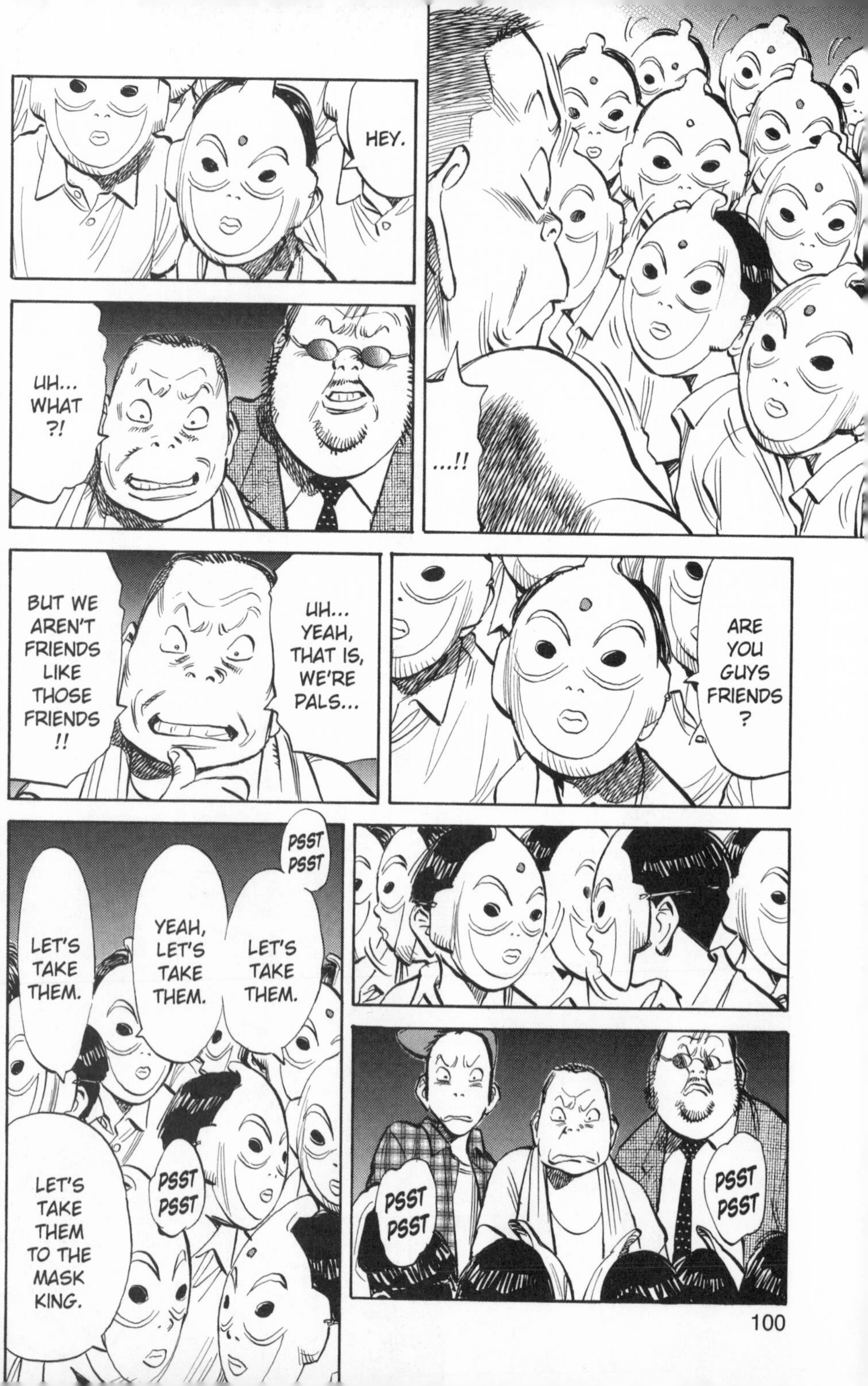
...!!
HEY.
UH... WHAT ?!
ARE YOU GUYS FRIENDS ?
UH... YEAH, THAT IS, WE'RE PALS...
BUT WE AREN'T FRIENDS LIKE THOSE FRIENDS !!
PSST PSST
PSST PSST
PSST PSST
LET'S TAKE THEM.
YEAH, LET'S TAKE THEM.
LET'S TAKE THEM.
PSST PSST
LET'S TAKE THEM TO THE MASK KING.

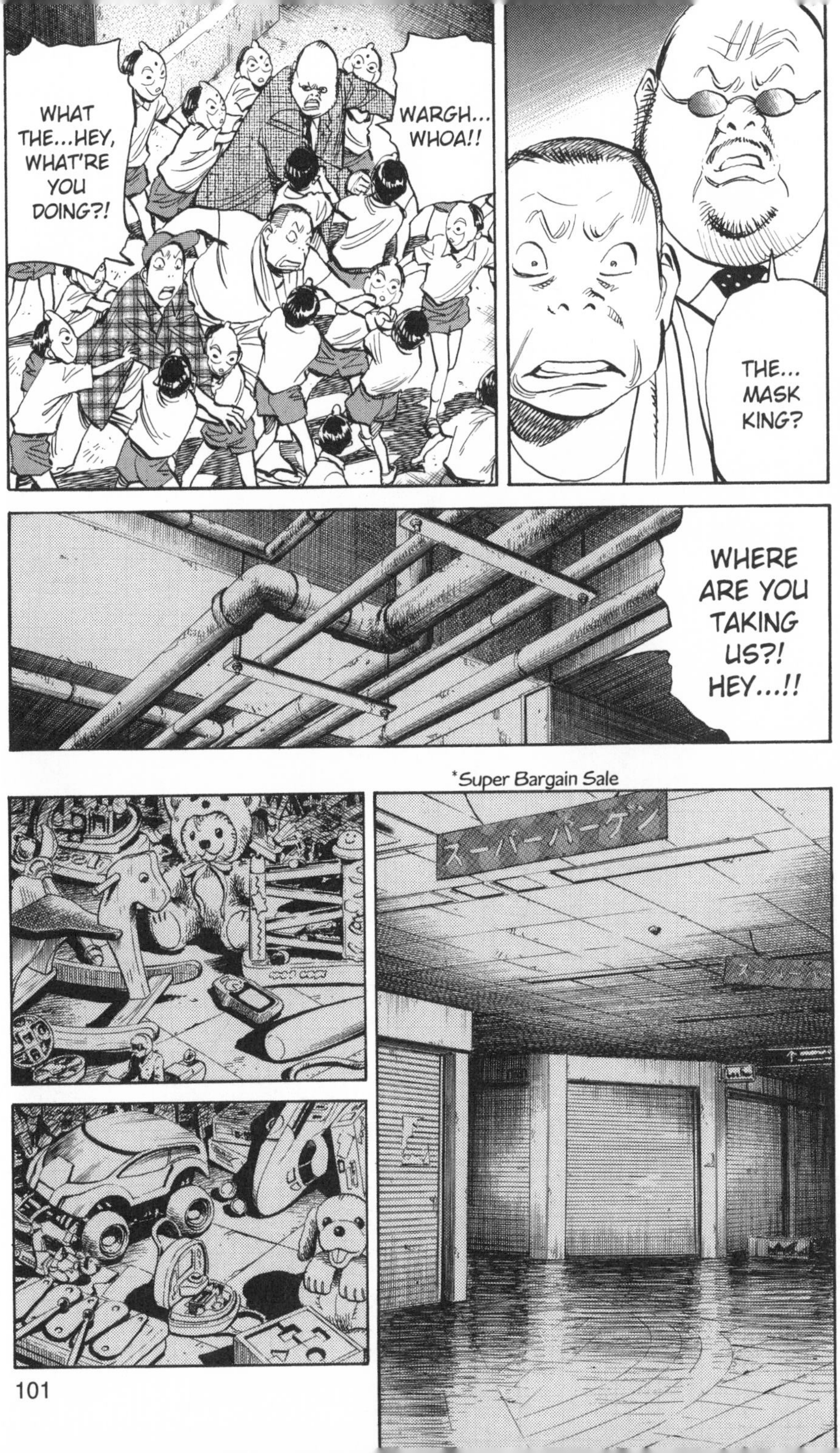
THE... MASK KING?
WARGH... WHOA!!
WHAT THE...HEY, WHAT'RE YOU DOING?!
WHERE ARE YOU TAKING US?! HEY...!!
スーパーバーゲン
*Super Bargain Sale

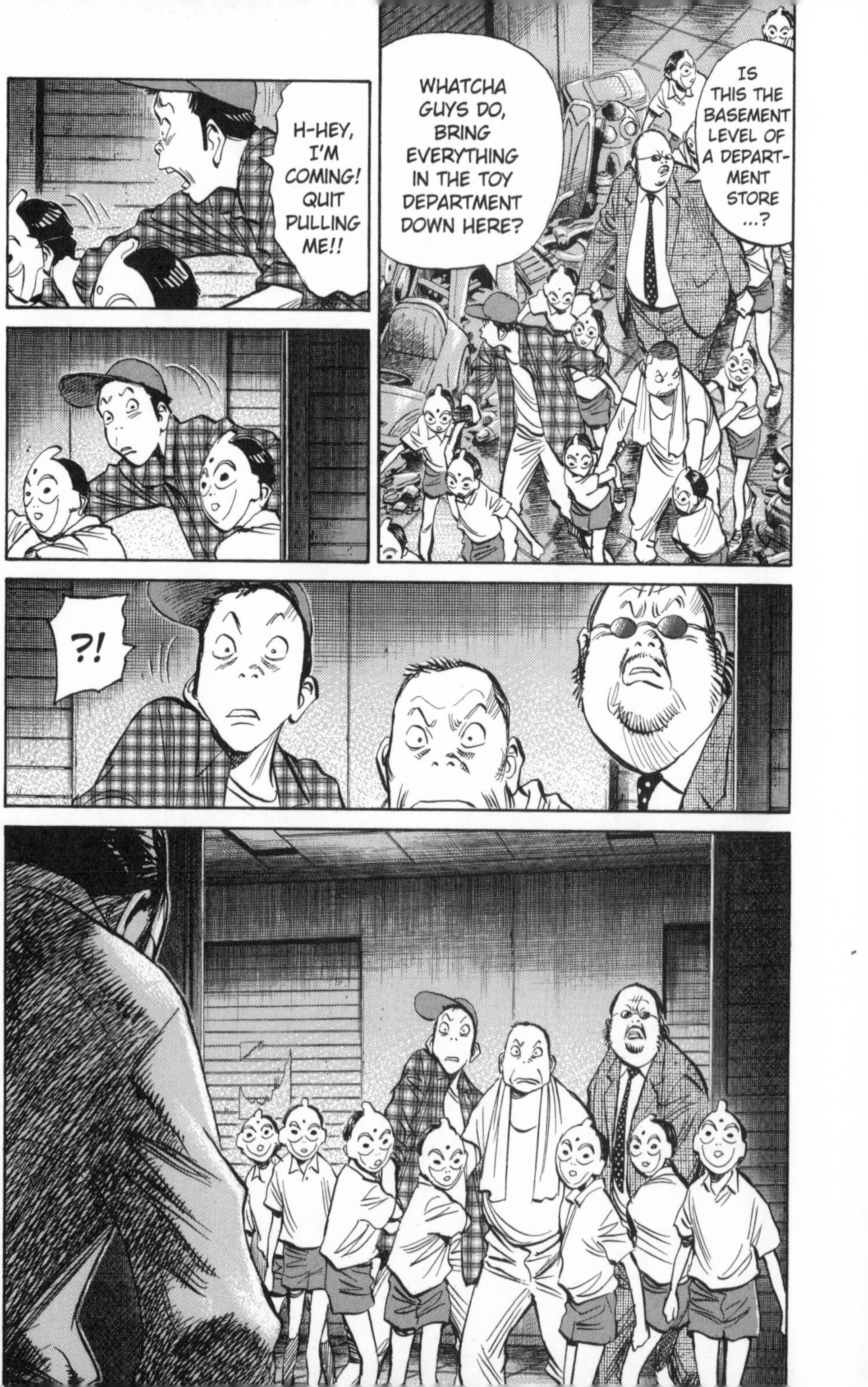
IS THIS THE BASEMENT LEVEL OF A DEPART-MENT STORE ...?
WHATCHA GUYS DO, BRING EVERYTHING IN THE TOY DEPARTMENT DOWN HERE?
H-HEY, I'M COMING! QUIT PULLING ME!!
?!

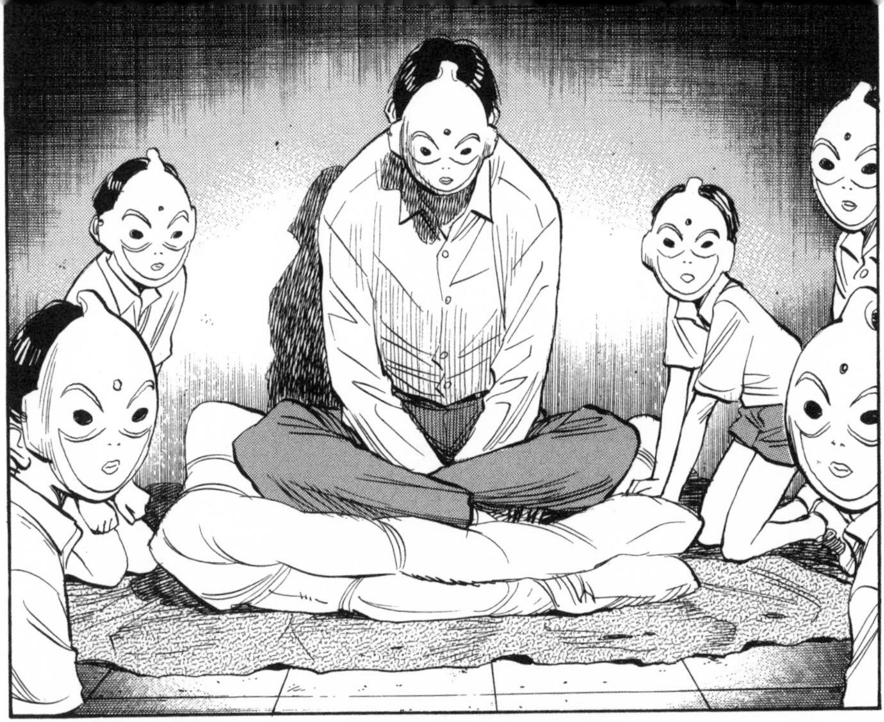

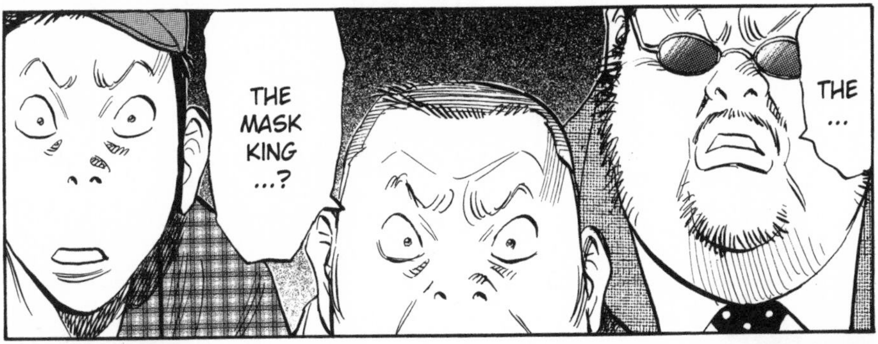
THE ...
THE MASK KING ...?

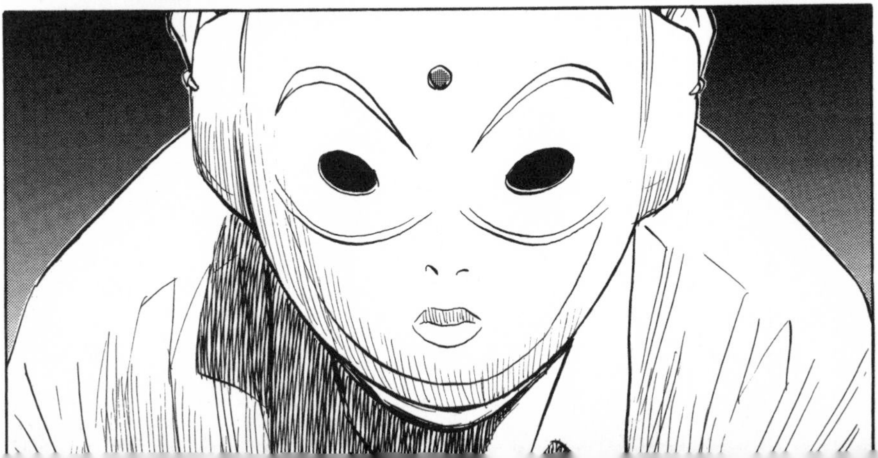

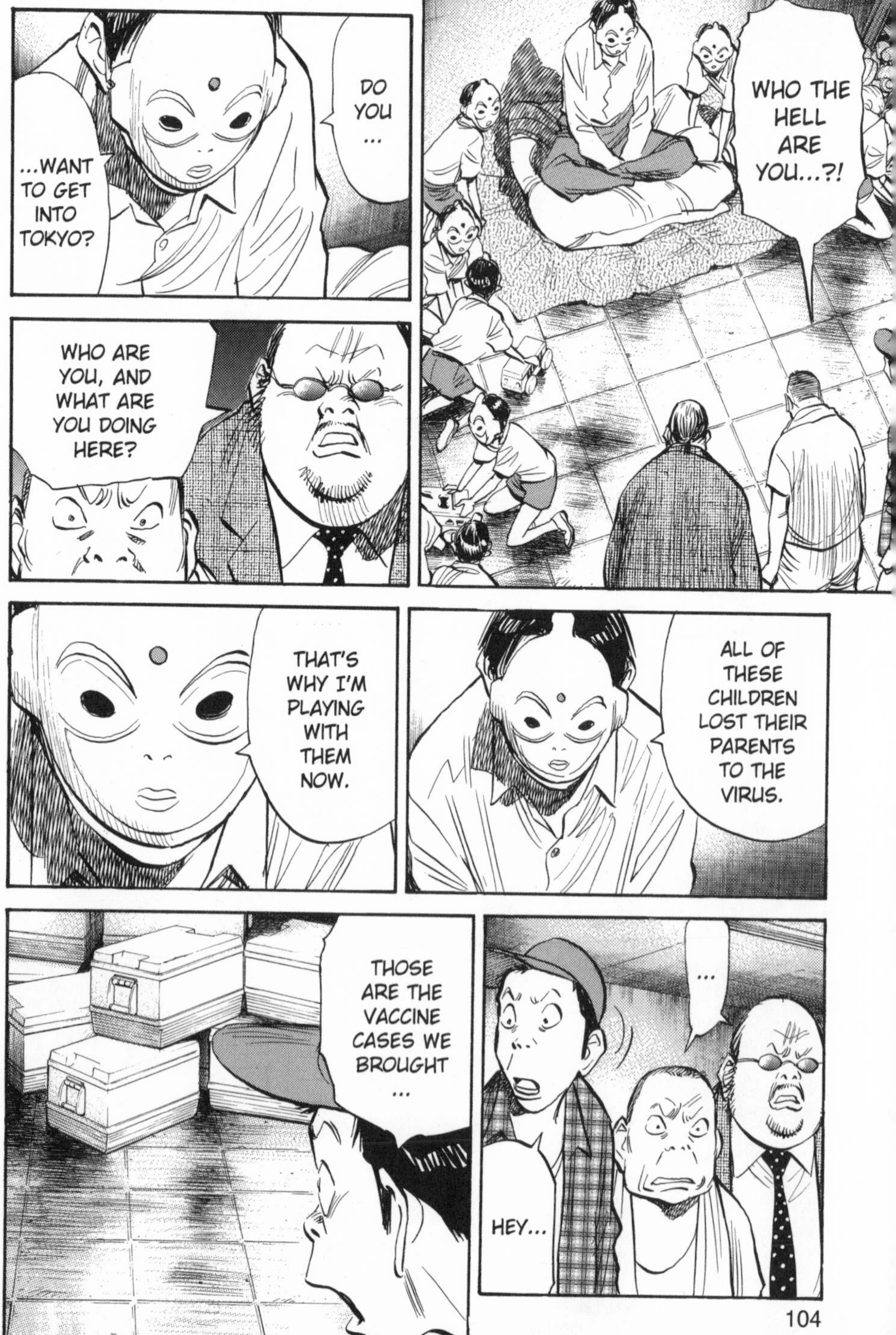
WHO THE HELL ARE YOU...?!
DO YOU ...
...WANT TO GET INTO TOKYO?
WHO ARE YOU, AND WHAT ARE YOU DOING HERE?
ALL OF THESE CHILDREN LOST THEIR PARENTS TO THE VIRUS.
THAT'S WHY I'M PLAYING WITH THEM NOW.
...
HEY...
THOSE ARE THE VACCINE CASES WE BROUGHT ...

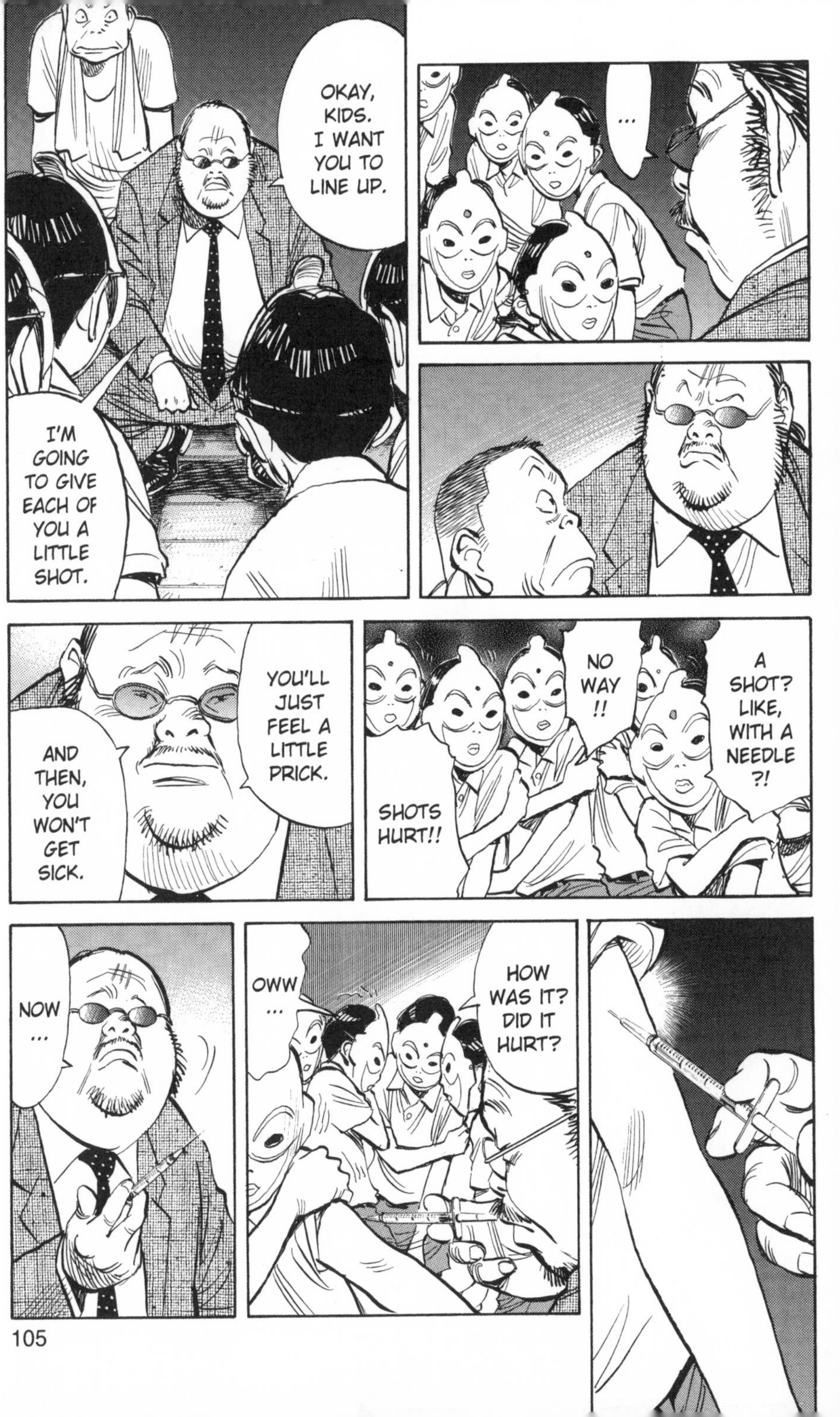
...
OKAY, KIDS. I WANT YOU TO LINE UP.
I'M GOING TO GIVE EACH OF YOU A LITTLE SHOT.
A SHOT? LIKE, WITH A NEEDLE?!
NO WAY!!
SHOTS HURT!!
YOU'LL JUST FEEL A LITTLE PRICK.
AND THEN, YOU WON'T GET SICK.
HOW WAS IT? DID IT HURT?
OWW...
NOW...

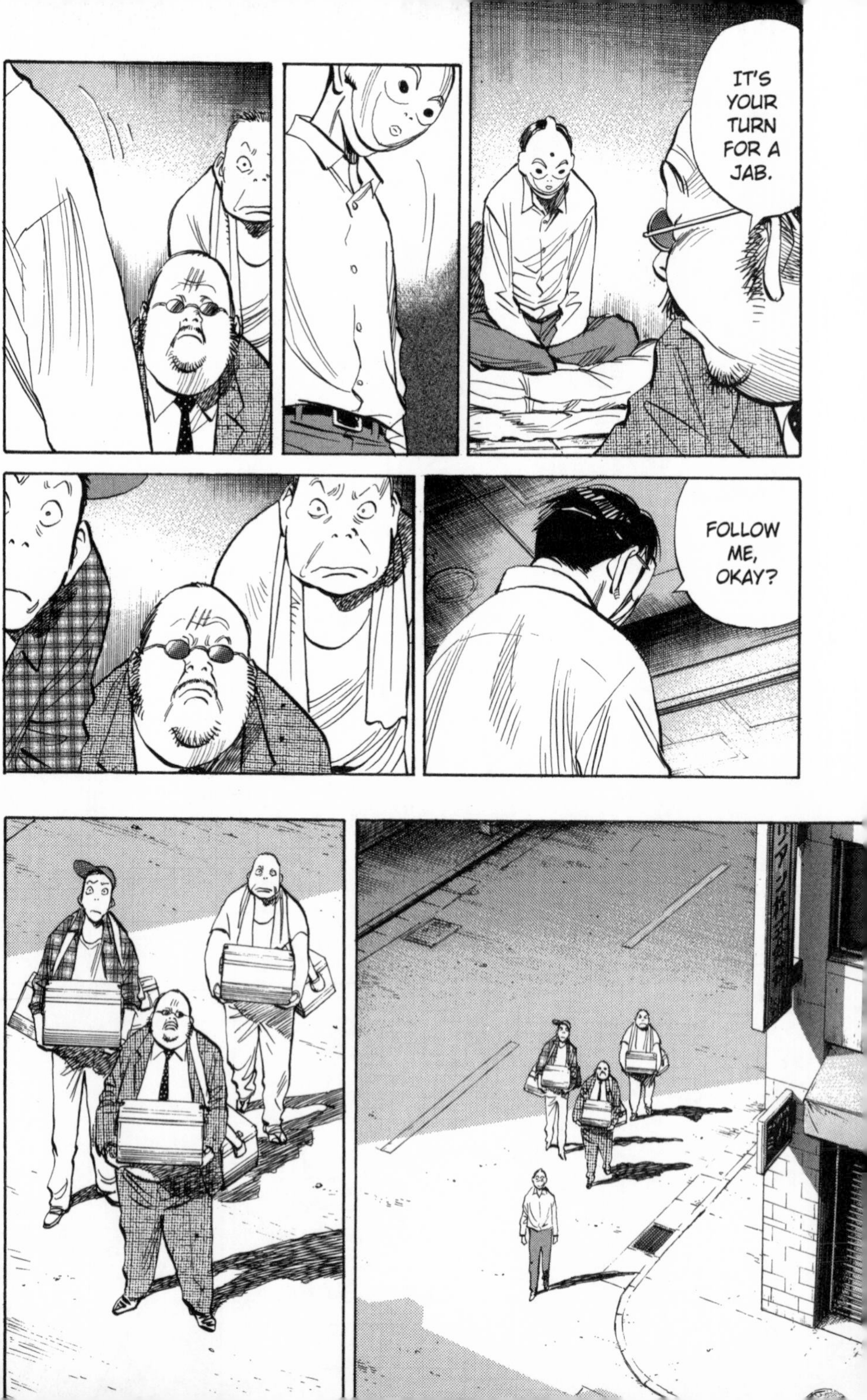
IT'S YOUR TURN FOR A JAB.
FOLLOW ME, OKAY?

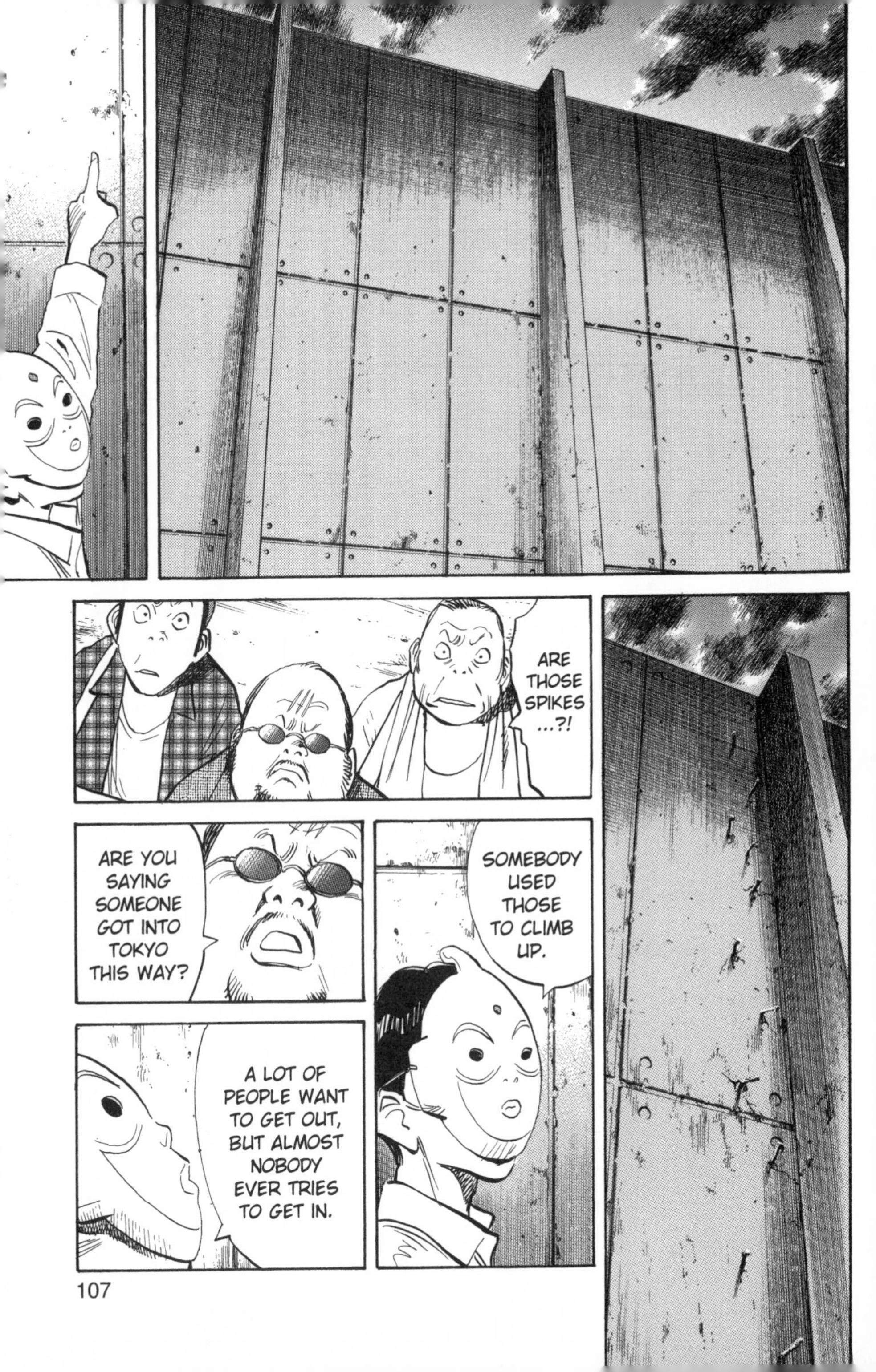
ARE THOSE SPIKES ...?!
SOMEBODY USED THOSE TO CLIMB UP.
ARE YOU SAYING SOMEONE GOT INTO TOKYO THIS WAY?
A LOT OF PEOPLE WANT TO GET OUT, BUT ALMOST NOBODY EVER TRIES TO GET IN.

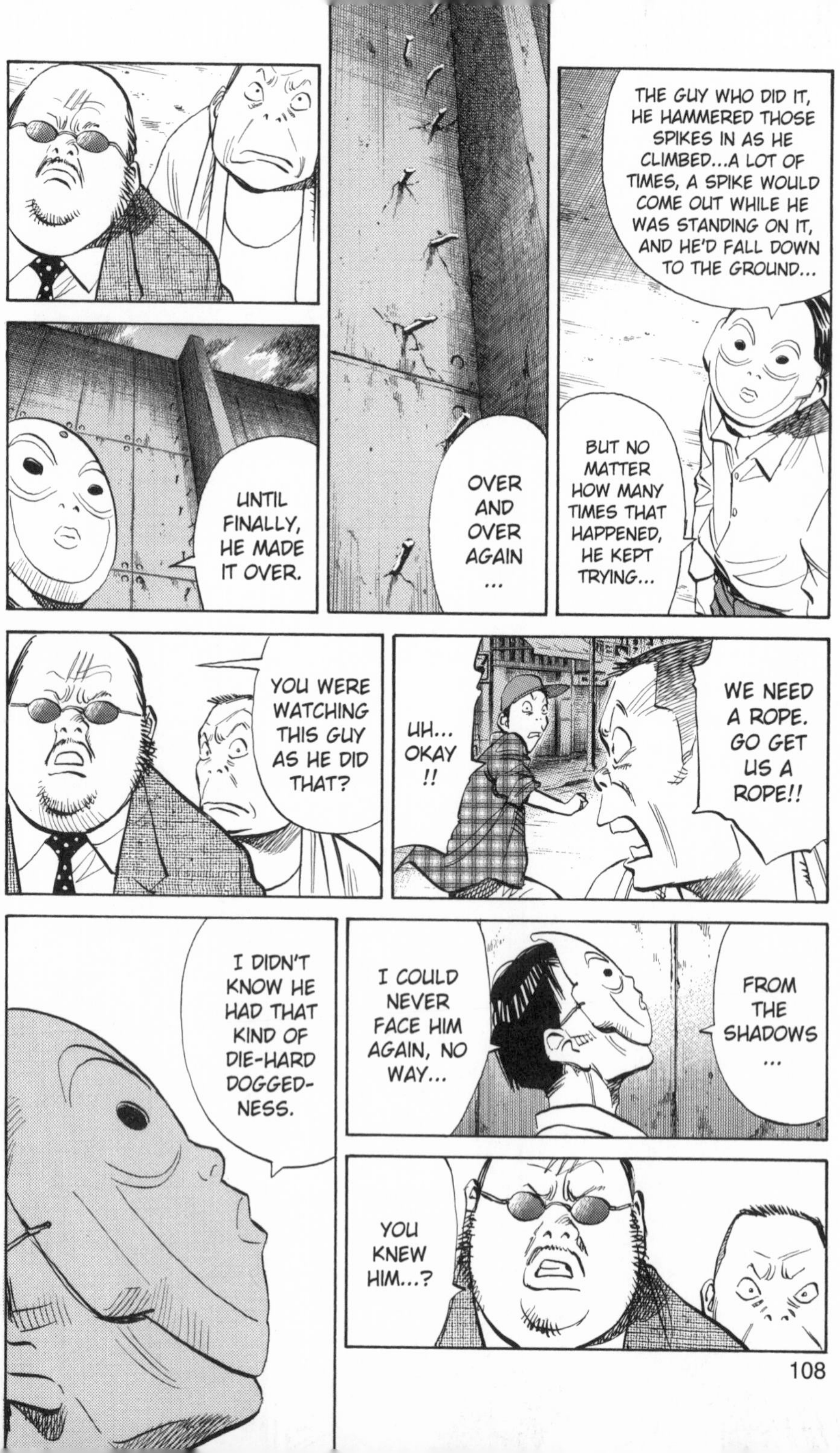
THE GUY WHO DID IT, HE HAMMERED THOSE SPIKES IN AS HE CLIMBED...A LOT OF TIMES, A SPIKE WOULD COME OUT WHILE HE WAS STANDING ON IT, AND HE'D FALL DOWN TO THE GROUND...
BUT NO MATTER HOW MANY TIMES THAT HAPPENED, HE KEPT TRYING...
OVER AND OVER AGAIN ...
UNTIL FINALLY, HE MADE IT OVER.
WE NEED A ROPE. GO GET US A ROPE!!
UH... OKAY !!
YOU WERE WATCHING THIS GUY AS HE DID THAT?
FROM THE SHADOWS ...
I COULD NEVER FACE HIM AGAIN, NO WAY...
YOU KNEW HIM...?
I DIDN'T KNOW HE HAD THAT KIND OF DIE-HARD DOGGED-NESS.

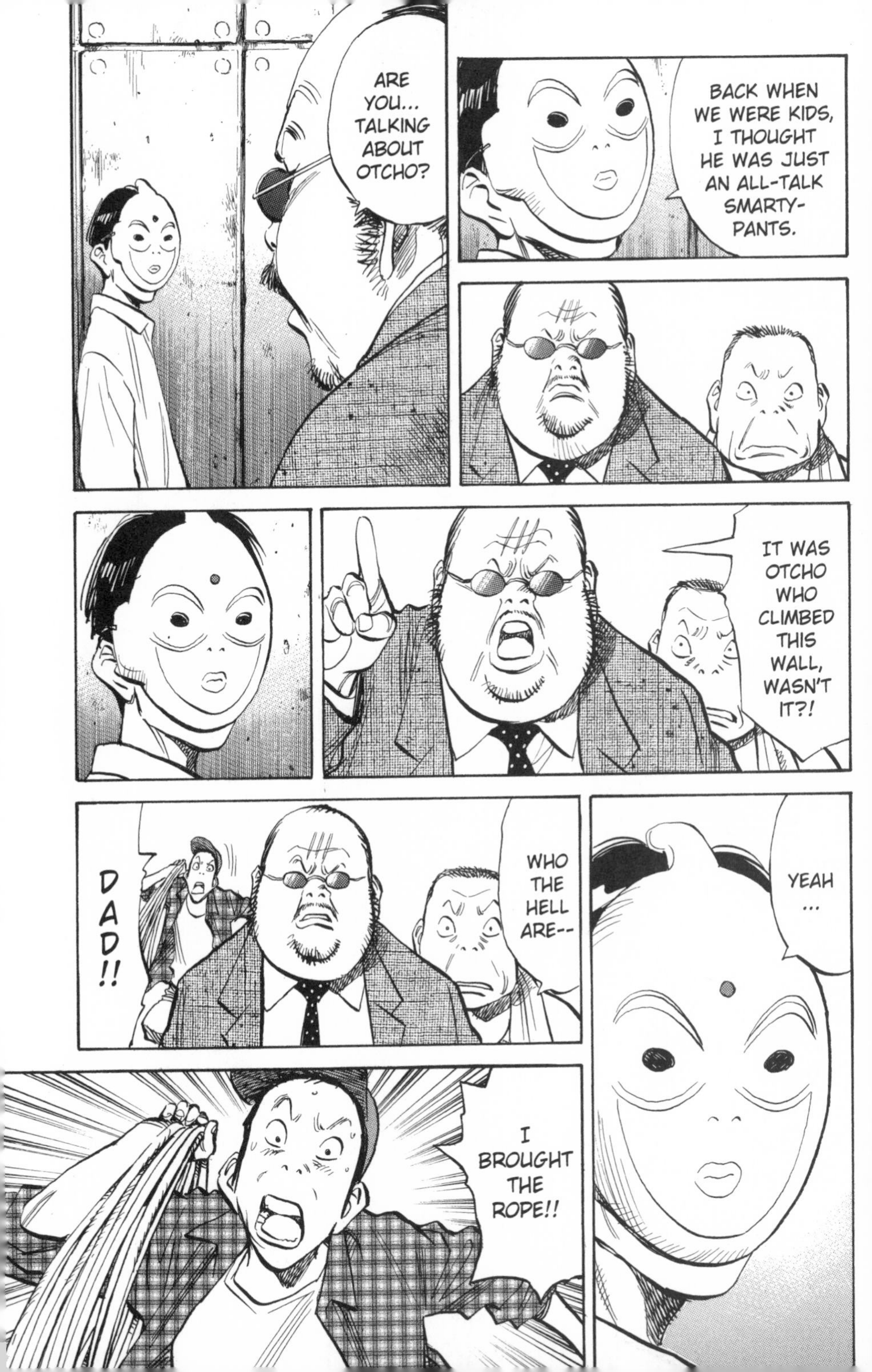
BACK WHEN WE WERE KIDS, I THOUGHT HE WAS JUST AN ALL-TALK SMARTY-PANTS.
ARE YOU... TALKING ABOUT OTCHO?
IT WAS OTCHO WHO CLIMBED THIS WALL, WASN'T IT?!
YEAH ...
WHO THE HELL ARE--
DAD!!
I BROUGHT THE ROPE!!

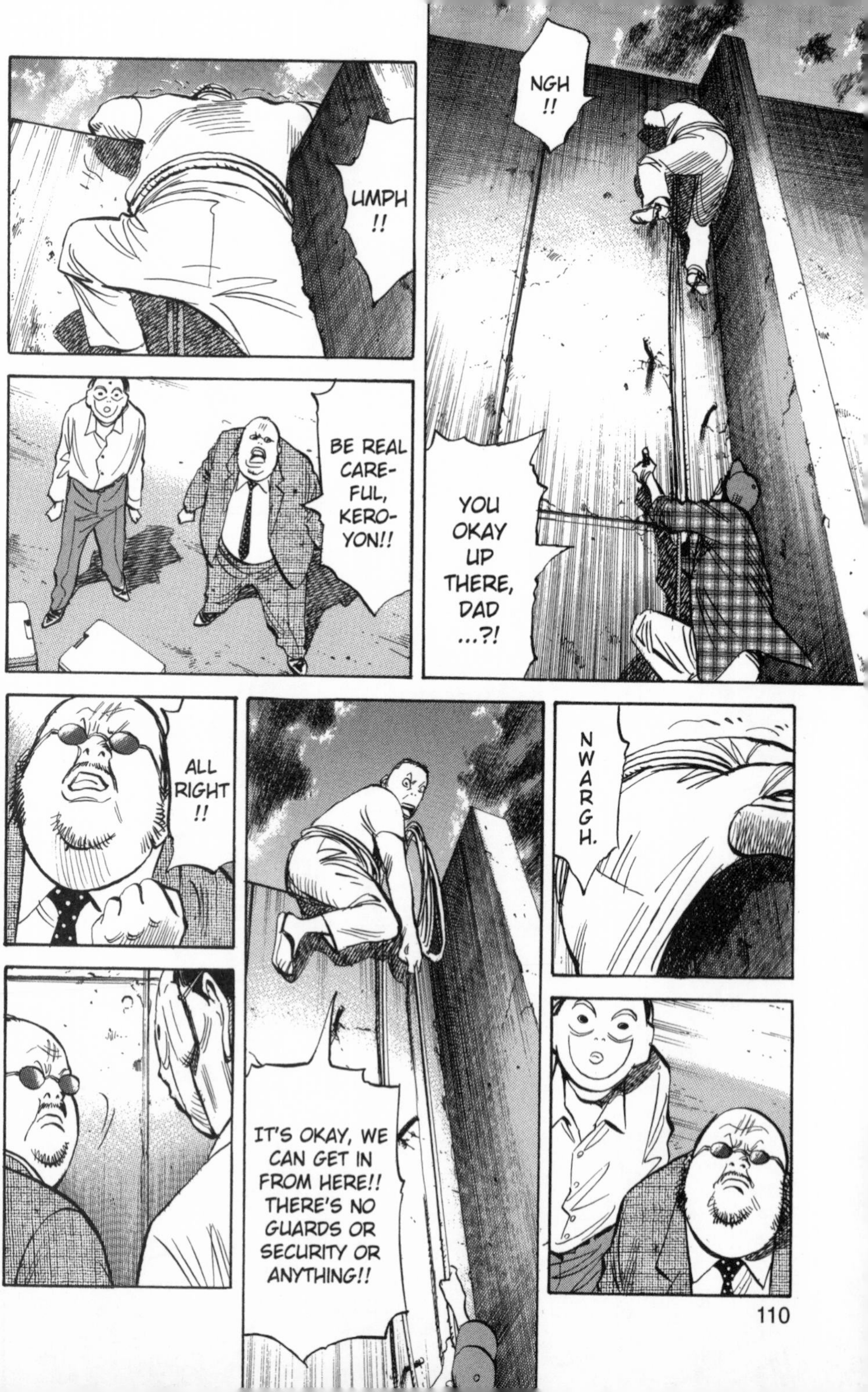
NGH !!
YOU OKAY UP THERE, DAD ...?!
UMPH !!
BE REAL CARE-FUL, KERO-YON!!
NWARGH.
IT'S OKAY, WE CAN GET IN FROM HERE!! THERE'S NO GUARDS OR SECURITY OR ANYTHING!!
ALL RIGHT !!

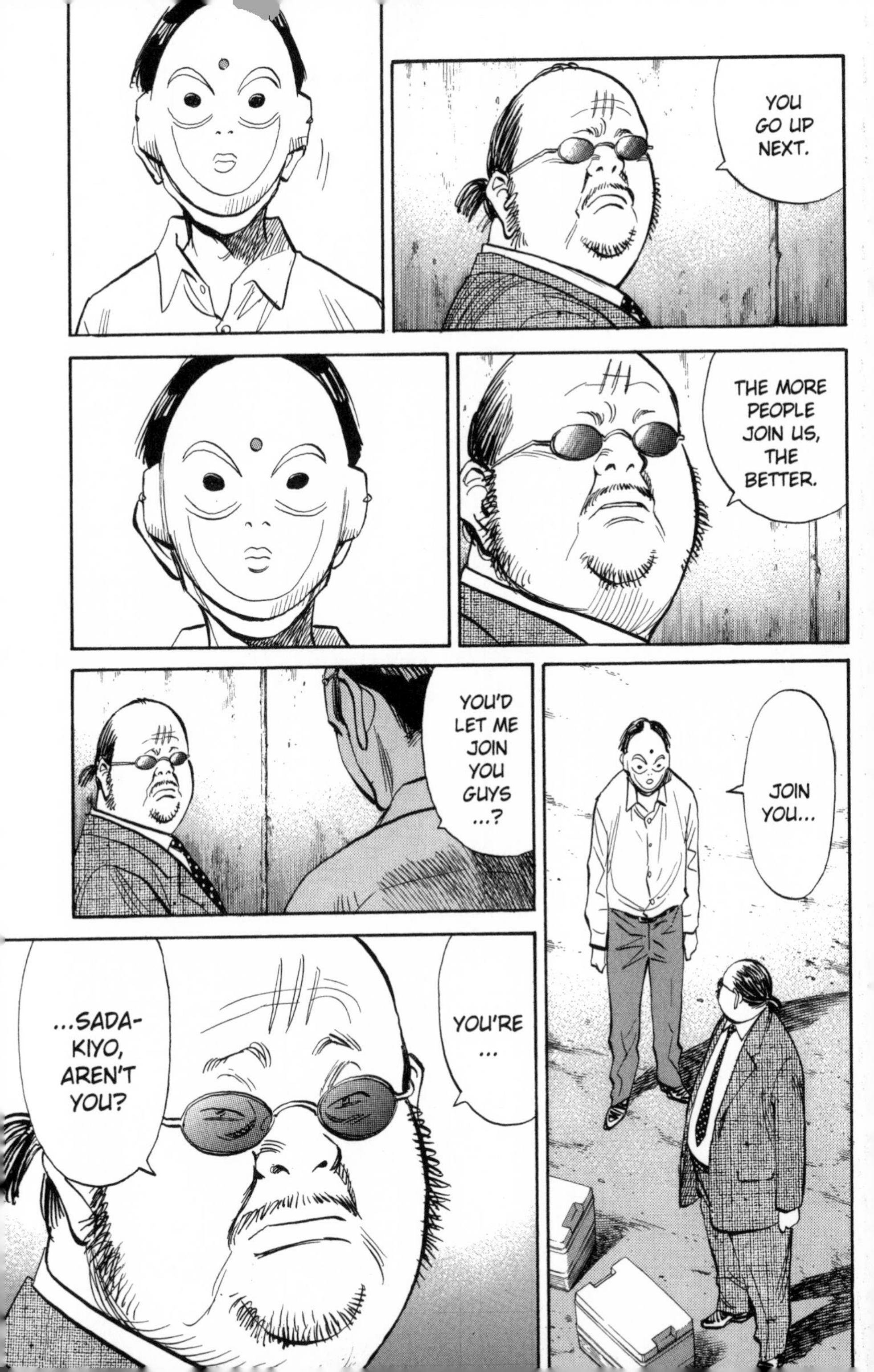
YOU GO UP NEXT.
THE MORE PEOPLE JOIN US, THE BETTER.
JOIN YOU...
YOU'D LET ME JOIN YOU GUYS ...?
YOU'RE ...
...SADA-KIYO, AREN'T YOU?

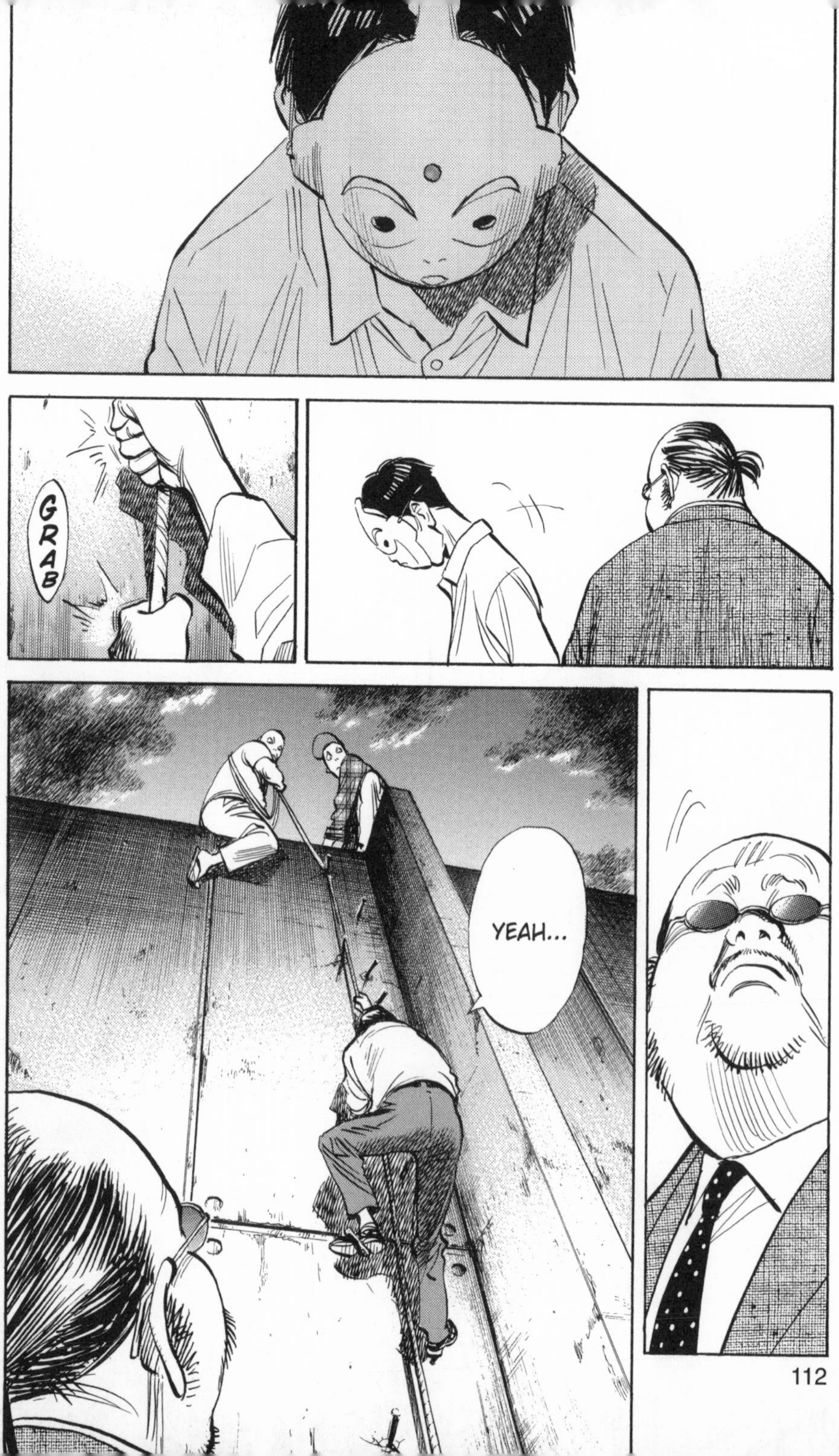
GRAB
YEAH...

Chapter 7 Don't Hand It to the Enemy

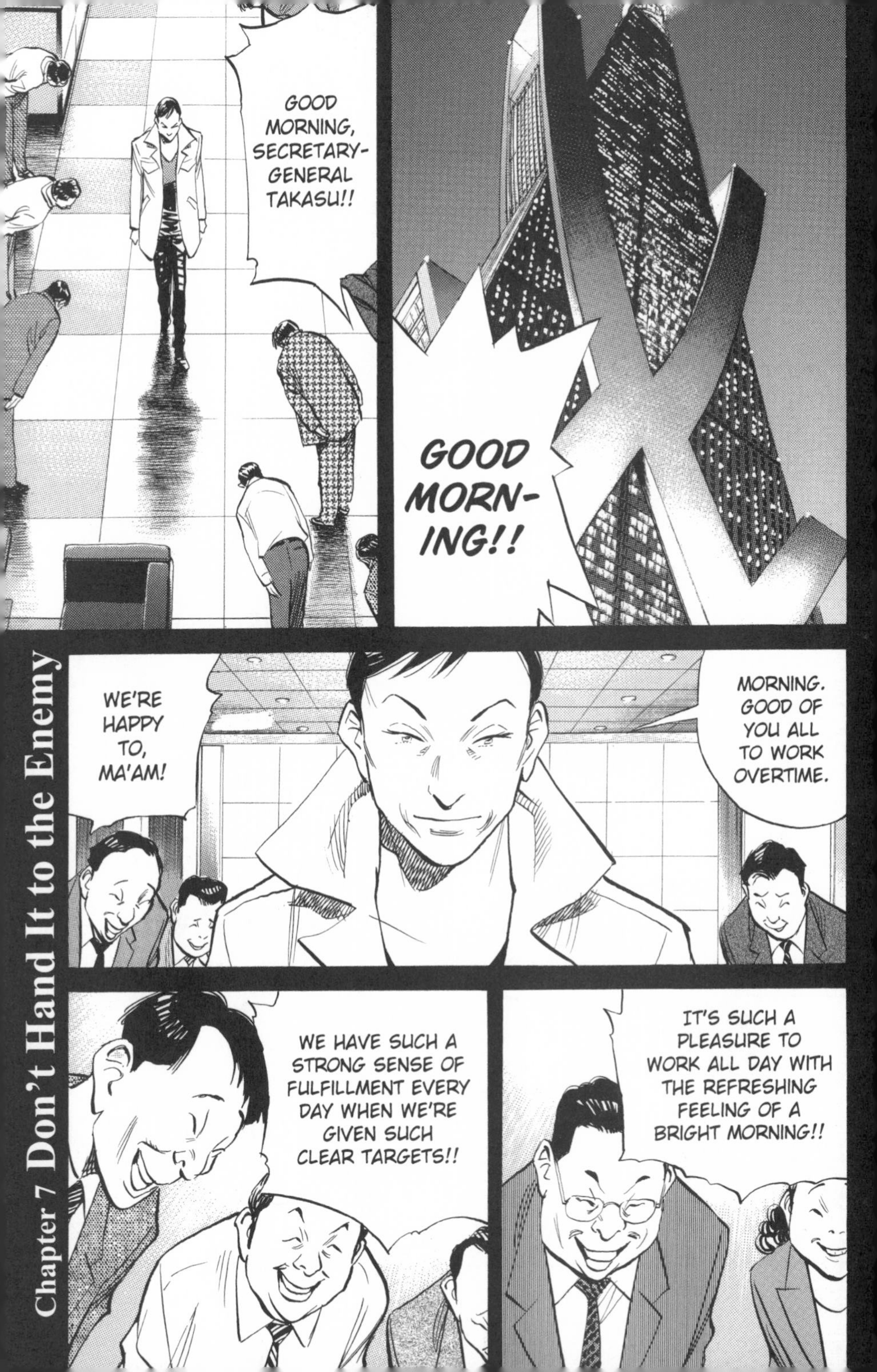
GOOD MORNING!!
GOOD MORNING, SECRETARY-GENERAL TAKASU!!
MORNING. GOOD OF YOU ALL TO WORK OVERTIME.
WE'RE HAPPY TO, MA'AM!
IT'S SUCH A PLEASURE TO WORK ALL DAY WITH THE REFRESHING FEELING OF A BRIGHT MORNING!!
WE HAVE SUCH A STRONG SENSE OF FULFILLMENT EVERY DAY WHEN WE'RE GIVEN SUCH CLEAR TARGETS!!

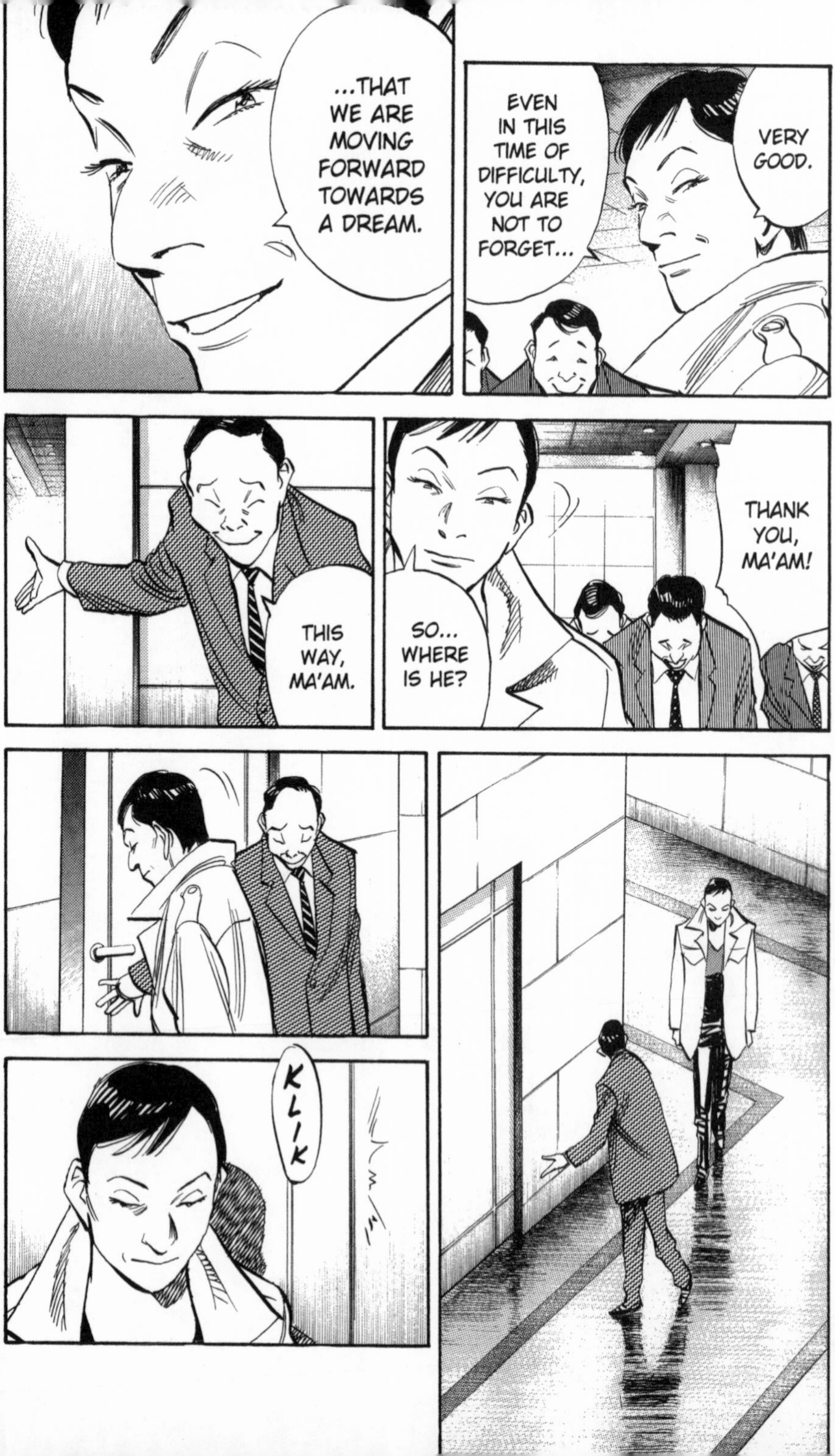
VERY GOOD.
EVEN IN THIS TIME OF DIFFICULTY, YOU ARE NOT TO FORGET...
...THAT WE ARE MOVING FORWARD TOWARDS A DREAM.
THANK YOU, MA'AM!
SO... WHERE IS HE?
THIS WAY, MA'AM.
KLIK

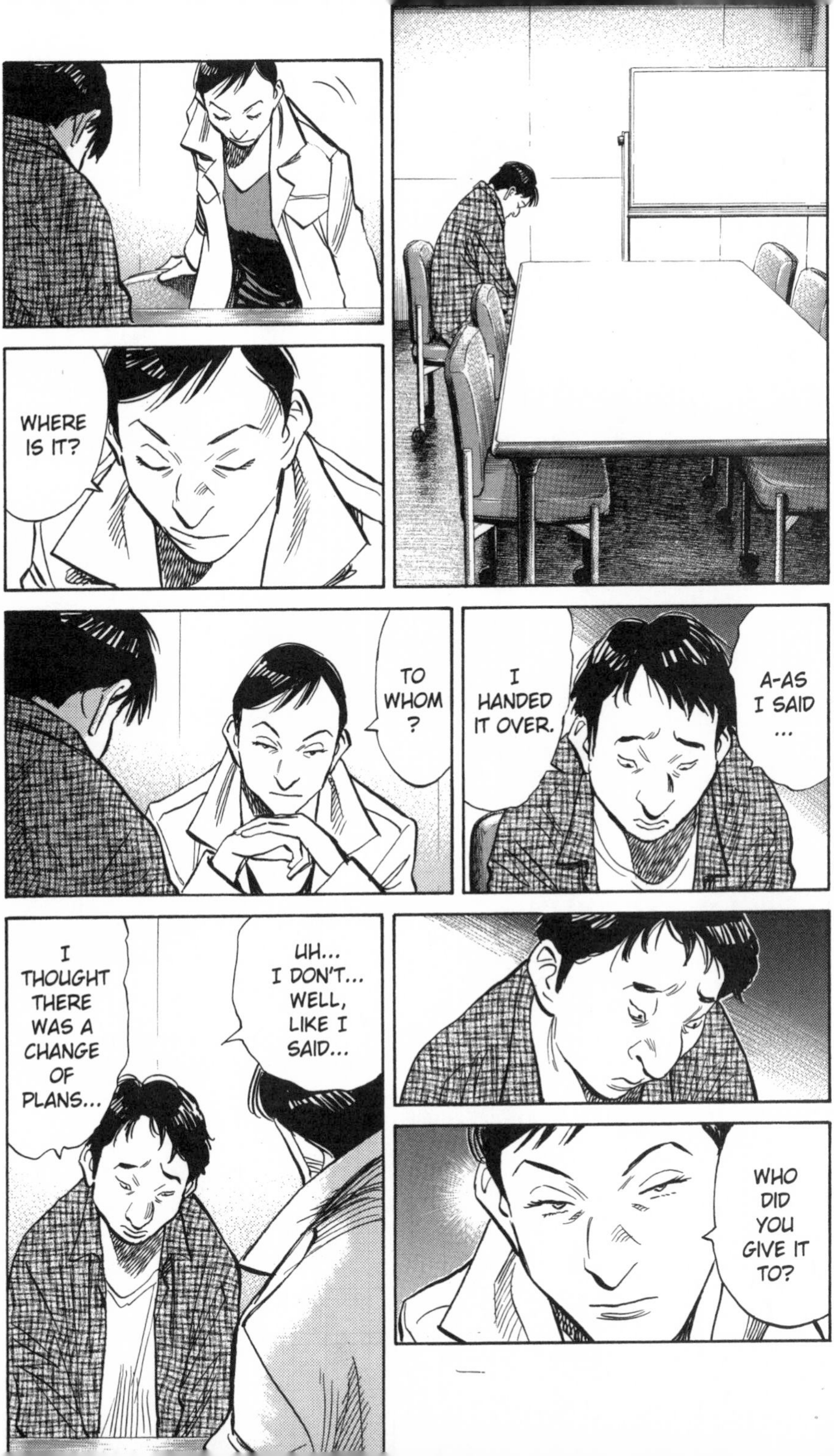
WHERE IS IT?
A-AS I SAID ...
I HANDED IT OVER.
TO WHOM ?
WHO DID YOU GIVE IT TO?
UH... I DON'T... WELL, LIKE I SAID...
I THOUGHT THERE WAS A CHANGE OF PLANS...

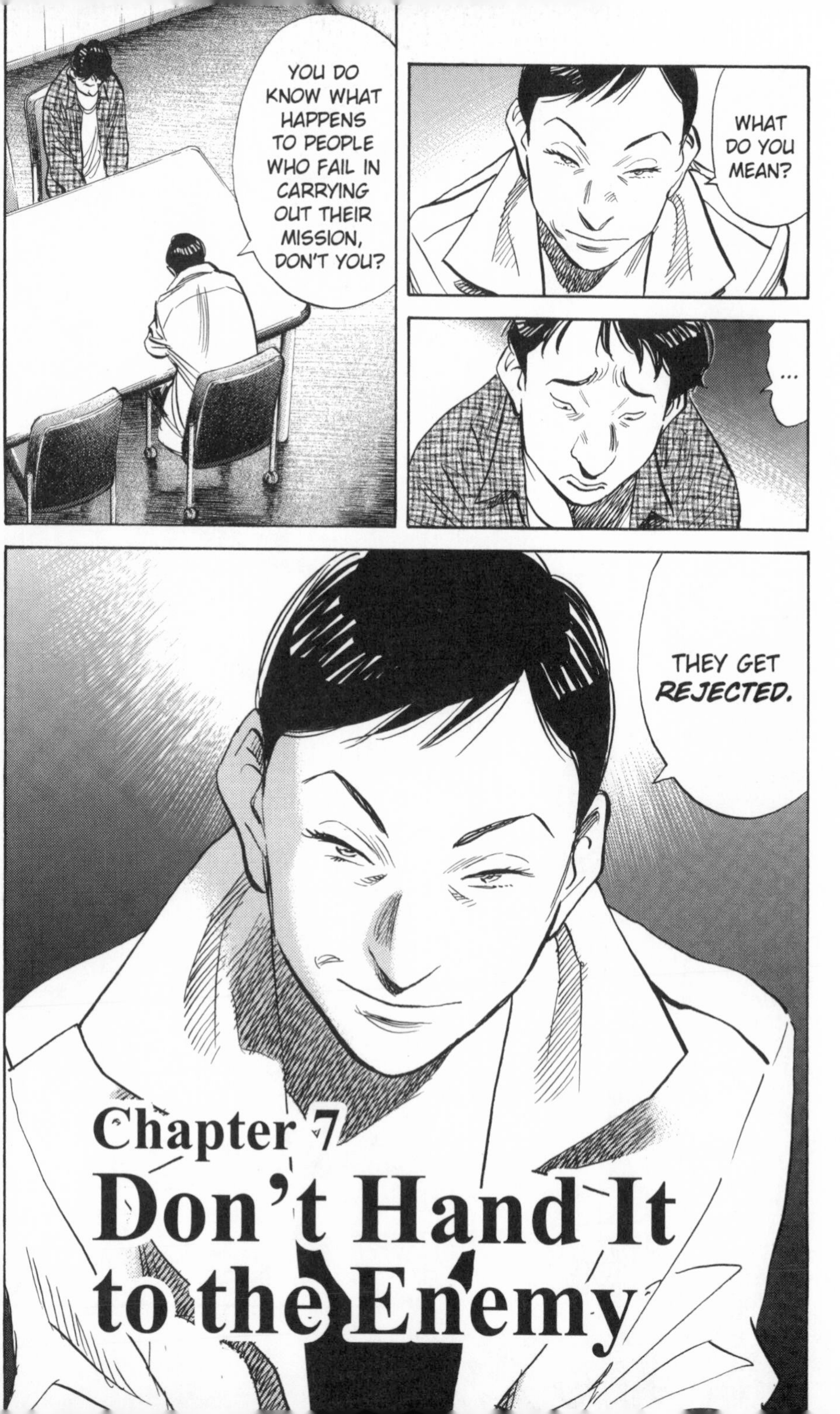
YOU DO KNOW WHAT HAPPENS TO PEOPLE WHO FAIL IN CARRYING OUT THEIR MISSION, DON'T YOU?
WHAT DO YOU MEAN?
...
THEY GET *REJECTED.*

Chapter 7
Don't Hand It to the Enemy

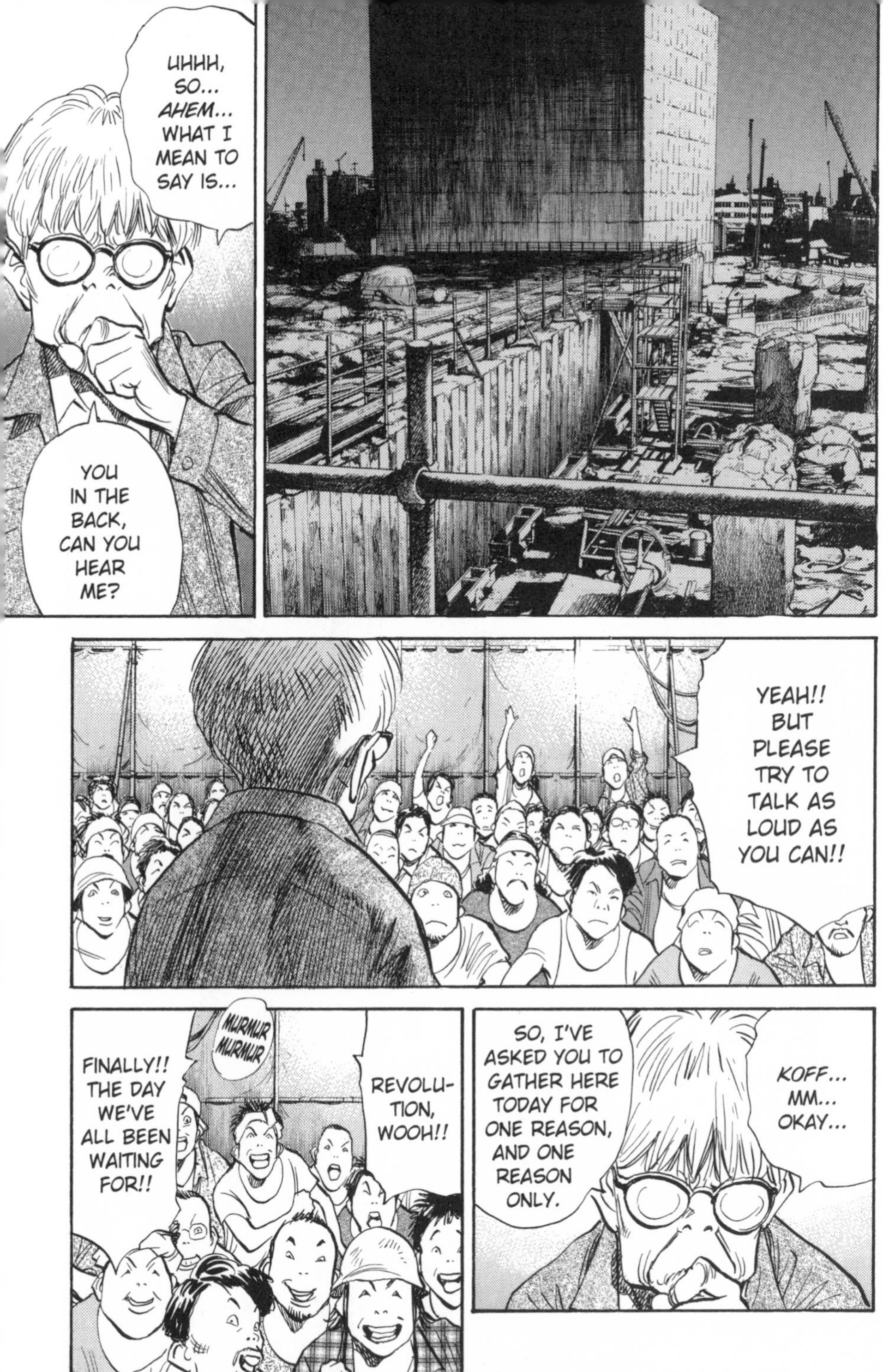
UHHH, SO... *AHEM*... WHAT I MEAN TO SAY IS...
YOU IN THE BACK, CAN YOU HEAR ME?
YEAH!! BUT PLEASE TRY TO TALK AS LOUD AS YOU CAN!!
KOFF... MM... OKAY...
SO, I'VE ASKED YOU TO GATHER HERE TODAY FOR ONE REASON, AND ONE REASON ONLY.
MURMUR MURMUR
REVOLU-TION, WOOH!!
FINALLY!! THE DAY WE'VE ALL BEEN WAITING FOR!!

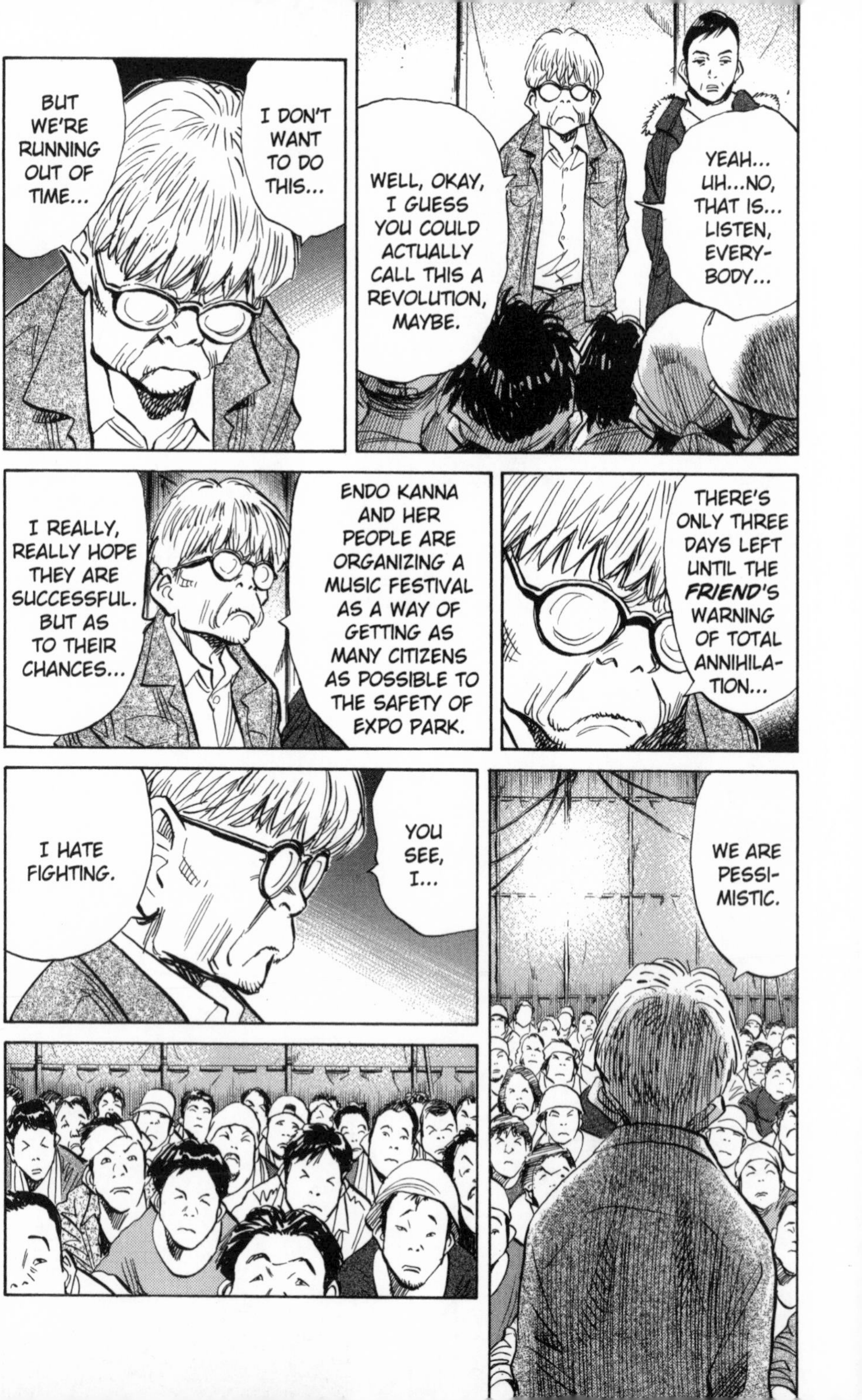
YEAH... UH...NO, THAT IS... LISTEN, EVERY-BODY...
WELL, OKAY, I GUESS YOU COULD ACTUALLY CALL THIS A REVOLUTION, MAYBE.
I DON'T WANT TO DO THIS...
BUT WE'RE RUNNING OUT OF TIME...
THERE'S ONLY THREE DAYS LEFT UNTIL THE ***FRIEND***'S WARNING OF TOTAL ANNIHILA-TION...
ENDO KANNA AND HER PEOPLE ARE ORGANIZING A MUSIC FESTIVAL AS A WAY OF GETTING AS MANY CITIZENS AS POSSIBLE TO THE SAFETY OF EXPO PARK.
I REALLY, REALLY HOPE THEY ARE SUCCESSFUL. BUT AS TO THEIR CHANCES...
WE ARE PESSI-MISTIC.
YOU SEE, I...
I HATE FIGHTING.

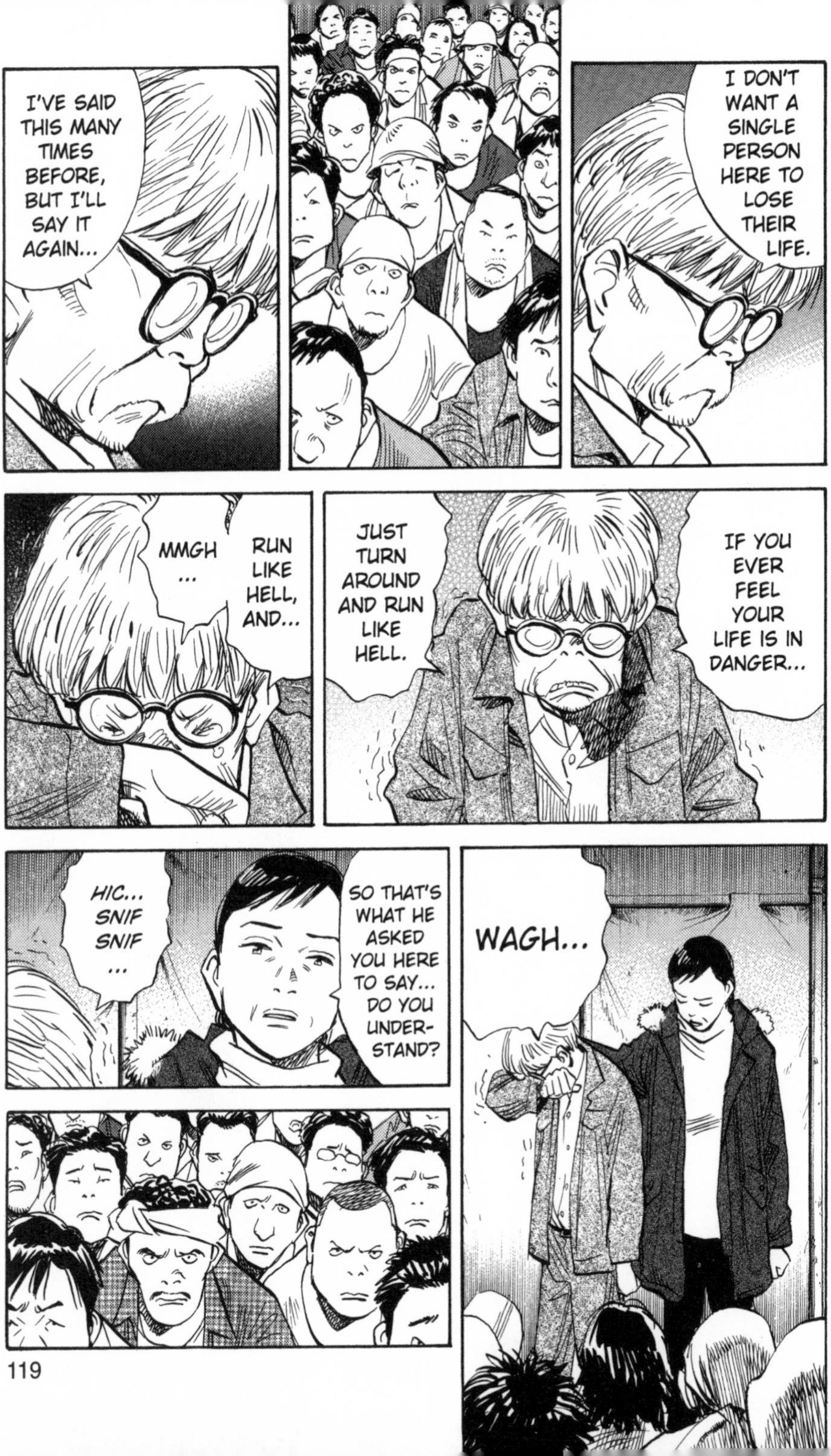
I DON'T WANT A SINGLE PERSON HERE TO LOSE THEIR LIFE.
I'VE SAID THIS MANY TIMES BEFORE, BUT I'LL SAY IT AGAIN...
IF YOU EVER FEEL YOUR LIFE IS IN DANGER...
JUST TURN AROUND AND RUN LIKE HELL.
RUN LIKE HELL, AND...
MMGH ...
WAGH...
SO THAT'S WHAT HE ASKED YOU HERE TO SAY... DO YOU UNDER-STAND?
HIC... SNIF SNIF ...

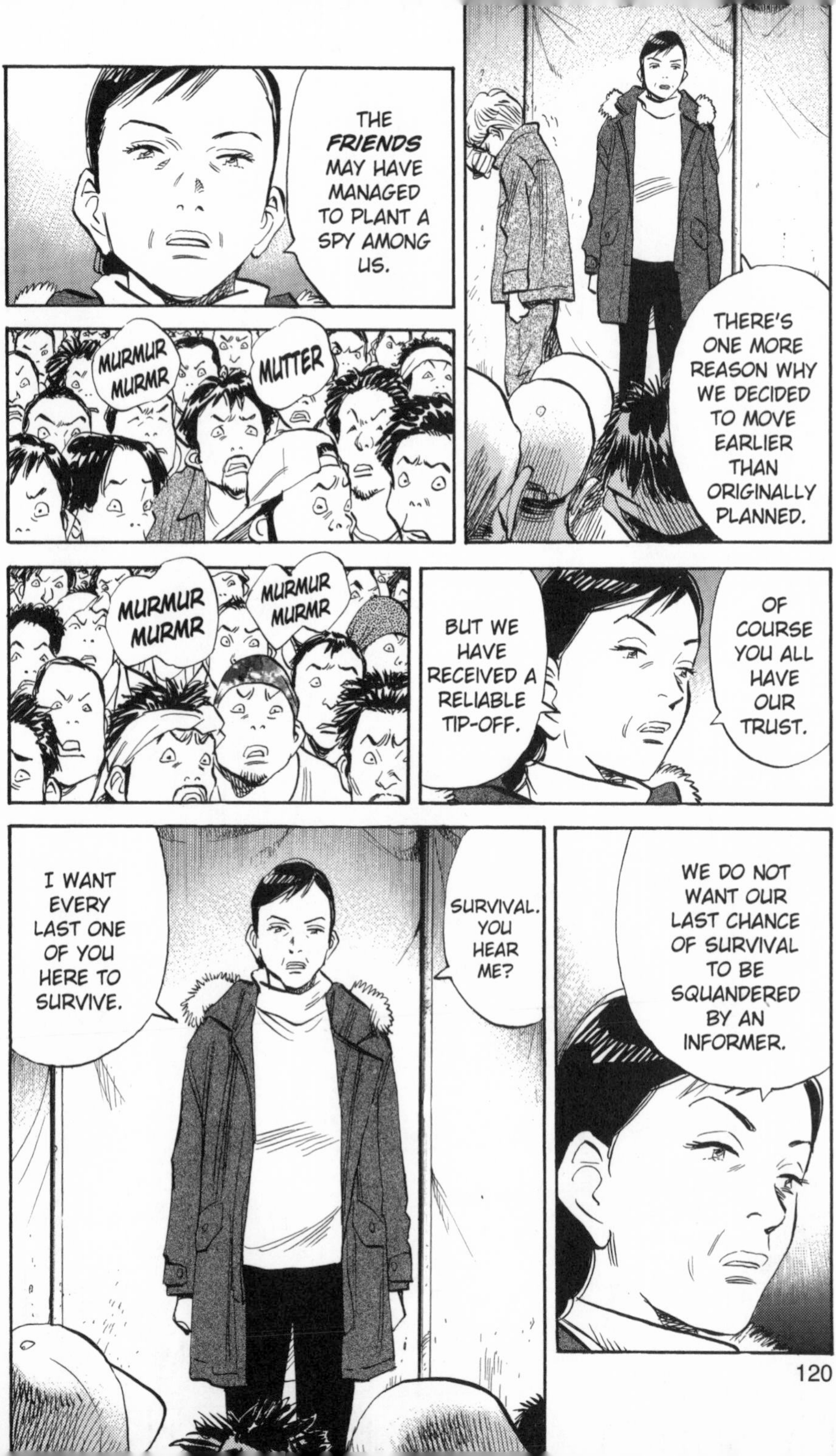
THERE'S ONE MORE REASON WHY WE DECIDED TO MOVE EARLIER THAN ORIGINALLY PLANNED.
THE *FRIENDS* MAY HAVE MANAGED TO PLANT A SPY AMONG US.
MUTTER
MURMUR MURMR
OF COURSE YOU ALL HAVE OUR TRUST.
BUT WE HAVE RECEIVED A RELIABLE TIP-OFF.
MURMUR MURMR
MURMUR MURMR
WE DO NOT WANT OUR LAST CHANCE OF SURVIVAL TO BE SQUANDERED BY AN INFORMER.
I WANT EVERY LAST ONE OF YOU HERE TO SURVIVE.
SURVIVAL. YOU HEAR ME?

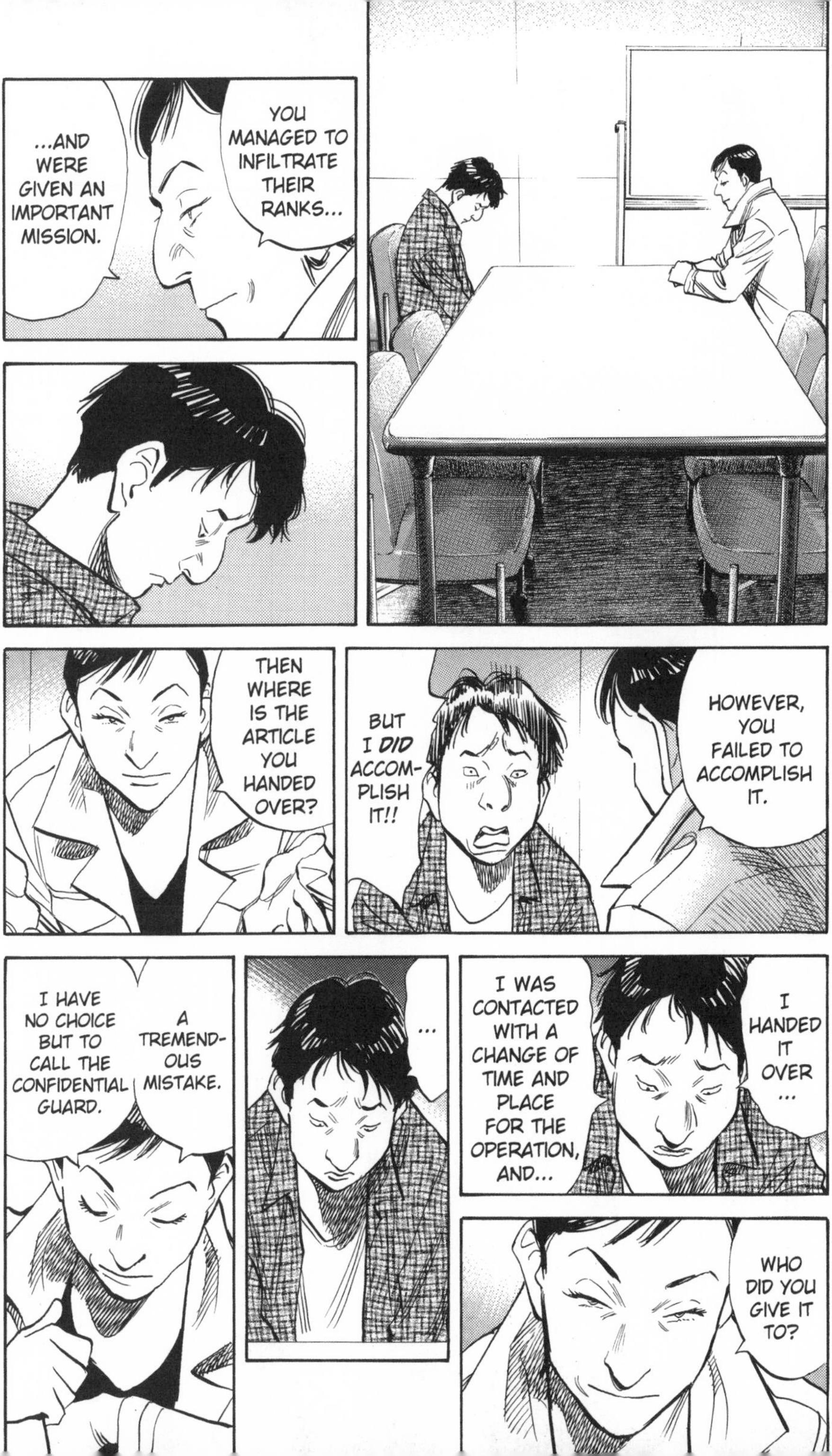
YOU MANAGED TO INFILTRATE THEIR RANKS...
...AND WERE GIVEN AN IMPORTANT MISSION.
HOWEVER, YOU FAILED TO ACCOMPLISH IT.
BUT I *DID* ACCOMPLISH IT!!
THEN WHERE IS THE ARTICLE YOU HANDED OVER?
I HANDED IT OVER...
I WAS CONTACTED WITH A CHANGE OF TIME AND PLACE FOR THE OPERATION, AND...
WHO DID YOU GIVE IT TO?
...
A TREMENDOUS MISTAKE.
I HAVE NO CHOICE BUT TO CALL THE CONFIDENTIAL GUARD.

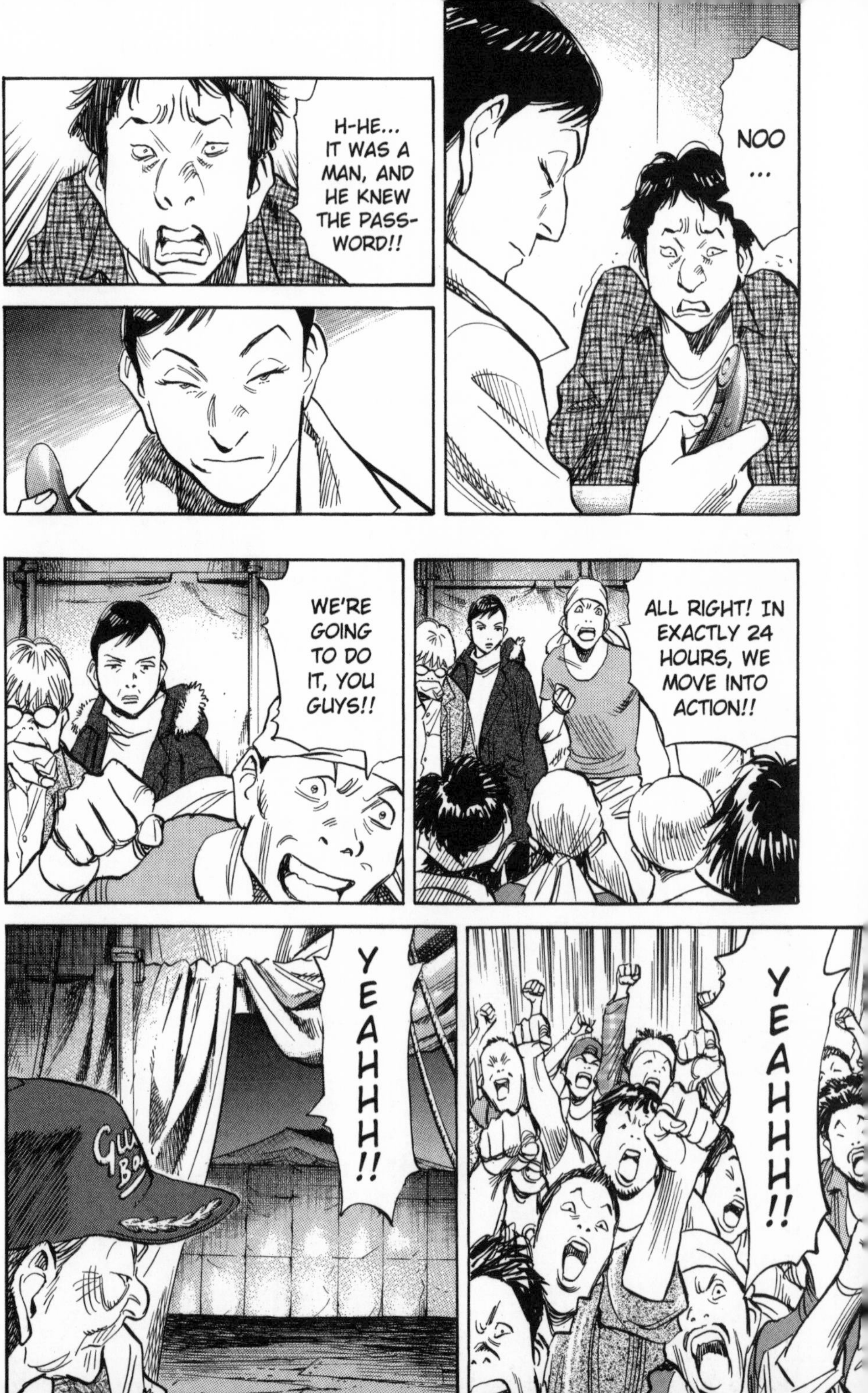
NOO ...
H-HE... IT WAS A MAN, AND HE KNEW THE PASS-WORD!!
ALL RIGHT! IN EXACTLY 24 HOURS, WE MOVE INTO ACTION!!
WE'RE GOING TO DO IT, YOU GUYS!!
YEAHHHH!!
YEAHHHH!!

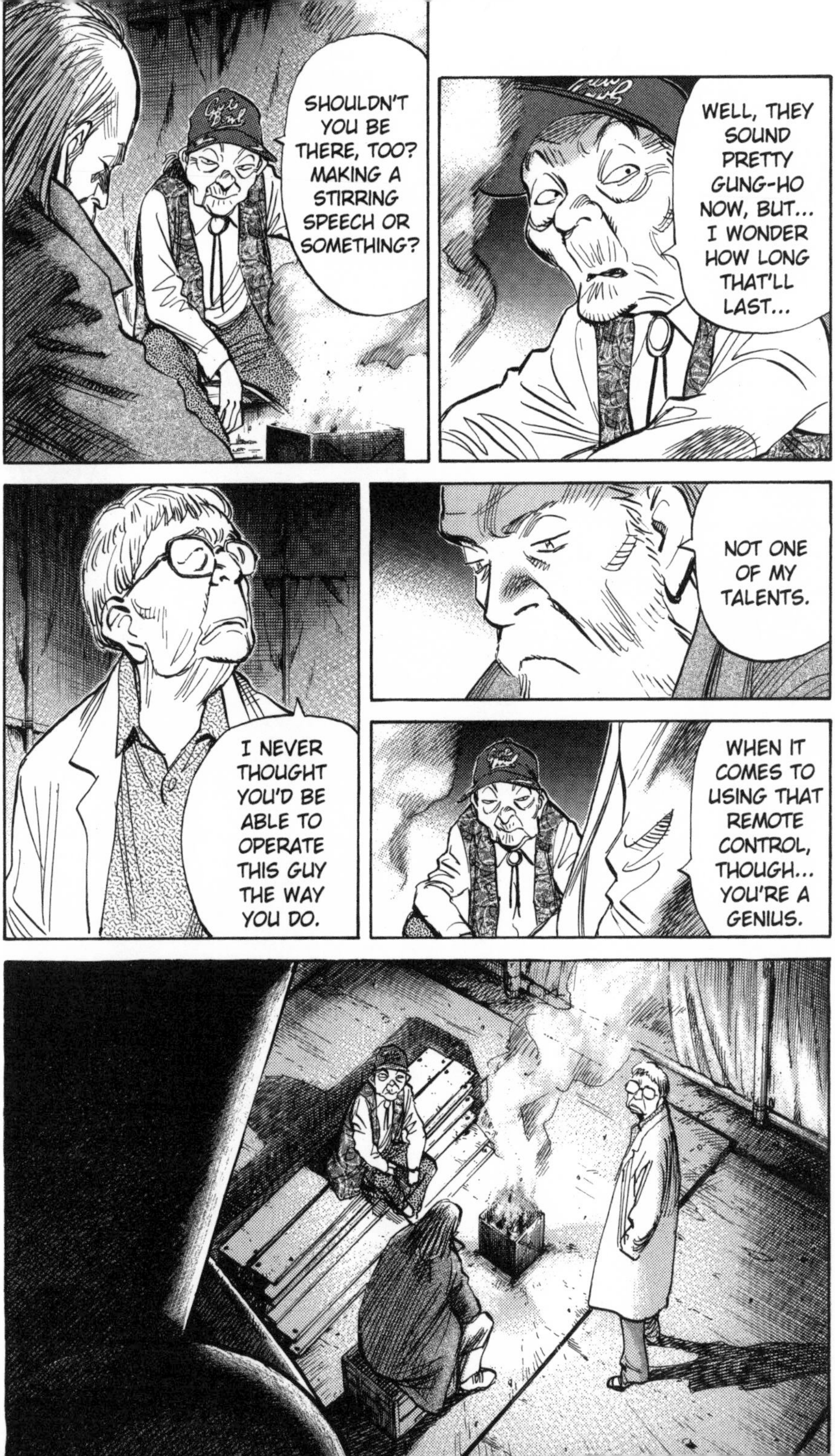
WELL, THEY SOUND PRETTY GUNG-HO NOW, BUT... I WONDER HOW LONG THAT'LL LAST...
SHOULDN'T YOU BE THERE, TOO? MAKING A STIRRING SPEECH OR SOMETHING?
NOT ONE OF MY TALENTS.
WHEN IT COMES TO USING THAT REMOTE CONTROL, THOUGH... YOU'RE A GENIUS.
I NEVER THOUGHT YOU'D BE ABLE TO OPERATE THIS GUY THE WAY YOU DO.

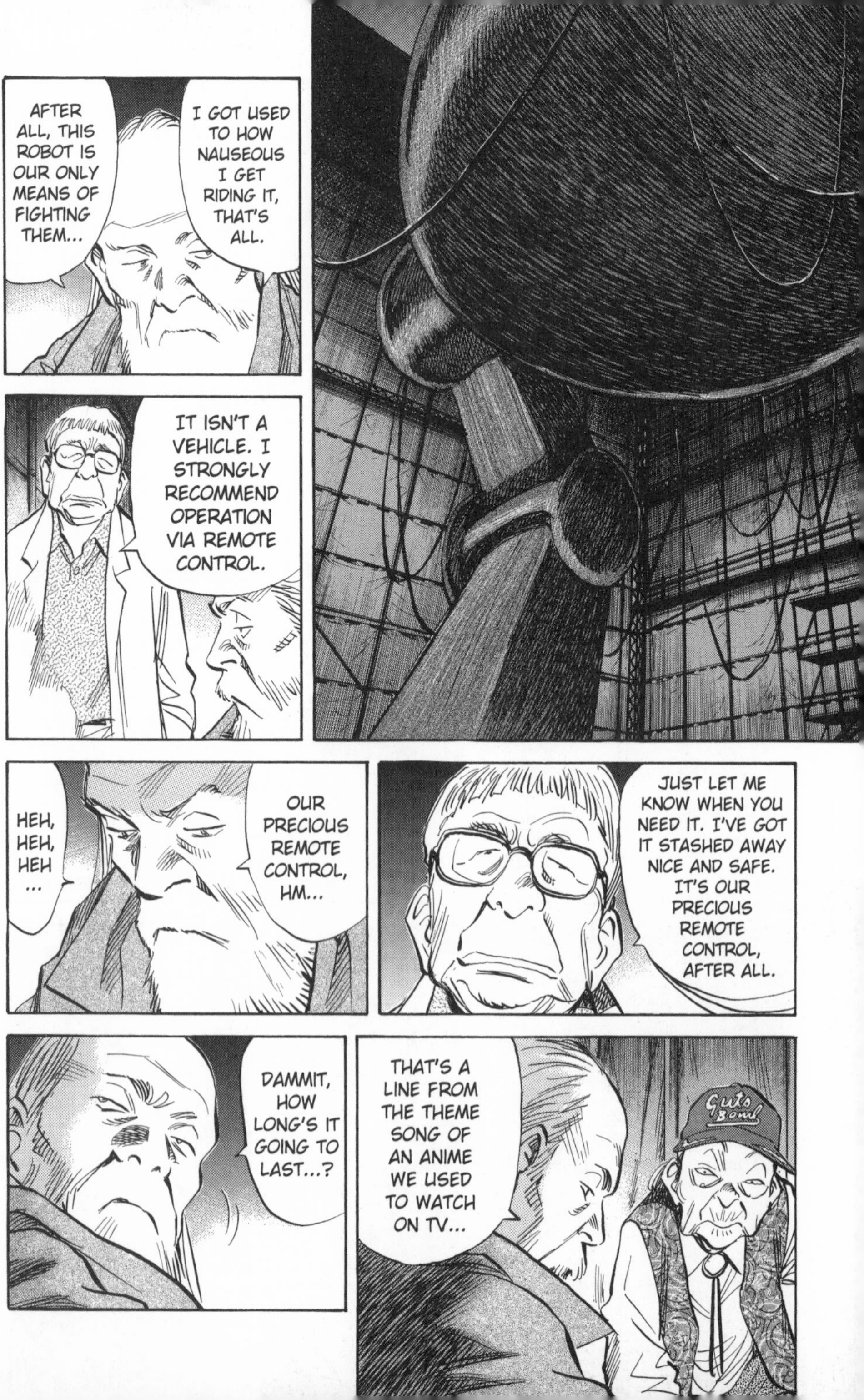
I GOT USED TO HOW NAUSEOUS I GET RIDING IT, THAT'S ALL.
AFTER ALL, THIS ROBOT IS OUR ONLY MEANS OF FIGHTING THEM...
IT ISN'T A VEHICLE. I STRONGLY RECOMMEND OPERATION VIA REMOTE CONTROL.
JUST LET ME KNOW WHEN YOU NEED IT. I'VE GOT IT STASHED AWAY NICE AND SAFE. IT'S OUR PRECIOUS REMOTE CONTROL, AFTER ALL.
OUR PRECIOUS REMOTE CONTROL, HM...
HEH, HEH, HEH...
THAT'S A LINE FROM THE THEME SONG OF AN ANIME WE USED TO WATCH ON TV...
DAMMIT, HOW LONG'S IT GOING TO LAST...?

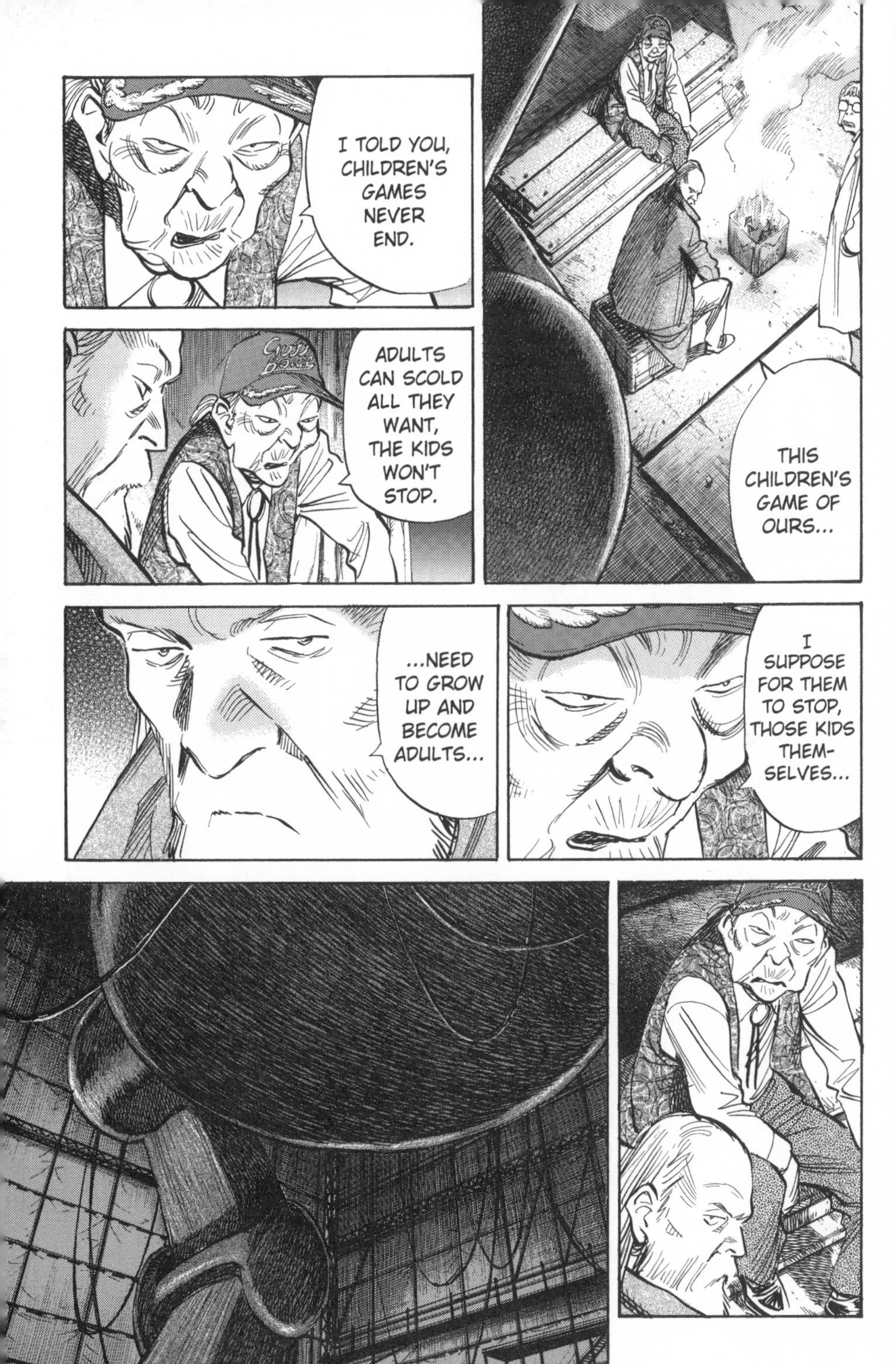
THIS CHILDREN'S GAME OF OURS...
I TOLD YOU, CHILDREN'S GAMES NEVER END.
ADULTS CAN SCOLD ALL THEY WANT, THE KIDS WON'T STOP.
I SUPPOSE FOR THEM TO STOP, THOSE KIDS THEM-SELVES...
...NEED TO GROW UP AND BECOME ADULTS...

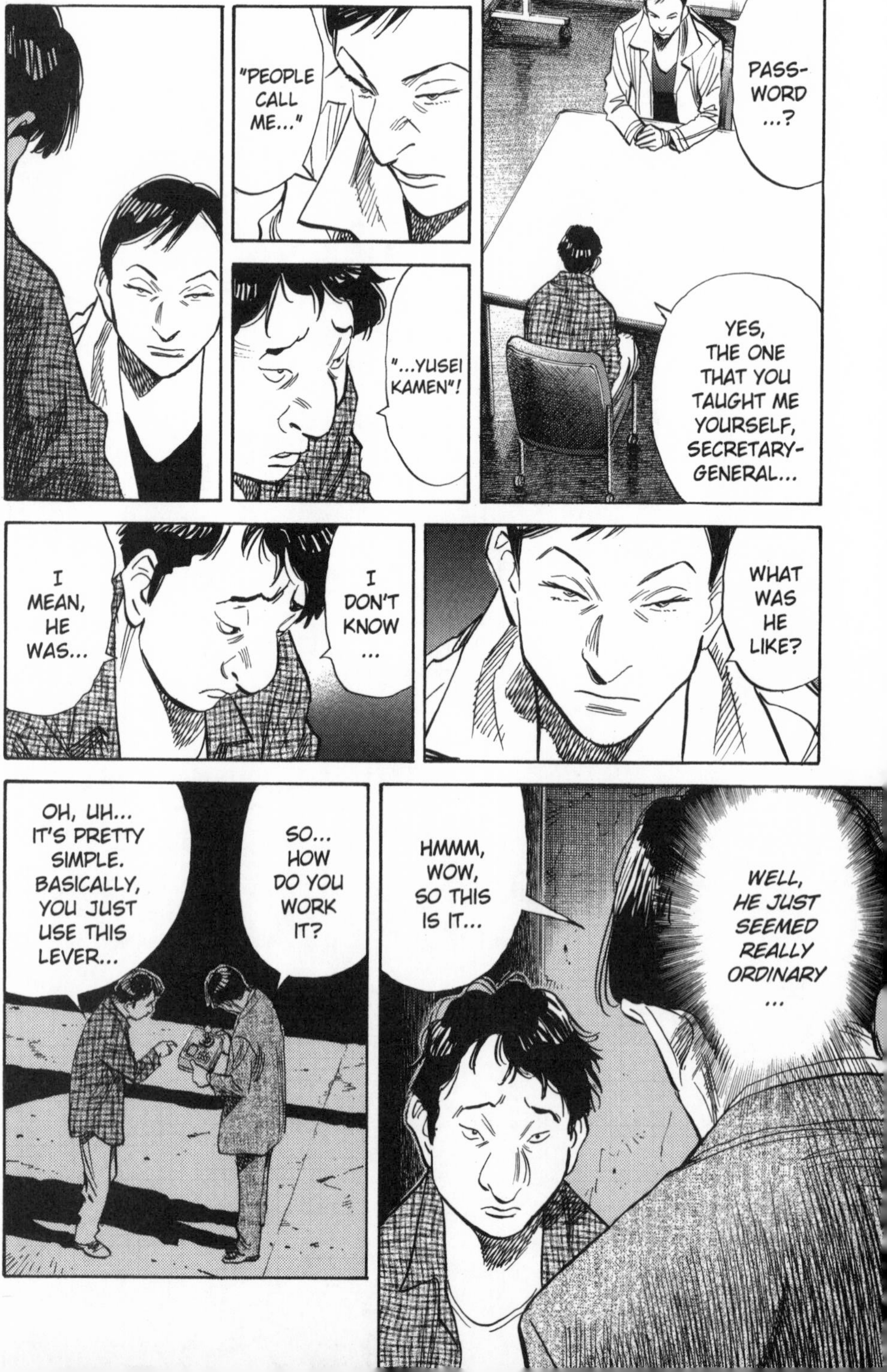
PASS-WORD...?
YES, THE ONE THAT YOU TAUGHT ME YOURSELF, SECRETARY-GENERAL...
"PEOPLE CALL ME..."
"...YUSEI KAMEN"!
WHAT WAS HE LIKE?
I DON'T KNOW...
I MEAN, HE WAS...
WELL, HE JUST SEEMED REALLY ORDINARY...
HMMM, WOW, SO THIS IS IT...
SO... HOW DO YOU WORK IT?
OH, UH... IT'S PRETTY SIMPLE. BASICALLY, YOU JUST USE THIS LEVER...

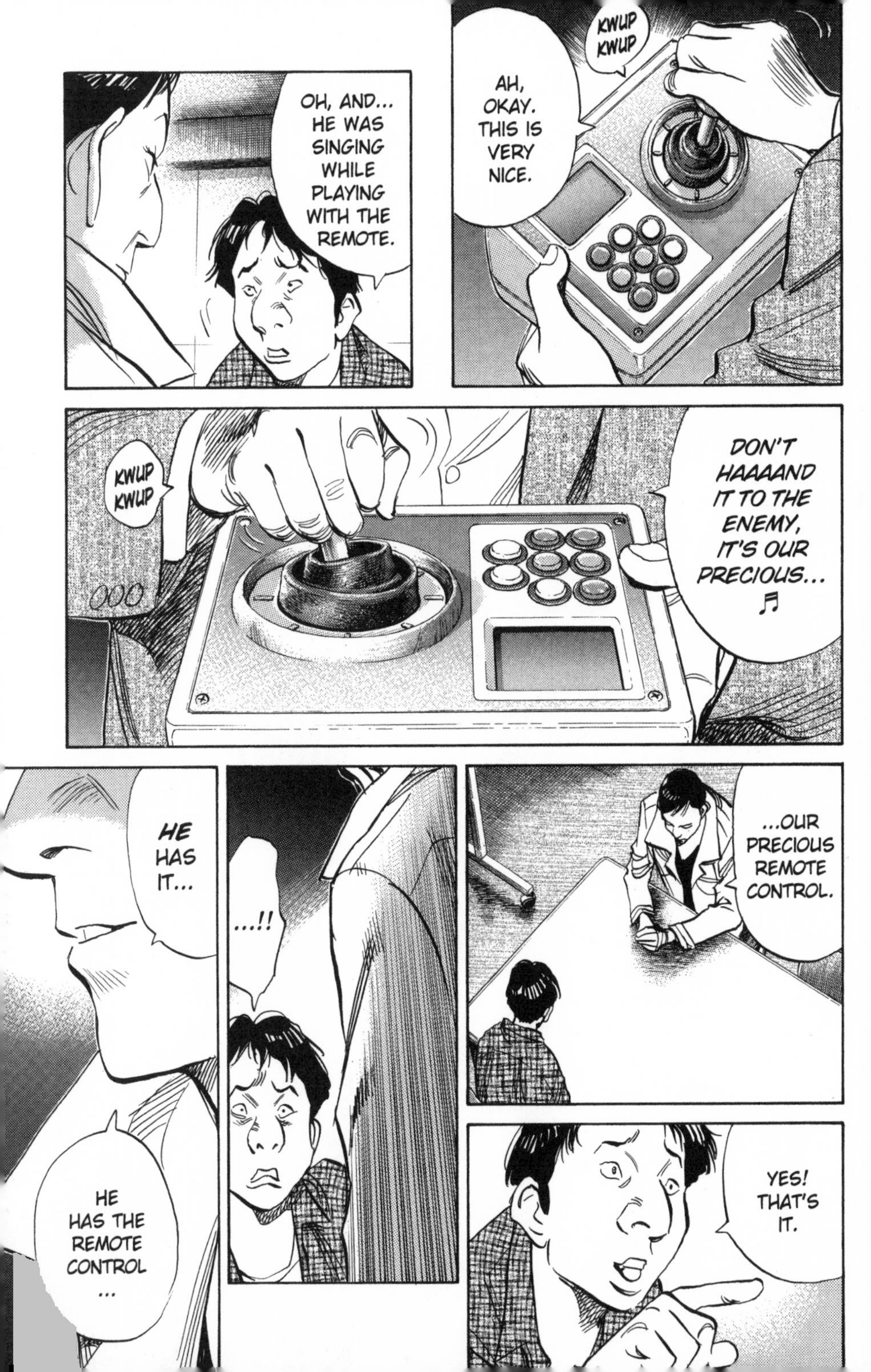
KWUP KWUP
AH, OKAY. THIS IS VERY NICE.
OH, AND... HE WAS SINGING WHILE PLAYING WITH THE REMOTE.
DON'T HAAAAND IT TO THE ENEMY, IT'S OUR PRECIOUS... ♬
KWUP KWUP
...OUR PRECIOUS REMOTE CONTROL.
YES! THAT'S IT.
...!!
HE HAS IT...
HE HAS THE REMOTE CONTROL ...

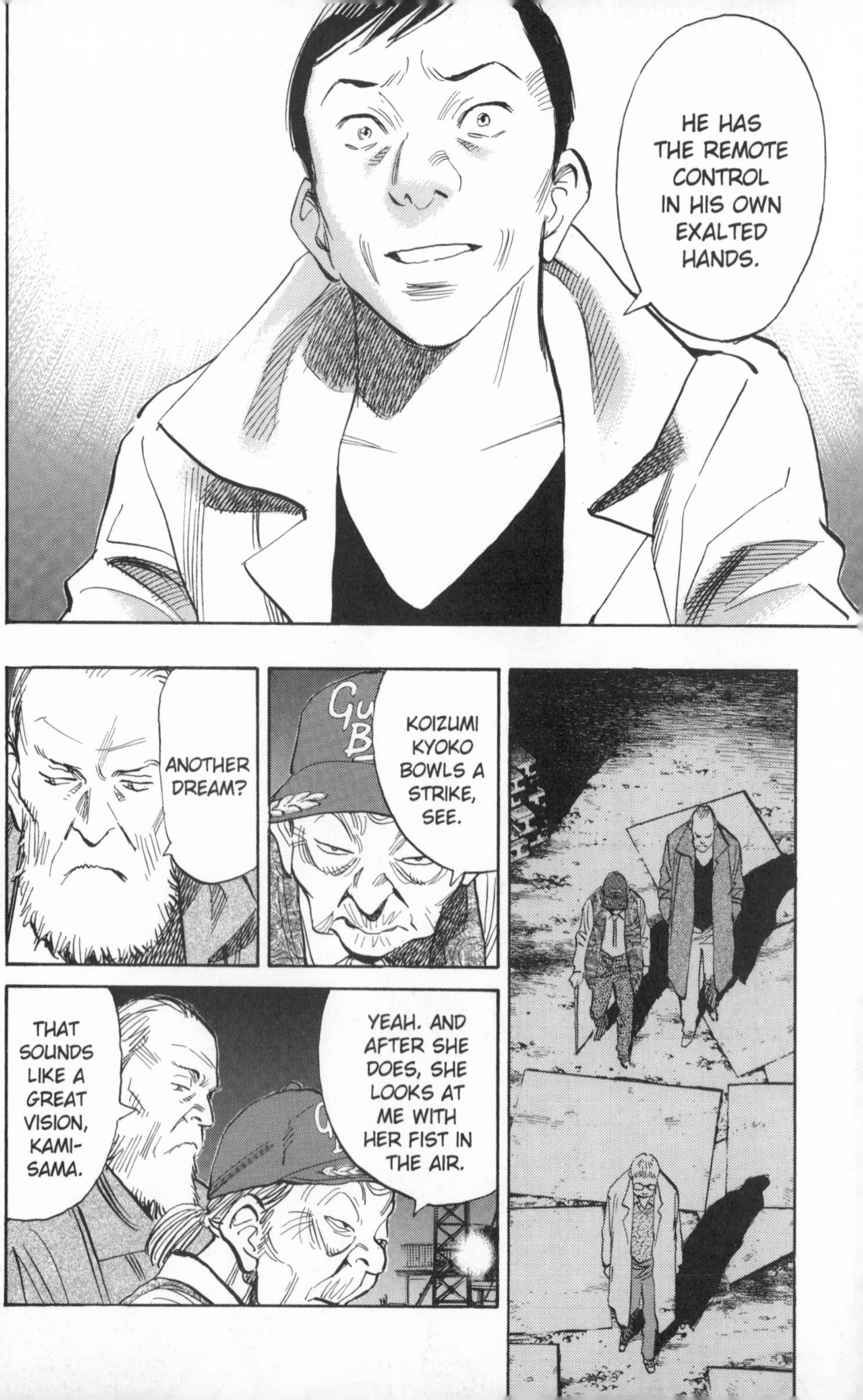
HE HAS THE REMOTE CONTROL IN HIS OWN EXALTED HANDS.
KOIZUMI KYOKO BOWLS A STRIKE, SEE.
ANOTHER DREAM?
YEAH. AND AFTER SHE DOES, SHE LOOKS AT ME WITH HER FIST IN THE AIR.
THAT SOUNDS LIKE A GREAT VISION, KAMI-SAMA.

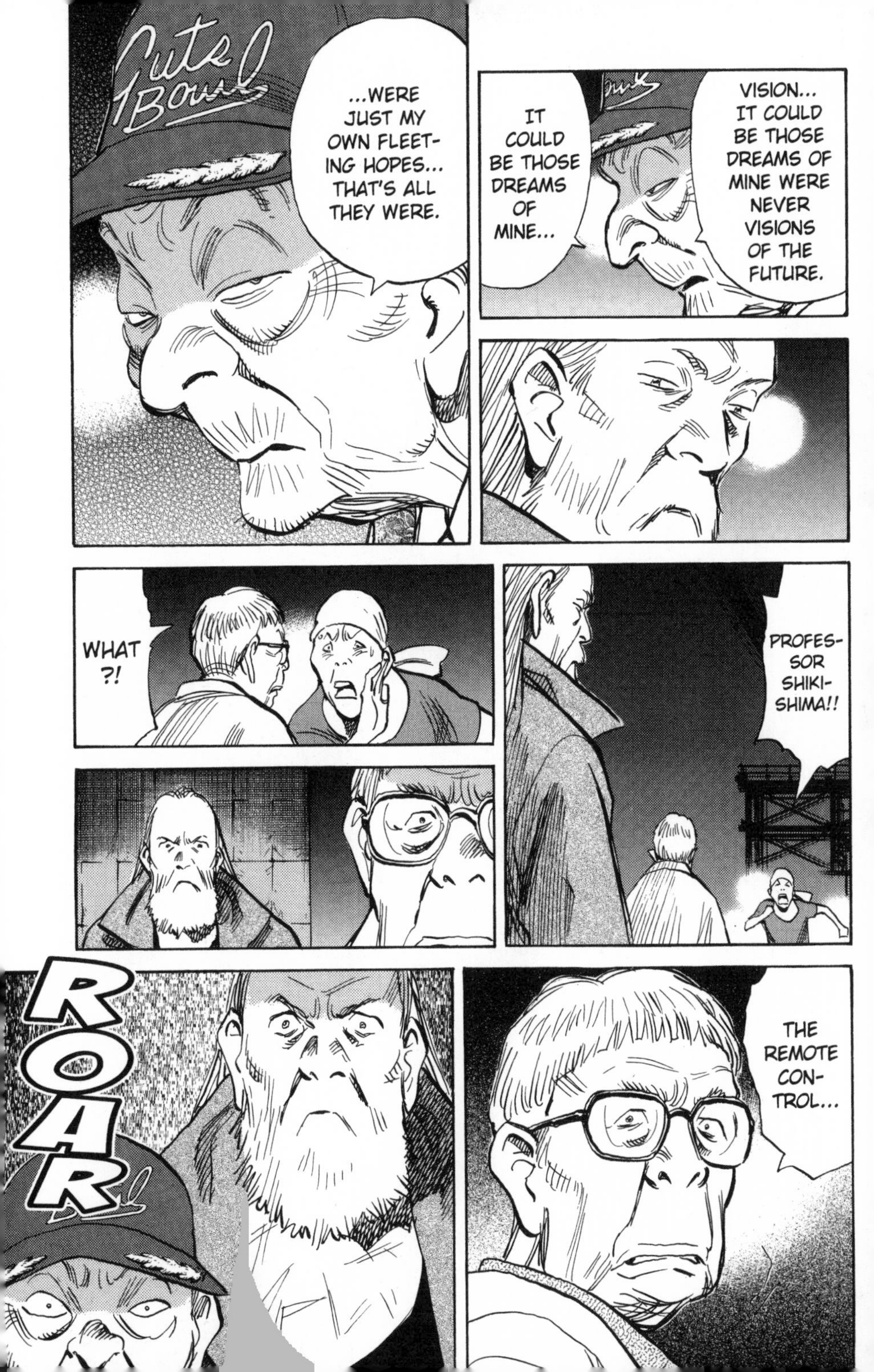
VISION... IT COULD BE THOSE DREAMS OF MINE WERE NEVER VISIONS OF THE FUTURE.
IT COULD BE THOSE DREAMS OF MINE...
...WERE JUST MY OWN FLEETING HOPES... THAT'S ALL THEY WERE.
PROFESSOR SHIKISHIMA!!
WHAT?!
THE REMOTE CONTROL...
ROAR

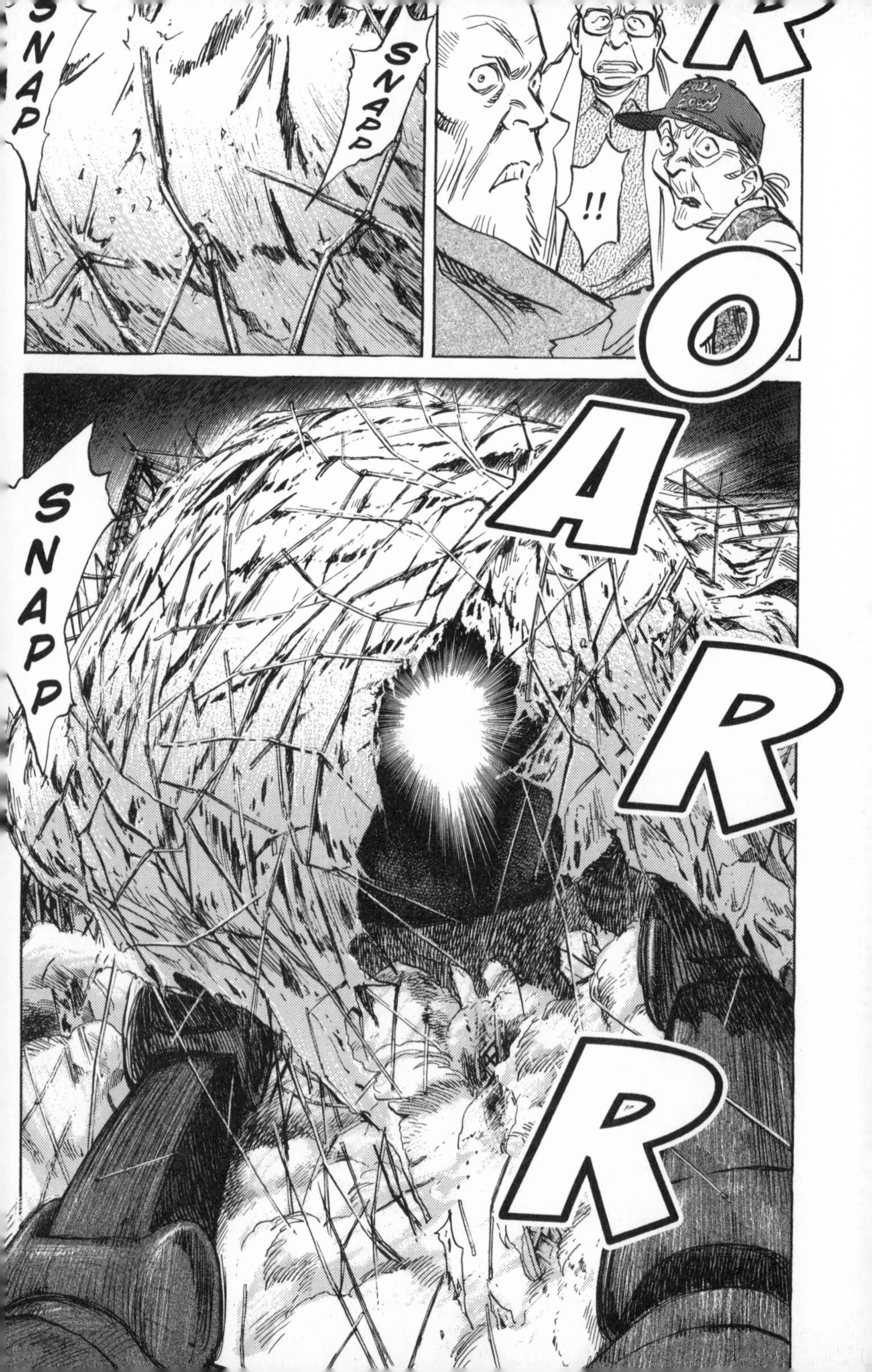
ROARR
!!
SNAPP
SNAP
SNAPP

Chapter 8 Legendary Detective Part 2

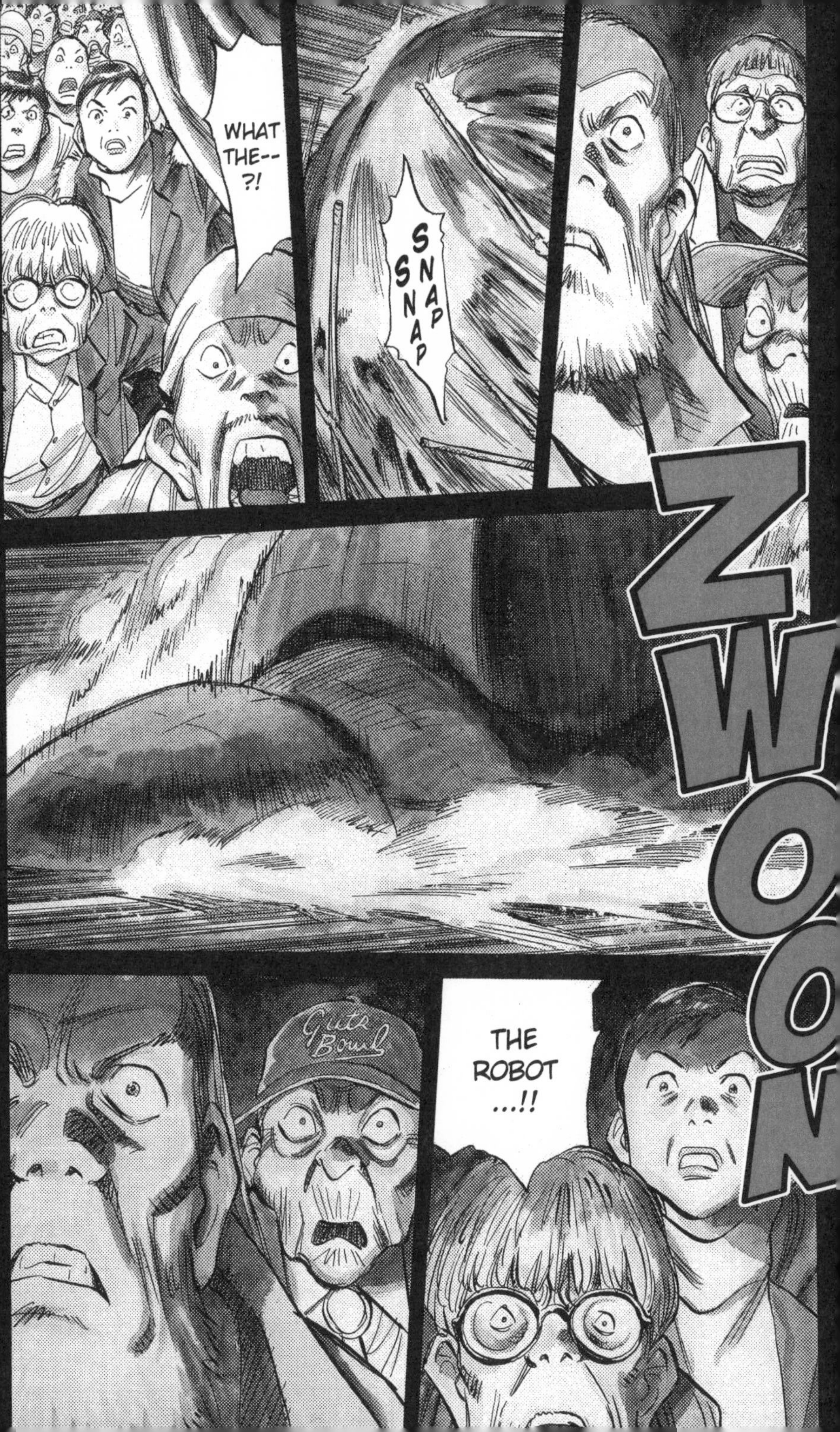
SNAP SNAP
WHAT THE-- ?!
ZWOOON
THE ROBOT ...!!

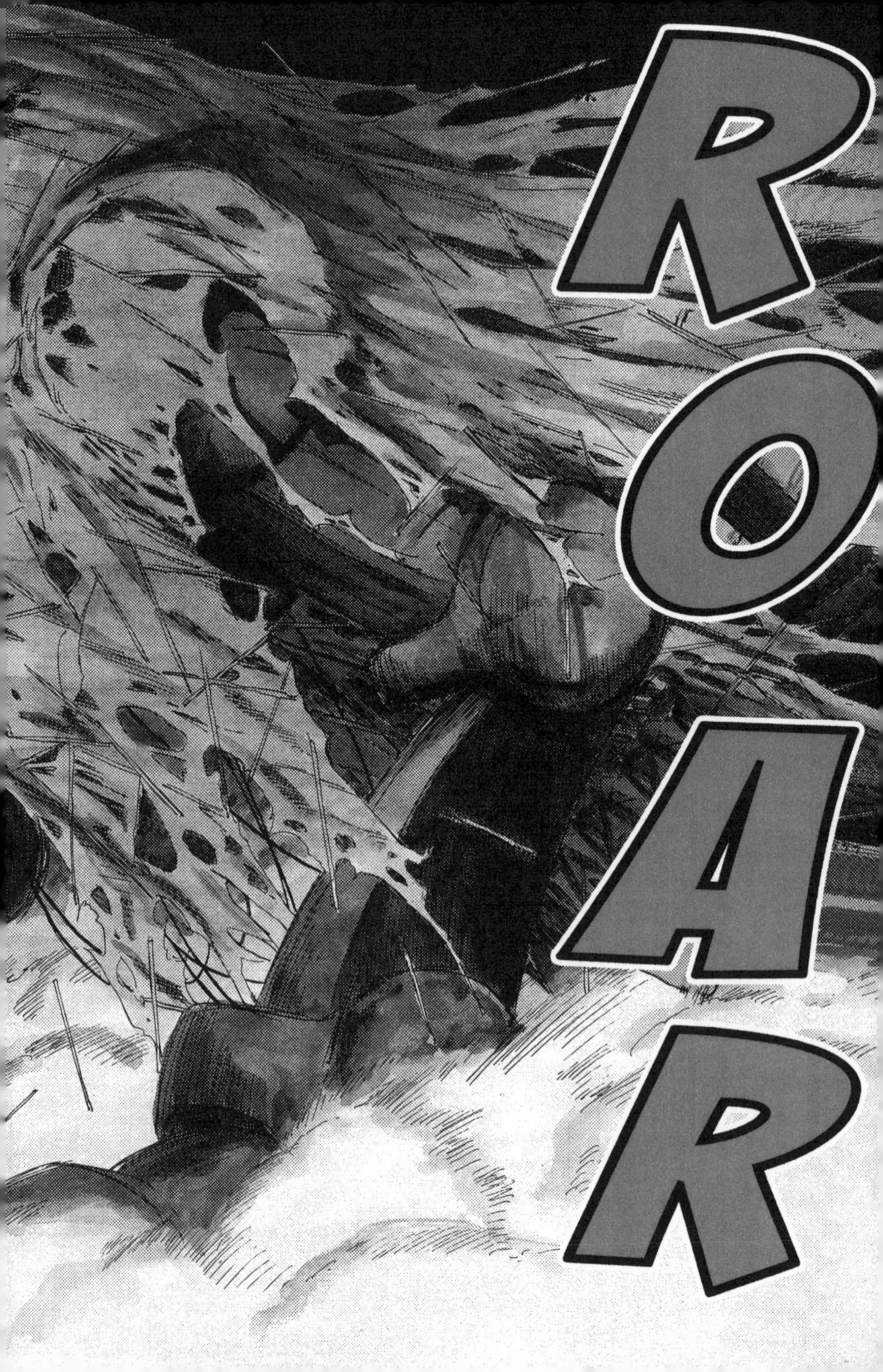
ROAR

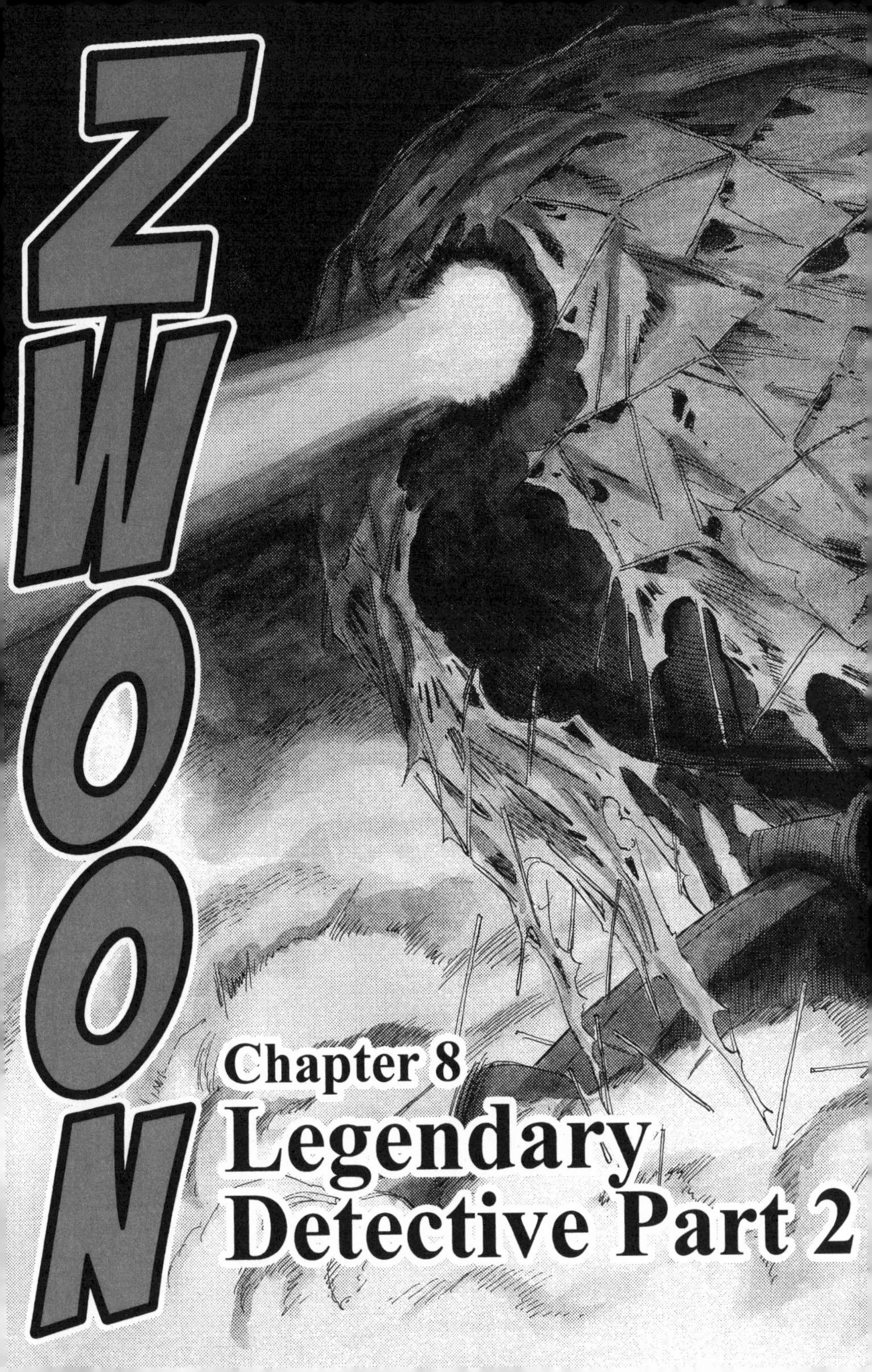
ZWOON
Chapter 8
Legendary Detective Part 2

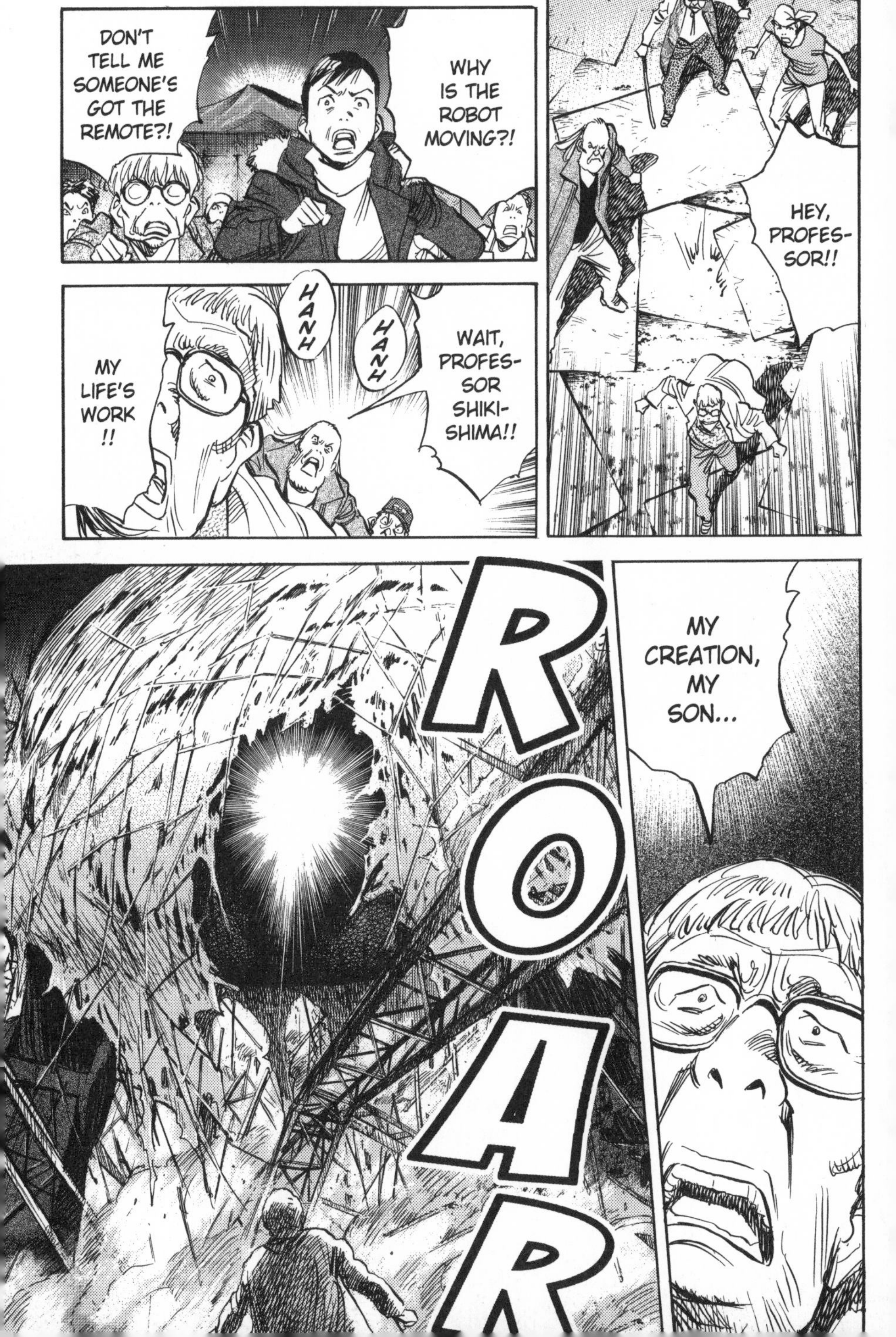
HEY, PROFES-SOR!!
WHY IS THE ROBOT MOVING?!
DON'T TELL ME SOMEONE'S GOT THE REMOTE?!
WAIT, PROFES-SOR SHIKI-SHIMA!!
HANH
HANH
MY LIFE'S WORK !!
MY CREATION, MY SON...
ROAR

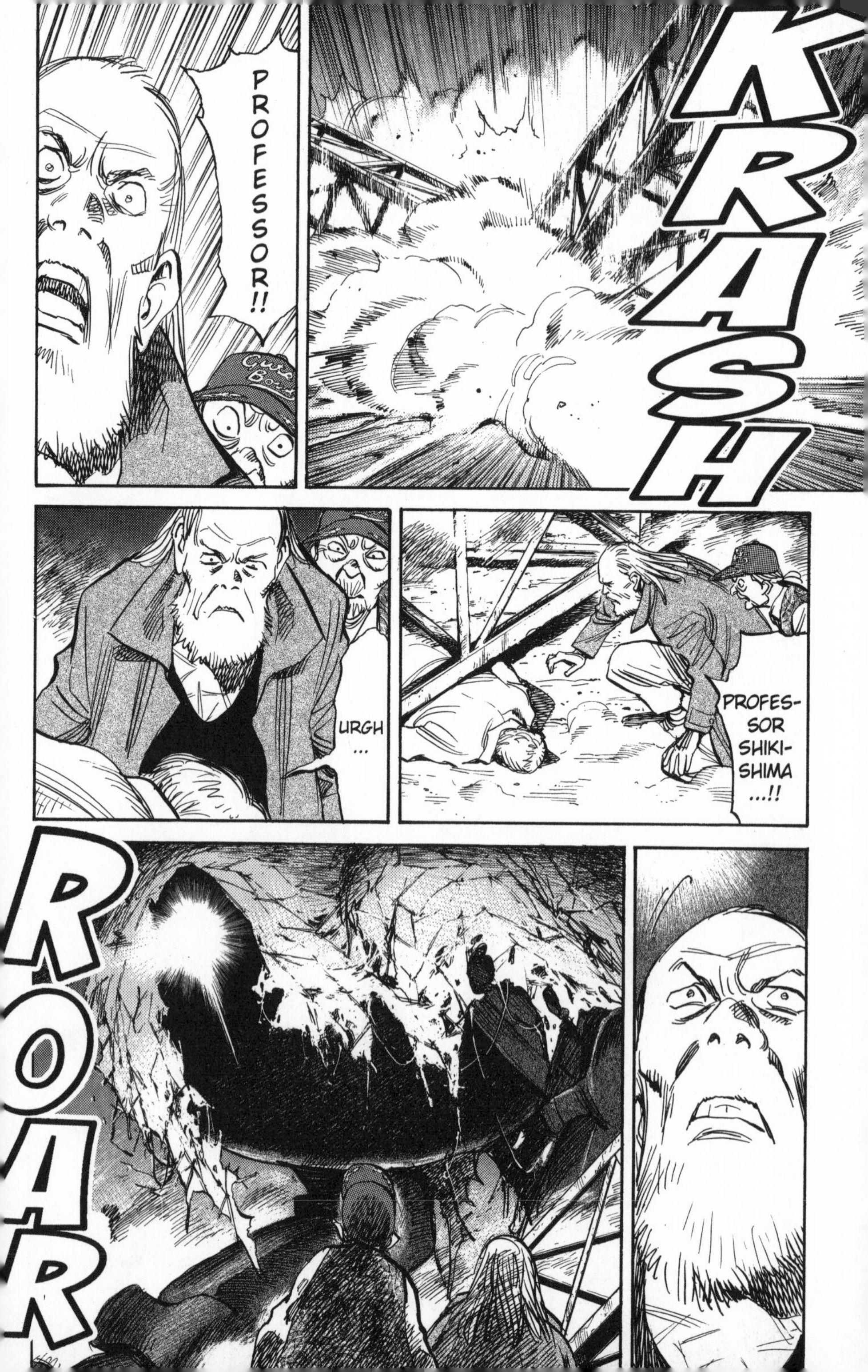
KRASH
PROFESSOR!!
PROFES-
SOR
SHIKI-
SHIMA
...!!
URGH
...
ROAR

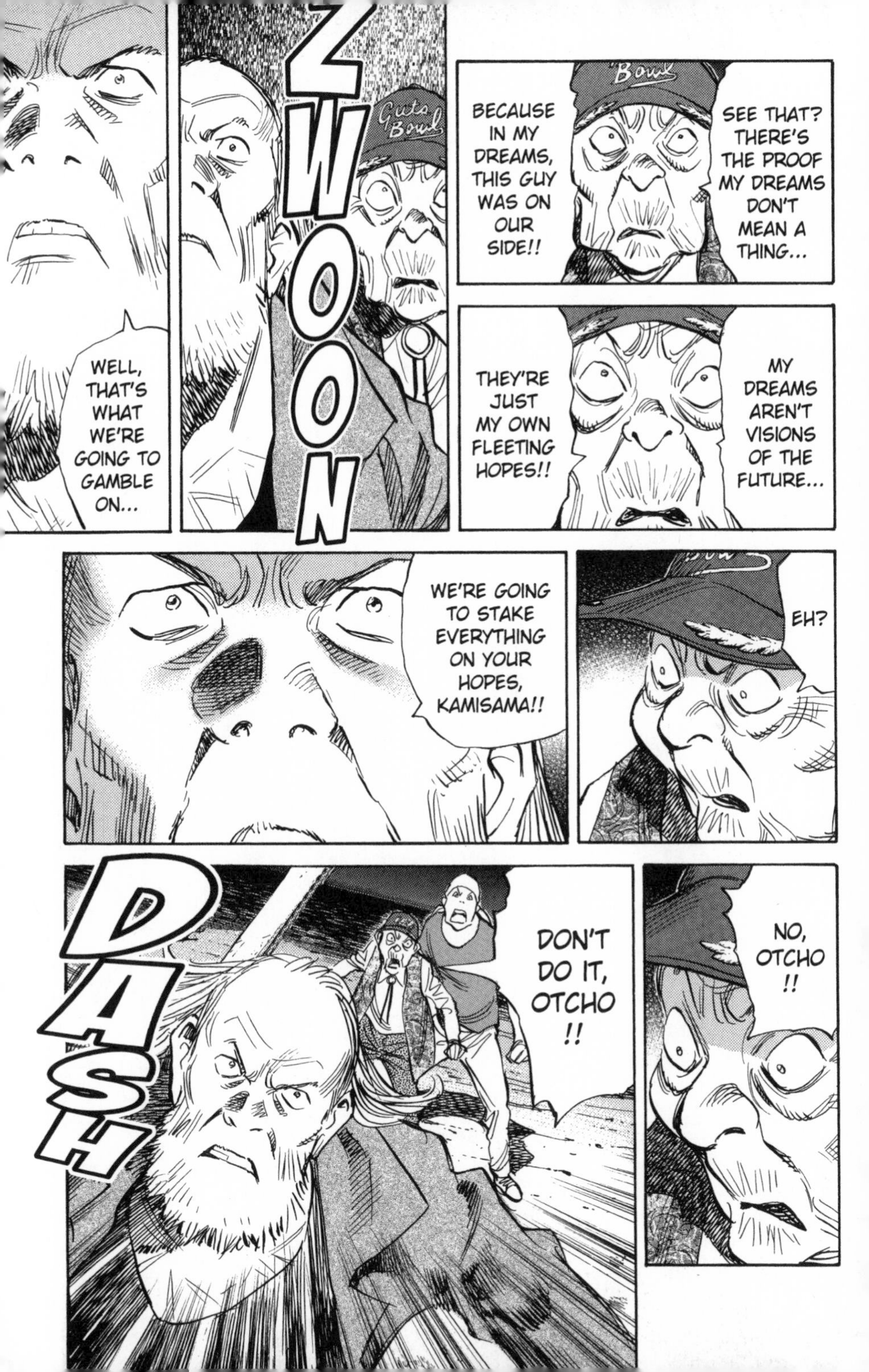
SEE THAT? THERE'S THE PROOF MY DREAMS DON'T MEAN A THING...
BECAUSE IN MY DREAMS, THIS GUY WAS ON OUR SIDE!!
MY DREAMS AREN'T VISIONS OF THE FUTURE...
THEY'RE JUST MY OWN FLEETING HOPES!!
ZWOON
WELL, THAT'S WHAT WE'RE GOING TO GAMBLE ON...
EH?
WE'RE GOING TO STAKE EVERYTHING ON YOUR HOPES, KAMISAMA!!
NO, OTCHO!!
DON'T DO IT, OTCHO!!
DASH

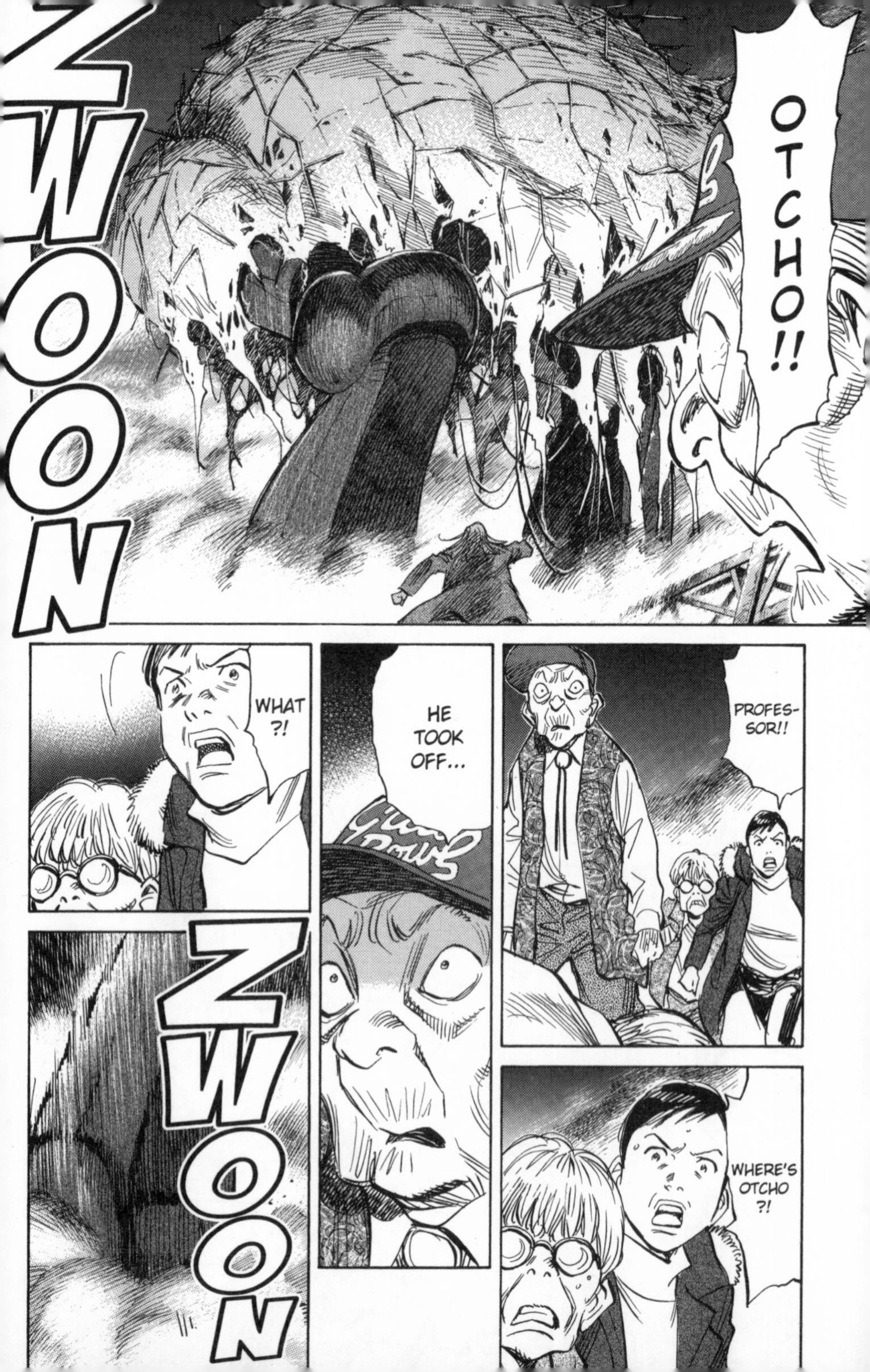
OTCHO!!
ZWOON
PROFES-SOR!!
WHERE'S OTCHO ?!
HE TOOK OFF...
WHAT ?!
ZWOON

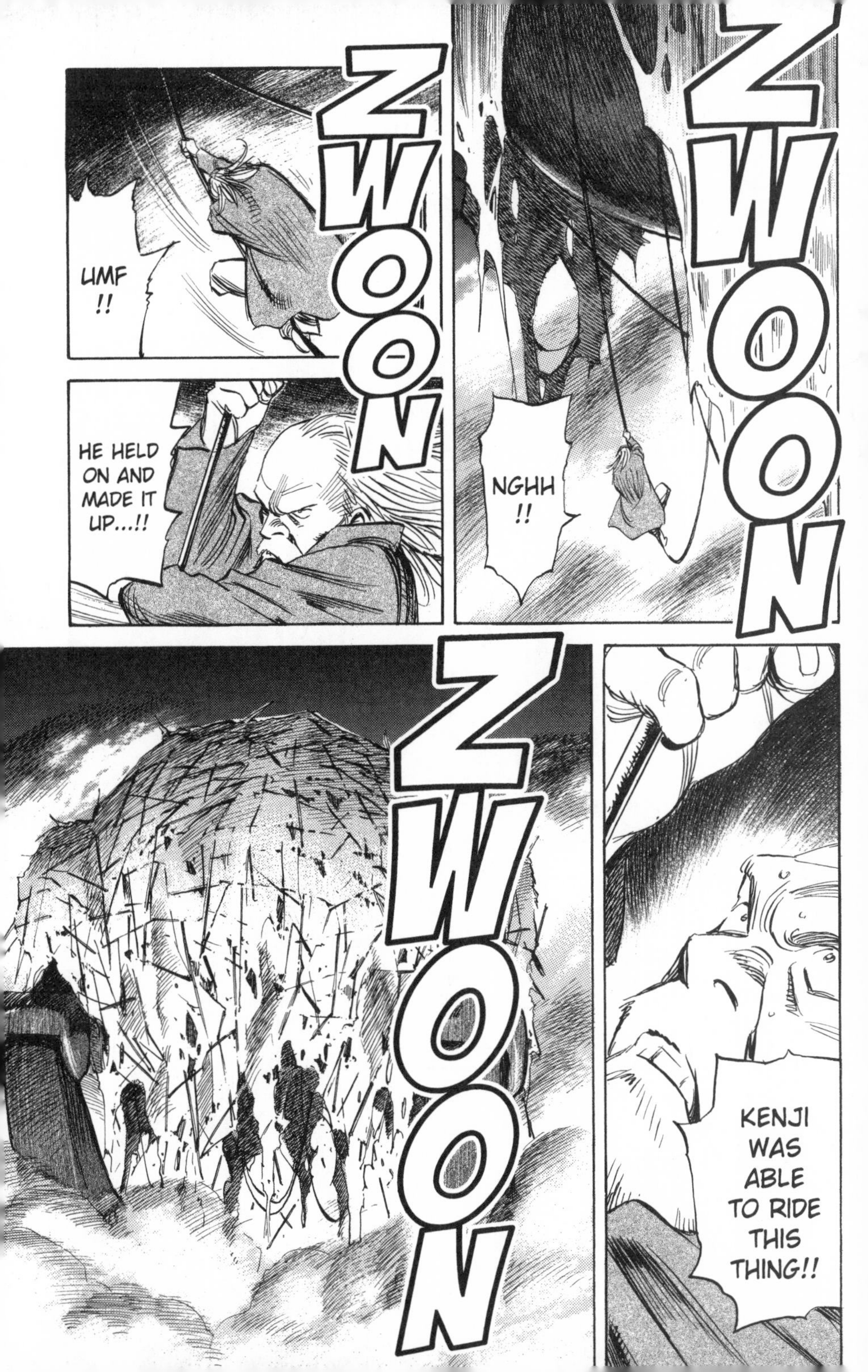
ZWOOON
NGHH !!
UMF !!
ZWOOON
HE HELD ON AND MADE IT UP...!!
KENJI WAS ABLE TO RIDE THIS THING!!
ZWOOON

UHHH...

BEAUTI-FUL...

PROFES-SOR!!

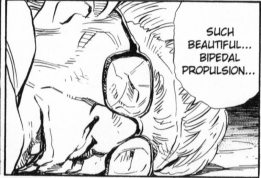

SUCH BEAUTIFUL... BIPEDAL PROPULSION...

IT'S ALREADY STARTED.

WHAT HAPPENS... TO OUR PLAN TO START THE UPRISING IN 24 HOURS...?

CALL EVERY-BODY TO ACTION.

HUH...?

PROFESSOR!!

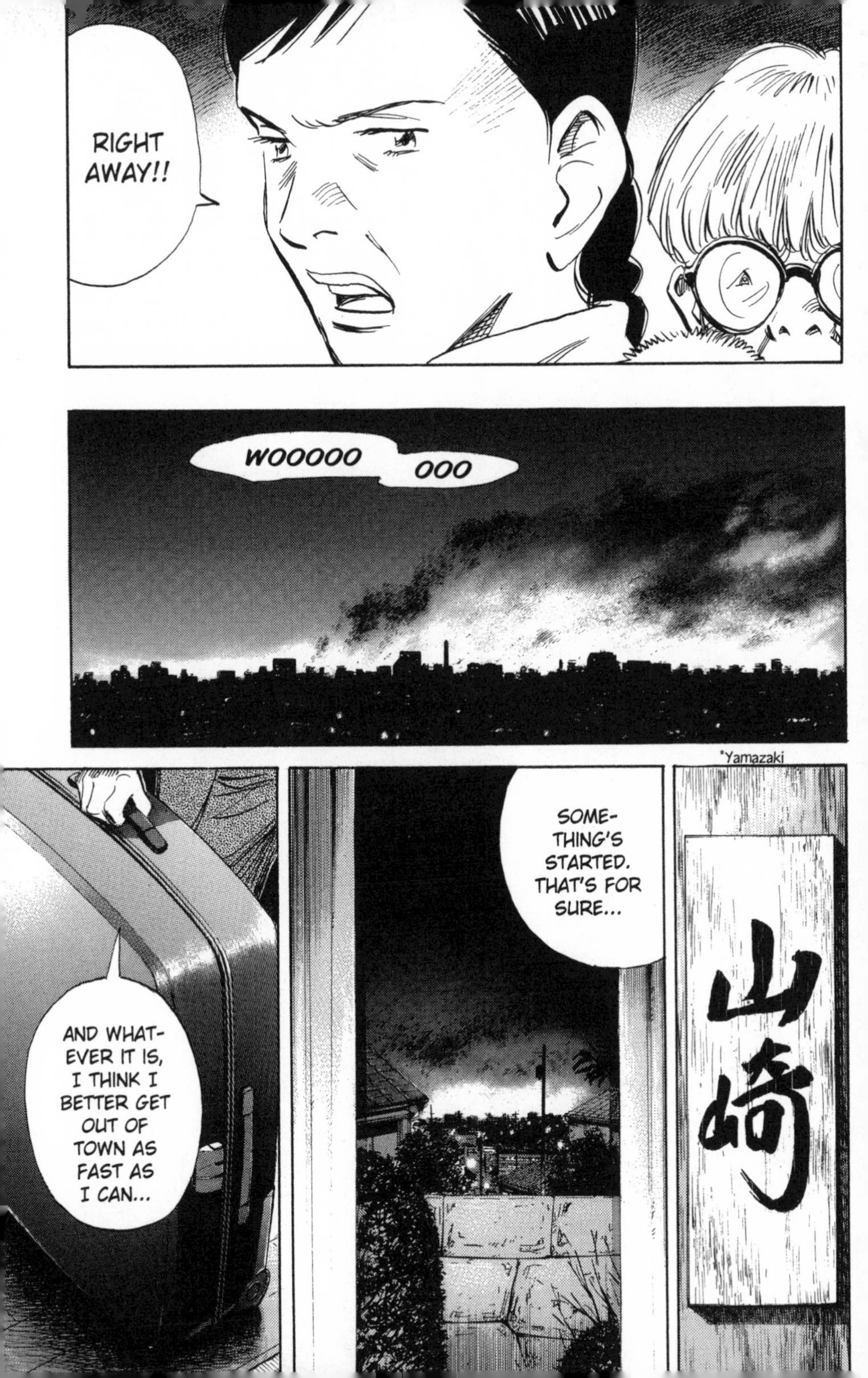
RIGHT AWAY!!
WOOOOO OOO
山崎
*Yamazaki
SOME-THING'S STARTED. THAT'S FOR SURE...
AND WHAT-EVER IT IS, I THINK I BETTER GET OUT OF TOWN AS FAST AS I CAN...

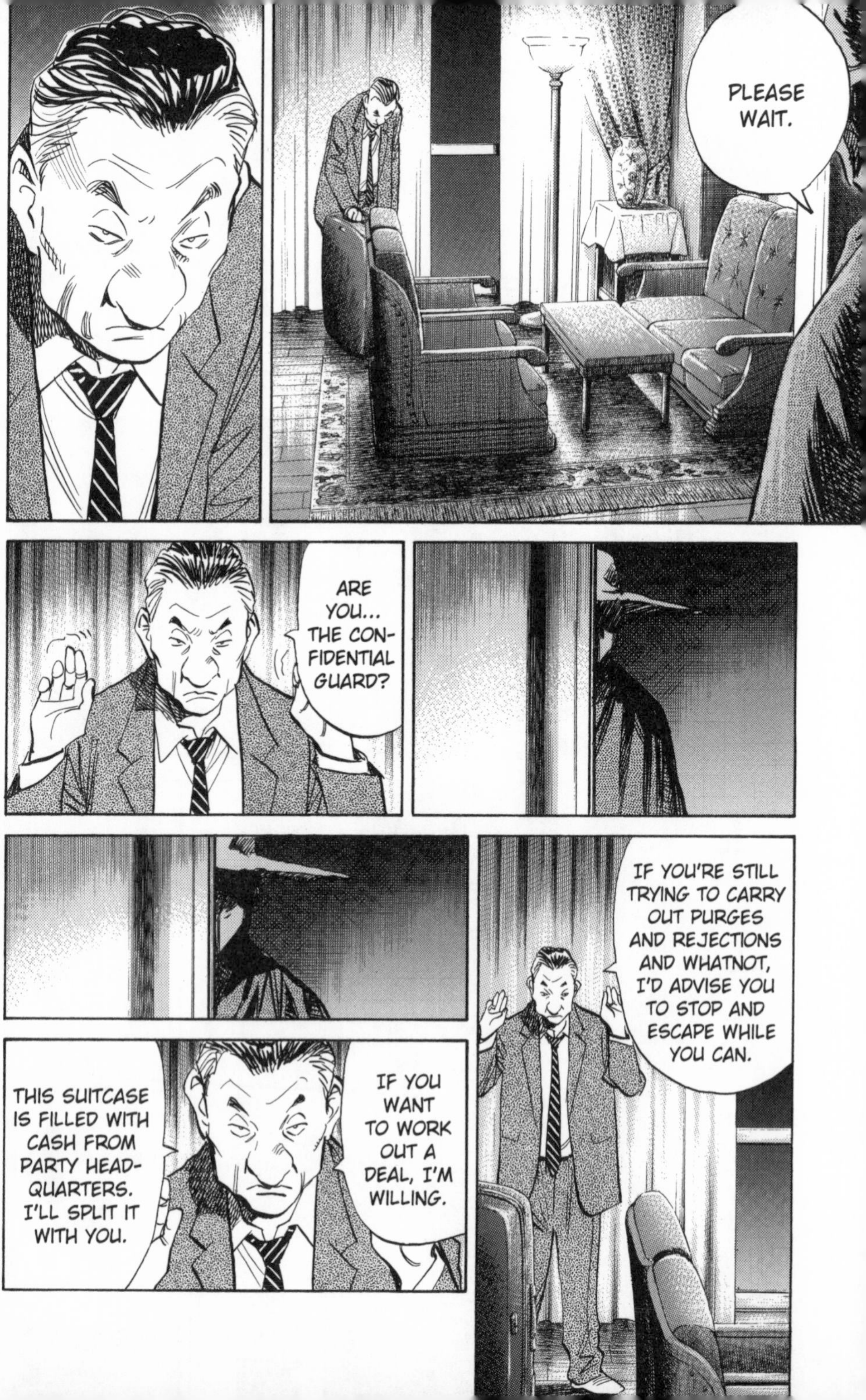
PLEASE WAIT.
ARE YOU... THE CON-FIDENTIAL GUARD?
IF YOU'RE STILL TRYING TO CARRY OUT PURGES AND REJECTIONS AND WHATNOT, I'D ADVISE YOU TO STOP AND ESCAPE WHILE YOU CAN.
IF YOU WANT TO WORK OUT A DEAL, I'M WILLING.
THIS SUITCASE IS FILLED WITH CASH FROM PARTY HEAD-QUARTERS. I'LL SPLIT IT WITH YOU.

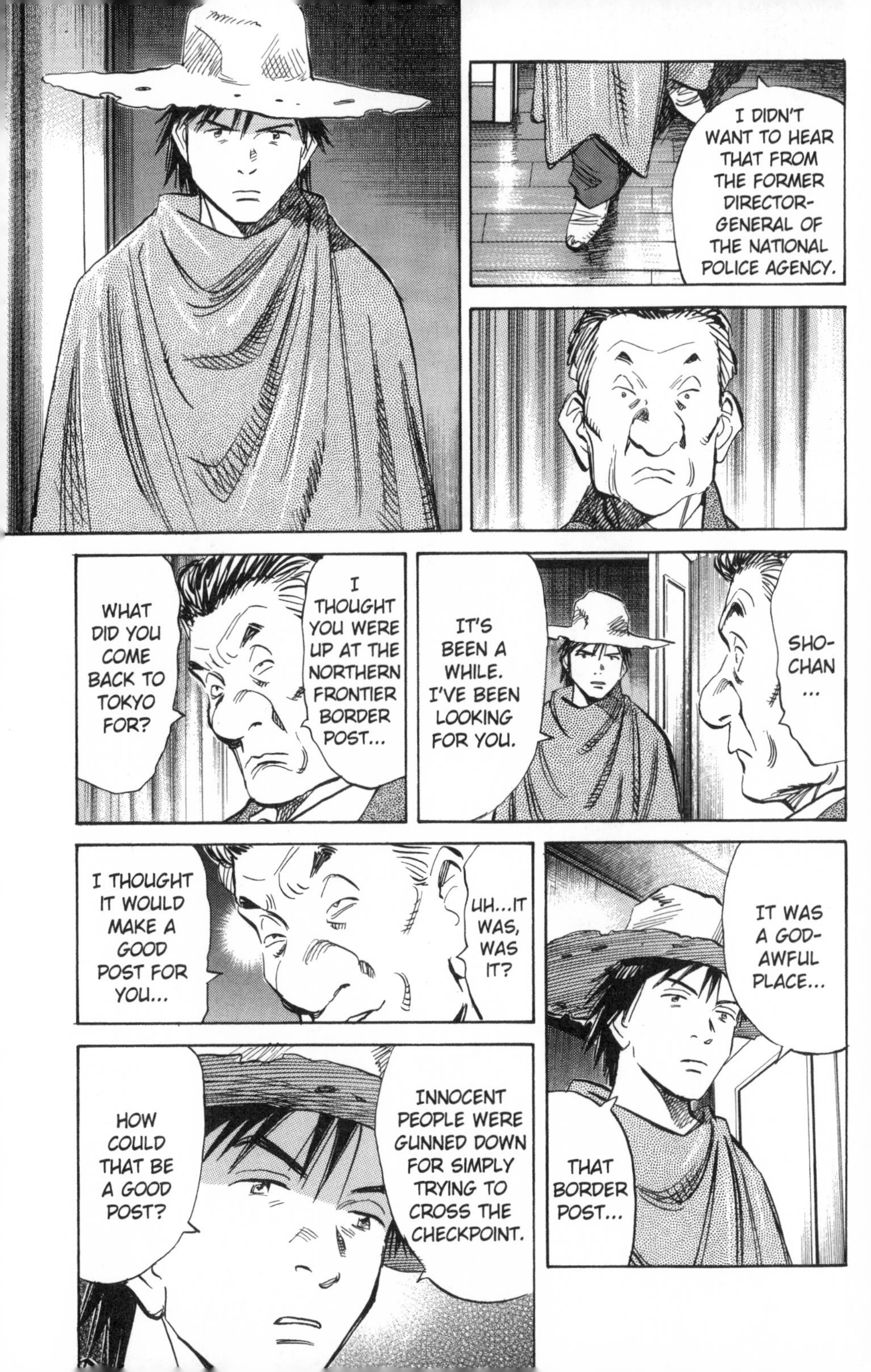
I DIDN'T WANT TO HEAR THAT FROM THE FORMER DIRECTOR-GENERAL OF THE NATIONAL POLICE AGENCY.
SHO-CHAN...
IT'S BEEN A WHILE. I'VE BEEN LOOKING FOR YOU.
I THOUGHT YOU WERE UP AT THE NORTHERN FRONTIER BORDER POST...
WHAT DID YOU COME BACK TO TOKYO FOR?
IT WAS A GOD-AWFUL PLACE...
THAT BORDER POST...
UH...IT WAS, WAS IT?
I THOUGHT IT WOULD MAKE A GOOD POST FOR YOU...
INNOCENT PEOPLE WERE GUNNED DOWN FOR SIMPLY TRYING TO CROSS THE CHECKPOINT.
HOW COULD THAT BE A GOOD POST?

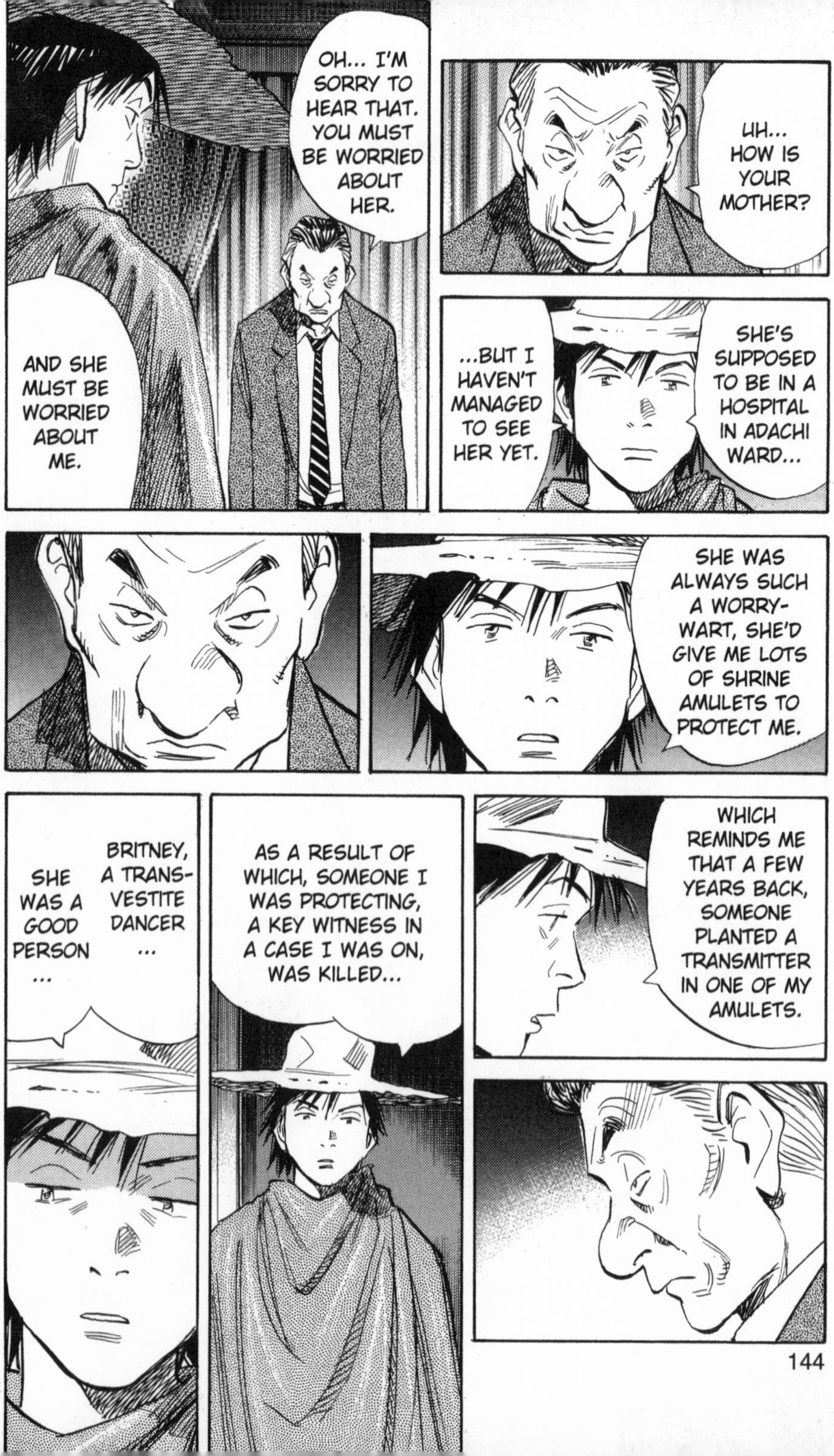
UH... HOW IS YOUR MOTHER?
SHE'S SUPPOSED TO BE IN A HOSPITAL IN ADACHI WARD...
...BUT I HAVEN'T MANAGED TO SEE HER YET.
OH... I'M SORRY TO HEAR THAT. YOU MUST BE WORRIED ABOUT HER.
AND SHE MUST BE WORRIED ABOUT ME.
SHE WAS ALWAYS SUCH A WORRY-WART, SHE'D GIVE ME LOTS OF SHRINE AMULETS TO PROTECT ME.
WHICH REMINDS ME THAT A FEW YEARS BACK, SOMEONE PLANTED A TRANSMITTER IN ONE OF MY AMULETS.
AS A RESULT OF WHICH, SOMEONE I WAS PROTECTING, A KEY WITNESS IN A CASE I WAS ON, WAS KILLED...
BRITNEY, A TRANS-VESTITE DANCER ...
SHE WAS A GOOD PERSON ...

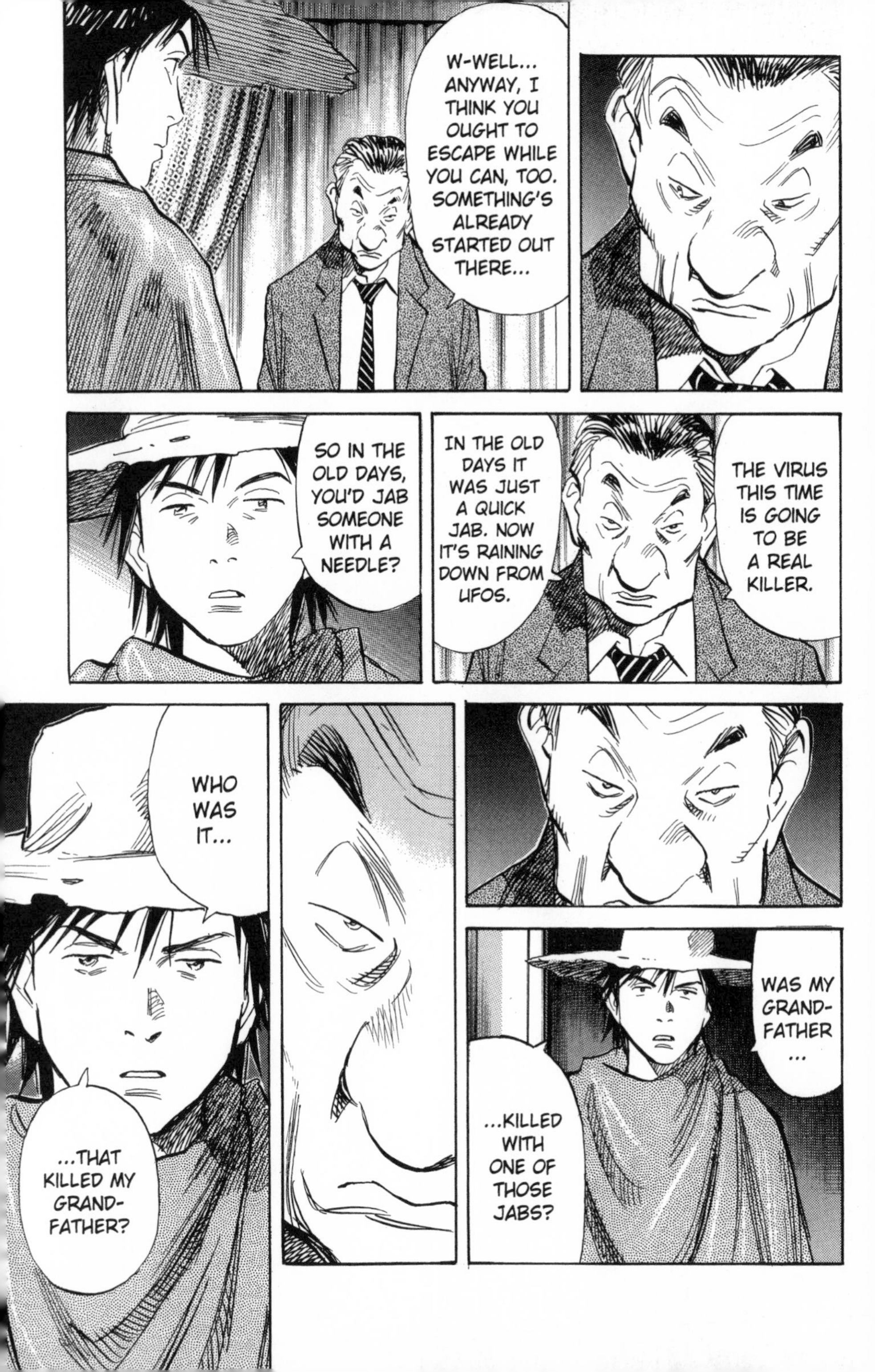
W-WELL... ANYWAY, I THINK YOU OUGHT TO ESCAPE WHILE YOU CAN, TOO. SOMETHING'S ALREADY STARTED OUT THERE...
THE VIRUS THIS TIME IS GOING TO BE A REAL KILLER.
IN THE OLD DAYS IT WAS JUST A QUICK JAB. NOW IT'S RAINING DOWN FROM UFOS.
SO IN THE OLD DAYS, YOU'D JAB SOMEONE WITH A NEEDLE?
WAS MY GRAND-FATHER...
...KILLED WITH ONE OF THOSE JABS?
WHO WAS IT...
...THAT KILLED MY GRAND-FATHER?

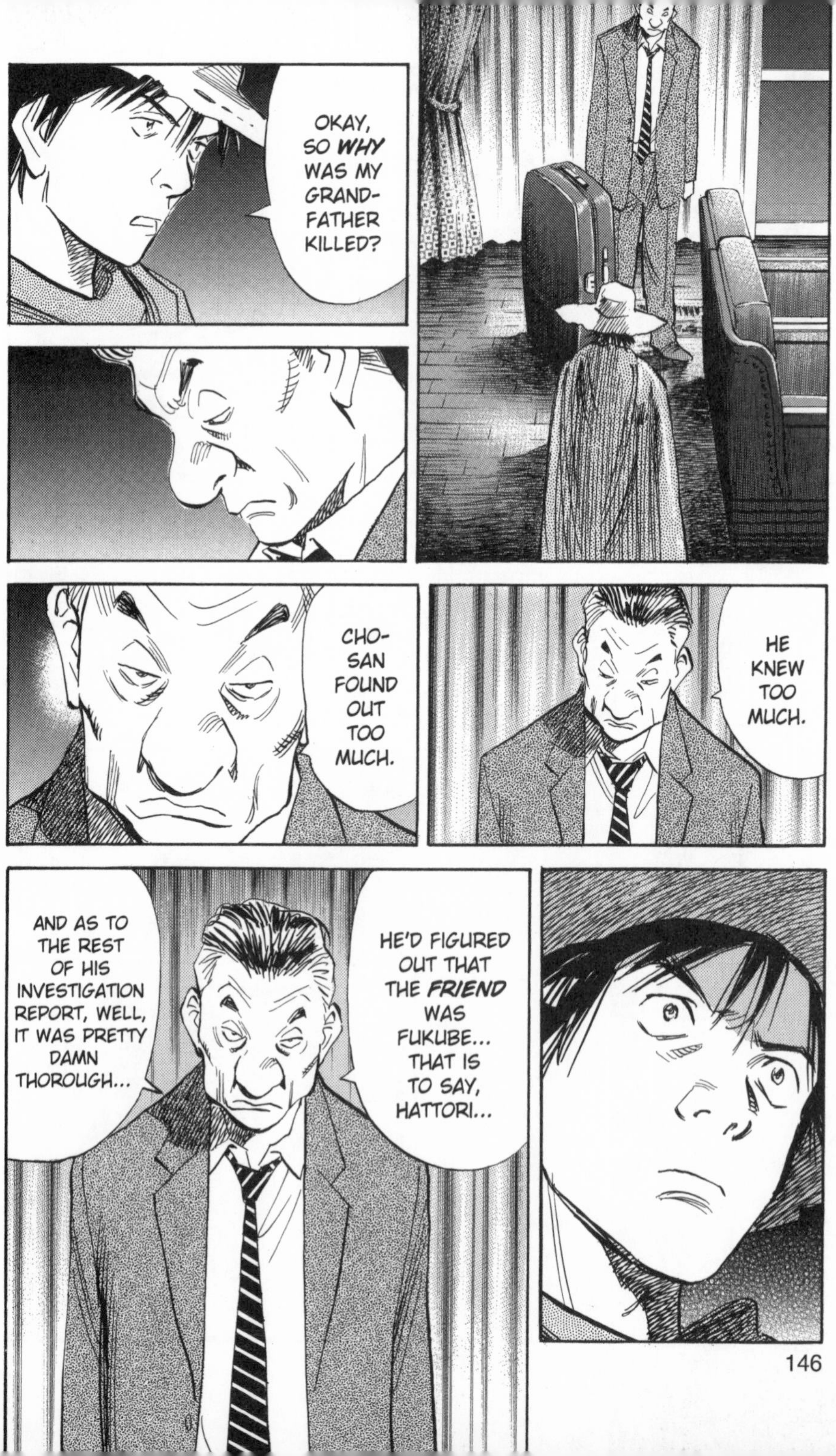
OKAY, SO *WHY* WAS MY GRAND-FATHER KILLED?
HE KNEW TOO MUCH.
CHO-SAN FOUND OUT TOO MUCH.
HE'D FIGURED OUT THAT THE *FRIEND* WAS FUKUBE... THAT IS TO SAY, HATTORI...
AND AS TO THE REST OF HIS INVESTIGATION REPORT, WELL, IT WAS PRETTY DAMN THOROUGH...

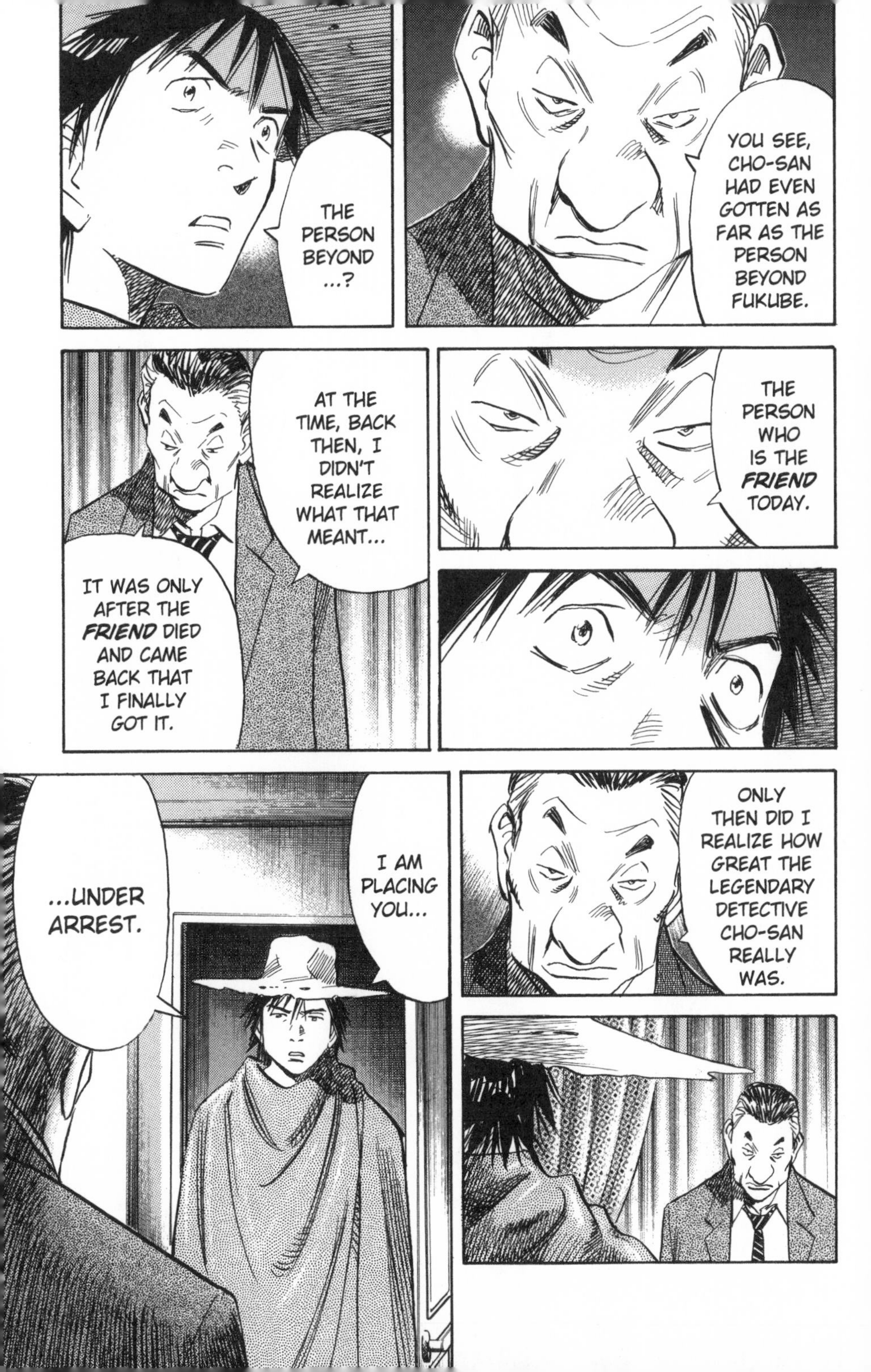
YOU SEE, CHO-SAN HAD EVEN GOTTEN AS FAR AS THE PERSON BEYOND FUKUBE.
THE PERSON BEYOND ...?
THE PERSON WHO IS THE *FRIEND* TODAY.
AT THE TIME, BACK THEN, I DIDN'T REALIZE WHAT THAT MEANT...
IT WAS ONLY AFTER THE *FRIEND* DIED AND CAME BACK THAT I FINALLY GOT IT.
ONLY THEN DID I REALIZE HOW GREAT THE LEGENDARY DETECTIVE CHO-SAN REALLY WAS.
I AM PLACING YOU...
...UNDER ARREST.

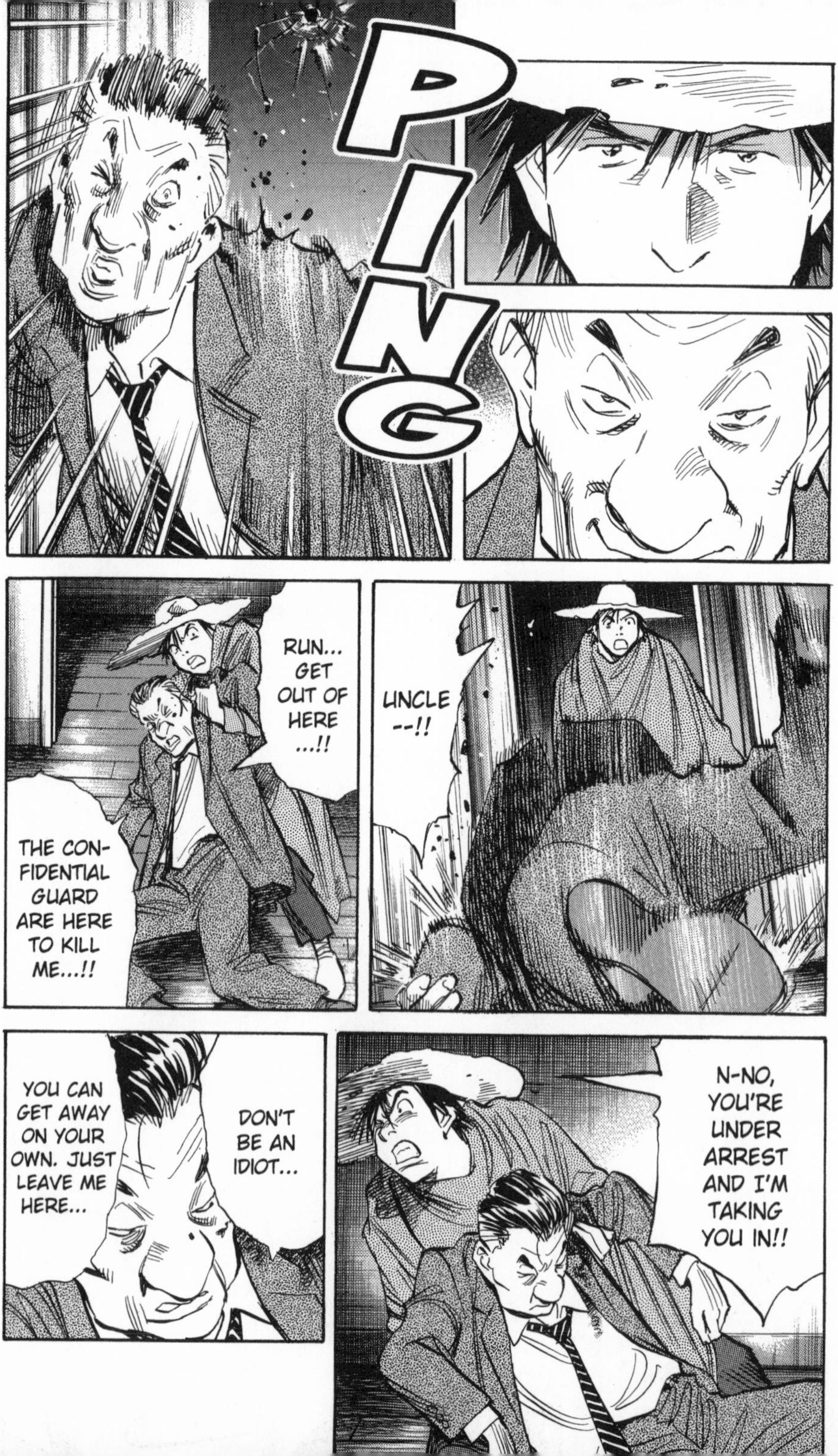
PING
UNCLE --!!
RUN... GET OUT OF HERE ...!!
THE CON-FIDENTIAL GUARD ARE HERE TO KILL ME...!!
N-NO, YOU'RE UNDER ARREST AND I'M TAKING YOU IN!!
DON'T BE AN IDIOT...
YOU CAN GET AWAY ON YOUR OWN. JUST LEAVE ME HERE...

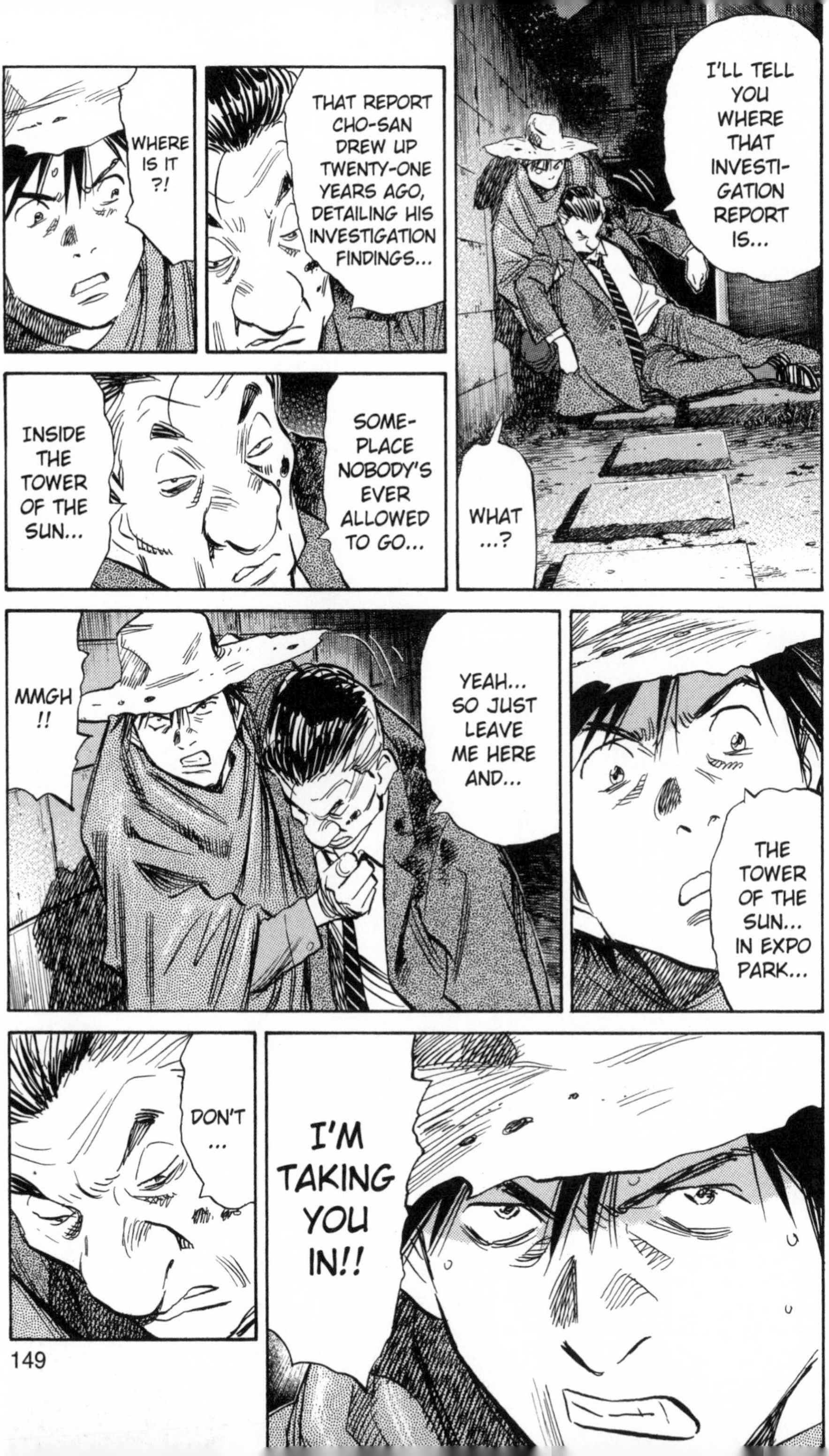
I'LL TELL YOU WHERE THAT INVESTIGATION REPORT IS...
WHAT ...?
THAT REPORT CHO-SAN DREW UP TWENTY-ONE YEARS AGO, DETAILING HIS INVESTIGATION FINDINGS...
WHERE IS IT ?!
SOME-PLACE NOBODY'S EVER ALLOWED TO GO...
INSIDE THE TOWER OF THE SUN...
THE TOWER OF THE SUN... IN EXPO PARK...
YEAH... SO JUST LEAVE ME HERE AND...
MMGH !!
I'M TAKING YOU IN!!
DON'T ...

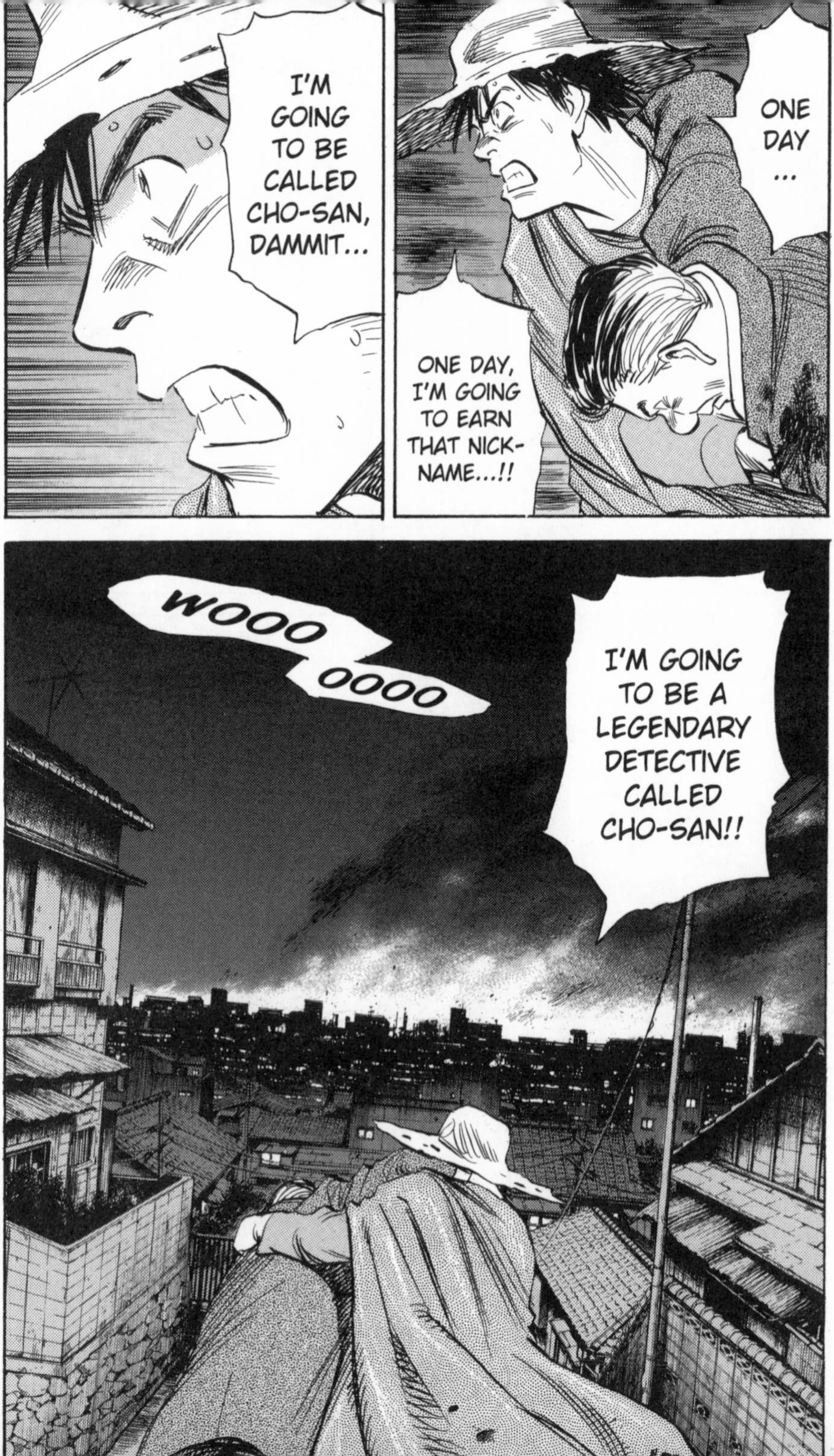
ONE DAY ...
ONE DAY, I'M GOING TO EARN THAT NICK-NAME...!!
I'M GOING TO BE CALLED CHO-SAN, DAMMIT...
I'M GOING TO BE A LEGENDARY DETECTIVE CALLED CHO-SAN!!
WOOOOOOOO

Chapter 9 Do Nothing

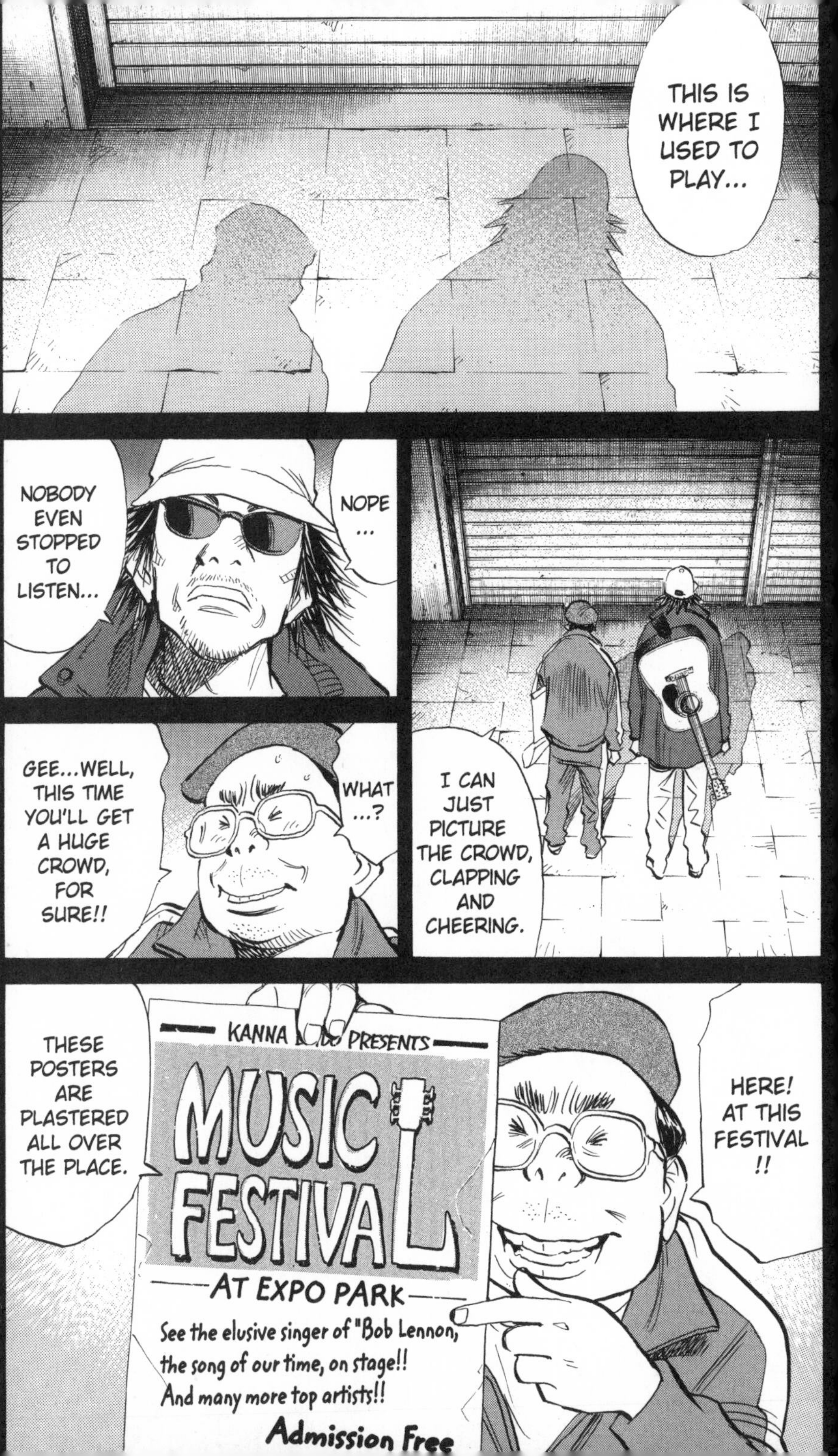
THIS IS WHERE I USED TO PLAY...
I CAN JUST PICTURE THE CROWD, CLAPPING AND CHEERING.
NOPE ...
NOBODY EVEN STOPPED TO LISTEN...
WHAT ...?
GEE...WELL, THIS TIME YOU'LL GET A HUGE CROWD, FOR SURE!!
HERE! AT THIS FESTIVAL !!
THESE POSTERS ARE PLASTERED ALL OVER THE PLACE.
KANNA PRESENTS
MUSIC FESTIVAL
AT EXPO PARK
See the elusive singer of "Bob Lennon, the song of our time, on stage!!
And many more top artists!!
Admission Free

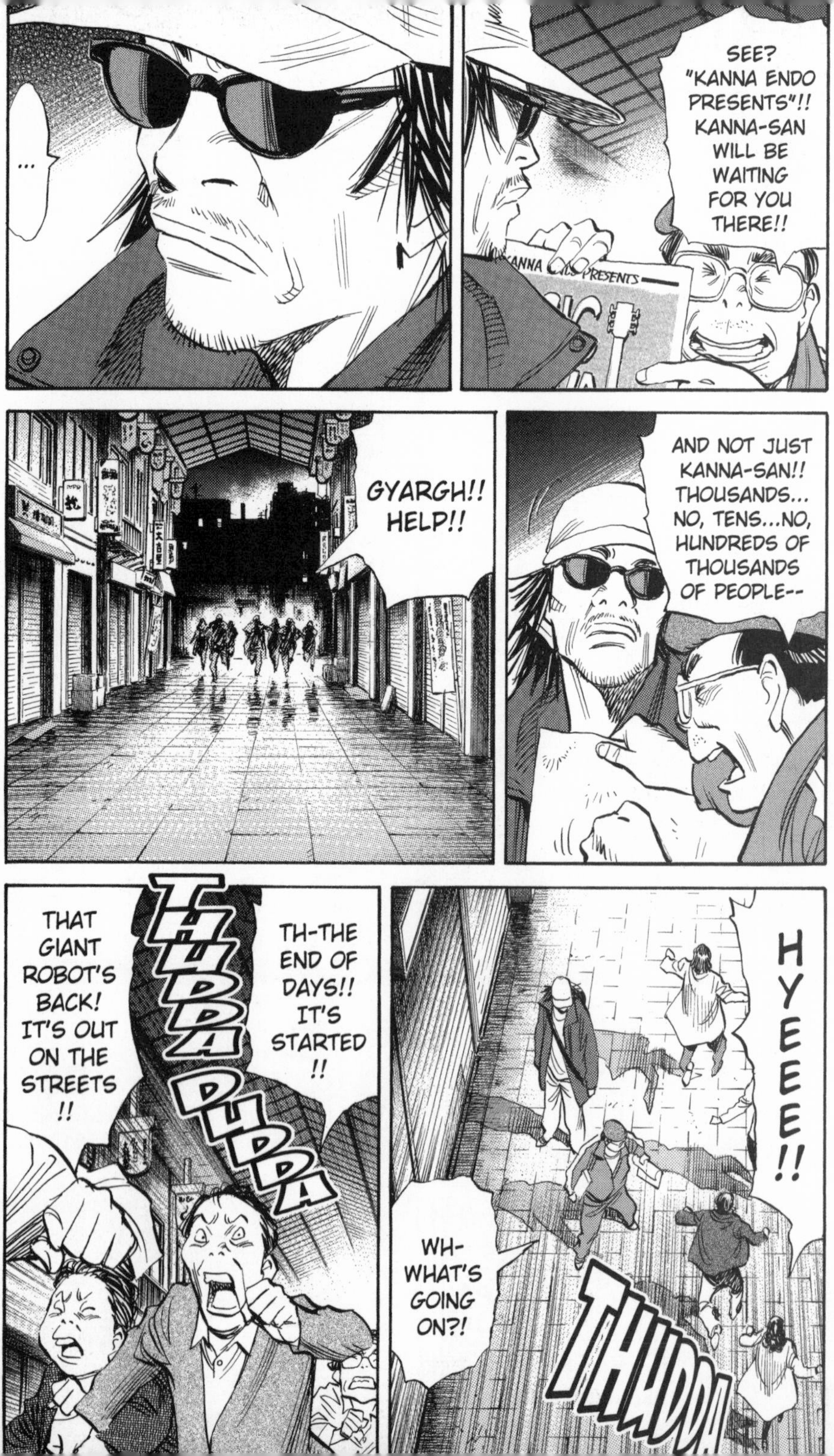
SEE? "KANNA ENDO PRESENTS"!! KANNA-SAN WILL BE WAITING FOR YOU THERE!!
...
AND NOT JUST KANNA-SAN!! THOUSANDS... NO, TENS...NO, HUNDREDS OF THOUSANDS OF PEOPLE--
GYARGH!! HELP!!
HYEEEE!!
WH- WHAT'S GOING ON?!
THUDDA
TH-THE END OF DAYS!! IT'S STARTED!!
THUDDA DUDDA
THAT GIANT ROBOT'S BACK! IT'S OUT ON THE STREETS!!

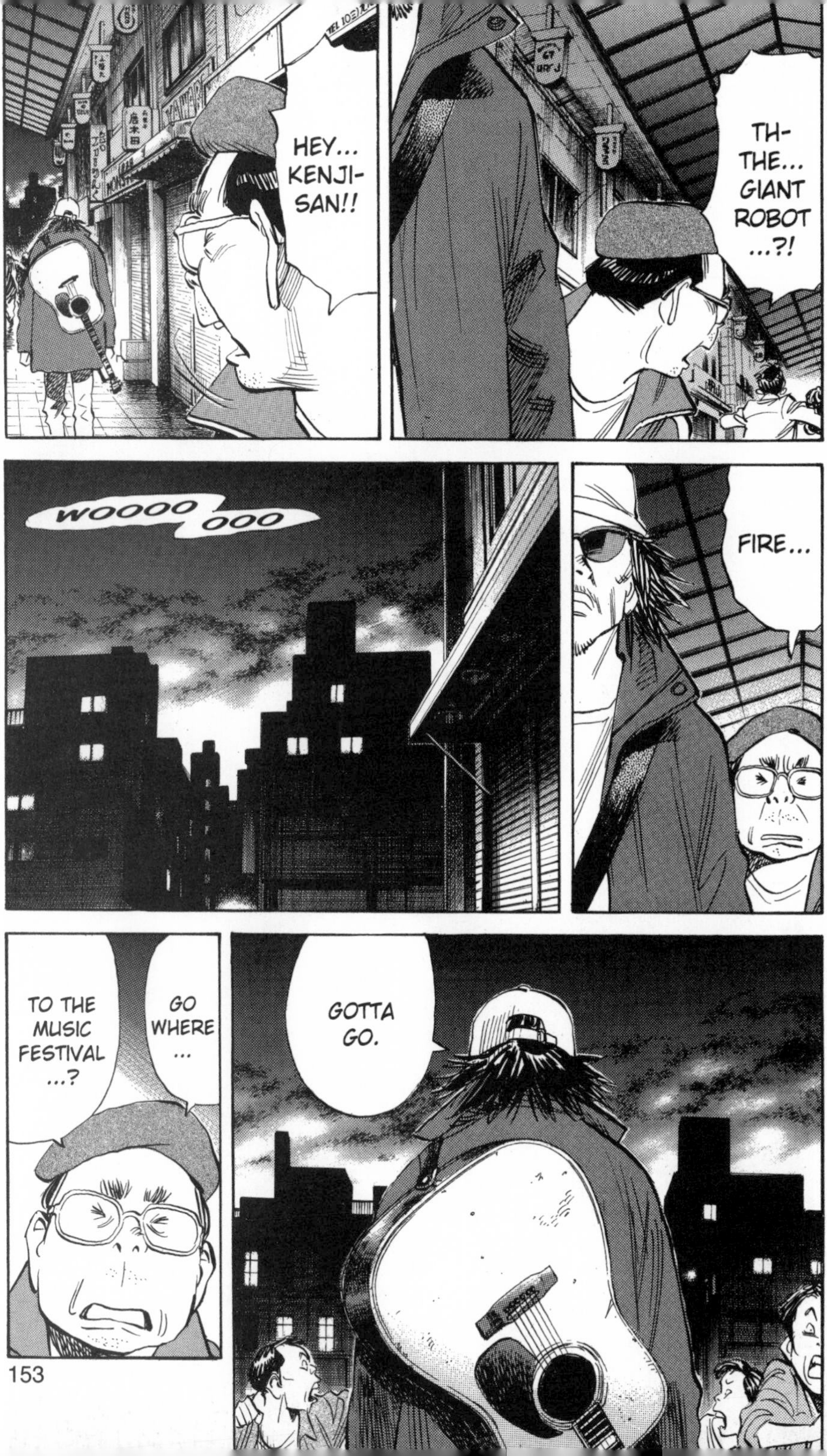
TH-THE... GIANT ROBOT ...?!
HEY... KENJI-SAN!!
FIRE...
WOOOO OOO
GOTTA GO.
GO WHERE ...
TO THE MUSIC FESTIVAL ...?

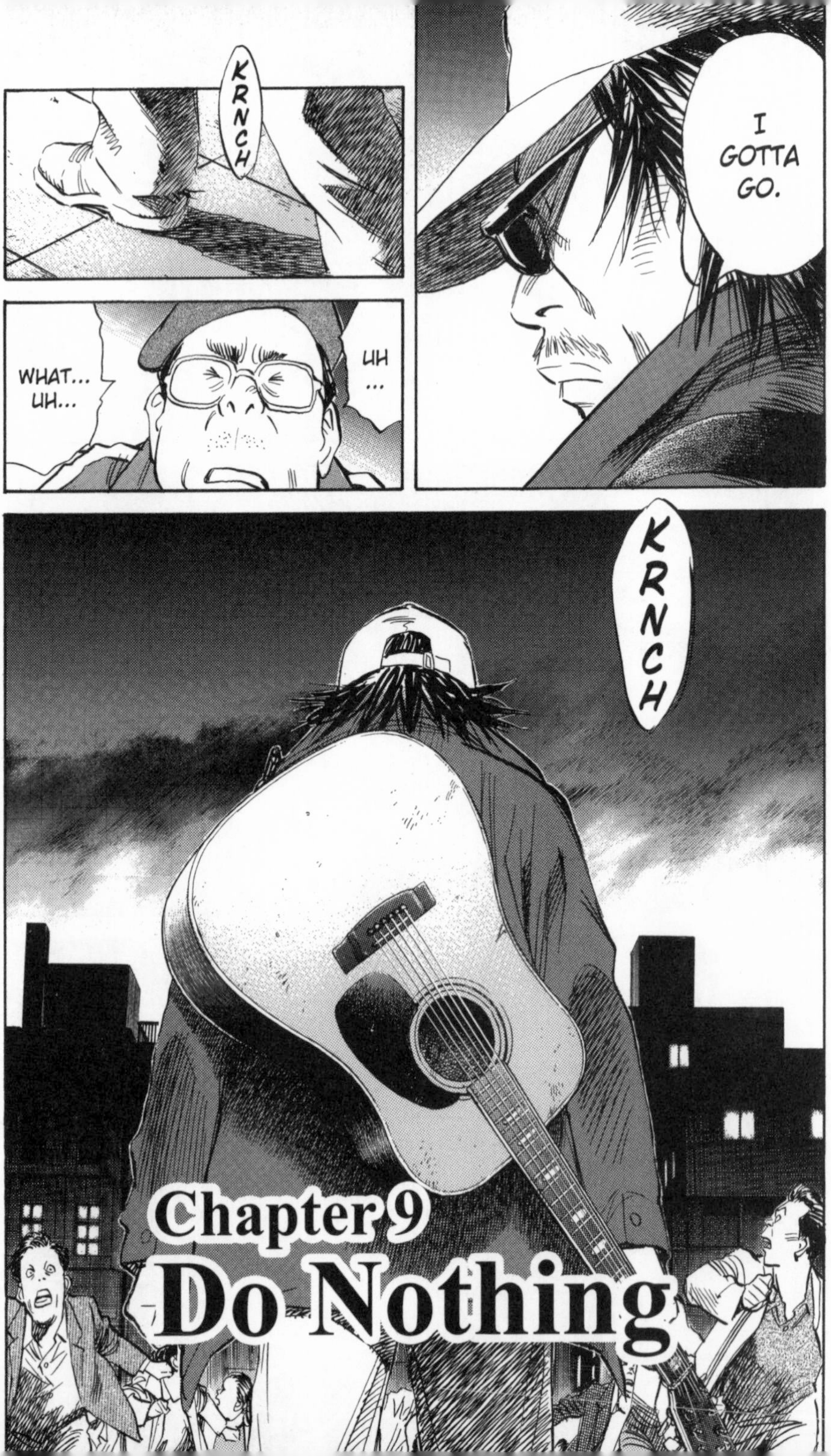
I GOTTA GO.
KRNCH
UH ...
WHAT... UH...
KRNCH

Chapter 9
Do Nothing

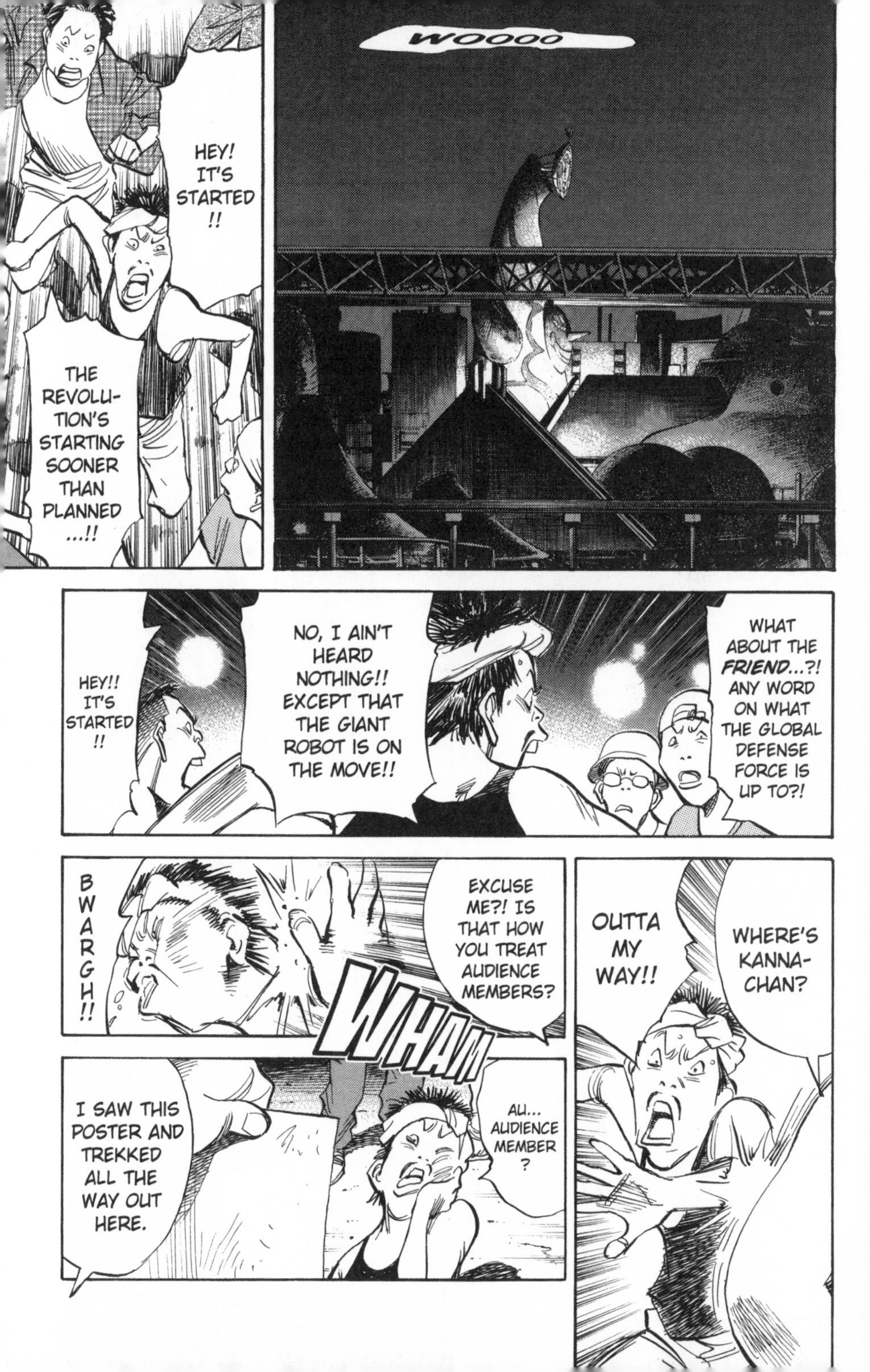
WOOOO
HEY! IT'S STARTED!!
THE REVOLUTION'S STARTING SOONER THAN PLANNED ...!!
WHAT ABOUT THE *FRIEND*...?! ANY WORD ON WHAT THE GLOBAL DEFENSE FORCE IS UP TO?!
NO, I AIN'T HEARD NOTHING!! EXCEPT THAT THE GIANT ROBOT IS ON THE MOVE!!
HEY!! IT'S STARTED!!
WHERE'S KANNA-CHAN?
OUTTA MY WAY!!
EXCUSE ME?! IS THAT HOW YOU TREAT AUDIENCE MEMBERS?
WHAM
BWARGH!!
AU... AUDIENCE MEMBER?
I SAW THIS POSTER AND TREKKED ALL THE WAY OUT HERE.

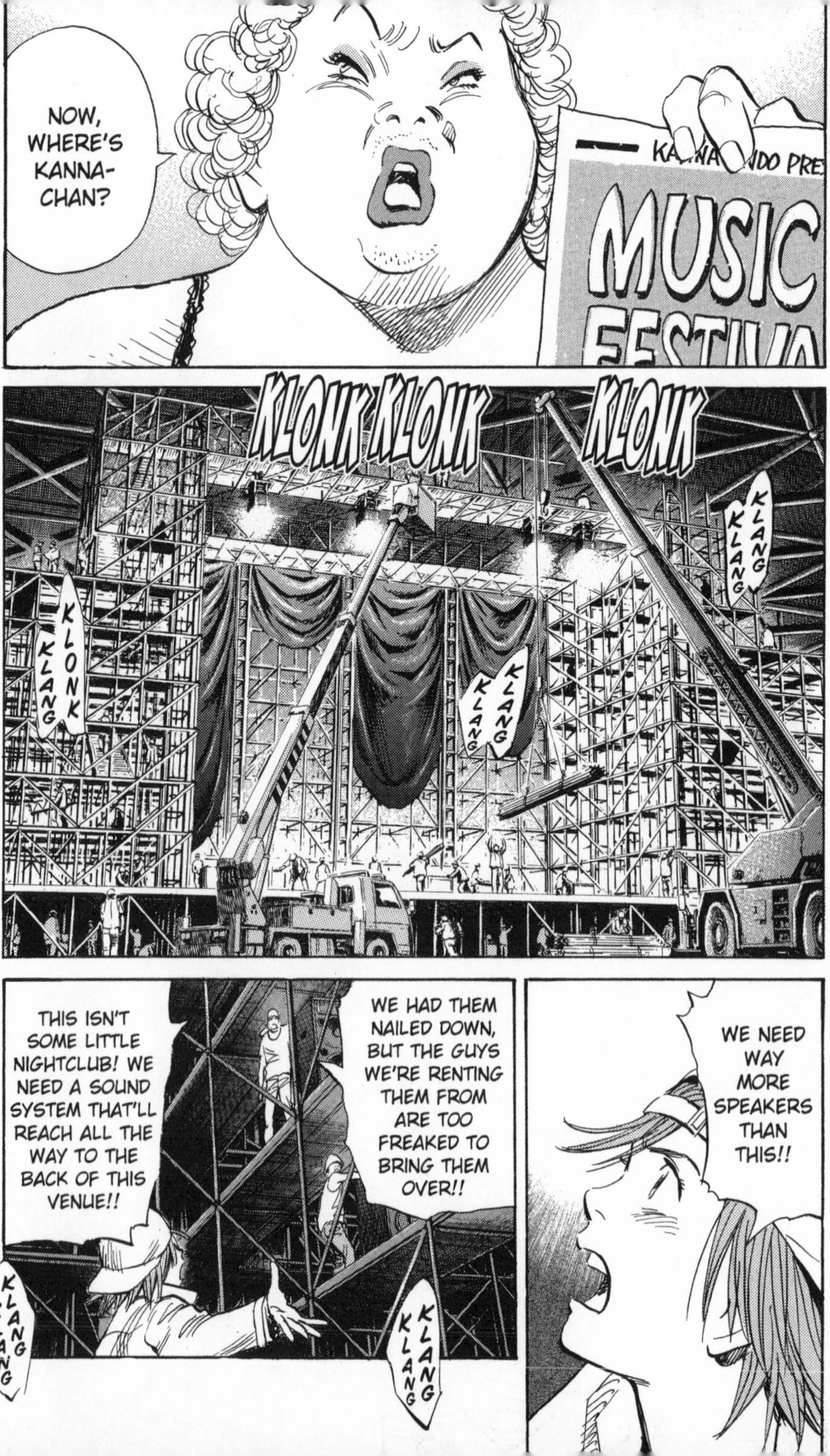
NOW, WHERE'S KANNA-CHAN?
MUSIC
KLONK KLONK
KLONK
KLANG KLANG
KLANG KLANG
KLONK KLANG
WE NEED WAY MORE SPEAKERS THAN THIS!!
WE HAD THEM NAILED DOWN, BUT THE GUYS WE'RE RENTING THEM FROM ARE TOO FREAKED TO BRING THEM OVER!!
THIS ISN'T SOME LITTLE NIGHTCLUB! WE NEED A SOUND SYSTEM THAT'LL REACH ALL THE WAY TO THE BACK OF THIS VENUE!!
KLANG KLANG
KLANG KLANG

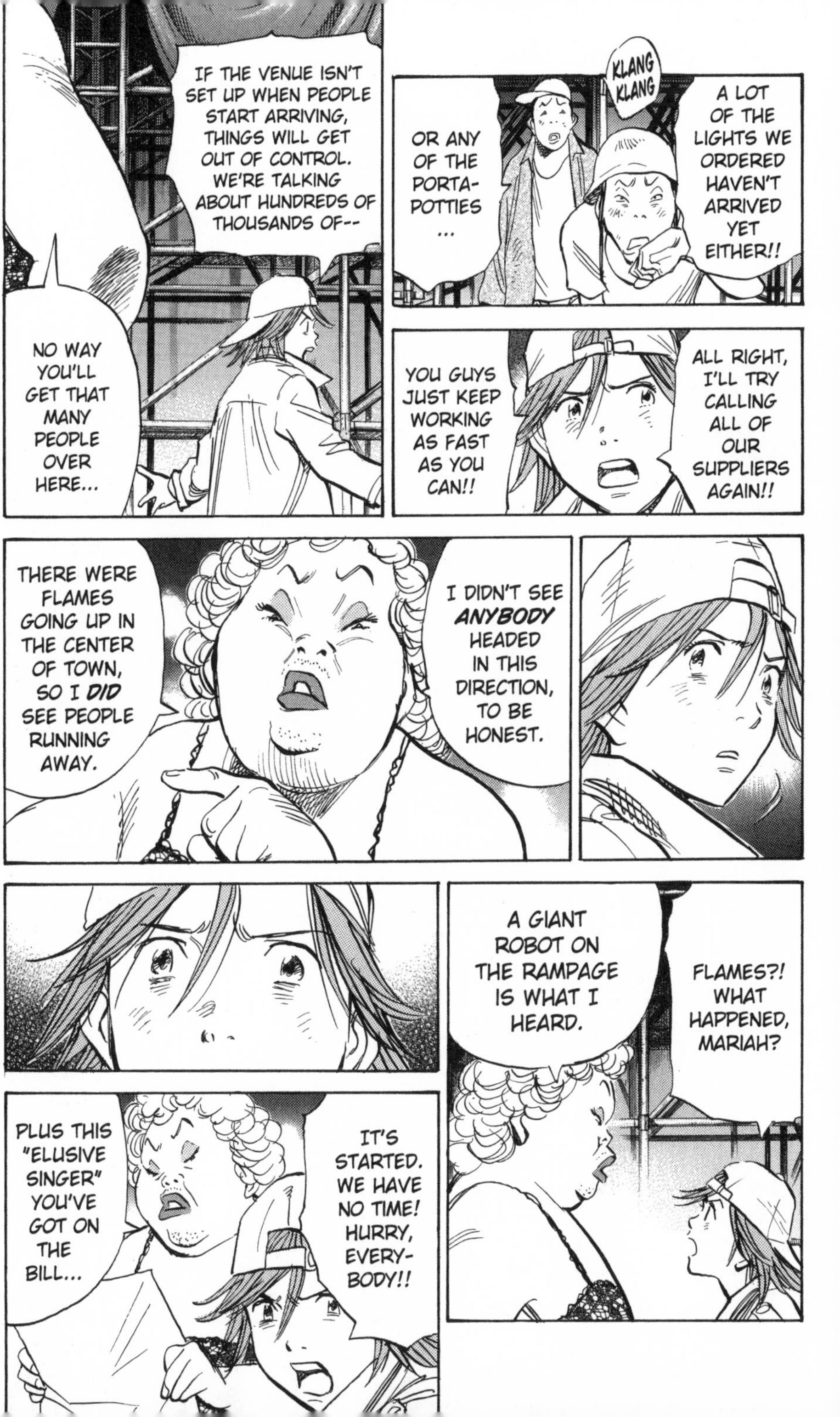
KLANG KLANG
A LOT OF THE LIGHTS WE ORDERED HAVEN'T ARRIVED YET EITHER!!
OR ANY OF THE PORTA-POTTIES ...
ALL RIGHT, I'LL TRY CALLING ALL OF OUR SUPPLIERS AGAIN!!
YOU GUYS JUST KEEP WORKING AS FAST AS YOU CAN!!
IF THE VENUE ISN'T SET UP WHEN PEOPLE START ARRIVING, THINGS WILL GET OUT OF CONTROL. WE'RE TALKING ABOUT HUNDREDS OF THOUSANDS OF--
NO WAY YOU'LL GET THAT MANY PEOPLE OVER HERE...
I DIDN'T SEE *ANYBODY* HEADED IN THIS DIRECTION, TO BE HONEST.
THERE WERE FLAMES GOING UP IN THE CENTER OF TOWN, SO I *DID* SEE PEOPLE RUNNING AWAY.
FLAMES?! WHAT HAPPENED, MARIAH?
A GIANT ROBOT ON THE RAMPAGE IS WHAT I HEARD.
IT'S STARTED. WE HAVE NO TIME! HURRY, EVERY-BODY!!
PLUS THIS "ELUSIVE SINGER" YOU'VE GOT ON THE BILL...

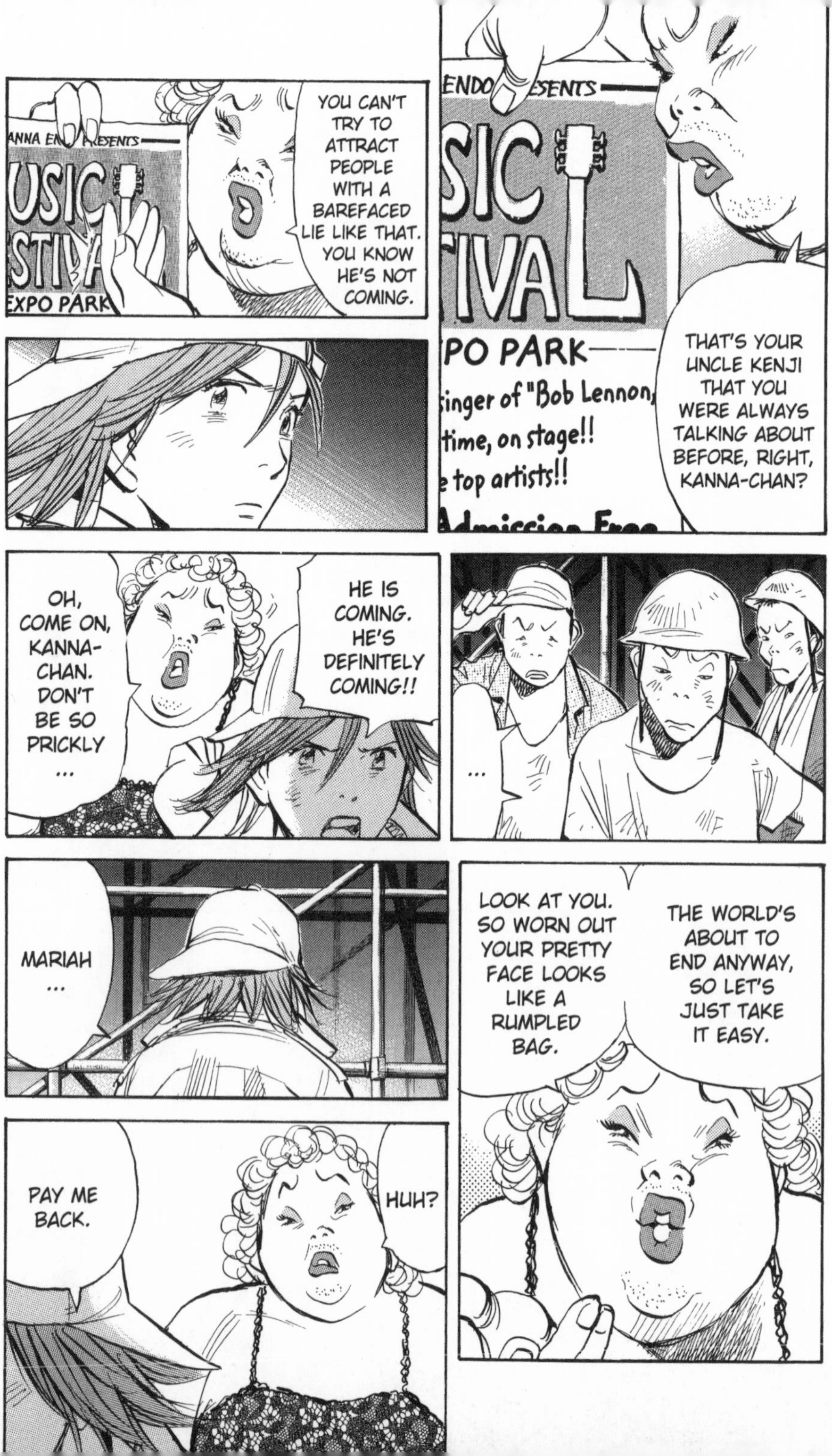
THAT'S YOUR UNCLE KENJI THAT YOU WERE ALWAYS TALKING ABOUT BEFORE, RIGHT, KANNA-CHAN?
YOU CAN'T TRY TO ATTRACT PEOPLE WITH A BAREFACED LIE LIKE THAT. YOU KNOW HE'S NOT COMING.
...
HE IS COMING. HE'S DEFINITELY COMING!!
OH, COME ON, KANNA-CHAN. DON'T BE SO PRICKLY ...
THE WORLD'S ABOUT TO END ANYWAY, SO LET'S JUST TAKE IT EASY.
LOOK AT YOU. SO WORN OUT YOUR PRETTY FACE LOOKS LIKE A RUMPLED BAG.
MARIAH ...
HUH?
PAY ME BACK.

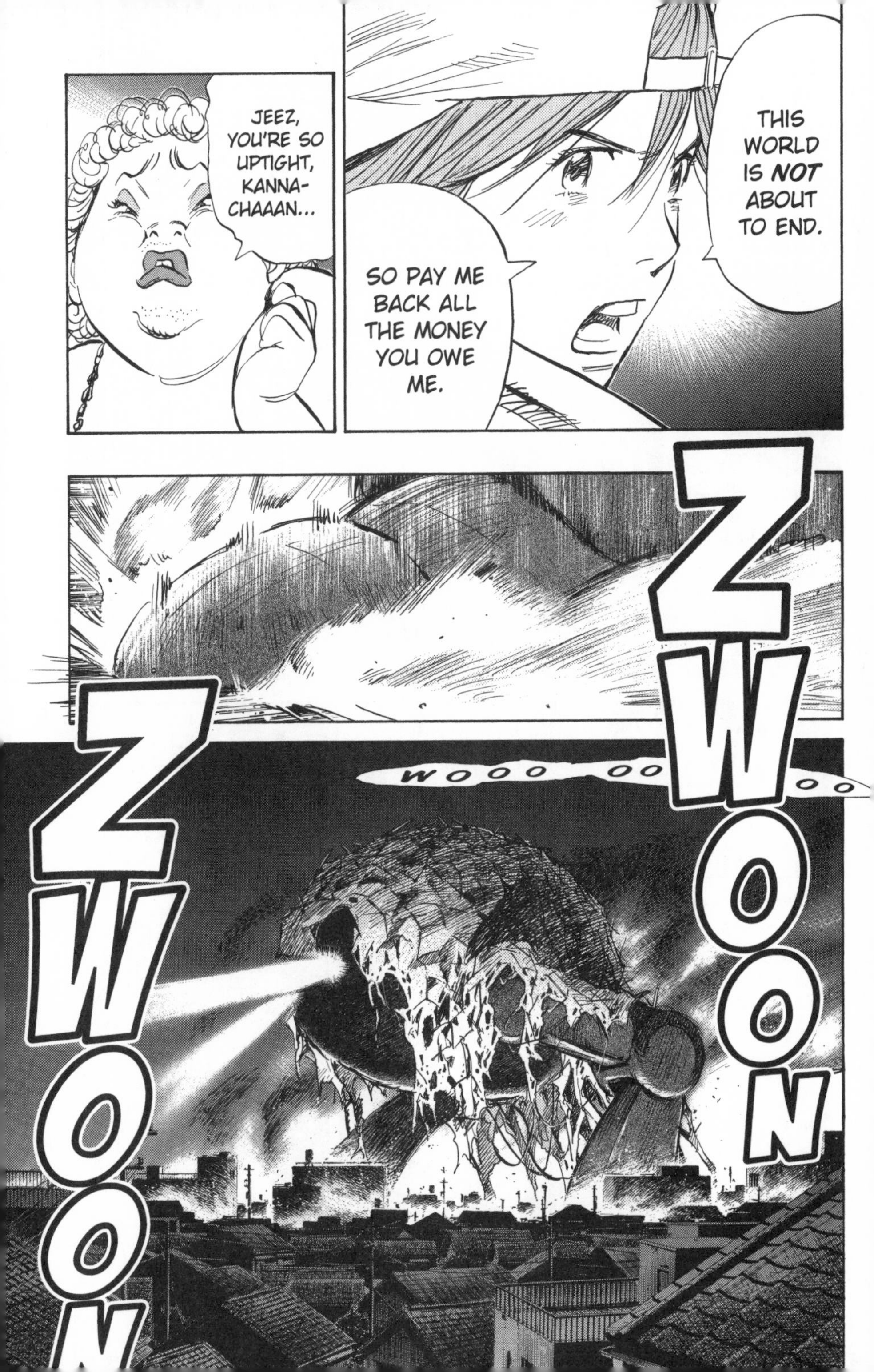
THIS WORLD IS **NOT** ABOUT TO END.
SO PAY ME BACK ALL THE MONEY YOU OWE ME.
JEEZ, YOU'RE SO UPTIGHT, KANNA-CHAAAN...
ZWOOON
WOOO OO OO
ZWOOON

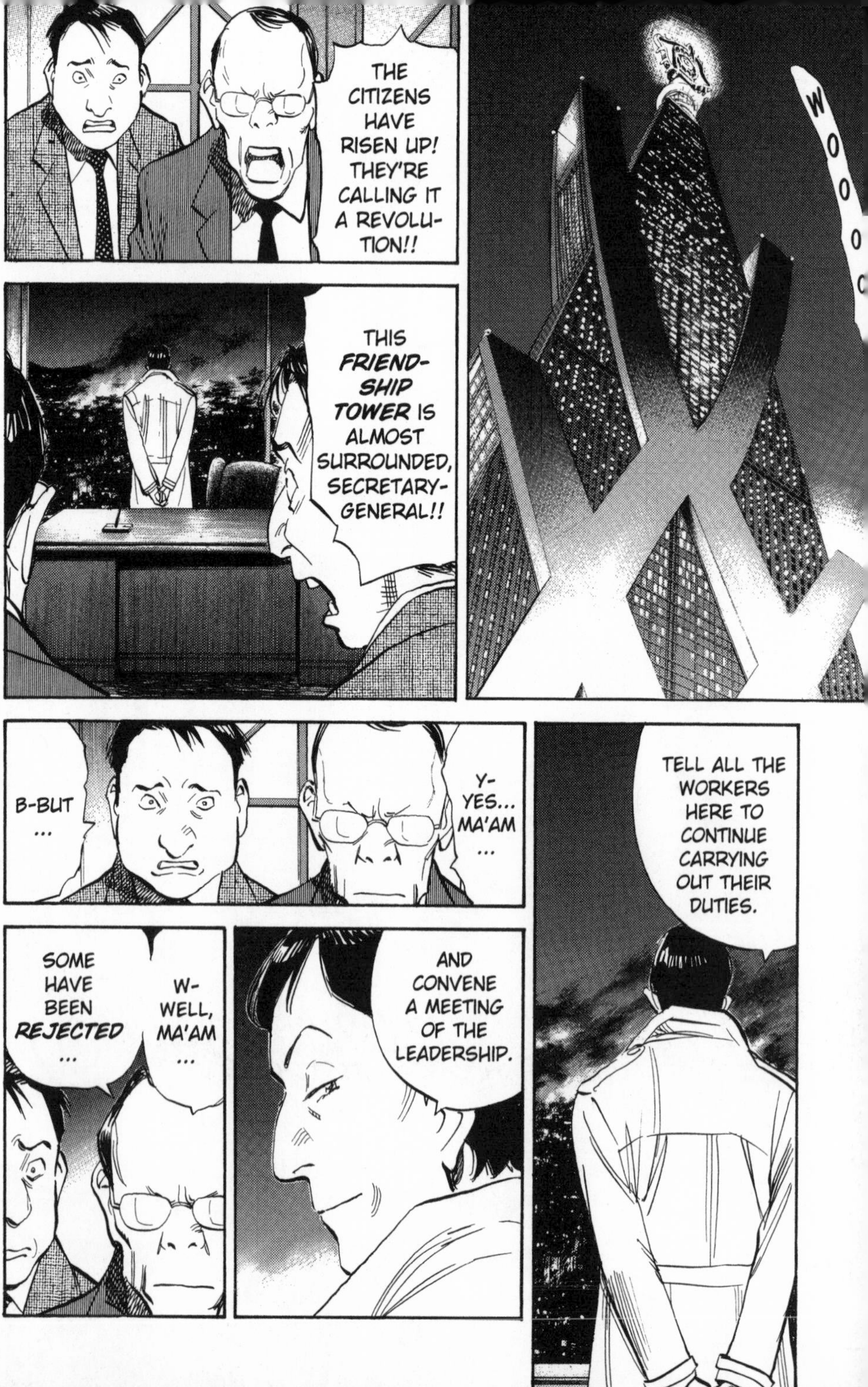
WOOOO
THE CITIZENS HAVE RISEN UP! THEY'RE CALLING IT A REVOLUTION!!
THIS ***FRIENDSHIP TOWER*** IS ALMOST SURROUNDED, SECRETARY-GENERAL!!
TELL ALL THE WORKERS HERE TO CONTINUE CARRYING OUT THEIR DUTIES.
Y-YES... MA'AM...
B-BUT...
AND CONVENE A MEETING OF THE LEADERSHIP.
W-WELL, MA'AM...
SOME HAVE BEEN ***REJECTED***...

...AND THE REST CANNOT BE REACHED.

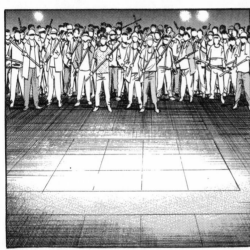

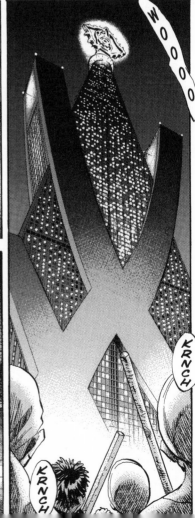

WOOOOO

KRNCH

KRNCH

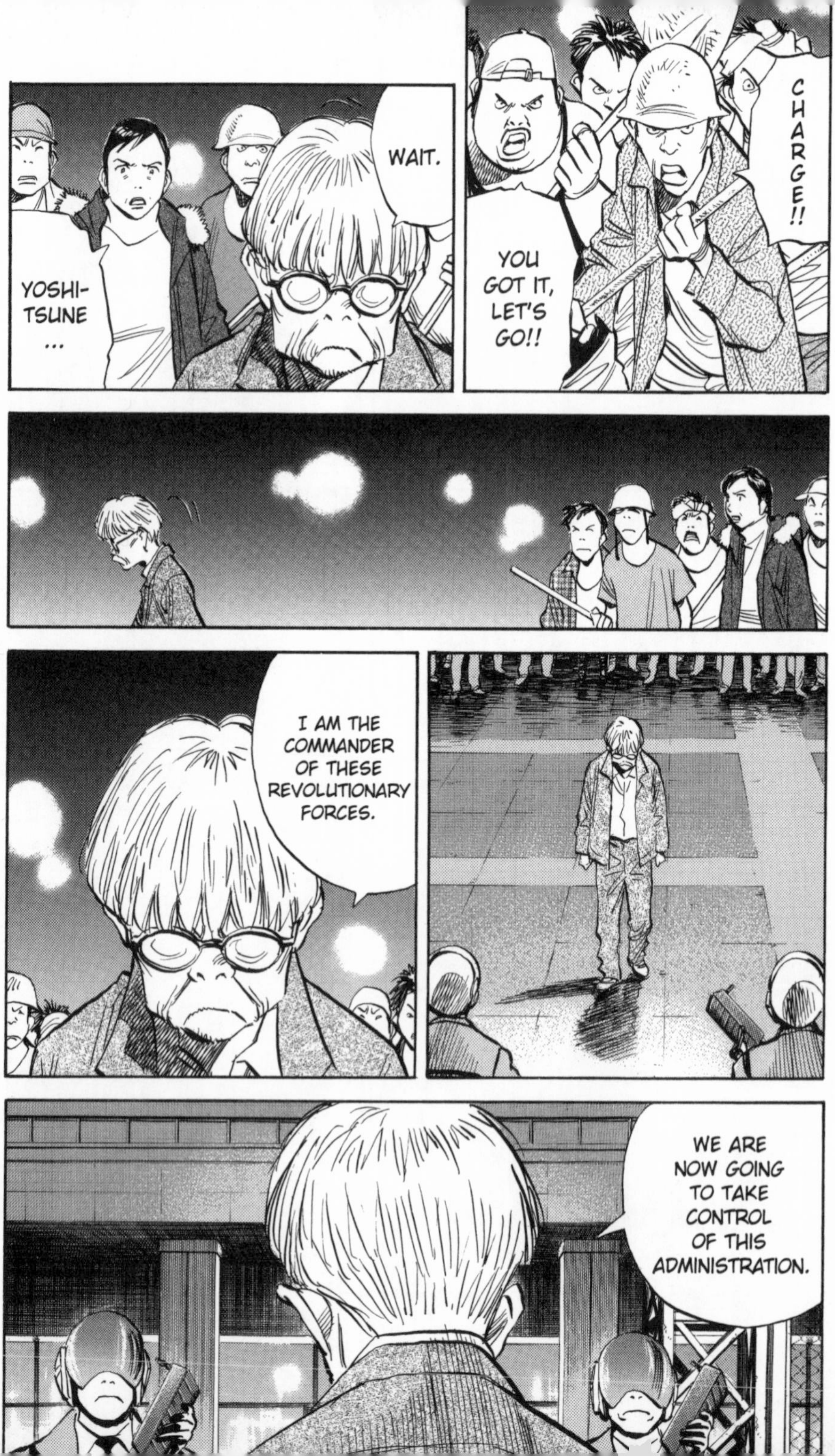
CHARGE!!
YOU GOT IT, LET'S GO!!
WAIT.
YOSHI-TSUNE ...
I AM THE COMMANDER OF THESE REVOLUTIONARY FORCES.
WE ARE NOW GOING TO TAKE CONTROL OF THIS ADMINISTRATION.

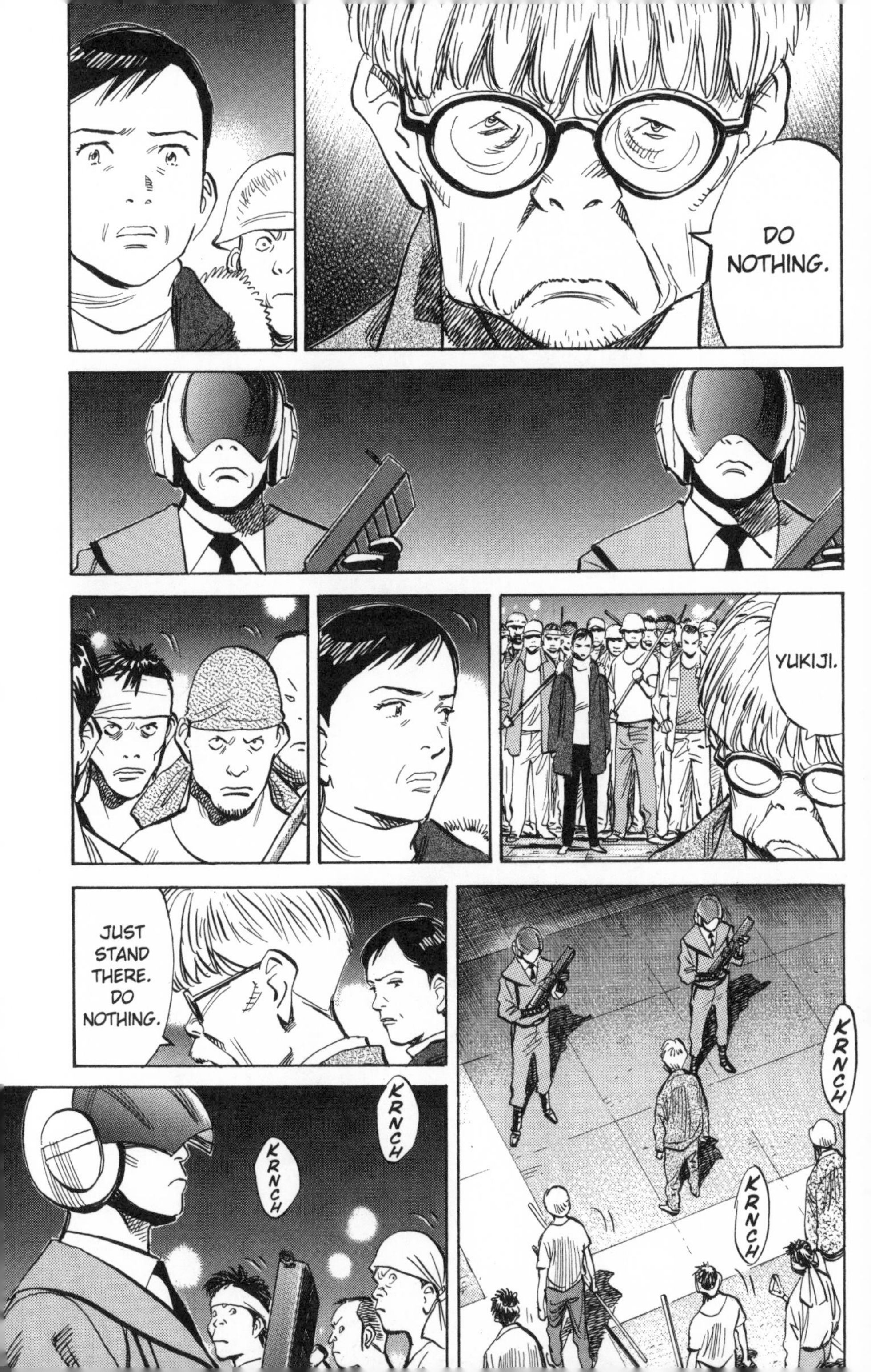
DO NOTHING.
YUKIJI.
KRNCH
KRNCH
JUST STAND THERE. DO NOTHING.
KRNCH
KRNCH

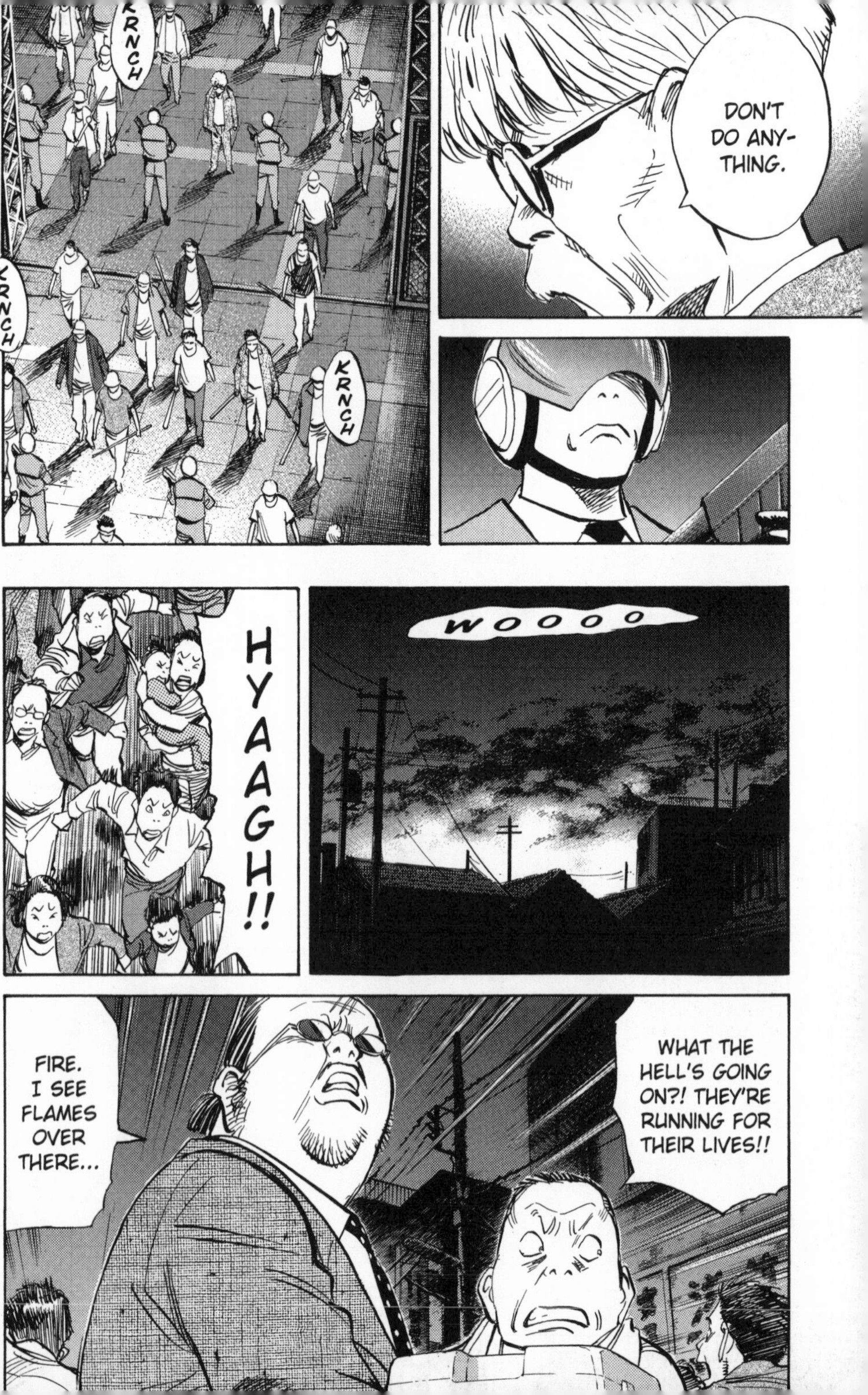
DON'T DO ANYTHING.
KRNCH
KRNCH
KRNCH
WOOOO
HYAAAGH!!
WHAT THE HELL'S GOING ON?! THEY'RE RUNNING FOR THEIR LIVES!!
FIRE. I SEE FLAMES OVER THERE...

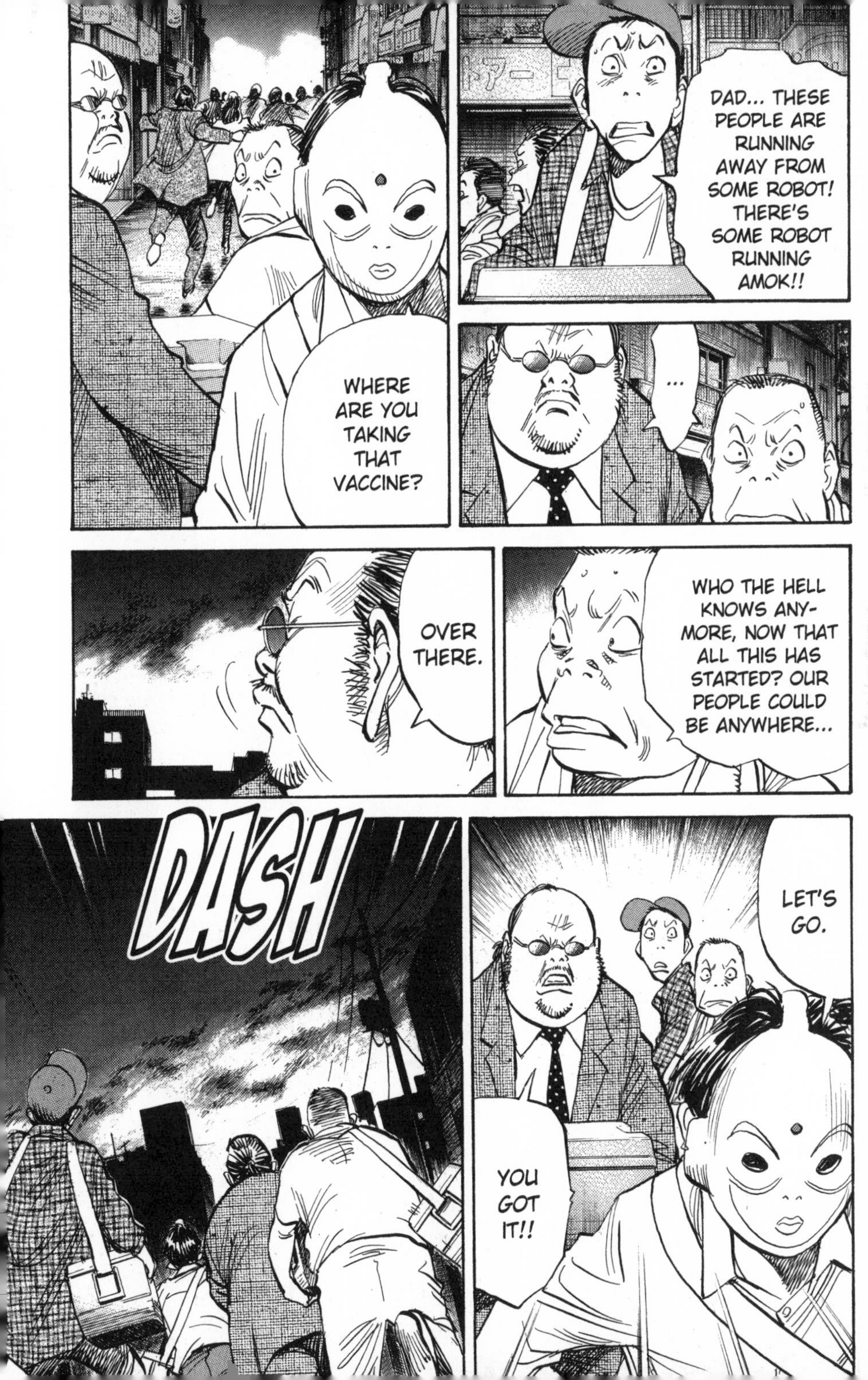
DAD... THESE PEOPLE ARE RUNNING AWAY FROM SOME ROBOT! THERE'S SOME ROBOT RUNNING AMOK!!
...
WHERE ARE YOU TAKING THAT VACCINE?
WHO THE HELL KNOWS ANY-MORE, NOW THAT ALL THIS HAS STARTED? OUR PEOPLE COULD BE ANYWHERE...
OVER THERE.
LET'S GO.
YOU GOT IT!!
DASH

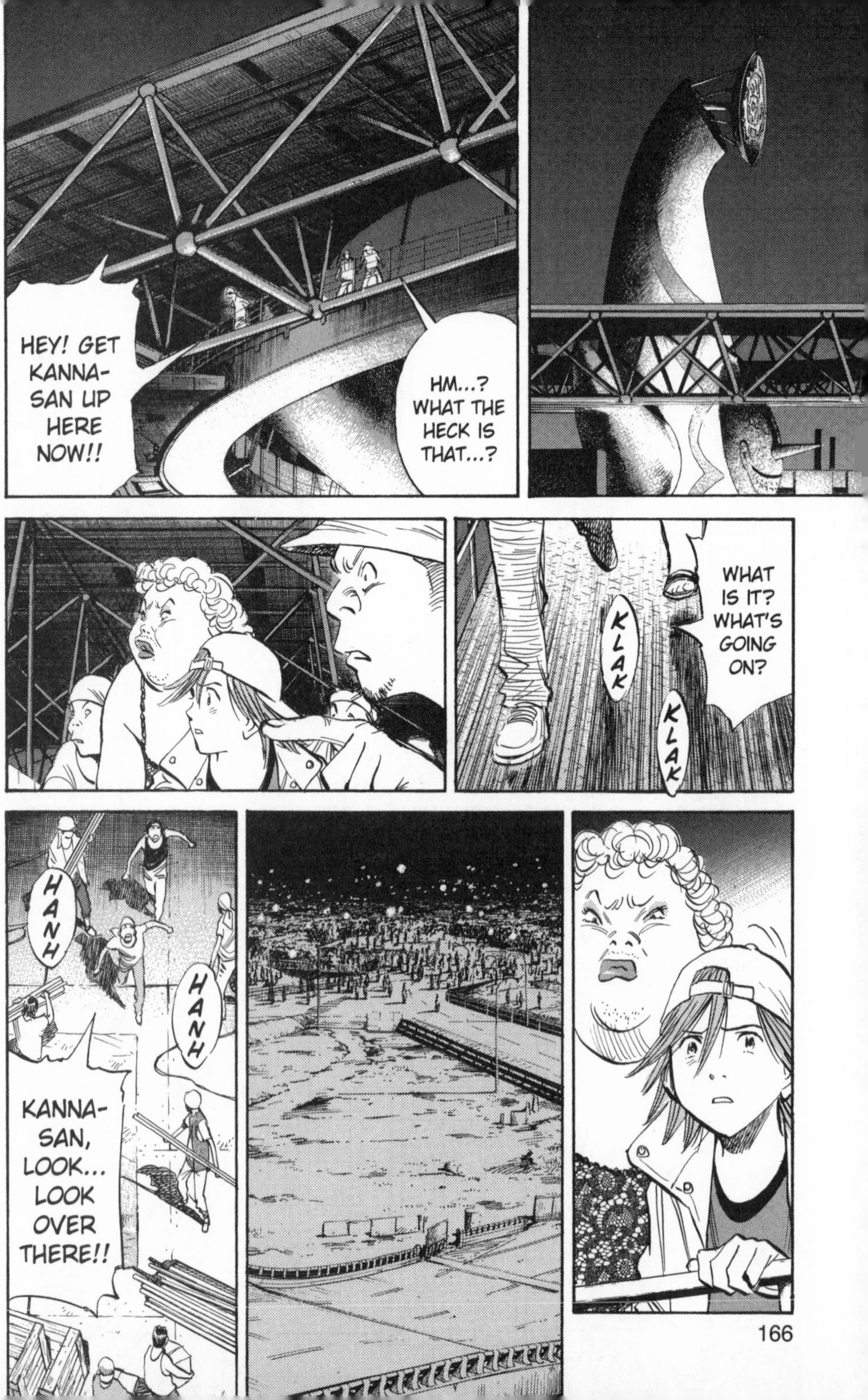
HM...? WHAT THE HECK IS THAT...?
HEY! GET KANNA-SAN UP HERE NOW!!
WHAT IS IT? WHAT'S GOING ON?
KLAK
KLAK
HANH
HANH
KANNA-SAN, LOOK... LOOK OVER THERE!!

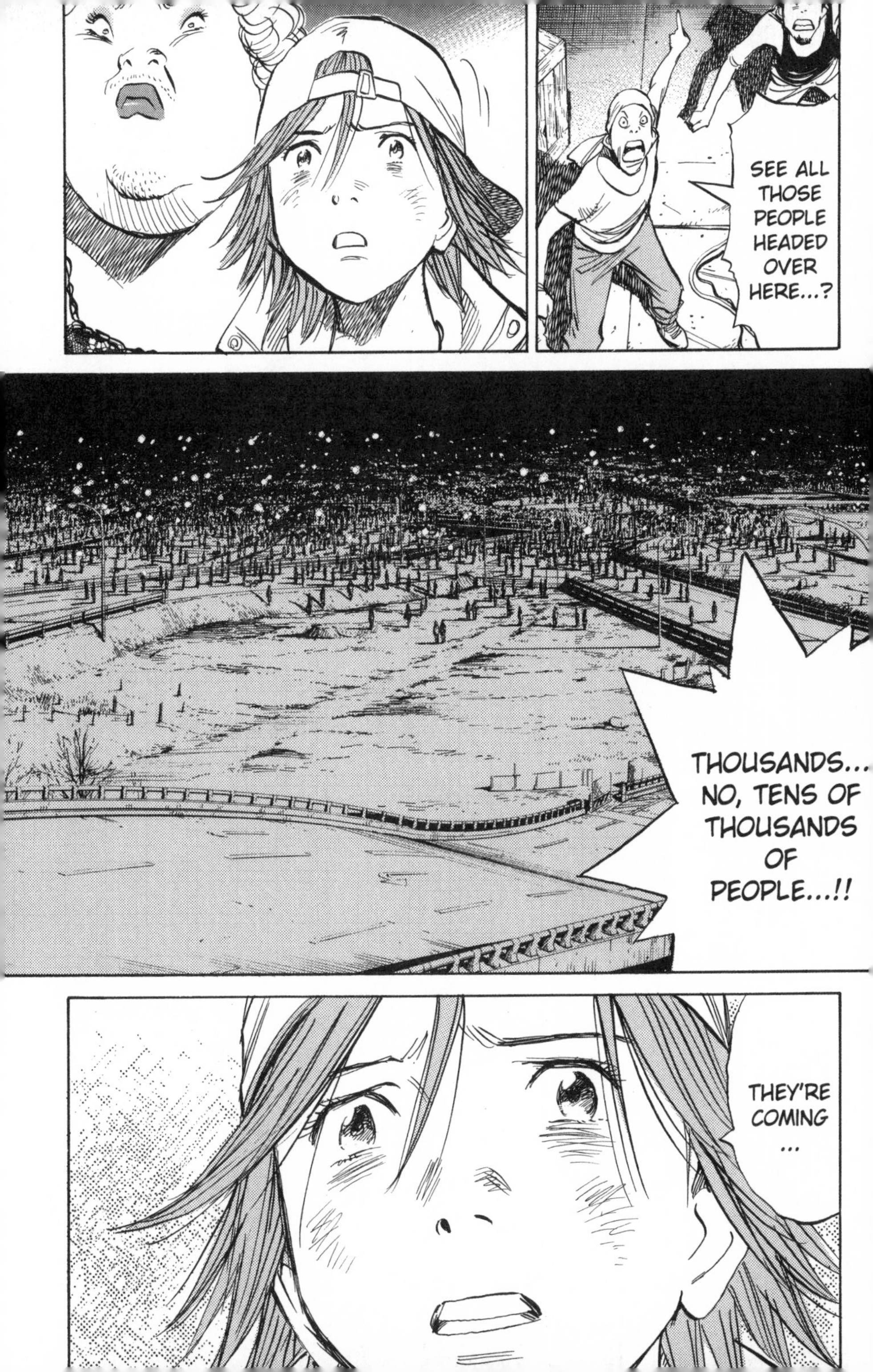
SEE ALL THOSE PEOPLE HEADED OVER HERE...?
THOUSANDS... NO, TENS OF THOUSANDS OF PEOPLE...!!
THEY'RE COMING ...

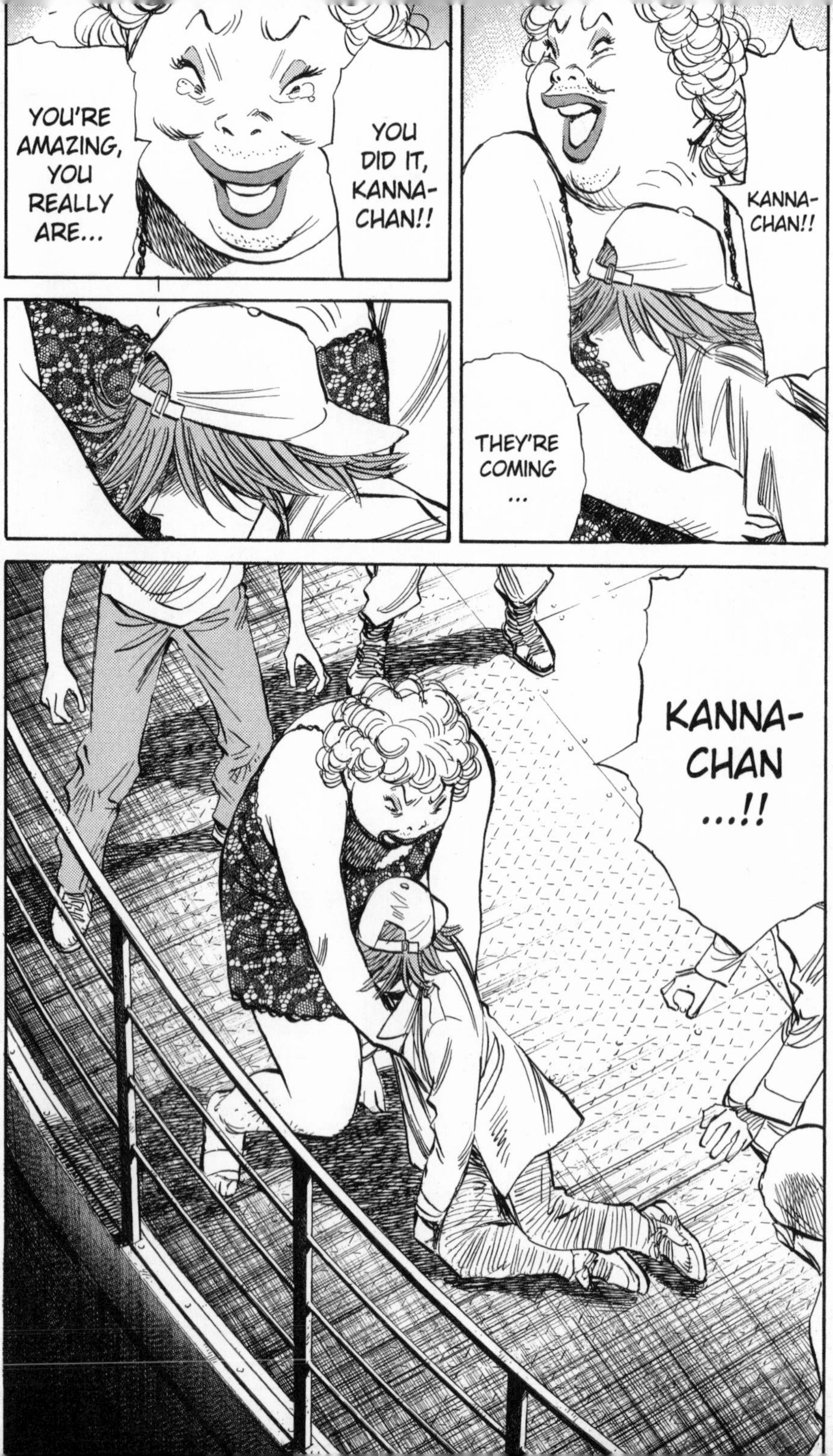
KANNA-CHAN!!
THEY'RE COMING ...
YOU DID IT, KANNA-CHAN!!
YOU'RE AMAZING, YOU REALLY ARE...
KANNA-CHAN ...!!

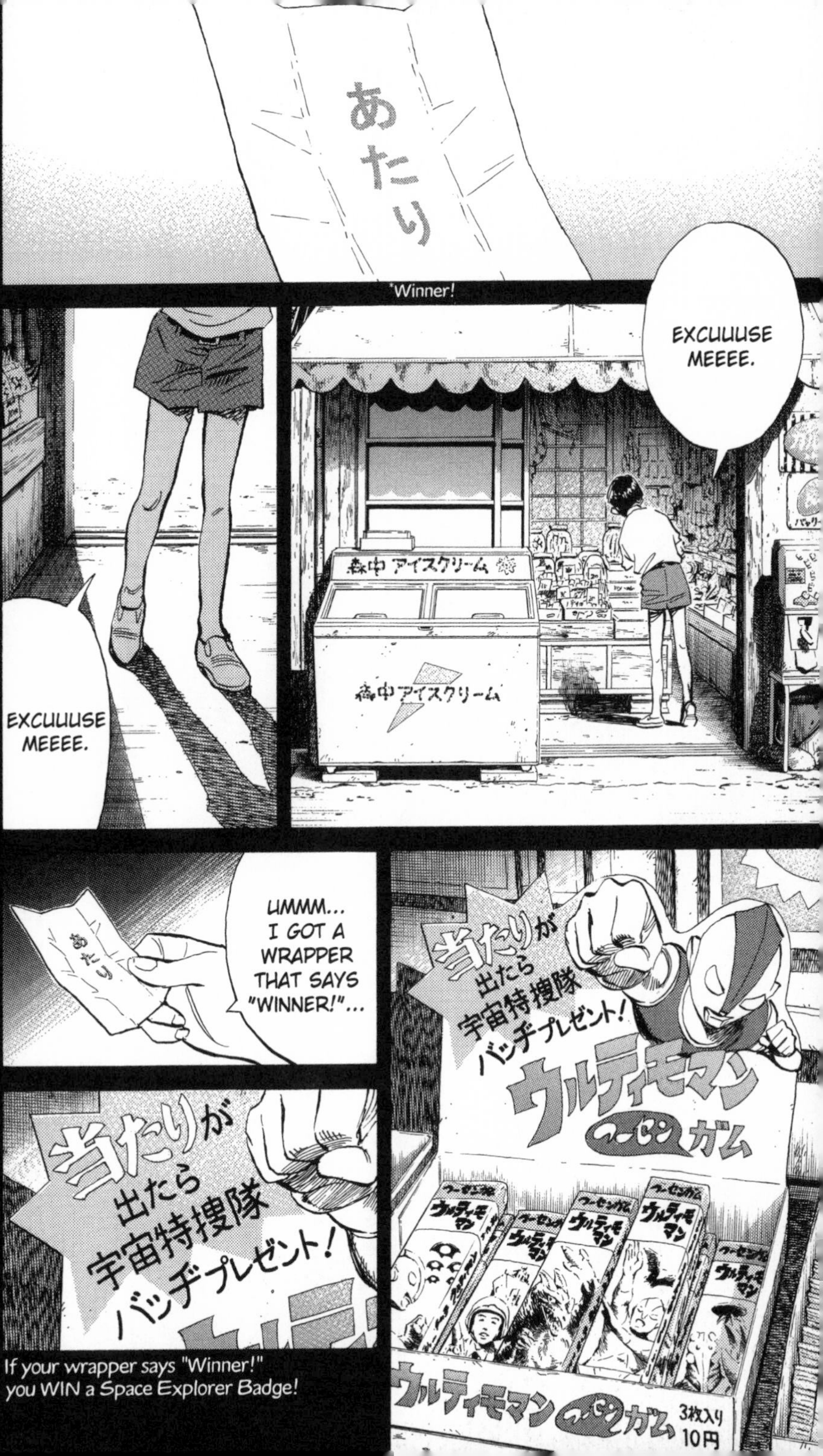
あたり
*Winner!
EXCUUUSE MEEEE.
EXCUUUSE MEEEE.
当たりが出たら宇宙特捜隊バッヂプレゼント！
ウルティモマン
フーセンガム
ウルティモマン フーセンガム 3枚入り 10円
UMMM... I GOT A WRAPPER THAT SAYS "WINNER!"...
あたり
当たりが出たら宇宙特捜隊バッヂプレゼント！
If your wrapper says "Winner!" you WIN a Space Explorer Badge!

UMMM...
I'LL PUT
IT RIGHT
HERE.

THE
SPACE
EXPLORER
BADGE...

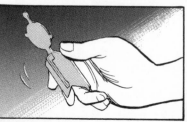

IT WAS
THE
EMBLEM
OF
JUSTICE...

Chapter 10
Beginning
of Justice

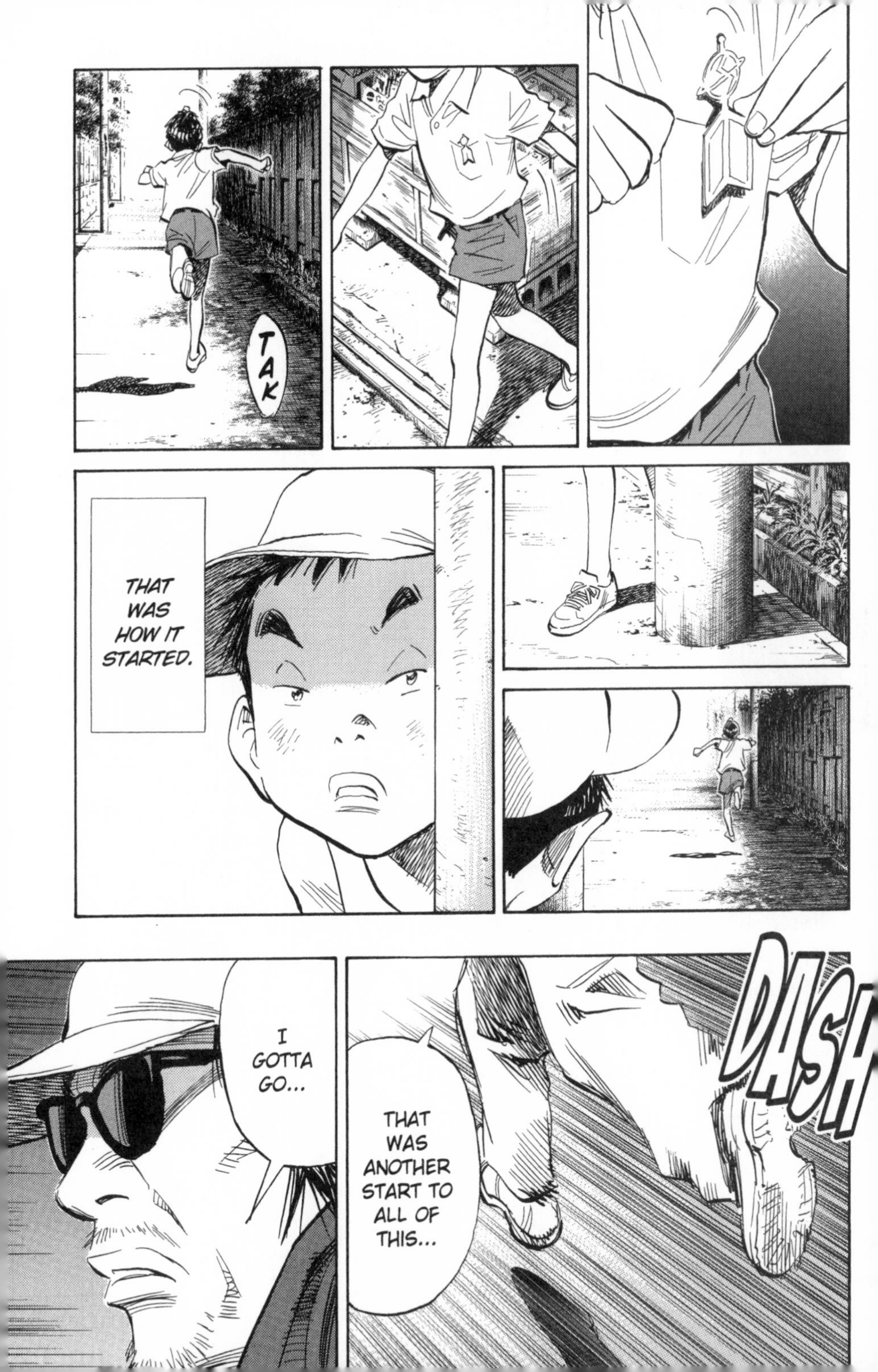
TAK
THAT WAS HOW IT STARTED.
DASH
THAT WAS ANOTHER START TO ALL OF THIS...
I GOTTA GO...

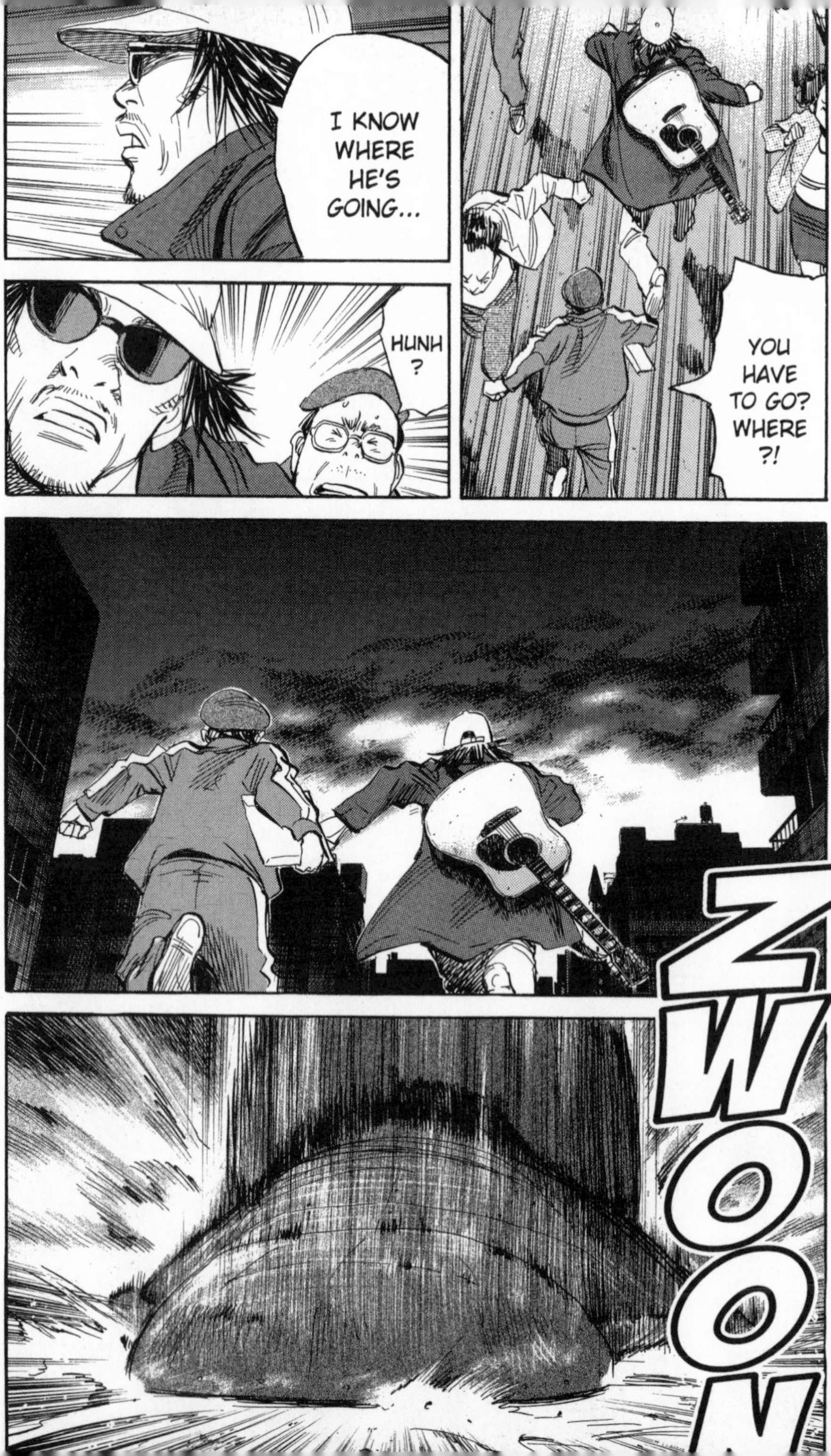
YOU HAVE TO GO? WHERE?!
I KNOW WHERE HE'S GOING...
HUNH?
ZWOON

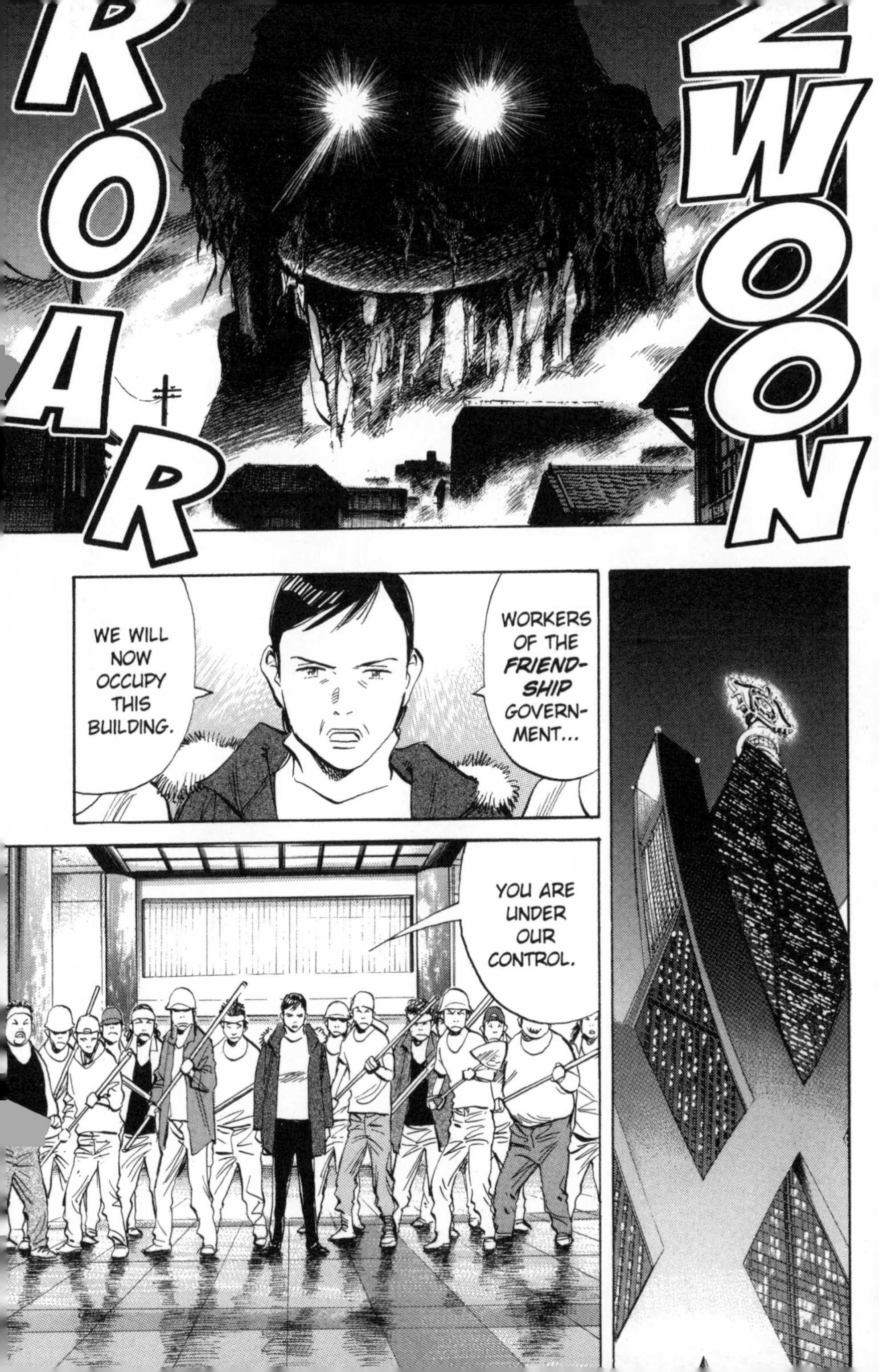
ZWOOON
ROAR
WORKERS OF THE *FRIENDSHIP* GOVERNMENT...
WE WILL NOW OCCUPY THIS BUILDING.
YOU ARE UNDER OUR CONTROL.

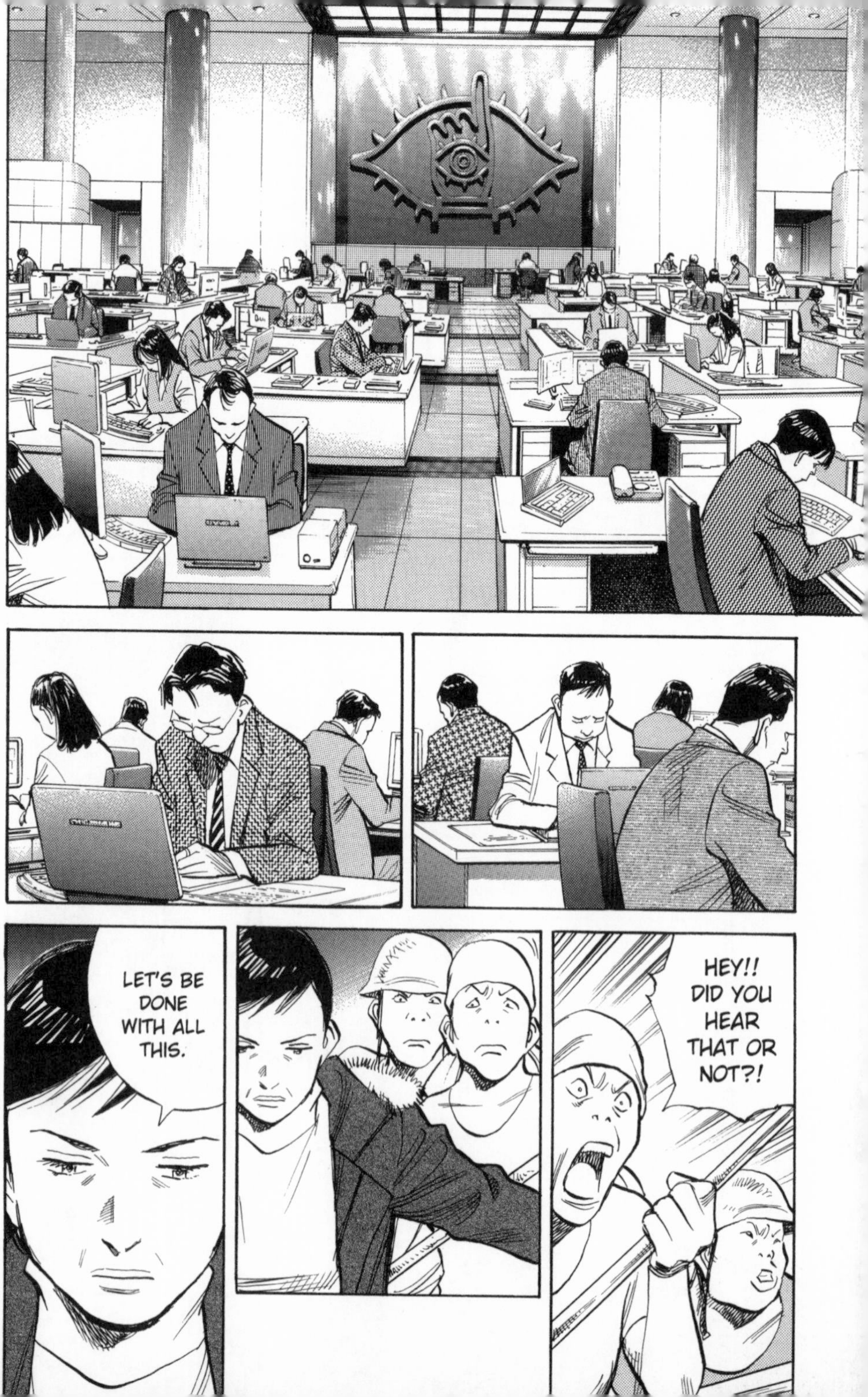
HEY!! DID YOU HEAR THAT OR NOT?!
LET'S BE DONE WITH ALL THIS.

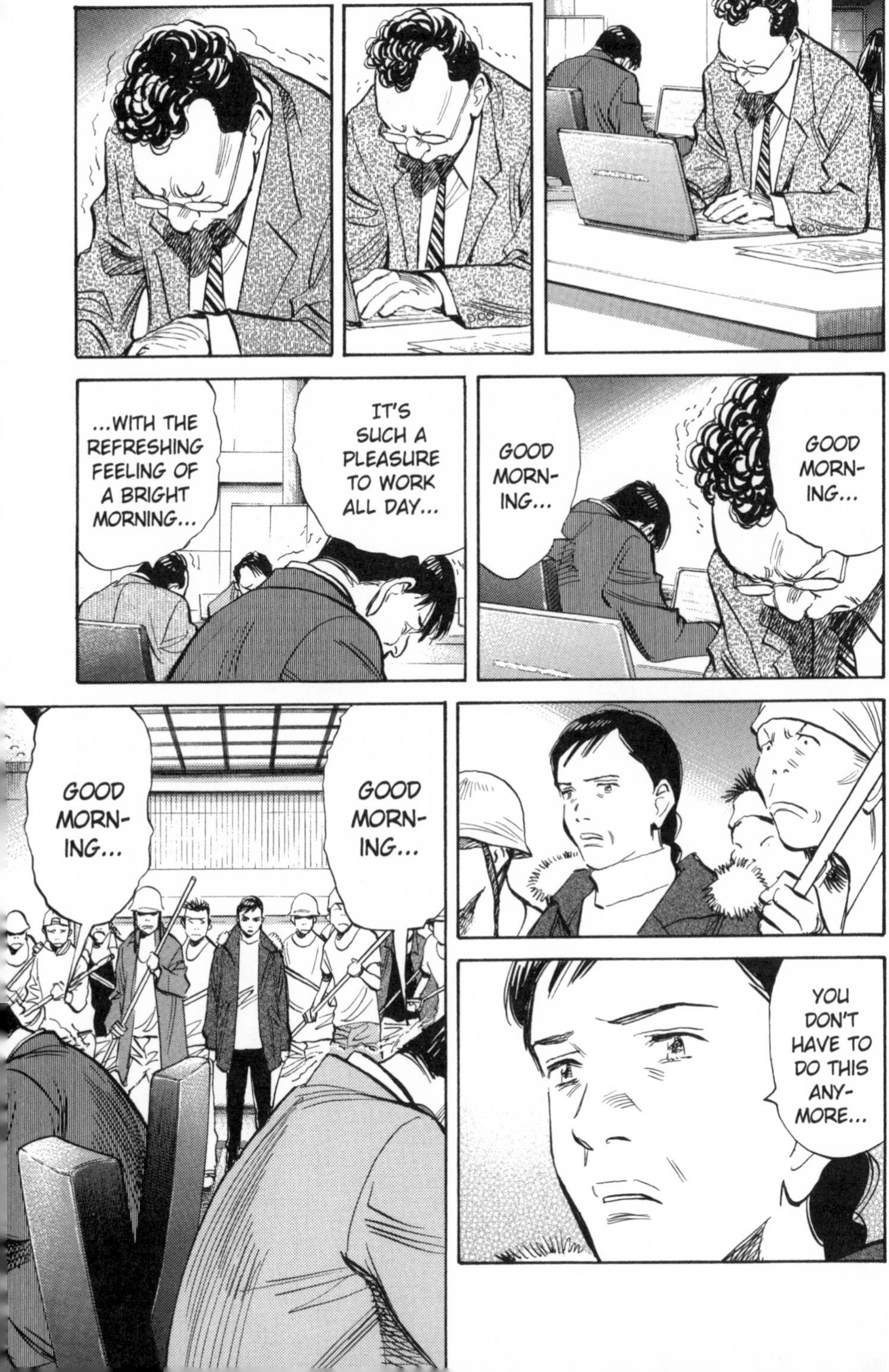
GOOD MORN-ING...
GOOD MORN-ING...
IT'S SUCH A PLEASURE TO WORK ALL DAY...
...WITH THE REFRESHING FEELING OF A BRIGHT MORNING...
YOU DON'T HAVE TO DO THIS ANY-MORE...
GOOD MORN-ING...
GOOD MORN-ING...

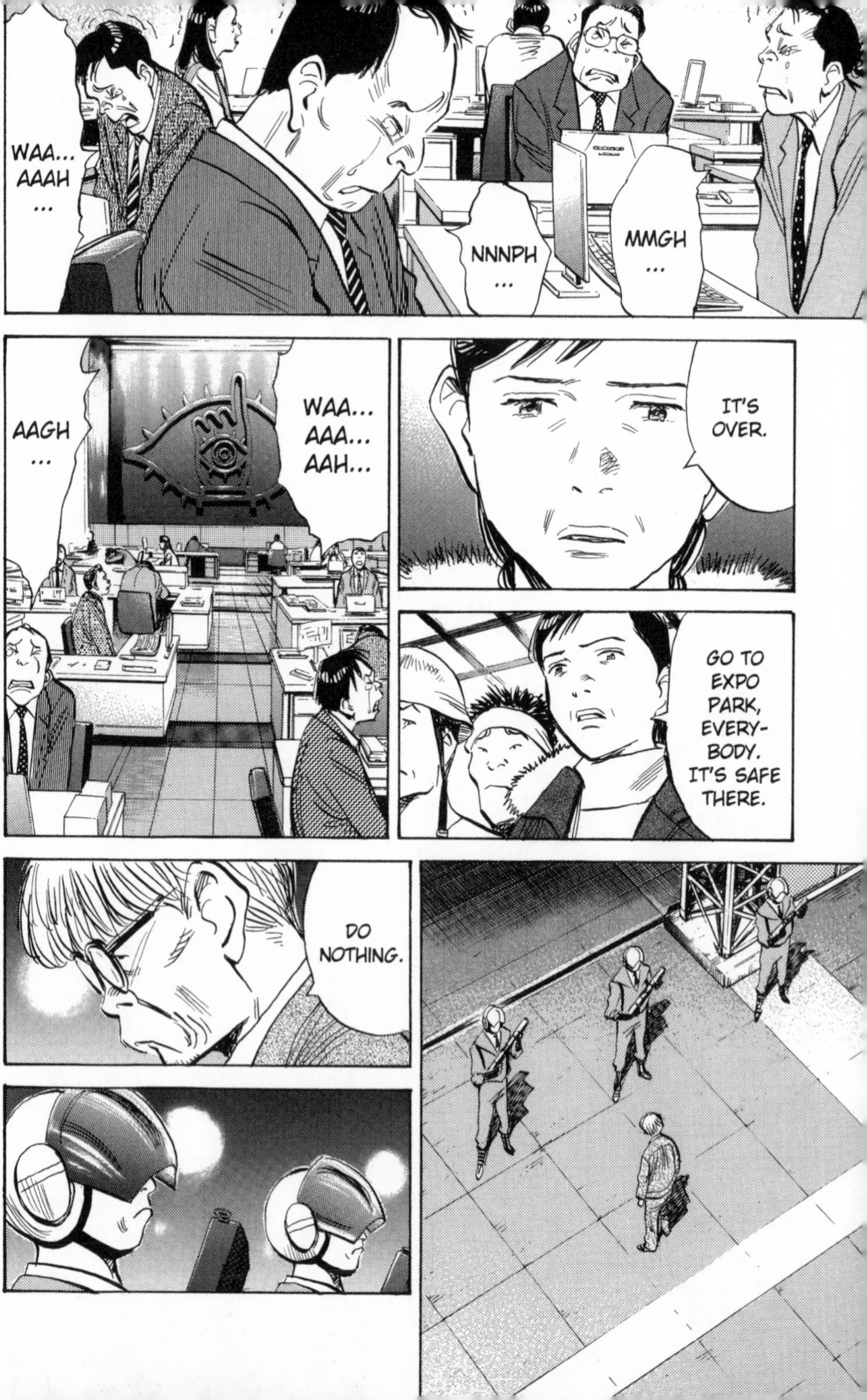
MMGH ...
NNNPH ...
WAA... AAAH ...
IT'S OVER.
GO TO EXPO PARK, EVERY-BODY. IT'S SAFE THERE.
WAA... AAA... AAH...
AAGH ...
DO NOTHING.

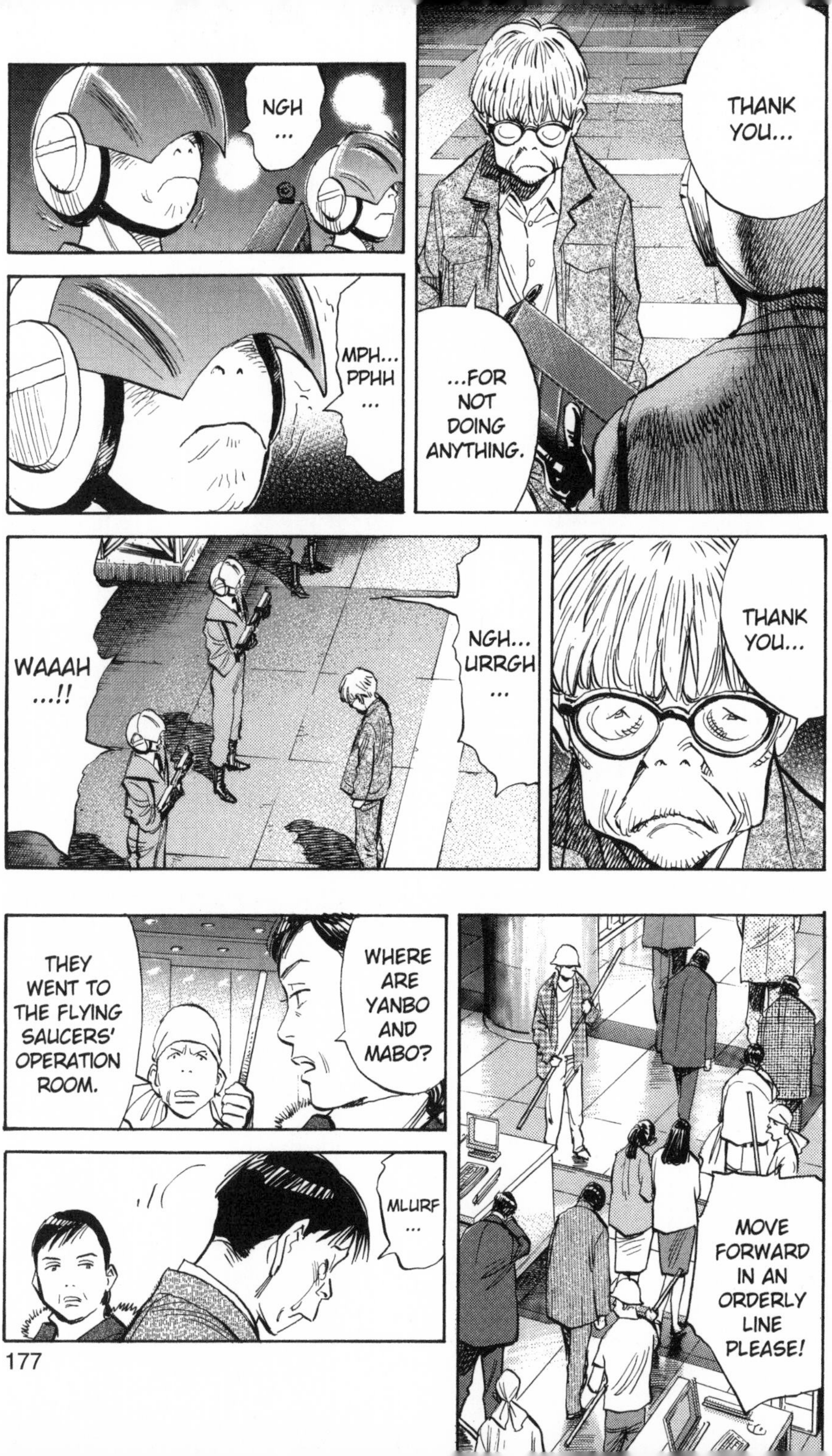
THANK YOU...
...FOR NOT DOING ANYTHING.
NGH ...
MPH... PPHH ...
THANK YOU...
NGH... URRGH ...
WAAAH ...!!
MOVE FORWARD IN AN ORDERLY LINE PLEASE!
WHERE ARE YANBO AND MABO?
THEY WENT TO THE FLYING SAUCERS' OPERATION ROOM.
MLURF ...

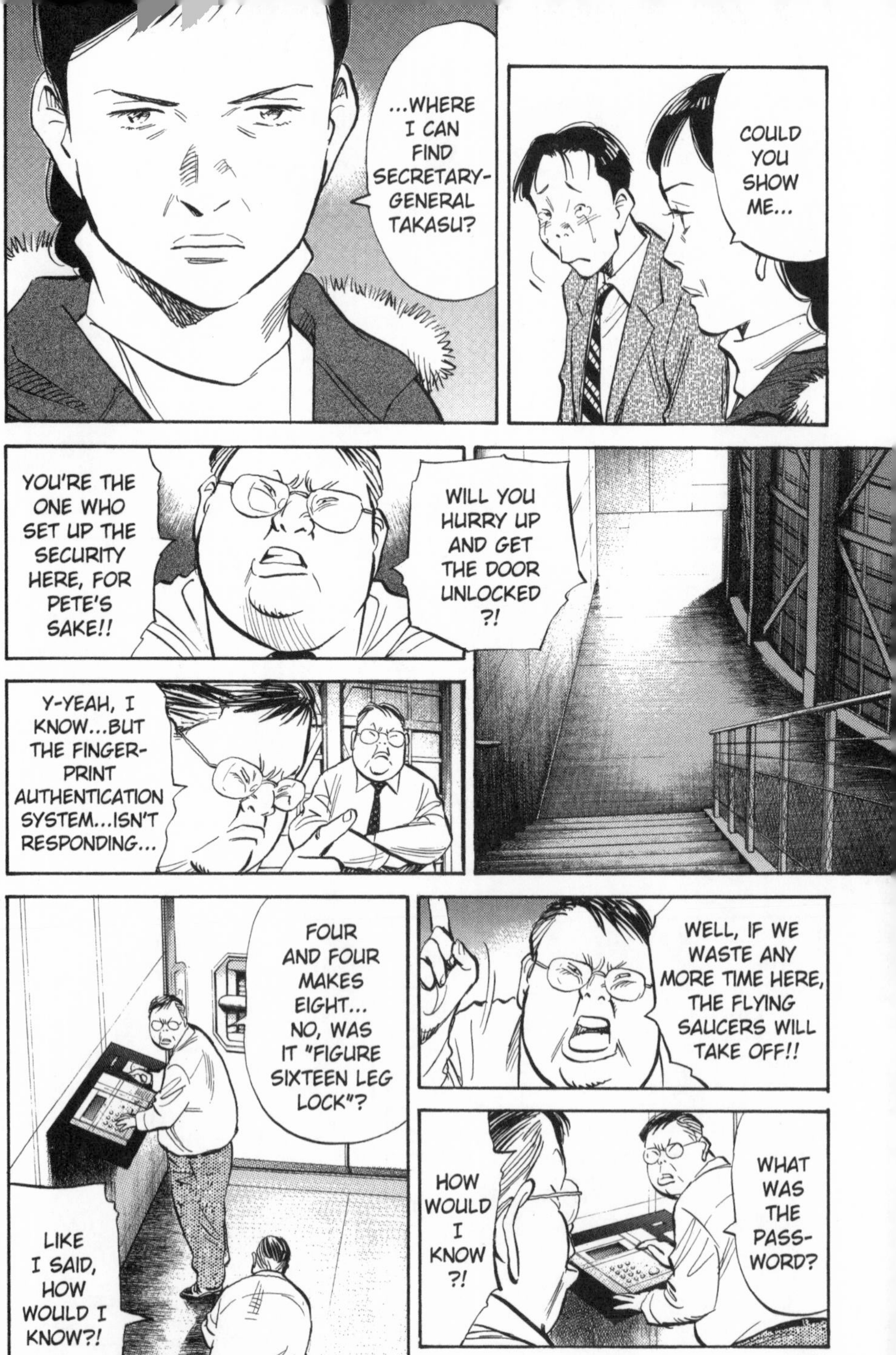
COULD YOU SHOW ME...
...WHERE I CAN FIND SECRETARY-GENERAL TAKASU?
WILL YOU HURRY UP AND GET THE DOOR UNLOCKED ?!
YOU'RE THE ONE WHO SET UP THE SECURITY HERE, FOR PETE'S SAKE!!
Y-YEAH, I KNOW...BUT THE FINGER-PRINT AUTHENTICATION SYSTEM...ISN'T RESPONDING...
WELL, IF WE WASTE ANY MORE TIME HERE, THE FLYING SAUCERS WILL TAKE OFF!!
WHAT WAS THE PASS-WORD?
HOW WOULD I KNOW ?!
FOUR AND FOUR MAKES EIGHT... NO, WAS IT "FIGURE SIXTEEN LEG LOCK"?
LIKE I SAID, HOW WOULD I KNOW?!

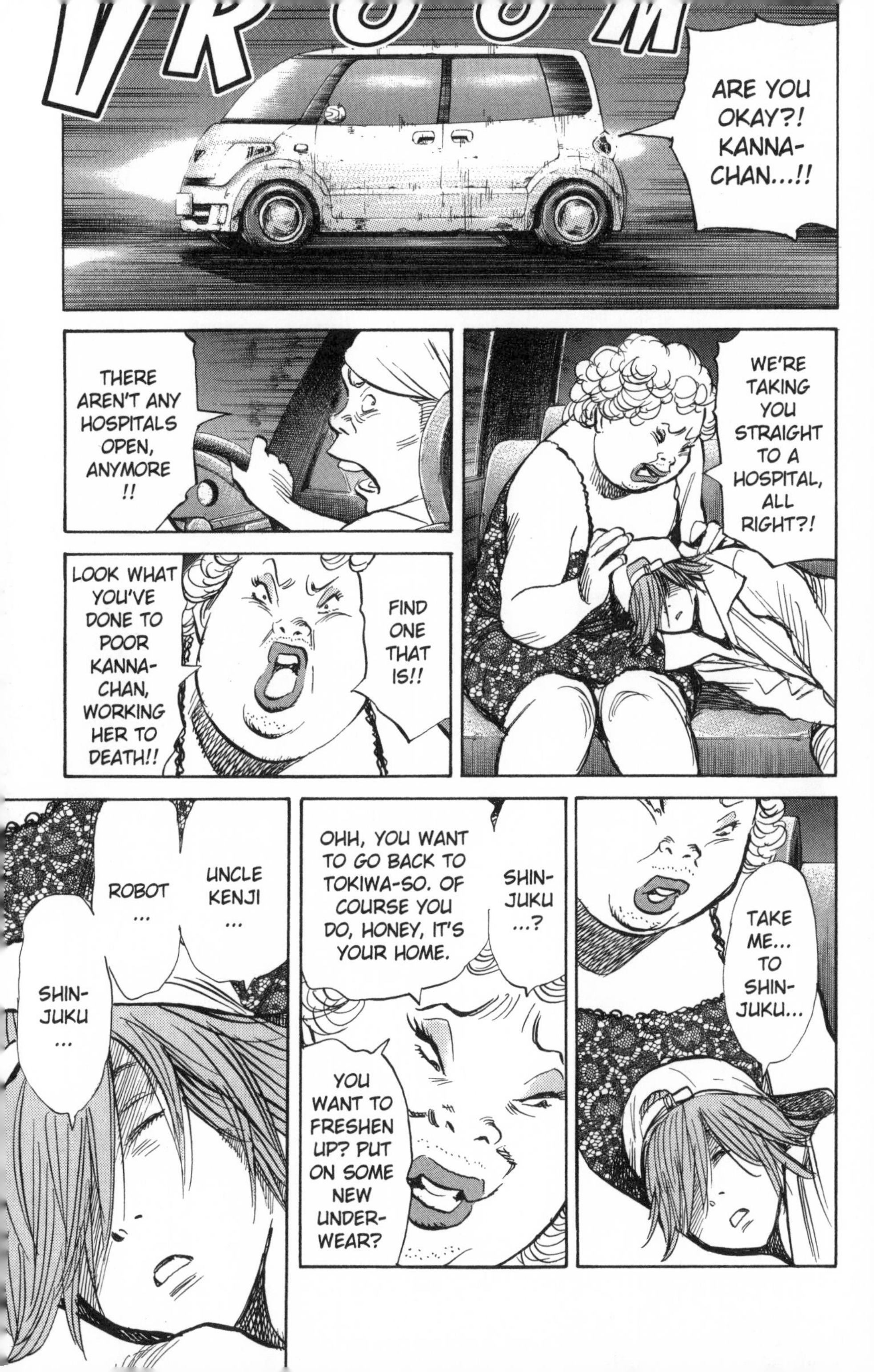
VROOOM
ARE YOU OKAY?! KANNA-CHAN...!!
WE'RE TAKING YOU STRAIGHT TO A HOSPITAL, ALL RIGHT?!
THERE AREN'T ANY HOSPITALS OPEN, ANYMORE!!
FIND ONE THAT IS!!
LOOK WHAT YOU'VE DONE TO POOR KANNA-CHAN, WORKING HER TO DEATH!!
TAKE ME... TO SHINJUKU...
SHINJUKU...?
OHH, YOU WANT TO GO BACK TO TOKIWA-SO. OF COURSE YOU DO, HONEY, IT'S YOUR HOME.
YOU WANT TO FRESHEN UP? PUT ON SOME NEW UNDERWEAR?
UNCLE KENJI...
ROBOT...
SHINJUKU...

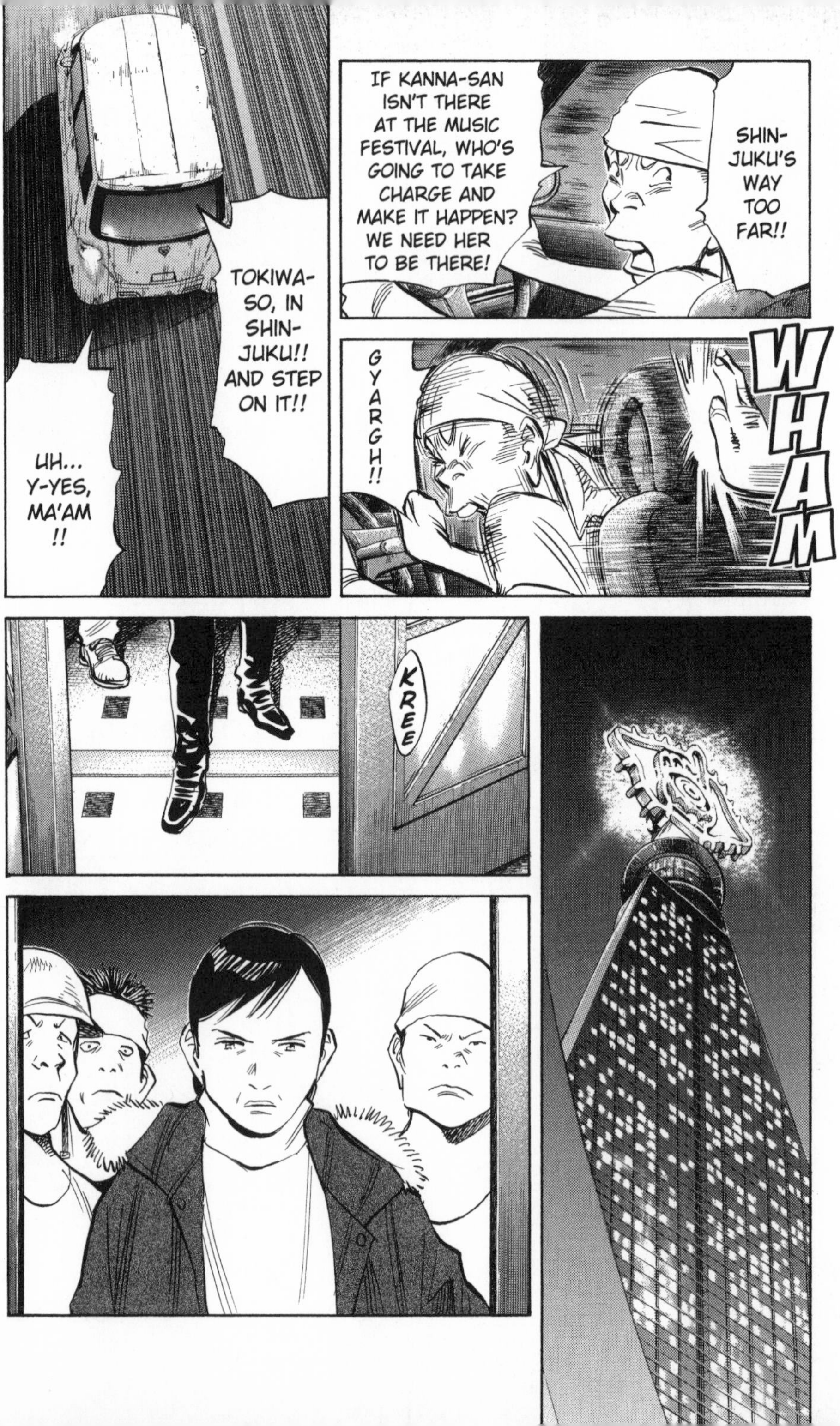
SHIN-JUKU'S WAY TOO FAR!!
IF KANNA-SAN ISN'T THERE AT THE MUSIC FESTIVAL, WHO'S GOING TO TAKE CHARGE AND MAKE IT HAPPEN? WE NEED HER TO BE THERE!
WHAM
GYARGH!!
TOKIWA-SO, IN SHIN-JUKU!! AND STEP ON IT!!
UH... Y-YES, MA'AM!!
KREE

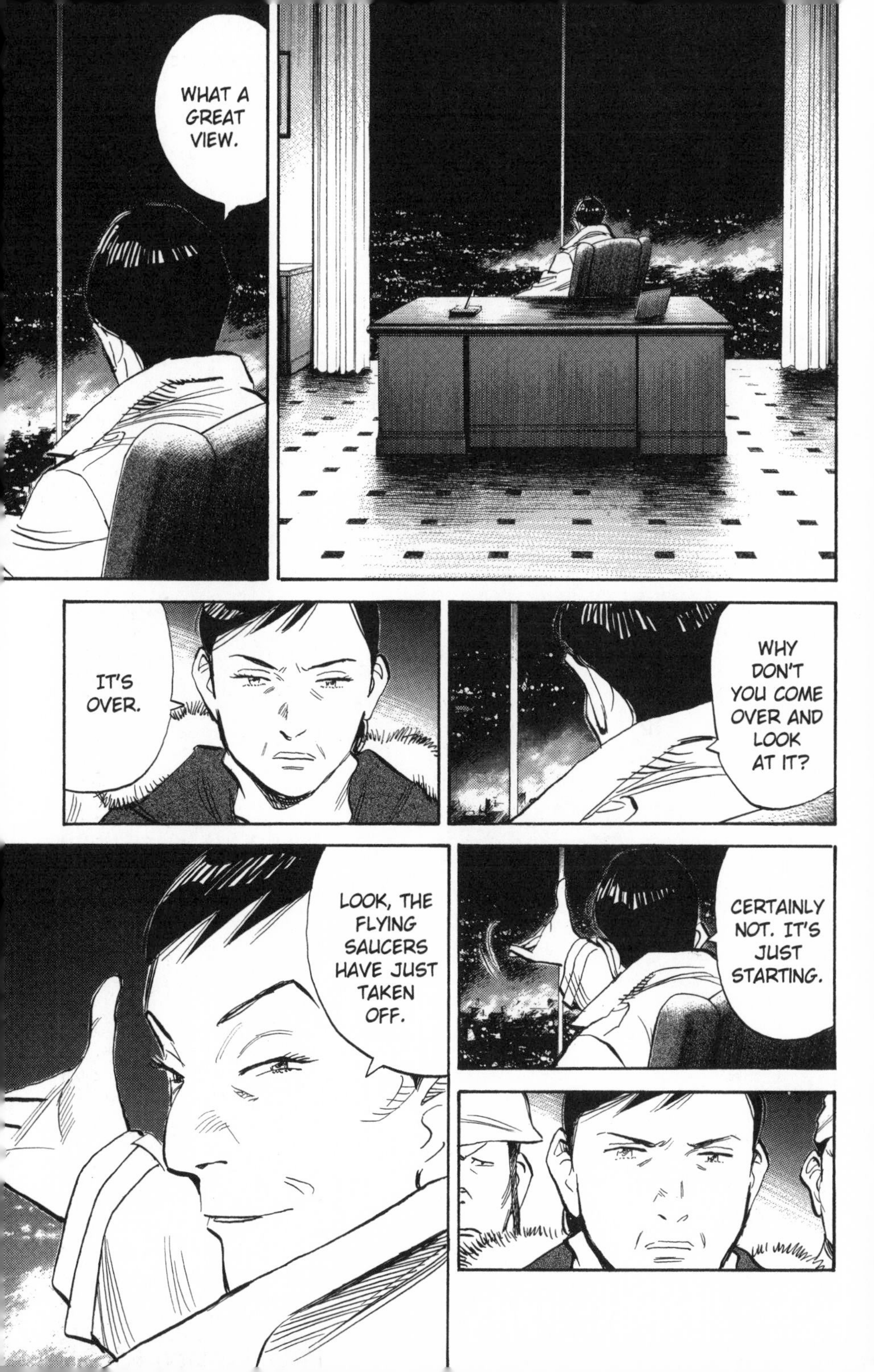
WHAT A GREAT VIEW.
WHY DON'T YOU COME OVER AND LOOK AT IT?
IT'S OVER.
CERTAINLY NOT. IT'S JUST STARTING.
LOOK, THE FLYING SAUCERS HAVE JUST TAKEN OFF.

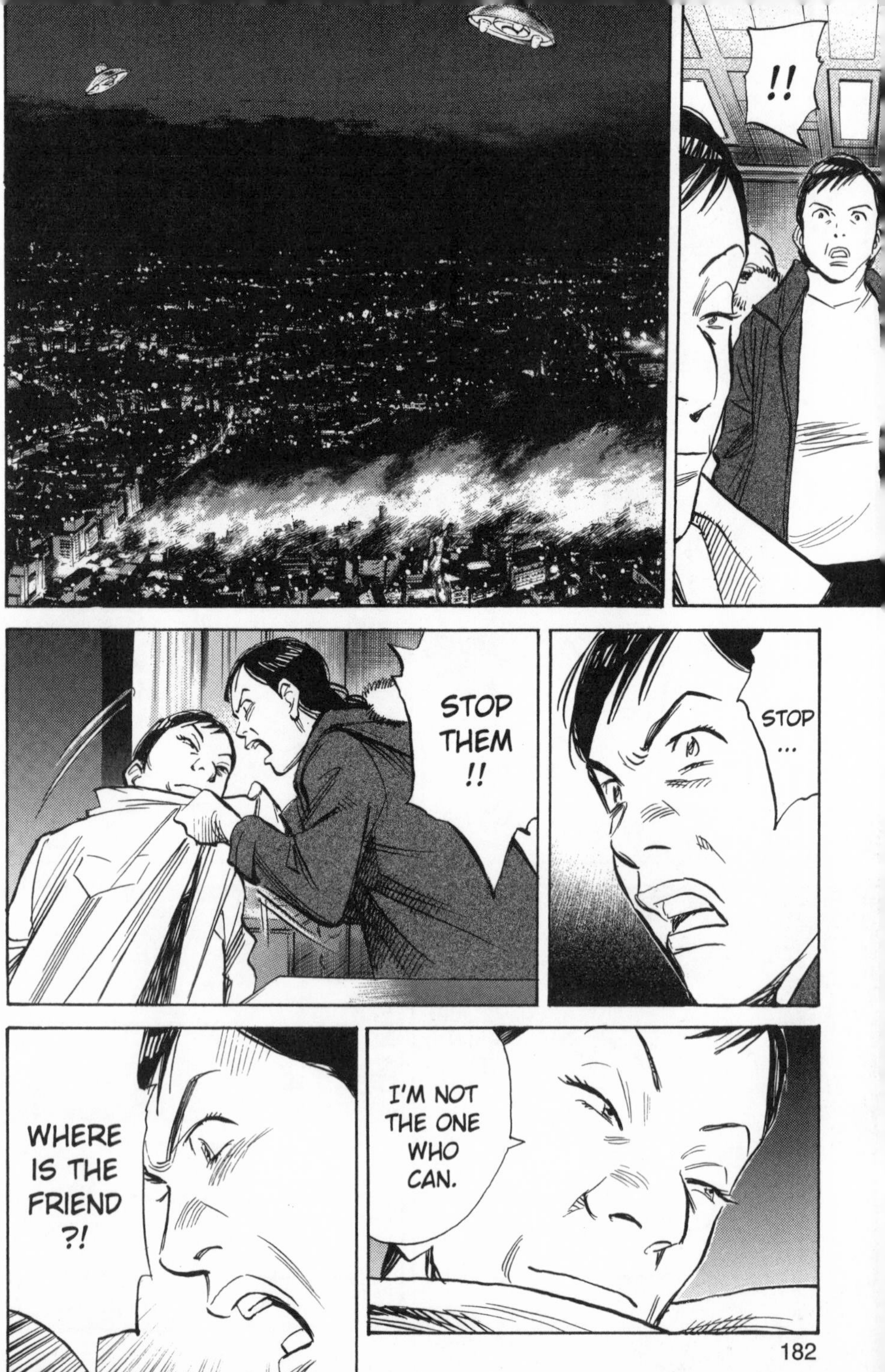
!!
STOP ...
STOP THEM !!
I'M NOT THE ONE WHO CAN.
WHERE IS THE FRIEND ?!

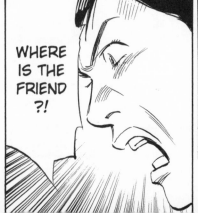

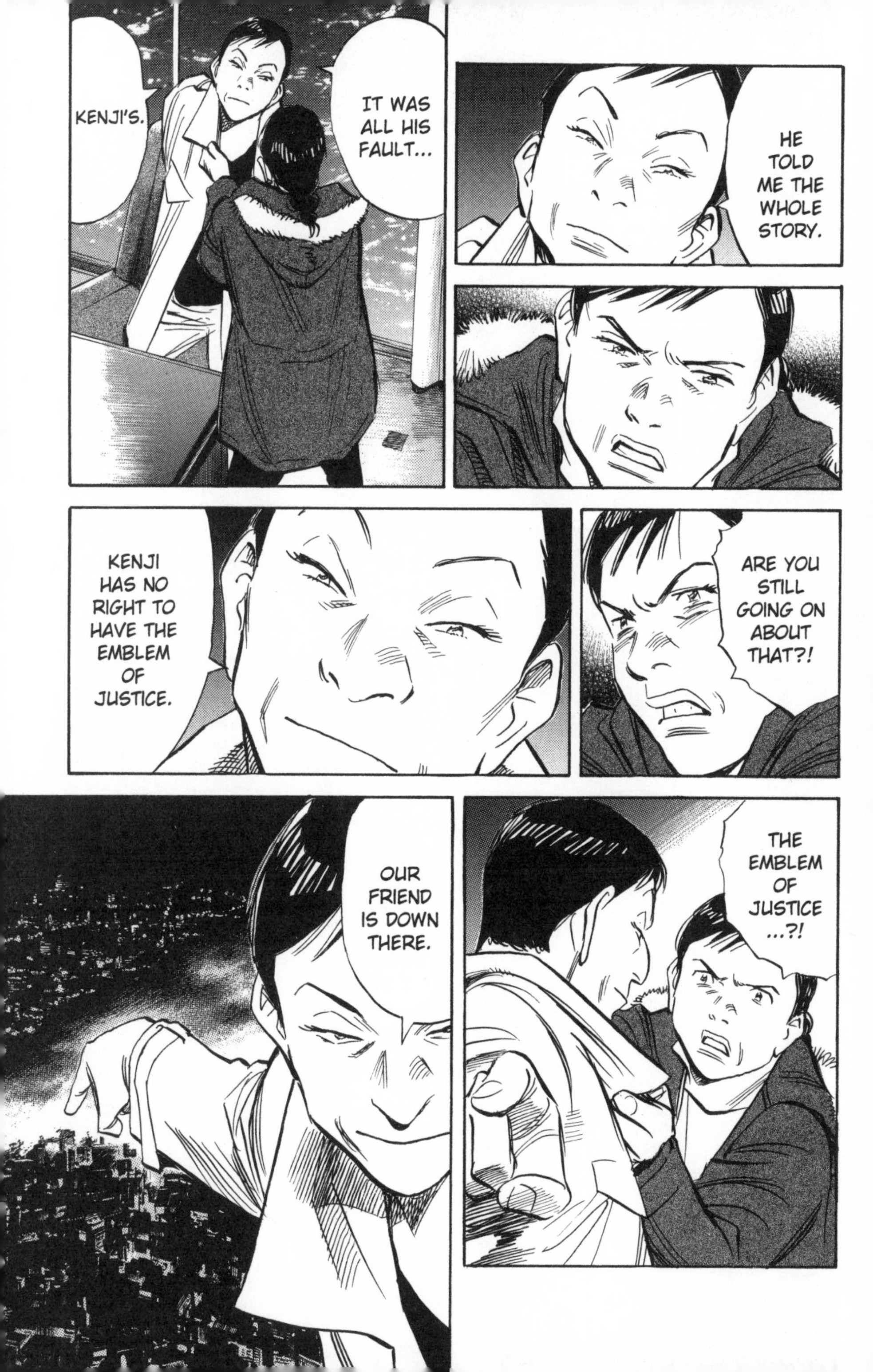
HE TOLD ME THE WHOLE STORY.
IT WAS ALL HIS FAULT...
KENJI'S.
ARE YOU STILL GOING ON ABOUT THAT?!
KENJI HAS NO RIGHT TO HAVE THE EMBLEM OF JUSTICE.
THE EMBLEM OF JUSTICE ...?!
OUR FRIEND IS DOWN THERE.

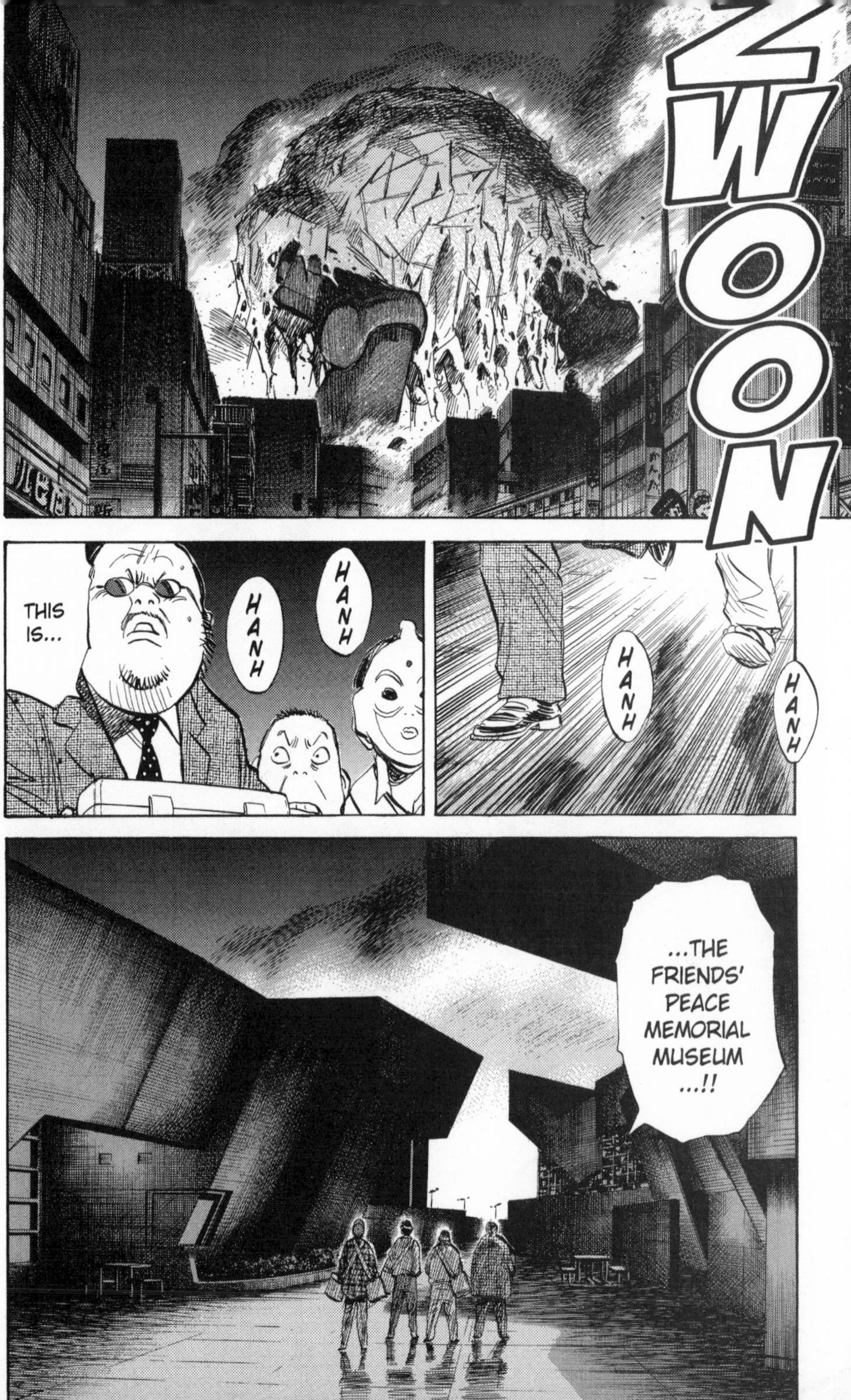
ZWOOON
HANH
HANH
HANH
HANH
THIS IS...
...THE FRIENDS' PEACE MEMORIAL MUSEUM ...!!

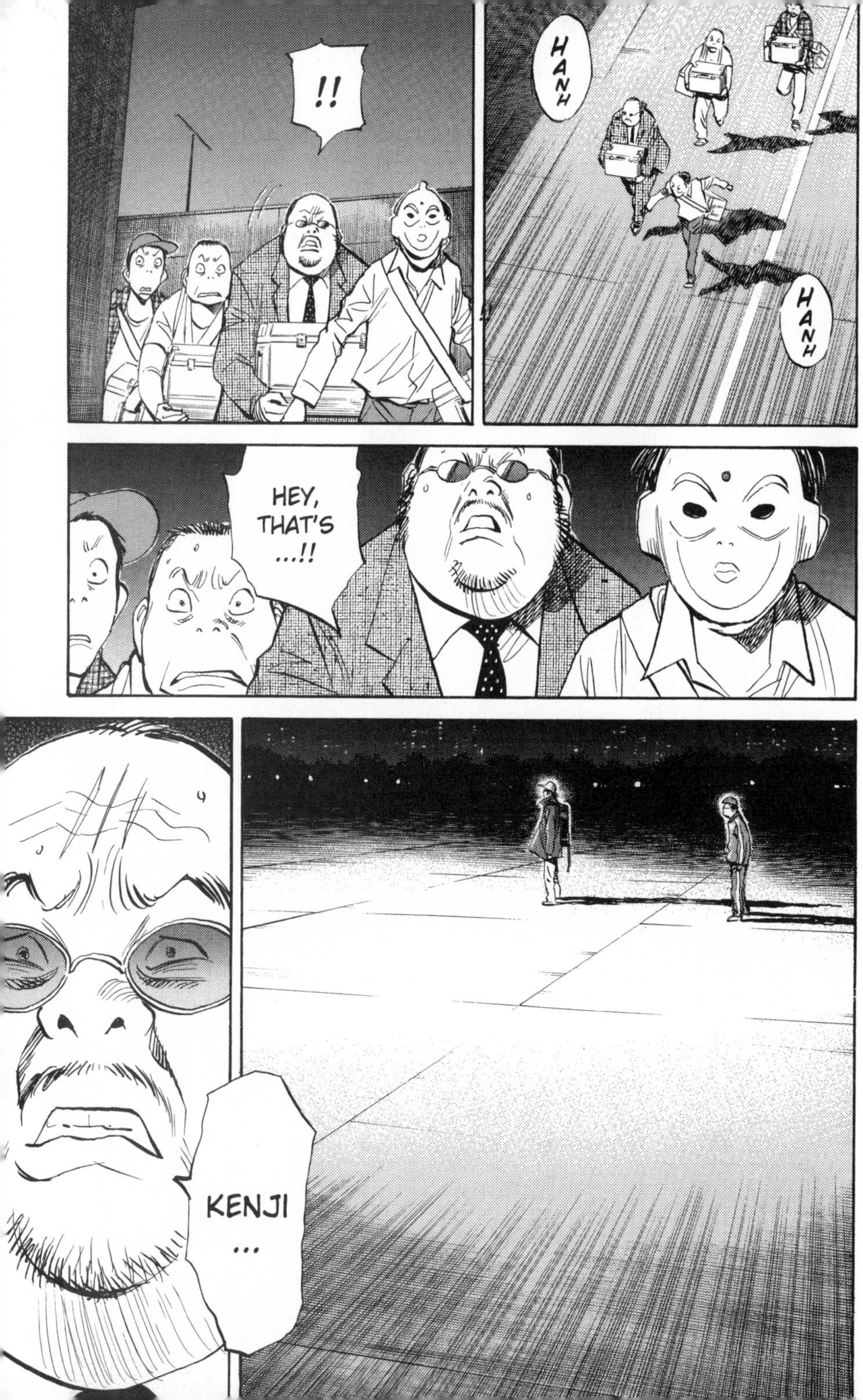
HANH
HANH
!!
HEY, THAT'S ...!!
KENJI ...

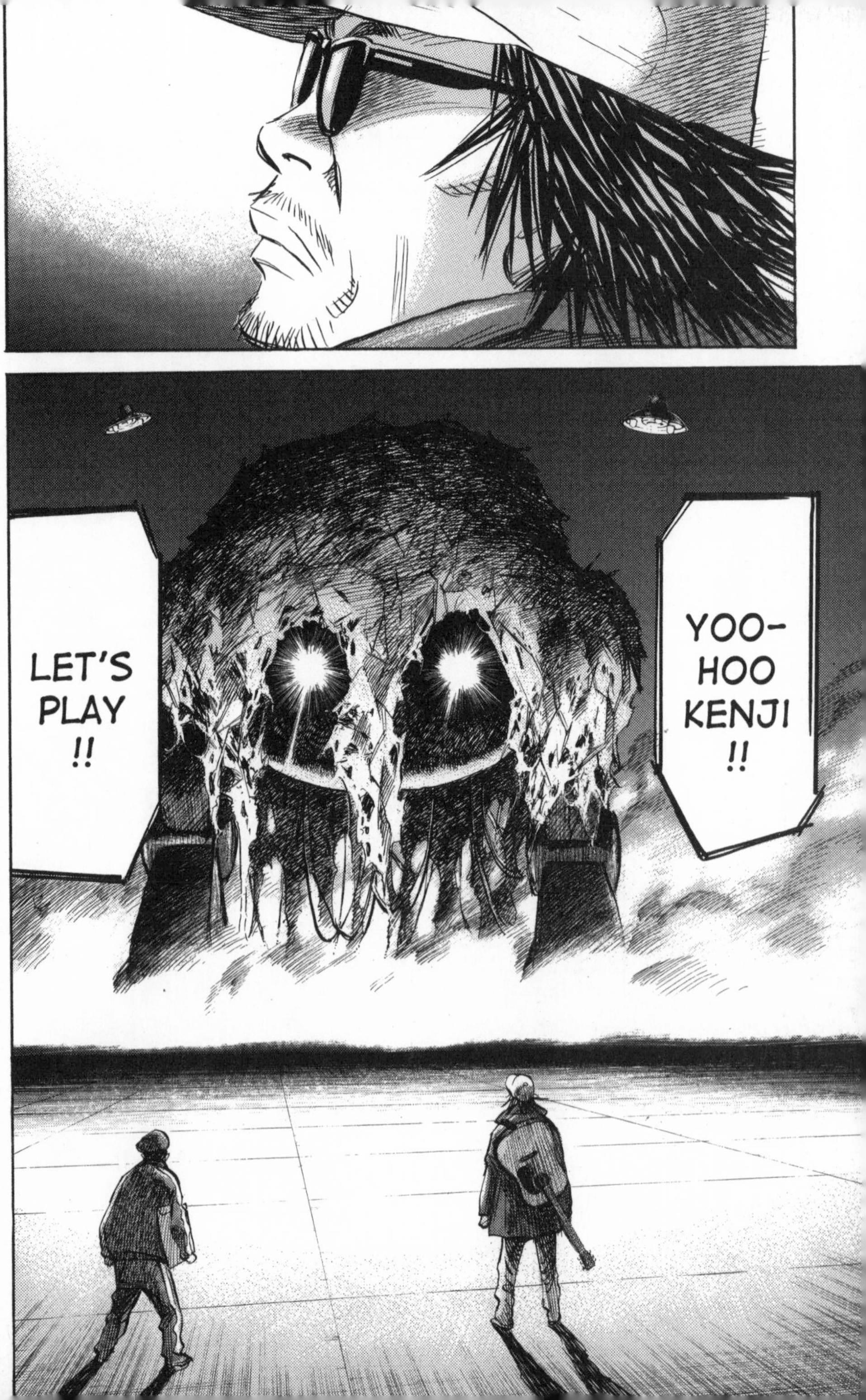
YOO-HOO KENJI !!
LET'S PLAY !!

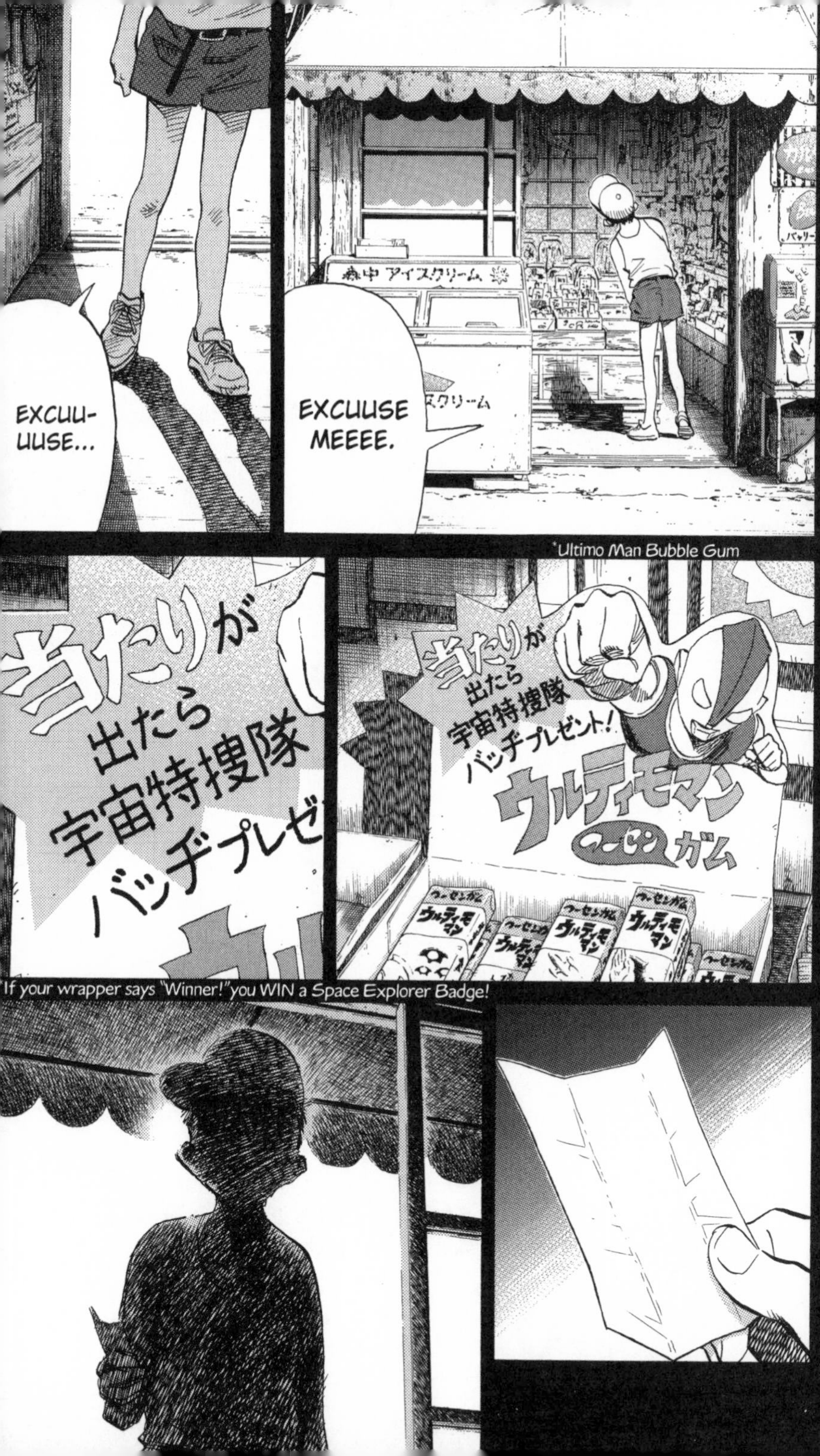
EXCUUSE MEEEE.
EXCUU-UUSE...
当たりが出たら宇宙特捜隊バッヂプレゼント！
ウルティモマン
フーセンガム
*Ultimo Man Bubble Gum
当たりが出たら宇宙特捜隊バッヂプレゼ
If your wrapper says "Winner!" you WIN a Space Explorer Badge!

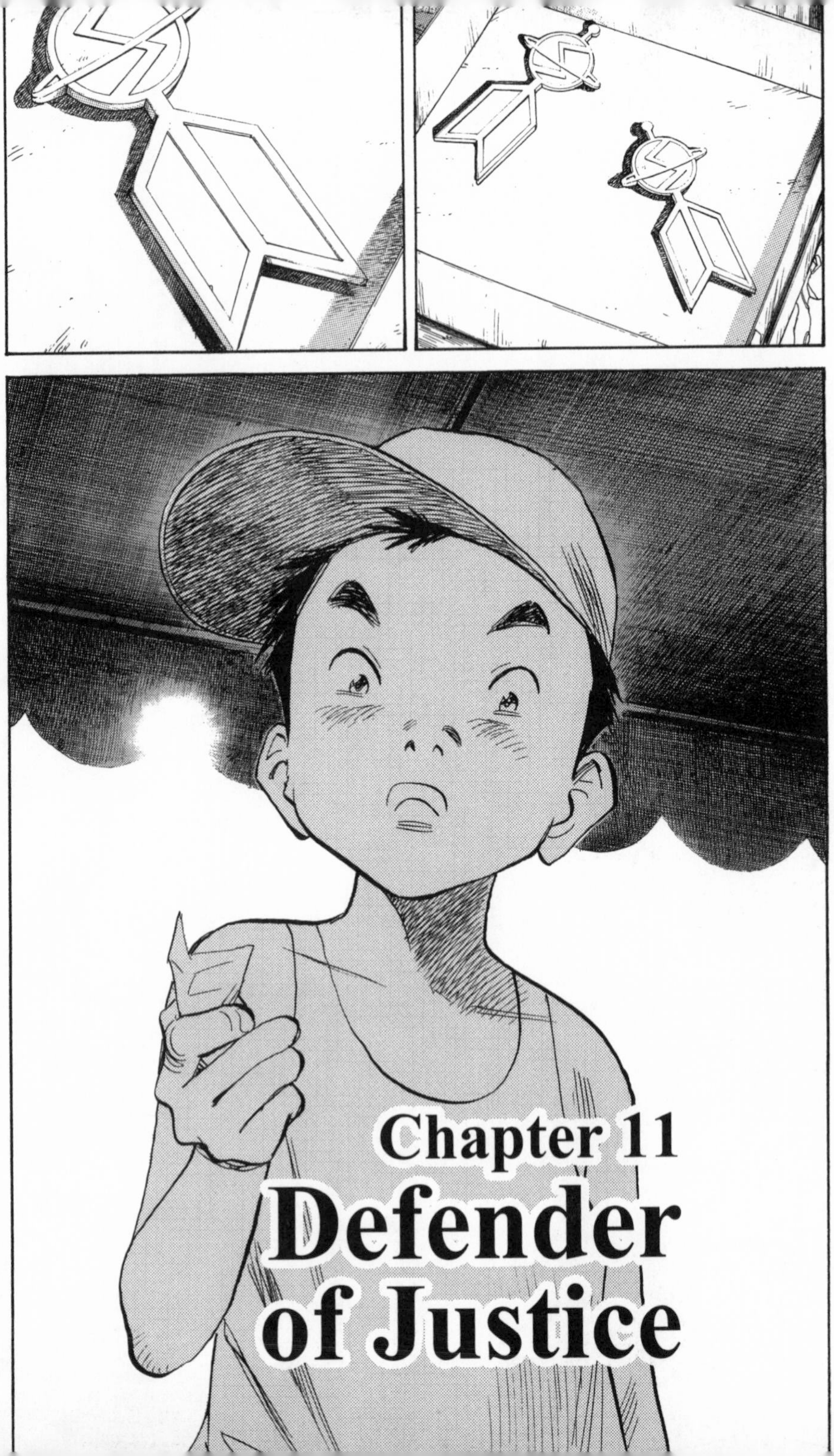
Chapter 11
Defender of Justice

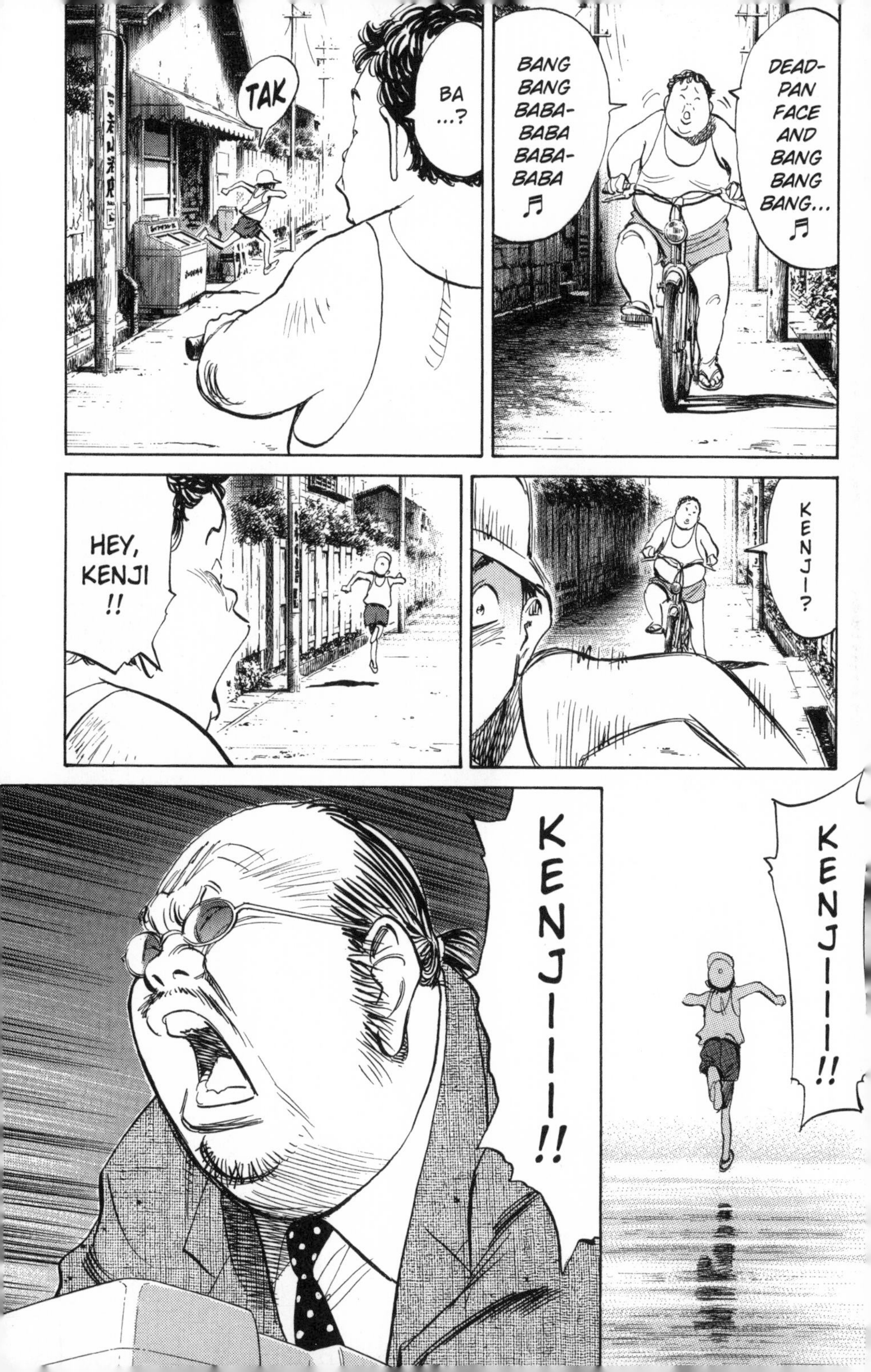
DEAD-PAN FACE AND BANG BANG BANG... ♬
BANG BANG BABA-BABA BABA-BABA ♬
BA ...?
TAK
KENJI?
HEY, KENJI !!
KENJIIII!!
KENJIIII!!

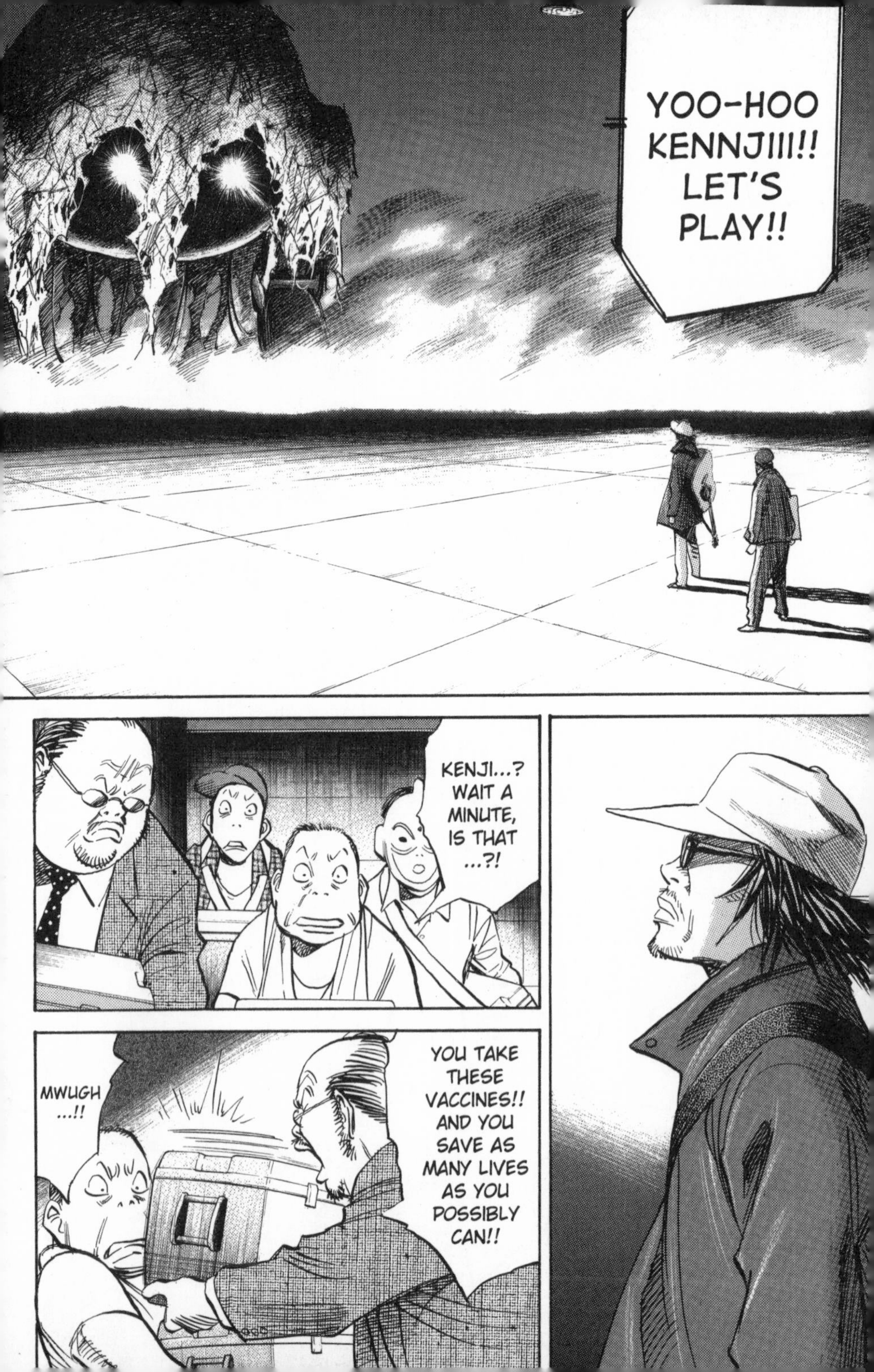
YOO-HOO KENNJIIII!! LET'S PLAY!!
KENJI...? WAIT A MINUTE, IS THAT ...?!
YOU TAKE THESE VACCINES!! AND YOU SAVE AS MANY LIVES AS YOU POSSIBLY CAN!!
MWUGH ...!!

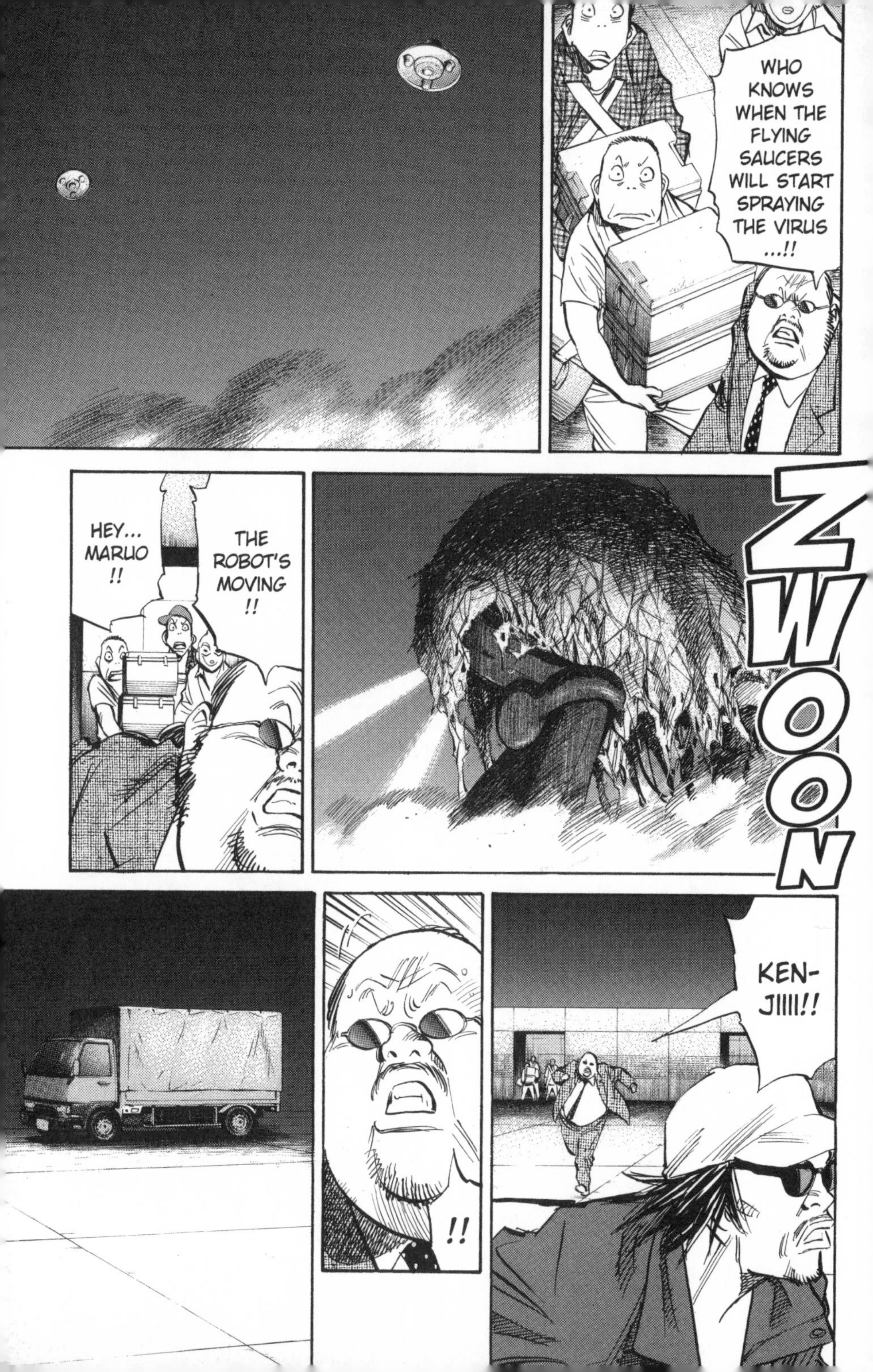
WHO KNOWS WHEN THE FLYING SAUCERS WILL START SPRAYING THE VIRUS ...!!
ZWOOON
THE ROBOT'S MOVING !!
HEY... MARUO !!
KEN-JIIII!!
!!

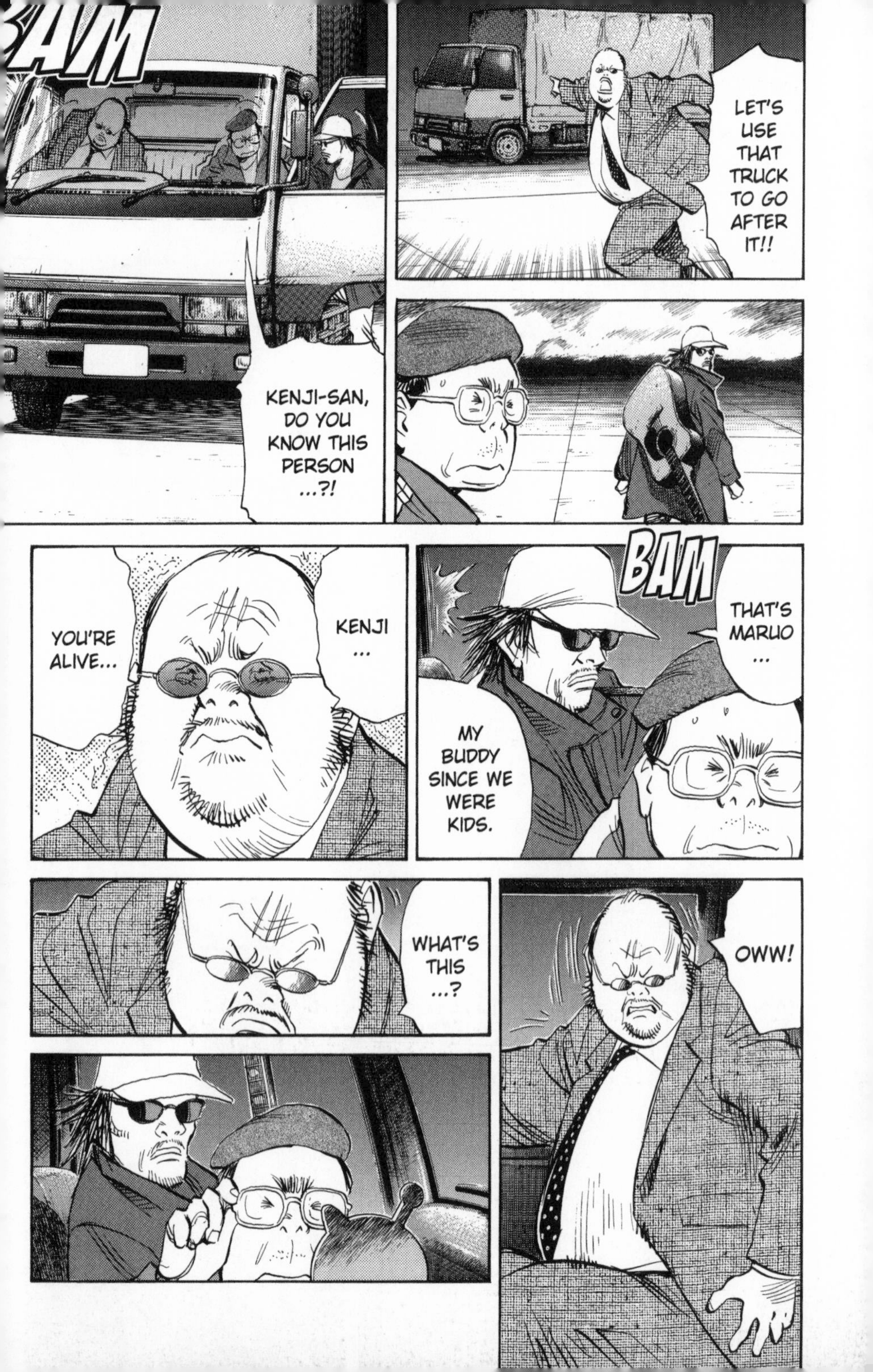
LET'S USE THAT TRUCK TO GO AFTER IT!!
KENJI-SAN, DO YOU KNOW THIS PERSON...?!
BAM
BAM
THAT'S MARUO...
MY BUDDY SINCE WE WERE KIDS.
KENJI...
YOU'RE ALIVE...
OWW!
WHAT'S THIS...?

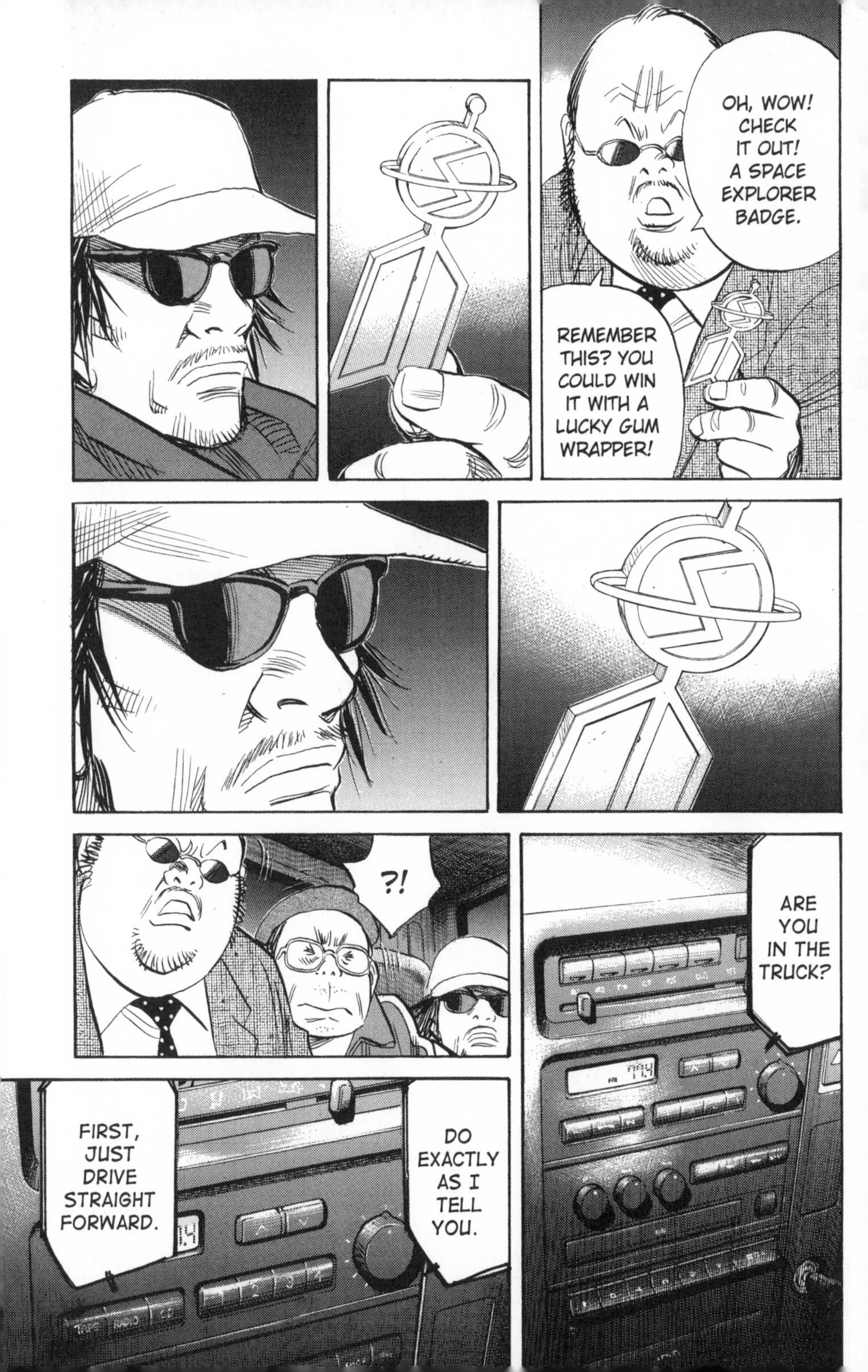
OH, WOW! CHECK IT OUT! A SPACE EXPLORER BADGE.
REMEMBER THIS? YOU COULD WIN IT WITH A LUCKY GUM WRAPPER!
ARE YOU IN THE TRUCK?
?!
DO EXACTLY AS I TELL YOU.
FIRST, JUST DRIVE STRAIGHT FORWARD.

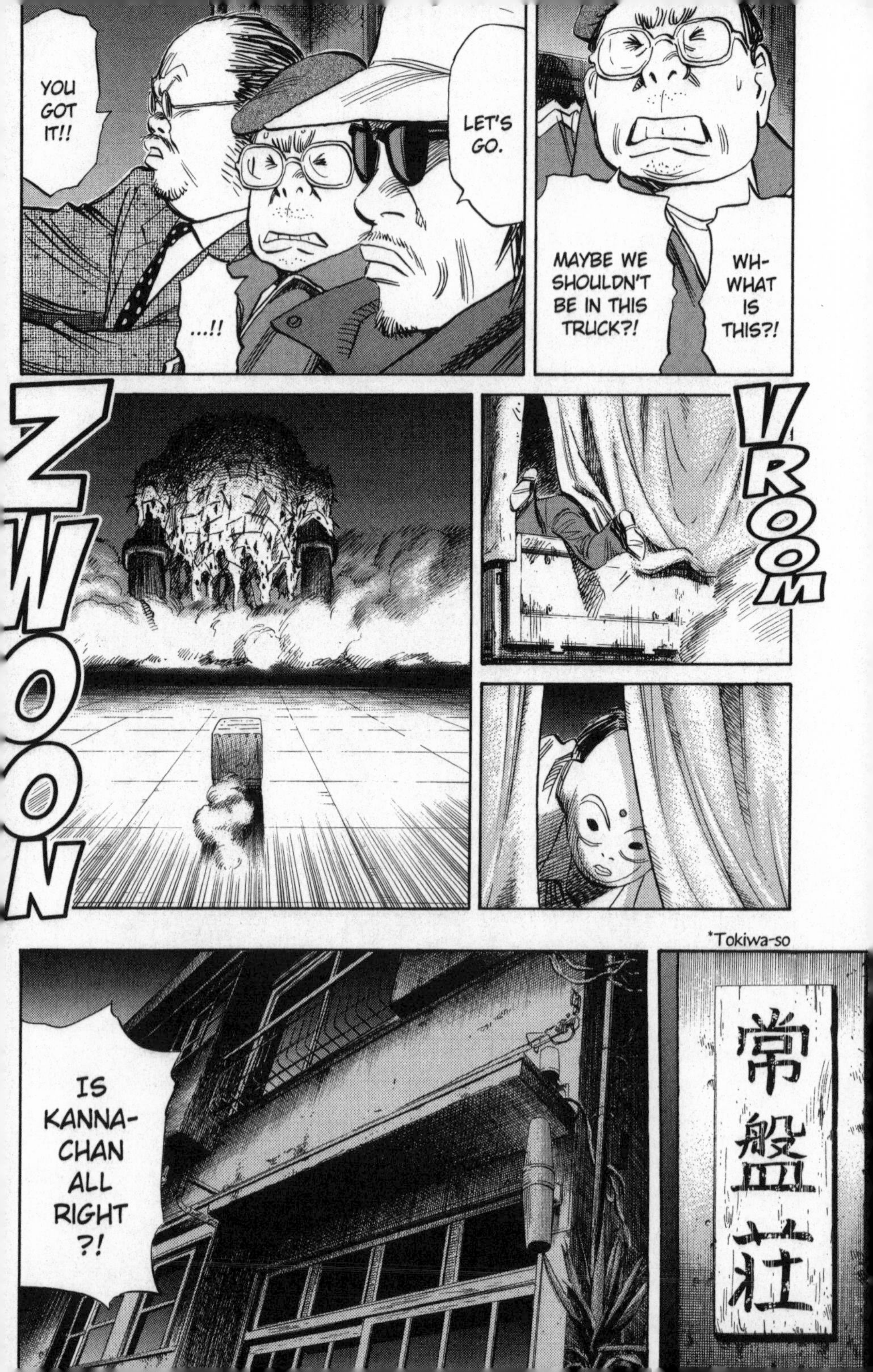
WH-WHAT IS THIS?!
MAYBE WE SHOULDN'T BE IN THIS TRUCK?!
LET'S GO.
YOU GOT IT!!
...!!
VROOM
ZWOON
*Tokiwa-so
常盤荘
IS KANNA-CHAN ALL RIGHT?!

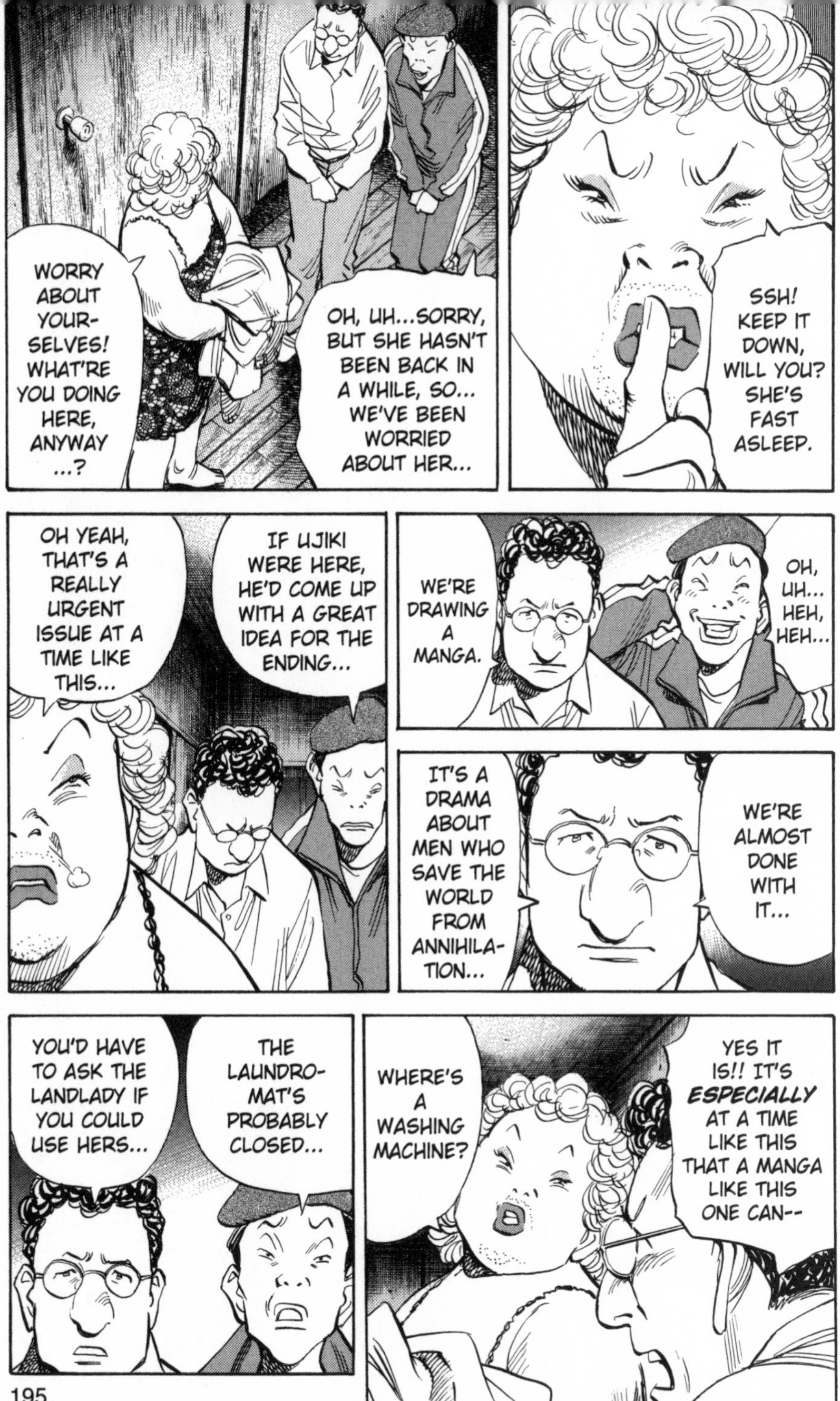
SSH! KEEP IT DOWN, WILL YOU? SHE'S FAST ASLEEP.
OH, UH...SORRY, BUT SHE HASN'T BEEN BACK IN A WHILE, SO... WE'VE BEEN WORRIED ABOUT HER...
WORRY ABOUT YOUR-SELVES! WHAT'RE YOU DOING HERE, ANYWAY ...?
OH, UH... HEH, HEH...
WE'RE DRAWING A MANGA.
WE'RE ALMOST DONE WITH IT...
IT'S A DRAMA ABOUT MEN WHO SAVE THE WORLD FROM ANNIHILA-TION...
IF UJIKI WERE HERE, HE'D COME UP WITH A GREAT IDEA FOR THE ENDING...
OH YEAH, THAT'S A REALLY URGENT ISSUE AT A TIME LIKE THIS...
YES IT IS!! IT'S ***ESPECIALLY*** AT A TIME LIKE THIS THAT A MANGA LIKE THIS ONE CAN--
WHERE'S A WASHING MACHINE?
THE LAUNDRO-MAT'S PROBABLY CLOSED...
YOU'D HAVE TO ASK THE LANDLADY IF YOU COULD USE HERS...

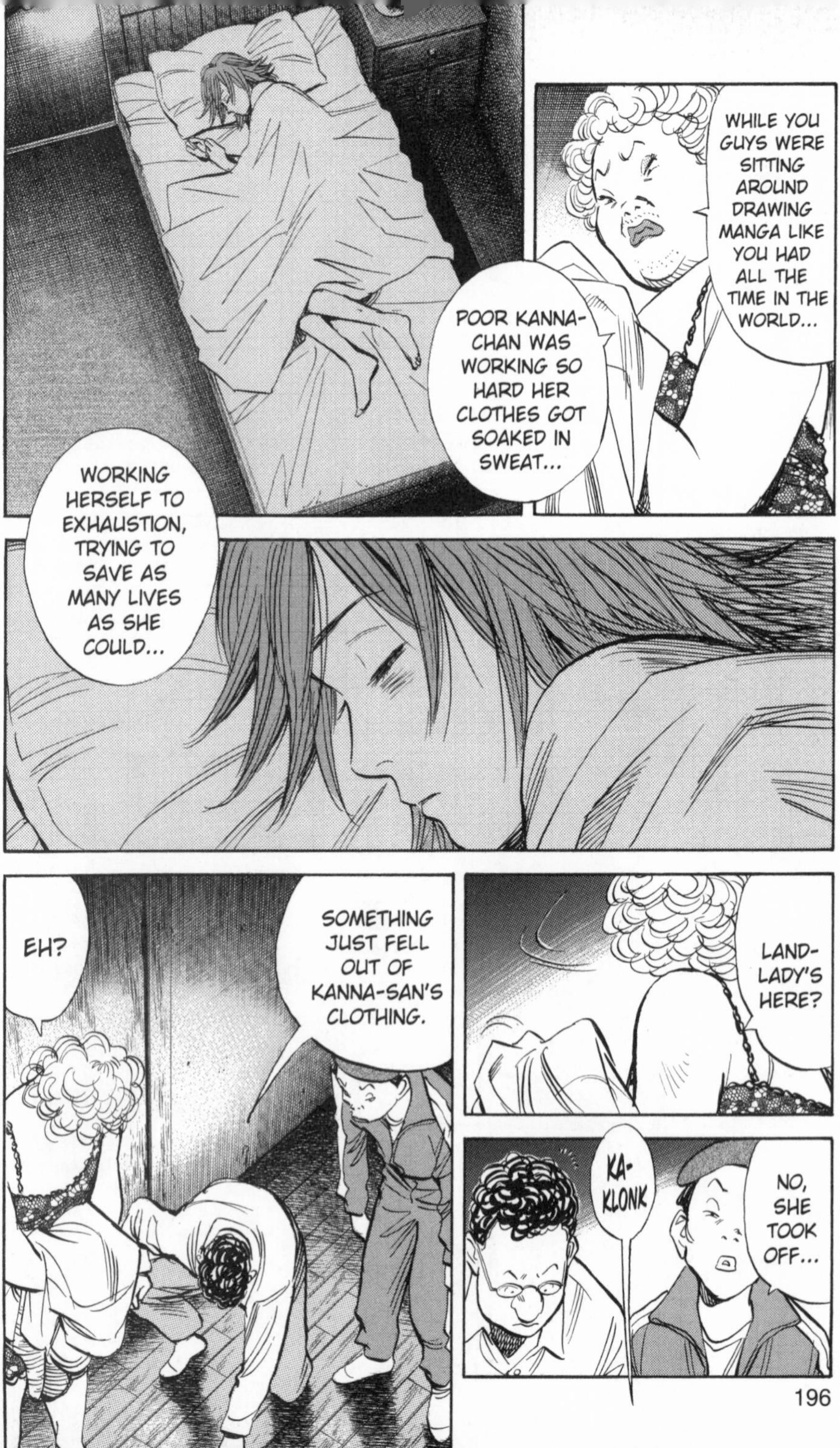
WHILE YOU GUYS WERE SITTING AROUND DRAWING MANGA LIKE YOU HAD ALL THE TIME IN THE WORLD...
POOR KANNA-CHAN WAS WORKING SO HARD HER CLOTHES GOT SOAKED IN SWEAT...
WORKING HERSELF TO EXHAUSTION, TRYING TO SAVE AS MANY LIVES AS SHE COULD...
LAND-LADY'S HERE?
NO, SHE TOOK OFF...
KA-KLONK
SOMETHING JUST FELL OUT OF KANNA-SAN'S CLOTHING.
EH?

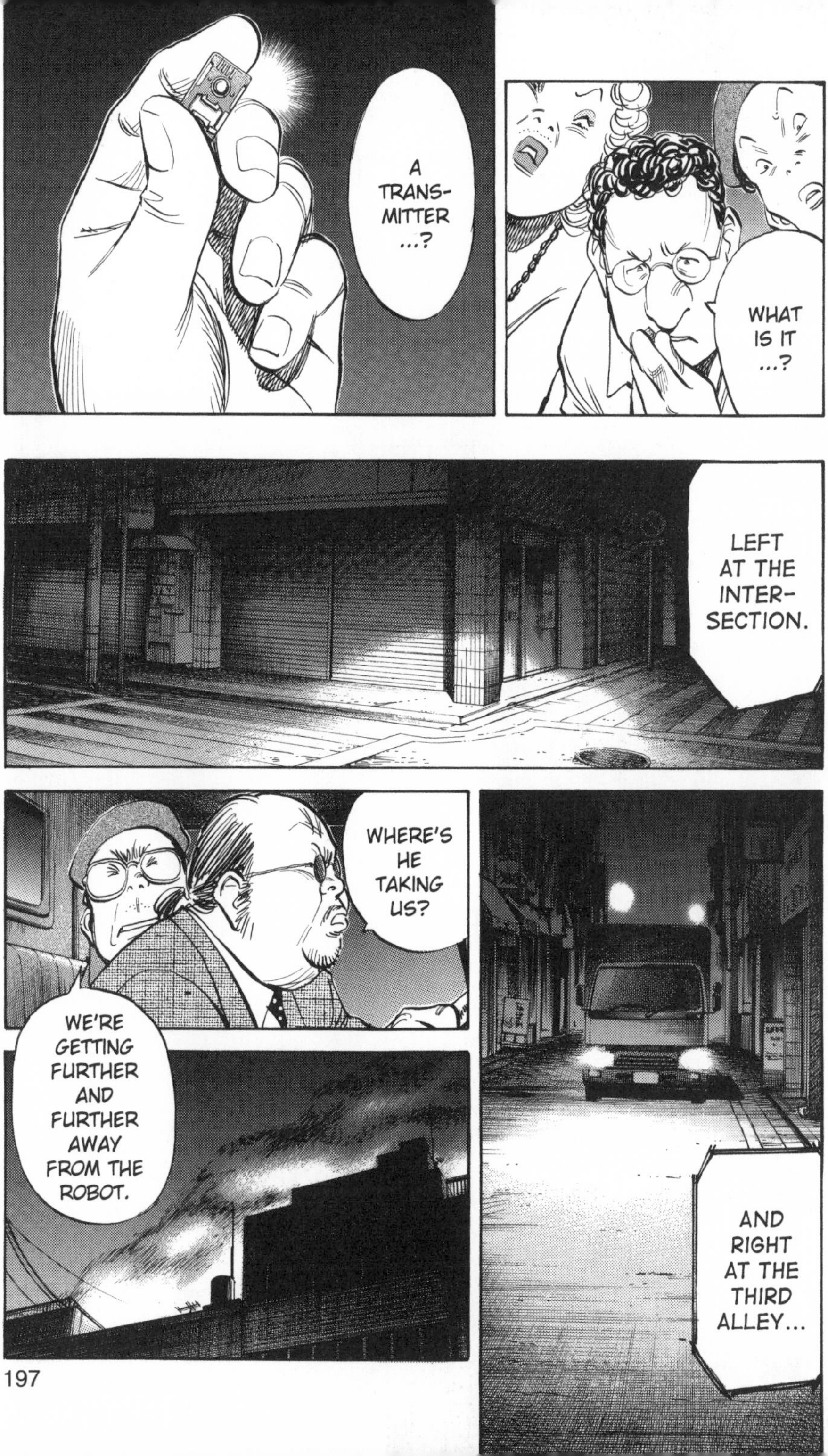
WHAT IS IT ...?
A TRANS-MITTER ...?
LEFT AT THE INTER-SECTION.
AND RIGHT AT THE THIRD ALLEY...
WHERE'S HE TAKING US?
WE'RE GETTING FURTHER AND FURTHER AWAY FROM THE ROBOT.

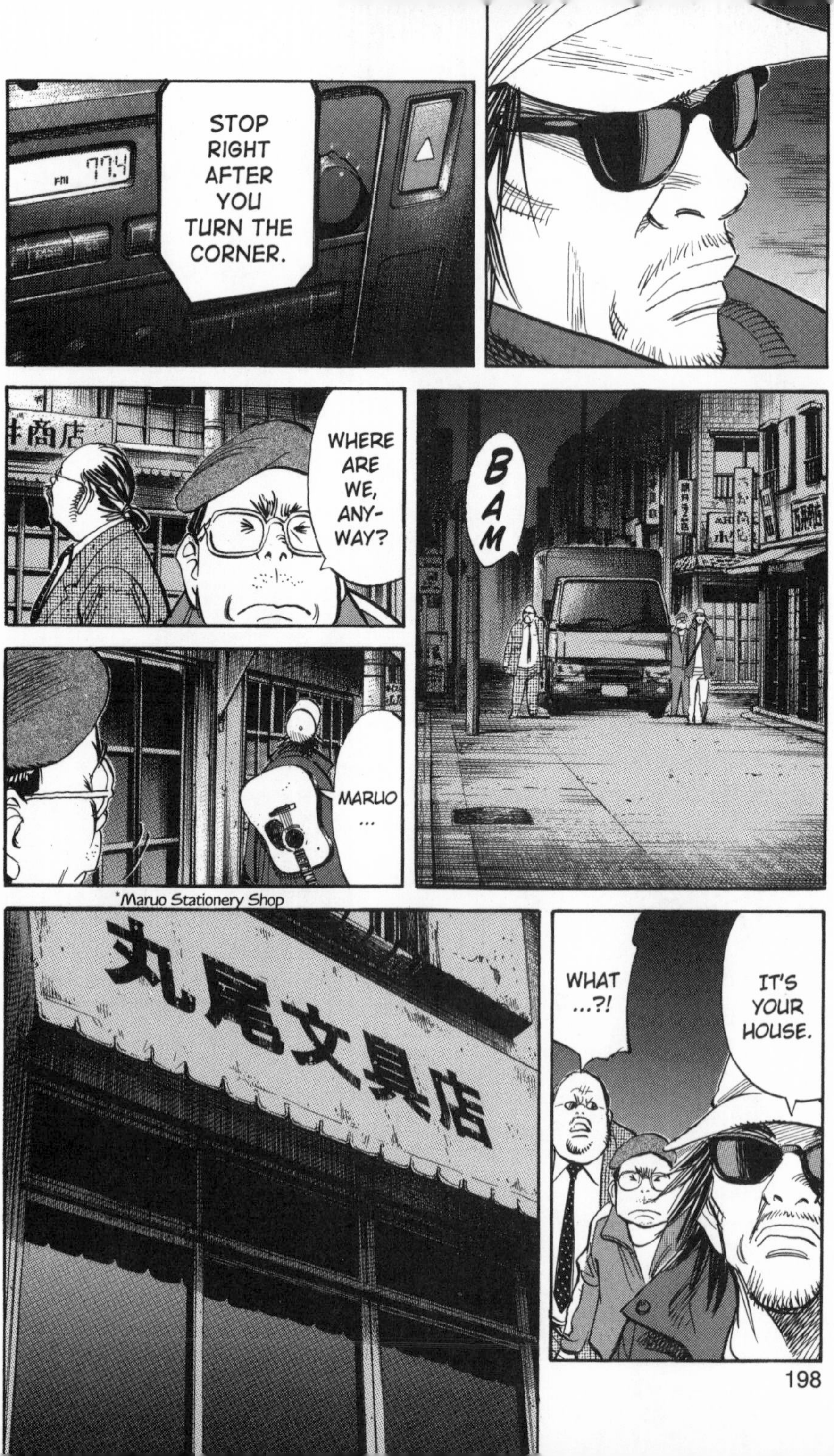
STOP RIGHT AFTER YOU TURN THE CORNER.
BAM
WHERE ARE WE, ANYWAY?
MARUO ...
*Maruo Stationery Shop
IT'S YOUR HOUSE.
WHAT ...?!
丸尾文具店

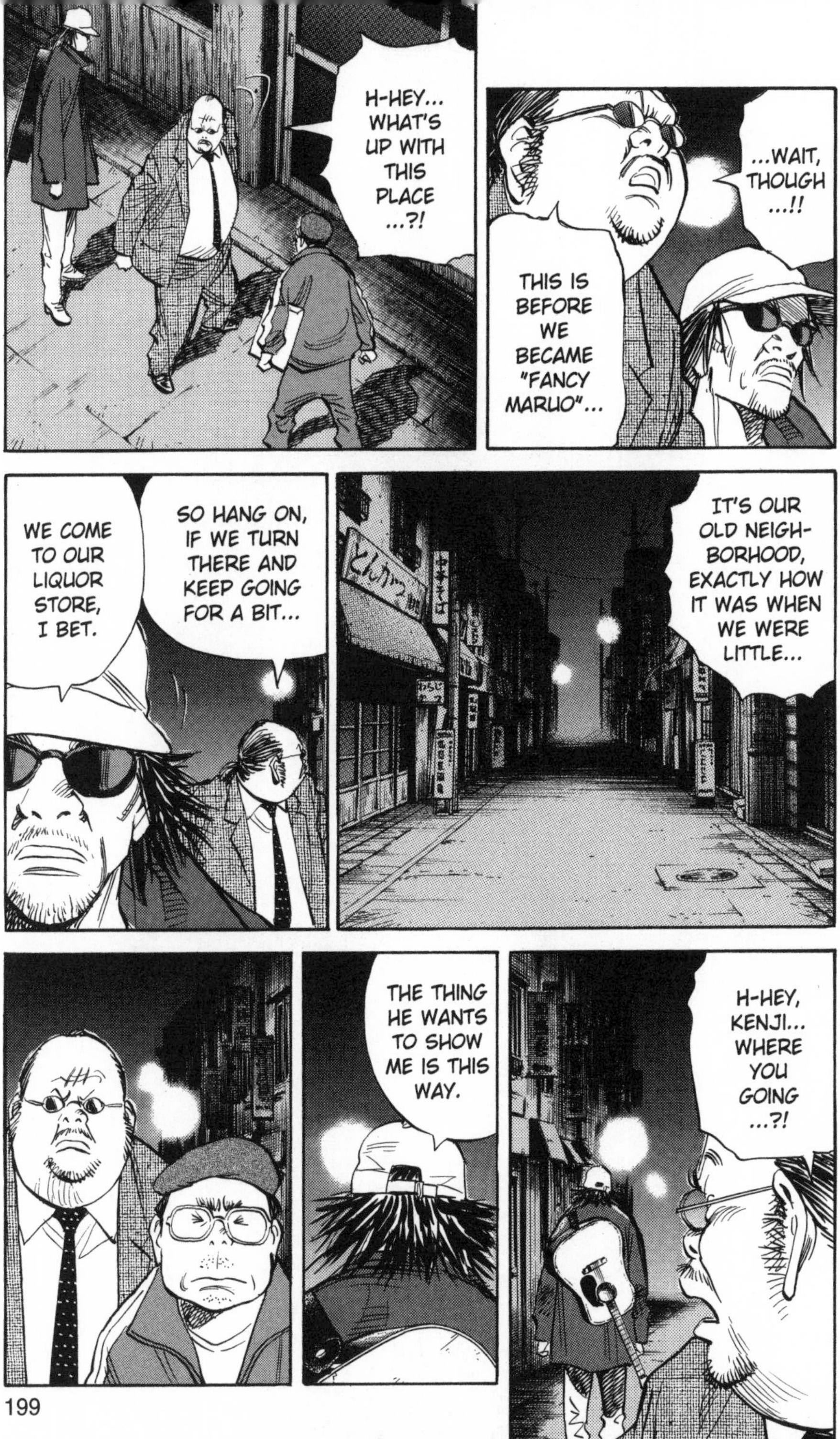
...WAIT, THOUGH ...!!
THIS IS BEFORE WE BECAME "FANCY MARUO"...
H-HEY... WHAT'S UP WITH THIS PLACE ...?!
IT'S OUR OLD NEIGH-BORHOOD, EXACTLY HOW IT WAS WHEN WE WERE LITTLE...
SO HANG ON, IF WE TURN THERE AND KEEP GOING FOR A BIT...
WE COME TO OUR LIQUOR STORE, I BET.
H-HEY, KENJI... WHERE YOU GOING ...?!
THE THING HE WANTS TO SHOW ME IS THIS WAY.

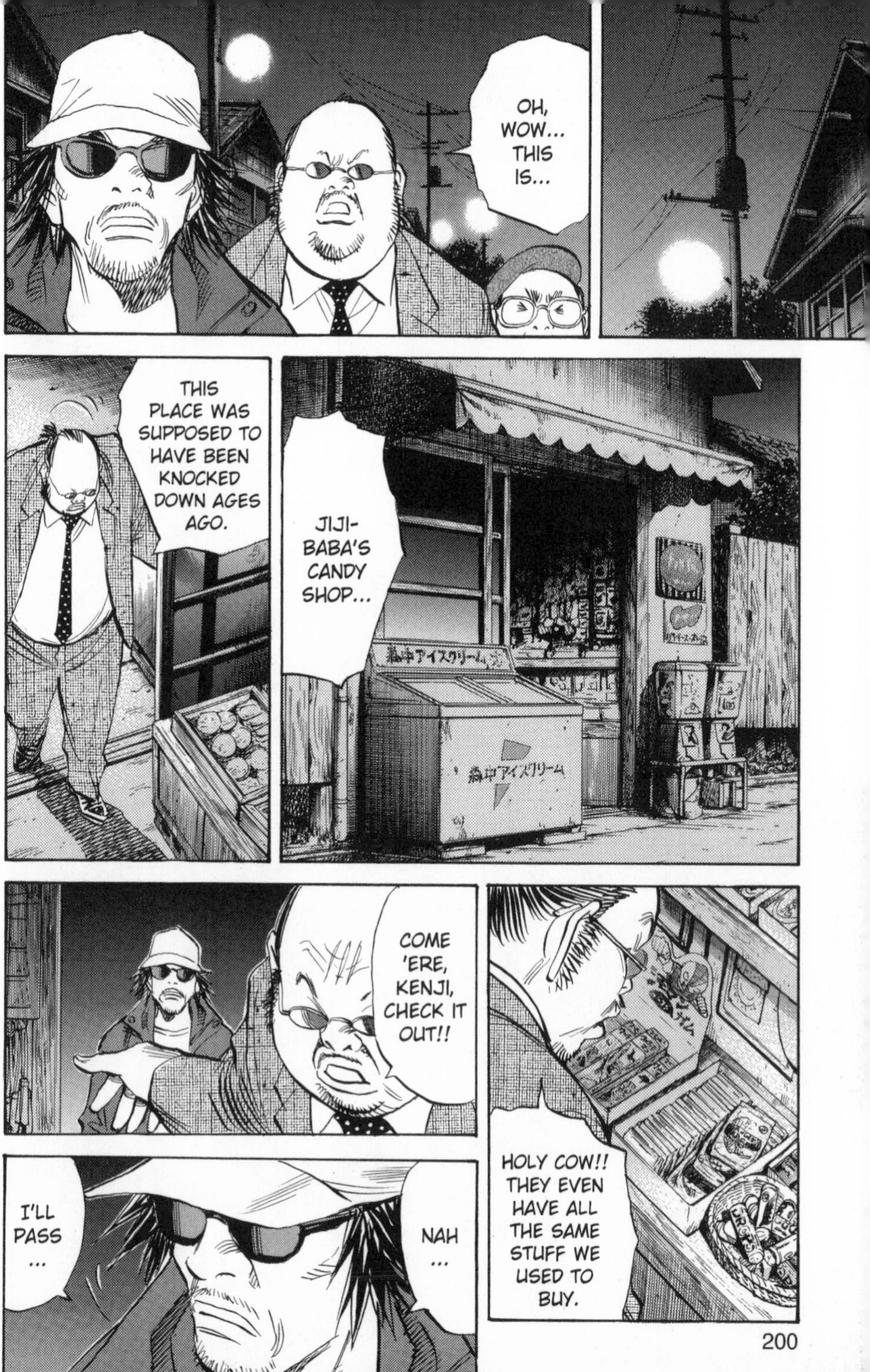
OH, WOW... THIS IS...
JIJI-BABA'S CANDY SHOP...
THIS PLACE WAS SUPPOSED TO HAVE BEEN KNOCKED DOWN AGES AGO.
HOLY COW!! THEY EVEN HAVE ALL THE SAME STUFF WE USED TO BUY.
COME 'ERE, KENJI, CHECK IT OUT!!
NAH ...
I'LL PASS ...

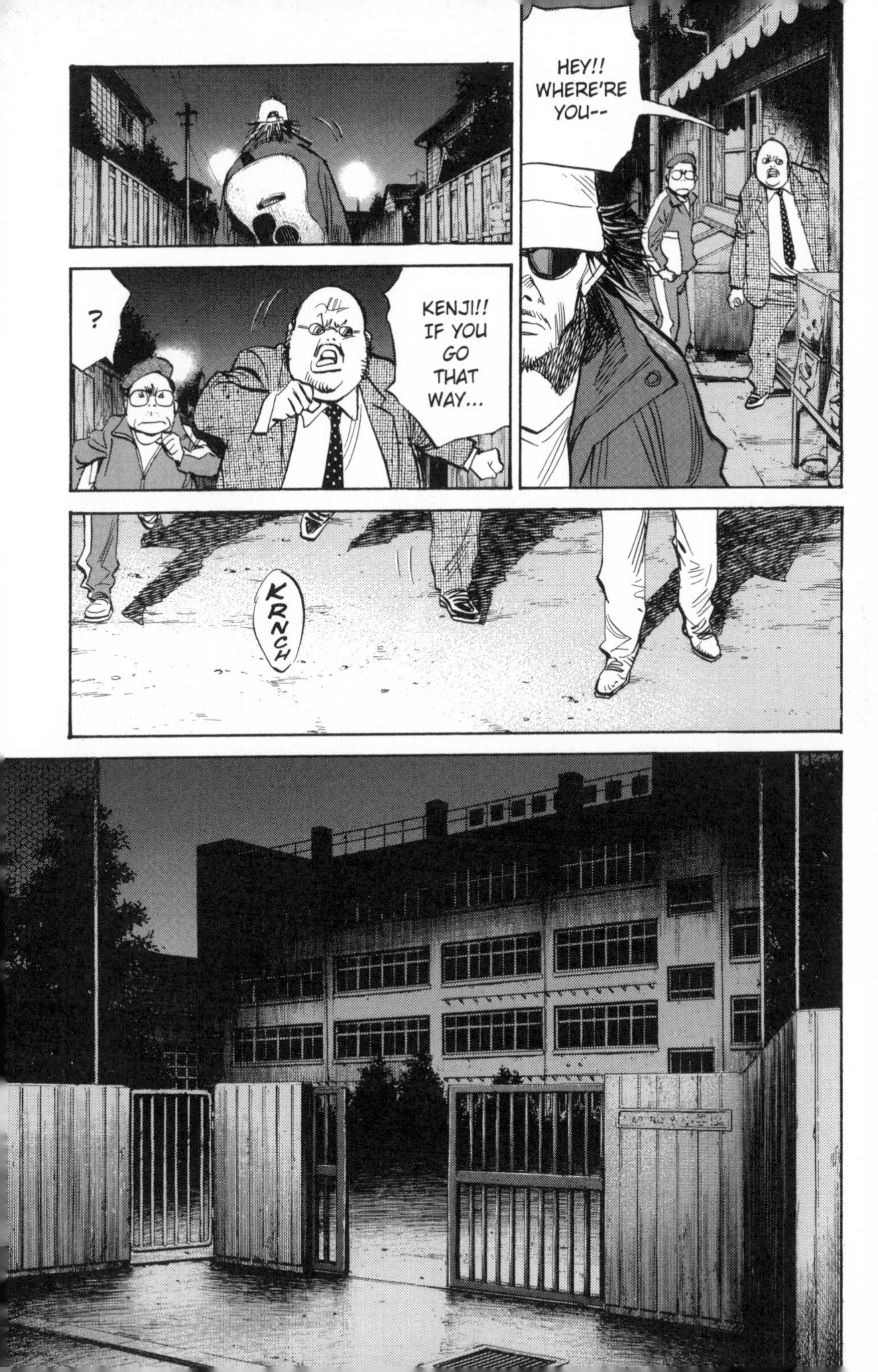
HEY!! WHERE'RE YOU--
KENJI!! IF YOU GO THAT WAY...
?
KRNCH

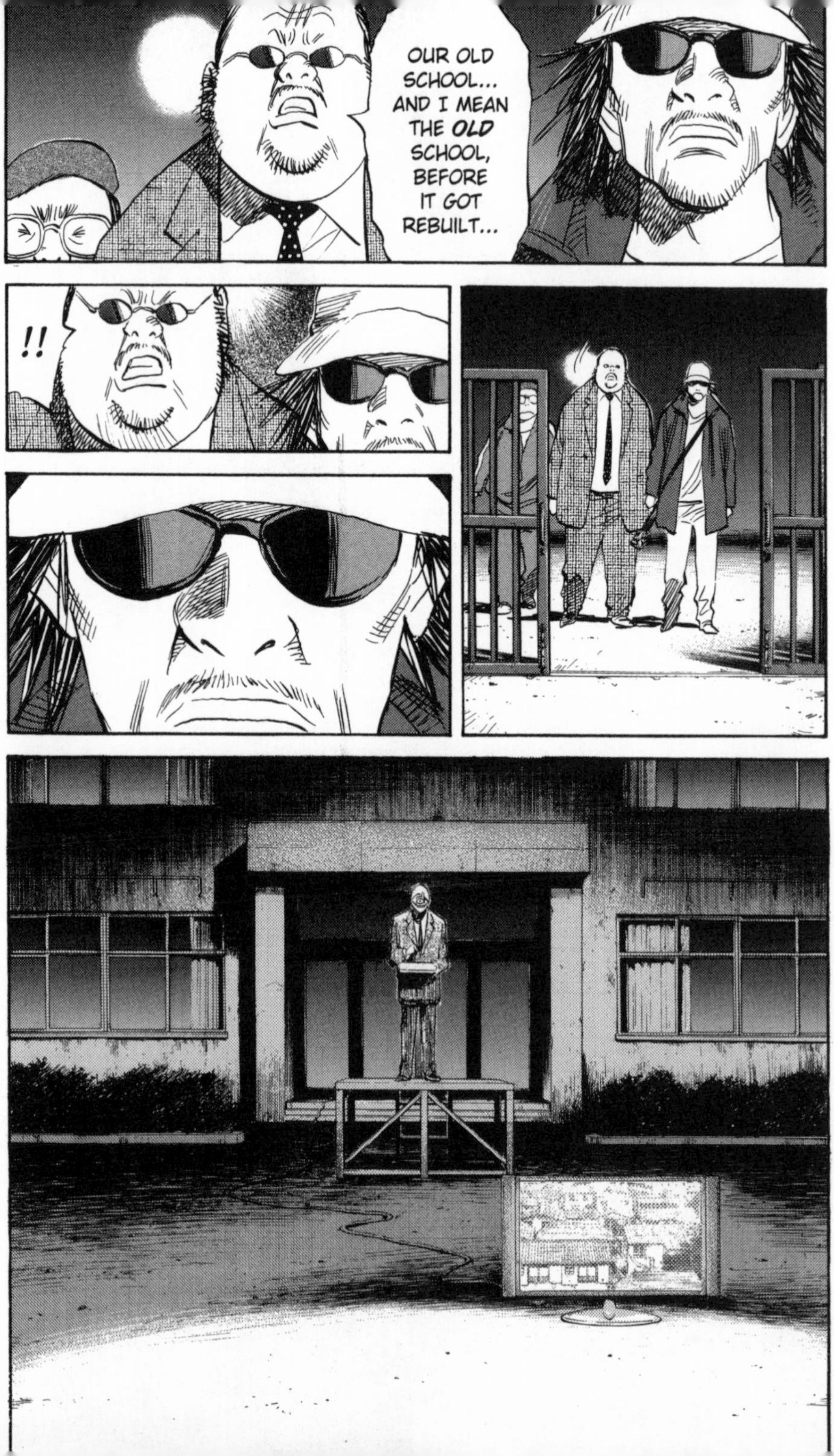
OUR OLD SCHOOL... AND I MEAN THE OLD SCHOOL, BEFORE IT GOT REBUILT...
!!

THE *FRIEND*...!!

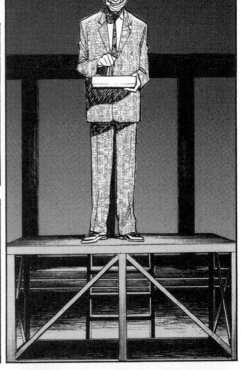

... KENJI.

HI... SO YOU CAME...

"MAN WHO SAVES THE WORLD," GIVE ME A BREAK.

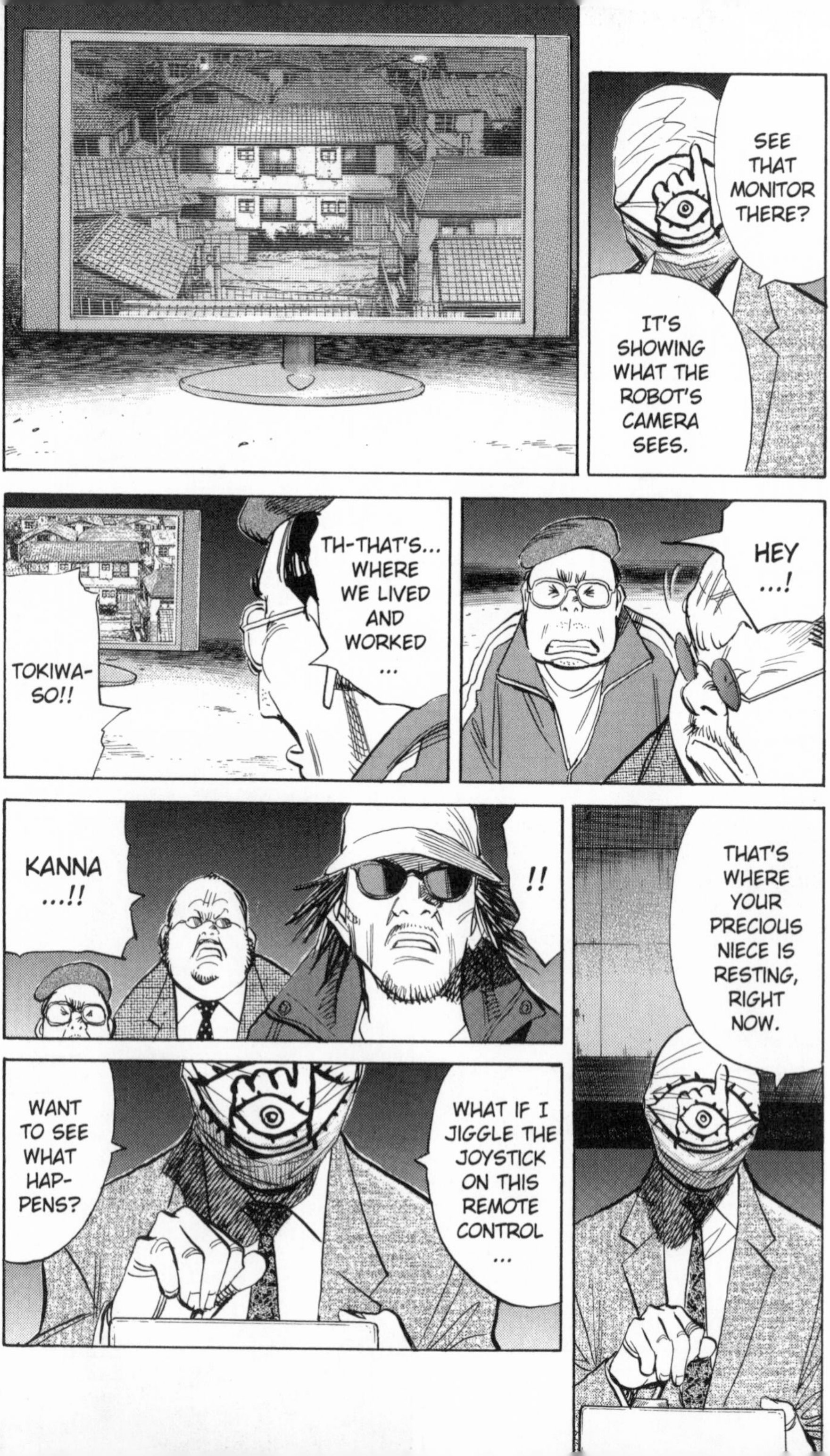
SEE THAT MONITOR THERE?
IT'S SHOWING WHAT THE ROBOT'S CAMERA SEES.
HEY ...!
TH-THAT'S... WHERE WE LIVED AND WORKED ...
TOKIWA-SO!!
THAT'S WHERE YOUR PRECIOUS NIECE IS RESTING, RIGHT NOW.
!!
KANNA ...!!
WHAT IF I JIGGLE THE JOYSTICK ON THIS REMOTE CONTROL ...
WANT TO SEE WHAT HAP-PENS?

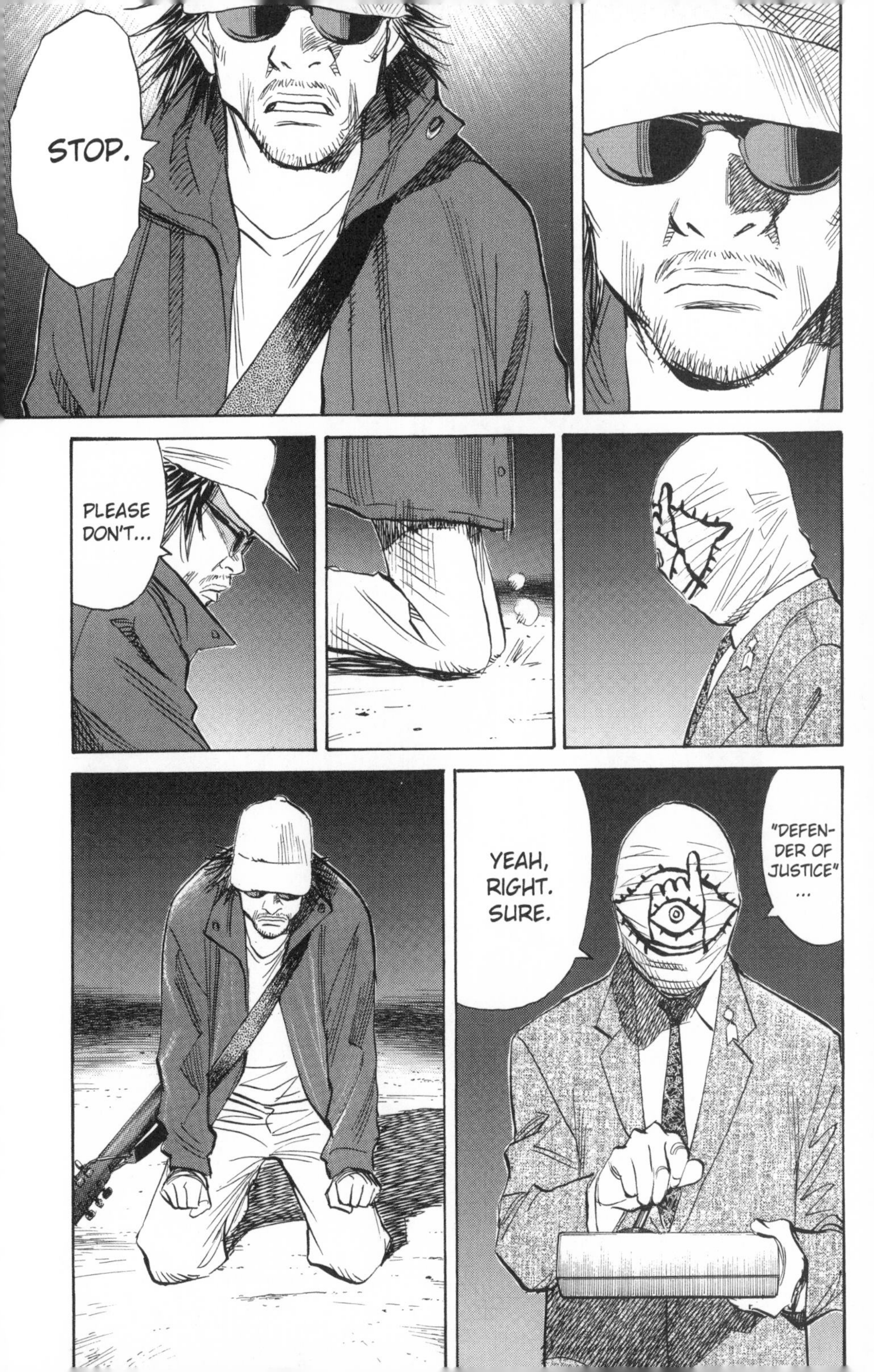
STOP.
PLEASE DON'T...
"DEFENDER OF JUSTICE"...
YEAH, RIGHT. SURE.

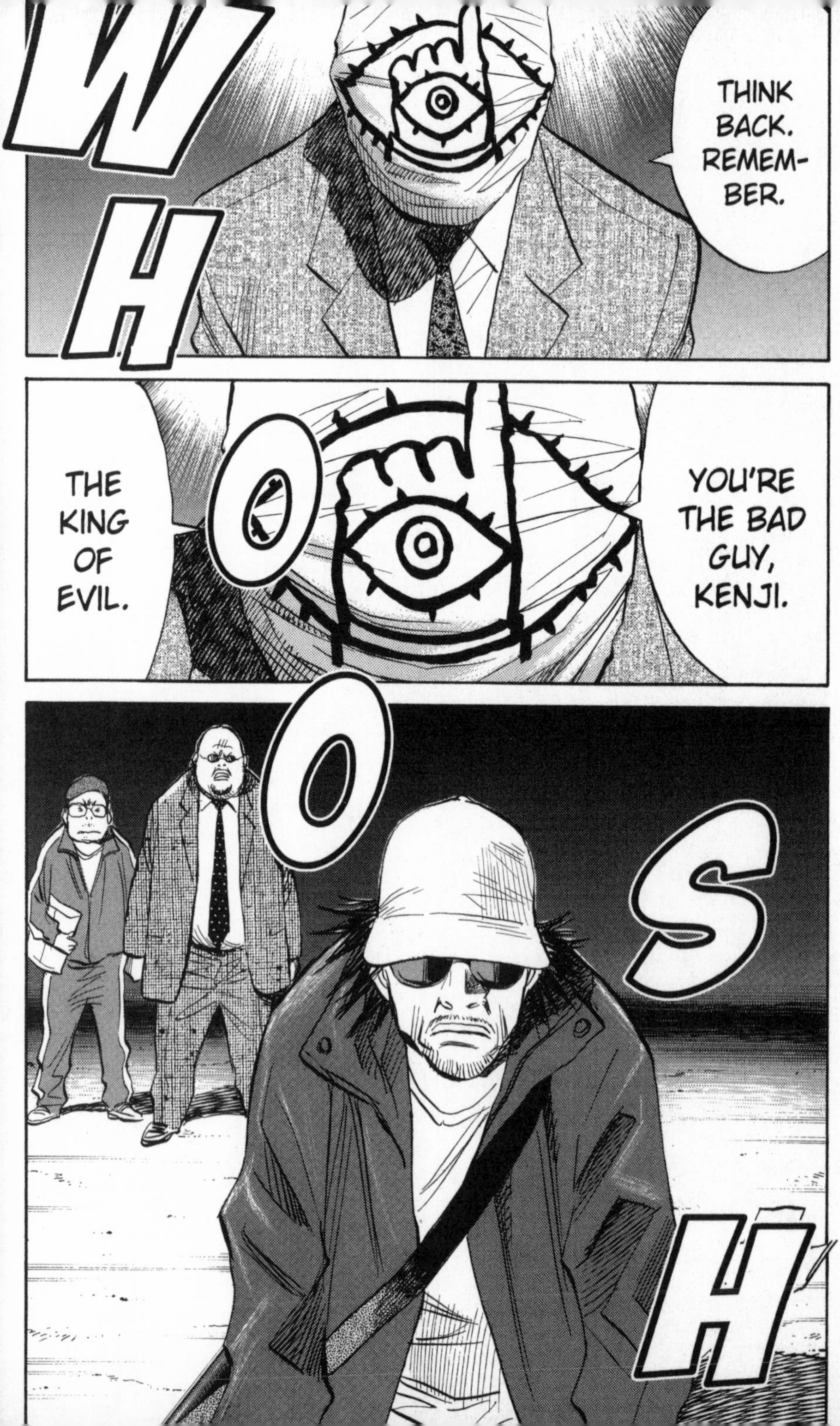
THINK BACK. REMEMBER.
YOU'RE THE BAD GUY, KENJI.
THE KING OF EVIL.
WHOOSH

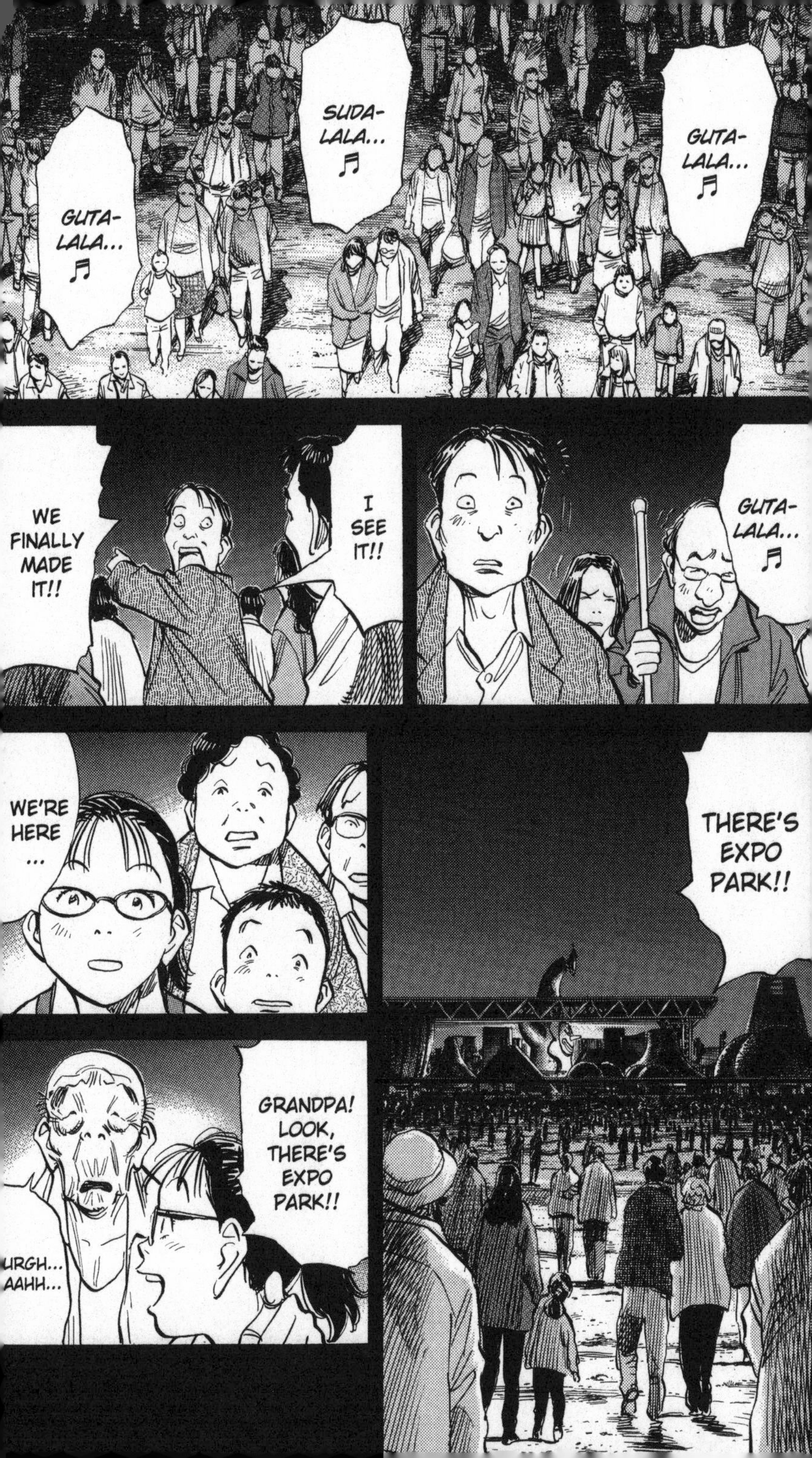
GUTA-LALA... ♬
SUDA-LALA... ♬
GUTA-LALA... ♬
GUTA-LALA... ♬
I SEE IT!!
WE FINALLY MADE IT!!
THERE'S EXPO PARK!!
WE'RE HERE ...
GRANDPA! LOOK, THERE'S EXPO PARK!!
URGH... AAHH...

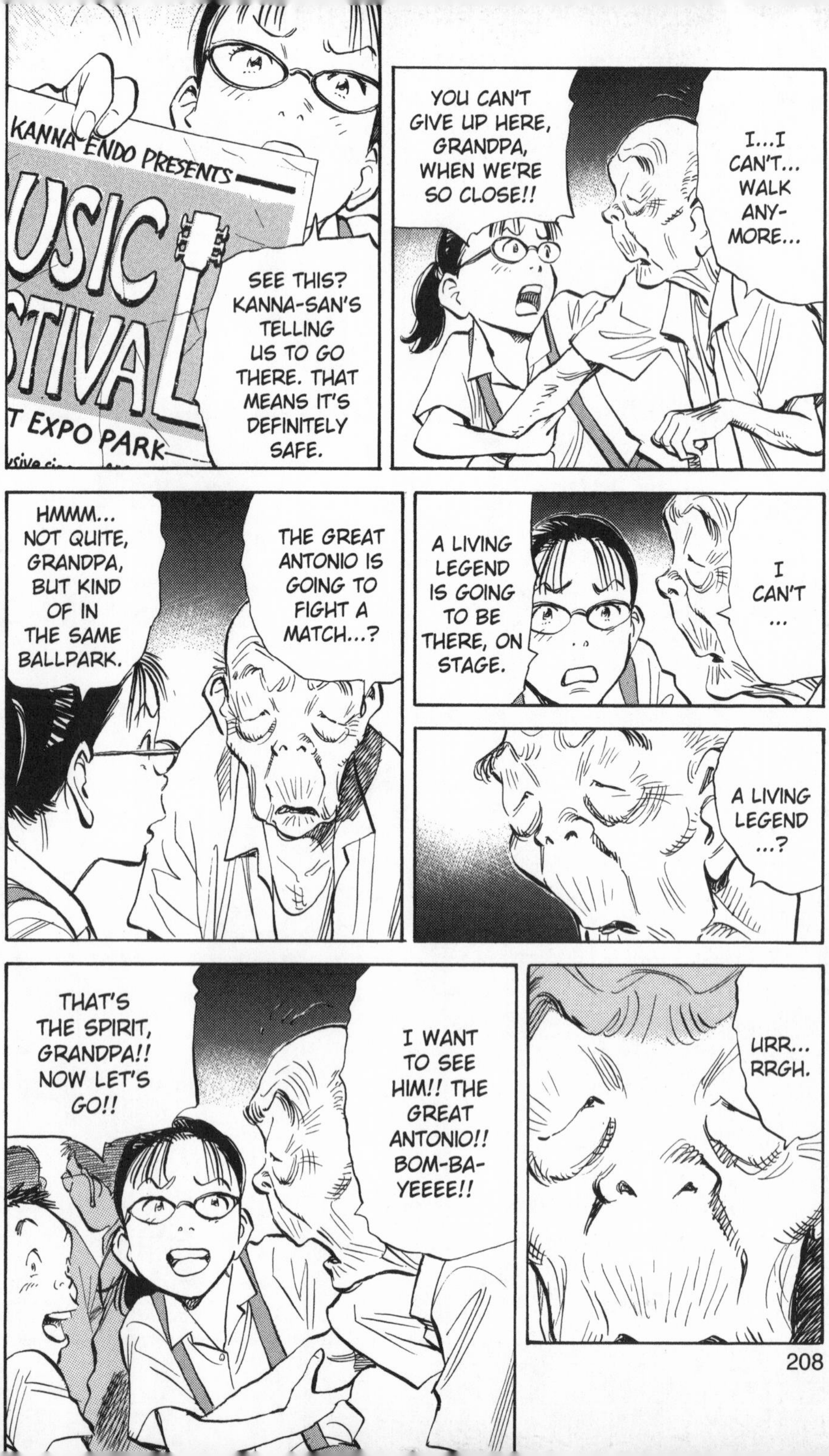
I...I CAN'T... WALK ANY-MORE...
YOU CAN'T GIVE UP HERE, GRANDPA, WHEN WE'RE SO CLOSE!!
KANNA ENDO PRESENTS
USIC
STIVAL
T EXPO PARK
SEE THIS? KANNA-SAN'S TELLING US TO GO THERE. THAT MEANS IT'S DEFINITELY SAFE.
I CAN'T ...
A LIVING LEGEND IS GOING TO BE THERE, ON STAGE.
A LIVING LEGEND ...?
THE GREAT ANTONIO IS GOING TO FIGHT A MATCH...?
HMMM... NOT QUITE, GRANDPA, BUT KIND OF IN THE SAME BALLPARK.
URR... RRGH.
I WANT TO SEE HIM!! THE GREAT ANTONIO!! BOM-BA-YEEEE!!
THAT'S THE SPIRIT, GRANDPA!! NOW LET'S GO!!

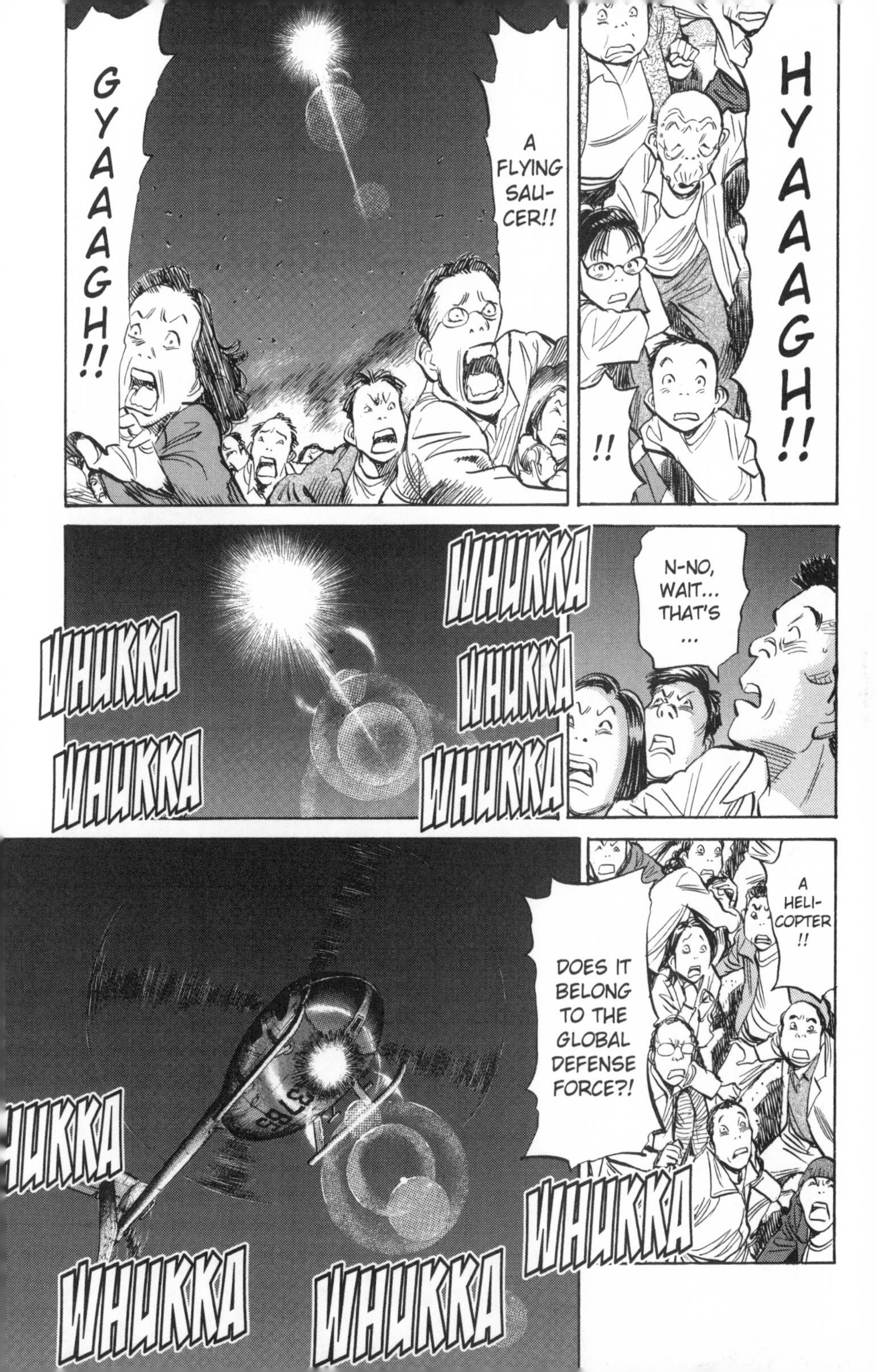
HYAAAAGH!!
!!
A FLYING SAUCER!!
GYAAAAGH!!
N-NO, WAIT... THAT'S ...
WHUKKA
WHUKKA
WHUKKA
WHUKKA
WHUKKA
A HELI-COPTER!!
DOES IT BELONG TO THE GLOBAL DEFENSE FORCE?!
WHUKKA
HUKKA
WHUKKA
WHUKKA

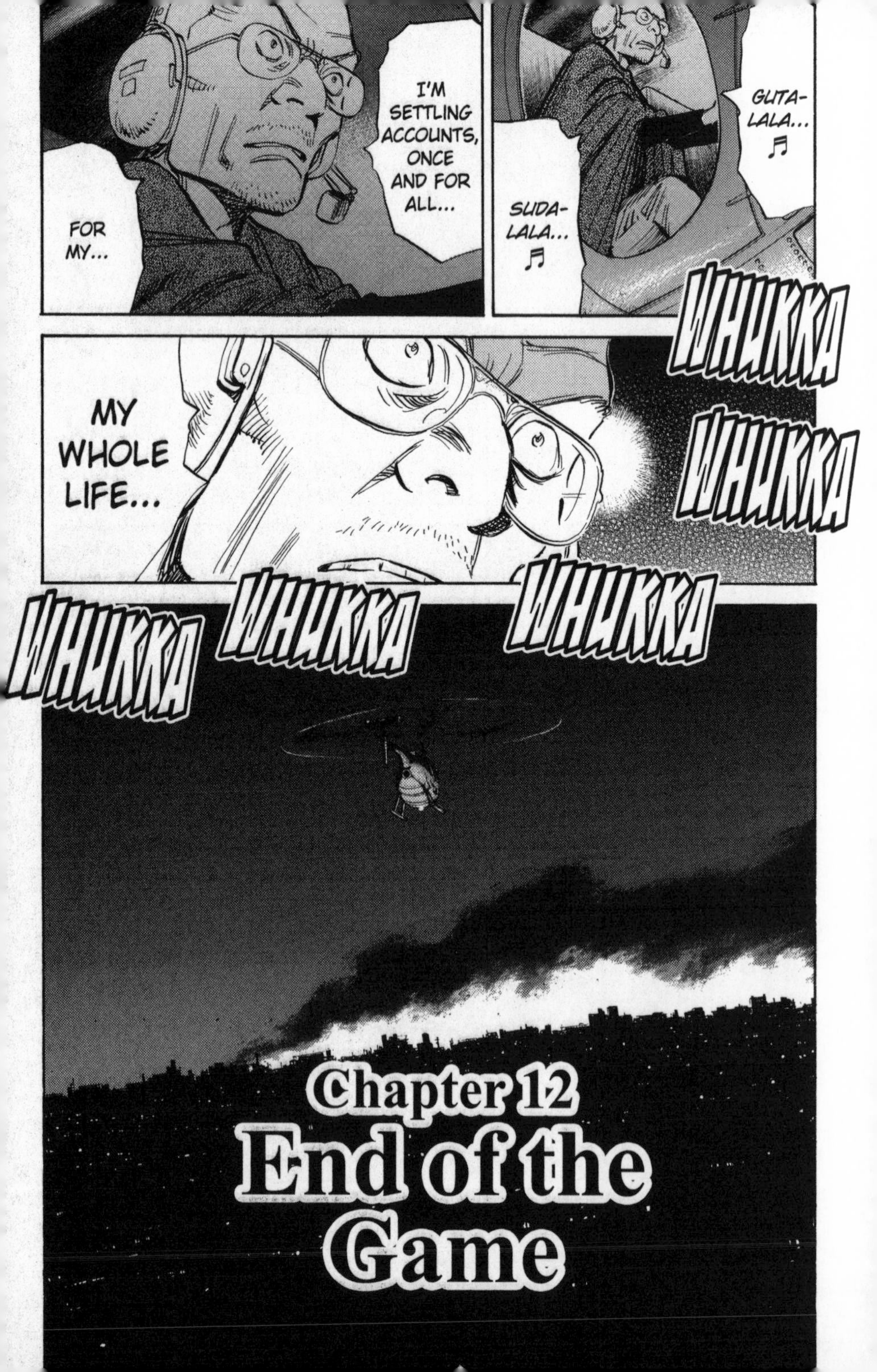
GUTA-LALA... ♬
SUDA-LALA... ♬
I'M SETTLING ACCOUNTS, ONCE AND FOR ALL...
FOR MY...
WHUKKA
WHUKKA
MY WHOLE LIFE...
WHUKKA
WHUKKA
WHUKKA

Chapter 12
End of the Game

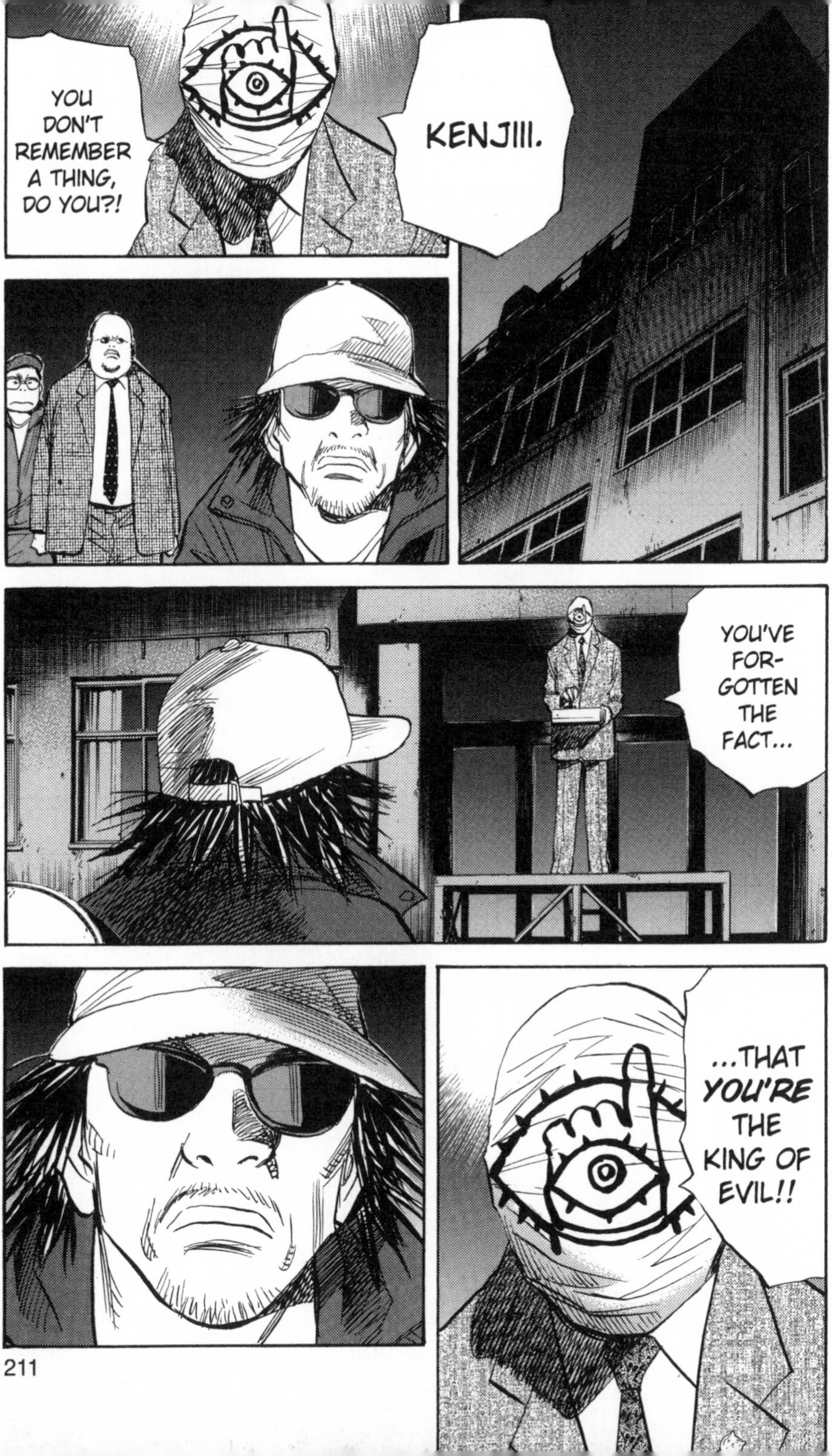
KENJIII.
YOU DON'T REMEMBER A THING, DO YOU?!
YOU'VE FOR-GOTTEN THE FACT...
...THAT *YOU'RE* THE KING OF EVIL!!

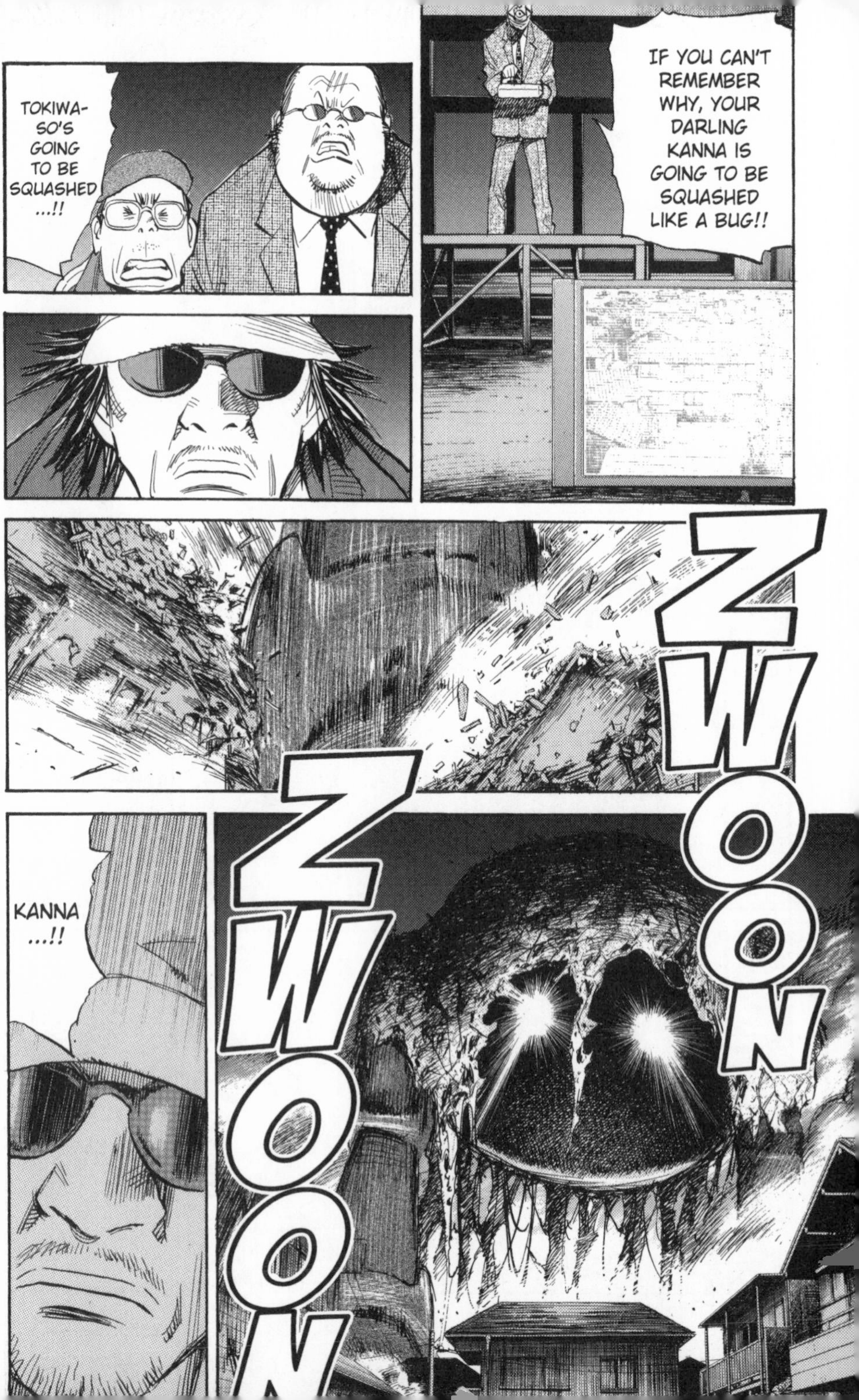
IF YOU CAN'T REMEMBER WHY, YOUR DARLING KANNA IS GOING TO BE SQUASHED LIKE A BUG!!
TOKIWA-SO'S GOING TO BE SQUASHED ...!!
ZWOOON
ZWOOON
KANNA ...!!

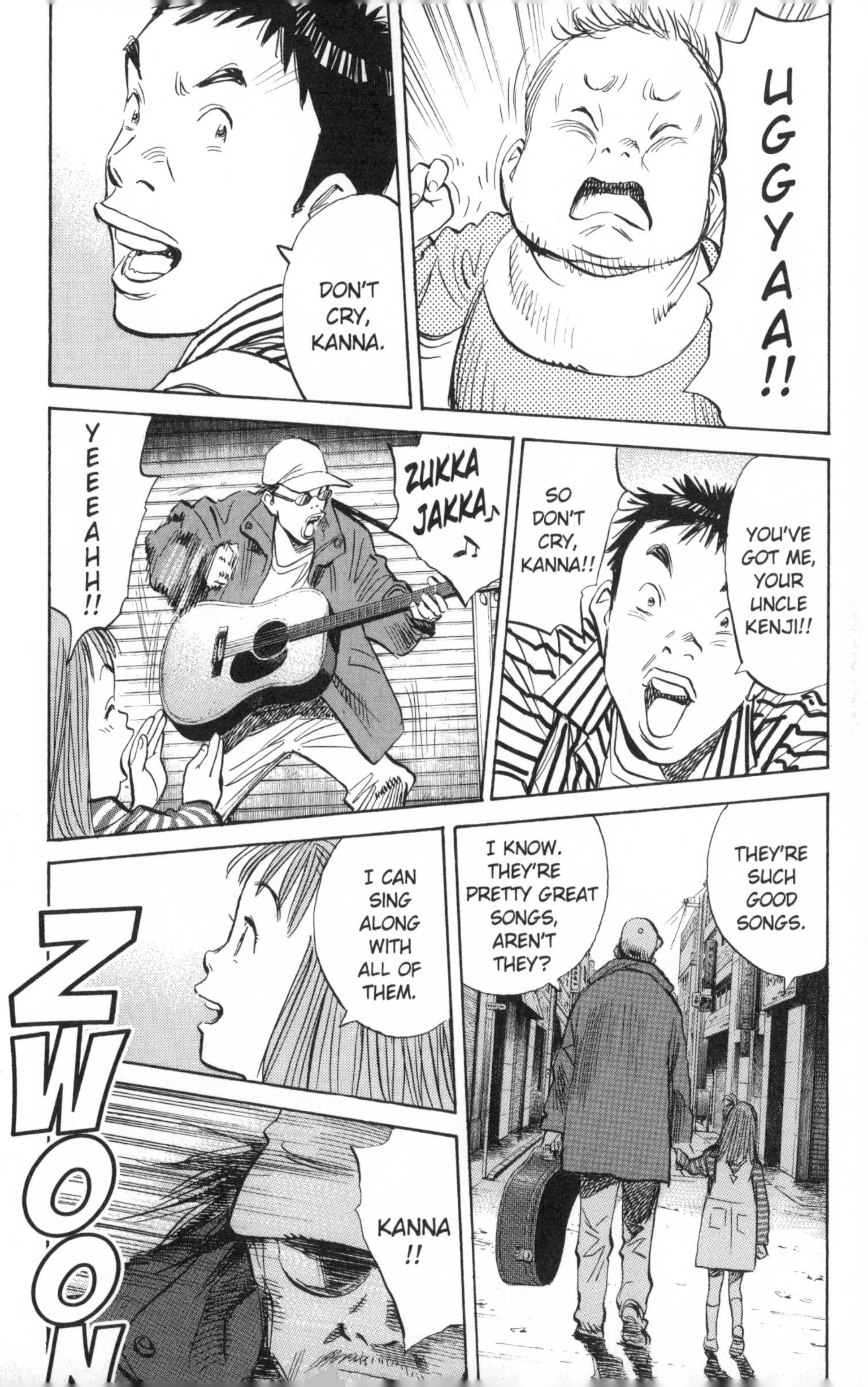
UGGYAA!!
DON'T CRY, KANNA.
YOU'VE GOT ME, YOUR UNCLE KENJI!!
SO DON'T CRY, KANNA!!
ZUKKA JAKKA♪ ♪
YEEEEAHH!!
THEY'RE SUCH GOOD SONGS.
I KNOW. THEY'RE PRETTY GREAT SONGS, AREN'T THEY?
I CAN SING ALONG WITH ALL OF THEM.
KANNA!!
ZWOOON

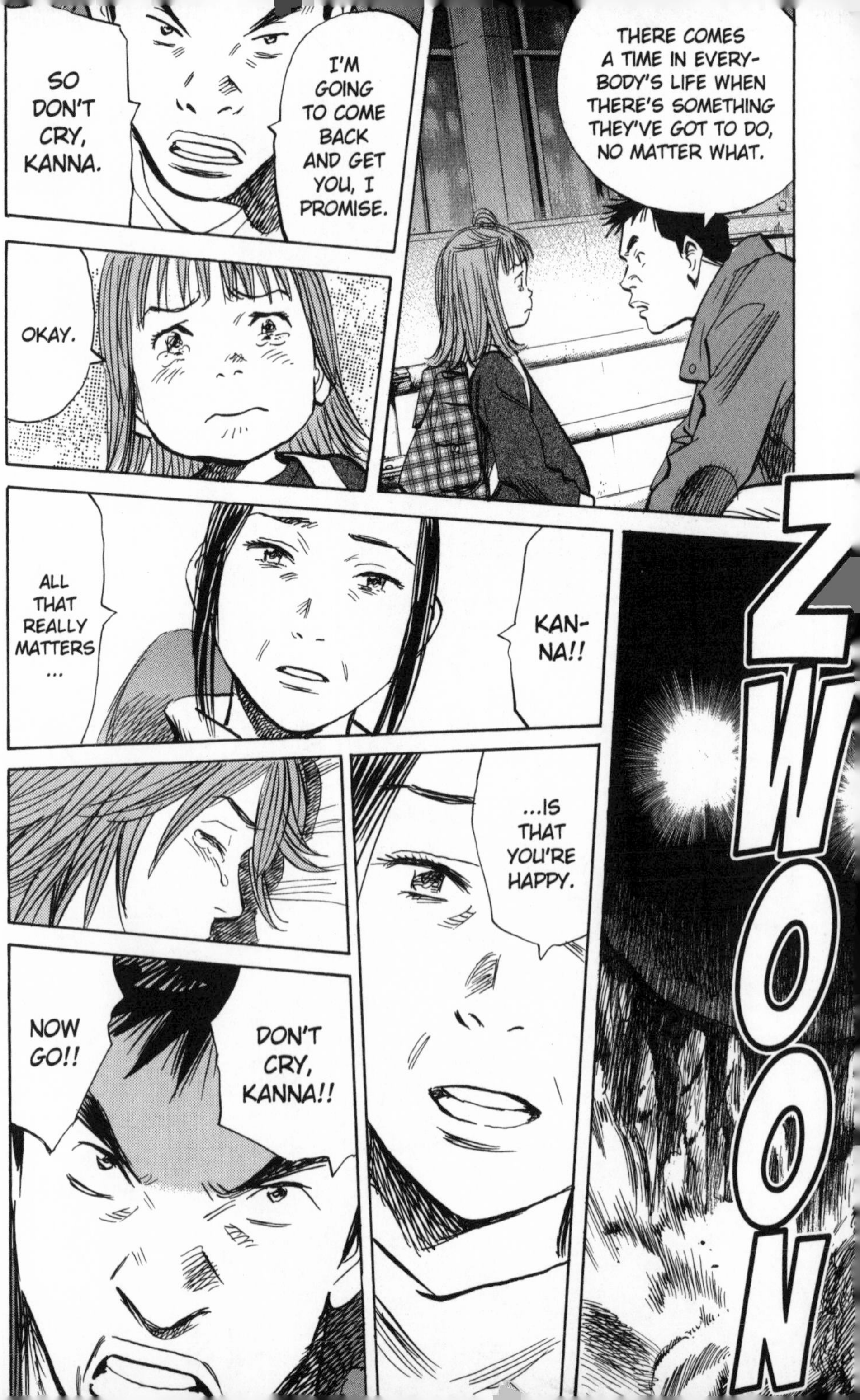
THERE COMES A TIME IN EVERYBODY'S LIFE WHEN THERE'S SOMETHING THEY'VE GOT TO DO, NO MATTER WHAT.
I'M GOING TO COME BACK AND GET YOU, I PROMISE.
SO DON'T CRY, KANNA.
OKAY.
ZWOOON
KAN-NA!!
ALL THAT REALLY MATTERS...
...IS THAT YOU'RE HAPPY.
DON'T CRY, KANNA!!
NOW GO!!

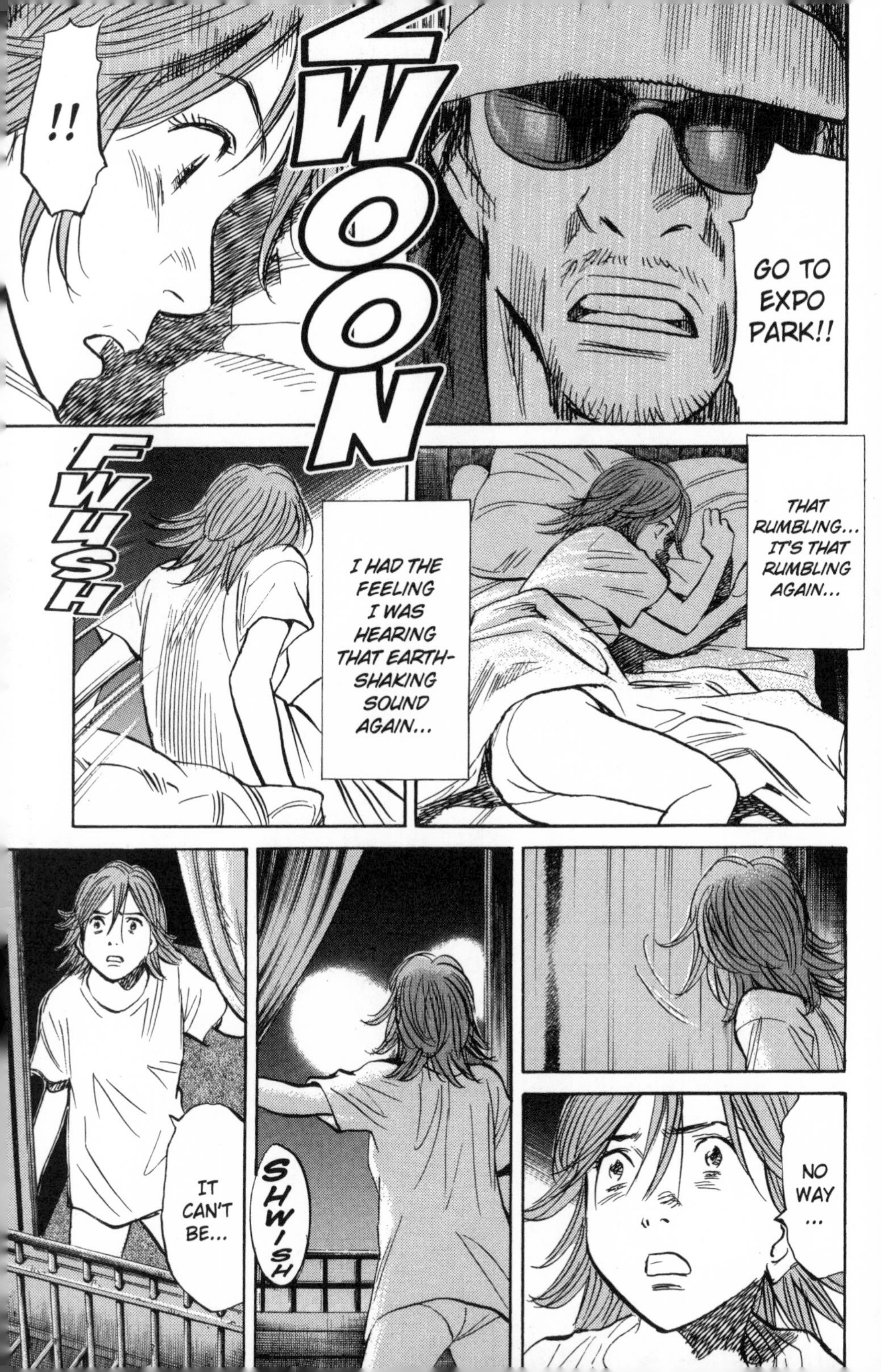
GO TO EXPO PARK!!
ZWOON
!!
THAT RUMBLING... IT'S THAT RUMBLING AGAIN...
I HAD THE FEELING I WAS HEARING THAT EARTH-SHAKING SOUND AGAIN...
FWUSH
NO WAY ...
SHWISH
IT CAN'T BE...

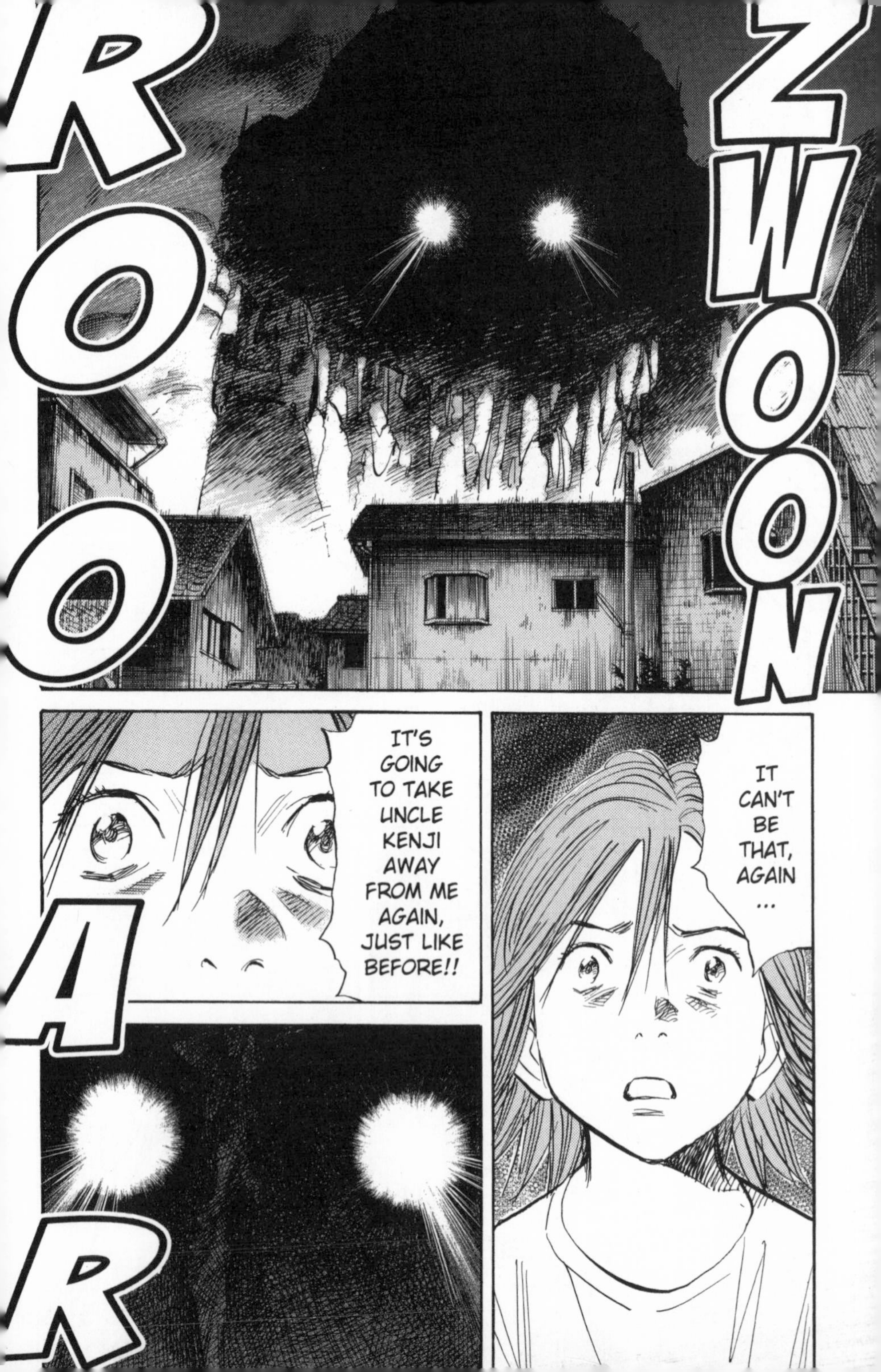
ZWOOON
ROOAR
IT CAN'T BE THAT, AGAIN...
IT'S GOING TO TAKE UNCLE KENJI AWAY FROM ME AGAIN, JUST LIKE BEFORE!!

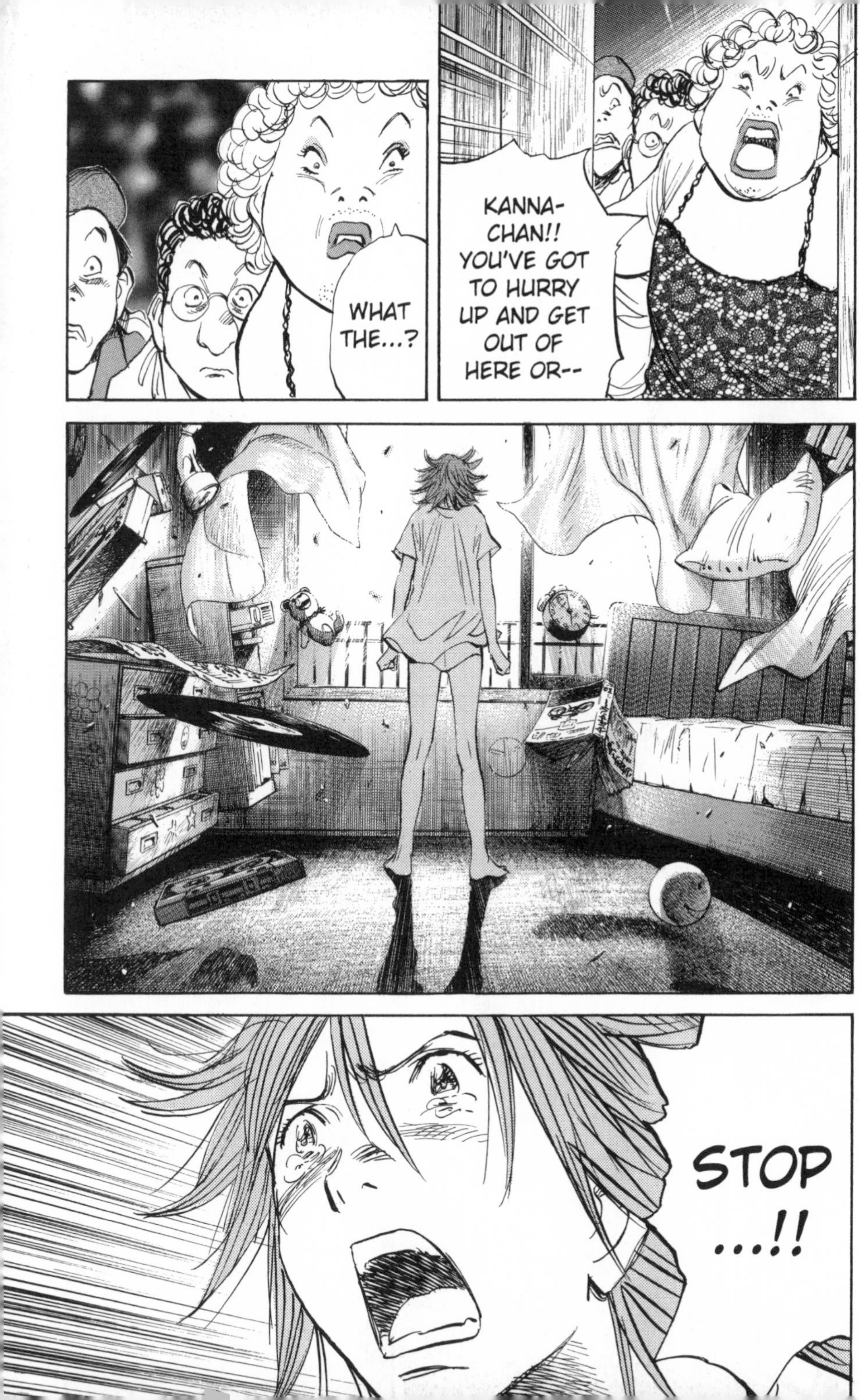
KANNA-CHAN!! YOU'VE GOT TO HURRY UP AND GET OUT OF HERE OR--
WHAT THE...?
STOP ...!!

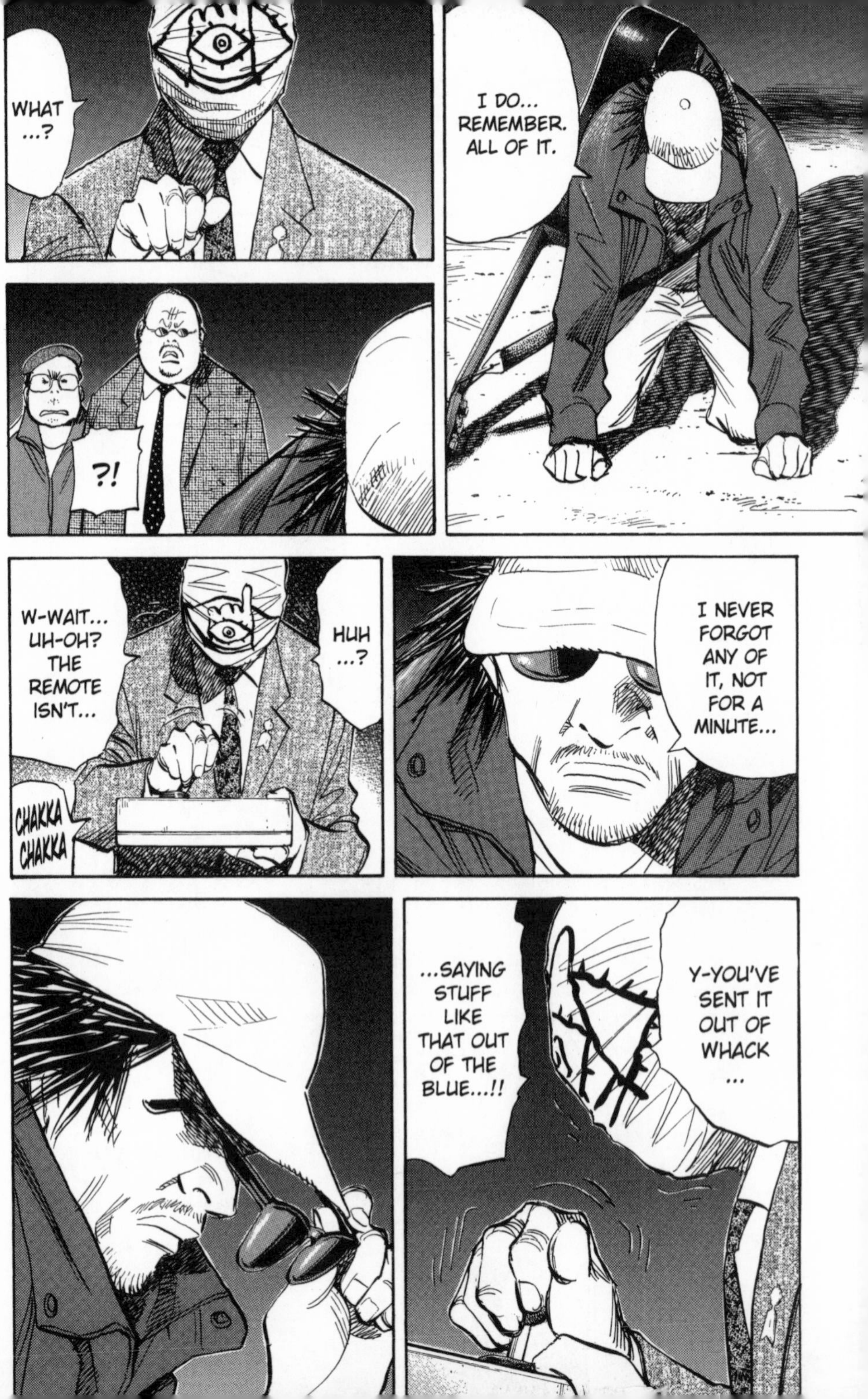
I DO... REMEMBER. ALL OF IT.
WHAT ...?
?!
I NEVER FORGOT ANY OF IT, NOT FOR A MINUTE...
HUH ...?
W-WAIT... UH-OH? THE REMOTE ISN'T...
CHAKKA CHAKKA
Y-YOU'VE SENT IT OUT OF WHACK ...
...SAYING STUFF LIKE THAT OUT OF THE BLUE...!!

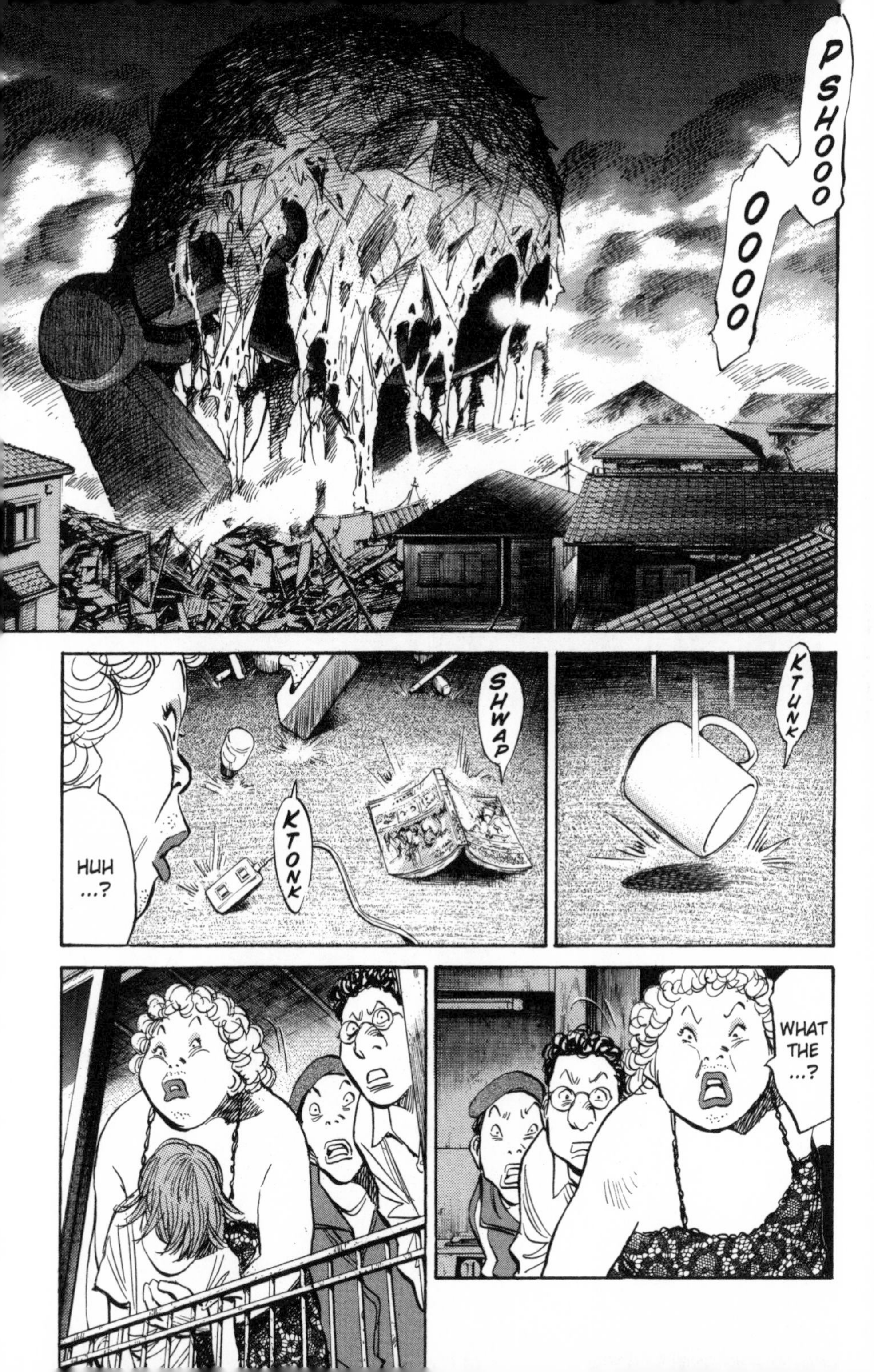
PSHOOOO
OOOOO
KTUNK
SHWAP
KTONK
HUH ...?
WHAT THE ...?

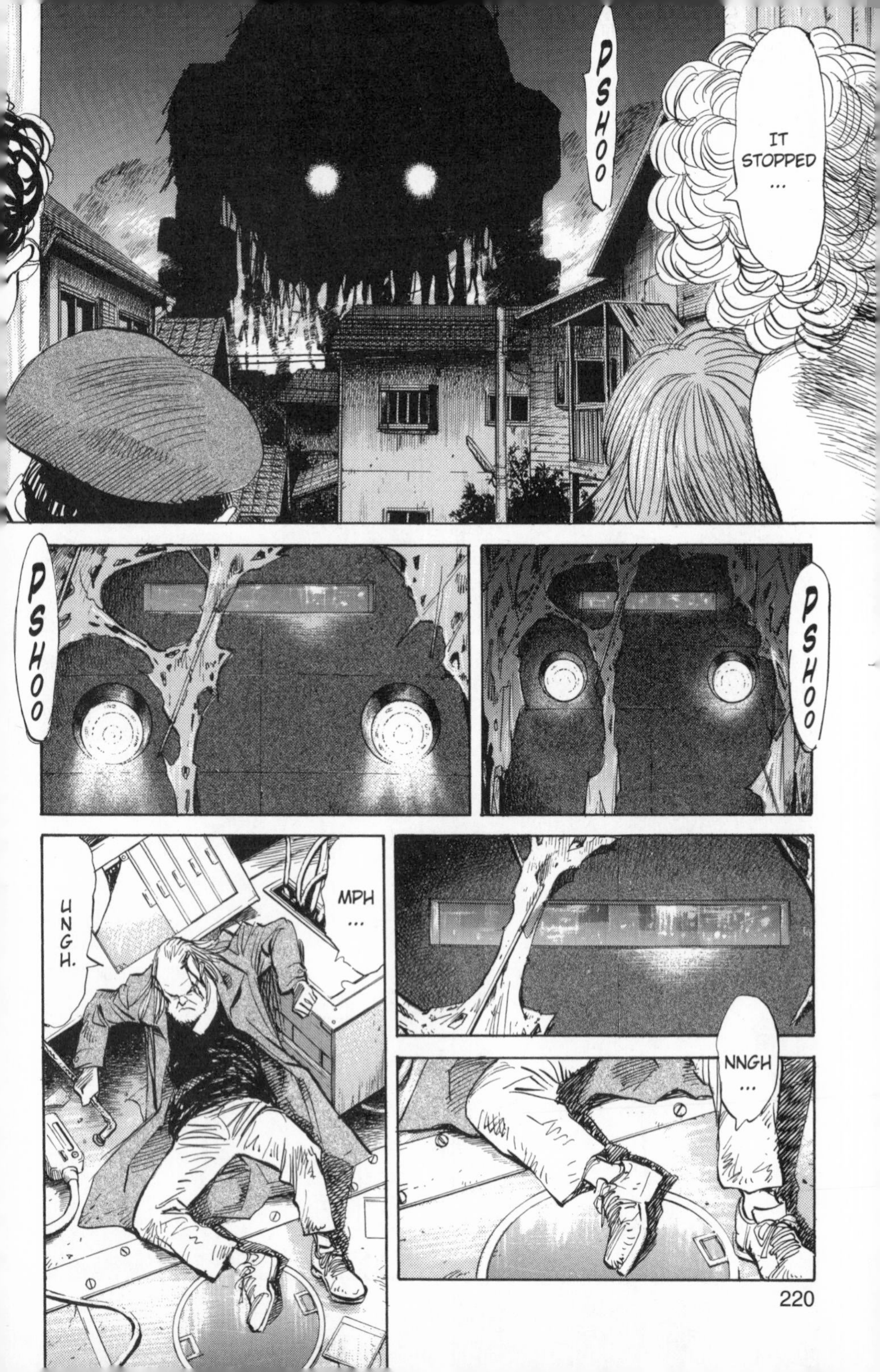
IT STOPPED ...
PSHOO
PSHOO
PSHOO
NNGH ...
MPH ...
UNGH.

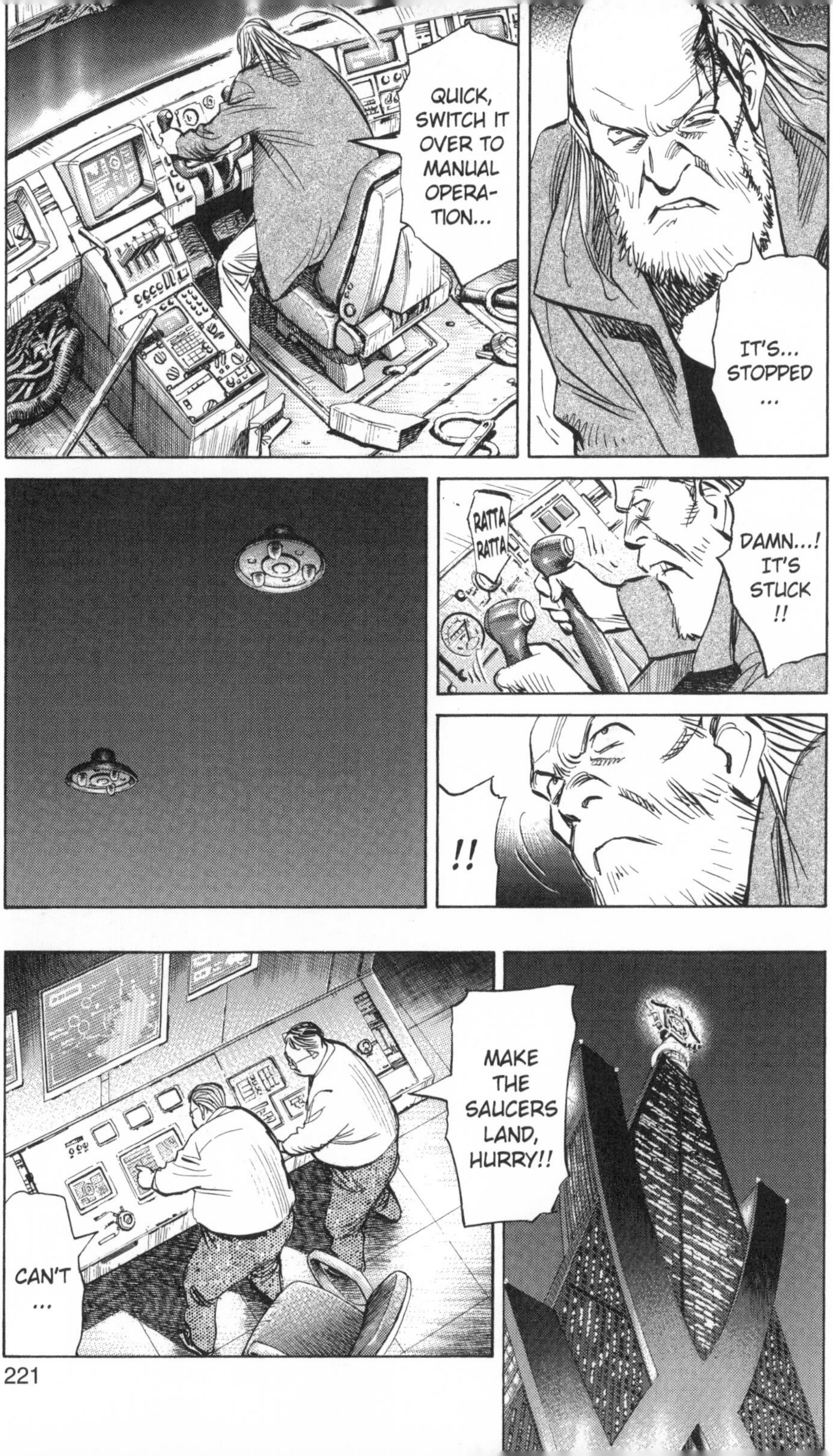
IT'S... STOPPED ...
QUICK, SWITCH IT OVER TO MANUAL OPERA-TION...
RATTA RATTA
DAMN...! IT'S STUCK !!
!!
MAKE THE SAUCERS LAND, HURRY!!
CAN'T ...

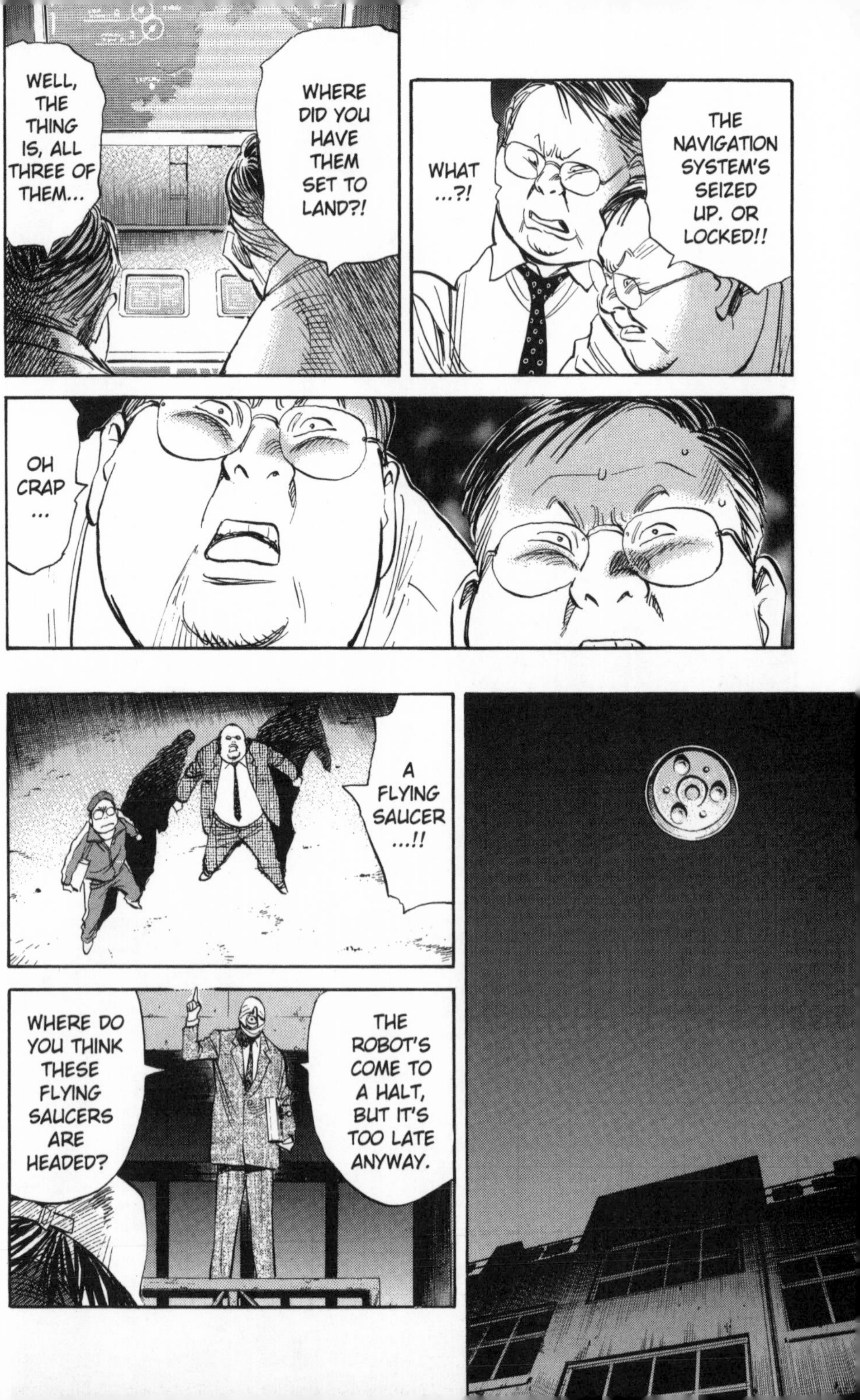
THE NAVIGATION SYSTEM'S SEIZED UP. OR LOCKED!!
WHAT ...?!
WHERE DID YOU HAVE THEM SET TO LAND?!
WELL, THE THING IS, ALL THREE OF THEM...
OH CRAP ...
A FLYING SAUCER ...!!
THE ROBOT'S COME TO A HALT, BUT IT'S TOO LATE ANYWAY.
WHERE DO YOU THINK THESE FLYING SAUCERS ARE HEADED?

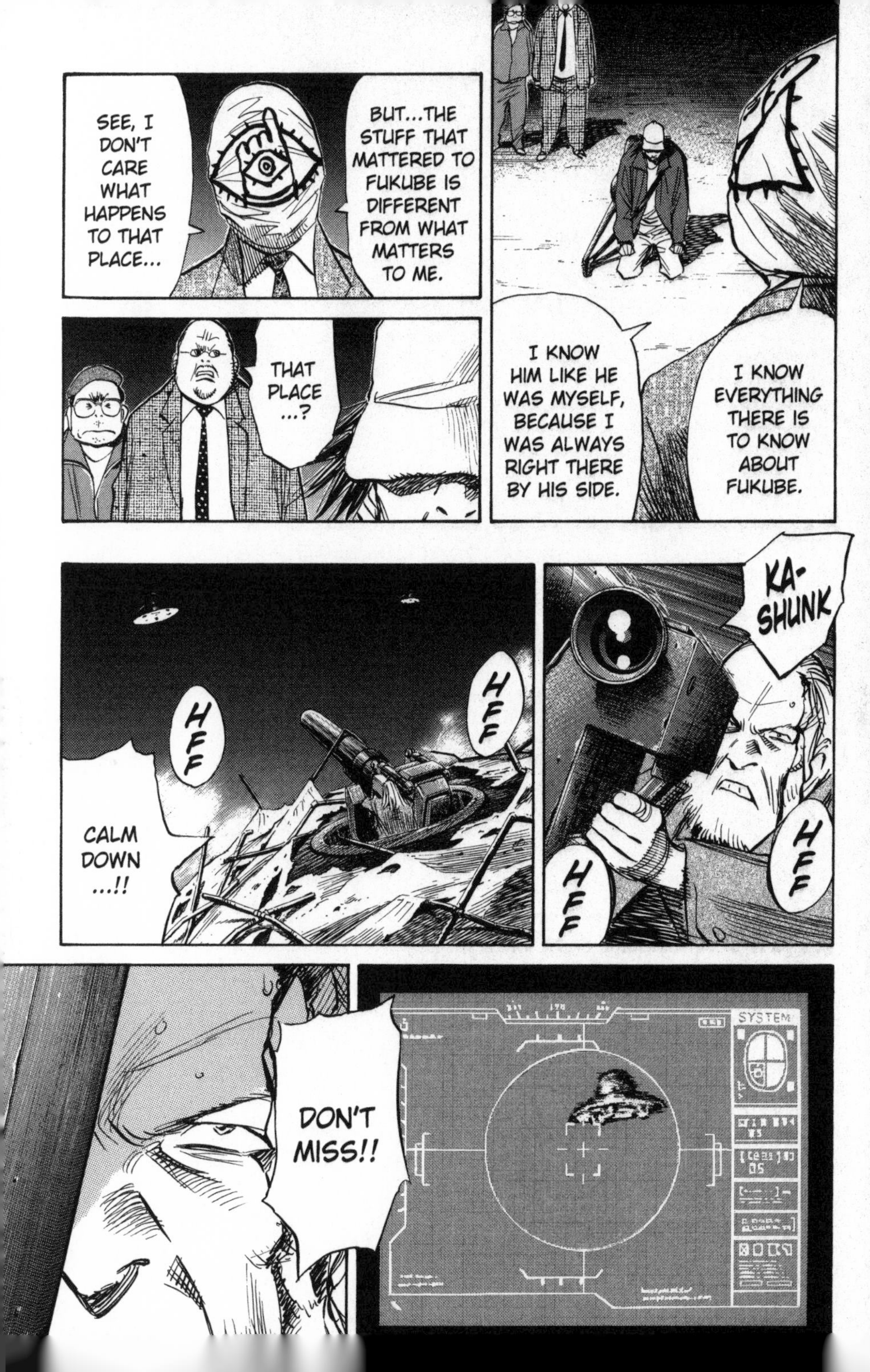
I KNOW EVERYTHING THERE IS TO KNOW ABOUT FUKUBE.
I KNOW HIM LIKE HE WAS MYSELF, BECAUSE I WAS ALWAYS RIGHT THERE BY HIS SIDE.
SEE, I DON'T CARE WHAT HAPPENS TO THAT PLACE...
BUT...THE STUFF THAT MATTERED TO FUKUBE IS DIFFERENT FROM WHAT MATTERS TO ME.
THAT PLACE ...?
KA-SHUNK
HFF
HFF
HFF
HFF
CALM DOWN ...!!
SYSTEM
DON'T MISS!!

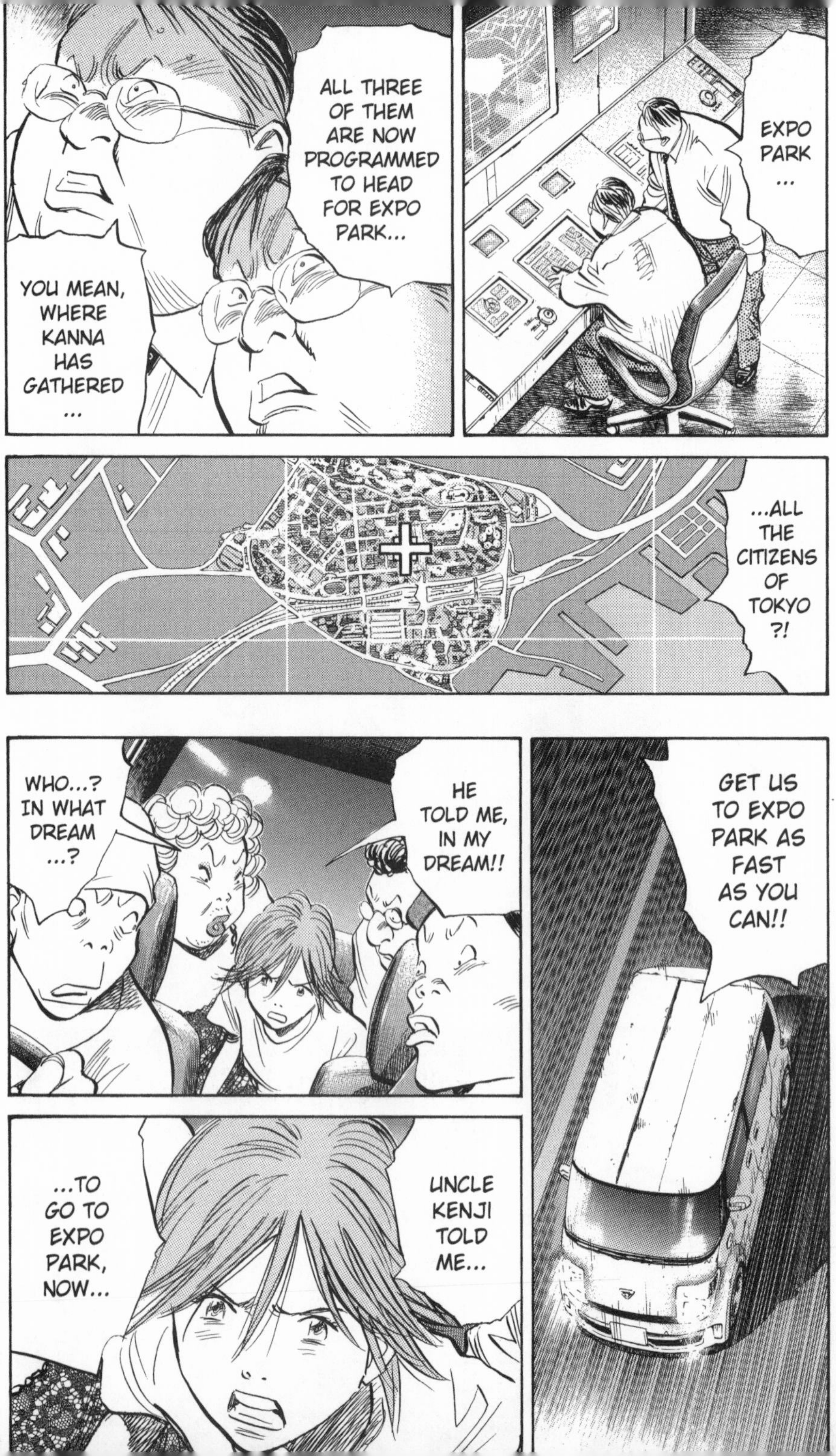
EXPO PARK ...
ALL THREE OF THEM ARE NOW PROGRAMMED TO HEAD FOR EXPO PARK...
YOU MEAN, WHERE KANNA HAS GATHERED ...
...ALL THE CITIZENS OF TOKYO ?!
GET US TO EXPO PARK AS FAST AS YOU CAN!!
HE TOLD ME, IN MY DREAM!!
WHO...? IN WHAT DREAM ...?
UNCLE KENJI TOLD ME...
...TO GO TO EXPO PARK, NOW...

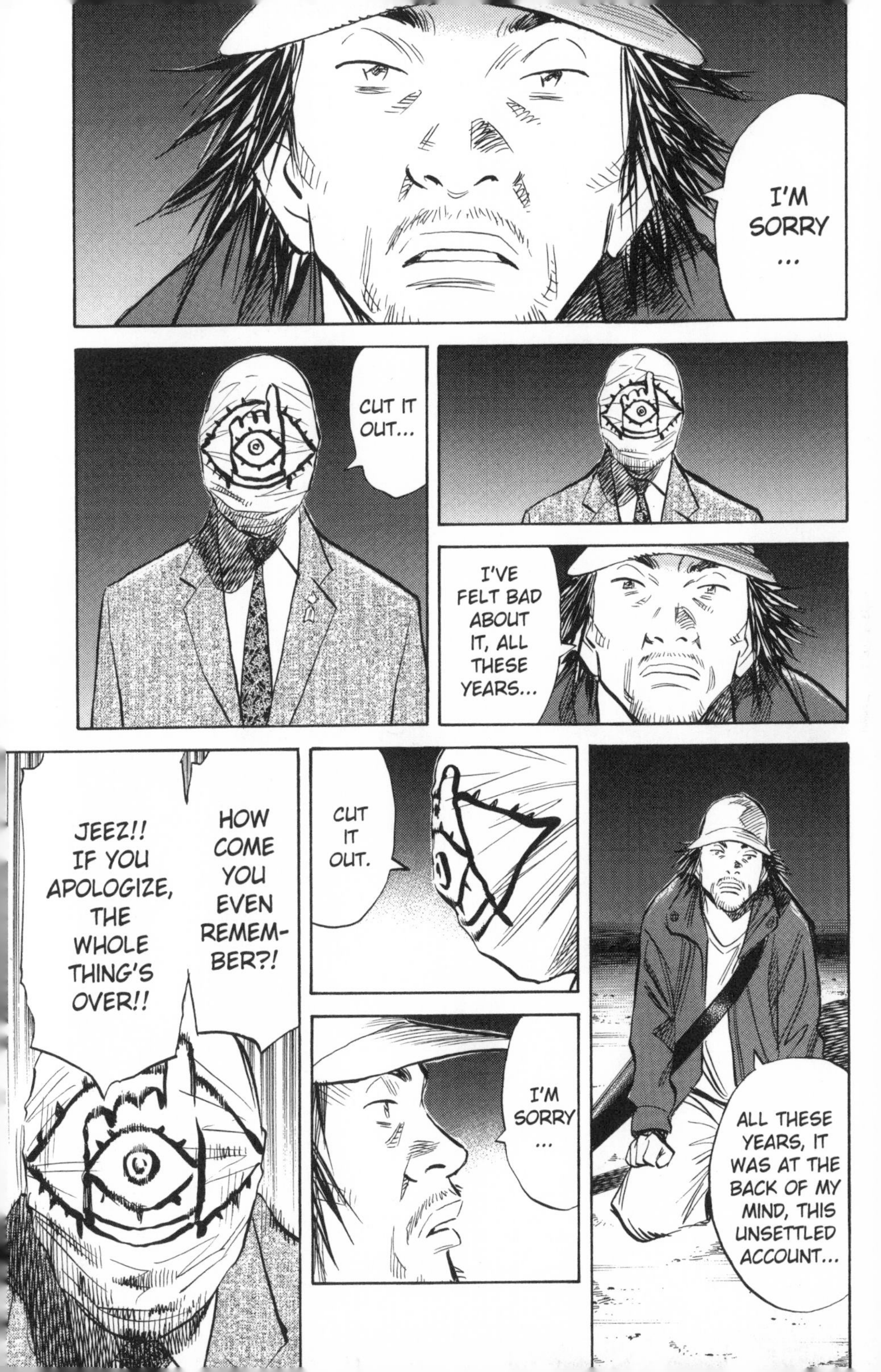
I'M SORRY ...
I'VE FELT BAD ABOUT IT, ALL THESE YEARS...
CUT IT OUT...
ALL THESE YEARS, IT WAS AT THE BACK OF MY MIND, THIS UNSETTLED ACCOUNT...
CUT IT OUT.
I'M SORRY ...
HOW COME YOU EVEN REMEM-BER?!
JEEZ!! IF YOU APOLOGIZE, THE WHOLE THING'S OVER!!

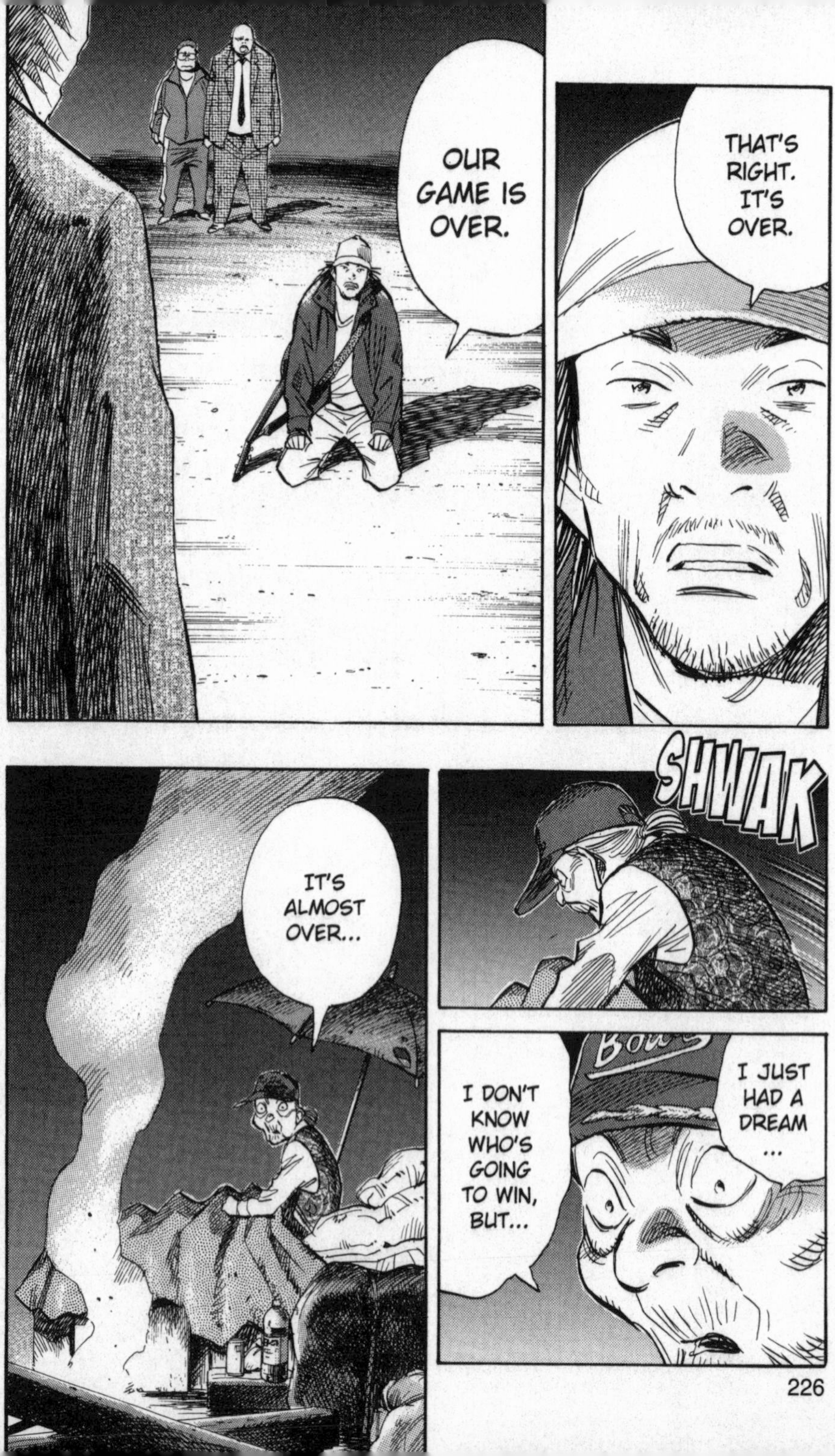
THAT'S RIGHT. IT'S OVER.
OUR GAME IS OVER.
SHWAK
I JUST HAD A DREAM...
I DON'T KNOW WHO'S GOING TO WIN, BUT...
IT'S ALMOST OVER...

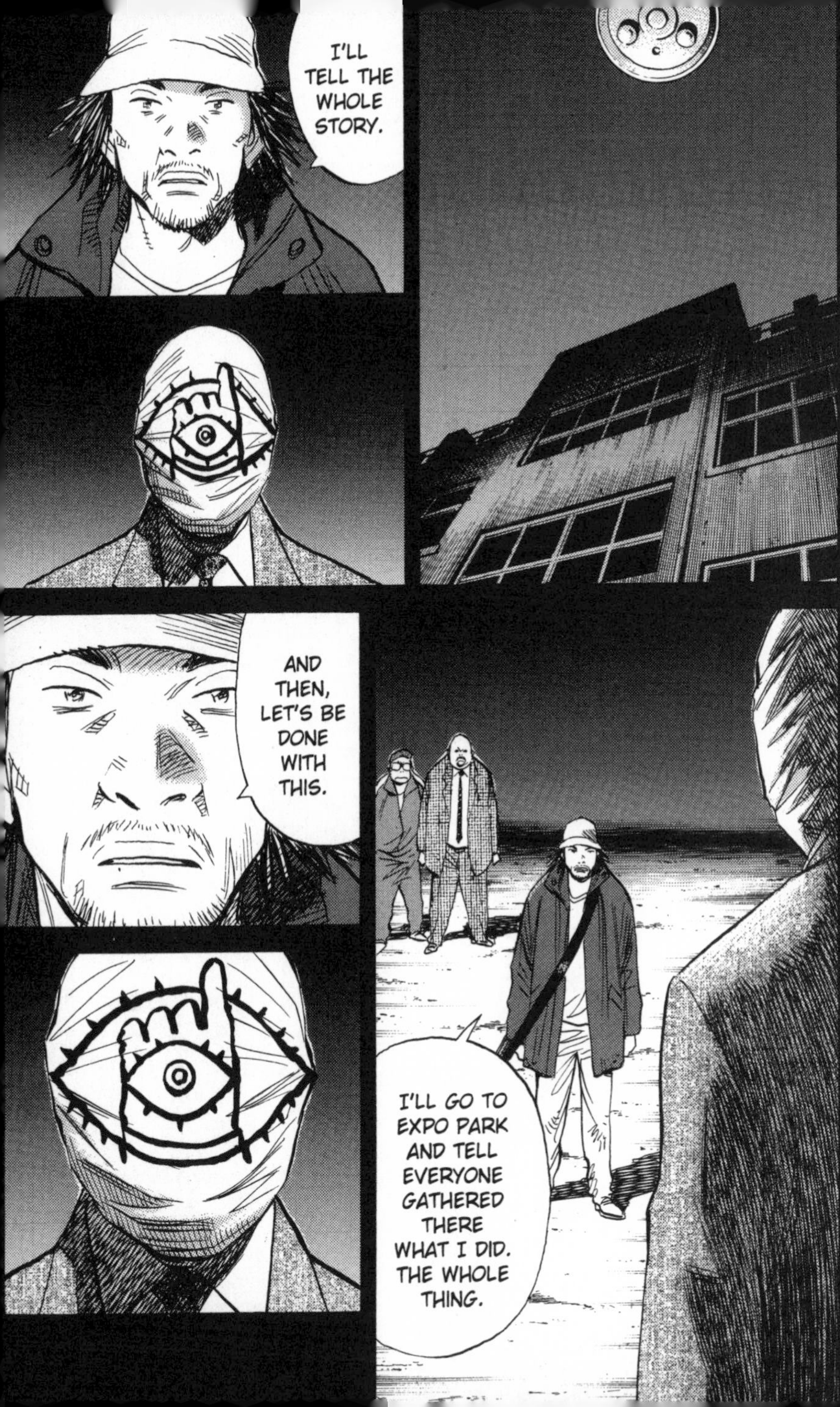
I'LL TELL THE WHOLE STORY.
I'LL GO TO EXPO PARK AND TELL EVERYONE GATHERED THERE WHAT I DID. THE WHOLE THING.
AND THEN, LET'S BE DONE WITH THIS.

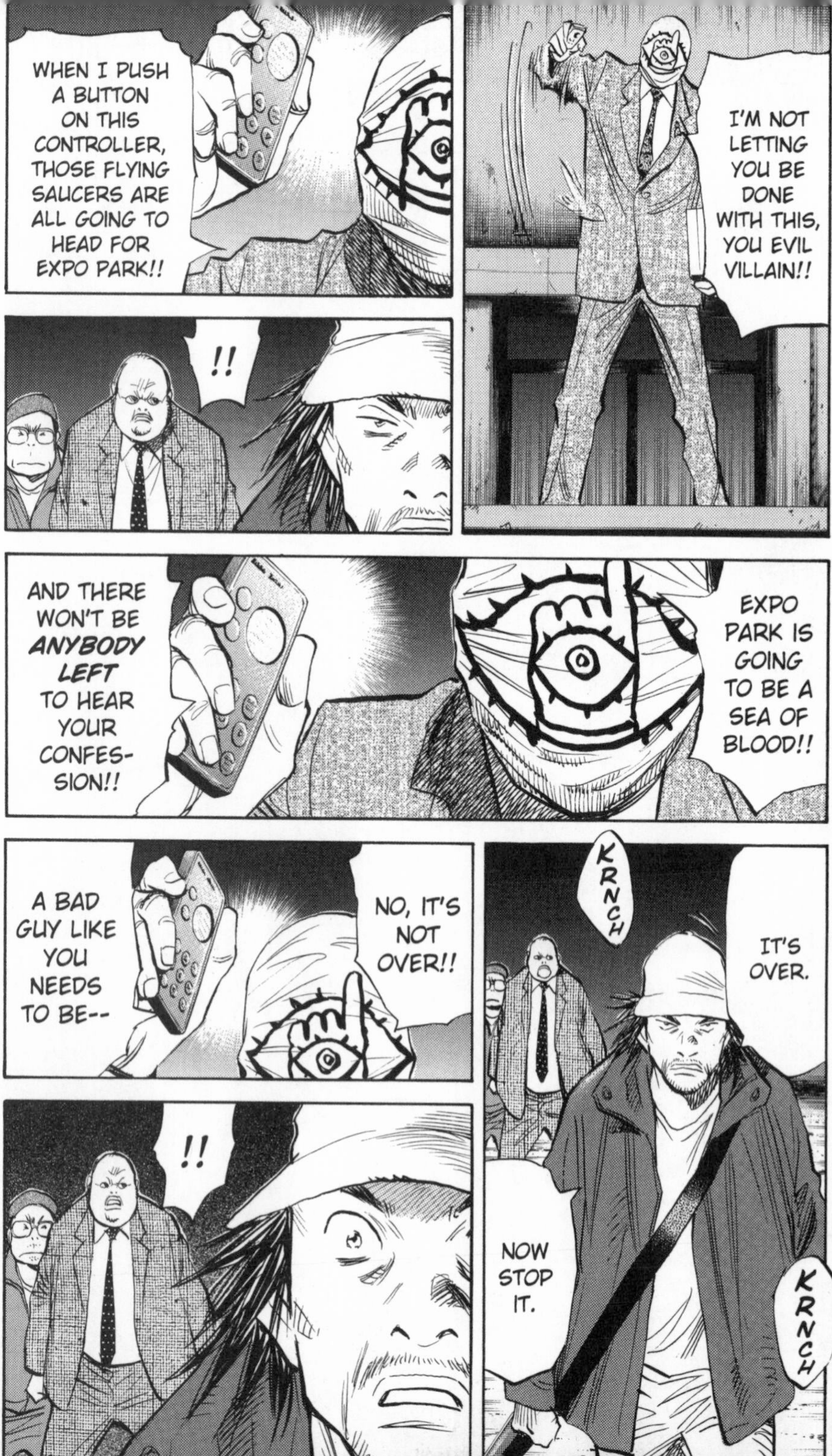
I'M NOT LETTING YOU BE DONE WITH THIS, YOU EVIL VILLAIN!!
WHEN I PUSH A BUTTON ON THIS CONTROLLER, THOSE FLYING SAUCERS ARE ALL GOING TO HEAD FOR EXPO PARK!!
!!
EXPO PARK IS GOING TO BE A SEA OF BLOOD!!
AND THERE WON'T BE ANYBODY LEFT TO HEAR YOUR CONFESSION!!
KRNCH
IT'S OVER.
KRNCH
NOW STOP IT.
NO, IT'S NOT OVER!!
A BAD GUY LIKE YOU NEEDS TO BE--
!!

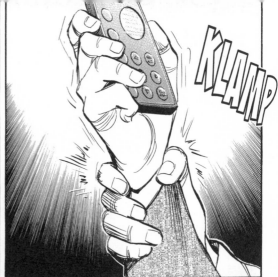

Chapter 13
Settling
Accounts

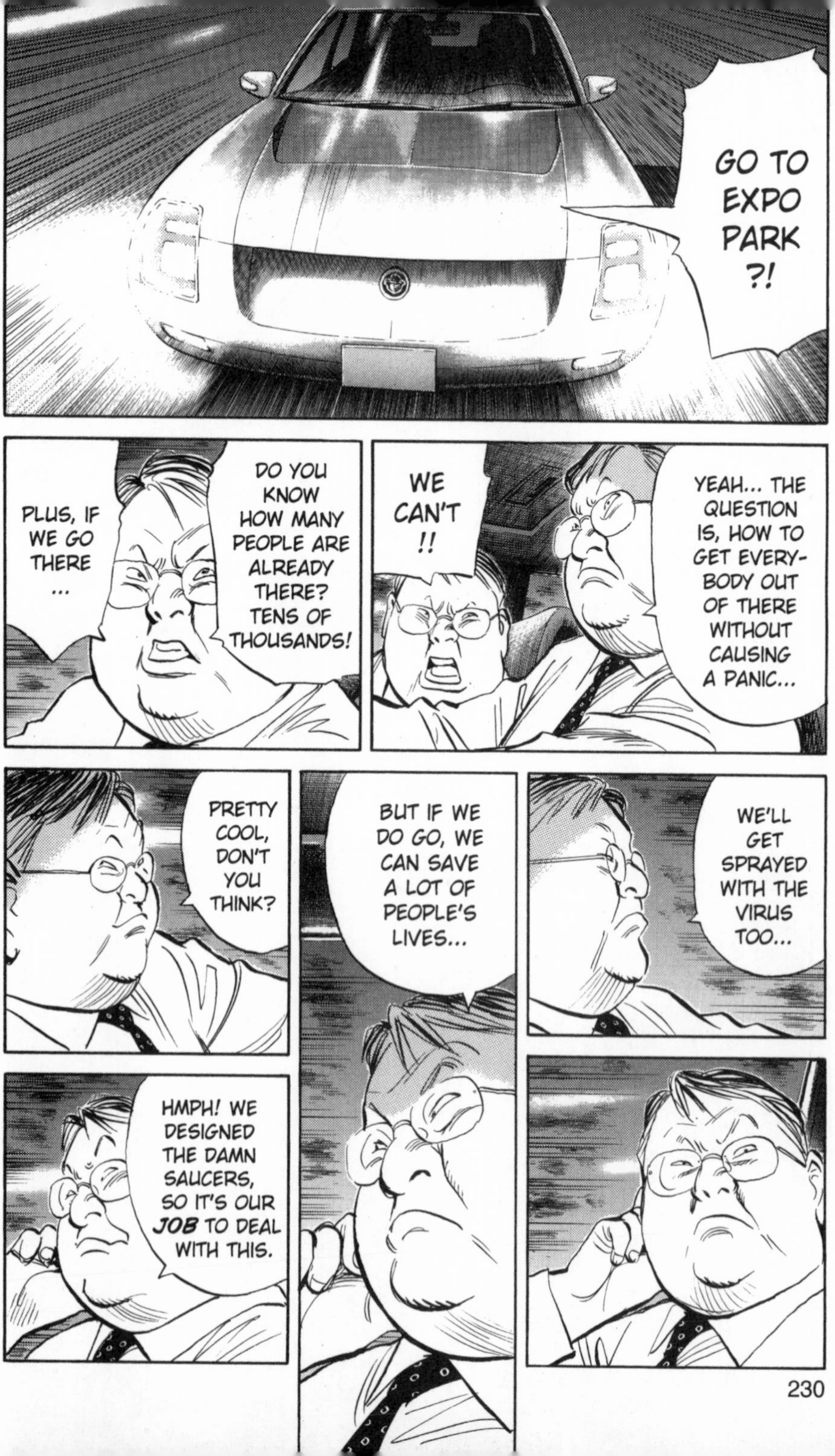
GO TO EXPO PARK ?!
YEAH... THE QUESTION IS, HOW TO GET EVERY-BODY OUT OF THERE WITHOUT CAUSING A PANIC...
WE CAN'T !!
DO YOU KNOW HOW MANY PEOPLE ARE ALREADY THERE? TENS OF THOUSANDS!
PLUS, IF WE GO THERE ...
WE'LL GET SPRAYED WITH THE VIRUS TOO...
BUT IF WE DO GO, WE CAN SAVE A LOT OF PEOPLE'S LIVES...
PRETTY COOL, DON'T YOU THINK?
HMPH! WE DESIGNED THE DAMN SAUCERS, SO IT'S OUR *JOB* TO DEAL WITH THIS.

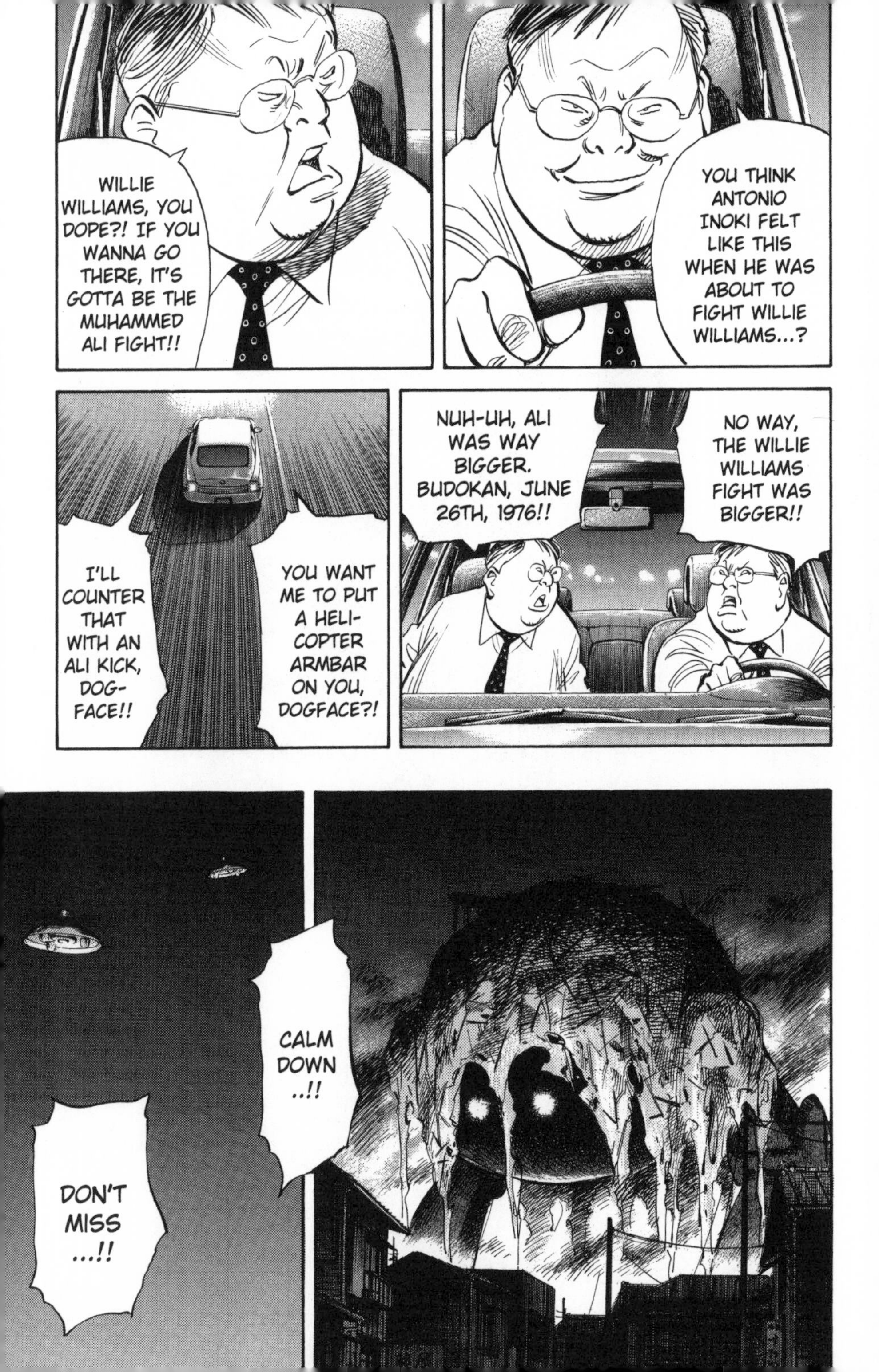
YOU THINK ANTONIO INOKI FELT LIKE THIS WHEN HE WAS ABOUT TO FIGHT WILLIE WILLIAMS...?
WILLIE WILLIAMS, YOU DOPE?! IF YOU WANNA GO THERE, IT'S GOTTA BE THE MUHAMMED ALI FIGHT!!
NO WAY, THE WILLIE WILLIAMS FIGHT WAS BIGGER!!
NUH-UH, ALI WAS WAY BIGGER. BUDOKAN, JUNE 26TH, 1976!!
YOU WANT ME TO PUT A HELI-COPTER ARMBAR ON YOU, DOGFACE?!
I'LL COUNTER THAT WITH AN ALI KICK, DOG-FACE!!
CALM DOWN ..!!
DON'T MISS ...!!

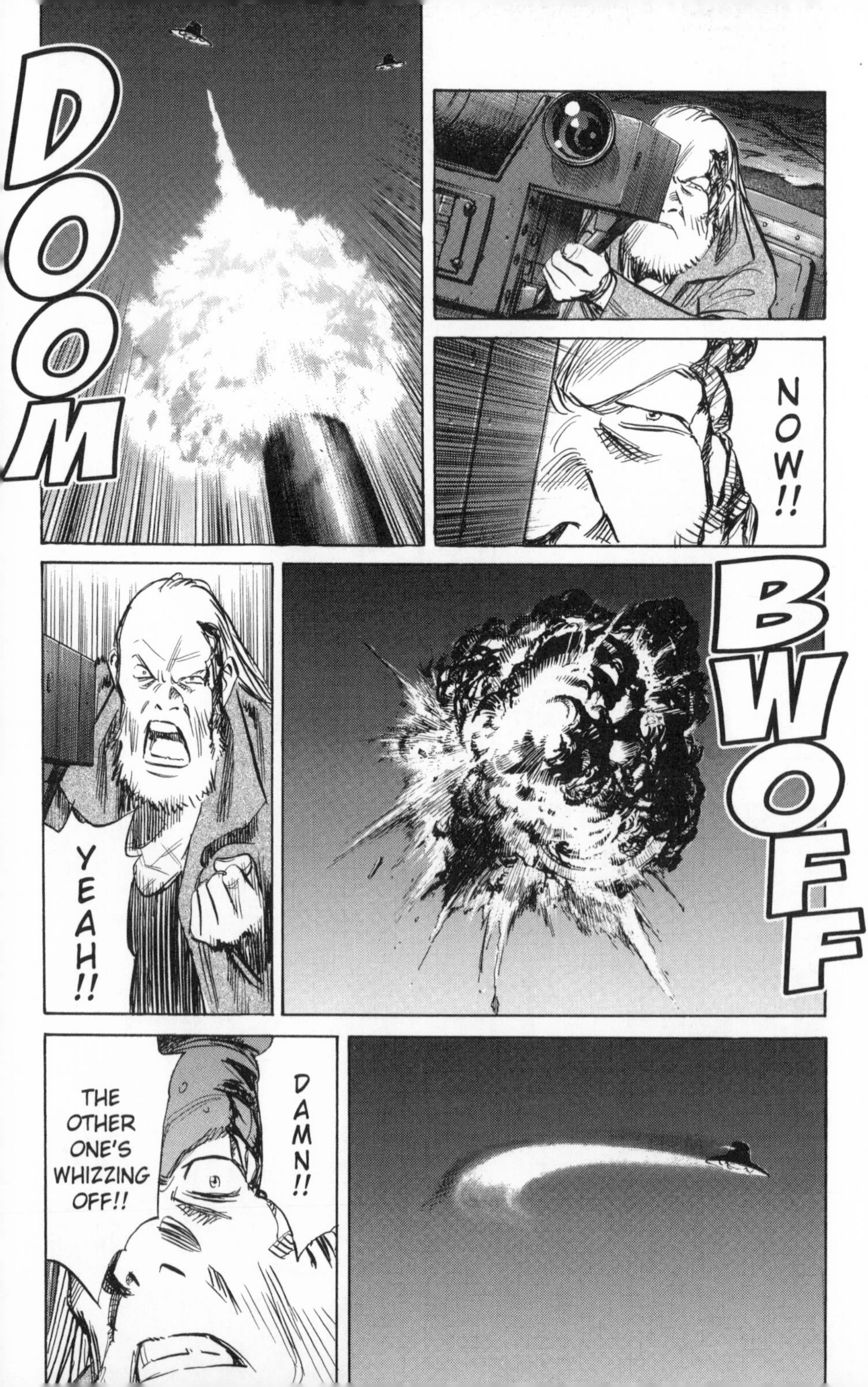
NOW!!
DOOM
BWOFF
YEAH!!
DAMN!!
THE OTHER ONE'S WHIZZING OFF!!

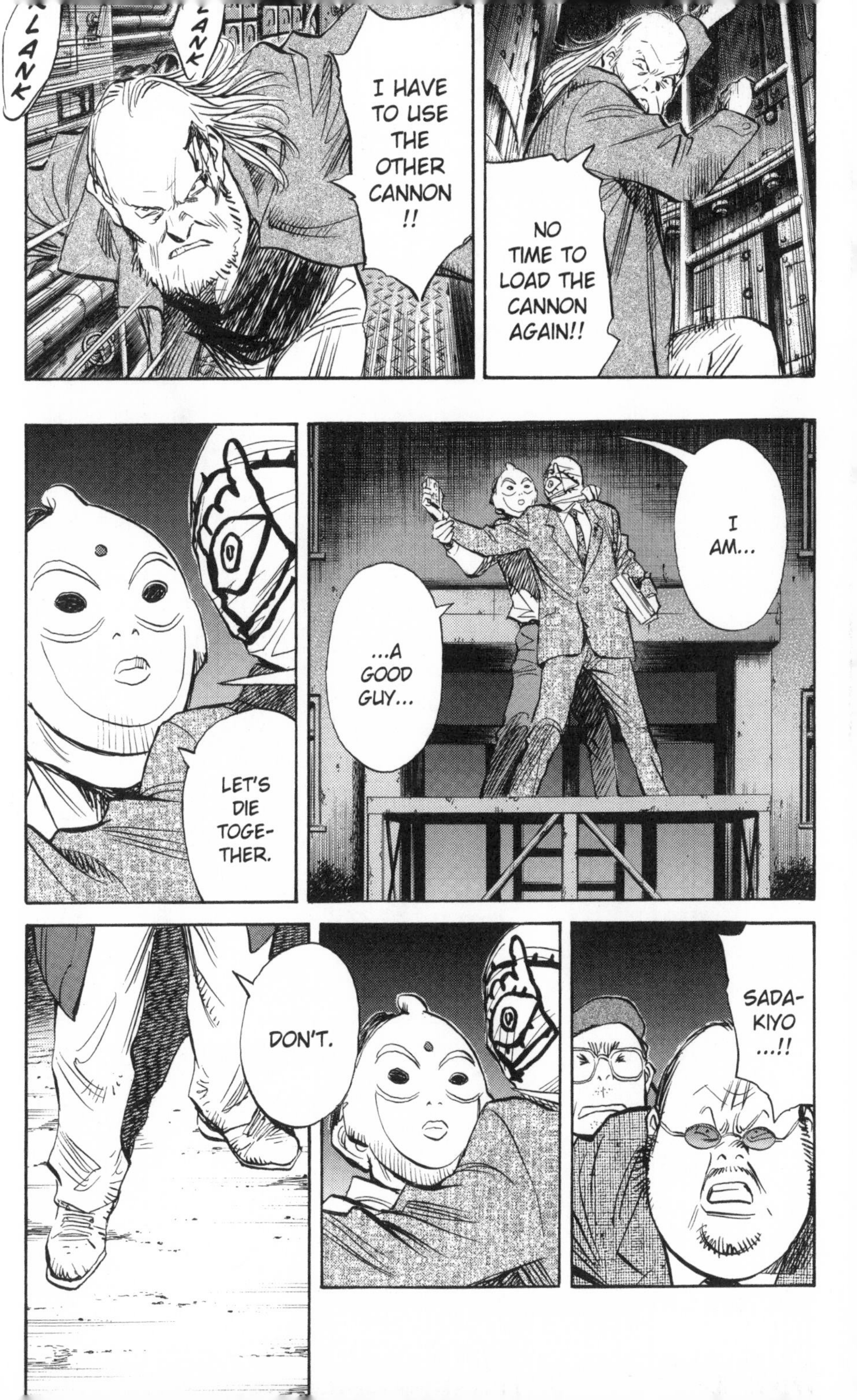
NO TIME TO LOAD THE CANNON AGAIN!!
LANK
I HAVE TO USE THE OTHER CANNON!!
LANK
I AM...
...A GOOD GUY...
LET'S DIE TOGE-THER.
SADA-KIYO...!!
DON'T.

LET'S JUST STOP.

YOU TOO, SADA-KIYO...

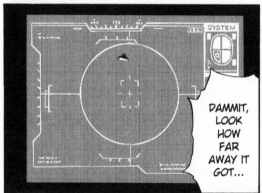

DAMMIT, LOOK HOW FAR AWAY IT GOT...

HANH

HANH

EQUANIMITY, LITTLE ANT.

HANH

HANH

LITTLE ANT...

234

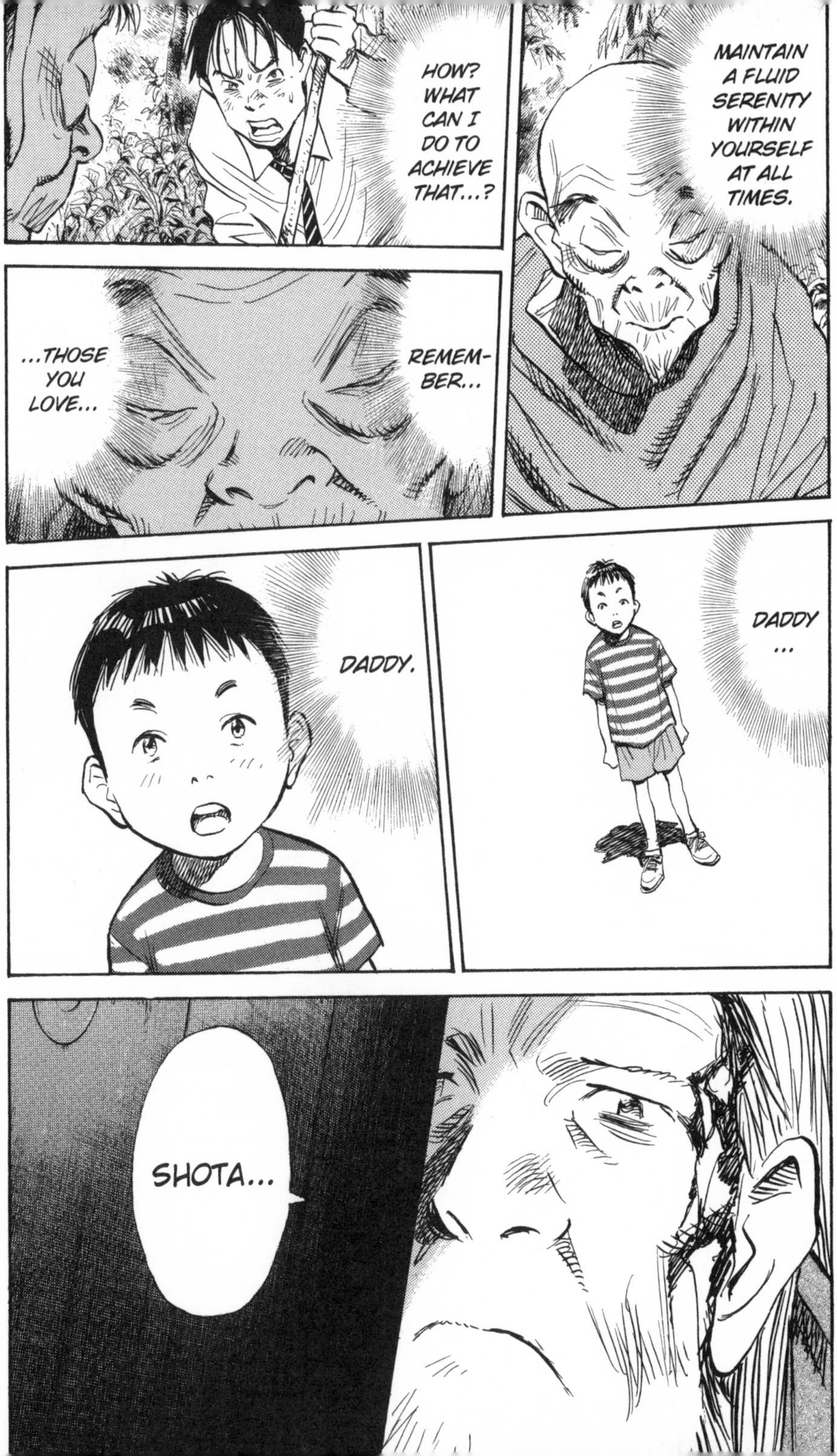

MAINTAIN A FLUID SERENITY WITHIN YOURSELF AT ALL TIMES.
HOW? WHAT CAN I DO TO ACHIEVE THAT...?
REMEMBER...
...THOSE YOU LOVE...
DADDY ...
DADDY.
SHOTA...

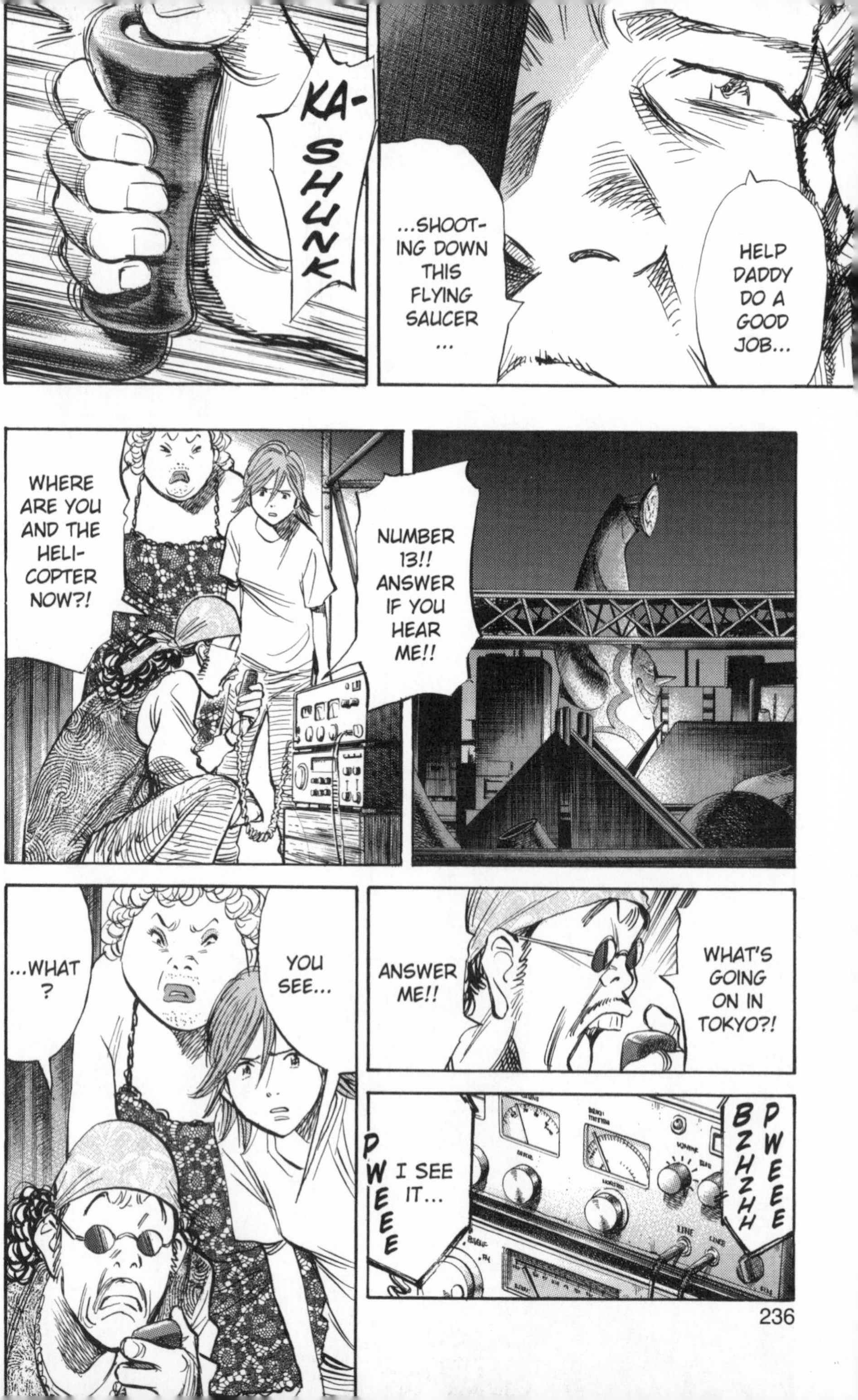
HELP DADDY DO A GOOD JOB...
...SHOOTING DOWN THIS FLYING SAUCER...
KA-SHUNK
NUMBER 13!! ANSWER IF YOU HEAR ME!!
WHERE ARE YOU AND THE HELICOPTER NOW?!
WHAT'S GOING ON IN TOKYO?!
ANSWER ME!!
PWEEE
BZHZHH
I SEE IT...
PWEEE
YOU SEE...
...WHAT?

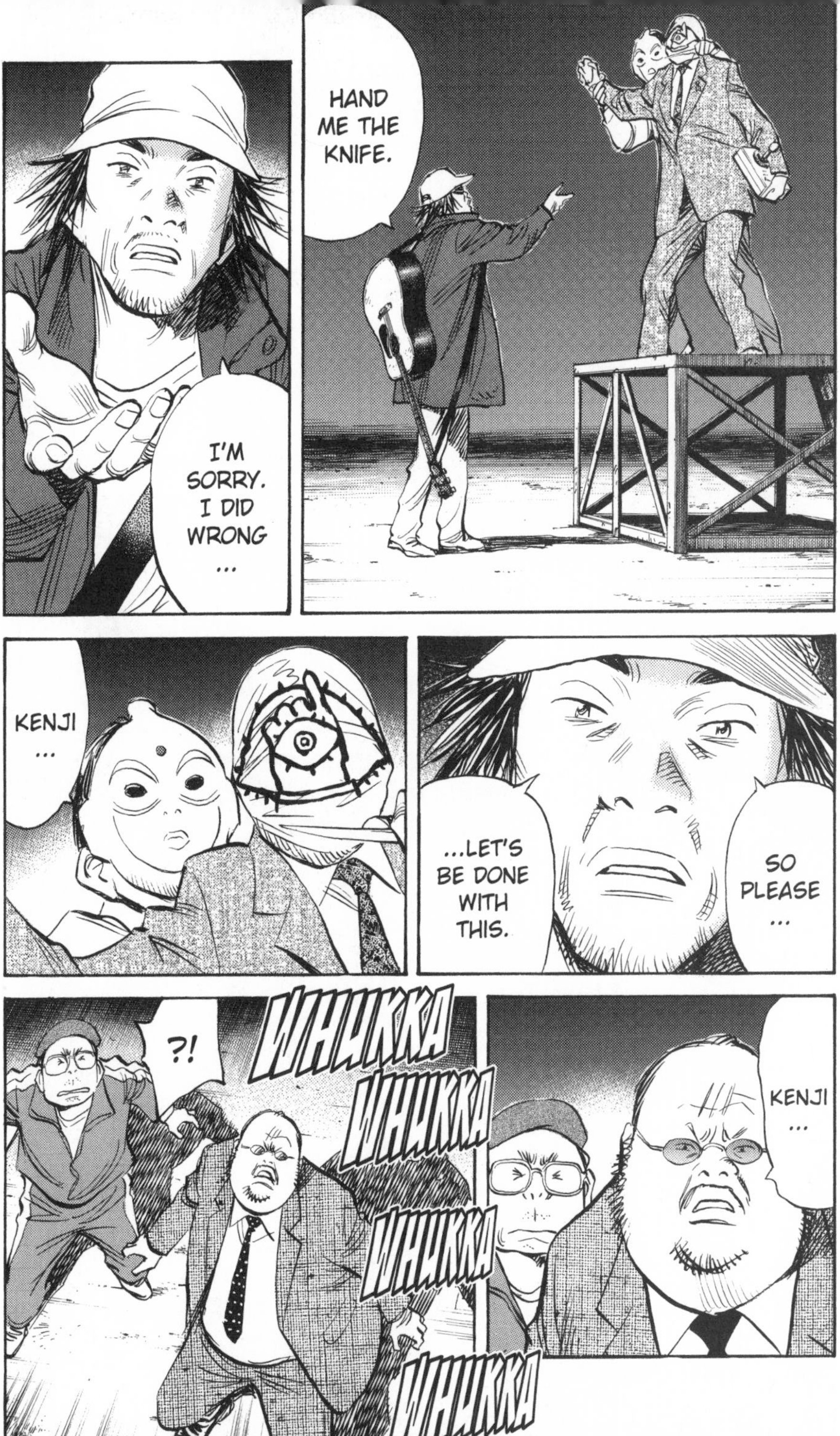
HAND ME THE KNIFE.
I'M SORRY. I DID WRONG ...
SO PLEASE ...
...LET'S BE DONE WITH THIS.
KENJI ...
KENJI ...
WHUKKA
WHUKKA
WHUKKA
WHUKKA
?!

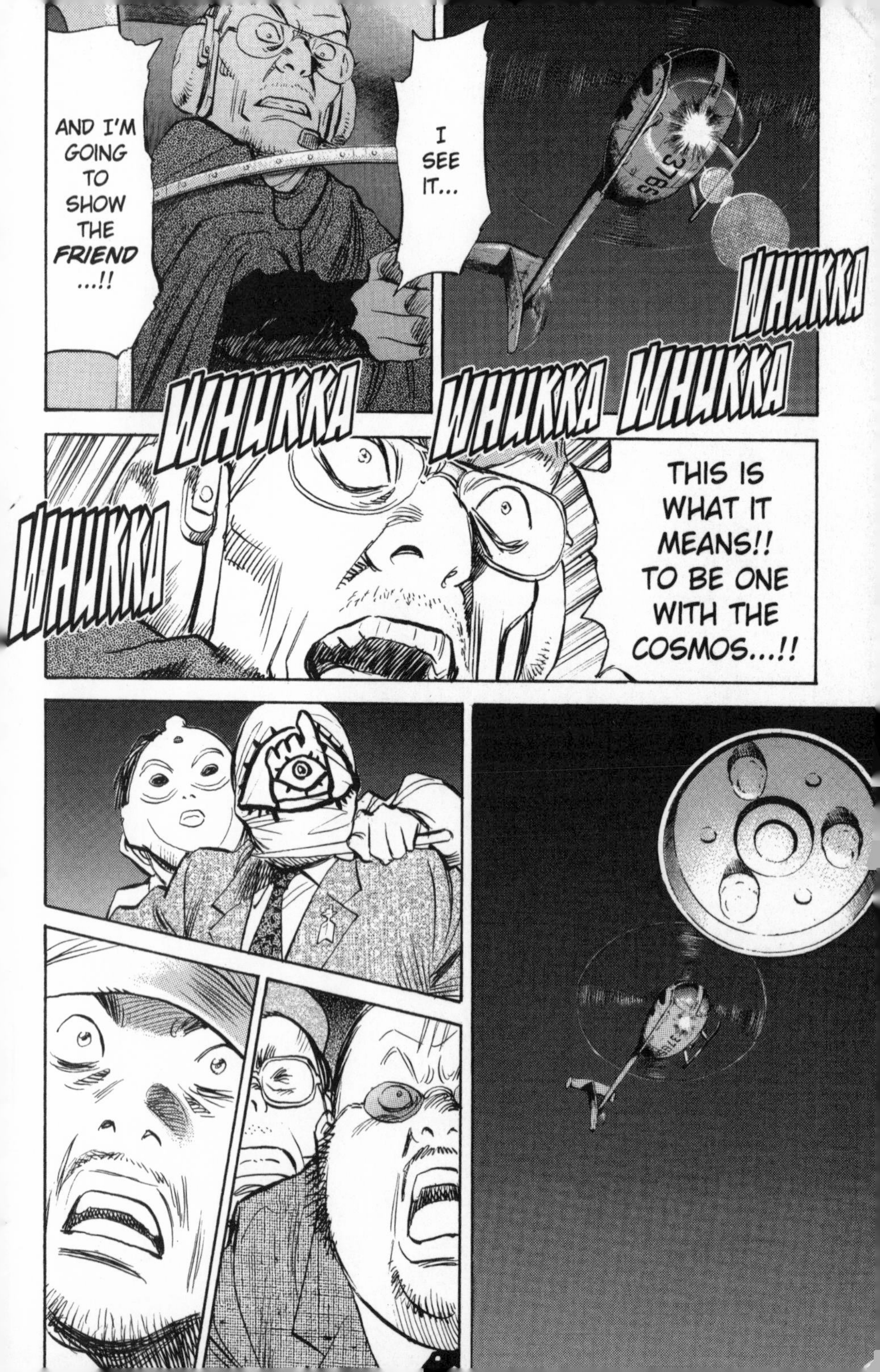
WHUKKA
WHUKKA
WHUKKA
I SEE IT...
AND I'M GOING TO SHOW THE *FRIEND* ...!!
WHUKKA
THIS IS WHAT IT MEANS!! TO BE ONE WITH THE COSMOS...!!
WHUKKA

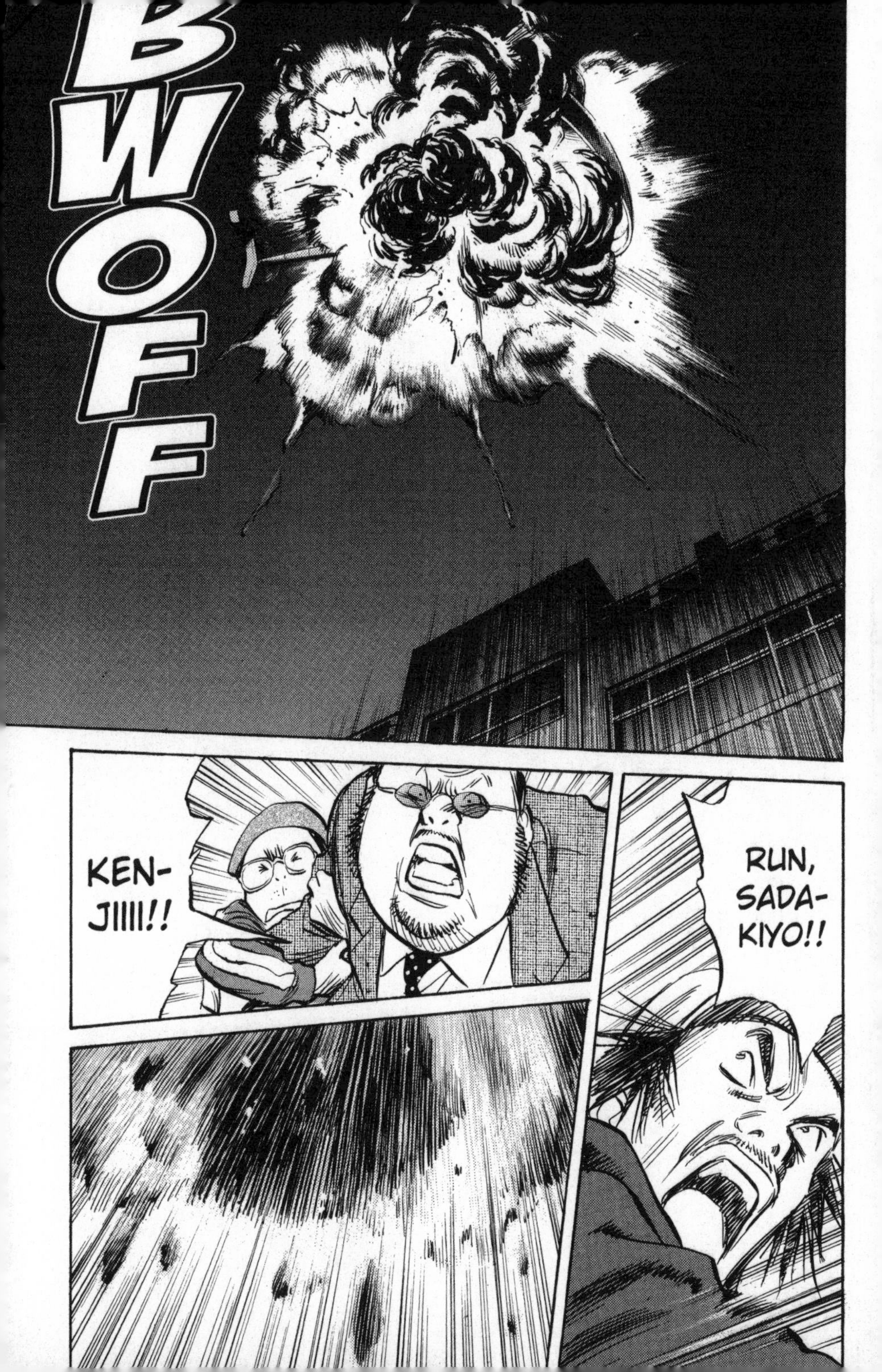
BWOFF
RUN, SADA-KIYO!!
KEN-JIIII!!

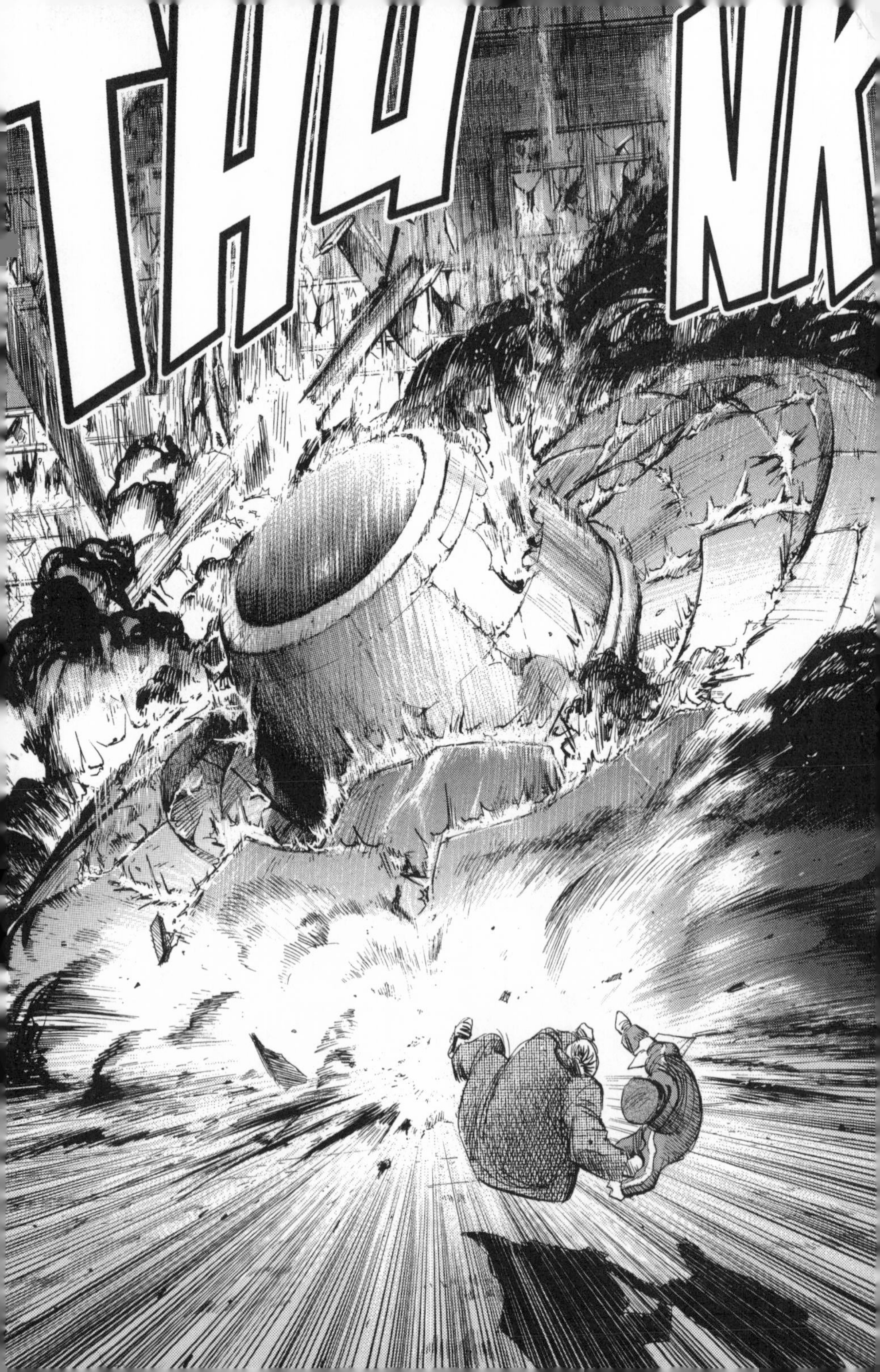
THUNK

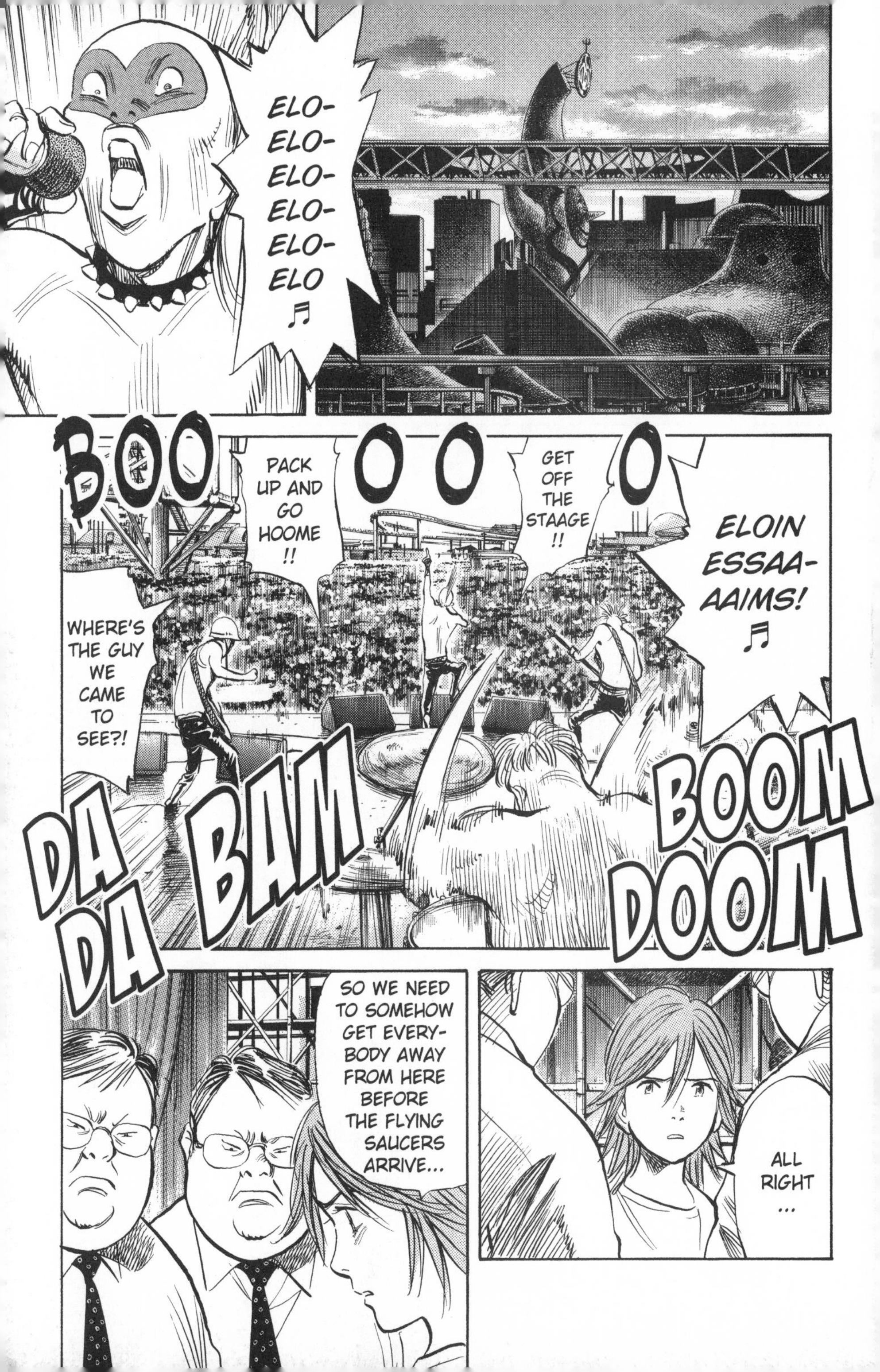

ELO-
ELO-
ELO-
ELO-
ELO-
ELO ♬
ELOIN ESSAA-AAIMS! ♬
GET OFF THE STAAGE !!
PACK UP AND GO HOOME !!
BOO O O O
WHERE'S THE GUY WE CAME TO SEE?!
BOOM DOOM
DA DA BAM
ALL RIGHT ...
SO WE NEED TO SOMEHOW GET EVERY-BODY AWAY FROM HERE BEFORE THE FLYING SAUCERS ARRIVE...

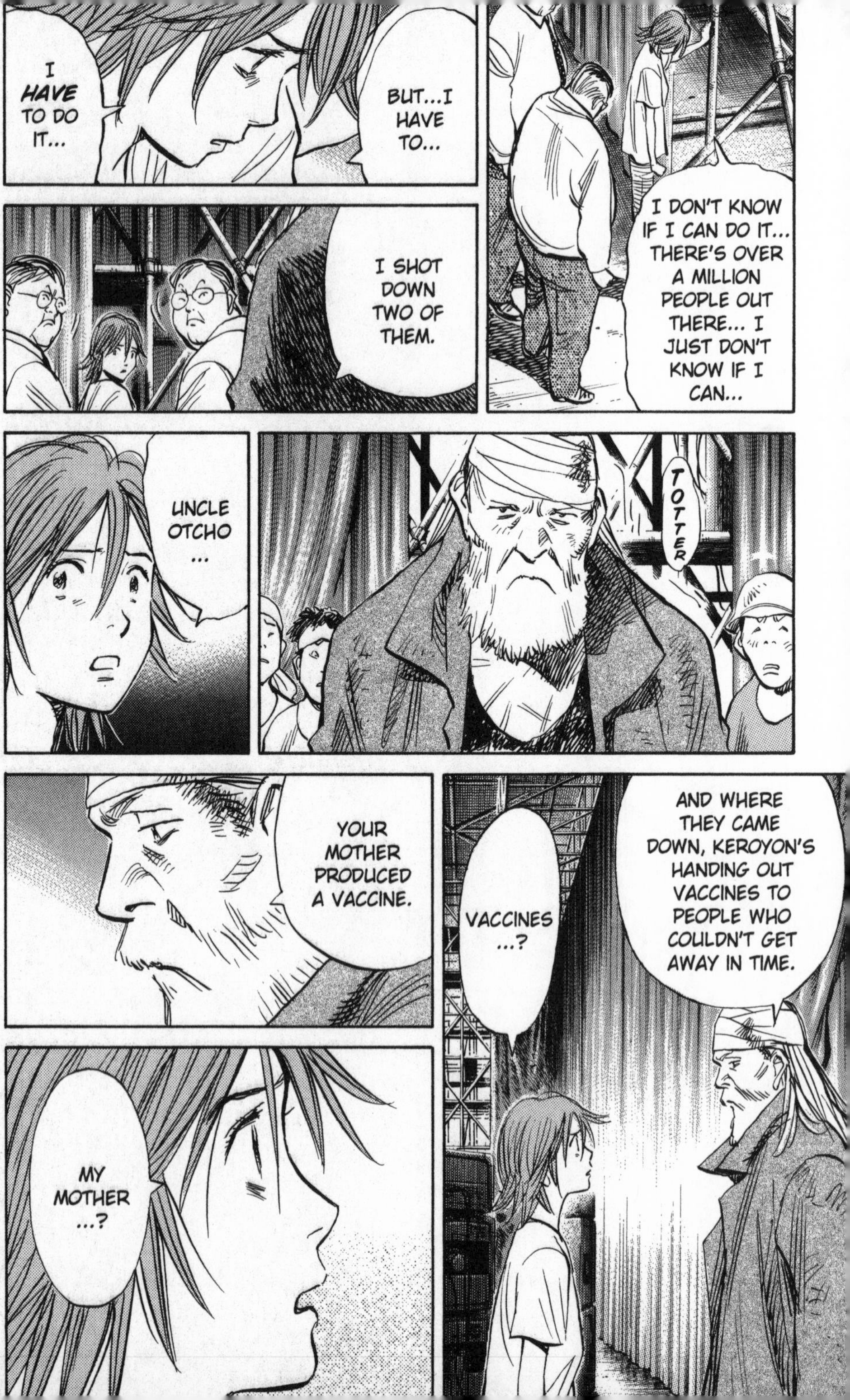
I DON'T KNOW IF I CAN DO IT... THERE'S OVER A MILLION PEOPLE OUT THERE... I JUST DON'T KNOW IF I CAN...
BUT...I HAVE TO...
I *HAVE* TO DO IT...
I SHOT DOWN TWO OF THEM.
TOTTER
UNCLE OTCHO...
AND WHERE THEY CAME DOWN, KEROYON'S HANDING OUT VACCINES TO PEOPLE WHO COULDN'T GET AWAY IN TIME.
VACCINES...?
YOUR MOTHER PRODUCED A VACCINE.
MY MOTHER...?

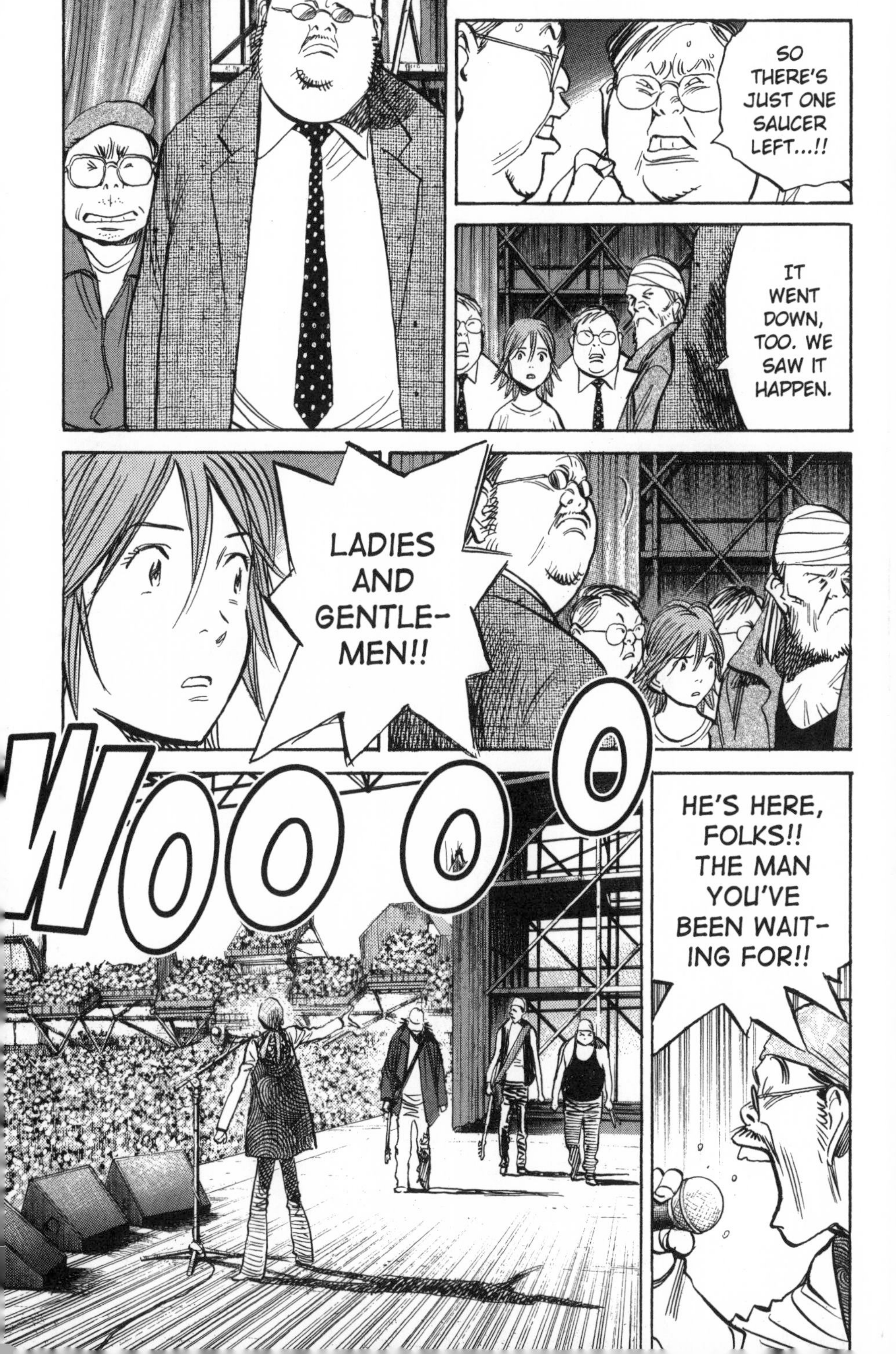
SO THERE'S JUST ONE SAUCER LEFT...!!
IT WENT DOWN, TOO. WE SAW IT HAPPEN.
LADIES AND GENTLE-MEN!!
HE'S HERE, FOLKS!! THE MAN YOU'VE BEEN WAIT-ING FOR!!
WOOOO

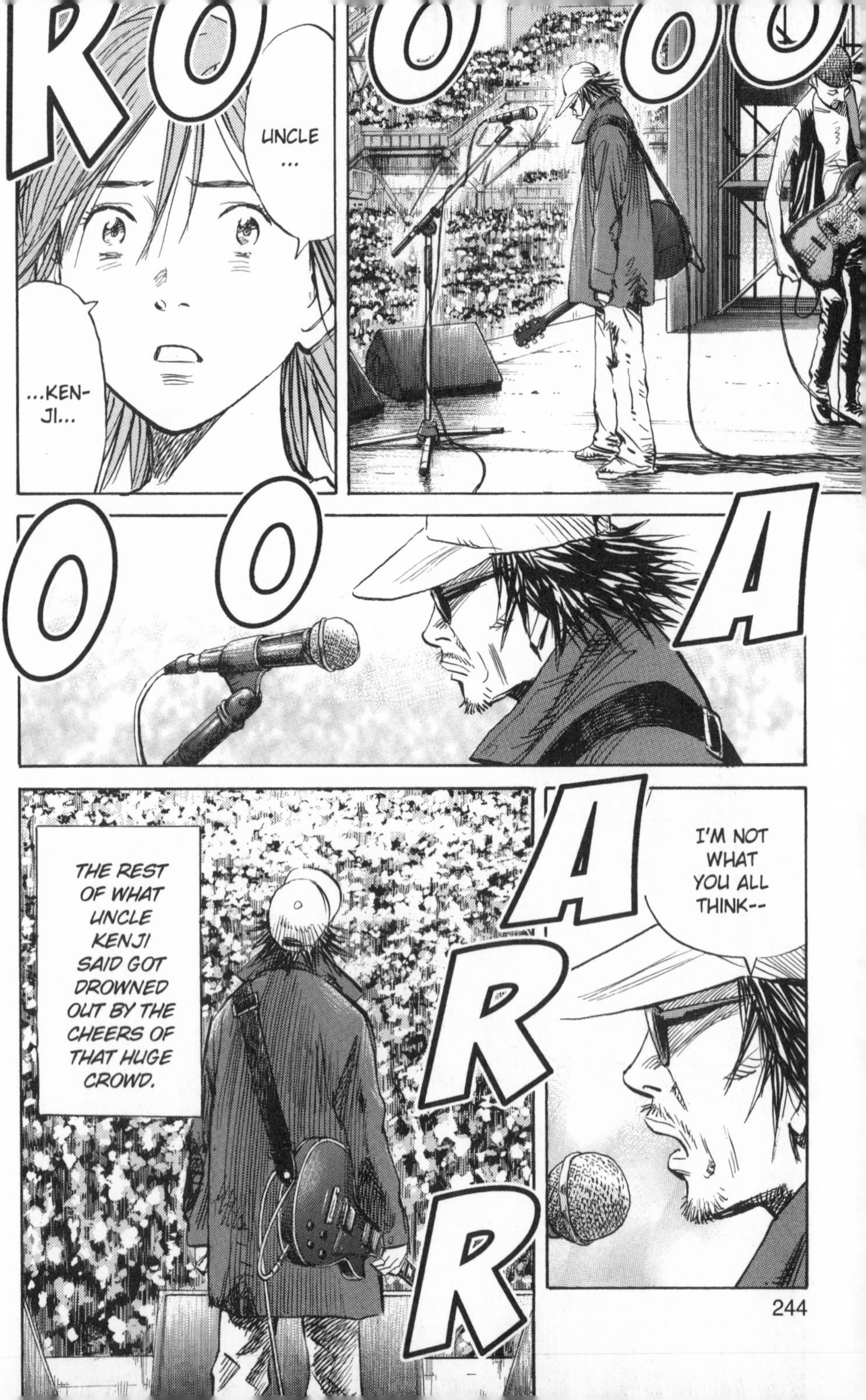
KOOOOOOAARR
UNCLE ...
...KENJI...
I'M NOT WHAT YOU ALL THINK--
THE REST OF WHAT UNCLE KENJI SAID GOT DROWNED OUT BY THE CHEERS OF THAT HUGE CROWD.

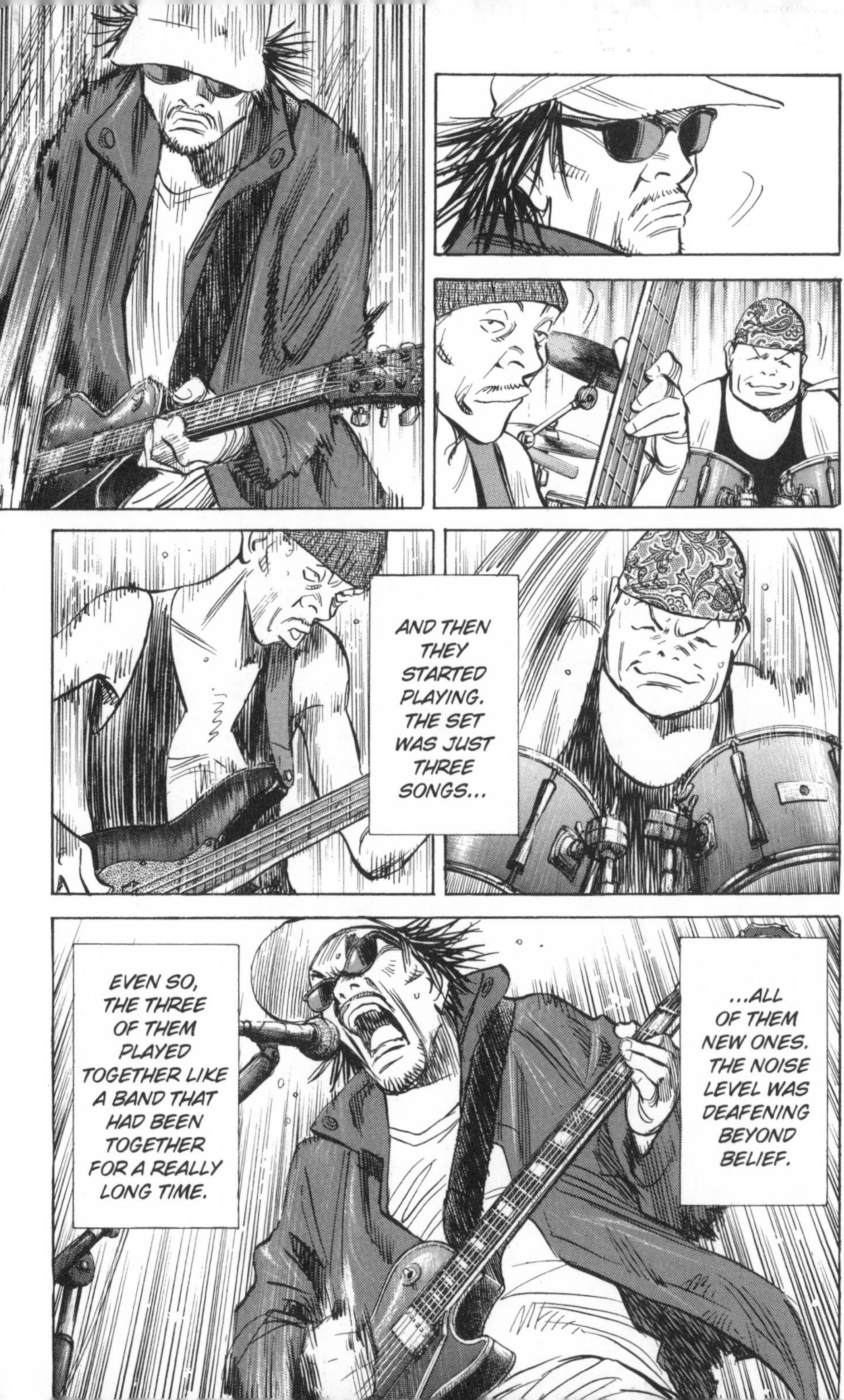
AND THEN THEY STARTED PLAYING. THE SET WAS JUST THREE SONGS...
...ALL OF THEM NEW ONES. THE NOISE LEVEL WAS DEAFENING BEYOND BELIEF.
EVEN SO, THE THREE OF THEM PLAYED TOGETHER LIKE A BAND THAT HAD BEEN TOGETHER FOR A REALLY LONG TIME.

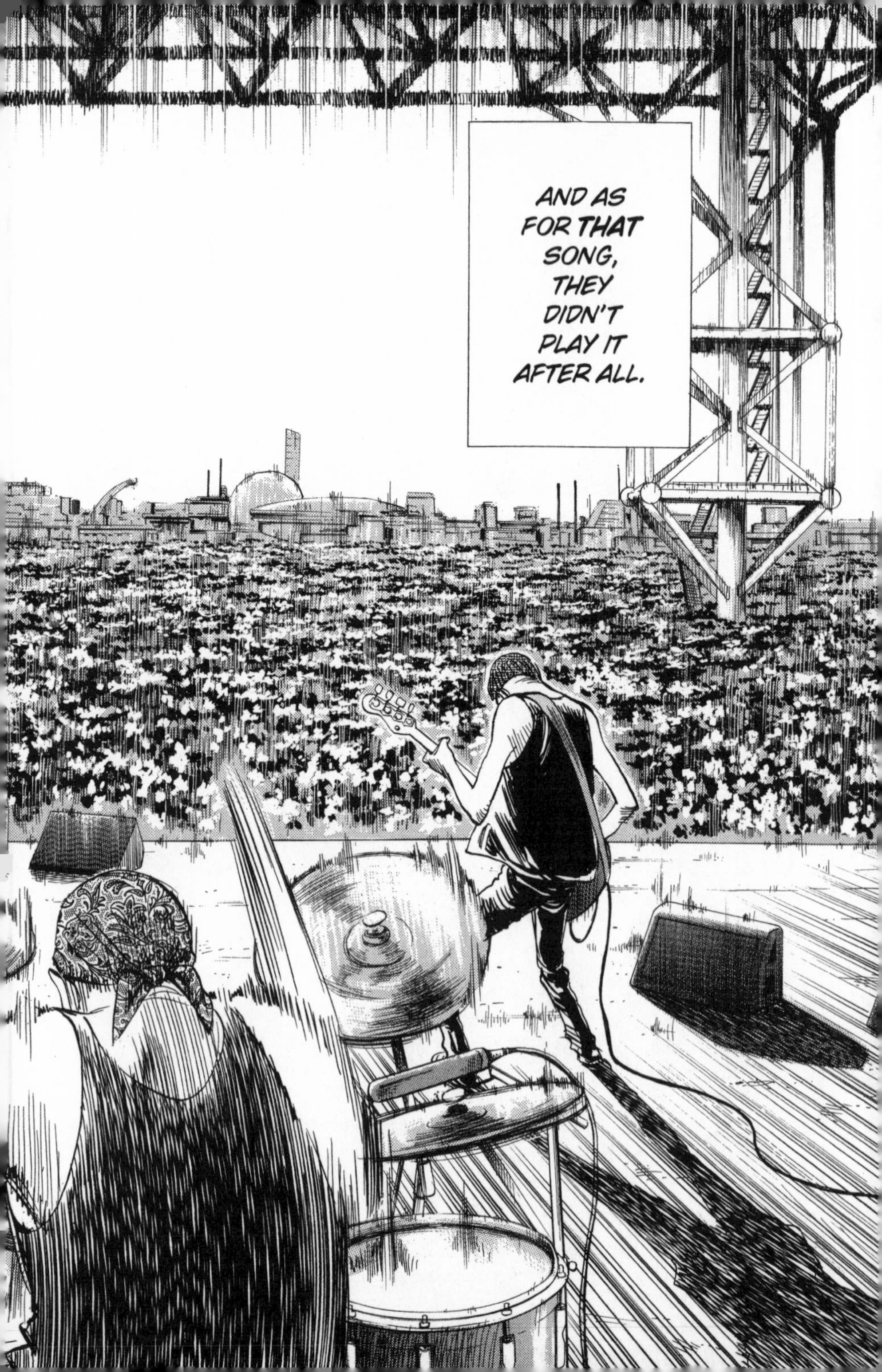
AND AS FOR THAT SONG, THEY DIDN'T PLAY IT AFTER ALL.

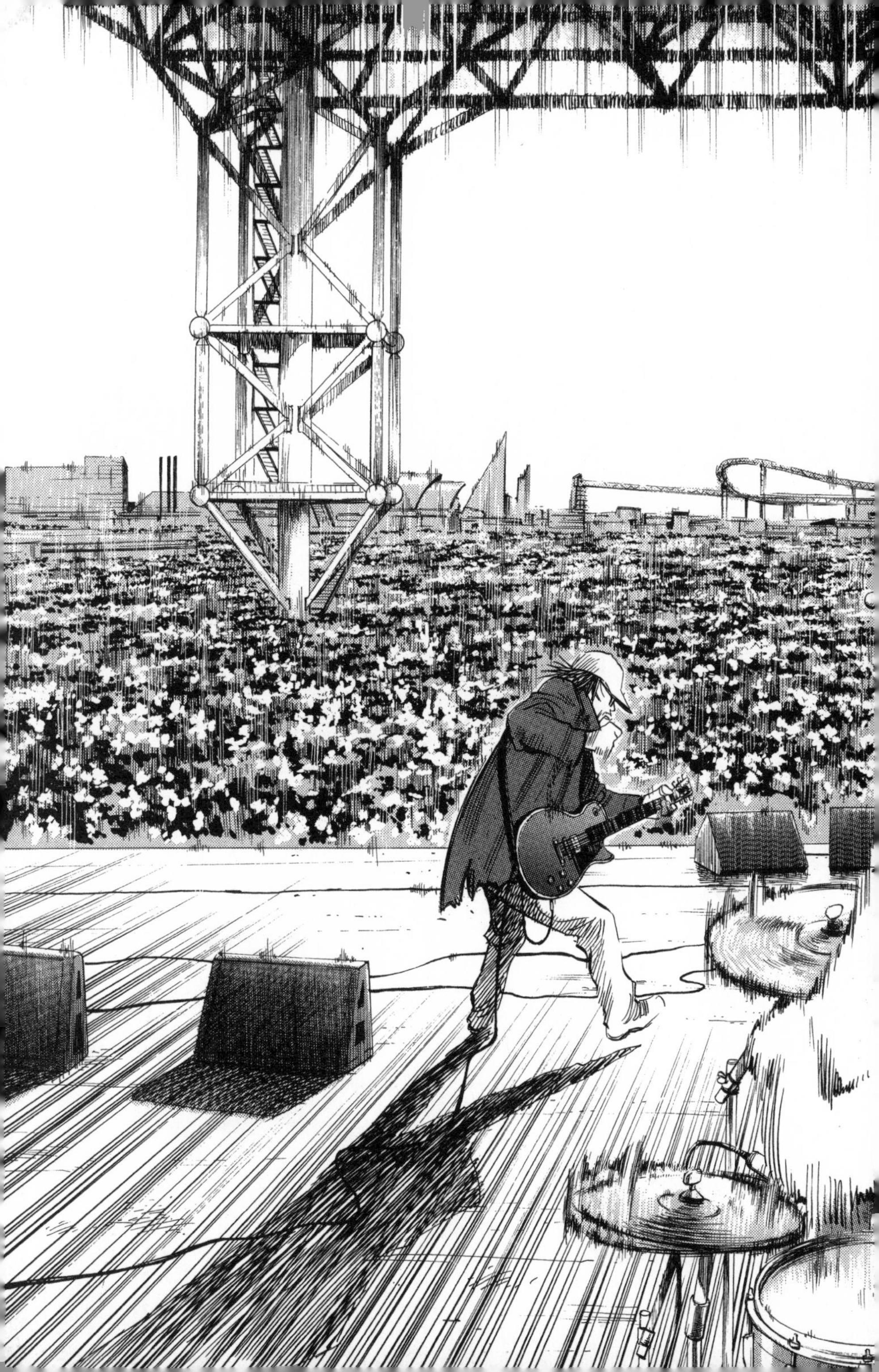

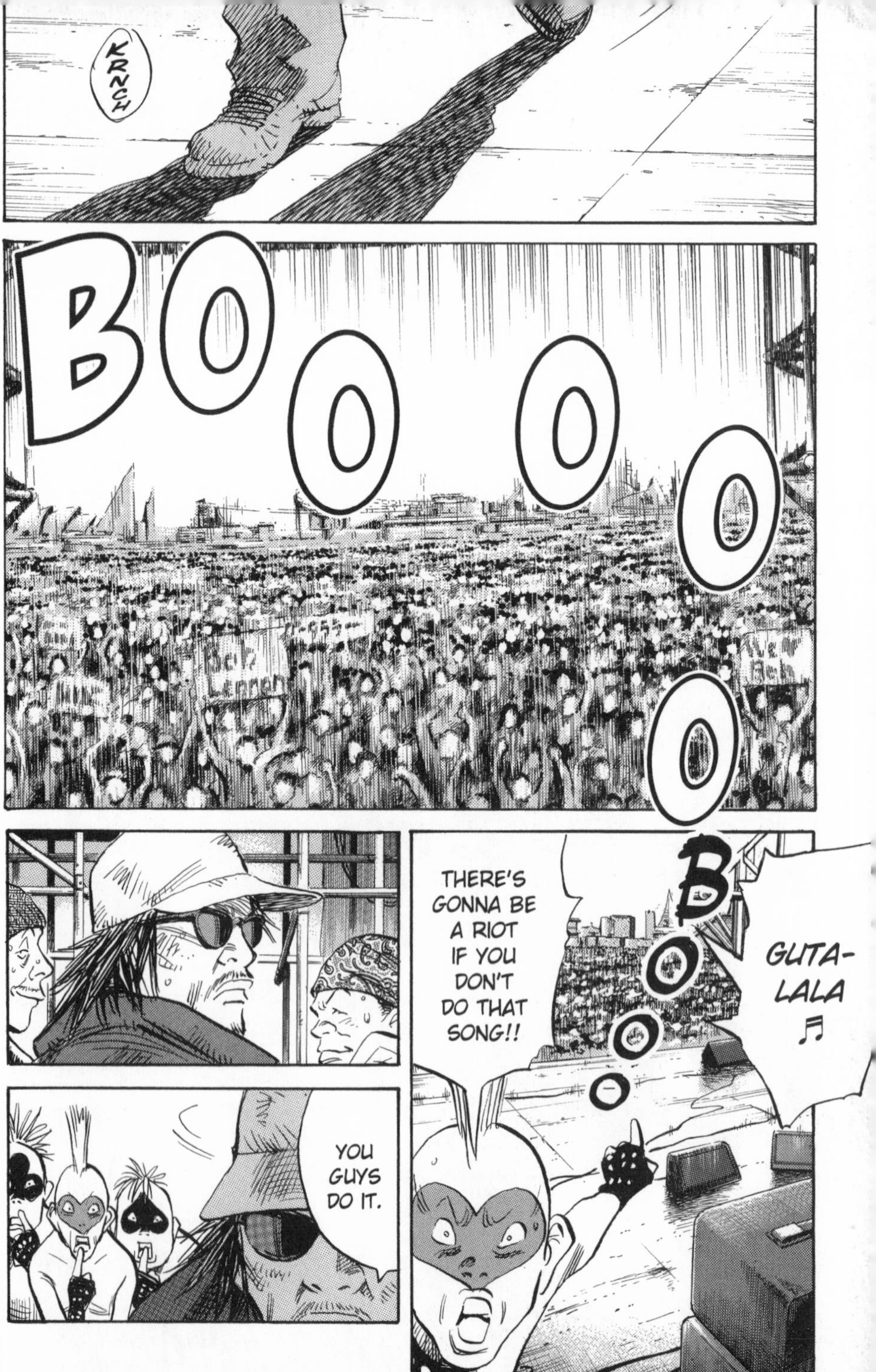
KRNCH
BOOOOOO
GUTA-LALA ♬
BOOOO
THERE'S GONNA BE A RIOT IF YOU DON'T DO THAT SONG!!
YOU GUYS DO IT.

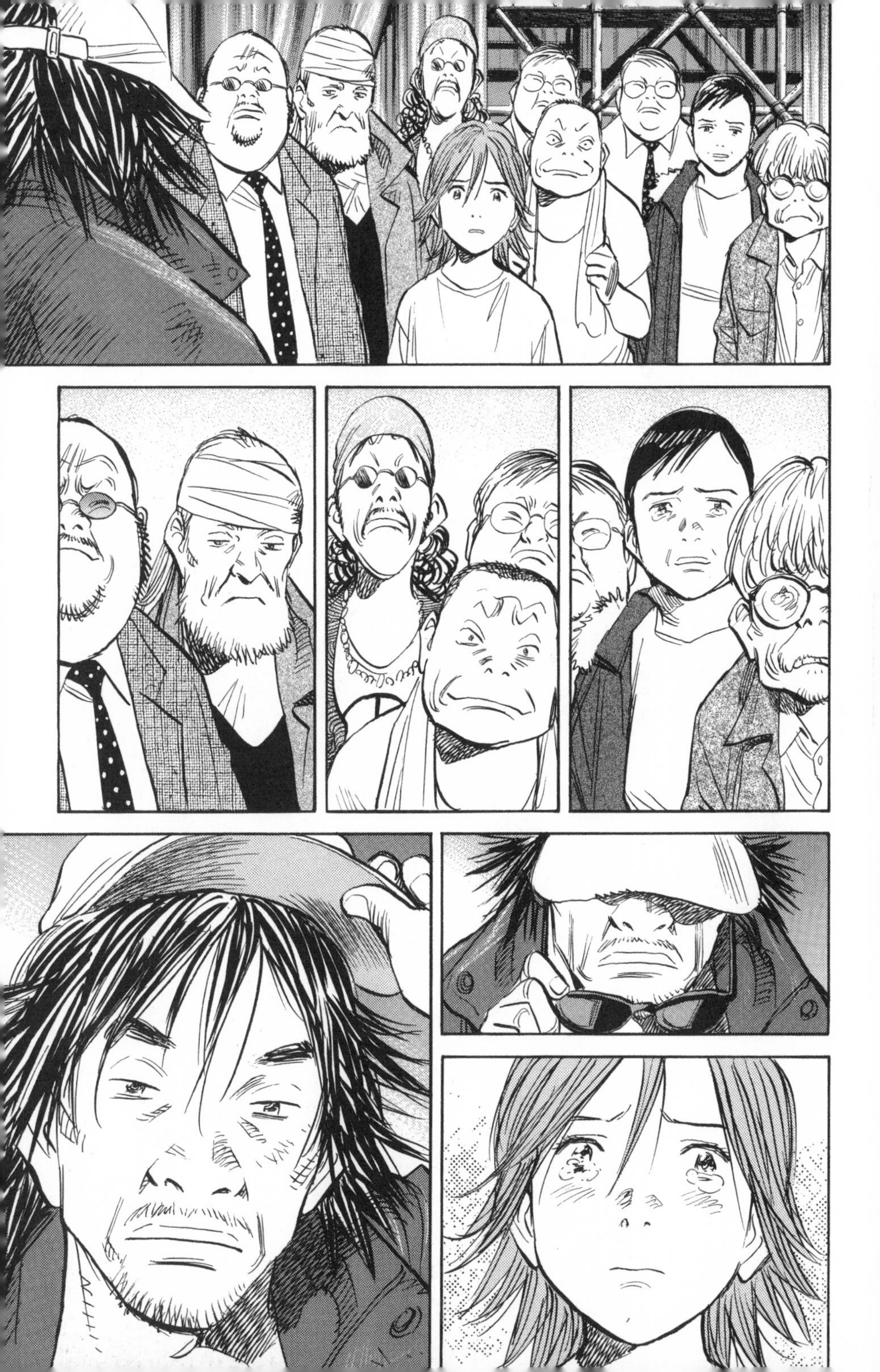

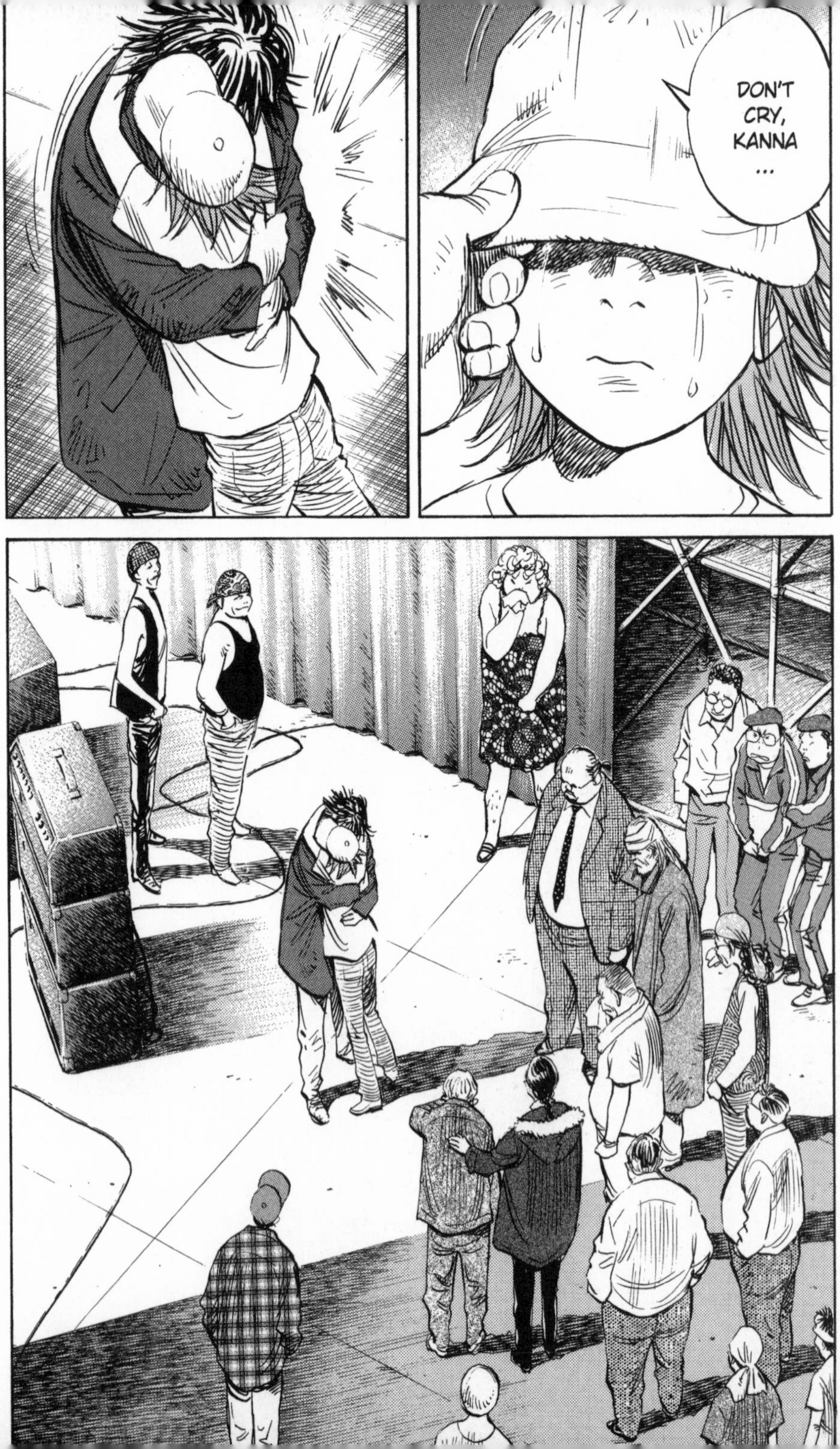
DON'T CRY, KANNA ...

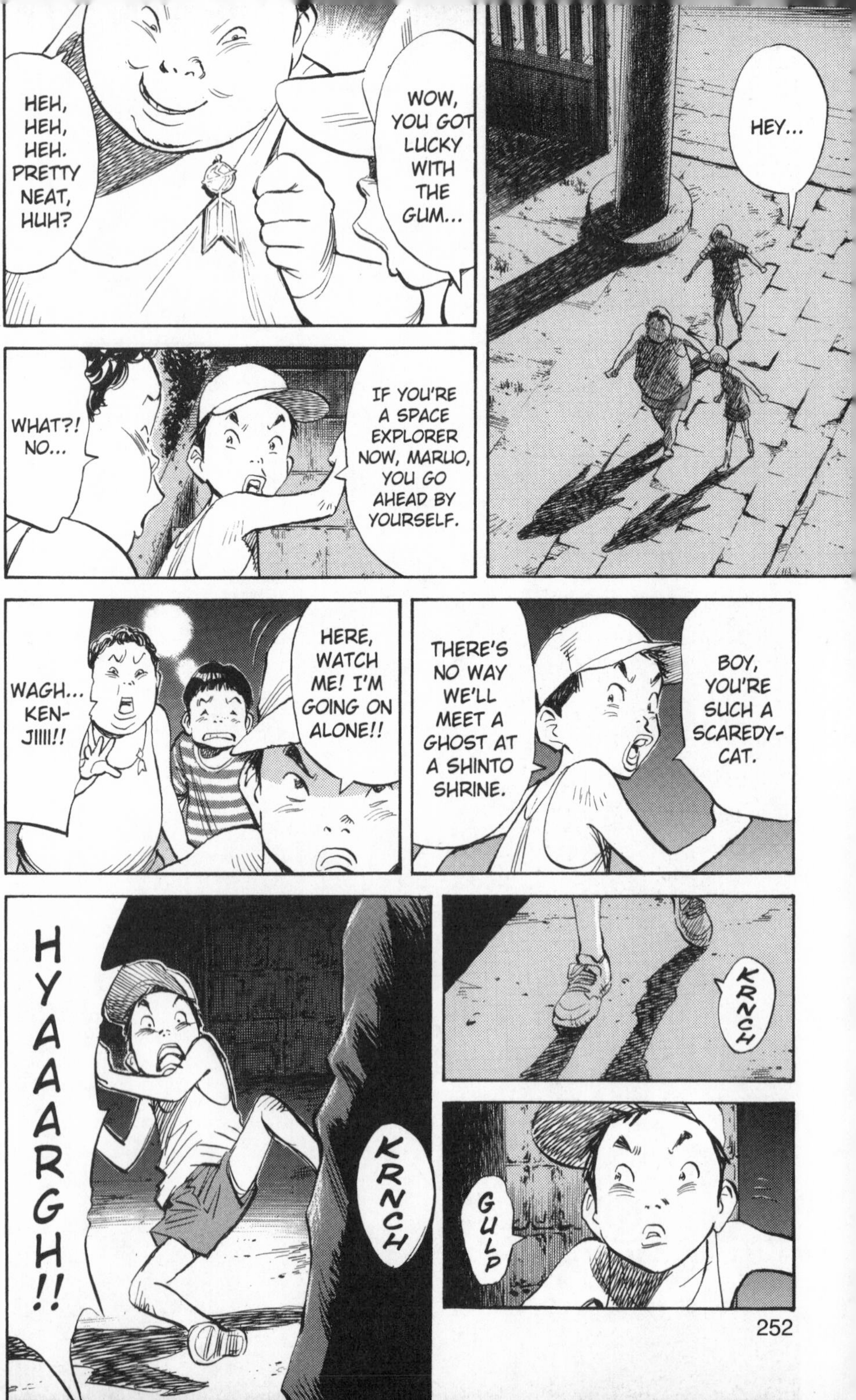
HEY...
WOW, YOU GOT LUCKY WITH THE GUM...
HEH, HEH, HEH. PRETTY NEAT, HUH?
IF YOU'RE A SPACE EXPLORER NOW, MARUO, YOU GO AHEAD BY YOURSELF.
WHAT?! NO...
BOY, YOU'RE SUCH A SCAREDY-CAT.
THERE'S NO WAY WE'LL MEET A GHOST AT A SHINTO SHRINE.
HERE, WATCH ME! I'M GOING ON ALONE!!
WAGH... KEN-JIIII!!
KRNCH
GULP
KRNCH
HYAAAARGH!!

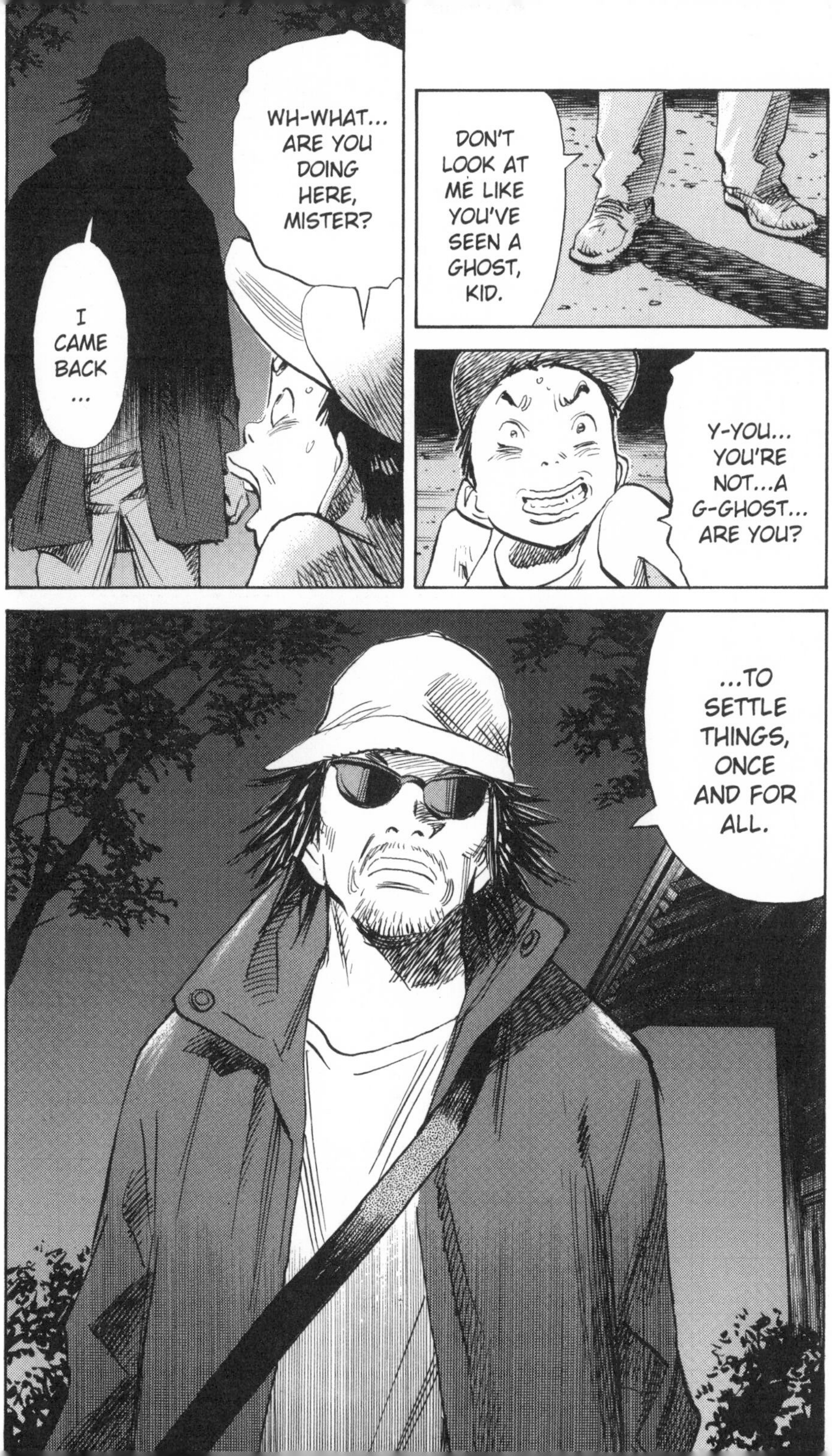
DON'T LOOK AT ME LIKE YOU'VE SEEN A GHOST, KID.
Y-YOU... YOU'RE NOT...A G-GHOST... ARE YOU?
WH-WHAT... ARE YOU DOING HERE, MISTER?
I CAME BACK ...
...TO SETTLE THINGS, ONCE AND FOR ALL.

Naoki Urasawa's
20th Century Boys
Volume 22

VIZ Signature Edition

STORY AND ART BY NAOKI URASAWA

20 SEIKI SHONEN 22 by Naoki URASAWA/Studio Nuts
© 2007 Naoki URASAWA/Studio Nuts
With the cooperation of Takashi NAGASAKI
All rights reserved. Original Japanese
edition published in 2007 by Shogakukan Inc., Tokyo.

English Adaptation/Akemi Wegmüller
Touch-up Art & Lettering/Freeman Wong
Cover & Interior Design/Sam Elzway
Editor/Andy Nakatani

Printed in the U.S.A.

Published by VIZ Media, LLC
P.O. Box 77010
San Francisco, CA 94107

10 9 8 7 6 5 4 3 2
First printing, September 2012
Second printing, August 2014

VIZ SIGNATURE
www.vizsignature.com

VIZ
media
www.viz.com